EDUCATION, LAW AND DIVER

Education is fundamentally concerned with realising the potential of every child, but an increasing social diversity presents enormous challenges for the state in terms of its commitment to providing an appropriate education for all. Factors such as ethnicity, disability and material deprivation are associated with inequality, social exclusion and the risk of low educational attainment. Diversity also reflects divergent cultural values and norms. In responding to the challenges posed by diversity, public education authorities are to some extent constrained by individual or group rights. This book examines the nature of these rights, including those under the European Convention on Human Rights, and the ways and contexts in which they operate. Their social effects are also considered. Areas discussed include the curriculum, special educational needs and choice of school. A key theme in the book is the promotion and enforcement of equal access to education, including higher education. Issues of multiculturalism, the social integration of minorities, religion in education and the recognition of children's independent rights are also discussed. The book centres on England and Wales and covers the evolving legislative framework, including the Education and Inspections Bill 2006, but relevant legal developments in other states are also highlighted.

Education, Law and Diversity

Neville Harris

·HART·
PUBLISHING

OXFORD AND PORTLAND, OREGON
2007

Published in North America (US and Canada) by
Hart Publishing
c/o International Specialized Book Services
920 NE 58th Avenue, Suite 300
Portland, OR 97213-3786
USA
Tel: +1-503-287-3093 or toll-free: (1)-800-944-6190
Fax: +1-503-280-8832
E-mail: mail@hartpub.co.uk
Website: www.isbs.com

Hart Publishing, 16C Worcester Place, Oxford, OX1 2JW
Telephone: +44 (0)1865 517530 Fax: +44 (0)1865 510710
E-mail: mail@hartpub.co.uk
Website: http://www.hartpub.co.uk

British Library Cataloguing in Publication Data
Data Available

ISBN-13: 978-1-84113-252-5 (paperback)
ISBN-10: 1-84113-252-7 (paperback)

Typeset by Forewords, Oxford
Printed and bound in Great Britain by
TJ International Ltd, Padstow, Cornwall

To Marie, Amy and Rosie and my parents

Preface

Education is so fundamental to human development and the process of social reproduction that its recognition as a basic human right is uncontroversial. The education of children and young people is among the most important central functions performed by the modern state, and the state's interest in the education of its future citizens continues to grow. Among the reasons for the increasing regulation and control of the education system in England and Wales over the past three decades, and its concomitantly intensifying politicisation, has been a growing governmental awareness that education is central to the realisation of a wide range of economic and social goals. Under the Conservative governments from 1979–97, education policy served economic and ideological agendas, through, for example, the development of a market based on competition and choice and the establishment of legal and moral frameworks for areas of the curriculum and discipline. Under the Labour government from 1997, improvements in education became the key to the achievement of social objectives, such as reducing social exclusion and the factors linked to it, including truancy and under-achievement, and increasing parental involvement and responsibility. Education is also regarded as having a critical role to play in maximising social cohesion at a time when a widening of social divisions is considered a significant risk. Both sets of governments have, in turn, recognised the importance of maximising educational attainment levels in order to bolster the 'skills economy'. Indeed, across the two political eras there have been many continuities in the underlying policy ideals and values. They include the importance attached to parental choice and diversity of provision.

There has been no let up in the use of law to control and manage closely the education of children and young people. However, the social environment in which it performs this role has been changing in recent years, in that the population is rapidly becoming more diverse, particularly ethnically and culturally. The way that the law is used to create educational structures and regulate the management of institutions and processes in the fulfilment of policy goals has always had the potential to bring it into conflict with the wishes and rights of particular citizens. Today, the education system engages with many issues on which, given the wide social, religious and ethnic diversity of much of England and Wales, national policy may increasingly struggle to reconcile the need to promote a common approach—in the interests of uniformity, equity and social cohesion—with that of recognising and upholding the cultural rights of the many and diverse minority communities. There is an underlying debate on how to strike the right balance in this regard, much of it centred on the need for greater integration and the role of a multicultural or intercultural approach. The way that this conflict plays out and receives legal resolution, both in the UK and elsewhere, is a dominant theme of this book.

This book aims to explore the relationship between education, law and diversity. Its conception of diversity is not, however, confined to ethnic, cultural and religious diversity. The social environment in which the education system operates is also marked by diversity on the basis of social class or income/wealth. Moreover, all aspects of social diversity have a strong association with inequality. Concern about how social disadvantage impacts upon access and choice to and within education has led to the introduction of a range of laws and policies to tackle inequity. Their implications and effects are a particular concern of the book.

The book begins, in Chapter 1, by examining aspects of diversity in England and Wales and explores the role of education and of politics in formulating education law and policy. Chapter 2 considers the notion of social rights and, in particular, that of education as a right, including its manifestation under international law and, in particular, the European Convention on Human Rights. The position of children and young people as independent holders, to varying degrees, of rights is also considered. Children's rights have rightly attracted enormous academic interest and constitute a vitally important subject area. This book also gives them attention, although necessarily concentrates on those of specific relevance to education.

Chapter 3 aims to provide an account of the way that the education system and its legal structure have been developing, up to and including the Education and Inspections Bill 2006. One feature of the evolving structural framework is yet another form of diversity, namely that reflected in the new categories of schools which have been introduced over the years, including academies and foundation schools and the controversial proposals for schools with 'trust' status. This diversity has contributed to the growing complexity of the schools system. Chapter 4 looks at equality of access to education, across schools and through to universities and other higher education institutions. It explores access from two main perspectives. First, it looks at anti-discrimination law, including the extension of the Disability Discrimination Act 1995 to schools, the new prohibitions concerning discrimination on the grounds of religion or belief and the whole question of positive discrimination. Secondly, it considers the effectiveness of the various legal and policy initiatives, both national and international, that are targeted at particular groups which experience disadvantage in accessing education. This includes discussion of the measures for widening access to higher education included within the Higher Education Act 2004.

Chapters 5 and 6 explore two large and discrete areas of education law where the greatest number of legal conflicts arise: school admission and special educational needs. The analysis in Chapter 5 includes an assessment of the social impact of school choice: does it, as some evidence suggests, increase social segregation? Chapter 6 also explores choice, but in this case in connection with parents' rights over the arrangements for their children who have special educational needs, a group comprising some one in six members of the school population but a very diverse group in itself. It examines how the law aims to maximise the inclusion of children with special educational needs in mainstream education. Inclusion and segregation and how the law both combats and contributes to them are pervasive themes in the book.

It is primarily in Chapter 7, dealing with the content of education, that the issue of multiculturalism and the related matter of 'common citizenship' are analysed. This chapter contains the most detailed exploration in the book of how cultural diversity is managed under the education system's statutory framework, including consideration of relevant human rights issues. It focuses on areas such as the National Curriculum, sex education, language, religious education, creationism and the freedoms of independent schools. Chapter 8 attempts to offer some general conclusions about the goals and challenges that diversity presents for education and its legal structures.

The organisation of material and themes for this book presented a significant challenge given the inter-relatedness of many of the issues, particularly those concerned with rights under the European Convention on Human Rights and the UN Convention on the Rights of the Child. Others can say whether I have succeeded in presenting something that approaches a coherent review of this broad subject. I acknowledge with thanks the information on various matters provided by Laura Lundy, Dominic McGoldrick, Helen Mountfield, Charlie Russo and Ben Vermeulen. I alone am responsible for any errors. I am also grateful to the publishers, and especially Mel Hamill and Richard Hart, for all their support. I must also record my appreciation for the administrative help provided by Joanne Riley of the School of Law at the University of Manchester. Finally, my wife Marie and daughters Amy and Rosie kept me in good cheer during the usual trials of book writing and as ever I owe them a huge debt.

This is an area of such rapid development that some of the legal content may already have been overtaken by changes. The book includes developments up to August 2006, but some updating occurred subsequently at proof.

Neville Harris
Manchester

Contents

List of Tables

List of Abbreviations

A2P1	Article 2 of Protocol 1 (or Article 2 of the First Protocol)
ADHD	Attention Deficit Hyperactivity Disorder
CEHR	Commission for Equality and Human Rights
CESCR	(UN) Committee on Economic, Social and Cultural Rights
CRE	Commission for Racial Equality
CTC	City Technology College
DDA	Disability Discrimination Act
DES	Department of Education and Science
DfEE	Department for Education and Employment
DfES	Department for Education and Skills
DRC	Disability Rights Commission
EA	Education Act
EAZ	Education action zone
ECHR	European Convention on Human Rights
ECJ	European Court of Justice
ECtHR	European Court of Human Rights
EiC	Excellence in Cities
ELR	Education Law Reports
ERA	Education Reform Act
ESF	Education Standards Fund
GCSE	General Certificate of Secondary Education
GM	Grant-maintained
GTC	General Teaching Council
HEFCE	Higher Education Funding Council for England
HRA	Human Rights Act
IAP	Independent appeal panel
ICCPR	International Covenant on Civil and Political Rights
ICECSR	International Covenant on Economic, Cultural and Social Rights
LEA	Local education authority
LSC	Learning and Skills Council
NCC	National Curriculum Council
OFFA	Office for Fair Access
Ofsted	Office for Standards in Education
PRU	Pupil referral unit
QCA	Qualifications and Curriculum Authority
RRA	Race Relations Act
SDA	Sex Discrimination Act
SEN	Special educational needs

SENDA	Special Educational Needs and Disability Act
SENDIST	Special Educational Needs and Disability Tribunal
SEU	Social Exclusion Unit
SSFA	School Standards and Framework Act
SRE	*Sex and Relationship Education*
STIs	Sexually transmitted infections
THEA	Teaching and Higher Education Act
UNCRC	United Nations Convention on the Rights of the Child

Table of Cases

Table of Legislation

Table of Statutory Instruments

National Legislation (Non-UK)

EC Legislation

International Treaties and Conventions

1

Diversity, Inclusion and the Role of Education

INTRODUCTION

SOCIAL DIVERSITY WITHIN the UK is increasing, and as it does so it is attracting ever more notice at all levels of government and administration and within national life. A report by the National Audit Office (NAO) has identified 'six key strands of diversity in the population' that government policy recognises, namely race, disability, gender, sexual orientation, age and religion/belief; but it also reports that government 'recognises and attends to other ways in which society is diverse, such as people with a primary language other than English and people with low incomes'.[1] People do not necessarily fall neatly into one of the categories, of course, as the concept of multiple identities recognises. Many people can be identified, or may identify themselves, with more than one category.[2] This extends the challenge for government in ensuring that policies across education and other areas of governance take proper account of social diversity, particularly if those policies aim to be equitable in their social impact. Moreover, as the NAO explains, the importance of designing public policies and delivering public services which properly recognise the needs of diverse groups stems in particular from the need for the government 'to promote social cohesion'.[3] It reflects a view on a general issue that has a particular relevance to education policy: that, in the way that it responds to and engages with diversity, public policy has the potential to underscore or reduce social divisions and the tensions that can arise from them. Some of the divisions are cultural; and, as the discussion in later chapters shows, there are crucial and difficult questions as to

---

[1] Comptroller and Auditor General, *Delivering Public Services to a Diverse Society*, HC 19-I Session 2004–2005 (London, TSO, 2004), para 1.6. Figures on diversity are shown below.

[2] See G Lewis and A Phoenix, '"Race, Ethnicity" and Identity' in K Woodward (ed), *Questioning Identity: Gender, Class, Ethnicity* (London, Routledge, 2004), at 115–49; 'Everyone has Multiple Identities' (at 130); K Woodward, 'Afterword' in ibid, 151–4, notes that multiple identities are a facet of diversity (at 154). See also A Vernon, 'The Dialectics of Multiple Identities and the Disabled People's Movement' (1999) 14 *Disability and Society* 385.

[3] Ibid, para 1.6.

how far recognition of the needs and group rights of diverse groups should go in the face of perceived threats to social cohesion arising from them. The wider public debate about multiculturalism is relevant to this issue and is discussed in Chapter 7.

Education has a longer and more direct experience of responding to diversity than many other areas of governance. As discussed later in the book, it was, for example, in the vanguard in the development of multicultural policies towards schooling in the 1970s and 1980s, albeit at a local rather than national level. Indeed, since long before then it has sought to accommodate religious difference through provision for denominational schools and parental opt-outs from religious education or worship at school. It has also engaged, to some extent, with the class structure, through the creation of comprehensive (non-selective) secondary schools, particularly during the 1960s and 1970s. It has also aimed to find effective ways of identifying, and differentiating from others, children with disabilities and other barriers to learning for whom standard educational provision is not always appropriate, but whose integration into mainstream schooling may be considered socially, psychologically and educationally important.

However, the perceived role of education is changing in a way that requires it to engage with issues of diversity in different ways. For example, education strategies to promote social inclusion acknowledge that particular social groups are more susceptible to poverty and social exclusion. Thus, for example, the progress of under-achieving groups, such as children of Gypsies and Travellers and people who spend time in custody, is being closely monitored,[4] while legislation aims to reduce or eliminate discrimination against disabled pupils in relation to admission to school, college or university or in respect of access to the benefits, facilities and services provided.[5] Extra resources have been targeted at a range of disadvantaged groups which face the greatest risk of social exclusion (a concept discussed below), including ethnic minorities with below average levels of educational attainment: for example, the Ethnic Minorities Achievement Grant involves committed public expenditure of over £150 million per annum.[6] Although the fact that the additional resources are linked only to specific programmes has raised doubts about their capacity to drive systematic overall improvement,[7] these kinds of initiatives, discussed more fully in Chapter 4, represent important ways in which the system has been made to address issues of diversity through positive, targeted support to complement the formal guarantees of equality that anti-discrimination legislation seeks to provide.

This book seeks to explore the ways in which diversity is engaged within the range of policies, institutional structures and legal provisions set in place by the

---

[4] See Chap 4. For example, Ofsted, *Provision and Support for Traveller Pupils* (HMI 455) (London, Ofsted, 2003) notes that Gypsy and Traveller children have overall attendance and attainment levels that fall below those of all other ethnic minorities.

[5] Disability Discrimination Act 1995, as amended by the Special Educational Needs and Disability Act 2001. See Chap 4

[6] DfEE, *Schools: Building Success* Cm 5050 (London, TSO, 2001), para 4.62. See Chap 4.

[7] L Platt, *Parallel Lives?* (London, CPAG, 2002), 151.

wide-ranging education reforms of recent decades. In doing so it is necessary to consider the ways in which these reforms and the attendant legal framework have affected various relationships, including those between different parts of the state and, in particular, between the state and individuals. One important issue concerns the position of parents and children as holders of rights under domestic legislation, for example in relation to access to education, including school choice and provision in respect of special educational needs. These are areas of potential conflict and, in the context of diversity and its impact on children's education, the potential clash between minorities' interests and wider normalising goals in relation to these and other aspects of education may be most acute. Cutting across these conflicts, potentially, is that between children's and parents' rights, which warrants particular attention.

EDUCATION AND DIVERSITY

Education in England and Wales operates in an ethnically and culturally diverse environment. The 2001 UK Census showed that, aside from 41 million people who described themselves as Christians, there were 1.5 million Muslims, 0.5 million Hindus, 0.3 million Sikhs and 0.25 million Jews, together with another 0.3 million of other faiths and 8.5 million of no faith.[8] Around one citizen in 12 belongs to a minority ethnic group and, as a Home Office report has put it, 'no community is truly homogenous.'[9] Ethnic and religious minorities are, however, more heavily concentrated in particular urban areas: for example, in Brent, Newham and Tower Hamlets in London over half the population is classed as Black and minority ethnic, with a range of religions, and in 12 other London districts the proportion exceeds one third, while of the 1,138 neighbourhoods (areas of population of between 30,000 and 50,000 people) across England and Wales as a whole, there are 56 where less than 50 per cent of the population is white British.[10] The non-white British population of England has been estimated as 7.1 million (as at mid-2003), an increase of over 500,000 since mid-2001.[11] In the 0–15 years age group in England, 84 per cent are classed as white British, compared with 39 per cent of this age group in Inner London.[12] In the North-East of England, which has the lowest non-white population, 88 per cent

---

[8] Cited in P Babbs, J Martin and P Hazelwindt (eds), *Focus on Social Inequalities, 2004 Edition* (London, TSO, 2004), Table 7.9.

[9] Home Office, *Strength in Diversity. Towards a Community Cohesion and Race Equality Strategy* (London, Home Office, 2004), paras 1.2 and 1.3.

[10] Ibid.

[11] Office for National Statistics, *Population Estimates By Ethnic Group (Experimental)*, News Release (London, ONS, 2006).

[12] Office for National Statistics, *Population Estimates By Ethnic Group (Experimental)*, (London, ONS, 2006), Table EE2, available at www.statistics.gov.uk/StatBase/Product.asp?vlnk=14238 (26 Jan 2006). These figures are for 2001.

Table 1: Estimated resident population of England aged 0-15 by ethnic group[a]

Ethnic group	Population (0–15 years) (thousands)
All groups	9,908.4
White:	
British	8,328.0
Irish	36.9
Other White	41.2
Mixed:	
White & Black Caribbean	19.1
White & Black African	35.5
White and Asian	88.4
Other Mixed	67.4
Asian or Asian British:	
Indian	237.2
Pakistani	249.8
Bangladeshi	107.3
Other Asian	56.8
Black or Black British:	
Black Caribbean	116.0
Black African	147.3
Other Black	37.0
Chinese or Other Ethnic Group:	
Chinese	40.5
Other	42.0

[a] See note 12. The broad categories are those used by the ONS.

of 0–15-year-olds were white British.[13] The extent of ethnic diversity among this age group can be discerned from the population data in table 1.

Data on school pupils' ethnicity[14] show that, in 2005, 19.5 per cent of primary school pupils and 15.9 per cent of secondary school pupils were classified as being of minority ethnic origin. The contrast with their teachers' ethnicity is quite stark: only 5 per cent of teachers were of minority ethnic origin, rising by

[13] Ibid.
[14] DfES, *National Statistics, First Release, Schools and Pupils in England, January 2005 (Final)*, SFR 42/2005 (London, DfES, 2005), table 5.

just 0.1 per cent by 2006.[15] This suggests that the current Training and Development Agency for Schools target of recruiting 9 per cent of all new teachers from minority ethnic communities by 2008[16] is far too ambitious. The largest minority grouping among pupils in 2005 comprised children of Asian origin, representing 7.5 per cent of all primary school pupils and 6.4 per cent of secondary school pupils, those of Pakistani origin being the largest contingent among this group, at 3.1 per cent of primary school and 2.4 per cent of secondary school pupils. The overall proportion of school pupils from minority ethnic backgrounds is expected to reach 20 per cent by 2010.[17] Of course, it would be wrong to assume that each of the ethnic and/or religious groups is itself homogenous in terms of lifestyle and social attitudes. Across their membership there may be variable levels of commitment to a faith and different values that affect attitudes towards particular aspects of life such as inter-faith marriage, abortion or the role of women.

There is also diversity in terms of sexuality, with an estimated 5–7 per cent of the population being homosexual or bisexual, and disability, which affects some 22 per cent of adults and 5 per cent of children (although, as shown in Chapter 6, around one in five children has a learning difficulty).[18]

Significant challenges are presented not merely as a result of the inherent social disadvantages and exclusion experienced by some of the minority ethnic communities or social groups (see below), but also because of the need for education to respond to diversity by developing policies and practices that recognise the cultural or religious rights of all groups and promote the kind of values concerned with respect for others that enable pluralistic societies to live peacefully and cohesively.[19] States' obligations in this regard are enshrined in international law, as discussed at various points in this book. The ECHR, the key provisions of which are incorporated into UK law via the Human Rights Act 1998, and the UN Convention on the Rights of the Child are of particular significance. The overriding theme of the obligations resting on the state, discussed in later chapters, is that, in the sphere of education, attention must be paid to the autonomy of these distinct communities and, in particular, regard must be paid to the cultural rights and religious freedoms within a pluralistic society.[20] This has a relevance to very many aspects of education, including the existence of faith schools, the curriculum (both religious and secular), school uniform and school admission policies. This dimension has assumed greatly increased importance as

---

[15] DfES, *National Statistics, First Release, School Workforce in England January 2006* (Provisional), SFR 18/2006 (London, DfES, 2006), table 10. In Jan 2006, 2.2 per cent of teachers were of Asian or Asian British origin and 1.7 per cent were Black or Black British: ibid.

[16] Noted in DfES, *Higher Standards, Better Schools for All*, Cm 6677 (London, DfES, 2005), para 8.14.

[17] Learning and Skills Council, *Moving Forward—the Learning and Skills Council's Annual Equality and Diversity Report 2002–2003* (Coventry, Learning and Skills Council, 2004), 19.

[18] Figures cited in Comptroller and Auditor General, *Delivering Public Services to a Diverse Society*, HC 19-I Session 2004–2005 (London, TSO, 2004), para 1.2.

[19] See generally M Cole (ed), *Education, Equality and Human Rights* (London, Routledge Falmer, 2000).

[20] See, eg, C Wright, D Weekes and A McGlaughlin, 'Race', Class and Gender in Exclusion from School* (London, Falmer, 2000).

a result of the Human Rights Act 1998, as illustrated by a range of decisions over the past few years, discussed throughout this book, including *Williamson*,[21] where the House of Lords had to decide whether there was a violation of the human rights of those who favoured the use of corporal punishment at a Christian Fellowship school which, with parental support, wanted to retain this sanction despite the attempt, via statute, to ban it.[22]

Religious groups' freedom as regards the operation of schools in accordance with their cultural values and the tenets of their faith, is discussed in Chapter 7. England and Wales, indeed the UK as a whole, has a long tradition of supporting, via public funding, denominational schools as components of the state education system. The right of religious groups to establish and run faith-based private schools (there are, for example, over 80 independent Muslim schools in Britain[23]) has also been acknowledged. State schools which are classed as denominational in character are assigned to one of three broad categories: voluntary aided, voluntary controlled or foundation (a category that also includes non-denominational schools).[24] Of 21,027 state primary and secondary schools in England in 2005, 4,313 were voluntary aided, 2,681 were voluntary controlled and 49 were religiously-affiliated foundation schools. The remaining 14,142 were non-denominational, and of them 13,154 were community schools.[25] Among

Table 2: Voluntary schools and religiously affiliated foundation primary and secondary schools in England (2005)[a]

Religious affiliation	Total number of schools
Church of England	4,669
Roman Catholic	2,064
Methodist	26
Other Christian	81
Jewish	36
Muslim	5
Sikh	2
Other	2

[a]   See note 25. By September 2006 there were eight maintained Muslim schools.

[21] *R (Williamson) v Secretary of State for Employment* [2005] UKHL 15; [2005] ELR 291; [2005] 2 AC 246.

[22] SSFA 1998, s 131. See further pp 396–99.

[23] Association of Muslim Social Scientists *et al*, *Muslims on Education. A Position Paper* (Richmond, Association of Muslim Social Scientists, 2004), para 2.5.2.

[24] See School Standards and Framework Act 1998, ss 20 and 21. Not all foundation schools are denominational. With regard to funding of state maintained denominational schools, see S Bailey (ed), *Cross on Local Government Law* (London, Sweet and Maxwell, 2005), paras 20–42–20–46. The different categories are explained in Chap 3.

[25] DfES, *National Statistics, First Release, Schools and Pupils in England, January 2005 (Final)*, SFR 42/2005 (London, DfES, 2005), table 8.

religiously affiliated schools, there is a preponderance of Church of England and Roman Catholic schools: see table 2.

The Government broadly supports faith schools, which it says have 'a record of delivering a high-quality of education to their pupils' and a 'clear ethos' that 'many parents welcome'.[26] It proclaims that since 1997 it has 'increased the range of faith schools in the maintained sector, including the first Muslim, Sikh and Greek Orthodox schools'.[27] Around one third of all schools in England are faith based. The religious character of these schools is reinforced by their power to discriminate in favour of people of the particular faith in question for appointment or promotion as teachers within the school, provided the school has been designated (by the Secretary of State) as having a religious character.[28] This power was formally extended to independent schools in 2003.[29] Regardless of a general acceptance that faith schools may play an important role in maintaining religious traditions that are of great importance to some individuals and communities and that the right of religious communities to run such schools is protected within the human rights framework, as noted in Chapter 5, opinions vary as to whether these schools either reinforce social divisions or in fact promote social cohesion by enabling minorities to feel more valued and secure.[30]

As discussed in Chapter 7, independent schools are not obliged to follow the National Curriculum. In the past, and certainly prior to the introduction of a new regulatory framework for independent schools under the Education Act 2002,[31] there have been concerns that some faith schools in the independent sector have adopted too narrow a curriculum.[32] In particular, official inspection has revealed that 'in a minority of independent schools with a religious basis there is still insufficient time allocated to the secular curriculum and the balance is unsatisfactory'.[33] The House of Commons Office of the Deputy Prime Minister Select Committee has recommended that as there may be a tendency for faith schools to be mono-cultural, no new faith schools should be approved unless the school is 'committed to promoting a multicultural agenda.' [34] A report by the

---

[26] DfEE, *Schools: Building Success* Cm 5050 (London, TSO, 2001), para 4.19.

[27] DfEE, *Schools: Achieving Success* (London, TSO, 2001), para 5.30.

[28] School Standards and Framework Act 1998, s 69(3) governs the designation of voluntary schools. The power of a school designated as having a religious character under s 69(3) to discriminate is in s 60 of this Act. It also permits discrimination in relation to remuneration and is also sanctioned in relation to people who attend religious worship in accordance with the tenets of the religion or religious denomination concerned or who give or are willing to give religious education at the school in accordance with those tenets.

[29] Independent Schools (Employment of Teachers in Schools with a Religious Character) Regulations 2003 (SI 2003/2037), inserting s 124B into the SSFA 1998. The designation procedure is set out in the Religious Character of Schools (Designation Procedure) (Independent Schools) (England) Regulations 2003 (SI 2003/2314).

[30] For a useful overview see also W Berliner, 'Wise and Wonderful?', *The Guardian*, 16 Mar 2004.

[31] EA 2002, Part 10. See Chap 7.

[32] See *R v Secretary of State for Education and Science ex p Talmud Torah Machzikei Hadass School Trust, The Times,* 12 Apr 1985.

[33] Office for Standards in Education, *Annual Report of Her Majesty's Chief Inspector of Schools: Standards and Quality in Education 2001/02* (London, Ofsted, 2003), para 445.

[34] Office of the Deputy Prime Minister Housing, Planning, Local Government and the Regions Committee, *Sixth Report of Session 2003–04, Social Cohesion Vol 1*, HC 45-I (London, TSO, 2004), para 61.

Association of Muslim Social Scientists and others challenges this view, however, arguing that 'mono-cultured schools are not necessarily insular and ignorant of other cultures.'[35] It argues that 'the objective of mainstreaming—the fostering of multi-culturally aware children who can engage with non-Muslims in later life—can still be achieved within a methodology that emphasises a separate cultural and religious identity'.[36] These issues are discussed in more depth in Chapter 7.

The education system often brings together the full range of social and cultural groups, yet its success in responding appropriately to diversity has been uneven. For example, some have argued that schools' failure to appreciate and adapt to cultural differences and the diverse needs of the different social groups is a factor in the disproportionately high rate of exclusion of African Caribbean pupils, boys in particular.[37] The relative paucity of teachers from ethnic minorities, noted above, is often seen as an exacerbating factor. The pressure generated by managerialism and market forces, which makes schools results-driven and likely to view '"need" . . . as both problematic and costly',[38] has also hindered progress. The marketisation of education is linked to the issue of choice, which may be founded on the legitimate, principled concerns of parents individually or in groups. As discussed in Chapters 5 and 6, there are rights of choice as to both school admission and special educational provision, but they tend to run up against the barrier of resource constraints that limit the state's duty to respond positively towards parents' religious, philosophical or cultural preferences. An example, discussed in Chapter 6, is the desire that a child with special educational needs is educated in a more expensive setting that meets the parents' wishes.[39] While the state's obligations under the ECHR (Article 2 of Protocol 1) require it to accord parental views due respect, the state is not subservient to the culturally or philosophically driven wishes of parents for the provision of particular forms of education for their child.[40] Thus in the *Belgian Linguistics* case, discussed in Chapters 2 and 7, the European Court of Human Rights upheld the power of the Flemish authorities to refuse French-speaking parents the right to French-medium teaching for their children, contrary to the parents' linguistic and cultural preferences, and to withhold financial support from schools that did not comply with the linguistic requirements, noting that 'the Contracting Parties do not recognise such a right to education as would require them to establish at their own expense, or to subsidise, education of any particular type or at any particular level'.[41]

---

[35] Association of Muslim Social Scientists, n 23 above, para 2.2.7.

[36] Ibid, para 4.1.5.

[37] For a useful review of the evidence see G Lewis, 'Discursive Histories, the Pursuit of Multiculturalism and Social Policy', in G Lewis, S Gewirtz and J Clarke, *Rethinking Social Policy* (London, Open University/Sage, 2000) 258–275.

[38] Wright, Weekes and McGlaughlin, n 20 above, 20.

[39] See, for example, *Simpson v UK* (1989) 64 DR 188.

[40] In *X, Y and Z v Germany*, Appl no 9411/81 (1982) 29 DR 224 the parents were unsuccessful in their claim to a particular form of scientific/mathematical education; and in *W and DM v U.K.* (1984) 37 DR 96 parents failed in their demands for places at single-sex selective schools rather than comprehensive schools with a different ethos.

[41] *Belgian Linguistics (No 2)*, 1 EHRR 252 (1979–80).

Facilities for education—including buildings and teachers—are expensive. It is noteworthy that, for example, although schools and LEAs are under a duty to ensure that a disabled child is not placed, by virtue of his or her disability, at a substantial disadvantage compared to other children without such disability, the statute falls short of requiring them to 'remove or alter a physical feature' or to 'provide auxiliary aids or services'.[42] To take another example, religious groups which prefer single-sex education for their children would find that the state is under no obligation to provide it. Although the state's duty under the Sex Discrimination Act 1975 to ensure equality of provision as between the sexes means that it could be unlawful for a local education authority to have a single-sex school for boys, but not one for girls, or to have an unequal number of single-sex places as between boys and girls,[43] this does not necessarily mean that the deficiency must be remedied by creating more single-sex education. The Court of Appeal, in holding that the Sex Discrimination Act 1975 did not prevent the closure of the only boys' school in Kettering even though single-sex education was available in the area to girls, held that the Act did not require the LEA to maintain provision that was unviable, because if the LEA did so it could not fulfil its statutory duty to ensure that the area had schools which were 'sufficient in number, character and equipment to afford for all pupils opportunities for education . . .'[44] Thus a pupil at the boys' school, whose pupil numbers were falling, was, for this reason, denied judicial review of the LEA's decision to close it. It would have been impossible for the under-subscribed school to maintain its curriculum, within normative resource constraints. In any event, while a religious desire for single-sex schooling would need to be taken into account in the school admission decision-making process,[45] it is unlikely to have primacy as a criterion for admission to a single-sex school unless there is an express provision in the admission policy that gives it a high priority.[46]

Cost is a particular factor where provision for members of another group is concerned, namely those children who have special educational needs. It will be seen in Chapter 6 that, in particular, while it is recognised that around one in six children has special educational needs, this generic label, used in the legislation that defines the duties owed towards such children,[47] in fact relates to children with wide-ranging forms of difficulty or disability in relation to learning, whose collective needs demand a very diverse range of provision. Indeed, there have even been recent attempts via litigation to press the case for gifted children to be treated as having such needs for the purposes of the statutory framework.[48] The

---

[42] Disability Discrimination Act 1995, s 28C(1), (2), as inserted by the Special Educational Needs and Disability Act 2001, s 13.

[43] Sex Discrimination Act 1975, ss 22, 23 and 25 See further *R v Secretary of State for Education and Science ex parte Keating* (1985) 84 LGR 469; *Equal Opportunities Commission v Birmingham City Council* [1989] 1 All ER 769; *R v Secretary of State for Education and Science ex parte Malik* [1992] COD 31; *R v Birmingham City Council ex parte Equal Opportunities Commission (No 2)* [1994] ELR 282 (CA).

[44] EA 1980, s 8; see now EA 1996, s 14, which refers to 'the opportunity of appropriate education'.

[45] *R (K) v London Borough of Newham* [2002] ELR 390.

[46] *Choudhury v Governors of Bishop Challoner Roman Catholic School* [1992] 3 All ER 277 (HL).

[47] Currently the EA 1996, Part IV, as amended. S 312 defines special educational needs: see Chap 6.

[48] See below pp 327–28.

needs and requirements of a minority of children with special educational needs are such that a 'statement' should be drawn up by a local education authority (LEA), specifying the provision required and identifying the child's needs.[49] Even children who do not require a statement may need an individual education plan to be drawn up by the school. This, then, is the area of educational provision where the most tailoring of provision to meet individual needs occurs. It is also an area where, as indicated above, needs and resources are most likely to come into conflict, not least because some of the best specialist provision for children with particular forms of disability, such as autism or psychological problems, is available in the private sector. The LEA could thereby face considerable extra expense in funding a placement.

While the law has long sought to accommodate the diverse needs of children with special educational needs, there is also, increasingly, a more general rejection of the 'one size fits all' approach to educational provision, particularly in the context of secondary education. The remark a few years ago by the Labour Party's former media director, Alistair Campbell, about 'bog standard' comprehensive schools still resonates. In addition to 'specialist school' status, which the Government wishes all secondary schools to acquire (see Chapter 3), there are opportunities for schools to be established as academies,[50] having a distinctive ethos, with sponsorship from private voluntary or faith groups. More flexibility has also been introduced into the curriculum via statutory amendments, particularly for those aged 14 or over;[51] and provision in learning support units for disaffected children is being extended. Schools that are deemed successful have been given the opportunity, via the Education Act 2002, to 'earn' greater autonomy, including exemption from particular curricular requirements, enabling them to adopt innovative thinking and a distinctive approach.[52] The theory is that allowing schools more autonomy provides them with an incentive to innovate and adapt provision to make it more consistent with the school's ethos and more adaptive to pupils' needs, thereby bringing about overall improvements in the drive for excellence for all children. The idea behind these kinds of developments is that as diversity of provision develops it will help the schools system in 'responding to individual needs and to different groups in society'.[53]

Yet it is not clear how far the education system can become more responsive to the needs of each individual pupil. While, for example, the curriculum is becoming more flexible, most school pupils will still be taught in accordance with the legislatively prescribed National Curriculum during most of their school years.[54] Moreover, there is still a strong emphasis on a common approach to the instilling of particular values, as reflected in the National Curriculum specifications for Citizenship and in the legislation and official guidance on sex and

[49] Ibid, s 324: see Chap 6.
[50] EA 1996, s 482, as substituted by the EA 2002, s 65.
[51] See Chap 7.
[52] EA 2002, ss 6–9; DfEE, *Schools: Achieving Success* (London, TSO, 2001), ch 5. See further Chap 3.
[53] Ibid (DfEE), para 5.7.
[54] The basic statutory framework is in the EA 2002, Part 6. See further Chap 7.

relationship education.[55] Indeed, this raises important questions concerned not only with cultural diversity, but also with the rights and autonomy of the child and the governance of childhood. This is discussed more fully in Chapter 2, but it can be noted here that, within the field of education, limits to the recognition of children's diversity and their autonomy are set by the ways in which pupils are categorised or labelled for legal and policy purposes. As Monk explains, attempts to respond to particular educational phenomena which are relativist in nature, such as a difficulty in learning or engagement in inappropriate behaviour, are made via legal constructs for the governance of childhood that tend to over-simplify the particular issues.[56] Thus, for example, responding to a child's behaviour may simply become a matter of deciding whether the child should or should not remain in a particular school rather than looking at the underlying causes of the behaviour, while for a child who experiences difficulty in learning, 'complex medical and psychosocial issues . . . are dramatically simplified so that a child is classified as a child either with or without a special educational need'.[57] Monk concludes that 'one of the challenges facing policy-makers is to develop reflexive structures that preclude oversimplification and systematic colonisation of the issues to include a genuine form of child responsiveness'.[58] Separately, he makes a similar point about sex education programmes operated by education or health professionals, which may reinforce the notion of the child 'as ideally non-sexual' or of acting in a healthy or unhealthy way.[59]

The question of identifying and responding to the needs of individual children, such as those with a special educational need or a disability, gives rise to what is referred to in debates about special and inclusive education as the 'dilemma of difference'. This comprises:

> the seemingly unavoidable choice between, on the one hand, identifying children's dif-
> ferences in order to provide for them differentially, with the risk of labelling and
> dividing, and, on the other hand, accentuating 'sameness' and offering common provi-
> sion, with the risk of not making available what is relevant to, and needed by,
> individual children.[60]

It shows that the way that the education system responds to diversity can be problematic. In particular, there in an argument that the systems that are set in place for responding to individual needs, which necessarily involve classifying particular children for statutory purposes as, for example, having special educational needs or a disability, might aim to enhance equality of opportunity for the individual, but can accentuate difference and thereby hinder social

---

[55] See Chap 7.

[56] D Monk, 'Theorising Education Law and Childhood: Constructing the Ideal Pupil' (2000) 21 *Br Journal of Sociology of Education* 355.

[57] Ibid, 364.

[58] Ibid, 367.

[59] D Monk, 'Health and Education: Conflicting Programmes for Sex Education' in E. Heinze (ed), *Of Innocence and Autonomy. Children, Sex and Human Rights* (Aldershot, Dartmoth, 2000) 179–194.

[60] L Terzi, 'Beyond the Dilemma of Difference: The Capability Approach to Disability and Special Educational Needs' (2005) 39(3) *Journal of the Philosophy of Education* 443, at 444.

inclusion.[61] Furthermore, while an individualised focus is clearly desirable, the prevalent view is that in relation to those with a disability it should not be based on the 'individual' or 'essentialist' model of disability but rather on the 'social' model, which is seen as consistent with the idea that being 'disabled' reflects a 'condition of society' rather than an individual's (presumed) incapability.[62] In the social model, disability is a social construct defined with reference to the disadvantage or restriction of activity that a person with a disability suffers within the current framework of social organisation, while the individual model is based on the idea that there is 'something wrong with the individual . . . cannot see, cannot hear, cannot walk, has Down's syndrome, has a mental illness, and so on'.[63]

There is an inherent tension here that Terzi argues can be resolved by looking at approaches to diversity through the prism of Sen's 'capability' approach.[64] It is appropriate to consider it here, because this approach specifically addresses the issue of equality in the context of human diversity and has a particular relevance to education.[65] Human diversity, according to Sen, arises from a range of factors: personal characteristics, such as physical or mental health or abilities, age and gender; external factors, such as family circumstances (wealth, culture, religion) and physical environment; and, in a person's capacity to achieve various 'functionings' which form a valued part of life and are critical to well-being, through the exercise of freedoms and choices.[66] Deakin and Browne apply the capability approach to the capacity to utilise a commodity, which is contingent upon both the individual's own personal resources and characteristics and social factors such as 'access to health care, education and other resources which equip them to enter into relations of exchange with others'.[67] Applying this approach specifically to disability, Terzi argues that it 'allows the overcoming of the duality between the individual and social models of disability and sees disability only instead as inherently relational'—in other words, relating both to individual impairment and the design of the relevant social institutions.[68] Terzi gives the example of the blind person whose visual impairment only becomes a disability in the context of computer use when Braille displays or speech output screen readers, which would enable the relevant functionings (work, leisure, consumer activity) to take place, are needed. Similarly, while dyslexia is disabling in the context of education that involves literacy (as, in fact, much of it does), it would not disadvantage a child in relation to physical education. Terzi argues that the

---

[61] See Chap 4.

[62] The social model is also contrasted with the medical model, which basically relates to the specific kind of disablement, as medically defined. See further Chap 4 at p 174.

[63] J Swain *et al*, *Controversial Issues in a Disabling Society* (Buckingham, Open University Press, 2003), 1.

[64] A Sen, *Inequality Re-examined* (Oxford, Clarendon Press, 1992).

[65] See M Walker, 'Towards a Capability-based Theory of Social Justice for Education Policy-making' (2006) 21 *Journal of Education Policy* 163.

[66] Sen, n 64 above, 1–28.

[67] S Deakin and J Browne, 'Social Rights and Market Order: Adapting the Capability Approach', in TK Hervey and J Kenner (eds), *Economic and Social Rights under the EU Charter of Fundamental Rights—A Legal Perspective* (Oxford, Hart, 2003), 27 at 34.

[68] Terzi, n 60 above, at 451.

capability approach promotes egalitarianism since it avoids unilateralist conceptions of disability, as for example related to biological or social causes, and instead enables disability to be perceived 'in the light of the distributive pattern of relevant capability', which has 'fundamental consequences for the design of educational policies and schooling systems'.[69]

What the capability approach shows us is that the education system caters for a far greater range of human diversity than that represented by the traditional labels. Indeed, those labels can be dangerous in placing an emphasis on a singular basis of identification when school pupils often have multiple identities. Some pupils may be officially classed as disabled, but because they may belong to more than one social group they may be at risk of multiple discrimination.[70] This was confirmed by a survey of disabled people which also examined the effect of their gender, ethnicity or sexuality on their treatment by others.[71] In fact, not all of the identities had equal impact upon personal experience. Some disabled school pupils, for example, reported that racism was the principal cause of negative school experiences, while '[d]isability was often the only issue which raised problems for lesbian and gay disabled people at school'.[72] The statement in the 2005 schools White Paper that 'all classes contain pupils with a range of abilities and attainments, different interests and motivation, and different home and background circumstances'[73] only begins to describe the diversity of the pupil population. That heterogeneity does justify attempts to focus on the needs of individual children, as in the White Paper's emphasis on 'personalised learning' and 'tailored teaching'. But it appears disingenuous, given the known limits to the flexibility that is possible in order to respond appropriately to the full range of pupils. As is illustrated by the case of provision for pupils with special educational needs, notwithstanding the extreme diversity of this group in itself, while there are statutory duties on schools to make the required provision to meet the individual's special educational needs,[74] policy and resource considerations often determine that broad brush approaches to definitions of need and especially provision to meet it are necessary, as noted above.

Recognition of diversity in the context of education is also encouraged by Article 29 of the UNCRC, which seems to address the individual child in its injunction to states to direct education towards, inter alia, 'the development of the child's personality, talents and mental and physical abilities their fullest potential'. However, it is only aspirational and cannot be enforced by individuals. Similarly, LEAs in England and Wales have a broad duty to secure that 'efficient primary education, secondary education and further education are available to meet the needs of the population of their area'[75] and to ensure that there are

---

[69] Ibid.

[70] See J Swain, S French and C Cameron, with A Vernon, 'A Dividing Society?', in Swain *et al*, above n 63, at 57–8.

[71] D Molloy *et al*, *Diversity in Disability*, DWP Research Report 188 (Leeds, Corporate Document Services, 2003).

[72] Ibid, 88–9.

[73] Department for Education and Skills, *Higher Standards, Better Schools for All*, Cm 6677 (London, TSO, 2005), para 4.37.

[74] EA 1996, s 317(1).

[75] Ibid, s 13.

sufficient schools to provide for all pupils the opportunity of an 'appropriate education', meaning:

> education which offers such variety of instruction and training as may be desirable in view of—
> (a) the pupils' different ages, abilities and aptitudes, and
> (b) the different periods for which they may be expected to remain at school.[76]

The statutory aims for the school curriculum, discussed in Chapter 7, similarly focus on ensuring that the curriculum promotes 'the spiritual, moral, cultural, mental and physical development of pupils at the school and of society'.[77] Yet, taken as a whole, and notwithstanding the various additional provisions aimed at curbing discrimination in relation to gender, race/ethnicity and disability, the law generally fails to address the full extent of diversity in the context of education, certainly in the broad 'capability' sense discussed above.

As we shall see in later chapters, pupils and their families face enormous difficulties in challenging any failures arising from the education system's inability to meet what they perceive to be their individual culturally-driven needs or philosophically-based wishes or to redress structural inequalities that affect them. Various areas of the education system have traditionally operated what Kymlicka and Norman refer to as 'difference-blind rules' and multicultural approaches which, by aiming to treat everyone the same regardless of background, in fact result in disadvantage to particular groups.[78] Examples, both discussed in Chapter 4, would be the university admissions system, which has increasingly come under pressure to reduce barriers to access stemming from social status or ethnic background, and headteachers' statutory power to exclude pupils as a disciplinary sanction.[79] Kymlicka and Norman argue that those who espouse multiculturalism and difference-blind institutions are under growing pressure to 'show that the status quo does not create injustices for minority groups and their members'.[80]

Among other specific problems for the law in acknowledging or responding to diversity is that of separating children's identities from those of their parents or adults in general. This brings into focus the whole issue of children's rights in and to education, which is a subject addressed further in Chapter 2 and in other chapters. Moreover, in a multicultural society where school pupils come from ethnically and culturally diverse family backgrounds, the interaction between home and school is a particularly important issue. As a Home Office report on religious discrimination explained, the school system is:

---

[76] Ibid, s 14(1)–(3).
[77] EA 2002, s 79(1).
[78] W Kymlicka and W Norman, 'Citizenship in Culturally Diverse Societies: Issues, Contexts, Concepts', in W Kymlicka and W Norman, *Citizenship in Diverse Societies* (Oxford, Oxford University Press, 2000), at 4.
[79] EA 2002, s 52.
[80] Ibid.

an arena within which family traditions and identities come into interaction with the beliefs and values of the wider and more diverse society. Such interaction can result in significant tensions for parents, children and teachers alike.[81]

Conflict can arise over, for example, the school curriculum. To cite just a few examples at this point, highlighted by the report's survey, there have been complaints arising from the problems some ethnic minorities have with regard to the use of early reading books where children have to recite the word 'pig' or with art classes involving the visual representation of living forms, which have resulted in some children feeling unable to take home artwork they had prepared in school.[82] This matter is explored in detail in Chapters 2 and 7, but a brief discussion is needed here.

We can take the example of a child's parents who want their child to be excused from mixed-sex drama lessons on religious grounds; the child wants to participate, not wanting to stand out from his or her peers; and the school considers the activity to be educationally beneficial. Let us also accept unquestioningly, for this purpose, the basic proposition that the education system follows what Jones refers to as an 'intercultural' approach, acknowledging 'minorities' rights to forms of schooling they find appropriate to their needs'.[83] In the case of the drama lessons, the conflict is not merely between the child's and the parents' separate rights to a particular form of education, but also between the majority's right to promote its cultural values and the minority group in question's right to preserve its own. In relation to sex education or religious education in England and Wales, the uneasy compromise has involved giving individual parents a statutory right to withdraw their child from the relevant classes.[84] The parents may well regard the education system as a threat to their cultural identity because of its potential role in the assimilation of their children into the dominant culture. However, some might argue that, as Merry explains, 'there is no reason to believe that learning about how others live or understanding different culturally specific notions of good will threaten a child's ability to remain firmly ensconced within her culture or to remain committed to its core values'.[85] Either way, this gives rise to difficult questions concerning competing liberal values, whereby the state recognises the rights, freedoms and choices of individuals and social groups, but at the same time seeks to promote overriding social objectives such as preparing children for life as citizens in wider society.[86] This inevitably gives rise to some limitation on the rights of minorities

[81] P Weller, A Feldman and K Purdam, *Religious Discrimination in England and Wales*, Home Office Research Study 220 (London, Home Office, 2001) 23.

[82] Ibid, Chap 3.

[83] C Jones, 'State Education and Minority Rights', in Minority Rights Group, *Education Rights and Minorities* (Florence, UNICEF, 1994) 7 at 8.

[84] EA 1996, s 405 and the SSFA 1998, s 71. See Chap 7.

[85] MS Merry, 'Cultural Coherence and the Schooling for Identity Maintenance' (2005) 39 *Journal of the Philosophy of Education* 477 at 484.

[86] See S Macedo, 'Liberal Civic Education and Religious Fundamentalism: The Case of God v John Rawls' (1995) 105 *Ethics* 468; C Glenn and J De Groof, *Finding the Right Balance. Freedom, Autonomy and Accountability in Education* (Utrecht, Lemma, 2002). See also A Bradney, 'Ethnicity, Religion and Sex Education' in N Harris (ed), *Children, Sex Education and the Law* (London, National Children's Bureau, 1996) 87–98.

within the national sphere, as explained in Kymlicka's liberal theory of minority rights. This asserts that immigrant communities should enjoy rights that enable them to preserve their cultural distinctiveness and pride whilst also enjoying the capacity to participate in economic and political institutions of the dominant society.[87] It also means that members of minority groups should have the freedom to distance themselves from aspects of their own community's culture, and thus to make choices.[88] Kymlicka envisages education policies as having a role in this process. But that role has come into question in both the UK and, especially, the United States, where some important litigation has arisen on this issue.[89]

It is also the case that upholding minority rights in education in reality involves recognising the rights of parents rather than those of children; indeed their respective interests are treated as indistinguishable. In one of the cases discussed in Chapter 7, *Wisconsin v Yoder*,[90] the US Supreme Court upheld the right of Amish parents to discontinue their children's public education beyond the eighth grade (the parents said it would conflict with their values and way of life) on the basis that, despite the importance of education to a democratic society, there was an infringement of the First Amendment prohibition on state interference with the free exercise of religion. Macedo comments that 'to allow Amish parents to withdraw their children from high school could thwart the children's ability to make adequately informed decisions about how to live their lives'.[91] The place of children's rights will, in itself, accord with the position of some faith groups in relation to the governance of childhood. The overall effect on children's rights in education in general is that the protection of minorities' rights may be an important factor in promoting and preserving parental rights and authority at the expense of the rights of the child. This issue is also discussed in later chapters.

Thus far the discussion has been concerned with aspects of social and cultural diversity and some of the key problems that the state education system experiences in responding to them. In order to understand why it is important that diversity is appropriately addressed by education law and policy it is necessary to examine more fully the role that the modern education system is expected to perform.

---

[87] W Kymlicka, *Multiculural Citizenship: A Liberal Theory of Minority Rights* (Oxford, Oxford University Press, 1995), 30–1.

[88] Ibid, 80–91.

[89] In particular, *Wisconsin v Yoder*, 406 US 205 (1972); *Mozert v Hawkins County Bd. of Education*, 827 F2d 1058 (6th Cir 1987). See Chap 7.

[90] 406 US 205 (1972).

[91] Macedo, above n 86, at 488. See also B Barry, *Culture and Equality* (Cambridge: Polity, 2001) 201.

THE ROLE OF EDUCATION

The state education system has developed from its humble beginnings under the Elementary Education Act 1870 into a major social institution. Formal education is a basic part of modern social organisation. In England some eight million children and young people are in full-time education in schools[92] for up to 189 days in each school year[93] and will spend at least 11 successive years of their life receiving formal education. The whole process of education and its entire institutional framework are today the subject of a detailed and elaborate legislative regime the complexity of which is growing as policy places an increasing emphasis on diversity of provision and public–private partnerships.[94] Yet it should not be forgotten that education is also regarded as a primary duty of parenthood. This moral imperative was acknowledged by Blackstone[95] and is reflected today both in the legal concept of parental responsibility[96] and in the statutory duty of the 'parent of every child of compulsory school age [to] cause him to receive efficient full-time education suitable . . . to his age, ability and aptitude, and . . . to any special educational needs he may have, either by regular attendance at school or otherwise'.[97] The importance of education is also reflected in its protection as a human right under international law,[98] including the ECHR, which provides in Article 2 of Protocol 1 that '[n]o-one may be denied the right to education'.[99] The recognition of education as a right is not incompatible with the parent's underlying responsibility, however. Indeed, with reference to the second sentence of the Article, which requires the state to respect parents' right to ensure that teaching and education is 'in conformity with their own religious and philosophical convictions', the European Court of Human Rights noted in *Kjeldsen* that it was 'in the discharge of a natural duty towards their children—parents being primarily responsible for the "education and teaching" of their children—that parents may require the State to respect their religious and philosophical convictions'.[100]

Yet the modern state is seen as having a fundamental role in ensuring that children receive an education that equips them for later life and reflects the

[92] Department for Education and Skills, *National Statistics First Release. Schools and Pupils in England. January 2005 (Final)*, SFR 42/2005 (London, DfES, 2005), table 1.
[93] The Education (School Day and School Year) (England) Regulations 1999 (SI 1999/3181), as amended by SI 2001/1429, provide for the school year to comprise 378 sessions, at two per day (with lunch break in the middle of the day).
[94] See Chap 3.
[95] '[I]t is not easy to imagine or allow, that a parent has conferred any considerable benefit upon his child, by bringing him into the world; if he afterwards entirely neglects his culture and education, and suffers him to grow up like a mere beast, to lead a life useless to others, and shameful to himself': W Blackstone, *Commentaries on the Laws of England* (London, W Walker, 1826), i, pt 451.
[96] Children Act 1989, s 3; R White, P Carr and N Lowe, *The Children Act in Practice* (3rd edn, London, Butterworths, 2002), para 3.38.
[97] EA 1996, s 7.
[98] See Chap 2.
[99] See further ibid.
[100] *Kjeldsen, Busk Madsen and Pedersen* 1 EHRR 711 (1976), at para 52, referring to the second sentence of Art 2 of Prot 1.

principal common values, social and moral, of the nation. In this regard, the UN Convention on the Rights of the Child (UNCRC) directs the state's attention to particular humanistic values to which education should be directed.[101] These provisions recognise the centrality of education to the social and intellectual development of children and its role in the process of socialisation. Durkheim said that:

> [s]ociety can survive only if there exists among its members a sufficient a sufficient degree of homogeneity; education perpetuates and reinforces this homogeneity by fixing in the child, from the beginning, the essential similarities that collective life demands.[102]

While the UNCRC identifies what are indeed common values that democratic societies would regard as part of the 'conscience collective' which Durkheim talked about, they also acknowledge the plurality and diversity of modern societies, not only in the provision made for the child's right to 'enjoy his or her own culture, to profess and practise his her own religion',[103] but also in the way that education should prepare pupils for life as a citizen. Although the right to education is considered in detail in Chapter 2, it is important to highlight here two matters to which, under Article 29(1) of the UNCRC, the education of the child should be directed by States Parties:

> (c) The development of respect for the child's parents, his or her cultural identity, language and values, for the national values of the country in which the child is living, the country from which he or she may originate, and for civilizations different from his or her own.

> (d) The preparation of the child for responsible life in a free society, in the spirit of understanding, peace, tolerance, equality of sexes, and friendship among all peoples, ethnic, national and religious groups and persons of indigenous origin.

These provisions acknowledge that while education can and does operate as a homogenising force within modern societies, individual societies are marked by diversity. Furthermore, education is clearly recognised as having the potential to reduce some of the tensions resulting from the divisions within them, including those arising from inequality. As with the ECHR, the UNCRC aims to protect the enjoyment of the Convention rights, including the rights concerned with education,[104] without discrimination on various grounds, including sex, race, ethnicity, property, religion and disability.[105] Having regard also to the duty to ensure education in conformity with parents' own religious and philosophical convictions, noted above,[106] it is clear that education must take account of social

---

[101] Art 29. See further Chap 2.
[102] E Durkheim, *Education and Sociology* (London, The Free Press, 1968) 70.
[103] UNCRC, Art 30.
[104] The child's right to education is protected by Art 28; see Chap 2.
[105] Art 2.
[106] Art 2 of Prot 1 (second sentence).

diversity in addition to the need for an inclusive society. The universality of these human rights provisions fits well with the ideology of social inclusion: all children must be educated, and, acknowledging the socialisation role of schooling, education must be directed at preparing the child for adult life as a responsible, informed and tolerant member of society.[107]

What the universality of these education rights fails fully to acknowledge, however, is the way that social factors affect the extent to which the benefits of educational provision can be realised and the fact that the various aims and objectives that are reflected in the posited international human rights norms tend by their nature to be aspirational and offer few guarantees concerning their realisation. Requiring education to seek to inculcate respect for persons of different racial origins, for example, while vitally important, is unlikely to prevent the social exclusion many children and adults from ethnic minorities experience—as, for example, in the disproportionate incidence of low educational attainment and heightened risk of exclusion from school among African Caribbean children and those of mixed white and black Caribbean origin in England, especially males, relative to most other groups.[108] Even the provision of free education, and the legally enforceable duty on parents to ensure that the child receives a suitable education (above), does not prevent substantial numbers of young people from missing out on education, such as through truanting. The most common characteristics among truants, apart from age (a majority are in the 14–16 age group) are that they tend to be from poorer backgrounds, live in local authority housing and have parents who are in low-skilled employment.[109] Truancy has a particularly detrimental impact on educational attainment,[110] compounding the educational disadvantage experienced by those from poorer backgrounds.[111] To cite another example, research has shown that children from homeless families, including those living in temporary accommodation, can also miss a significant amount of schooling due to the disrupted pattern of living and strained social circumstances and that 'homelessness generally has an adverse effect on education progress'.[112] Thus problems with education form part of the cycle of deprivation that affects the socially disadvantaged.

It was noted earlier that Article 29 of the UNCRC also calls on States Parties to direct the child's education towards the development of, inter alia, the child's talents and abilities to their 'fullest potential'. If this is to be achieved within a

---

[107] See UNCRC, *The Aims of Education*, CRC/GC/2001/1 (General Comments) (Geneva, United Nations, 2001).

[108] See generally L Platt, *Parallel Lives?* (London, CPAG, 2002) and DfES, *Permanent and Fixed Period Exclusions from Schools and Exclusion Appeals in England, 2004/05*, SFR 24/2006 (London, DfES, 2006), Chart B and Tables 4 and 7. The exclusion rate is highest among Gypsy/Roma and Travellers of Irish Heritage, although the numbers recorded for the latter group are small, so caution is needed.

[109] P Babb, J Martin and P Haezewindt (eds), *Focus on Social Inequalities, 2004 Edition* (London, TSO, 2004) 14.

[110] See M Morris and S Rutt, *An Analysis of Pupil Attendance Data in Excellence in Cities (EIC) Areas and Non-EIC EAZs*, Research Report RR 657 (London, DfES, 2005).

[111] E Tanner *et al*, *The Costs of Education* (London, CPAG, 2003), 1.

[112] S Power, G Whitty and D Youdell, *No Place to Learn. Homelessness and Education* (London, Shelter, 1995) 57.

diverse and unequal society significant measures will need to be taken. The most significant of those introduced in England and Wales are discussed in Chapter 4. The underlying policy commitment to achieve the goal of realising the potential of all regardless of their background is reflected in the Education and Inspections Bill 2006, which aims to impose a general duty on LEAs to exercise their functions relating to education with a view to 'promoting high standards' and 'promoting the fulfilment by every child concerned of his educational potential'.[113] Some progress in improving educational attainment levels among young people has occurred since Labour was returned to power in 1997. For example, the proportion of 11-year-olds in England reaching the expected attainment level for their age in reading rose from 67 per cent that year to 83 per cent in 2004; and the proportion of pupils reaching five or more A*–C grades at GCSE rose from 46.3 per cent to 55.7 per cent between 1997–8 and 2004–5.[114] However, by 2004, there were still as many as 25 per cent of 16-year-olds who left school without a single GCSE graded above a D; and 6 per cent of the age group left without any qualifications at all.[115] But it is the 'achievement gap' between those from different backgrounds that is the biggest cause of concern and the Government has committed itself to closing it.[116]

The principal factors in the achievement gap are poverty and deprivation and, in relation to some groups, ethnicity. Indeed, according a recent UNICEF report, '[t]he social and economic circumstances of parents is an overwhelming indicator of educational achievement, such that, among all OECD countries, differences between children's achievements within a country are significantly wider than those between countries'.[117] In England, approximately 17 per cent of pupils at nursery or primary schools, 14 per cent of pupils at secondary schools and 34 per cent of pupils at special schools are eligible for free school meals,[118] which LEAs (or in some cases school governing bodies) are under a duty to ensure are provided to those in receipt of various income-related welfare benefits or tax credits.[119] In 2003, of those 11-year-olds who attended a school where at least one third of pupils were in receipt of free school meals, around 40 per cent failed to reach the expected level of attainment (level 4) in Mathematics

---

[113] Education and Inspections Bill 2006 (as first published), cl 1, inserting EA 1996, s 13A. This duty will apply in respect of children of compulsory school age, being educated at school or otherwise, and those above that age but under 20 who are being educated at a school: ibid.

[114] DfES, *Statistical First Release 46/2005, GCSE and Equivalent Results for Young People in England, 2004–05 (Provisional)* (London, DfES, 2005).

[115] G Palmer *et al*, *Monitoring Poverty and Social Exclusion 2004* (York, Joseph Rowntree Foundation, 2004) 22.

[116] HM Treasury, *Child Poverty Review* (July 2004), available at www.hm-treasury.gov.uk (5 Jan 2005), para 5.23.

[117] G Lansdown, *The Evolving Capacities of the Child* (Florence, UNICEF, 2005) 19–20.

[118] DfES, *National Statistics, First Release, Schools and Pupils in England, January 2005 (Final)*, SFR 42/2005 (London, DfES, 2005), tables 3a–3c.

[119] EA 1996, ss 512, 512ZA, 512ZB and 512A; the Education (Prescribed Tax Credits) (England) Order 2003 (SI 2003/383) and same (Wales) Order 2003 (SI 2003/879) (W.10); the Education (Transfer of Functions Concerning School Lunches, etc) (England) (No.2) Order 1999 (SI 1999/2164), as amended, and the same (Wales) (No2) Order 1999 (SI 1999/1779).

or English, compared to approximately 25 per cent across all schools.[120] More complete figures for the numbers who reached the expected level of attainment for their age group at age 11 in English, Mathematics and Science in 2002 show that the average attainment gap between the proportion of children receiving free school meals and other children in each of these subjects was 11 per cent, 8 per cent and 7 per cent respectively; by age 14 (end of key stage 3), the gap had widened to 14 per cent, 12 per cent and 16 per cent respectively.[121] In schools in the areas of greatest socio-economic disadvantage, the pupils are 50 per cent or less likely to achieve five or more GCSE passes at grades A*–C than the national average.[122] At 'A' level, around 43 per cent of pupils from the higher socio-economic groups pass two or more subjects, while among those from lower socio-economic backgrounds the equivalent rate is 19 per cent.[123] Similar disparities appear in the progress of pupils from different ethnic groups, with those defined as Black Caribbean, Black Other or Mixed White/Black Caribbean performing significantly less well than other groups (apart from Roma and other Travellers) up to and including GCSE.[124] Black boys are a particular concern in this regard, leading the chairman of the Commission for Racial Equality, Trevor Phillips, to make the controversial suggestion that they should be taught separately with a view to raising their levels of achievement.[125] Girls outperform boys in National Curriculum assessments and at GCSE across all ethnic groups, apart from Roma at GCSE.[126] Overall, in 2004–5 only 52 per cent of boys obtained at least five GCSE passes at grades A*–C compared with 62 per cent of girls.[127]

These kinds of disparities, which led the UN Committee on the Rights of the Child to highlight 'the sharp differences in educational outcomes for children according to their socio-economic background and to other factors such as gender, disability, ethnic origin or care status' and to recommend that the UK

---

[120] Palmer *et al*, n 115 above, 23. (It is assumed that special schools, catering for those with various forms of learning difficulty, were excluded from these figures.) Almost all of the data showing educational attainment among disadvantaged pupils is based on pupils receiving free school meals, even though '[c]omparing these students with others is an extremely crude way of measuring the attainment gap': J Blanden and S McNally, 'Minding the Gap: Child Poverty and Educational Attainment' (2006) 123 *Poverty* 10.

[121] Department for Education and Skills, *Statistics of Education. Pupils Progress by Pupil Characteristics: 2002* (London, DfES, 2003), tables 19 and 20.

[122] Cited in J Flaherty, J Veit-Wilson and P Dornan, *Poverty: the Facts* (5th edn, London, CPAG, 2004) 153. Ironically, analysis of Census findings has revealed that areas with the highest proportion of young people with no qualifications are in general those with the lowest number of available teachers per head of population: Joseph Rowntree Foundation, 'The Relationship between Poverty, Affluence and Area', *Findings*, Sep 2005, 3.

[123] Department for Education and Skills, *The Future of Higher Education*, Cm 5735 (London, TSO, 2003), para 6.3.

[124] Department for Education and Skills, *National Curriculum Assessment, GCSE and Equivalent Attainment and Post-16 Attainment by Pupil Characteristics in England 2004* (London, DfES (National Statistics), 2005), tables 1–3. See also Babb *et al*, n 109 above, 11.

[125] See Anon, 'Boost for Campaign to Segregate Black Boys', *The Times*, 2 June 2005.

[126] Department for Education and Skills, n 124 above, tables 1–3; Babb *et al*, n 109 above, 11.

[127] DfES, National Statistics First Release, *GCSE and Equivalent Results and Associated Value Added Measures for Young People in England 2004/05 (Revised)* (London, DFES, 2006), table 1.

Government take 'all necessary measures' to eliminate them,[128] are not unique to this country. For example, a report by the Council of Europe notes that right across the continent, '[s]tudents from low income families and students from families that are poor for a long time show lower performance in standardised achievement tests than students from high income families'.[129] In Central European countries, 66 per cent of the poor have not progressed beyond primary education level.[130] In the Netherlands, pupils of Turkish or Moroccan origin have lower than average attainment levels, higher than average truancy rates and are more likely to leave school early, while in Germany pupils of migrant origin are more than twice as likely as non-migrants to leave school without any formal qualifications.[131] In the United States, where similar disparities exist, the No Child Left Behind Act 2001 is designed to ensure, through measures such as prescribed standards, annual state-wide progress objectives, monitoring of different social groups' progress, corrective central powers and parental rights to transfer their children from persistently failing schools, that the impact of factors such as poverty, race/ethnicity and disability on educational attainment is significantly lessened. The aim is that all groups of state school pupils reach appropriate levels of proficiency in reading and mathematics within 12 years of the enactment of the legislation.[132] States must set tests aligned to standards they are required to determine in particular subjects and the tests must identify the progress made by minority ethnic groups, pupils with disabilities, those from poor families and those with limited proficiency in English. Thus it is increasingly recognised both by individual nations and in international fora, such as the UN Committee on the Rights of the Child,[133] that there is a need to address the barriers to educational attainment that affect the social disadvantaged.

Education and Social Exclusion

While the education system cannot eliminate social and economic inequalities by itself, it can contribute to their reduction. Gewirth explains how education is a prime means for the development of 'productive agency', meaning the capacity for self-support and self-sufficiency, and 'additive values' (intellectual, cultural, aesthetic and so on) that promote individual well-being.[134] Education policies

---

[128] UN Committee on the Rights of the Child, *Concluding Observations: United Kingdom of Great Britain and Northern Ireland*, CRC/C/15/Add.188, 9 Oct 2002, para 47.

[129] A Furlong, B Stadler and A Azzopardi, *Vulnerable Youth: Perspectives on Vulnerability in Education, Employment and Leisure in Europe* (Strasbourg, Council of Europe, 2000) 21.

[130] N Vandycke, *Access to Education for the Poor In Europe and Central Asia. Preliminary Evidence and Policy Implications* (Washington, DC, World Bank, 2001) 7.

[131] Ibid, 22.

[132] For critical analysis of the policy, see PE Peterson and MR West (eds), *No Child Left Behind? The Politics and Practice of Accountability* (Washington, DC, Brookings Institution Press, 2003).

[133] See L Lundy, 'Schoolchildren and Health: The Role of International Human Rights Law' in N Harris and P Meredith (eds), *Children, Education and Health. International Perspectives on Law and Policy* (Aldershot, Ashgate, 2005), 3.

[134] A Gewirth, *The Community of Rights* (Chicago, University of Chicago Press, 1996) 132, 149–50.

(he cites the Project Head Start policy for children in the US in the 1960s) can have an 'equalizing impact'.[135] In fact, across Western societies the role of the education system has been broadened over the past 50 years in response to social changes that are associated with such inequalities. Lawrence, for example, explains how the social and political problems of the 1960s and 1970s in the US presented challenges to education as schools were increasingly expected to assist young people 'in personal and social adjustment'.[136] He notes that in the 1960s new laws were enacted supporting education and that the legislation had among its goals 'the use of school to address social problems such as poverty, unemployment, crime, violence, and racial discrimination'.[137] Lawrence points out that some in the US have been critical of what they see as unrealistic expectations which arise from these responsibilities placed upon the education system; but he has nevertheless found evidence that schools have had some success in dealing with problems such as disruption and violence through a range of strategies. He notes that, for example, some teaching strategies have proven 'effective in helping at-risk students perform better academically and avoid involvement in delinquent behaviour'.[138] However, Whitty is cautious about the capacity of the education system to 'reverse long standing patterns of social disadvantage', arguing that schools 'can make a difference, but they cannot buck social trends on their own'.[139]

In the UK, which is witnessing wide-ranging social problems affecting young people, such as crime, violence and drug misuse, and where evidence of under-achievement within some social sectors has come to greater prominence, education is also being assigned a key role as an agent of social change and as a means to broadening social participation as a citizen.[140] Moreover, the functions of the education system are being extended to give it a wider community role, such as in the provision of childcare or other community services.[141] Many of the post-1997 Labour Government's extensive education reforms have been driven by a wide-ranging policy agenda that has focused on reducing social exclusion and realising the idea of 'a fairer, more inclusive society where nobody is held back by disadvantage or lack of opportunity'.[142]

'Social exclusion' is a term that has 'no universally agreed definition', despite being widely used in Europe.[143] It is not specifically defined in the *Opportunity for All* annual reports[144] by which the Government has charted the progress of its

[135] Ibid, 155–62.
[136] R Lawrence, *School Crime and Juvenile Justice* (New York, Oxford University Press, 1998) 8.
[137] Ibid.
[138] Ibid, 139.
[139] G Whitty, *Making Sense of Education Policy* (London, Paul Chapman, 2005) 124.
[140] See, eg, H Glennester, 'Tackling poverty at its roots? Education' in C Oppenheim (ed), *An Inclusive Society* (London, IPPR, 1998) 137–50.
[141] EA 2002, ss 14–17, 27 and 28. For background see DfEE, *Schools: Achieving Success* (London, TSO, 2001), ch 8 and N Harris, '"Extended Schools": A Legal Framework for Childcare Provision in Schools' (2001) 2 *Education Law* 194.
[142] See Secretary of State for Work and Pensions, *Opportunity for all. Fifth Annual Report 2003*, Cm 5956 (London, TSO, 2003) vii.
[143] N Ardill, 'The Social Exclusion Trap', *Legal Action*, Aug 2005, 7–8.
[144] Eg *Seventh Report 2005* Cm 6673 (London, TSO, 2005).

policies against a range of indicators, some of which have been linked to specific targets, such as the proportion of pupils reaching the expected attainment level by a particular age, reduction in the numbers excluded from school and an increase in the staying-on rate for pupils above compulsory school age (targets that have in fact been progressively abandoned). However, the reports describe social exclusion as occurring 'where different factors combine to trap individuals and areas in a spiral of disadvantage'.[145] In the case of education, the downward spiral affects socially disadvantaged children and young people, whose educational achievements are below average which in turns accentuates their social exclusion by intensifying and prolonging it. Poverty is the main source of social disadvantage and is identified as the main barrier to social inclusion. It also features prominently in the definition of social exclusion adopted by the Council of Europe, although the Council also notes that:

> [s]ocial exclusion also strikes or risks to strike persons who without being poor are denied access to certain rights or services as a result of long periods of illness, the breakdown of their families, violence, release from prison or marginal behaviour as a result of for example alcoholism or drug addiction.[146]

The Council's definition does not, however, refer specifically to problems particularly associated with childhood: some are merely implicit (such as abuse or exclusion from school), while others are omitted (such as educational under-achievement and learning difficulties).

Researchers have explored the relationship between social exclusion and poverty. Social exclusion may be viewed as a state affecting the individual, whether as an acute form of poverty or as a 'less acute but more widely experienced condition'.[147] Dean explains, however, that poverty may be seen as concerned with the distribution of incomes, goods and services within a society, while social exclusion is quite distinct and concerned with 'processes' that create marginalisation.[148] He concludes that social exclusion is not necessarily dependent upon poverty, but in practice 'the two tend to occur together'.[149] Howarth and Kenway identify the processes that create social exclusion: the labour market, the welfare state, the legal system, the political system, the family and the community.[150] Seen in these terms, education may be a part of the problem, as a process that contributes to social exclusion; but, equally, it can also be seen as an important part of the solution, by ameliorating the effects of wider social problems. The Government's approach has emphasised the need to deal with the barriers to social exclusion, such as poor educational achievement or a

---

[145] Eg Secretary of State for Social Security, *Opportunity for All: Tackling Poverty and Social Exclusion*, Cm 4445 (London, TSO, 1999), ch 2, para 7.

[146] Council of Europe, *Explanatory Report to the European Social Charter (ETS No.163)*, available at http://conventions.coe.int/treaty/en/Reports/HTML/163.htm, para 114.

[147] C Howarth and P Kenway, 'A Multi-dimensional Approach to Social Exclusion Indicators' in C Oppenheim, *An Inclusive Society* (London, IPPR, 1998) 79 at 80.

[148] H Dean, *Welfare Rights and Social Policy* (Harlow, Prentice Hall, 2002), 24.

[149] Ibid.

[150] Howarth and Kenway, n 147 above, at 80–1.

failure to remain within the education system. This includes efforts to tackle truancy and exclusion from school.[151] Glennester comments that while '[w]e should be extremely careful about offering easy solutions or suggesting that education can solve the problem of poverty', it is possible for 'carefully thought out quality interventions targeted at low performers, both adults and children, especially in poor areas . . . over the long haul . . . [to] make a difference'.[152] The Government has in fact identified a number of policy priorities for children and young people. It aims to ensure a 'high quality education wherever they go to school' and 'additional help in the pre-school years'; combating family poverty and social exclusion through policies to tackle worklessness; 'increasing support for families and improving the environment in which children grow up'; and supporting vulnerable young people making the 'difficult transition to adult life'.[153] Among the groups that have been found to be particularly in need of targeting is that comprising teenage mothers, given that 73.3 per cent of 16–19-year-old mothers were not in education, employment or training in 2003, the highest rate since 1999.[154] Another group facing educational disadvantage and highlighting the link between it and difficult social circumstances comprises young people in care, whose levels of attainment are well below average.[155] As we shall see in subsequent chapters, an enormous range of policies have been set in place across discrete areas of education, including school admissions and school transport, to combat the effects of social exclusion experienced by these groups and by and other social and ethnic minority groups.

Equality: of Outcome or of Opportunity?

It has nevertheless been argued that, by focussing on social inclusion and participation, the Government has in fact managed to avoid the issue of inequality, particularly income inequality.[156] It is more accurate to say that, in terms of economic redistribution, the Labour Government has steered a middle course, consonant with the so-called 'Third Way'. This involves making the system work actively to move people from welfare dependence and poverty, through education, training and support. It forms a middle course between, at one extreme, a simple redistribution of welfare in their favour or, at the other, minimal support or the bare safety net of residual welfare.[157] It therefore places an emphasis on improving 'equality of opportunity' rather than 'equality of outcome'.[158]

---

[151] Social Exclusion Unit, *Truancy and School Exclusion*, Cm 3957 (London, TSO, 1998).

[152] Glennester, above n 140, 148.

[153] Secretary of State for Social Security (1999), above n 145, 5.

[154] Secretary of State for Work and Pensions, *Opportunity for All. Fifth Annual Report 2003*, Cm 5956 (London, TSO, 2003) 166.

[155] Social Exclusion Unit, *A Better Education for Children in Care* (London, Social Exclusion Unit, 2003); NCH, *Close the Gap for Children in Care* (London, NCH, 2005). See Chap 4.

[156] D Byrne, *Social Exclusion* (Milton Keynes, Open University Press, 1999).

[157] Secretary of State for Social Security and Minister for Welfare Reform, *New Ambitions for our Country—A New Contract for Welfare*, Cm 3805 (London, TSO, 1998), paras 5 and 6.

[158] R Plant, 'Supply Side Citizenship' (1999) 6 *Journal of Social Security Law* 124 at 132.

A forthright exposition of this approach was made in a paper for the Institute of Public Policy Research by the then Schools Minister, David Millibrand in 2003. He argues that:

> schooling has unique power to contribute to equality of opportunity . . . [it] cannot create an equal society on its own; but unless we make the necessary changes in school-ing, and specifically in the way that we organise teaching and learning, then we will not make a more equal society.[159]

Millibrand acknowledges that despite overall improvements in *average* attainment levels, the low achievers have made relatively weaker progress than others, so that there remains a gap, one that is linked to social class. Some of the evidence on this position was cited above. While acknowledging that poverty, reduced parental expectations and neighbourhood characteristics (such as crime levels) are important factors in under-achievement, Millibrand argues that so too is the quality of schooling. He argues that education should be based around the concept of 'personalised learning', tailored to the individual needs of the student, a theme that has been developed in both the Government's five year plan published towards the end of 2004 and its White Paper on schools published in late 2005.[160] Other necessary components of quality in education should be effective assessment for learning, a flexible curriculum, good teaching, harnessing information and computer technology, and more effective school organisation. Millibrand's paper significantly downplays the disparities between schools' performance; indeed, it stresses that '[t]he extent of variation in performance of students within schools is four times greater at age 15 than variation in performance between schools'.[161] It also ignores the issue of choice of school, instead focussing on the potential for *all* schools to meet pupils' individual needs. As part of the 'social democratic settlement for our country', there is to be an education system in which every school has 'the legal and financial flexibility to adapt provision to local needs'.[162] The framework for the realisation of this vision, the foundations of which were set in place in the Education Act 2002, is extended by proposals in the 2005 White Paper and the Education and Inspections Bill 2006.[163]

The basis for Labour's approach is therefore that flexibility and diversity of provision hold the key to equality, fairness and a Benthamite vision of the greatest good for the greatest number. The way of tackling inequality of opportunity (there is no reference to equality of outcome) is not to deal with certain unequal structural factors such as access to private schooling or selection on the basis of academic ability, but rather, and somewhat idealistically, to

---

[159] D Millibrand, *Opportunity for All: How Schooling Can Help* (London, IPPR, 2003) 1.

[160] DfES, *Department for Education and Skills: Five Year Strategy for Teachers and Learners*, Cm 6272 (London, TSO, 2004); HM Government, *Higher Standards, Better Schools for All*, Cm 6677 (London, TSO, 2005). See Chap 7.

[161] Ibid, 7.

[162] Ibid, 12.

[163] See Chap 3.

attempt to ensure 'excellence for everyone'.[164] Towards that end, policies, reinforced by strict regulation and statutory enforcement mechanisms, aim to ensure that schools must be 'excellent, improving or both'.[165] The idea that equality in education is dependent upon securing equality of provision is rejected on the basis that such a goal has tended to result in uniformity and to rest inappropriately on the assumption that all children have the same level of ability.[166] The principle adopted is therefore that a child should have the right to provision that develops his or her talents to the full. This necessarily means that there must be diversity of provision, but it would meet the requirement of equality if the necessary political commitment and legal framework combined to maximise standards universally. It would thereby accord with Rawls's notion that 'those who are at the same level of talent and ability and have the same willingness to use them, should have the same prospects of success regardless of their initial place in the social system, that is, irrespective of the income class into which they were born'.[167]

But what of the barriers to educational equality resulting from the wide diversity of children's social and economic circumstances, including family background? Brighouse argues that it is possible to 'insulate the child's prospects' from social factors, including the ability of the parents to support the child's education (and without undermining the cultural integrity and values of the family).[168] The relevant means involve requiring the child to attend school or equivalent provision for most of the day and 'equalizing the resources devoted to each child's schooling, subject to the requirement that more be spent on less-able and disabled children'.[169] Brighouse, in a detailed examination of the theories concerned with educational equality, argues that equal educational opportunity is dependent on three key factors.[170] The first two are that the quality of educational inputs should reflect neither the wealth of children's parents nor their decision-making ability (both of which would, of course, be linked to the parents' own educational attainment and social class). The other is discrimination in the allocation of resources in favour of children with various disabilities (in the broad sense) and against those who are free of them. Positive discrimination in the allocation of resources need not undermine the idea that government should treat all citizens with equal concern and respect, which is fundamental to the case for educational equality. Brighouse takes the view that although the equality principle rests on the idea that devoting more resources to one person's education than to another's results in disparate levels of opportunity to acquire intrinsic rewards, thereby appearing to confer more value on the first person's life and thus suggest inequality of respect as between the two, 'there are reasons, grounded in equal respect for persons, for allowing resources to be

---

[164] DfEE, *Excellence in Schools*, Cm 3681 (London, TSO, 1997) 38.
[165] Ibid, 12, para 19.
[166] Ibid, 11, para 12.
[167] J Rawls, *A Theory of Justice* (Cambridge, Mass, Harvard University Press, 1971) 73.
[168] H Brighouse, *School Choice and Social Justice* (Oxford, Oxford University Press) 160.
[169] Ibid.
[170] Ibid, 163.

distributed to the advantage of some.'[171] This same argument can be applied to positive discrimination and targeted provision in favour of various social or socio-economic groups whose educational under-achievement is most marked, such as Black Caribbean boys. Similarly, certain minority ethnic and socio-economic groups are under-represented in higher education as a whole,[172] and recent evidence has emerged of their uneven distribution across the university sector, with 53 institutions having less than 5 per cent of ethnic minority students across the student body, while 20 others have more than 40 per cent.[173] Policies to counter such phenomena[174] can become politically contro-versial; those on the libertarian and anti-collectivist right will sometimes see them as involving an unacceptable level of central coercion that conflicts with notions of freedom.[175] On the other hand, it is said that they prefer equality of opportunity to equality of outcome, because the former 'does not presuppose any particular social arrangements as desirable'.[176]

What Whitty refers to as 'compensatory mechanisms',[177] involving targeting of support, do, however, involve redistribution. Those who benefit from educational policies directed at improving social justice or social inclusion tend to be precisely the groups from relatively deprived backgrounds whose educational disadvantages have been exacerbated by previous market-orientated education reforms based on competition and choice.[178] Even proponents of such aims nonetheless see risks in Labour's policy of targeted support. Gewirtz, for example, argues that the additional resources enjoyed by schools in education action zones, which have been established in areas of social disadvantage and under-achievement,[179] can contribute to improved educational attainment; but the zones may not be able to 'interrupt the processes of segregation and polarization that markets seem to produce', because 'there is a possibility that any improvements will be at the expense of neighbouring schools which may lose teachers attracted by the better pay in zone schools and students attracted by better resources'.[180] In fact, subsequent research has failed so far to reveal such effects, including the anticipated improvement of pupil performance.[181] The social justice case for another of the diverse forms of provision, specialist schools (these are secondary schools able to specialise in a specific subject, or two subjects, and to select up to 10 per cent of their annual intake on the basis of

---

[171] Ibid, 121.

[172] D Leslie, A Abbott and D Blackeby, 'Why are Ethnic Minority Applicants Less Likely to be Accessing Education?' (2002) 56 *Higher Education Quarterly* 65. See also T Modood and M Shiner, *Ethnic Minorities and Higher Education* (London, Policy Studies Institute, 1994).

[173] P Curtis, 'Segregation, 2006 Style', *The Guardian Education*, 3 Jan 2006, 1–2, reporting a survey drawing on Higher Education Statistics Agency (HESA) figures for 2003–4.

[174] See further pp 180–6 below.

[175] See V George and P Wilding, *Ideology and Welfare* (Routledge and Kegan Paul, 1985) 24–25.

[176] Ibid, 24.

[177] G Whitty, *Making Sense of Education Policy* (London, Paul Chapman, 2005) 108.

[178] See Chap 5.

[179] See pp 105–08 below.

[180] S Gewirtz, 'Social Justice, New Labour and School Reform' in G Lewis, S Gewirtz and J Clarke, *Rethinking Social Policy* (Milton Keynes, Open University/Sage, 2000) 307 at 311.

[181] S Power *et al*, 'Paving a "Third Way"? A Policy Trajectory Analysis of Education Action Zones' (2004) 19 *Research Papers in Education* 461.

aptitude in the specialist area), which could expect to receive an additional £100,000 of matched funding towards capital expenditure, is even more problematic.[182] The Government aimed to increase the number of specialist schools from around 400 in 2001 to 1,500 by 2006,[183] but in fact that number has been exceeded.[184] The Government's justification for targeted extra support for these schools is based on the idea that their success will lead to improvements across the system: '[f]ar from concentrating success in a few schools, diversity is about motivating individual schools, spreading excellence, sharing success and working collaboratively. This is at the heart of specialist schools'.[185] Gorard and Taylor, however, warn that the ability of specialist schools to engage in various forms of selection of pupils[186] contributes to raised levels of socio-economic segregation among pupil intakes. They therefore warn that policy-makers 'need to weigh up the purported advantages of specialist schools in urban areas with preferential funding against the potential disadvantages in terms of equity'.[187] This is the danger, for in the attempt to introduce the greater diversity in the education system that specialist schools bring, '[t]he yet to be resolved question is whether such diversity can be delivered without creating gainers and losers, and whether "parity of esteem" can be achieved by different forms of education'.[188]

Social and Economic Costs and Benefits

In giving education a key role in widening social inclusion, the educational reform agenda has not merely been motivated by the altruistic belief that 'everyone should have the opportunity to achieve their potential'.[189] The economic and social returns are also acknowledged. So far as the former are concerned, the White Paper stated that it was 'economically inefficient to waste the talents of even one single person'.[190] The potential economic benefits of a better educated society have been recognised by UNICEF, in the recommendation that if developing countries tackle the barriers to girls' education it will ultimately aid their economic growth and reduce poverty.[191] The UN Committee on Economic, Social and Cultural Rights has said that '[i]ncreasingly, education is recognized as one of the best financial investments States can make'.[192] In the

---

[182] S Gorard and C Taylor, 'The Composition of Specialist Schools in England: Track Record and Future Prospect' (2001) 21 *School Leadership & Management* 365 at 368.

[183] DfEE, *Schools: Building on Success*, Cm 5050 (London, TSO, 2001), para 4.14.

[184] See Chap 5.

[185] DfEE *Schools: Achieving Success*, Cm 5230 (London, TSO, 2001), para 5.5

[186] This issue is discussed at 293–5 below.

[187] Above n 182, at 380.

[188] G Smith and T Smith, 'Excellence, Diversity and Inequality in Education', in G Finnister (ed), *Tackling Child Poverty in the UK. An End in Sight?* (London, CPAG, 2001) 51 at 54.

[189] Department for Education and Employment, *Excellence in Schools*, Cm 3681 (London, TSO, 1997) 1.

[190] Ibid.

[191] UNICEF, *The State of the World's Children 2004* (New York, UNICEF, 2004).

[192] Committee on Economic, Social and Cultural Rights, 21st session, 15 Nov–3 Dec 1999, *Implementation of the International Covenant on Economic, Social and Cultural Rights. General Comment No. 13, The Right to Education*, E/C.12/1999/10 (Geneva, United Nations, Office of the Commissioner for Human Rights, 1999), para 1.

UK, the Government has emphasised the economic benefits of better educational opportunities, most particularly in the context of the drive to increase participation rates in higher education and promote lifelong learning in order to 'close the skills gap . . . [and] underpin innovation and enterprise in the economy and society'.[193] The twin aims of 'economic prosperity and social cohesion'[194] underlie the push for improvements—'excellence for everyone'[195]—via educational reform. As the report by the Commission on Social Justice that formed part of the intellectual underpinning of New Labour's policies stated: '[t]he social benefits of learning have been central to civic life since the Ancient Greeks. The *economic* centrality of education and training is now widely accepted'.[196] Research for the Department for Work and Pensions has concluded that the evidence that education improves the individual's employability and reduces inequality shows that 'there are society wide benefits stemming from greater investment in education and training'.[197] It argues that economic research suggests that:

> attempts to identify the extent to which education and qualifications affect relative economic performance . . . have begun to reveal the importance of human capital . . . [There is] a general link with an increase in the stock of human capital leading to output growth.[198]

Similarly, a study for the World Bank has reported that 'education, as a prime component of human capital, is conducive to long term economic growth and development' and there is a 'virtuous circle, whereby increased growth generates resources for investment in education, which in turn fosters economic growth'; an accumulation of human capital in itself is not, however, a sufficient condition for growth.[199]

The social costs arising from exclusion and truancy in terms of the greater risk of criminality,[200] unemployment and homelessness,[201] are accompanied by calculable economic costs to the state. In particular, there is the extra cost of home tuition or a specialist placement and, in some cases, the involvement of

---

[193] Department for Education and Skills, *The Future of Higher Education*, Cm 5735 (London, TSO, 2003), para 1.24.

[194] Secretary of State for Education and Employment, *Excellence in Schools*, Cm 3681 (London, TSO, 1997), ch 1, para 1.

[195] Ibid, ch 1, para 19.

[196] Commission on Social Justice, *Social Justice. Strategies for National Renewal* (London, Vintage, 1994) 120 (original emphasis).

[197] P Elias, T Hogarth and G Pierre, *The Wider Benefits of Education and Training: a Comparative Longitudinal Study*, DWP Research Report 178 (Leeds, Corporate Document Services, 2002) 25.

[198] Ibid, 18–19.

[199] N Vandycke, *Access to Education for the Poor in Europe and Central Asia. Preliminary Evidence and Policy Implications* (Washington, DC, World Bank, 2001) 5.

[200] However, truancy, exclusion and entry into crime may all have the same root cause, namely a problematic childhood, owing to poor or abusive parenting: S Asquith, 'Children, Crime and Society' in M Hill and J Aldgate (eds), *Child Welfare Services. Developments in Law, Policy, Practice and Research* (London, Jessica Kingsley, 1996) 75–89.

[201] Social Exclusion Unit, *Truancy and Social Exclusion*, Cm 3937 (London, TSO, 1998).

social services, educational psychologists or other professional services in supporting the child and his or her family.[202] Overall, therefore, there is evidence to justify the Labour Government's claim that as it increases the proportion of national income spent on education (at the start of its programme of reforms it pledged an investment of an additional £19bn for educational improvement,[203] and annual expenditure on education rose from £35 billion in 1997–8 to £51 billion in 2004–5[204]), it will be able to 'decrease it on meeting the bills of past social and economic failure'.[205] Effective educational provision for children with special educational needs can help to offset some of the additional social and economic costs arising from support needs and the inherently weaker than average employment prospects.[206] It has been estimated, for example, that the lifetime cost to the public purse in the case of a child with autism could, depending on the severity of his or her condition, be £3 million, and it has been argued that 'even moderate improvements in educational provision could result in major savings in later living costs' as well as facilitating the realisation of creative potential.[207]

EDUCATION AND POLITICS

One final introductory issue that needs to be mentioned is the important influence of politics and political ideology in the shaping of education reform. This moulding of the system to meet political and associated policy objectives is highlighted in the detailed review of the institutional framework in Chapter 3 and the discussion of discrete areas of provision elsewhere. It will be seen that the influence of these factors has become increasingly pronounced over the past three decades, which represent a period of intense legislative activity in this field. The education system has been subjected to wave after wave of new policy initiatives and a tide of regulation. To some, the position the education system finds itself in today epitomises the new managerialism that has swept across the public services. Education is more closely audited, assessed and centrally controlled than at any time in history. This has formed an important part of the centralisation of power over the direction of education policy and the management of the system to meet various political and economic goals. The relationship between law and politics in the context of education reform is important to an understanding of the way that the politicisation of education

---

[202] C Parsons *et al*, *Excluding Primary School Children* (London, Family Policy Studies Centre, 1994); C Parsons *et al*, *Exclusion from School: The Public Cost* (London, Commission for Racial Equality, 1996).

[203] See Secretary of State for Social Security, above n 145, 6.

[204] In real terms, this represented a 29 per cent increase in expenditure per pupil over this period: DfES, *Higher Standards, Better Schools for All*, Cm 6677 (London, TSO, 2005), para 1.4.

[205] Secretary of State for Education and Employment, *Excellence in Schools*, Cm 3681 (London, TSO, 1997), ch 1, para 15.

[206] Ie, in comparison with those who do not have special educational needs.

[207] D Boyle and E Burton, *Making Sense of* SEN (London, New Philanthropy Capital, 2004) 46.

during the past 30 years has shaped its legal framework and the structures of control and regulation within the system. Moreover, the increasing importance accorded to civic rights and obligations both within education policy and also more widely, and the emergent tensions between human rights and state power which are being felt in the field of education as elsewhere,[208] mean that the law has an important role not merely as an instrument of policy implementation but also in defining the boundaries within which the politics of education are played out.

The instrumentality of law in the process of policy implementation over the previous two decades meant that when Tony Blair, on becoming prime minister, proclaimed that 'education, education, education' were his three priorities for government, change to the legislative landscape was inevitable. The first of Labour's reforms occurred via the short Education (Schools) Act 1997, which provided for the phasing out of the assisted places scheme.[209] Under the scheme, introduced under the Education Act 1980 and covered by regulations, parents from poorer backgrounds could qualify for support with fees and incidental expenses if their child secured admission to a participating independent school. The education of around 40,000 children each year was supported in this way. The incoming Labour Government's argument was that the £145 million per annum expended on the scheme was needed to fund the reduced sizes for infant classes,[210] but it was an overtly political measure designed to cut off the flow of resources from the public to the private sector and to reinforce the message that state education would be made desirable for all. The School Standards and Framework Act 1998, the Teaching and Higher Education Act 1998 and the Education Acts of 2002 and 2005 have maintained the trend of continual legislative reform while undermining any assumption that the Labour Government's proclamation in the 1997 White Paper on schools that 'standards matter more than structures'[211] meant that the process of structural reform would be slowed or halted. The current Education and Inspections Bill, discussed in subsequent chapters, continues the trend. Within the seemingly constant process of education reform that has occurred throughout the past three decades, the prominence of the issues of social diversity, equality and inclusion has in fact varied enormously, as later chapters will explain.

Consideration of the political dimension to education reminds us that the direction of education policy is highly susceptible to changes of government. Nonetheless, it is difficult to see how the future election of a government that is

---

[208] See C Harvey (ed), *Human Rights in the Commmunity* (Oxford, Hart, 2004). In relation to education specifically, see N Harris, 'Education: Hard or Soft Lessons in Human Rights?' in ibid, at 81–112.

[209] Via the Education (Schools) Act 1997, which provided for the phasing out of the scheme.

[210] HC Debs, vol 295, col 592, 5 June 1997, Mr S Byers MP. The phasing out of the scheme meant that pupils who held a funded place lost this financial support when their primary education ended and they moved to the secondary stage at an "all-through" (ages 5–18) school. They unsuccessfully claimed that pre-election promises by Labour gave rise to a legitimate expectation regarding continuing support: *R v Secretary of State for Education and Employment ex parte Begbie* [2000] ELR 445.

[211] DfEE, *Excellence in Schools*, Cm 3681 (London, TSO, 1997), ch 1, para 17.

committed to a more limited role for the state in relation to provision, but with arguably an equally tight focus on the direction of policy and levels of expenditure and efficiency, would herald a change in the central role and involvement of government in education. Only if a wholesale privatisation of education occurred would we see such a change. However, although the role of the private sector has grown (for example, through private finance initiatives or in the sphere of further education and training), it seems unlikely that such a wholesale privatisation would have anywhere near sufficient popular support to make it realisable. Instead, if there is a shift to the right there is likely to be a return towards the neo-liberalist agendas of the past, namely reinforcement of choice and markets through parent 'passports' similar in effect to the education voucher scheme proposed by the Institute for Economic Affairs in the 1970s and attempted, in limited form, via nursery education vouchers worth up to £1,000 under the Conservatives' Nursery Education and Grant-maintained Schools Act 1996, since repealed. Such schemes would, however, revive debate on the potentially socially divisive and stratifying effects of individual choice, which are discussed in Chapter 5.

CONCLUSION

Over the past 30 years central government has secured an ever tighter grip on the direction and implementation of education policy and on expenditure, but many of the education system's basic structures have been left intact. To that extent, the system has proved resistant to some of the key features of postmodernity, such as a steering rather that controlling state and contingent rather than fixed structures[212] (albeit there are bodies such as education action forums[213] that represent a contingent response illustrative of a more flexible state apparatus). In the modern state, governance through regulation, incentivisation (through market elements and competition) and surveillance of activity (facilitated by vast amounts of data on performance and other matters) represent changes in the way that all areas of government activity, including service delivery, are conducted.[214] These changes have affected education, particularly in the push for raised standards and greater social inclusion.

An important question is whether, if and when the time comes for the political pendulum to swing in a different direction, the social inclusion agenda to the post-1997 Labour Government's legislative reforms and policies, built around ideas of social justice, equality of opportunity and a degree of respect for the human rights of individuals and diverse social groups, has become so firmly embedded in the public conscience as to make it as permanent as rights and

---

[212] See D Richards and MJ Smith, *Governance and Public Policy in the UK* (Oxford, Oxford University Press, 2002).

[213] See Chap 3.

[214] Ibid, 279–80.

duties concerned with parental choice appear to have become. The answer to this question lies in large part in the impact that these policy themes have had since 1997. Subsequent chapters will examine this issue. To the extent that education is integral to concerns about social division along racial, religious, cultural lines and is included in calls for policies that promote integration, the role of education law and policy and the way that basic individual or group rights are accommodated are particularly important. The concerns are central to many debates across western societies. In the Netherlands, for example, there is reported to be a 'feeling that the education system somehow must make up for problematic trends in society such as segregation, individualization, lack of social cohesion etc'.[215] As later chapters will discuss, this has become one of the crucial issues surrounding education and, indeed, other areas of public policy in the UK at the present time.

The multicultural, multifaith and socio-economically diverse society is well established in Britain and, in the sphere of education, there is quite a lengthy experience of adapting and developing education policies and provision in response to pluralism and the divisions produced by social stratification. However, there is now unprecedented pressure on government to find a means not only of fulfilling the normative goal of maximising equality of opportunity in and through education, but also of finding a fair balance between individual rights and the realisation of collective goals. Moreover, as the discussion of social rights in the next chapter shows, education is strongly associated with notions of citizenship which, as with the rights underpinning it, is seen as a contingent notion that includes elements of responsibility and active participation. Education is central to the achievement of the goal of maximising individual capacity for such participation, but its effectiveness is increasingly seen as in part dependent upon citizen involvement, especially parental participation. Thus the challenge is how to universalise engagement with education in a way that supports notions of citizenship, thereby strengthening the social fabric, without undermining notions of liberty and freedom that are reflected in many of the state's human rights obligations, to which the next chapter gives attention.

[215] BP Vermeulen and CW Norrlander, 'The Legal Right of Students in the Netherlands' in C Russo and J De Groof (eds), *The Legal Rights of Students* (Scarecrow, forthcoming).

2

The Right to Education

INTRODUCTION

THE RIGHT TO education is a social right that arises from, and is correlative to, a positive duty to provide a child with learning that, while
assumed by society and associated with the principle of parental
responsibility, rests with and is carried out by the state. And like other universal
services to which all are guaranteed access by right, its provision has a
redistributive effect.[1] The right to education fits into the welfare/interest theory
of rights (in part because it is seen as compatible with the idea that children are
rights holders), under which the right to education is protecting an interest (in
being educated) the importance of which has warranted the imposition of duties
for the benefit of the interest holder.[2] In theory, the duty should be enforceable
by the rights holder,[3] although, in practice, enforcement is problematic (see
below). Even in the Soviet Union, where state control was more or less total and
all aspects of education were centrally dictated, a basic right to education was
prescribed.[4] There, as in the UK today, education was provided, or at least regulated, by the state and, in practice, the right to education meant a right to
whatever form of education the state had deemed necessary or desirable. In other
words, the normative basis of education that the notion of a right to education
implies is premised on the assumption that all children should receive an education of a particular type or content. Nonetheless, various qualifications to this
principle are necessary.

First, while the education of the child is today very much towards the latter
end of the private ordering–public regulation continuum applicable to child
welfare,[5] parents have moral and legal claims to determine aspects of the process
of education, in addition to legal responsibilities concerning school attendance

---

[1] See the discussion of social and economic rights in D Feldman, *Civil Liberties and Human Rights
in England and Wales* (2nd edn, Oxford, Oxford University Press, 2002) 13–14.

[2] Under the will or choice theory, however, the rights holder has the choice whether to enforce the
duty or waive it: see DW Archard, *Children, Family and the State* (Aldershot, Ashgate, 2003) 4–5.

[3] Ibid.

[4] Starting with the Constitution of the Union of Soviet Republics 1936, Art 121.

[5] See G Douglas and N Lowe, 'Becoming a Parent in English Law' (1992) 102 *LQR* 414.

and good behaviour. Indeed, under the Irish Constitution, 'the State acknowledges that the primary and natural educator of the child is the Family and guarantees to respect the inalienable right and duty of parents to provide, according to their means, for the religious and moral, intellectual, physical and social education of their children'.[6] The parent may exercise this right by sending the child to a state or private school or educating him or her at home.[7] It was noted in Chapter 1 how, under the ECHR, the state must respect 'the right of parents to ensure such education and teaching in conformity with their own religious and philosophical convictions'.[8] There is clearly a tension in this relationship between the state and the parent, arising from the potential conflict between the former's power and authority and the latter's basic rights. In essence, the conflict, such as has arisen over, for example, matters such as the use of corporal punishment in school in furtherance of religious ideals, is about the content and meaning of the right to education. The growth of individual 'consumer' rights in education and the development of a home–school 'partnership' approach (see below) since the 1980s have represented a shift towards the private interest, with parents able to exercise a degree of choice and with the opportunity to assert their preferences in areas tied to their own cultural values, such as single-sex schooling, religious education and sex education. In some instances the conflict may require resolution with reference to international human rights norms, particularly as enshrined in the ECHR.

Secondly, education may involve an applied process, but its universal provision occurs within an institutional framework the scale, shape and maintenance of which in turn are ultimately dependent upon finite resources. The conditioning of the right to education under the ECHR as a result of resource limitations facing the state, which impact upon factors such as quality and choice, was clearly marked out by the judgment of the ECtHR in the *Belgian Linguistics* case, discussed below. In particular, as noted in Chapter 1, the Court confirmed that 'the Contracting Parties do not recognise such a right to education as would require them to establish at their own expense, or to subsidise, education of any particular type or at any particular level'.[9]

Thirdly, however, there has been a clear trend in England and Wales over the past two decades towards increased diversity in the education system, as discussed in Chapter 3. Whether the underlying policy objective has been to harness popular support for greater 'consumer' choice or to support social inclusion, the impression that is intended to be created is of a more flexible and socially responsive education system. At the same time, a growing emphasis on the need for education for citizenship and to inculcate more social and sexual responsibility, set against a continuing background of central curricular control, has prompted an uneasy compromise between individual education rights, including those of minority groups, and the state's power to determine educational content and act in the national or general societal interest.

---

[6] Irish Constitution, Art 42(2).
[7] Ibid, Art 42(3).
[8] Art 2 of Prot 1 (second sentence).
[9] *Belgian Linguistics (No 2)* (1979–80) 1 EHRR 252, para 3.

THE NATURE OF THE RIGHT TO EDUCATION

The Scope of the Right

As concepts, education and rights are generic terms capable of different meanings in various contexts. Read together, they coalesce into a basic human right, recognised in a range of international instruments, not least the European Convention on Human Rights (ECHR), the Universal Declaration of Human Rights, the UN Convention on the Rights of the Child (UNCRC), the Charter of Fundamental Rights of the European Union[10] and the new Constitution for Europe.[11] The Universal Declaration proclaims that '[e]veryone has the right to education',[12] and this is mirrored in the Charter of Fundamental Rights of the European Union.[13] The ECHR provides, in Article 2 of the First Protocol, that '[n]o-one shall be denied the right to education'. Under the International Covenant on Economic, Social and Cultural Rights (ICESCR) the States Parties 'recognize the right of everyone to education'[14] and the parties to the UNCRC recognise 'the right of the child to education'.[15]

Two fundamental principles are enshrined under the various international treaty obligations. First, there is the principle of universality—that education, or at least elementary (or primary) education, must be available, free of charge, to all. Indeed, generally it is provided that education should be compulsory for those of primary school age.[16] Secondly, there should be equal access to education for everyone. The latter is reflected in the ECHR which, as discussed later, ties the right to education to requirement that Convention rights be enjoyed without discrimination.[17] Discrimination in the context of education is also, for example, covered by the UNESCO Convention against Discrimination in Education.[18] As we shall see, most of the international instruments prescribe broad aims and values attached to the education right. For example, several provide that education should promote understanding and friendship between those of different race or religious background and that it should be aimed at developing the person's or child's personality to the full.

Universal access also extends beyond primary school level. Secondary education is to be made 'available and accessible to every child' under the

---

[10] Agreed in Nice, December 2000.

[11] The Constitution provides for a right to education in Art II–74, but does not come into effect unless ratified by each of the Member States and it has already been rejected by the Netherlands and Denmark. For a detailed review of both national and international instruments, apart from the last two EU provisions, see D Hodgson, *The Human Right to Education* (Aldershot, Ashgate, 1998).

[12] Art 26(1).

[13] Art 14(1).

[14] Art 13(1).

[15] Art 28(1).

[16] Universal Declaration of Human Rights, Art 26(1); ICESCR, Art 13(2)(a); UNCRC, Art 28(1)(a).

[17] ECHR Art 14.

[18] See H Cullen, 'Education Rights or Minority Rights?' (1993) 7 *International Journal of Law and the Family* 143.

UNCRC,[19] and 'generally available and accessible to all' under the ICESCR.[20] The Universal Declaration, while not referring specifically to secondary education, provides that 'technical and professional education' should be made generally available.[21] Under the UNCRC, in furtherance of access to secondary education, states are required to 'take appropriate measures such as the introduction of free education and offering financial assistance in case of need'.[22] This appears to go further than the ICESCR, which calls for the employment of 'every appropriate means, and in particular . . . the progressive introduction of free education'.[23] However, although the UNCRC seems to make unconditional the duty to ensure access to and availability of secondary education, Article 4, which calls for states parties to undertake all appropriate legislative, administrative and other measures for the implementation of the Convention rights, provides that, '[w]ith regard to economic, social and cultural rights, [states] shall undertake such measures to the maximum extent of their available resources', which will not be limitless. As Fortin comments, 'article 4 clearly acknowledges that the resource implications of such provisions may rule out their immediate or even long term fulfilment'.[24] This may be particularly true of special arrangements that involve extra costs, such as provision for those with disabilities. A similar position was confirmed by the European Committee of Social Rights in response to a complaint brought by Autism-Europe in respect of the arrangements in France for the education of children with autism.[25] It was alleged that there were qualitative and quantitative shortfalls in the provision of both mainstream and specialist education for such children which violated, in a discriminatory way, Articles 15 and 17 of the European Social Charter. These Articles concern, respectively, measures to provide people with disabilities with education and the right to education through the provision of adequate institutions and services. The Committee noted the flexibility that was needed where the realisation of a right was 'exceptionally complex and particularly expensive to resolve'; however, it clearly found this a case where even the greater latitude that was necessary, given the particular form of education and costs involved, did not justify the failure to make suitable provision. The Committee emphasised that the realisation of the relevant rights should occur within 'a reasonable time, with measurable progress and to an extent consistent with maximum available resources', which had not happened.[26] The question of how much time and how much leeway should be shown over resourcing of provision to meet social rights obligations remains uncertain, however. Even in relation to standard educational provision there might still be circumstances where, because of resource constraints, there is no access to a particular form of education—as, for example, in the *Ali* case, where there were

---

[19] Art 28(1)(b).

[20] Art 13(2)(b).

[21] Art 26(1).

[22] Art 28(1)(b).

[23] Art 13(2)(b).

[24] J Fortin, *Children's Rights and the Developing Law* (2nd edn, London, Lexis Nexis Butterworth, 2002) 44.

[25] *Autism-Europe v France*, Complaint No 13/2002 (2003), European Committee of Social Rights.

[26] Ibid, paras 53 and 54.

inadequate primary school places as a result of financial constraints and teacher shortages in Tower Hamlets.[27] Moreover, the authority of the state to make choices about expenditure is acknowledged, as in the ECtHR's observation in *Belgian Linguistics*, noted above.[28]

So far as higher education is concerned, all of the above international instruments refer to it, but concede that not everyone may have the necessary capacity or ability to benefit from it. The UNCRC and the ICESCR say it should be accessible to all on the basis of 'capacity',[29] and the Universal Declaration says should be 'equally accessible to all on the basis of merit'.[30] The ECHR does not mention equality of access to education specifically but promotes it via the non-discrimination duty in Article 14, which is mirrored in the UNCRC and elsewhere.[31] The Strasbourg case law indicates that access to higher education may be restricted to those 'who have attained the academic level required to most benefit from the courses offered'.[32] In relation to financial support for participation in higher education, only the ICESCR alludes to it with its reference to 'the progressive introduction of free education'.[33] In *Douglas*,[34] Scott Baker LJ referred to the decision of the ECtHR in *Petrovic v Austria*,[35] where it was held that the state was under no duty (under Article 8 of the ECHR) to provide a parental leave allowance (accordingly, Article 14 had no application). He said that, similarly, the state was under no duty to provide a student loan to support the right to education under A2P1; and so Article 14 could not be invoked by the student, who had claimed that the cut-off age of 55 years for eligibility under the student support regulations violated those provisions. Scott Baker LJ said that the arrangements concerning student loans were 'a facilitator of education but they are one stage removed from the education itself'.[36] The absence of this financial support might 'make it more difficult for a student to avail himself of his Art 2 rights but they are not so closely related as to prevent him from doing so'.[37]

The various rights and co-relative duties concerning education reflect the fact that within modern societies education is generally seen as fundamental to human welfare, since it not only gives the individual an important means to self-fulfilment and maximisation of personal potential, but also contributes to a collective economic and social benefits through the inculcation of skills and provision of enlightenment. Landsdown argues that in many states where the right to education is not guaranteed in practice and where provision is substandard or non-existent (citing UNICEF figures in the late 1990s showing

---

[27] *R v Inner London EducationAuthority ex parte Ali* (1990) 2 Admin LR 822. See p 41 below.
[28] *Belgian Linguistics (No 2)* (1979–80) 1 EHRR 252. See p 36 above.
[29] UNCRC Art 28(1)(c); ICESCR Art 13(2)(c).
[30] Art 26(1).
[31] UNCRC, Art 2; see also ICESCR, Art 2(2);
[32] *X v UK* App no 8844/80 (1980) 23 DR 228 at 229.
[33] Art 13(2)(c).
[34] *R (Douglas) v North Tyneside Metropolitan Borough Council and Secretary of State for Education and Skills* [2004] ELR 117.
[35] (2002) 33 EHRR 14.
[36] *R (Douglas) v North Tyneside*, n 34 above, at para [57].
[37] Ibid.

that 130 million children of school age worldwide had no access to basic education), there is not only an impact on health and the economy, but also 'impeded progress towards democracy'.[38] Fabre says that 'one can convincingly argue that the right to adequate education is necessary for people to participate in the democratic process and for such process to function',[39] while Hodgson regards 'a proper education' as 'a prerequisite to a more reasoned exercise of political and civil liberties'.[40] In this regard, the UN Committee on Economic, Social and Cultural Rights (CESCR) has referred to the right to education as 'an empowerment right'.[41] The fact that education is critical to the proper enjoyment of economic, political and cultural rights is certainly implied in the statutory requirement in England that the curriculum for a maintained (state) school should prepare pupils 'for the opportunities, responsibilities and experiences of later life' and that, at the third key stage (ages 11–14), Citizenship is to be a National Curriculum foundation subject.[42] The prescribed content of Citizenship includes 'the legal and human rights and responsibilities underpinning society'; 'central and local government, the public services they offer and how they are financed, and the opportunities to contribute'; 'the key characteristics of parliamentary and other forms of government'; and 'the electoral system and the importance of voting'.[43]

Social Rights and Citizenship

The inter-dependence of social, civil and political rights was part of TH Marshall's theories about citizenship, whose three elements correspond with these areas. In *Citizenship and Social Class*, first published in 1950,[44] Marshall identified citizenship as being dependent upon civil rights (such as equality before the law and access to legal remedies), political rights (such as the right to vote in a fair election) and social rights, namely rights to welfare. The importance of the social rights of citizenship would lie in their capacity for the inclusion of the individual in society, not least because the fullest enjoyment of the civil and political rights is conditional upon the welfare that social rights aim to guarantee. Independent citizenship depends upon having the necessary social and economic resources to participate economically, socially and politically.[45] While rights to

---

[38] G Landsdown, 'Progress in Implementing the Rights in the Convention' in S Hart *et al*, *Children's Rights in Education* (London, Jessica Kingsley, 2001) 37 at 40.

[39] C Fabre, *Social Rights under the Constitution* (Oxford, Oxford University Press, 2000) 184.

[40] D Hodgson, *The Human Right to Education* (Aldershot, Ashgate, 1998) 18.

[41] Committee on Economic, Social and Cultural Rights, 21st session, 15 Nov–3 Dec 1999 *Implementation of the International Covenant on Economic, Social and Cultural Rights. General Comment No. 13, The Right to Education* E/C12/1999/10 (Geneva, United Nations, 1999), para 1.

[42] Education Act 2002, ss 78(1)(b) and 84(3)(h)(i).

[43] Prescribed content on Department for Education and Skills website (26 Apr 2004), available at www.dfes.gov.uk.

[44] Included in TH Marshall and T Bottomore, *Citizenship and Social Class* (London, Pluto Press, 1992).

[45] R Plant, 'Citizenship, Rights and Welfare' in A Coote (ed), *The Welfare of Citizens: Developing New Social Rights* (London, IPPR/Rivers Oram Press, 1992) 15 at 21.

income maintenance (social security), which are traditionally perceived as tied to the central aim of the welfare state, hold the key to social and economic participation, the right to education is no less important in that respect. As Heater explains:

> A citizen is a person furnished with knowledge of public affairs, instilled with attitudes of civic virtue and equipped with skills to participate in the civil and political arenas. The acquisition and enhancement of these attributes is in truth a lifelong undertaking: even so, a firm foundation must be laid down in schools to ensure both their early and systematic learning.[46]

Social rights should therefore aim to ensure that, on the basis of equality of opportunity, there is 'access to educational, training and employment opportunities to facilitate participation by the individual in civil society to the limits and extent of his or her ability'.[47] The idea that equality is inherent in the very notion of social rights is important, especially in the light of criticisms that Marshall's concept of citizenship did not address issues of social diversity or pluralism.[48]

One of the difficulties, however, arises from the fact that, in the area of education, provision itself is unequal in terms of quality and availability. This is partly because of local variations in funding, expenditure and costs. For example, teacher shortages have been a problem in areas of London and the South East, as recruitment is hindered by high living costs. A case in 1990 arose from a shortage of primary school places in Tower Hamlets due to a shortfall in teacher recruitment. In the borough, which had a high concentration of children of Bangladeshi origin, there were nearly 300 children who did not have a school place. The parents claimed that an infringement of a private law right arose from the LEA's breach of duty to ensure that there were 'sufficient' schools, a duty defined in the Education Act 1944 as requiring there to be schools that were sufficient 'in number, character and equipment to afford for all pupils opportunities for education offering such variety of instruction and training as may be desirable having regard to their ages, abilities, and aptitudes . . .'[49] Woolf J held that the LEA's duty was a 'target' duty only and did not give rise to an enforceable private law right.[50] The LEA was not acting unlawfully if it was doing all it reasonably could to fulfil its duty with the finite resources available to it.

This case illustrates two important factors about the right to education as a social right. First, it shows the difficulty faced by the individual in enforcing it, a fact that will be further illustrated with reference to post Human Rights Act 1998

---

[46] D Heater, *Citizenship. The Civic Ideal in World History, Politics and Education* (3rd edn, Manchester, Manchester University Press, 2004) 343.

[47] KD Ewing, 'Social Rights and Constitutional Law' [1999] PL 104, 106.

[48] R Lister, *The Female Citizen* (Liverpool, Liverpool University Press, 1989); K O'Donovan, 'Gender Blindness or Justice Engendered' in R Blackburn (ed), *Rights of Citizenship* (London, Mansell, 1993) 12; A Philips, *Democracy and Difference* (London, Polity, 1993).

[49] Education Act 1944, s 8(1).

[50] *R v Inner London Education Authority ex p Ali and Murshid* [1990] 2 Admin LR 822. See further N Harris, 'Education By Right? Breach of the Duty to Provide "Sufficient" Schools' (1990) 53 *MLR* 525.

cases below. Plant argues that there is an assumption that 'the general provision of public services is what social rights require, but equally it is clear that these have not led, by and large, to individually enforceable rights'.[51] On that basis, he argues, social rights 'are actually a bit of a sham'.[52] Enforceable rights, he says, can be a means of empowerment of the citizen. But, as we shall see in relation to decisions on provision for children with special educational needs, which are often contested by parents, outcomes can be somewhat hit and miss. For example, while there is a statutory duty on LEAs to arrange the educational provision specified in a child's statement of special educational needs,[53] the advantage to the parent or child is diminished by the difficulty in securing that the provision they have chosen is specified. Dean views the substantive social rights in areas such as education, health or social care as 'tenuous'[54] on the basis that the rights that arise out of the state's obligations in such areas are imprecise and uncertain. In relation to education, parents have some limited rights over choice of school and to information about provision, but little control over the content of their children's education. Children with special educational needs 'have a right to have their needs assessed, but not necessarily to command the resources necessary to satisfy their needs'.[55] A fundamental reason for the ambiguous status of the right to education that Dean seems to be identifying is that '[e]ducation is not so much a right for either children or their parents as an obligation, and it is not clear that the education system has ever existed to serve the interests of children or their parents'.[56]

Dean's approach may be somewhat at odds with the consumerist notion of education rights that developed during the 1980s and 1990s, and perhaps even more so with the notion of education as a human right that has come to greater prominence as a result of the Human Rights Act 1998. Nonetheless, it is true that there remain fundamental parental obligations linked to education. In some respects, the state could be seen as acting as an agent for the parent in fulfilling a basic moral and legal duty. That would be consistent with the parent's continuing right to educate his or her child otherwise than at school, for example at home, and the fact that parents and the state have parallel duties to ensure that a child receives an 'efficient' education 'suitable' to his or her 'age, ability and aptitude'.[57] The state's duty, imposed on LEAs, arises when a child under compulsory school age will not receive suitable education because of 'illness, exclusion from school or otherwise'; the LEA must make arrangements for suitable full-time or part-time provision. In a case, *ex parte T*, where the LEA sought to cut the provision for a girl with chronic fatigue syndrome (ME) from five to three hours per week due to budgetary constraints, the House of Lords held that the statute

---

[51] R Plant, n 45 above, at 26.
[52] Ibid.
[53] Education Act 1996, s 324(5)(a). See Chap 6.
[54] H Dean, *Welfare Rights and Social Policy* (Harlow, Prentice Hall, 2002) 155.
[55] Ibid.
[56] Ibid.
[57] Education Act 1996, ss 7 and 19; see further *R v East Sussex County Council ex parte T* [1998] ELR 251 (HL), per Lord Brown-Wilkinson at 256. Under s 7 the parent may fulfil his or her duty to cause the child to receive efficient education 'either by regular attendance at school or otherwise'.

did not suggest that resource considerations were relevant to the question of what was 'suitable education'.[58] Lord Browne-Wilkinson, who gave the only substantive judgment, drew support from the fact that the content of the parallel parental duty to ensure the child received a suitable education 'cannot vary according to the resources of the parent'.[59] This case therefore contrasts with the Tower Hamlets case above by virtue of the differences in the nature of the respective duties. Woolf LJ was clear in the earlier case that the statutory duty to ensure that there were sufficient schools did not give rise to an enforceable right for the individual, whereas the House of Lords in *ex parte T* considered that the statutory obligation to ensure a suitable education meant that the LEA owed a 'statutory duty to each sick child individually and not to sick children as a class'.[60] This decision shows that some education rights *are* enforceable as strict duties.[61] It has been argued that this reinforces the possibly of construing them as property rights.[62] Carney and Hanks, however, discussing Reich's argument in favour of welfare entitlement as a form of 'new property',[63] contends that the property metaphor is dependent upon the capacity for individualism and that this makes the new property concept 'highly problematic as a foundation for the welfare state'.[64] In education, though, there is arguably more scope for individualism than in many other areas of state welfare provision. This and the fact that there has been a trend towards the commodification of education (see below) suggests that this is an area that warrants further analysis by property law theorists.

The second problem with education as a social right is that scarcity places the individual in a competitive situation that, as Stychin explains, limits the potential of certain social rights to ensure social inclusion on the basis of equality.[65] Some parents are better able, due to wealth or the cultural capital derived from their own privileged educational backgrounds, to derive benefit from the rights that are available—to enforce access or choice. Moreover, social and economic barriers operate in relation to participation in particular levels of education. For example, in higher education, entry to which remains highly competitive in relation to a majority of courses, Black Caribbean people and people from

---

[58] At 256E–F.

[59] At 256H, referring to EA 1993, s 298 (now EA 1996, s 19, discussed in Chap 4).

[60] At 257A–B.

[61] In *ex parte T*, n 57 above, the authority had a duty to ensure that the claimant had a 'suitable education'. It could, however, take account of its resources in deciding which form of 'suitable education' to provide. See I Hare, 'Social Rights as Fundamental Human Rights' in B Hepple (ed), *Social and Labour Rights in a Global Context* (Cambridge, Cambridge University Press, 2002) 153 at 172.

[62] T Kaye, '"Education, Education, Education". Commodity for Sale or Property Right?' in F Meisel and PJ Cook (eds), *Property and Protection* (Oxford, Hart, 2000) 61–86.

[63] C Reich, 'The new property' (1965) 73 *Yale Law Journal* 733.

[64] T Carney and P Hanks, *Social Security in Australia* (Melbourne, Oxford University Press, 1994) 106.

[65] C Stychin, 'Consumption, Capitalism and the Citizen: Sexual and Equality Rights Discourse in the European Union' in J Shaw (ed), *Social Law and Policy in an Evolving European Union* (Oxford, Hart, 2000) 258 at 262.

families of manual workers are under-represented among students.[66] These difficulties suggest that efforts to strengthen social rights through a constitutional framework are unlikely in themselves to guarantee social inclusion. As we saw in Chapter 1, young people of Moroccan or Turkish origin in the Netherlands are at a much greater risk of social exclusion that others as a result of under-attainment, early school leaving or truancy. The fact that the right to education is enshrined within the Dutch Constitution[67] does not appear to give it enhanced potency as a social right. Fabre nonetheless defends the constitutionalisation of social rights, on the basis that although they cannot by themselves solve problems such as social deprivation and bring about social justice they provide important protections, particularly when welfare states are under economic or political strain.[68]

The development of a quasi-market for education during the 1980s, discussed in Chapter 5, was in part based on the introduction of a range of rights over choice of school and access to information. Furthermore, parental rights in other contentious areas such as special educational needs and school discipline extended the notion of education as a product. While the commodification of education and the unleashing of elements of individualism and consumer empowerment within a market framework wrapped the relevant education rights in a mantle of economic rights (to be enforced through the exercise of civil rights), the essential character of education as a social right continued. Nonetheless, the market values of individualism, choice and competition were seen as inimical to the ideals of equality and social cohesion that are associated with the social citizenship paradigm.[69] It was against this background that calls grew for the strengthening of the social rights of citizenship through a constitutional framework[70] or, in any event, for the reduction of the barriers to the effective exercise of their rights by individuals.[71] The aim was not so much to extend the potential for each individual to satisfy his or her wants or needs within a competitive market, because that alone could not remove the underlying structural barriers to citizenship for all.[72] Indeed, it is said that markets serve to widen social and economic inequalities and that, in part through a redistribution of society's wealth in order to underpin social citizenship rights,[73] the aim should be to give the individual an economic and social status that is far less dependent

---

[66] D Leslie, A Abbott and D Blackeby, 'Why are Ethnic Minority Applicants Less Likely to be Accessing Education?' (2002) 56 *Higher Education Quarterly* 65. See also T Modood and M Shiner, *Ethnic Minorities and Higher Education* (London, Policy Studies Institute, 1994).

[67] Art 23.

[68] C Fabre, *Social Rights under the Constitution* (Oxford, Oxford University Press, 2000).

[69] A Furlong (ed), B Stadler and A Azzopardi, *Vulnerable Youth: Perspectives on Vulnerability in Education, Employment and Leisure in Europe* (Strasbourg, Council of Europe, 2000) 17.

[70] Eg N Lewis and M Seneviratne, 'A Social Charter for Britain' in Coote (ed), above n 45, ch 2.

[71] See P Golding (ed), *Excluding the Poor* (London, Child Poverty Action Group, 1986); R Lister, *The Exclusive Society* (London, CPAG, 1990); J Le Grand, 'The State of Welfare' in J Hills (ed), *The State of Welfare: The Welfare State in Britain since 1984* (Oxford, Clarendon Press, 1991) 358–60. See also Commission on Social Justice, *Social Justice: Strategies for National Renewal* (London, Vintage, 1994).

[72] C Stychin, n 65 above, at 260.

[73] D Heater, above n 46, 275.

on the operation of the market and one that involves more direct recognition of the right of social participation.[74] In reality though, the evidence is that, despite the rhetoric of consumer empowerment that pervaded the reforms during the period of educational restructuring under the Conservatives in the 1980s and 1990s, including the enactment of new rights of redress (such as appeal rights over choice of school, special educational needs and permanent exclusion from school), it was procedural rights rather that substantive rights that were advanced during that era.[75] It was always going to be the case that the wider collective interests of the community would need to be balanced against the rights of individual education consumers. In the interests of social justice and effective and efficient universal provision (and the necessity for significant elements of central planning and resource allocation) the rights of the individual would therefore have to be limited.[76]

Social rights therefore remain inherently weak at the core. Their value is reduced by their susceptibility to economic and political pressures. Significant extensions of social rights are associated with increased provision by the state that is viewed not merely by those on the right but also the social democratic left as unsustainable in economic terms. Furthermore, the moral underpinning of the notion of social justice is reinforced by the idea that what is socially desirable is the encouragement and support of self-sufficiency. The solution under Labour's 'Third Way', noted in Chapter 1, has been to develop policies aimed at balancing rights and responsibilities, so that individuals are subjected to elements of compulsion and support for the improvement of their education, training or employability. An emphasis is placed on equality of opportunity rather than equality of outcome. Thus, within education, the goal has, for example, been to maximise the numbers actually participating by stiffening the penalties on parents who fail to fulfil their duty to ensure their children are educated, while encouraging young people to stay on in education post-16 through the provision of financial support in the form of educational maintenance allowances (EMAs).[77] In some public policy areas, notably welfare to work, the stick has been more prominent than the carrot.[78] Even the EMAs are subject to strict conditions concerning attendance and participation in education. Thus while

---

[74] See generally the discussion in P Taylor-Gooby and R Lawson, 'Where do We Go from Here? The New Order in Welfare' in P Taylor-Gooby and R Lawson (eds), *Markets and Managers: New Issues in the Delivery of Welfare* (Milton Keynes, Open University Press, 1993) 132–49. A Vincent and R Plant, *Philosophy, Politics and Citizenship* (Oxford, Basil Blackwell, 1984); P Golding (ed), *Excluding the Poor* (London, Child Poverty Action Group, 1986); R Lister, *The Exclusive Society. Citizenship and the Poor* (London, CPAG, 1990); C Oppenheim (ed), *An Inclusive Society: Strategies for Tackling Poverty* (London, IPPR, 1998); N Harris, 'Exclusion-Inclusion: Tensions in Education Law and Policy' (2000/2001) 5 *Contemporary Issues in Law* 127.

[75] See N Harris, 'The Three Rs: Rights, Remedies and Regulation. The Legal Frontiers of Education in the 1990s' (1998) XXI *Liverpool Law Rev* 7.

[76] N Harris, *Law and Education: Regulation, Consumerism and the Education System* (London, Sweet and Maxwell, 1993), ch 8, especially at 262–3.

[77] See Chap 4.

[78] R Lister, 'Citizenship, Exclusion and "the Third Way": Reflections on T.H. Marshall' (2000) 7 *Journal of Social Security Law* 70, at 87. N Harris *et al.*, *Social Security Law in Context* (Oxford, OUP, 2000), especially chs 1 (Harris) and 10 (Lundy). See also R Lister, 'Vocabularies of Citizenship and Gender: the UK' (1998) 18 *Critical Social Policy* 309.

ideas about citizenship may have supported the growth of welfarism in the first few post-war decades and provided a justification for strengthening social rights in order to promote social integration,[79] the concept itself has also been amenable to attempts to promote the reciprocal obligations and responsibilities that may be attached to it.[80] Plant argues that citizenship thereby becomes 'an achievement rather than a status'.[81] While the level of state intervention and redistribution required is clearly greater than a market/consumer-based system would involve, there is still the underlying problem of social inequality that the enforcement of social responsibility seems as likely to sustain as to remove.[82] Increased fines or even imprisonment of parents in respect of their child's truancy[83] may ultimately improve the educational opportunities of some children; but others will be even more disadvantaged by the sanctions imposed on an already disadvantaged family.

Social Rights and Cultural Diversity

One of the most problematic aspects of education rights as social rights arise from social, ethnic or religious diversity, noted in Chapter 1. Perhaps more so than any other sphere of state activity, education is able to influence significantly the way that children from diverse religious, cultural and social backgrounds perceive the world in which they are growing up. We saw in Chapter 1 that there is considerable scope for conflict between the family and the state, even if not always played out through protest or attempts at legal redress. The cultural integrity of the family and social groupings is potentially weakened by their having to surrender autonomy over educational matters to the state. That is not to deny the fact that those cultural rights enjoy a degree of protection within the framework of human rights (see below), for example in the state's duty (under the ECHR), in the exercise of any functions which it assumes in relation to education and to teaching, to 'respect the right of parents to ensure such education and teaching in conformity with their own religious and philosophical convictions',[84] or even (under the Universal Declaration, which does not contain rights enforceable by the individual) 'a prior right to choose the kind of education that shall be given to their child'.[85] As we saw in Chapter 1, the UNCRC also goes as far as to respect cultural integrity by providing that education should be directed at, inter alia, 'respect for the child's parents, his or

---

[79] See D Harris, *Justifying State Welfare* (Oxford, Basil Blackwell, 1985).

[80] See, eg, Secretary of State for Social Security/Minister of Welfare Reform, *New ambitions for our country. A New Contract for Welfare* Cm 3805 (London, TSO, 1998). For a critique, see Lister (2000), above n 78, 75. See generally M Bulmer and AM Rees (eds), *Citizenship Today: The Contemporary Relevance of TH Marshall* (London, University College London Press, 1996).

[81] R Plant, 'Supply Side Citizenship' (1999) 6(3) *Journal of Social Security Law* 124, 125.

[82] Eg P Alcock, 'Welfare and Self-Interest' in F Field *et al*, *Stakeholder Welfare* (London, IEA, 1996) 47 at 52–3.

[83] See Chap 4 at p 143.

[84] ECHR, Art 2 of Prot 1 (second sentence).

[85] Universal Declaration of Human Rights, Art 26(3).

her own cultural identity, language and values'.[86] Nonetheless, the fact that various international instruments require states parties to ensure that education inculcates tolerance, understanding and friendship towards all racial, ethnic or religious groups,[87] plus (under the UNCRC) respect for 'the national values of the country in which the child is living . . . and for civilizations different from his or her own',[88] does not guarantee minority groups the protection they might seek from inroads into their cultural autonomy. Indeed, the state's duty under the UNCRC to direct the education of the child towards 'the preparation of the child for responsible life in a free society' may be inconsistent with the child's religious upbringing within a strict faith community, a conflict of a kind that is particularly well illustrated by the case of Amish people in the United States referred to in Chapter 1 and discussed in detail in Chapter 7 (albeit that the US has not in fact ratified the Convention).[89] Moreover, while it is true that not only religious freedom but also the right of a child from a minority group to 'enjoy his or her own culture' and 'to use his or her own language' is protected by the UNCRC, that does not guarantee a right to be taught in one's mother tongue or freedom from the assimilatory effects of schooling, particularly in the state sector.[90]

The modern state is faced by a difficult problem. According proper respect to the rights of minorities to have their children educated in a way that protects their community's traditions, culture and ethnic or religious identity involves acknowledging a right to segregation. Yet it might be considered in the interests of society as a whole for there to be more integration, because it is said that segregation is clearly divisive and tends to reinforce social and cultural barriers between different communities. This issue has been the subject of an ongoing and at times very intense debate over the past few years. The debate has centred on the role of multiculturalism. In the context of education, it is relevant to issues such as faith schools, school uniform and the effects of choice of school, although it is of particular relevance to the curriculum. It is the subject of discussion in Chapter 7, where the schools system's capacity to respond to cultural diversity is assessed with particular reference to the content of school education, including religious education and sex education.

---

[86] Art 29(1)(d).

[87] Universal Declaration on Human Rights (1948), Art 26(2), International Covenant on Economic, Social and Cultural Rights (1966) Art 13(1) (the only one that refers to ethnic groups as opposed merely to religious or racial groups), UNCRC, Art 29(1)(d). See aso the Framework Convention for the Protection of National Minorities, discussed in Chap 7.

[88] UNCRC, Art 29(1)(c).

[89] See pp 391–4.

[90] See below and also Chap 7. See further H Cullen, 'Education Rights or Minority Rights?' (1993) 7 *International Journal of Law and the Family* 143. Kilkelly notes that 'notwithstanding that pluralism in education for minorities requires that policies designed to assimilate minorities be prohibited [citing Art 5 of the Framework Convention for the Protection of National Minorities, 1995 (ETS No.157)], the Court [of Human Rights] has shown a tolerance for assimilation policies which appears to be out of line with its insistence on pluralism in other matters': U Kilkelly, *The Child and the European Convention on Human Rights* (Aldershot, Ashgate, 1999) 81.

THE RIGHT TO EDUCATION AS A RIGHT OF THE CHILD

We have seen already that international law recognises the child's right to education. In stating that '[n]o-one shall be denied the right to education' or that the state should 'recognize the right of everyone to education',[91] the ECHR and the ICESCR respectively are not restricting the right to persons of any particular age, although it is assumed that the state has the power and authority to prescribe the age at which education should start. The UNCRC refers specifically to the right to primary education but does not specifically mention nursery or pre-school education.[92]

The major problem with the child's enjoyment of the right to education flows from the fact the child's parents also hold rights over his or her education. This is the case under UK education law but also under the ECHR. There is a dichotomy in Article 2 of the First Protocol to the Convention, which confers a right on the *child* to education but, in its second sentence, upholds the right of the *parents* to have their religious and philosophical convictions respected in the matter of teaching.[93] Parental rights over a child's education not only have the potential to generate intra-familial conflict but may also weaken some of the rights of the child in this context. The fact that education law in the UK has conferred a range of rights on parents exclusively, especially those (discussed in later chapters) concerned with the exercise of choice (for example, choice of school, the content of special educational provision or the child's receipt of sex education in school) or remedies (such as appeal rights over school admission or permanent exclusion), has caused parental rights to predominate in this sphere. Indeed, in her report on the UK in 2000, the UN's Special Rapporteur on the right to education referred to 'the inherited legal status of the child as the object of a legally recognised relationship between the school and the child's parents rather than the subject of the right to education and of . . . rights in education'.[94]

Many have remarked on the contrast between child law in general and the law of education in this respect, pointing not merely to the absence of independent procedural or substantive education rights for children but also, for example, to the absence of general welfare principles under education law equivalent to those,

---

[91] ECHR, Art 2 of Prot 1; CESRC, Art 13(1).

[92] Arts 28 and 29.

[93] See *Eriksson v Sweden* (1990) 12 EHRR 183, para 93.

[94] UN Commission on Human Rights, *Report submitted by Katarina Tomaševski, Special Rapporteur on the right to education, Addendum. Mission to the United Kingdom 18–22 October 1999*, E/CN4/2000/6/Add 2 (Centre for Human Rights, Geneva, 2000), available at www.unhcr.ch/Huridcoda, para 90. On the exclusion of children's rights in education, see eg C Hamilton, 'Rights of the Child: a Right to Education and a Right in Education' in C Bridge (ed), *Family Law Towards the Millennium: Essays for P.M. Bromley* (London, Butterworths, 1997) 201–33; P Meredith, 'Children's Rights in Education' in J Fionda (ed), *Legal Concepts of Childhood* (Oxford, Hart, 2001) 203–22; N Harris, 'Education Law: Excluding the Child' (2000) 12(1) *Education and the Law* 31; and J Fortin, *Children's Rights and the Developing Law* (London, Lexis Nexis Butterworths, 2003).

including the paramountcy and best interests principles or the duty to consider the ascertainable wishes or feelings of the child, that are expected to underpin decision-making under the Children Act 1989.[95] Theoretical concerns about the failure of education law to accord due recognition to children's independent rights are matched by empirical evidence that children are often marginalised in the decision-making process and that, while their participation in certain decision-making fora may not always be in their best interests (for example, where comments on children's educational difficulties or mental problems might undermine confidence and self-esteem), its exclusion is often unjustified. Monk makes the salient point that, in any event, proceedings under the Children Act 1989 do not always take proper account of the wishes and feelings of the child and that, accordingly, 'presenting the Act as a model for "rights in education" is, at best, highly problematic'.[96] He says that the private law sphere of child law, where the interests of the child tend to be tied in with those of the family, the preservation of which is given primacy, parallels education law and that this is unsurprising, as both the family and the school 'represent sites of childhood regulation, surveillance and control'.[97]

Yet, the dominant emphasis placed on the parent's rights rather than those of the child by education law constitutes an important part of the dichotomy between the two areas of law. This dominance is predicated on two assumptions: first, that the interests of parents and children as regards the latter's education are as one; and, secondly, that children's ability to act with competence over decisions concerning their education is in question and, consequently, there is a risk of damaging their future prospects and harming their long term interests.[98] The basis of each of these assumptions is open to criticism, especially in the case of older children whose competence is recognised in other legal spheres, such as the *Gillick*-competent child in relation to health care;[99] or the child whose age and understanding gives them the right to be consulted over decisions concerning their care,[100] or, as provided for by Article 12 of the UNCRC, more generally.[101] Why, for example, should the law assume, as it does, that a girl or boy of 15 or 16 is not competent to decide whether he or she should receive sex education at school and leave the parent free to withdraw the child from sex education lessons

---

[95] Art 3 of the UNCRC requires 'the best interests of the child' to be a 'primary consideration' in all actions concerning children undertaken by public or private social welfare institutions, courts of law, administrative authorities or legislative bodies. There is no equivalent within education law to the principle in s 1(1) of the Children Act 1989, which provides that when a court is determining any question relating to, inter alia, the upbringing of a child 'the child's welfare shall be the court's paramount consideration'. S 1(1) applies only within the context of litigation: see R White, P Carr and N Lowe, *The Children Act in Practice* (3rd edn, London, Butterworths Lexis Nexis, 2002), paras 2.13–2.15.

[96] D Monk, 'Children's Rights in Education—Making sense of the Contradictions' (2002) 14 *Child & Family Law Quarterly* 45, at 48.

[97] Ibid, 49.

[98] P Meredith, 'Children's Rights and Education' in J Fionda (ed), *Legal Concepts of Childhood* (Oxford, Hart, 2001) 203–22, at 206.

[99] See J Fortin, *Children's Rights and the Developing Law* (2nd edn, London, LexisNexis, 2003), ch 5.

[100] Children Act 1989 s 1(3).

[101] See p 53 below.

regardless of the child's wishes?[102] It has, in fact, been observed that in many countries the education system fails to 'respect children's right to participate in decision-making in accordance with their own evolving capacities'.[103] The notion of 'evolving capacities' is incorporated within UNCRC Article 12, as discussed below, but also in Article 5, which affirms that the parent's responsibilities and rights to provide 'in a manner consistent with the evolving capacities of the child, appropriate direction and guidance in the exercise by the child of the rights recognized in the . . . Convention', which include the rights concerning education.[104]

Perhaps one should not lose sight of the fact that the law is also seeking to reconcile the potential conflict between the state and the family by (at least in relation to particular matters, such as sex education or religious education) giving primacy to the cultural integrity and religious or moral values of the particular family rather than the wider social interests that the state seeks to uphold. In striking what it sees as an appropriate balance, the independent interests of the individual child seem difficult to accommodate. Perhaps, ultimately, what is happening is that the state education system is not merely fulfilling an important social function in providing an education service, but, as noted above, is also acting in an agency capacity for what is an essential element in the upbringing of a child, ensuring his or her education, the responsibility for which ultimately still rests with the parent. Discipline and education are considered aspects of parental responsibility;[105] and the basis for disciplinary authority over school pupils was for many years considered to be the *in loco parentis* principle. In *Ryan v Fildes*, for example, Tucker J said that 'when a parent sends his child to school, he delegates to the teacher the taking of such steps as are necessary to maintain disciplime with regard to the child committed to the teacher's care'.[106] By the time of the Elton Report in 1989 the *in loco parentis* principle as a basis for teachers' disciplinary authority was being questioned,[107] and today most aspects of teachers' disciplinary authority are legislatively based and controlled.[108] In recent years there has been an attempt to reassert notions of parental responsibility over matters such as school attendance and children's behaviour, through increased penalties for truancy,[109] the use of home–school agreements[110] and the introduction of parenting contracts and parenting orders.[111] These developments reinforce the idea that educational provision is

---

[102] Education Act 1996, s 405. See pp 406–10 below.

[103] G Lansdown, *The Evolving Capacities of the Child* (Florence, UNICEF, 2005) 59.

[104] Arts 28 and 29, noted above.

[105] C Barton and G Douglas, *Law and Parenthood* (London, Butterworths, 1995) 114–16.

[106] [1938] 3 All ER 517 at 521D–E.

[107] Lord Elton, *Discipline in Schools. Report of the Committee of Enquiry Chaired by Lord Elton* (London, HMSO, 1989), para 72.

[108] See generally N Harris and K Eden with A Blair, *Challenges to School Exclusion* (London, Routledge Falmer, 2000), ch 3; and see further the Education and Inspections Bill 2006, Part 7, ch 1, which will reinforce schools' and teachers' disciplinary authority.

[109] See p 143 below.

[110] See the School Standards and Framework Act 1998, ss 110 and 111.

[111] Under the Anti-social Behaviour Act 2003: see p 143 (n 13) below.

made on the basis of a kind of contract between parents and state, sometimes expressed in the language of 'partnership' (eg, '[p]artnership with parents plays a key role . . . in enabling children and young people with [special educational needs] to achieve their potential'[112]). Indeed, it is consistent with the idea of a 'welfare contract' based on a balance of rights and responsibilities that the Labour Government has promoted since 1997.[113] However, it is a 'contract' to which the child has seemingly not been a party.

The Education Act 1997, for example, made provision for 'home–school partnership documents' intended to formalise the relationship between parent and school by incorporating a statement of the school's and the parents' respective responsibilities for the education of the child. It would have permitted school admission arrangements to enable a child to be denied admission on the ground that the parent had not signed the declaration acknowledging and accepting his or her responsibilities under the agreement.[114] The Act provided that the partnership document could not create obligations in respect of whose breach liability could arise in contract or tort.[115] It did not provide for the child to be a party to this agreement, even though it was the child's education for which the school would be responsible. This has since been remedied: the 1997 Act provisions were replaced under the School Standards and Framework Act 1998 with two important changes. First, the power to deny admission to a school on the basis of the parent's failure to sign the declaration was omitted. Secondly, the child, once a registered pupil, could now be invited by the governing body of the school to sign the parental declaration 'as a sign that he acknowledges and accepts the school's expectations of its pupils', but only where the governing body considers that the pupil 'has a sufficient understanding of the home–school agreement as it relates to him'. [116] This recognition of the child's capacity is significant; moreover, an Ofsted survey has found that schools uniformly support the involvement of children as signatories and that pupils are keen to sign: '[f]or many pupils it is the first document they are asked to sign and they feel very "grown-up" and take it very seriously. The pupils' commitment is very important to the success of the home–school agreement'.[117] In terms of its recognition of the child's independent rights, however, this development is somewhat limited, treating them as merely an adjunct to those of the parent. For one thing, the child has to sign the *parental* declaration rather than there being a separate pupil declaration. Moreover, in so doing he or she is, according to the 1998 Act, indicating acceptance of the school's expectations of pupils; there is no mention made of acceptance of the obligations owed to its pupils by the school.

---

[112] Department for Education and Skills, *Special Educational Needs Code of Practice* (London, DfES, 2001), para 2.1.

[113] Secretary of State for Social Security and Minister for Welfare Reform, *New Ambitions for our Country. A New Contract for Welfare*, Cm 3805 (London, TSO, 1998).

[114] Education Act 1997, s 13. This section (inserting two new ss, 413A and 413B, into the Education Act 1996) was never brought into force and was repealed by the School Standards and Framework Act 1998.

[115] Ibid.

[116] SSFA 1998, s 110(5).

[117] Cited in DfES, *Home-School Agreements*, web-based guidance available at www.dfes.gov.uk.

It is in the area of decision-making that the right of the child to education becomes particularly problematic. A range of potential decisions falls to be made about the education of individual children. The parent's interest in such decisions is recognised both by international and national law and, irrespective of whether the ultimate aim of the law is to safeguard the child's educational interests, the fact remains that parents are the presumed actors. As noted above and in Chapter 1, the ECHR confers on parents the right to a degree of influence over their children's education by providing that in the exercise by the state of any functions which it assumes in relation to education and to teaching, respect must be paid to 'the right of parents to ensure such education and teaching in conformity with their own religious and philosophical convictions'.[118] National law has also recognised parents' vested interest in their children's education. Since the 1944 Act the Secretary of State and LEAs have been under a duty (now in section 9 of the Education Act 1996) to have regard to the general principle that 'pupils are to be educated in accordance with the wishes of their parents, so far as that is compatible with the provision of efficient instruction and training and the avoidance of unreasonable public expenditure'.[119] The terms in which this duty is expressed (which were incorporated into the UK's reservation to the right to education in Article 2 of the First Protocol to the ECHR) has limited its potency as a guarantor of parental choice.[120] In *Watt v Kesteven County Council*, for example, Denning LJ said[121] that a local education authority is entitled 'to have regard to other things as well, and also to make exceptions to the general principle if it thinks fit to do so. It cannot therefore be said that a county council is at fault simply because it does not see fit to comply with the parent's wishes'; and in a much more recent case, David Pannnick QC (sitting as a High Court judge) confirmed that it was 'well established that s 9 does not require the local education authority to give priority to parental wishes, so long as they are properly considered and taken into account'.[122] Nonetheless, the principle that education should broadly conform to the wishes of the parents conveys a more

---

[118] ECHR, Art 2 of Prot 1.

[119] Education Act 1996, s 9; previously Education Act 1944, s 76.

[120] See Chap 5 at 237–43.

[121] [1955] 1 QB 408 (CA), at 424.

[122] *R v West Sussex County Council ex p S* [1999] ELR 40 at 45A–B. See also *Darling and Jones v Ministry of Education* (1962) *The Times* 7 Apr 1962; *Wood v Ealing LBC* [1967] Ch 346; *Cumings v Birkenhead Corporation* [1972] Ch 12; *Harvey v Strathclyde Regional District Council* (1988) *The Times* 13 Oct 1988 (referring to the equivalent provision in Scotland); *R v London Borough of Lambeth ex p G* [1994] ELR 207. In *Cumings* (above) the father of a boy who attended a Roman Catholic primary school complained that his son had been allocated a place by the LEA at a Roman Catholic secondary school, contrary to his wishes. The CA held that for the purposes of the 1944 Act (s 76) duty, parental wishes were not the sole or overriding consideration, for there were other things to which the LEA might have regard which might outweigh the wishes of the parents. See further Chap 5. The principle in s 9 may in particular be a factor to be considered in conjunction with parental choice of special educational provision and school placement: see *B v Gloucestershire County Council and the Special Educational Needs Tribunal* [1998] ELR 539; *S and S v Bracknell Forest Borough Council and the Special Educational Needs Tribunal* [1999] ELR 51; *W-R v Solihull Metropolitan Borough Council and Wall* [1999] ELR 528; *C v Buckinghamshire County Council and the Special Educational Needs Tribunal* [1999] ELR 179; *B v London Borough of Harrow* [2000] ELR 109 (HL); *S v Metropolitan Borough of Dudley and Another* [2000] ELR 330. See Chap 6 at 345–7.

general recognition of parental rights as opposed to those of the child, which carries through into various specific areas, including those involving appeal rights, such as preference for school admission[123] or special educational needs placements.[124]

All of the above provisions were first established before the UK ratified the UNCRC, Article 12 of which requires states to 'assure to the child who is capable of forming his or her own views the right to express those views freely in all matters affecting the child', with the child's views to be given 'due weight in accordance with the age and maturity of the child'. Lundy has conceptualised this right with reference to 'space' (the opportunity to express a view), 'voice' (enabling children to express their views), 'audience' (the view must be listened to) and 'influence' (acting on the view where appropriate to do so).[125] In 1995 the UK was criticised by the UN Committee on the Rights of the Child for its failure to uphold Article 12 in several key areas of educational decision-making, including the withdrawal of the child from sex education; the process of exclusion from school, including the fact that the child has no independent right of appeal against permanent exclusion;[126] and other decisions, which were not in fact specified in the report but which might justifiably have included preference as to school admission and withdrawal from religious education or collective worship. In relation to all these decisions the parents alone have rights under the present legislation (but sixth formers will soon have a withdrawal right regarding collective worship). The Committee said that in all of these 'the child is not systematically invited to express his/her opinion and those opinions may not be given due weight, as required by Article 12'.[127] Paying close attention to the evidence presented by the Children's Rights Development Unit in *UK Agenda for Children*,[128] the UN Committee also expressed concern about a failure to ensure implementation of the general 'best interests' principle in Article 3 of the Convention.[129] The Committee has returned to these issues in its second report, in 2002.[130]

Commenting on the failure to accord due recognition to the rights of the child in the field of education, and especially the right to express views and for them to be duly considered, Dame Brenda Hale, writing in 1997, said:

> in every other area of dispute about a child's upbringing, there is a formal requirement to discover the child's views and give due consideration to them, having regard to his age and understanding. Education looms large in a child's life... It is curious that a sys-

---

[123] School Standards and Framework Act 1998, ss 86 and 94.
[124] Education Act 1996, s 326 and Sched 27.
[125] L Lundy, '"Voice" is Not Enough: the Implications of Article 12 of the United Nations Convention on the Rights of the Child for Education', paper presented at the SLSA conference, University of Liverpool, 31 Mar 2005.
[126] See nn 201 and 202 and accompanying text, below.
[127] UN Committee on the Rights of the Child, *Concluding Observations of the Committee on the Rights of the Child: United Kingdom*, CRC/C/15/Add 34 (Geneva, Centre for Human Rights, 1995), para 216. For the new worship opt out for sixth formers see p 437 n 561 below.
[128] (London, CRDU, 1994).
[129] UN, above n 127, para 213.
[130] See below, p 56.

tem which is so radical in other respects has been slower than others to recognise his independent status.[131]

There are two particular reasons why this failure is regrettable. First, it should not be assumed that in every case the parent will be able to safeguard the child's best interests. As Fortin says in relation to the exclusion appeal process, for example, there will be cases where 'parents are too uninterested or nervous to pursue an appeal on their child's behalf, or where they are incapable of presenting the child's case satisfactorily or objectively'.[132] Moreover, the *Special Educational Needs Code of Practice*, a revised edition of which came into force in January 2002, addresses the need to involve the child in various aspects of needs assessment and decision-making. It recognises that parents whose experience of co-operation with professionals has been disappointing or made them feel marginalised might be unwilling to involve their children in decision-making, lest the authorities place undue weight on the views of their child. The parents may feel that their child is 'ill-equipped to grasp the relevant factors' or they and their child 'may have different views about the origins of and provision for a special educational need'.[133] One of the grounds for the Government's opposition to a Private Member's Bill in the 1990s which aimed to establish an independent appeal right for children alongside that of the parent in respect of special educational needs decisions was precisely because of the risk of the parent and child disagreeing.[134] A separation of interests is recognised under child care law under the Children Act 1989, which accords the child separate procedural rights and makes provision for independent representation for the child, in addition to requiring the court to have regard to 'the ascertainable wishes and feelings of the child concerned (considered in the light of his age and understanding)'.[135] One of the effects of doing so under education law might be to ensure that the child's interests become more central within the decision-making process; even allowing for the fact that the law permits wider issues, such as the interests of other pupils or of the school as a whole, to be considered by independent appeal panels considering an appeal against an exclusion, the child's interests are not always sufficiently well recognised in these cases.[136]

Problems would still arise where there was a conflict between the child's and parent's wishes. This would be especially sensitive where cultural or religious matters were in question. As Cullen says, '[p]arents may oppose participation in activities thought to be contrary to family beliefs, whereas children, through

---

[131] Foreword, in N Harris, *Special Educational Needs and Access to Justice* (Bristol, Jordans, 1997), p vi.

[132] J Fortin, *Children's Rights and the Developing Law* (2nd edn, London, LexisNexis Butterworths, 2003) 183.

[133] Department for Education and Skills, *Special Educational Needs Code of Practice* (London, DfES, 2001), para 3.5. See also the Welsh code: Welsh Assembly Government, *Special Educational Needs Code of Practice for Wales* (Cardiff, National Assembly for Wales, 2004), para 3.5.

[134] HL Debs, Vol. 575, col. 1155, 11 Dec 1996, per Lord Henley. See Harris, n 131 above, at 5–6.

[135] S 1(3)(a).

[136] See N Harris and K Eden with A Blair, *Challenges to School Exclusion* (London, RoutledgeFalmer, 2000); C Hamilton, 'Rights of the Child: a Right to Education and a Right in Education' in C Bridge (ed), *Family Law Towards the Millennium: Essays for P.M. Bromley* (London, Butterworths, 1997) 201.

curiosity or a desire for acceptance, wish to share in the activities of fellow students'.[137] In *Begum*,[138] the claimant was aged nearly 14 at the time that she decided she wished on religious grounds to wear the jilbab to school. The school's ban on this form of dress led to her claim that her rights under Article 9 (freedom to manifest her religion) had been violated. Baroness Hale made the general comment that it was

> not surprising to find adolescents making different moral judgments from those of their parents. It is part of growing up. The fact that they are not yet fully adult may help to justify interference with the choices they have made. It cannot be assumed, as it can with adults, that these choices are the product of a fully developed adult autonomy.[139]

But her Ladyship felt that there was sufficient autonomy for there to be an interference with the claimant's choice as regards her own religious beliefs and how they were expressed or manifested.[140] Archard argues that in a culturally diverse society, children's education should prepare them sufficiently to make their own choices, when an adult, about how to live their lives; permitting the parents' values and beliefs to hold sway could deny the child 'the right to an open future'.[141] At least in the context of its educational function, the state would seek to protect that right.[142]

Secondly, it must clearly be the case that decisions about children are likely to be more appropriate if they take account of the child's wishes and feelings, because a particular form of educational provision is likely to be more effective if it is accepted by the child and includes support for particular difficulties that the child may be best placed to identify. As Sachs J said in the Constitutional Court of South Africa, in a case where the South African Parliament's ban on corporal punishment was challenged on religious grounds and where the interests of the pupils, many of whom 'would have been in their late teens and capable of articulate expression', had not been represented by a '*curator ad litem*' to ensure that the children's voice or voices could be heard, the children's 'actual experiences and opinions would not necessarily have been decisive, but they would have enriched the dialogue, and the factual and experiential foundations for the balancing exercise in this difficult matter would have been more secure'.[143] The *Special Educational Needs Code of Practice* in force in England makes a similar point, in stating that '[c]hildren and young people with special educational needs have a unique knowledge of their own needs and

---

[137] Cullen, above n 90, 160.
[138] *R (Begum) v Headteacher and Governors of Denbigh High School* [2006] UKHL 15.
[139] Ibid, at para 93.
[140] Ibid.
[141] DW Archard, *Children, Family and The State* (Aldershot, Ashgate, 2003) 131–2.
[142] Ibid, 134–42, discussing the justification for such an approach.
[143] *Christian Education South Africa v Minister of Education* (Case CCT 4/00) [2001] 1 LRC 441, at para 53.

circumstances and their own views about what sort of help they would like to help them make the most of their education'.[144]

Progress towards recognising children as independent holders of rights in the field of education has been somewhat slow in England, lagging behind the rather more enlightened approach adopted in Scotland, where there is now a children's rights framework to statutory educational provision. In particular, the Standards in Scotland's Schools Act 2000 provides that '[i]t shall be the right of every child of school age to be provided with school education by, or by virtue of arrangements made, or entered into, by, an education authority'.[145] There is nothing akin to this in the English legislation. This was specifically noted by the UNCRC in its second report on the UK's implementation of the Convention.[146] The Committee also expressed the concern that, in education, 'schoolchildren are not systematically consulted in matters that affect them', and it recommended that the UK take further steps 'to promote, facilitate and monitor systematic, meaningful and effective participation of all groups of children in society, including in schools, for example through school councils'.[147] It welcomed developments in Scotland to reflect Article 12 of the Convention. It presumably had in mind section 2 of the Standards in Scotland's Schools Act 2000, which provides that in carrying out its duty to ensure that 'education is directed to the development of the personality, talents and mental and physical abilities of the child or young person to their fullest potential' (which thereby incorporates Article 29(1)(a) of the UNCRC), an education authority must 'have due regard, so far as is reasonably practicable, to the views (if there is a wish to express them) of the child or young person in decisions that significantly affect that child or young person, taking account of the child or young person's age and maturity'. The Committee considered that legislation was needed throughout the UK to reflect Article 12 and ensure that there was respect for 'children's rights to express their views and have them given due weight in all matters concerning their education, including school discipline'.[148]

Against a background of continuous debate about how children's interests can best be represented in decision-making and political processes[149] and a general policy trend involving the establishment of a range of mechanisms for

---

[144] Department for Education and Skills, *Special Educational Needs Code of Practice* (London, DfES, 2001), para 3.2. See also Welsh Assembly Government, *Special Educational Needs Code of Practice for Wales* (Cardiff, National Assembly for Wales, 2004), para 3.2.

[145] Standards in Scotland's Schools Act 2000, s 1. See also Scottish Executive, *Improving Our Schools—the Consultation* (Edinburgh, The Scottish Executive, 2000).

[146] Committee on the Rights of the Child, *Concluding Observations of the Committee on the Rights of the Child: United Kingdom*, CRC/C/15/Add 188 (Geneva, Centre for Human Rights, 2002).

[147] Ibid, paras 29 and 30.

[148] Ibid, para 48.

[149] See, eg, M Rosenbaum and P Newell, *Taking Children Seriously* (London, Calouste Gulbenkian Foundation, 1991); R Hodgkin and P Newell, *Effective Government Structures for Children* (London, Calouste Gulbenkian Foundation, 1996); J Fortin, *Children's Rights and the Developing Law* (2nd edn, London, LexisNexis, 2003), ch 6; R Hodgkin, 'Child Impact Analysis', in R Hodgkin (ed), *Child Impact Statements 1997/98. An Experiment in Child Proofing UK Parliamentary Bills* (London, National Children's Bureau, 1999) 1.

consultation with children over local and national policy issues,[150] including the creation of the office of Children's Commissioner for England with express responsibilities in this area,[151] there has been steady progress of late in the field of education. Take, for example, the question of discipline policy within schools, referred to by the UN Committee. The Conservative Government's guidance on school discipline policies in 1994 advised that pupils should be involved in discussions about the school's discipline policy,[152] but the present Government's guidance on *School Inclusion*, introduced in 1999, identified this as a 'key principle', stating that 'pupils can help to re-inforce school behaviour policies by active involvement in anti-bullying and harassment policies, and contributing ideas through Schools' Councils and in class discussions'.[153] The Government chose not to make explicit provision in the School Standards and Framework Act 1998 to require that pupils be consulted over school behaviour policies, disciplinary measures and home–school agreements; and it opposed an amendment to the Bill to that effect proposed by Baroness David.[154] The Government instead saw this as 'a matter for individual schools in the light of their particular circumstances... Schools require flexibility, and that is best left to guidance rather than wording on the face of the Bill'.[155] The Government's approach on this matter was mirrored in its second report to the UN Committee on the Rights of the Child.[156]

---

[150] Eg, the examination by the Social Exclusion Unit's Policy Action Team 12 on Young People on ways in which children and young people can influence policy design and delivery, noted in Secretary of State for Social Security, *Opportunity for All. Tackling poverty and social exclusion*, Cm 4445 (London, TSO, 1999), ch 3, para 75. Note also the consultation of children and young people (including 500 in England) by Save the Children in the context of the review of the implementation of the UN Convention on the Rights of the Child leading up to the UK's second report, even though only the consultation in Scotland was specifically referred to in the report itself. (This led Gerison Lansdown of the Children's Rights Office to conclude that 'the commitment to consulting with children and young people was little more than cosmetic': 'Children's Rights: A response to the 2nd UK Government Report to the Committee on the Rights of the Child', paper presented at the NYAS annual conference, 27–28 Jan 2000, 5.) For details of the Scottish consultation, see HM Government, *United Nations Convention on the Rights of the Child. Second Report by the United Kingdom* (London, TSO, 1999), Annex C; and Save the Children, *'Its Our Education': Young People's Views on Improving Their Schools* (London, Save the Children, 1999). The Green Paper, Department of Health, *Every Child Matters*, Cm 5860 (London, TSO, 2003), covering a range of issues (including education) relevant to children, was issued for consultation in a special version for children and young people.

[151] Under the Children Act 2004, s 2, the Children's Commissioner in England is under a general duty, inter alia, to promote awareness of the views of children in general, and in particular among persons exercising functions or engaged in activities affecting children and on the part of the Secretary of State (whom the Commissioner is to advise on such matters). Children's views with which the Commissioner is, in particular, to be concerned are to include those on their physical and mental health, their protection from harm or neglect, their education and training, their contribution to society and their social and economic well being.

[152] Department for Education, Circular 8/94, *Pupil Behaviour and Discipline* (London, Department for Education, 1994), paras 19 and 21.

[153] DfEE, Circular 10/99, *School Inclusion: Pupil Support* (London, DfEE, 1999), para 2.1; see now DfES, *Advice on Whole School Behaviour and Attendance Policy* (London, DfES, 2003), paras 38–9.

[154] HL Debs, Vol. 590, Col. 697, 8 June 1998.

[155] Ibid, col. 698, per Lord Whitty.

[156] HM Government, *United Nations Convention on the Rights of the Child. Second Report by the United Kingdom* (London, TSO, 1999), para 9.33.5.

An important advance, however, occurred with the introduction via the Education Act 2002, section 176, of a new duty on LEAs and governing bodies of maintained schools to have regard to guidance given to them by the Secretary of State 'about consultation with pupils in connection with the taking of decisions affecting them'.[157] The guidance must 'provide for a pupil's views to be considered in the light of his age and understanding'.[158] The guidance was issued in April 2004[159] and, although it could perhaps be criticised for being fairly short on concrete measures for involving pupils (for which the defence might be that it is best if schools are left to develop their own strategies), it does stress in clear terms the benefits of pupil participation for both young people and schools themselves. These include the reinforcement of citizenship education, raised self-esteem and the idea that children and young people are 'major stakeholders in society with important contributions to make to the design and delivery of services they receive, including education'.[160] It also acknowledges what could be one of the most challenging aspects of this initiative, namely ensuring that there is equality of opportunity to participate and be heard regardless of ethnicity, gender, disability or other excluding factor.[161] A duty to listen to children's views on aspects of their education may not go so far as to meet the ideal of children's participation as part of a 'power-sharing framework'[162] or as an 'agent of change',[163] as has been advocated, nor does it provide a firm structural basis for pupil participation such as is found under the legislation in a number of other European countries.[164] Moreoever, such participation might be viewed, cynically, as 'little more than a form of behaviour management and social control'.[165] Nonetheless, it could be important in fostering a cultural change within schools, whereby children are actively engaged in aspects of policy-making and thereby gain a greater sense of attachment to or 'ownership' of those policies. It might also increase the proportion of pupils feeling a sense of 'belonging' to a school, which, according to one research paper, stands at only 17 per cent in the UK compared with 30 per cent in France.[166]

However, there is the danger that the establishment of various national and local consultation and participation mechanisms, to which has been added consultation by a children's services authority during the preparation of a

---

[157] Education Act 2002, s 176(1).

[158] Ibid, s 176(2).

[159] Department for Education and Skills, *Working Together: Giving Children and Young People a Say*, DfES guidance 0134/2004 (London, DfES, 2004).

[160] Ibid, para 2.1.

[161] Ibid, para 3.1.

[162] Y Penny Lancaster, 'Listening to Young Children: Promoting the Voices of Children under the Age of Eight' in Rt Hon Lord Justice Thorpe (ed), *Hearing the Children* (Bristol, Family Law, 2004) 147 at 153.

[163] R Davie, 'Partnership with Children: The Advancing Trend' in R Davie, G Upton and V Varma (eds), *The Voice of the Child: A Handbook for Professionals* (London, Falmer, 1996) 1 at 9.

[164] See S Varnham, 'Citizenship in Schools: the Gap between Theory and Practice' (2005) 17 *Education & the Law* 53.

[165] D Monk, 'Children's Rights in Education—Making sense of the Contradictions' (2002) 14 *Child & Family Law Quarterly* 45, at 56.

[166] C Haydon and C Blaya, 'Children at the Margins' (2005) 26 *Policy Studies* 67 at 70.

children and young people's plan under the Children Act 2004,[167] leads to a sense of complacency about respect for children's independent interests and a false perception that somehow inclusiveness and the upholding of rights are guaranteed. A recent UNICEF report has highlighted diverse ways in which children would have the capacity to become involved in helping to shape various aspects of their education, such as curriculum design; effective teaching methods; developing school codes of behaviour, non-discrimination and non-violence; and classroom design and décor.[168] Kirby *et al* found that young people's participation in various organisations, including schools, in the UK often occurs on a one-off or isolated basis rather than being part of an embedded process.[169] There is a risk that mechanisms for participation could become discredited and viewed with cynicism by children and young people if they failed to influence policy.[170] Policies will also need to be underpinned by making children and young people aware of their rights under the UNCRC (as Article 42 requires), including those in Article 12, and by promoting the participation of pupils as members of school councils, local youth forums or 'associate members' of committees of school governing bodies (albeit that all associate members are excluded from having voting rights unless aged 18 at the date of their appointment).[171] Participation in schools councils has not specifically been legislated for in England, but has been in Wales.[172] It could have been adopted as part of citizenship education in England, but according to Sir Bernard Crick, whose committee's recommendations on this subject were influential in the shaping of Citizenship as a National Curriculum subject,[173] there were concerns 'as to what the DfES might make of trying to lay down in regulations for a schools council, their power or limits'.[174] The Welsh regulations[175] require each governing body of a school to establish a school council, comprised exclusively of pupils, whose purpose is to be the discussion of matters relating to the school, the pupils' education and other

---

[167] The Children and Young People's Plan (England) Regulations 2005 (SI 2005/2149), reg 7. The plan must set out the 'improvements which the authority intend to make . . . to the well-being of children and relevant young persons' in relation to various matters, including 'education, training and recreation', 'the contribution made by them to society', and 'social and economic well-being': ibid, reg 4. See also the Children Act 2004, s 17.

[168] G Lansdown, *The Evolving Capacities of the Child* (Florence, UNICEF, 2005) 59.

[169] P Kirby *et al*, *Building a Culture of Participation: Involving Young People in Policy, Service Planning, Delivery and Evaluation. Research Report* (London, DfES, 2003) 3.

[170] See P Anderson, 'School Students' Views on School Councils and Daily Life at School' (2000) 14 *Children & Society* 121; J Moorhead, 'Kids Rule', *The Guardian* (Education), 24 Oct 2000, 2; M Baginsky and D Hannam, *Schools Councils. The View of Students and Teachers* (London, NSPCC, 1999).

[171] The School Governance (Constitution) (England) Regulations 2003 (SI 2003/348), reg 11 and Sched 6, para 1 permit the governing body to include 'associate members' on committees of the governing body, but not as governors. The School Governance (Procedure) (England) Regulations 2003 (SI 2003/1377), reg 22 enables associate members to be given voting rights (save in respect of admissions; pupil discipline; the election or appointment of governors; and budget and financial commitments of the governing body), but provides that a person who was aged under 18 at the date of his or her appointment may not vote.

[172] The Schools Council (Wales) Regulations 2005 (SI 2005/3200 (W236)).

[173] See Chap 7.

[174] House of Commons Select Committee on Education and Skills, *Citizenship Education: Oral Evidence, 24 October 2005*, HC 581–I (London, TSO, 2005), Q11.

[175] Above n 172.

matters of concern of interest to them; and they place the governors and head teacher under a duty to consider and provide a response to any matter communicated to them by the school council. There seems no good reason why there should not be equivalent provision made in England.

Despite the claim in the section 176 consultation guidance that it supports Article 12 of the UNCRC, it is clear from the document that what is contemplated is enabling pupils collectively to influence policy formulation rather than giving a voice to the individual pupil over a particular education decision that relates to him or her. The guidance states that it

> is not aimed at diminishing the ability of decision-makers to apply established policies in cases related to individual pupils. It is, however, asking them to take account of children's and young people's views when setting and revising policies.[176]

However, no similar duty to that in section 176 is being proposed in relation to other decision makers in education, such as LEAs. Indeed, under the Education and Inspections Bill 2006 LEAs will be placed under a new statutory duty to consider representations by parents alone as to how the authority has exercised its functions concerning the ensuring of sufficient schools in their area to provide all pupils with the opportunity of an appropriate education.[177] Moreover, under the original wording of the proposed new duty on school governing bodies to consult with pupils and parents before making a statement of the school's behaviour policy only 'a sample of the registered pupils' needed to be consulted,[178] compared with parents in general.

When one searches for specific provisions recognising *individual* pupils as having rights to present their views concerning their education and for those views specifically to be taken into account, one finds them somewhat thin on the ground. It is clear that applications for school admission and appeals over refusals of choice of school are considered to be made by the parent. The legislation refers specifically to these as rights of parents, without mentioning the child.[179] There is no requirement to consult with or consider the views of the child: the separate Codes of Practice on admissions and admission appeals, regard to which must be had by the relevant decision makers or adjudicators when exercising their respective functions,[180] make no mention of participation by the child in the relevant processes.[181] The appeal code simply states that '[t]he parent is appealing on behalf of his or her child over a matter that is very important to the child's future'.[182] This carries through into any subsequent

[176] Department for Education and Skills, *Working Together: Giving Children and Young People a Say*, DfES guidance 0134/2004 (London, DfES, 2004), para 1.3.

[177] Education and Inspections Bill 2006 (as first published), cl 3, inserting s 14A into the EA 1996, which refers to the duty of the LEA under EA 1996, s 14 (on which see below p 91).

[178] Cl 75(3). An amendment has now removed the words 'a sample of the'.

[179] SSFA 1998, ss 86 and 94.

[180] SSFA 1998, s 84(3). This duty is to be strengthened under the Education and Inspections Bill: see Chap 5.

[181] DfES, *School Admissions Code of Practice*, DfES/0031/2003 (London, DfES, 2003); DfES, *School Admission Appeals Code of Practice*, DfES/0030/2003 (London, DfES, 2003).

[182] Ibid, para 4.26.

challenge via judicial review. In *R v London Borough of Richmond ex p JC*[183] an application for judicial review of an admission decision and the appeal panel's subsequent rejection of an appeal was made in the name of the child, aged 5. Kennedy LJ said (Ward LJ concurring) that such challenges should be made in the name of the parent, not the child, save in exceptional circumstances where the child might have a sufficient interest to bring the application in his or her own name.[184] Although the principal objection to bringing an application in the child's name appears to have been that it could constitute an 'abuse' of the legal aid system, Ward LJ concluded from the statute's reference to an appeal by 'the parent of the child' that '[i]t is therefore the parent's appeal, not the child's'.[185] This is also consistent with the case law on special educational needs appeals; the right to appeal to the SENDIST is conferred on the parent, and thus the right of further appeal to the High Court is construed accordingly.[186] In a subsequent admission case, Newman J considered that the 'rationale of the judgment [in *ex parte JC*] is that it is the parents' legal right and its enforcement by the parents is sufficient to protect the child's interest' and that 'exceptional circumstances' justifying an application in the child's name would be where 'the child's interest is not protected by the action of the parents'.[187] It is not clear when exactly the courts would accept that to be the case, however. For example, if the parent decided not to appeal and but the child was so concerned about not securing a place at his or her preferred school that he or she wished that an appeal should proceed, would the courts really permit the challenge to go ahead contrary to the wishes of the parent (even assuming that the child was in a position to obtain legal assistance)? Also adding to the rather confused messages here is Newman J's acknowledgment that the Article 6 ECHR right in question (concerning the independence and impartiality of the admission appeal panel) would be a right of the child,[188] whilst its protection would be conferred on the parent 'in connection with the panel proceedings which were his suit'.[189]

The issue also arose in a case in 2003 where a judicial review challenge was mounted in the name of two pupils to a decision to close their Church of

---

[183] [2001] ELR 21 (CA).

[184] At paras 31 and 69.

[185] At para 69. The relevant statutory provision then was the Education Act 1996, s 423(1). See now SSFA 1998, s 94(1), which adopts the same wording.

[186] See, in particular, *S v Special Educational Needs Tribunal and the City of Westminster* [1996] ELR 228 (CA). In *London Borough of Wandsworth v Mrs K and Special Educational Needs and Disability Tribunal* [2003] ELR 554, Newman J refused to grant leave for a child with special educational needs to be joined as a party to proceedings in which the LEA was challenging the SEN tribunal's decision that applied behavioural analysis, descriptions of facilities and staffing arrangements as specified in part 3 of the child's statement of SEN as educational provision (having the effect of putting the LEA under a statutory duty to ensure that it was all delivered).

[187] *R (B) v Head Teacher of Alperton Community School and Others; R v Head Teacher of Wembley High School and Others ex p T; R v Governing Body of Cardinal Newman High School and Others ex p C* [2001] ELR 359, at para [15].

[188] See also *S, T and P v London Borough of Breant and Others* [2002] ELR 556 at para [30] (per Schiemann LJ). In fact he concluded that the right to education was not a civil right and so was not protected by Art 6: see below.

[189] N 187 above para [16].

England primary school in Otley.[190] Scott Baker J held that both parents and children had an interest in a school closure or reorganisation decision, but that normally the parents would have the 'the real primary interest' in bringing the case.[191] He was mindful of the fact that the relevant legislation gave parents, but not children, the right to be consulted over the changes and to lodge objections to them. Nevertheless, Scott Baker J considered that the court would not regard the bringing of the application in the child's name as an abuse of the legal aid system unless there was clear evidence to that effect, which he felt was not the case. This contrasts with the presumption that it would amount to an abuse, unless shown otherwise, according to the Court of Appeal in *ex parte JC* (above). However, in an appeal decision over permission to apply for judicial review in the Otley case Sedley LJ said that Kennedy LJ's comments in *ex parte JC* were obiter, and he said that it was 'a defensible proposition that pupils may have a sufficient interest to seek judicial review of a decision affecting their schooling'.[192] Oddly, this issue appears not to have been considered or mentioned in any of the numerous school exclusion judicial review decisions in cases brought over the past decade, funded by legal aid. One reason may be the fundamental importance of the decision to the child him/herself for the child's reputation and long term future; an exclusion is perhaps considered to be potentially more damaging in those respects than a failure to secure a place at the school of one's choice. Another could be an underlying assumption that the child has not been well served by the parent; the child's behaviour at school may be partly attributed to a lack of parental control or competence, an assumption that also underlies the measures within the Anti-social Behaviour Act 2003 that seek to make the parent accountable for their child's behaviour at school (and elsewhere).[193]

The individual child's right to education is not therefore backed by independent procedural rights, because the parent alone is considered competent to enforce them. This has led to the participation of children in the various decision-making processes being somewhat marginalised in the past.[194] However, it would not now be consistent with the Government's drive to educate and involve pupils as citizens with rights and responsibilities for this to continue to be the position. In fact, over the past few years greater opportunities for the inclusion of the individual child in the decision-making process have been established. The *Special Educational Needs Code of Practice*, noted above, has an entire chapter on 'pupil participation',[195] focussing on ways that individual pupils' views and experience can be fed into a range of decision-making and assessment processes; for example, pupils should be encouraged to discuss any barriers to their learning.[196] When new special educational needs appeal

[190] *R (WB and KA) v Leeds School Organisation Committee* [2003] ELR 67.
[191] At para [37].
[192] *R (B) v Leeds School Organisation Committee* [2002] EWCA Civ 884.
[193] See Chap 4 at p 143 n 13.
[194] See N Harris, *Special Educational Needs and Access to Justice* (Bristol, Jordans, 1997); N Harris and K Eden, with A Blair, *Challenges to School Exclusion* (London, RoutledgeFalmer, 2000).
[195] DfES, *Special Educational Needs Code of Practice* (London, DfES, 2001), ch 3.
[196] Ibid, para 3.16.

regulations were introduced in 2001[197] they conferred some new rights on children. The parent's statement of his or her case 'may include the views of the child',[198] and if the LEA's statement of its case indicates that the LEA opposes the appeal it must state, inter alia, 'the views of the child concerning the issues raised by the appeal, or the reasons why the authority has not ascertained those views'.[199] The child now has a specific right to attend the hearing, although any person (including a child) could be excluded by the tribunal if likely to disrupt the proceedings or 'make it difficult for any person to adduce the evidence or make the representations necessary for the proper conduct of the appeal'.[200] There is also now a clear rule that the tribunal 'may permit the child to give evidence and to address the tribunal on the subject matter of the appeal'.[201] While the child is still not a party to the appeal and there is no specific provision enabling the child to be independently represented at the hearing (other than by the parent or vicariously via the parent's representative), the above amendments have resulted in the child's improved status in these proceedings. Effective participation of the child will, however, largely hinge on the approach adopted by the tribunal, which has a sensitive task.

In the area of permanent exclusion from school, again the pupil (if aged under 18) does not have a statutory right to take his or her case to the governing body's discipline committee and, if not reinstated by the governors, to appeal as a party to the statutory appeal proceedings to an independent appeal panel.[202] Sedley LJ stated in one exclusion case that 'the governing body and appeal committee are required to afford an opportunity to the pupil's parent, *clearly acting on behalf of the pupil*, to make oral representations'.[203] The child's rights are thus to be upheld only through the agency of the parent. The Secretary of State's guidance, to which LEAs, schools and appeal panels have to have regard,[204] stresses that an appeal panel should permit a pupil aged under 18 to attend, and speak on his or her own behalf, 'if he or she wishes to do so and the parent agrees'. [205] The child's opportunity to participate is consistent with a clear line of judicial authority.[206]

---

[197] Special Educational Needs Tribunal Regulations 2001 (SI 2001/600), as amended by the Special Educational Needs Tribunal (Amendment) Regulations 2002 (SI 2002/2787).

[198] Ibid, reg 9(1).

[199] Ibid, reg 13(2).

[200] Ibid, reg 30(2) and (4).

[201] Ibid, reg 30(7).

[202] These procedures are governed by the Education Act 2002 s 52 and the Education (Pupil Exclusions and Appeals) (Maintained Schools) (England) Regulations 2002 (SI 2002/3178) (as amended), reg 7. See also the Education (Pupil Exclusions and Appeals) (Pupil Referral Units) (England) Regulations 2002 (SI 2002/3179). Both of these sets of regulations came into force on 20 Jan 2003.

[203] Emphasis added. *R v Head Teacher and Independent Appeal Committee of Dunraven School ex parte B* [2000] ELR 156, at 183C

[204] SSFA 1998, s 68, now repealed and replaced by SI 2002/3178, reg 7, and see also SI 2002/3179.

[205] DfES, *Improving Behaviour and Attendance: Guidance on Exclusion from Schools and Pupil Referral Units* (DfES), available only at www.teachernet.gov.uk/wholeschool/behaviour/exclusion/guidance, para 103.

[206] The courts have accepted that it is not always possible to question the culprit (eg, if he or she has left the school premises: see *R v Roman Catholic Schools ex parte S* [1998] ELR 304; *R v Board of Governors and Appeal Committee of Bryn Elian High School ex parte Whippe* [1999] ELR 380). In other cases though, it might be a denial of natural justice: eg, *R v Laurelhill High School ex parte K*, 6

However, the parent effectively has a veto. Moreover, the rights of the child or young person (if he or she is aged under 18) are dependent on the application of the guidance, whereas the participation rights of the parent (or the young person if aged 18-plus) are set out in the regulations.[207]

Evidence of the child's participation in exclusion appeal hearings was provided by a research study of exclusion appeals led by the author in the late 1990s.[208] It found that the excluded child attended only a minority of hearings (just 40 per cent of those observed or 46 per cent of the hearings of the cases reported by parents). This was rather surprising in view of the prevalent view among the parents that the child should attend because the child's perspective would help the panel to understand not only the events leading to the exclusion but also the reasons behind them. Although a majority of panel members and LEAs considered the child's attendance at the hearing to be a matter of fairness and an aid to evaluation of the case, there was a concern about the attendance of young children and children liable to be unduly distressed by the experience. The researchers found that, even where the child was present at the hearing, it was unusual for him or her to be asked for his or her views or version of events; and where the child did not attend his or her views were presented to the panel by others (such as parents, teachers or social workers) in only half the cases. Overall, the child made an oral contribution in fewer than one third of the hearings that were observed. Nearly two thirds of the children permanently excluded from school each year, very nearly 80 per cent of whom are boys, are in the 13–15 age group[209] and, in the research study, three quarters of appeals concerned children in this age group. Most children of this age would be reasonably well able to give their views, suggesting that encouragement should be given to the child's attendance and participation. Yet parents have generally not been informed that hearing the child's views and his or her explanation of the events might be helpful to the panel.

Feb 1997 (unreported) (NI)). See also *Goss v Lopez*, 419 US 565; 95 SCt 729 (1975) where the Supreme Court remarked that it would be a 'strange disciplinary system in an educational institution if no communication was sought by the disciplinarian with the student in an effort to inform him of his dereliction and to let him tell his side of the story in order to make sure that an injustice is not done': per White J at III. It was a denial of due process of law, contrary to the 14th Amendment to the US Constitution, where the student was not given an opportunity to present his version of events. However, the UK courts have held that it is not always necessary for an appeal panel to hear from the excluded pupil directly. In *R (S) v Head Teacher of C High School and Others* [2002] ELR 73 it was held that the appeal panel had been entitled to consider an alleged verbal confession by the culprit introduced by the head teacher at the hearing. Richards J said (at paras [25]–[28]) that the claimant had had a fair opportunity at the hearing to challenge the evidence. In *R (B) v Head Teacher of Alperton Community School and Others; R v Head Teacher of Wembley High School and Others ex p T; R v Governing Body of Cardinal Newman High School and Others ex p C* [2001] ELR 359, Newman J held (at para [31]) that the pupil had a right to be heard, but this could be through his or her parent. See also *R v Head Teacher and Independent Appeal Committee of Dunraven School ex parte B* [2000] ELR 156 (CA).

[207] N 202 above.

[208] N Harris and K Eden with A Blair, *Challenges to School Exclusion* (London, RoutledgeFalmer, 2000).

[209] Department for Education and Skills, *Permanent and Fixed Period Exclusions from Schools and Exclusion Appeals in England, 2004/05* SFR 24/2006 (London, DfES, 2005), table 4. These official statistics do not include details of the ages of children who are the subject of appeals.

Other matters of concern as issues of children's rights are the act of exclusion itself,[210] the making of alternative provision for excluded children and the ways in which the reinstatement of an excluded child whose parent's appeal is successful are managed. All of these matters have been the subject of legal arguments based around Article 2 of the First Protocol to the ECHR on the ground that, inter alia, the right to education has been prejudicised by the child's exclusion from mainstream education. The relevant cases are discussed in Chapter 4. In addition, one of the problems that the issue of exclusion highlights is the potential conflict between the competing rights of individual children within a school community. Excluding one pupil might be damaging to his or her education but could assist the education of others at the school by removing a source of disruption or, in the case of a bully, fear. This is recognised by the guidance, which refers to situations where the exclusion was unreasonable in the particular circumstances but reinstatement is not practicable because it is 'not in the best interests of those concerned'.[211] This is consistent with a Court of Appeal judgment in 1996,[212] where the governing body reinstated two pupils responsible for firing an air pistol in the school yard, a pellet from which struck another pupil. Kennedy LJ said, 'where, as here, there was a child victim the overall case did require some serious investigation of the effect that the proposed setting aside of the head's decision would have on the injured boy'.[213] Although the injury was caused inadvertently, it was held that the governors had not properly considered the impact of the reinstatement of the two pupils on the victim or on the school as a whole. A similar approach was adopted by the Court of Appeal in a more recent case[214] arising from the exclusion of a male pupil (D), following an investigation into an alleged rape of a female pupil, K, by a group of five boys in a classroom during lunchtime. D had left the room before the rape actually occurred but had touched the girl's bottom and had not alerted anyone to the continuing attack upon the girl. Simon Brown LJ said that the decision taken by the majority of the appeal panel to uphold the exclusion 'was entirely reasonable, a "permissible option" . . . K and her parents would surely have been devastated had she been required to face these boys for the remainder of her schooldays'.[215]

Finally, the emergence of private law rights in tort arising from the public provision of education has added an important dimension to the notion of the child's right to education. In two judgments, both concerning negligence claims brought by pupils with special educational needs, the House of Lords accepted that a common law duty of care arose in connection with the performance of ordinary professional duties concerning the education of the child. These decisions are referred to in Chapter 6, but a few aspects need to be mentioned

---

[210] See C Hamilton, 'Rights of the Child: a Right to Education and a Right in Education' in C Bridge (ed), *Family Law Towards the Millennium: Essays for P.M. Bromley* (London, Butterworths, 1997) 201; N Harris, 'Education Law: Excluding the Child' (2000) 12 *Education and the Law* 31.

[211] N 205 above, para 129.

[212] *R v London Borough of Camden and the Governors of Hampstead School ex parte H* [1996] ELR 360.

[213] At 378B.

[214] *R (DR) v Head Teacher and Governing Body of S School* [2003] ELR 104 (CA).

[215] At paras 49–51.

here. In the first of the House of Lords' decisions, *X and Others (Minors) v Bedfordshire County Council (Etc)*,[216] Lord Browne-Wilkinson, giving the lead judgment, said:

> In my judgment a school which accepts a pupil assumes responsibility not only for his physical well-being but also for his educational needs. The head teacher, being responsible for the school, himself comes under a duty of care to exercise the reasonable skills of a headmaster in relation to such educational needs.[217]

He said that the duty included taking appropriate steps to deal with a pupil's under-performance where evidence of it came to light. In the second case, *Phelps v London Borough of Hillingdon,* [218] the court confirmed this duty and also held that educational psychologists owed a common law duty of care when assessing a child for, for example, dyslexia and possibly when giving advice to parents. Lord Nicholls, however, distinguished cases where there is 'manifest incompetence or negligence comprising specific, identifiable mistakes', such as where a teacher 'carelessly teaches the wrong syllabus for an external examination', from a more general claim that a child did not receive an adequate education at the school or was not properly taught, where a range of external factors contribute to the child's performance.[219] Although the court in both cases decided that there could be no liability for breach of statutory duties and the exercise of 'statutory discretions' over educational matters, as opposed to day-to-day professional duties which gave rise to a duty of care (above), Lord Slynn nevertheless commented in *Phelps* that the relevant statutory duties were 'of the greatest importance . . . A failure to fulfil the duties by an authority either generally or in a particular case can have a serious effect on a child's education, his well-being and his future life'.[220] What we see, therefore, is that in so far as education rights are often co-relative to duties resting with LEAs and others, the duty of care in relation to education, which appears to extend to welfare or disciplinary functions concerned with preventing or limiting bullying,[221] gives rise to a right enjoyed by the individual child (with a possible claim to damages for breach), although likely to be exercised through the parent as his or her 'next friend'.

THE EUROPEAN CONVENTION ON HUMAN RIGHTS

Discussion of the ECHR occurs throughout this book. The Human Rights Act 1998 necessitates the application of several key Convention rights and obligations

---

[216] [1995] ELR 404; [2005] 2 AC 633 (HL).

[217] [1995] ELR 404 at 451B–C.

[218] *Phelps v London Borough of Hillingdon, Anderton v Clwyd County Council; G v London Borough of Bromely; Jarvis v Hampshire County Council* [2000] ELR 499; [2000] 3 WLR 776; [2000] 4 All ER 504 (HL).

[219] [2000] ELR 499, at 532A–D.

[220] Ibid, at 514D.

[221] See, eg, *Bradford-Smart v West Sussex County Council* [2002] ELR 139 (CA).

to many areas of educational provision and decision-making. The remaining part of this chapter focuses on the one education-specific provision in the Convention, Article 2 of the First Protocol (A2P1), in order to consider what its application tells us about the notion of education as a right, and highlights other Convention Articles that are of relevance to issues covered in later chapters. The application of these provisions in the UK courts is noted in several places, but is mostly considered in later chapters.[222]

Article 2 of the First Protocol

A2P1 provides:

> No-one shall be denied the right to education. In the exercise of any functions which it assumes in relation to education and to teaching, the State must respect the right of parents to ensure such education and teaching in conformity with their own religious and philosophical convictions.

As noted above, the second sentence, which is mirrored in the Charter of Fundamental Rights of the European Union (which adds respect for 'peda-gogical' convictions to those convictions referred to in A2P1 ECHR, but which is only declaratory[223]) is subject to a reservation by the UK: the principle in the sentence is accepted only so far as is compatible with 'the provision of efficient instruction and training and the avoidance of unreasonable public expend-iture'.[224] The effect of the reservation and the provision in English education law on which it is based has been referred to above.

The Article is expressed in such general language that it is not even clear from the wording whether it applies to all levels of education, including further and higher education. The Strasbourg case law holds that A2P1 is concerned primarily with elementary education and not necessarily advanced studies.[225] In *Karus v Italy*,[226] however, the Commission reiterated this view but seemed to accept that A2P1 was relevant to the application by a university student complaining about differential fees and other matters. In *Douglas v North Tyneside Metropolitan Borough Council and the Secretary of State for Education and Skills* in the Court of Appeal, Scott Baker LJ, in reviewing the Strasbourg authorities (although not, as it happens, *Karus*), said he could 'see no reason in principle for concluding that the . . . right should cease at any particular stage in

---

[222] See also N Harris, 'Education: Hard or Soft Lessons in Human Rights?' in C Harvey (ed), *Human Rights in the Community* (Oxford, Hart, 2005) 81–112.

[223] Charter of Fundamental Rights of the European Union, Art 14(3).

[224] As regards the possible invalidity of the UK's reservation, however, see K Williams and B Rainey, 'Language, Education and the European Convention on Human Rights in the Twenty-first Century' (2002) 22 *Legal Studies* 625, 641.

[225] See *Sulak v Turkey* (1996) 84 DR 101 and *Yasinik v Turkey* (1993) 74 DR 14. See also *X v UK*, App no 5962/72 (1975) 2 DR 50. See further K Starmer, *European Human Rights Law* (London, LAG, 1999) 568; K Kerrigan and P Plowden, 'Human Rights and Higher Education' (2002) 3 *Education Law Journal* 16.

[226] App no 29043/95, decision of 20 May 1998.

the education process . . . Art 2 of Protocol 1 does apply to tertiary education.'[227] More recently, in *Leyla Şahin v Turkey*, the ECtHR stated that 'it would be hard to imagine that institutions of higher education existing at a given time do not come within the scope of the first sentence of Article 2 of Protocol 1';[228] and so the point can now be regarded as settled. The Court has also held that the right to education is a 'right guaranteed equally to pupils in State and independent schools, no distinction being made between them'.[229]

It is clearly consistent with the notion of a right to education that a person has access to an institution that provides it. In *Timishev v Russia*, for example, the applicant's children, aged 7 and 9, were not permitted by the authorities to continue at the school which they had attended for two years, because their father, a Chechen migrant, did not have registered residence and a migrant's card.[230] Russia's Education Act guaranteed a right to be educated irrespective of place of residence and the decision was therefore contrary to Russian law. The Court noted that 'the right to education guarantees access to elementary education which is of primordial importance for a child's development'.[231] The Court found that the children were denied the right to education provided for by the domestic law and their exclusion from school was 'therefore incompatible with the requirements of Article 2 of Protocol No.1'.[232] While this judgment implied that a breach of domestic law governing access to education necessarily implies a breach of the Convention, the House of Lords in *Ali* (discussed in detail in Chapter 4) has come to a different conclusions about that,[233] and Lords Hoffmann and Bingham of Cornhill explicitly rejected such a view.[234] Lord Hoffmann's interpretation of the Court's conclusion in *Timishev* was that there was found to be a breach of the Convention 'because it was a failure to provide education' and that 'the court's reference to domestic law was to rebut an argument that such a failure could be justified, in accordance with [*Belgian Lingustics*], as being part of the Russian domestic educational system'.[235] The *Ali* case was essentially about the lawfulness of a boy's exclusion from school when he was a possible suspect in respect of arson there; and Baroness Hale of Richmond, while in the minority in concluding that the exclusion was contrary to the Convention, nevertheless acknowledged that '[n]ot every act of unlawful exclusion is incompatible with the right contained in article 2 of the First Protocol'.[236]

---

[227] *R (Douglas) v North Tyneside Metropolitan Borough Council and the Secretary of State for Education and Skills* [2004] ELR 117 (CA), at paras 43 and 44; the other judges (Thorpe and Jonathan Parker LJJ) agreed. For discussion of the case see P Plowden and K Kerrigan, 'From Payground to Campus: Recognising a Right to Tertiary Education' (2004) 5 *Education Law* 70.

[228] App no 44774/98, 10 Nov 2005, at para 137; and see also para 141; affirmed in *Mürsel Eren v Turkey*, App no 60856/00, judgment of 7 Feb 2006, para 41.

[229] *Costello-Roberts v United Kingdom*, App no 13134/87 [1994] ELR 1, para 27.

[230] *Timishev v Russia*, App nos 55762/00 and 55974/00, 13 Dec 2005.

[231] Ibid, para 64.

[232] Ibid, para 66.

[233] *Ali v Headteacher and Governors of Lord Grey School* [2006] UKHL 14; [2006] 2 WLR 690.

[234] Ibid, at paras 24 and 58–60 respectively.

[235] Ibid, para 60.

[236] Ibid, para 82.

In the case of a university, access may be restricted to persons 'who have attained the academic level required to most benefit from the courses offered'.[237] In *Mürsel Eren v Turkey*[238] the applicant believed he had met the entry requirements for university when he obtained a high mark in the examinations in 1997. However, the central body (the ÖSYM) that determined whether a person passed the requirements for entry to university decided that his examination results should be annulled because they were so inconsistently better than those obtained at his previous examination attempts from 1994–6, an improvement that in its view could not be explained. The European Court of Human Rights, by a majority of six to one, held that Turkey could not point to any legal basis for the ÖSYM's discretion to annul results on the ground that a student could not explain his or her success. Moreover, it found that such a wide discretion would create 'such legal uncertainty as to be incompatible with the rule of law, one of the basic principles of a democratic society enshrined in the Convention'.[239] The ÖSYM's regulations in any event gave rise to a legitimate expectation on the part of the candidate that if he or she satisfied the conditions for admission, he or she had a right to attend university; overriding those rules would damage the legal protection against arbitrary interference by public authorities that they were designed to afford.[240] The Court found the authorities' decision 'lacked a legal and rational basis, resulting in arbitrariness', given that there was no evidence of cheating by the applicant and in view of the fact that the applicant had attended a private course in preparation for the examinations.[241] There had therefore been a breach of A2P1.

The fact that A2P1 leaves open the meaning of 'education' and, in particular, the question as to precisely what minimum level of provision, aims or content would be consistent with the notion of education for the purposes of the Article, means that there is wide scope for interpretation.[242] The judgment of the European Court of Human Rights (ECtHR) in *Belgian Linguistics*[243] has yielded the most influential guidance on this matter. The Court held that within the ambit of the right to education were access to educational institutions, provision of education in the national language or languages, and official recognition of studies that have been successfully completed.[244] The state's duty under the second sentence of A2P1 to respect the religious and philosophical convictions of

---

[237] *X v UK* App no 8844/80, (1980) 23 DR 228 at 229.
[238] App no 60856/00, Judgment 7 Feb 2006.
[239] Ibid, para 46.
[240] Ibid, para 49.
[241] Ibid, para 50.
[242] Cf the interpretation of the Education Article of the State Constitution (Art 11.1) in New York, which provides for the maintenance of 'free common schools, wherein all the children of this state may be educated', by the Supreme Court of New York in *Campaign for Fiscal Equity et al. v State of New York et al*, 719 NYS 2d 475(1995). It was alleged that the funding of public schools was inadequate in relation to the education of minorities. The court considered whether a basic test of whether a 'sound basic education' was provided to all and referred, inter alia, to the essential components of that as including teachers, appropriate curricula, adequate books and school buildings, support for those with additional needs and suitable class sizes.
[243] *Belgian Linguistics (No 2)* (1979–80) 1 EHRR 252
[244] Ibid, paras 3 and 4.

parents with regard to the teaching of their children applied 'not only to the content of the curriculum and the manner of its teaching, but to other factors such as the organising and financing of public education, and matters relating to internal administration such as discipline'.[245] Subsequent judgments on sex education and corporal punishment confirmed the state's competence over such matters.[246] In *Kjeldsen*, for example, the Court held:

> the setting and planning of the curriculum fall in principle within the competence of the Contracting State. This mainly involves questions of expediency on which it is not for the Court to rule and whose solution may legitimately vary according to the country and era.[247]

Generally, and in the absence of any clear evidence that parental convictions have been subjected to unjustified interference, the ECtHR would refrain from intervention. In *Valsamis v Greece*,[248] for example, a girl who was a member of the Jehovah's Witness sect was suspended from school for refusing to take part in a national day parade commemorating the war between Fascist Italy and Greece. National law permitted children to be excused from participation in religious education or observance but from not national events such as the parade. The girl and her parents claimed that their rights under the second sentence of A2P1, based on their pacificist beliefs, had been denied. The Court said that it was not for it 'to rule on the expediency of other educational methods which, in the applicants' view, would be better suited to the aim of perpetuating historical memory among the younger generation'.[249]

These cases illustrate that the right to education cannot be considered an absolute right. As Lord Bingham of Cornhill commented in *Ali v Headteacher and Governors of Lord Grey School*, the Convention's guarantee in A2P1 is 'in comparison with other Convention guarantees, a weak one'.[250] It is well known that states are allowed a 'margin of appreciation' in implementing the Convention provisions. Moreover, as noted above when discussing social rights and correlative state obligations, it is acknowledged that welfare provision does not occur in an economic and political vacuum. It is inevitable that regard will be had to the necessity to manage resources with a degree of economic efficiency and to operate within a politically mandated policy framework. As noted above, in *Belgian Linguistics* the Court observed that 'the Contracting Parties do not recognise such a right to education as would require them to establish at their own expense, or to subsidise, education of any particular type or at any particular level'.[251] Thus in that case the Court held that the state was entitled to adopt its linguistic policy and was not denying the French-speaking parents the right to

---

[245] Citing *Campbell and Cosans v UK* (1982) 4 EHRR 293; *Kjeldsen, Busk Madsen and Pedersen v Denmark* (1979–80) 1 EHRR 711; and *Valsamis v Greece* (1997) 24 EHRR 294.
[246] See *Kjeldsen, Busk Madsen and Pedersen v Denmark* and *Campbell and Cosans*, both n 245 above.
[247] *Kjeldsen*, n 245 above, para 53.
[248] Case No 74/1995/580/666 (1996) 24 EHRR 294; [1998] ELR 430.
[249] At para 32.
[250] [2006] UKHL 14; [2006] 2 WLR 690, at para 24.
[251] *Belgian Linguistics (No 2)* (1979–80) 1 EHRR 252, para 3.

education by failing to uphold their linguistically and culturally based wishes concerning the language in which their children were taught and by withholding financial support from schools that did not operate in accordance with the Flemish linguistic requirements. The Court noted that the signatories to the Convention all possessed and continued to possess an established education system, so the Article was not concerned with requiring the creation of such as system, but merely guaranteeing people 'the right . . . to avail themselves of instruction existing at a given time'.[252] As Hare explains, the right to education guarantees 'equal access to existing facilities and imposes no obligation to provide further educational resources'.[253] Moreover, it is the negative formulation of the first sentence of A2P1 that underlines the state's exemption from having to commit resources at a particular level.[254] (In the case of the UK, there is also the reservation that applies to the second sentence of the Article, noted above, so that the avoidance of unreasonable public expenditure can be a ground for limiting adherence to parental wishes.) Resource constraints were also acknowledged in *X v UK*,[255] where the Commission accepted that there was no positive obligation on the state to fund a specific form of educational provision in furtherance of the religious or philosophical beliefs of particular citizens, and *Simpson v UK*,[256] where the Commission, in finding that no breach of the first sentence of A2P1 had occurred as a result of the local education authority's decision to refuse to fund the placement of a boy with dyslexia at an independent school preferred by his parents, but to place him at a mainstream comprehensive school, said that the state enjoyed 'a wide measure of discretion . . . as to how to make the best use possible of the resources available to them in the interests of disabled children generally'.[257] Not surprisingly, it has also been held that the state has no obligation to subsidise private education.[258] However, if one religion benefited from such funding to the exclusion of others that might amount to unlawful discrimination for the purposes of Article 14 (below).[259]

[252] Ibid.

[253] I Hare, 'Social Rights as Fundamental Human Rights' in B Hepple (ed), *Social and Labour Rights in a Global* Context (Cambridge, Cambridge University Press, 2002) 153 at 167.

[254] *Belgian Linguistics (No 2)*, n 251 above, 280–2. See E Palmer, 'Resource Allocation, Welfare Rights—Mapping the Boundaries of Judicial Control in Public Administrative Law' (2000) 20 *Oxford Journal of Legal Studies* 17.

[255] App no 7782/77 (1978) 14 DR 179.

[256] (1989) 64 DR 188.

[257] Ibid, at para 2. See also *SP v United Kingdom*, App no 28915/95, European Commission of Human Rights, 17 Jan 1987, and *Coster v United Kingdom*, App no 24876/94 (2001) 33 EHRR 479, paras 134–7. In *Leyla Şahin v Turkey*, App no 44774/98, 10 Nov 2005, para 154, the Grand Chamber stated that 'the regulation of educational institutions may vary in time and place, *inter alia*, according to the needs and resources of the community and the distinctive features of the different levels of education. Consequently, the Contracting States enjoy a certain margin or appreciation in this sphere . . .'

[258] *W and KL v Sweden*, App no 10228/82 (1985) 45 DR 143. As regards Canada, see *Adler v Ontario* [1996] 3 SCR 609, [1996] CanLII 148 (SCC), where Jewish and other parents complained that while they had a right to send their children to a private school on religious grounds, the state of Ontario had no duty to fund the school.

[259] Cf *Adler* n 258 above, where the court held that Ontario's restriction of public funding for schools to non-denomination public schools and Catholic private schools did not unlawfully discriminate against Jewish and Protestant parents under the Canadian Charter of Rights and Freedoms.

While the duty to 'respect' parental views has been held to go further than requiring the state to 'acknowledge' them or 'take [them] into account',[260] this does not mean that the state is under a strict obligation to ensure that specific forms of education preferred by particular parents are provided.[261] For example, in various decisions the Commission of Human Rights failed to regard parental views on special education as amounting to philosophical convictions for the purposes of A2P1,[262] and rejected convictions-based complaints relating to methods of mathematics teaching in Germany and the ethos of comprehensive schooling in England.[263] Whether the recent decision by the Court in *Cyprus v Turkey*[264] heralds a move to accord greater respect for parental education rights in the future remains to be seen. Here Greek Cypriots living in northern (Turkish) Cyprus complained that their children were not taught in Greek beyond the primary school stage. This was held to amount to a breach of A2P1,[265] as it was not feasible for the parents to transfer their children to the (Greek) south for teaching in the medium of Greek, because of the potential impact on their family life.[266] This decision supports the principle, articulated in another judgment, that, although in a democracy majority views tend to hold sway, 'a balance must be achieved which ensures the fair and proper treatment of minorities and avoids any abuse of a dominant position'.[267]

With parents having to assert that their religious or philosophical convictions are not being respected, the Court will need to weigh in the balance not only resource considerations but also the overall objectives behind the policy adopted by the state. For example, in *Leyla Şahin v Turkey*,[268] where a medical student at Istanbul University challenged the university's ban on the wearing of the Islamic headscarf, partly on the ground that the ban affected her right of access to the education provided at the university in breach of A2P1, the ECtHR placed considerable weight on the purpose of the restriction, which was to preserve the secular character of educational institutions (consistent with the secularist nature of the constitutional state of Turkey).[269] The court will also need to make

---

[260] *Valsamis v Greece*, above n 245, at para (27).

[261] See, eg, *X, Y and Z v The Federal Republic of Germany*, App no 9411/81 (1982) 29 DR 224, where the parents wanted a particular form of scientific and mathematical education for their child, and *W and DM, M and HI v UK*, App no 10228/82 (1984) 37 DR 96, where the parents preferred a place for their child at a single-sex selective school rather than a comprehensive school and said they were philosophically opposed to aims and ideals of comprehensive education.

[262] *P and LD v UK*, App no 14135/88 (1989) 62 DR 292; *Graeme v UK*, App no 13887/88 (1990) 64 DR 158; *Klerks v Netherlands*, App no 25212/94 (1995) 82 DR 41. See also *W and KL v Sweden*, App no 14688/83, above n 258, *Simpson v UK*, App no 14688/89 (1989) 64 DR 188; *Cohen v UK*, App no 25959/94 (1996) 21 EHRR CD 104. For discussion of UK case law on special educational needs placements where the Human Rights Act 1998 has been argued, see Chap 6 at pp 336, 347–8.

[263] *X, Y and Z v Federal Repulic of Germany*, App no 9411/81 (1982) 29 DR 224; *W and DM, M and HI v UK*, App no 10228/82 (1984) 37 DR 96.

[264] App no 25781/94 (2002) 35 EHRR 731.

[265] Ibid, para 280.

[266] Ibid, para 278.

[267] *Young, James and Webster v United Kingdom* (1982) 4 EHRR 38, at para 63.

[268] App no 44774/98, 10 Nov 2005. See further Chap 4.

[269] Ibid, at para 158. The factors relevant to the A2P1 complaint were considered (see para 157) to be not capable of being divorced from those bearing upon the separate claim under Art 9, discussed below. In both cases the ban was considered to be proportionate given that the measures did not

qualitative judgments about the convictions themselves, assuming that they are religious or philosophical within the terms of the Convention, as was not found to be the case with regard to the linguistic preferences for teaching in *Belgian Linguistics*.[270] In *Kjeldsen*,[271] for example, the complainants asserted their objections to compulsory sex education for their children in Denmark on the ground that it conflicted with their Christian beliefs and values. Here, however, the cogency of the convictions did not defeat the state's authority to make sex education compulsory in schools in the public interest, provided the 'information or knowledge is conveyed in an objective, critical and pluralistic manner' and not via 'indoctrination that might be considered as not respecting parents' religious and philosophical convictions'.[272] The Court placed some weight on the fact that the parents had the option of sending their children to private schools or educating them at home.[273] Parents have the right under the Convention to arrange and pay for the child's private education.[274]

The Court's decision in *Campbell and Cosans v UK*[275] stands in contrast to that in *Kjeldsen*, because the philosophical convictions that were advanced, namely that corporal punishment was wrong and should not be administered to their children in school, were considered to be sufficiently important to justify interference with the state's authority. The convictions amounted to:

> a weighty and substantial aspect of human life and behaviour, namely the integrity of the person, the propriety or otherwise of the infliction of corporal punishment and the exclusion of the distress which the risk of such punishment entails.[276]

The parents' convictions were deemed worthy of respect in a democratic society, consistent with human dignity and not in conflict with the child's fundamental right to education. Yet in *Valsamis v Greece*,[277] the essential facts of which were outlined above, the majority of the Court found no violation of A2P1, because there was 'nothing, either in the purposes of the parade, or in the arrangements

---

prevent students from observing their religion. The relevant issues had as far as possible been weighed up in the decision-making process, and there were procedural safeguards in policy-making that protected students' interests. In addition, the Court found that the applicant would reasonably have been aware that if she wore the headscarf she would be refused admission to lectures and examinations: ibid, para 160. See further p 159 below.

[270] See K Williams and B Rainey, 'Language, Education and the European Convention on Human Rights in the Twenty-first Century' (2002) 22 *Legal Studies* 625.

[271] N 245 above.

[272] Ibid, at 731, para 53. See also *Campbell and Cosans v UK* (1982) 4 EHRR 293, and *Valsamis v Greece*, n 245 above.

[273] An obligation on home-educating parents in the UK to assist the authorities in evaluating their children's education was held not to be inconsistent with the parent's right under Art 2 of Prot 1: see *Family H v UK*, App no 10233/83 (1984) 37 DR 105.

[274] *Jordebo v Sweden*, App no 11533/85 (1987) 51 DR 125. The right to establish a private school is also recognised: *Verein Gemeinsam Lernen v Austria*, App no 23419/94 (1995) 82 DR 41; (1995) 20 EHRR CD 78.

[275] N 245 above.

[276] Para 36.

[277] Case No 74/1995/580/666 (1996) 24 EHRR 294; [1998] ELR 430.

for it, which could offend the applicants' pacifist convictions to an extent prohibited by the second sentence of [A2P1]'. [278] The fact that the parents could educate their children within the family about matters pertaining to their convictions on matters of war and peace was noted by the court, in a similar approach to that taken in *Kjeldsen*. It is, however, difficult to reconcile this decision with that in *Campbell and Cosans*.[279] The views expressed in the minority judgments in *Valsamis*, to the effect that the parade did symbolise a view of war and armed conflict that could be regarded as inimical to the religious or philosophical convictions of the parents, seem to have some cogency, as does the minority's conclusion that, unless unfounded or unreasonable, the parents' views should be respected. The minority also considered that Article 9 (on freedom of religion: see below) was also violated.

As Kilkelly says, the ECtHR has established 'a threshold whereby only those views which are serious, important and coherent will require respect under [A2P1]'.[280] Yet there is no clear guidance on how that threshold would be applied to determine whether individual parental rights or the state's authority to act in what it perceives to be the national interest should prevail. It may be that decisions over corporal punishment affect particularly closely the integrity of the individual and potentially represent an especially severe interference by the state, and one that coulld fall within the remit of a separate important Convention right.[281] But might it not be the importance of the particular convictions centred on the religious or philosophical beliefs of the complainant that is the relevant issue rather than the subject matter? In other words, is it possible to judge the matter solely in accordance with an objective test based around a notional shared societal view of what amounts to a serious or important view. Is it not the fact that society as a whole might think differently from particular groups of parents with minority beliefs that underlies the very right enshrined in A2P1? Of course, not merely is a question of collective beliefs or values in play, as another reason for the state to consider itself to be acting in the national interest is its public responsibility to allocate resources and manage the education system efficiently. The UK's reservation to the second sentence of A2P1, noted above, expressly reflects that approach. Referring to the issue of mother tongue teaching, Williams and Rainey argue that, even if it were considered that choice of language for education could amount to a conviction recognised by A2P1, the state could still legitimately deny it on sound resource grounds.[282] A similar point is made by

---

[278] Ibid, para (31). The Court did, however, find a violation of Art 13 (right to a remedy). Cullen argues that as the case law holds that an applicant must have an 'arguable case' under another Convention right in order to sustain an Art 13 challenge, the claims in the case under Art 9 must have been considered to have some merit: H Cullen, '*R (Williamson) v Secretary of State for Education and Employment*—Accommodation of Religion in Education' (2004) 16 *Child & Family Law Quarterly* 231 at 237.

[279] As also noted by Cullen, ibid.

[280] U Kilkenny, *The Child and the European Convention on Human Rights* (Aldershot, Ashgate, 1999), 77.

[281] Namely Art 3, which proscribes torture or inhuman or degrading treatment or punishment: see DJ Harris *et al*, *Law of the European Convention on Human Rights* (London, Butterworths, 1995), 546.

[282] N 270 above, 641.

Kilkenny[283] in relation to views by individual parents on special educational needs and provision, where questions of resources frequently arise because of the relatively high cost of the specialist provision and the potential strain it causes on education budgets as a whole.

Article 14

A2P1 must be read in conjunction with Article 14, which provides that Convention rights and freedoms:

> shall be secured without discrimination on any ground such as sex, race, colour, language, religion, political or other opinion, national or social origin, association with a national minority, property, birth or other status.

The test for whether Article 14 has been violated, as articulated by Lord Bingham of Cornhill,[284] depends first on whether the facts of the case fall within the ambit of a Convention right such as that in A2P1. Put another way, the substantive right must be 'engaged'.[285] If so, then, secondly, there must be a difference in treatment compared with that given to others; and, thirdly, it must relate to one or more of the factors proscribed under Article 14 (above). Fourthly, the others who were treated more favourably must have been in an analogous situation to the complainant. Finally, the question is whether the difference in treatment was objectively justifiable in the sense of having a legitimate aim and bearing a reasonable relationship of proportionality to that aim.

The effect of A2P1 and Article 14, when read together, should mean that, leaving aside legitimate entry qualifications, access to institutions must occur without discrimination on various grounds. In *Douglas* (above), the fact that students aged 55 or over did not have the additional support of access to a loan to support their studies that was available to younger students was held not in itself to limit access:

> The right of access is not *necessarily* affected by the absence of a loan . . . any differential treatment is in the funding of students and not with who goes on the course. The funding arrangements are one stage removed from the course itself.[286]

However, as noted above, differential, discriminatory treatment which can be shown by the state to have a reasonable and objective justification may, in any

---

[283] Kilkenny, above n 280, 79–80.

[284] In *A and Others v Secretary of State for the Home Department* [2004] UKHL 56, [2005] 2 WLR 87, at para 45ff.

[285] See, eg, *Leyla Şahin v Turkey*, App no 44774/98, 10 Nov 2005, where access to higher education was held to be within the scope of the Art 2 of Prot 1 right, which was engaged, in a case brought by a university student who was denied access while wearing the Islamic headscarf. Art 9 (freedom of religious expression, etc) was also engaged. There was, however, held to be no infringement of these substantive rights, nor of Art 14.

[286] *R (Douglas) v North Tyneside Metropolitan Borough Council and Secretary of State for Education and Skills* [2004] ELR 117, per Scott LJ at para 60 (original emphasis).

event, be sanctioned.[287] In *Karus v Italy*[288] the applicant was a German national who was admitted to the University of Bari in Italy as a student. As an international student, her fees at the university were higher than those for most Italian nationals (whose fees were assessed in the light of their means and other factors by the university's administrative authorities), although such a student could apply for a reduction, but of only up to 50 per cent, by applying for a certificate from her consultate. The applicant applied for validation of her previous studies, to be exempt from certain examinations at the university. After some delay she heard from the university that she would have to take and pass all her basic German grammar and language examinations again. She decided in the light of this to abandon her studies in Italy. In relation to her complaint that the differential treatment constituted a breach of Article 14 read together with A2P1, the Commission held that the difference in treatment over fees had an objective and reasonable basis because it would be difficult for the university authorities to assess foreign students' means. Moreover, the 50 per cent maximum fees reduction also had an objective and reasonable justification:

> namely the much higher degree of probability that foreign students will leave Italy on completion of their studies, whereas students of Italian nationality are, as a general proposition, more likely to remain in Italy where, by applying the knowledge and skills which they have acquired at public expense, they will be able to make a valuable contribution to Italian society and in this manner repay, albeit in an indirect and unquantifable way, the financial investment from which they have benefited.[289]

In judging whether there is legitimate justification for the discrimination, the aim and effect of the measure in question will need to considered. Positive discrimination may, for example, be legitimate if it aims to redress pre-existing inequality.

A further factor will be whether the means that are employed are proportionate to the aim or aims. In *Angeleni v Sweden*[290] the state excused from attendance at Christian-orientated religious knowledge lessons children from other religious communities, but did not excuse atheists from them. Children of other denominations would be expected to learn about religion from their own community. This could not be the case with atheists. The overriding aim of the state's policy was to ensure that, via either schooling or their communities, all children would receive 'sufficient factual religious knowledge'.[291] The Commission of Human Rights concluded that the policy aim was a legitimate aim for the purposes of Article 14 of the Convention, and the difference in

---

[287] See K Starmer, *European Human Rights Law* (London, LAG, 1999) 687–90. A similar test was held, by the UN Human Rights Committee, to apply to discrimination under Art 26 International Covenant on Civil and Political Rights (entitlement to equal protection of the law) in *Waldman v Canada* (Comm No 694/1996, 3 Nov 1999, 67/D/694/1996), a case concerned with the same issue as *Adler v Ontario*, nn 258 and 259 above.

[288] App no 29043/95, 20 May 1998 (Commission of Human Rights).

[289] Ibid, 'The Law', Part 2.

[290] (1988) 10 EHRR 123.

[291] Ibid, para 4.

treatment therefore had an objective and reasonable justification.[292] Similarly, in *Belgian Linguistics* all but one of the complaints of discrimination by French-speaking children who were denied mother tongue teaching in Flemish schools in Belgium were rejected by the ECtHR on the ground that the objective of the state's policy that the medium of instruction should be Flemish, namely linguistic unity, amounted to a legitimate aim and the action of the authorities was proportionate to it.[293] The pragmatism that is evident in the way that the Strasbourg judges approach their evaluation of the discriminatory effects of particular state education policies is further illustrated by the decision in *X v UK*, where accepted as a legitimate justification for the state's discrimination against integrated schools in Northern Ireland, by not providing full funding, was that state control over the fully funded (denominational) schools was greater.[294]

Other Convention Rights

The right to education under A2P1 interacts with several other Convention rights. In *Kjeldsen* the Court said that the two sentences of A2P1 'must be read not only in the light of each other but also, in particular, Arts 8, 9 and 10 of the Convention'.[295] The application of these provisions in the domestic case law, especially post-2000, will be considered in later chapters, but their relevance to the right to education needs to be assessed here.

Article 8(1) provides that '[e]veryone has the right to respect for his private and family life, his home and his correspondence'. Article 8(2) prohibits interference by a public authority[296] with the exercise of that right

> except such as is in accordance with the law and is necessary in a democratic society in the interests of national security, public safety or the economic well-being of the country, for the prevention of disorder or crime, for the protection of health or morals, or for the protection of the rights and freedoms of others.

The European Court of Human Rights has held that an interference with this right will be 'necessary in a democratic society' for one of the legitimate aims if it answers 'a pressing social need' and if it is proportionate to the legitimate aim in question.[297] The general position is that the 'margin of appreciation' enjoyed by states in the implementation of their social and economic policies is wide. But '[w]here general social and economic policy considerations have arisen in the context of Article 8 itself, the scope of the margin of appreciation depends upon

---

[292] Ibid.

[293] *Belgian Linguistics (No 2)* (1979–80) 1 EHRR 252.

[294] App no 7782/77 (1978) 14 DR 179. See also *Verein Gemeinsam Lernen v Austria*, App no 23419/94 (1995) 82 DR 41; (1995) 20 EHRR CD 78.

[295] *Kjeldsen, Busk Madsen and Pedersen v Denmark* (1979–80) 1 EHRR 711, paras 52 and 54.

[296] In the UK, a 'public authority' is prohibited from acting in a way which is incompatible with a Convention right: Human Rights Act 1998, s 6(1). The meaning of public authority in the context of education is discussed in Chap 4 at pp 149–51.

[297] See *Connors v United Kingdom*, App no 6674601, 27 May 2004, para 81; and *Smith and Grady v United Kingdom*, Application nos 33985/96 and 33986/96, 27 September 1999, para 88ff.

the context of the case, with particular significance attaching to the extent of the intrusion into the personal sphere of the applicant'.[298] In *S v United Kingdom*, school uniform requirements, challenged by a parent (not on religious or philosophical grounds), were held by the Europen Commission of Human Rights to be not serious enough a constraint to give rise to a violation of Article 8.[299] In *Costello-Roberts v UK*,[300] which concerned the use of corporal punishment in school, the Court said that 'the sending of a child to school necessarily involves some degree of interference with his or her private life'. The Court held that a violation of Article 8 would need to entail sufficiently adverse effects for a person's physical or moral integrity.[301] The fact that A2P1 calls for respect for parents' religious and philosophical convictions acknowledges that many aspects of education are highly pertinent to personal or family integrity, as we have seen from the cases concerned with sex education, corporal punishment and the language that forms the medium of teaching. Moreover, interference with a child's education in other contexts, such as where a Gypsy family is evicted from land by a local authority, could form part of a more general interference with the Article 8 right.[302] In the English courts Article 8 has been argued by complainants (mostly without success) in cases concerned with school admissions,[303] ballots on grammar school status,[304] exclusion from school,[305] corporal punishment[306] and special educational needs.[307] In *Kjeldsen* the Court commented that 'it seems very difficult for many subjects taught at school not to have, to a greater or lesser extent, some philosophical complexion or implications [and the] same is true of religious affinities'.[308] In holding that the state was 'forbidden to pursue an aim of indoctrination that might be considered as not respecting parents' religious and philosophical convictions', the Court said that such an interpretation was consistent with Article 8, amongst other provisions. Arguments based on a breach of Article 8 were rejected in *Belgian Linguistics* on the ground that if the parents, in order to ensure their children were taught in French, sent them to another region for that purpose it would be their individual choice rather than an interference by the state. In *Simpson v UK* (above)[309] the Commission regarded as too hypothetical in nature a complaint that sending a dyslexic child who had a 'delicate' personality to a large comprehensive school would infringe Article 8 by causing a deterioration in the boy's mental condition

---

[298] *Connors*, n 297 above, at para 82.

[299] App no 11674/85, (1986) 46 DR 245, 'The Law', para 1.

[300] Case No 89/1991/341/414 [1994] ELR 1; (1986) 8 EHRR 235.

[301] Ibid, para 36. See *X and Y v Netherlands*, Series A No. 91, paras 22–27.

[302] See *Connors*, n 297 above, at para 85ff.

[303] *R (O) v St James RC Primary School Appeal Panel* [2001] ELR 469; *R (K) v London Borough of Newham, R v London Borough of Richmond ex p JC* [2001] ELR 21. See Chap 5.

[304] *R v Secretary of State for Education and Employment ex p RCO* [2000] ELR 307.

[305] *R (B) v Head Teacher of Alperton Community School and Others; R v Head Teacher of Wembley High School and Others ex parte T; R v The Governing Body of Cardinal Newman High School and Others ex parte C* [2001] ELR 359.

[306] *R (Williamson) v Secretary of State for Education and Employment* [2003] ELR 176 (CA).

[307] *CB v London Borough of Merton and Special Educational Needs Tribunal*, [2002] EWHC 877 (Admin); [2002] ELR 441. See Chap 6.

[308] *Kjeldsen, Busk Madsen and Pedersen v Denmark* (1979–80) 1 EHRR 711 (1976), para 53.

[309] *Simpson v UK*, App no 14688/89 (1989) 64 DR 188, 'The Law', at para 4.

and ability to be educated. As discussed in Chapter 4, Article 8 has also been invoked, unsuccessfully, to challenge a refusal of asylum that would result in a child with cerebral palsy who was receiving specialist educational provision in London having to return to the Lebanon where facilities were inferior.[310]

Article 9 provides for freedom of thought, conscience and religion and, inter alia, for the individual's freedom 'either alone or in community with others and in public or private, to manifest his religion or belief, in worship, teaching, practice and observance', subject to such limitations as are 'prescribed by law and are necessary in a democratic society in the interests of public safety, for the protection of public order, health or morals, or for the rights and freedoms of others'.[311] The precise effect of this provision will be discussed in Chapter 7, which looks at its impact in the context of the curriculum and multiculturalism. As regards the scope of the provision, it may be noted here that both the Court in *Valsamis* (above) and the Commission in *Arrowsmith v UK*[312] acknowledged that a belief in pacifism fell within the ambit of Article 9.[313] In *Kokkinakis v Greece* the ECtHR stated that freedom of thought, conscience and religion as enshrined in Article 9 was 'also a precious asset for atheists, sceptics and the unconcerned'.[314] Article 9 was raised in support of the parents' case in *Kjeldsen* (above), the parents being persons with strong Christian beliefs—a fact which is important because, whatever the nature of the belief (it might, for example, include veganism), it will require respect only if it is serious as well as coherent rather than a 'mere opinion',[315] although 'the State's duty of neutrality and impartiality is incompatible with any power on the State's part to assess the legitimacy of religious beliefs or the ways in which those beliefs are expressed'.[316]

Article 9 has a potential application to many aspects of education, especially the curriculum, discipline and the clothing worn to school (as in the recent UK cases of *Begum*[317] and *Williamson*,[318] discussed in Chapter 7). It was, for example, the principal basis for the challenge in *Leyla Şahin v Turkey* [319] to the ban on the wearing of the Islamic headscarf at Istanbul University, noted above. The applicant failed on the ground that the authorities were held to be entitled to take steps, in accordance with the constitutional position in Turkey, to preserve the secular nature of the institution in order to promote the values of pluralism, respect for the rights of others and equality before the law of men and women.

---

[310] *Dbies and Others v Secretary of State for the Home Department* [2005] EWCA Civ 584.

[311] Art 9(2).

[312] App no 7050/75 (1978) 19 DR 5.

[313] For a list of those beliefs recognised in the cases, see K Starmer, *European Human Rights Law* (London, LAG Books, 1999), para 27.5.

[314] (1994) 17 EHRR 387, at para 31.

[315] *McFeeley v UK*, App no 8317/78 (1981) 3 EHRR 161. Veganism was regarded by the Commission as within the scope of Art 9 in *X v UK*, App no 18187/91, 10 Feb 1993.

[316] See *Leyla Şahin v Turkey*, App no 44774/98, 10 Nov 2005, para 107; and *Refah Partisi (Welfare Party) v Turkey*, App nos 41340/98, 41342/98, 41343/98 and 41344/98 (2004) 37 EHRR 1, para 91.

[317] *R (Begum) v Headteacher and Governors of Denbigh High School* [2006] UKHL 15; [2006] 2 WLR 719.

[318] *R (Williamson) v Secretary of State for Education and Employment* [2005] UKHL 15, [2005] ELR 291; [2005] 2 AC 246.

[319] App no 44774/98, 10 Nov 2005 (Grand Chamber).

The ECtHR accepted that the ban was for a legitimate purpose and was proportionate as regards the means employed and objectives pursued. The justification
for a school's ban on the wearing of the jilbab that was considered in *Begum*,
where that garment was not sanctioned by the school's uniform policy although
another form of Muslim dress (the shalwar kameeze) was, is discussed in
Chapters 4 and 7, but it may be noted here that in that case Lord Hoffmann
considered that the difference between the national contexts of Turkey and the
UK that had exercised Brooke LJ in the Court of Appeal when considering the
effect of *Şahin*[320] was irrelevant because the decision of the authority in question
was not made at the national level. Lord Hoffmann concluded that '[i]n applying
the principles of *Şahin v Turkey* the justification must be sought at the local level
and it is there that an area of judgment, comparable to the margin of
appreciation, must be allowed to the school'.[321]

Justification, however, becomes a relevant consideration only if an interference
has taken place. There were differing views among their Lordships in *Begum* as to
whether the school's refusal to permit a Muslim pupil to wear the jilbab to school
amounted to an interference for the purposes of Article 9. The issue of
interference with freedom of religion or the right to manifest one's belief has
arisen in other contexts, notably that of employment or the slaughter of animals
(the relevant Strasbourg jurisprudence is reviewed by Lords Bingham of Cornhill
and Hoffmann in *Begum* and by the Grand Chamber in *Şahin*), with the ultimate
test being whether in the particular circumstances the person in question has the
freedom to manifest his or her beliefs in practice,[322] which leaves the position
that, according to Lord Bingham, 'interference is not easily established'.[323] In
Begum, the majority found that there was no interference because the applicant
had had the right to attend another school at which she could have worn the
jilbab.[324] It appears to be more difficult to argue that there has been an
interference where one has voluntarily entered into a commitment, such as a job
or place at a school or university, knowing of the religious restrictions that apply,
as in *Karaduman v Turkey*,[325] where the applicant complained about having to be
photographed without her headscarf which was necessary for her graduation, or
in *Begum* itself, where the complainant had been aware of the school's uniform
policy when she joined the school, but had found it unacceptable two years later
when her beliefs had become more fundamentalist.

The Article 9 right should protect a child from compulsory participation in
collective worship or religious education, so that the statutory opt-out (albeit

[320] In this case it was the Chamber judgment: *Leyla Şahin v Turkey*, App no 44774/98 [2004] ELR 520. The Grand Chamber judgment (above n 316) was at one with the Chamber judgment on this point.
[321] *R (Begum) v Headteacher and Governors of Denbigh High School* [2006] UKHL 15; [2006] 2 WLR 719, at para 64.
[322] *R (Williamson) v Secretary of State for Education and Employment* [2005] UKHL 15, [2005] ELR 291; [2005] 2 AC 246, per Lord Nicholls of Birkenhead at para 38.
[323] *R (Begum) v Headteacher and Governors of Denbigh High School* [2006] UKHL 15; [2006] 2 WLR 719 at para 24, per Lord Bingham of Cornhill.
[324] Lord Nicholls of Birkenhead and Baroness Hale of Richmond dissented on this point.
[325] (1993) 74 DR 93.

conferred on the parent[326]), discussed in Chapter 7, seems to uphold that right. It means that if non-Christian parents or children object to collective worship that is, in accordance with the statutory requirement in England, 'wholly or mainly of a broadly Christian character',[327] a claim of breach of Article 9 would be barred by reason of the existence of a right of withdrawal and to make alternative arrangements. But, on the basis that Article 9 is engaged, it has been argued that the requirement could nonetheless be discriminatory contrary to Article 14.[328] If, on the other hand, the parents favour participation in religious education, their preference will warrant recognition under A2P1, but that could conflict with the child's right under Article 9[329] (and, indeed, under Article 12 UNCRC[330]). As Fortin says, '[t]he Strasbourg institutions have not considered what rights, if any, children might have if they disagreed with their parents regarding decisions over religion'.[331]

Another way in which Article 9 may be relevant to education concerns the freedom to manifest one's religion through teaching. The term 'teaching' has not been fully elucidated judicially in this context; but leaving aside the issue of whether proseltysing is included (as was so held in *Arrowsmith*[332] as long as it is not 'improper proselytism'[333]), it not surprisingly is regarded as relevant to school education.[334] In *Dahlab v Switzerland*, for example, the ECtHR noted the possibly proseltysing effect of the wearing of the Islamic headscarf by a teacher of a class of small children.[335] Children are protected from indoctrination by the right to respect for their parents' religious and philosophical beliefs by A2P1, as considered in *Kjeldsen* (above). Indeed, in *Valsamis*, the majority decision linked together the parents' right under the second sentence of A2P1 with the right of the child under Article 9.[336] As the Court had found that the obligation to take part in a school parade did not amount to a failure to respect the girl's parents' religious convictions, it 'did not amount to an interference with her freedom of religion either'.[337]

Another relevant provision with a bearing on the right to education is Article 10, which provides for the right to freedom of expression, including 'freedom to

---

[326] SSFA 1998, s 71.

[327] School Standards and Framework Act 1998, sched 20, para 3(2). See also *R v Secretary of State for Education ex p R and D* [1994] ELR 495.

[328] C Hamilton, 'Freedom of Religion and Religious Worship in Schools' in J de Groof and J Fiers (eds), *The Legal Status of Minorities in Education* (Leuven, Acco, 1996), 165.

[329] E Craig, 'Accommodation of Diversity in Education—a Human Rights Agenda?' (2003) 15 *Child & Family Law Quarterly* 279 at 293.

[330] H Cullen, '*R (Williamson) v Secretary of State for Education and Employment*—Accommodation of Religion in Education' (2004) *Child & Family Law Quarterly* 231 at 241.

[331] J Fortin, *Children's Rights and the Developing Law* (2nd edn, London, LexisNexis, 2003) 356.

[332] Above n 312.

[333] Ibid, at 17.

[334] See C Evans, *Freedom of Religion under the European Convention on Human Rights* (Oxford, Oxford University Press, 2001) 110.

[335] App no 42393/98. See also *Karaduman v Turkey*, App no 16278/90 and C Langenfeld and S Mohsen, 'Germany: the Teacher Head Scarf Case' (2005) 3 *International Journal of Constitutional Law* 86.

[336] That it was a right enjoyed by the child, in the context of education, was acknowledged in *Angeleni v Sweden*, App no 10491/83 (1988) 10 EHRR CD 123.

[337] *Valsamis v Greece*, above n 245, para (37).

hold opinions and to receive and impart information and ideas without interference by public authority . . .' Although Article 10 may protect the right of pupils to express themselves through words, conduct and even dress or bodily adornment, the right may be interfered with by a restriction 'prescribed by law'.[338] As head teachers have a statutory power to define what is to be considered acceptable or unacceptable behaviour and to 'regulate the conduct of pupils' through school rules or otherwise,[339] it seems likely that curbs on expression that is inconsistent with strictures within the scope of that authority would be upheld. In *S v United Kingdom* the European Commission of Human Rights held that a school's requirements on pupils' uniforms did not violate pupils' right to freedom of expression under Article 10, since wearing the uniform did not prevent the child from expressing a particular opinion or idea, and pupils could express themselves freely outside school.[340] Any restriction on individual freedom of expression would also have to be 'necessary in a democratic society, in the interests of . . . [inter alia] public safety . . . the prevention of disorder or crime, [and] for the protection of health or morals' (Article 10(2)). Many of the more extreme, outlandish, disruptive or obscene expressions of individuality by pupils would seem to be outside the protection of Article 10. However, the restrictions themselves need to be 'proportionate to the legitimate aim pursued'.[341] In *Vogt v Germany*,[342] the dismissal of a secondary school teacher engaged in various political activities was sought to be justified because she had failed to meet a statutory requirement that civil servants maintain loyalty to the Constitution. The Court felt, however (albeit by only a 10 to nine majority), that to dismiss her when she had made no anti-constitutional statements and had not adopted an anti-constitutional stance was disproportionate to the legitimate aim pursued.[343] However, in *Cyprus v Turkey*,[344] the Court found that there was 'excessive censorship' in northern Cyprus of school textbooks intended for use by Greek Cypriots and an interference with the Article 10 right was not justified.[345] Bearing in mind that Article 10(2) states that freedom of expression 'carries with it duties and responsibilities', the Court might well accept that the protection from indoctrination that is aimed at via the statutory requirement in England that the LEA, governing body and head teacher must forbid 'the promotion of partisan political views in the teaching of any subject in the school'[346] is not inconsistent with Article 10. Indeed, as Article 17 aims to prevent a Convention right from being interpreted as conferring a right to destroy or limit *any* Convention right or freedoms, it could be argued that the right to education provided in an objective manner, as upheld by *Kjeldsen*, may not be undermined by the exercise of the right of freedom of expression under Article 10. In *X v*

---

[338] Art 10(2).
[339] School Standards and Framework Act 1998, s 61(4).
[340] App no 11674/85, (1986) 46 DR 245, 'The Law', para 2.
[341] *Sunday Times v United Kingdom (No 2)* (1992) 14 EHRR 229, at para 50.
[342] Case No 7/1994/454/535 (1995) 21 EHRR 205; [1996] ELR 232.
[343] See ibid, para (61).
[344] App no 25781/94 (2002) 35 EHRR 731.
[345] Ibid, para 254.
[346] Education Act 1996, s 406(1).

UK[347] a teacher's right under Article 10 was found by the Commission not to have been violated when he was forbidden to display religious and anti-abortion stickers on his clothes and briefcase, because a teacher should have regard to the right of parents to have their religious and philosophical convictions respected under A2P1.

A final matter concerning the nature of the right to education concerns its treatment for the purposes of Article 6(1) of the Convention.[348] This provision states that '[i]n the determination of his civil rights and obligations or of any criminal charge against him, everyone is entitled to a fair and public hearing within a reasonable time by an independent and impartial tribunal established by law'. In these cases, a pivotal question concerns the status of the right to education under A2P1. Is it a 'civil right' for the purposes of Article 6(1)? If not, then determinations relating to a person's right to education would not be protected by its fair trial requirement, although in the UK would nevertheless be protected by ordinary principles of fairness or natural justice at common law.[349]

The Commission stated in *Simpson v UK*[350] that the right not to be denied an elementary education fell 'squarely within the domain of public law, having no private law analogy and repercussions on private rights or obligations' and so was not a 'civil right'. Thus the applicant's complaint under Article 6 about the special educational needs appeal procedures then in operation failed. In a subsequent admissibility decision, *Lalu Hanuman v UK*,[351] where a university student had sought to impugn his university's academic appeals procedures with reference to Article 6, the Court (declaring the complaint inadmissible) again held that no civil right was in issue, which is somewhat at odds with the clear private law contractual relationship between universities and students recognised by the Court of Appeal in the UK.[352] In *R (Varma) v HRH the Duke of Kent*,[353] a case arising from a student's unsuccessful complaint to the university visitor following the university's decision that his registration should be terminated for his insufficient academic progress, Collins J dismissed the student's complaint of a violation of Article 6 arising from unfairness in the procedure adopted by the visitor. The essential difficulty for the claimant was, again, the view that no civil right was at stake. Collins J cited the ECtHR's decision in *Van Marice v*

---

[347] (1979) 16 DR 101.

[348] Note that Art 6(2), which provides for the right to the presumption of innocence until proved guilty in the case of anyone charged with a criminal offence, was used to challenge strict liability for a truancy offence under the 1996 Act in *Barnfather v London Borough of Islington Education Authority and the Secretary of State for Education and Skills* [2003] ELR 263 (QBD).

[349] See, eg, *R (N) v The Head Teacher of X School and Others* [2001] EWHC Admin 747; [2002] ELR 187; *R (A) v Governing Body of K School and the Independent Appeal Panel of the London Borough of Enfield* [2002] EWHC Admin 395; [2002] ELR 631; *R (MB) v Independent Appeal panel of SMBC* [2002] EWHC Admin 1509; [2002] ELR 676; *R (T by her mother and litigation friend A) v Head Teacher of Elliott School and Others* [2002] EWCA Civ 1349; [2003] ELR 160; *R (S) v The Governing Body of YP School* [2002] EWHC Admin 2975.

[350] *Simpson v UK*, App no 14688/89 (1989) 64 DR 188, 'The Law', para 1.

[351] App no 56965/00 (admissibility decision) [2000] ELR 685.

[352] *Clark v University of Lincolnshire and Humberside* [2000] 3 All ER 752; [2000] ELR 345 (CA); *Moran v University College Salford (No.2)* [1994] ELR 187.

[353] [2004] EWHC Admin 1705; [2004] ELR 616.

Netherlands,[354] where the appeal board's consideration of accountants' registration was 'akin to a school or university examination and so far removed from the exercise of a judicial function as to fall outside Art 6'.[355] He acknowledged, though, that in a case where a visitor was dealing with an appeal concerning dismissal from employment, as in *Page*, Article 6 would apply.[356] Clearly, a civil right would be at issue. Indeed, there was a case in 2003, *Mohtasham*, [357] which was not referred to by Collins J, where the dispute centred on whether the claimant had been engaged as a research associate at King's College, and the court was prepared to consider an Article 6 argument in relation to the protracted nature of the visitor's procedure. The fact that university visitors lack true independence from their university has been regarded as contrary to the principle of impartiality in Article 6,[358] and is one of the main reasons why the visitor's jurisdiction over student complaints has been abolished, under the Higher Education Act 2004, which specifically provides for the establishment of an independently operated student complaints scheme.[359] In *Varma*, Collins J acknowledged visitors' lack of independence and indicated, obiter, that the view of the House of Lords in *Page*, that a visitor's decision is not amenable to judicial review, 'may require reconsideration' in the light of Article 6.[360]

The approach adopted in *Simpson* has also been applied by the UK courts in several decisions concerned with school admission and exclusion.[361] However, there was a hint in a Court of Appeal judgment in 2002[362] of a more flexible approach in the future. This was a case where the complaint was that the Secretary of State's guidance to independent appeal panels compromised the panels' independence and that the LEA, which organised appeals and appointed panel members, was an interested party to a decision. The court stated, obiter, that it was a 'tenable assumption' that the conclusion that no civil right was involved might now be viewed differently for the purposes of domestic human rights law, and possibly even by the ECtHR.[363] Nonetheless, in a subsequent decision in the High Court the orthodox view prevailed.[364] One of the factors

---

[354] (1986) 8 EHRR 483.

[355] *Varma*, n 353 above, at para 25.

[356] Ibid, referring specifically to the situation in *R v Lord President of the Privy Council ex p Page* [1993] AC 682.

[357] *R (Mohtasham) v Visitor of King's College, London* [2003] EWHC Admin 2372; [2004] ELR 29.

[358] T Birtwistle, 'Should Multiple Systems for Academic Appeals Remain? The Sole Role of the Visitor' (2000) 1 *Education Law Journal* 135.

[359] Higher Education Act 2004, Part 2. The scheme is operated by the Office of the Independent Adjudicator for Higher Education, which is the designated operator. See also Department for Education and Skills, *The Future of Higher Education*, Cm 5735 (London, TSO, 2003), paras 4.11–4.12.

[360] *Varma*, n 353 above, at para 26. See also *R (McBride) v Visitor of the University of London* [2004] EWHC Admin 104.

[361] See in particular *R (B) v Head Teacher of Alperton Community School and Others; R v Head Teacher of Wembley High School and Others ex p T; R v Governing Body of Cardinal Newman High School and Others ex p C* [2001] ELR 359, Admin Ct, followed, on the Art 6 point, in *R (S) v Head Teacher of C High School and Others* [2002[ELR 73.

[362] *S, T and P v London Borough of Brent and Others* [2002] EWCA Civ 693; [2002] ELR 556 (CA).

[363] Ibid, at para [30] per Schiemann LJ

[364] *A v Headteacher and Governors of The Lord Grey School* [2003] EWHC 1533 (QB).

that is seen as characterising public law rights is the element of discretion involved in the decision in question.[365] The most contentious areas of decision-making in education cases concern matters such as admissions, discipline issues, special educational provision and transport to or from school, all of which involve discretion, albeit exercised within a statutory and local policy framework. The English courts will need to make something of a jurisprudential leap if they are to construe the right to education as a civil right.

CONCLUSION

This chapter has examined the nature of the right to education, highlighting the difficulties inherent in the realisation of a right of the individual that arises out of a duty on the state that is essentially collectivist in nature. The state has wide social and economic goals to achieve through educational provision to all children. While it undeniably owes a duty to the individual child, in part as a consequence of its assumption of the responsibility for a child's education, these wider social and economic goals predominate. As a consequence, the state's authority and power over education results in a fairly severe curtailment of the individual's rights, and the state education system as a whole is in general fairly unresponsive to the wishes of individual parents or particular groups. This demonstrates a seemingly inherent problem with social rights arising from the fact that the matters to which they relate, including education, are highly susceptible to economic pressures, which have intensified with the search for greater economic efficiency since the late 1970s. These rights are highly conditional and far from absolute. Even the firm commitment given under the ECHR to uphold the right to education and to accord respect to individual parents' philosophical and religious beliefs in this context is shown in reality to protect principles rather than confer real entitlements. As we shall see in later chapters, the UK courts have adopted both a pragmatic and yet cautious approach to the advancement of human rights in education.

In relation to the rights of members of minority groups in the context of education, there are instabilities in the balancing of the state's wider role and the rights of the individual or particular ethnic groups, a position which brings into play much wider issues concerning integration and pluralism that are the concern of all modern western democracies. In the context of education, they arise from the interconnectivity of education rights and cultural rights in general; and, in particular, from the centrality of educational matters to the cultural and religious values of particular minority groups. This chapter has aimed to raise awareness of some of the surrounding issues. Later chapters will look at this matter in more detail, in a range of specific contexts.

The position of children collectively, particularly in relation to participation

---

[365] See the House of Lords' decision in the homelessness case of *Begum v London Borough of Tower Hamlets* [2003] UKHL 5; [2003] UKHRR 419.

opportunities, has been discussed in this chapter. Despite the increasing, if slow, recognition of the benefits of such collective participation and the conferment of some new rights, the position of children as a class or group may require further consideration by policy makers in the light of the new Equality and Human Rights Commission's duties, under the Equality Act 2006, to promote understanding of the importance of good relations between groups and to work towards the elimination of, inter alia, prejudice against and hostility towards members of groups.[366] As groups can be defined by, inter alia, age,[367] children could be a group for this purpose.[368] This implies a need to work towards greater respect for children as a group, but, given that groups can be defined also by race and religion of belief,[369] for respect between different groups of children. It is worth stressing, in this context, the relevance of the UNCRC's argument that 'children are capable of playing a unique role in bridging many of the differences that have historically separated groups of people from one another'.[370]

The Education and Inspections Bill 2006 provides for an Office of Children's Rights Director as a member of the new Office of Standards in Education, Children's Services and Skills (which will replace Ofsted).[371] This has symbolic importance but comes against a background of education law in England and Wales being long regarded by many, including the UNCRC, as seriously deficient in terms of recognition of the independent rights of the child. We saw that the first sentence of A2P1 of the ECHR, calling on states to prevent denial of the right to education, is a right of the child and that children have a range of other rights related specifically to education under the UNCRC. On the other hand, parents not only retain legal responsibility for their children's education but are also holders of such rights of preference or choice as are conferred by the ECHR in A2P1 or by domestic education law, with its continuing consumerist focus. They are also the presumed actors in relation to appeals and other forms of redress. The underlying assumption that children's and their parents' interests necessarily coincide may be questionable. Moreover, the primacy given to the parent runs the risk of compromising the rights of the child as, for example, articulated in the UNCRC. It is problematic for effective decision-making by authorities because it runs the risk that the voice of the child will not be properly heard or listened to, despite the widespread and informed view that children and young people often have a good insight into their educational needs. Although there have been advances of late in the opportunities afforded by education law for participation by children and young people, there remains significant room for improvement.

---

[366] Equality Act 2006, s 10(1).

[367] Ibid, s 10(2)(a).

[368] See Children's Legal Centre, 'Equality Bill: Child Impact Assessment' (2005) 220 *Childright* 17 at 18. Equality Bill, cl 10.

[369] Equality Act 2006, s 10(2)(e) and (f).

[370] UNCRC, *The Aims of Education,* CRC/GC/2001/1 (General Comments) (Geneva, United Nations, 2001), App, para 4.

[371] Cl 106. The Director's remit will be limited primarily to welfare of boarding children and care standards: see Cl 106(3).

3

Educational Provision: The Changing Legal Framework

INTRODUCTION

OVER THE PAST quarter of a century the education system in England and Wales has developed a complex institutional framework underpinned by extensive legislation. The increasing politicisation of this sphere of activity since the 1960s, noted in Chapter 1, has led to almost continual reform, shifting the balance of control and changing and diversifying the schools and other institutions responsible for educational provision. At the time of writing, further reforms are in prospect under the Education and Inspections Bill 2006. While subsequent chapters explore in depth discrete areas of provision which impact directly upon parents and children and give rise to key issues concerning social and cultural diversity—namely equal access to education, choice of school, special educational needs and provision and the content of education—this chapter aims to map out the changes to the system as a whole, to provide a broader political and legal context to the operation of the specific measures discussed later. This review concentrates on roles and structures under key pieces of legislation, particularly those under New Labour post-1997. As this book is primarily about the education of children and young people at school, the ensuing review of developments makes only passing references to further and higher education.

It will also be seen that there is no discussion of education in Scotland or Northern Ireland. The Scottish education system is different and separate from that in the rest of Great Britain and has its own legislative framework comprised in various Education (Scotland) Acts. These were, in the past, made by the UK Parliament and some parts of them remain in force, but the Scotland Act 1998 has given the new Scottish Parliament authority to enact its own primary legislation; and although certain matters, such as social security, finance and the economy, are reserved to the UK Parliament, education is not one of them. Education policy-making and central administration in Scotland fall within the remit of the Scottish Executive, whose ministers are empowered to promulgate secondary legislation. An example is the Education (National Priorities) (Scotland) Order 2000,[1] made in furtherance of the Executive's duty under the Standards in Scotland's Schools Act 2000 to 'define . . . priorities in educational objectives for school education provided for Scotland'.[2] The education system of Northern Ireland has also developed separately and had its own legislative framework and administration long before the Northern Ireland Act 1998, which aimed to give legislative effect to the Belfast Agreement concluded between the various political factions and the UK and Republic of Ireland governments, set in place a new constitutional framework for devolved government (albeit suspended at the time of writing).[3]

In the case of England and Wales there was essentially a single education system prior to the Government of Wales Act 1998. Although policy-making and central administration in England and Wales respectively were the responsibility of the Department for Education and Employment (as it was then known) in London and the Welsh Office based in Cardiff, policies often had joint application, as did the legislative framework, although education in Wales for the most part was the subject of discrete secondary legislation. The Government of Wales Act 1998 has not given the Assembly comparable legislative power to that given to the Scottish Parliament, so primary legislation for Wales still has to be made at Westminster. But secondary legislation is now formally made by the Welsh Assembly and, despite continuing areas of commonality, education policy in Wales is increasing divergent from that in England.[4] The UK Government has published formal proposals to devolve further legislative power to the Welsh Assembly.[5] Although many legislative provisions on education in Wales are now separate from, although they often mirror, those covering England, there are still some common provisions.

In the shaping of the current education system in England and Wales, three separate eras of reform can be discerned. The reforms that have been introduced under New Labour post-1997 have by no means eradicated all traces of those which preceded them. The first of the two earlier phases began with the Education Act 1944, strongly associated with RA Butler, the Minister of Education who steered this landmark legislation through Parliament. Butler's reputation in this context is perhaps as much derived from the legislation's subsequent longevity as his with political skilfulness in maintaining a broad consensus over its provisions. The 1944 Act incorporated a basic division of primary and secondary stages of education, an accommodation of denominational schools within the state sector, and confirmation of the role of LEAs. That phase was followed by the era of marketisation and managerialism, competition and control, that began with the Conservatives' Education Act 1980 and took

---

[1] SI 2000/443.

[2] Standards in Scotland's Schools Act 2000, s 4(1).

[3] See B Hadfield, 'The Nature of Devolution in Scotland and Northern Ireland', (1999) 3 *Edinburgh Law Review* 3; L Lundy, 'Education Law under Devolution: The Case of Northern Ireland' (2000) *Education Law Journal* 81.

[4] Eg, the National Curriculum: see Chap 7.

[5] The Wales Office, *Better Governance for Wales*, Cm 6582 (London, TSO, 2005).

hold with the Education Reform Act 1988. Much of the present legislative framework has been created in the third phase, from 1997, and it is of particular relevance to this book's themes since it is the only one of the three periods (notwithstanding Labour's comprehensivisation of secondary education in the 1960s) in which there has been anything approaching a concerted effort by government to address issues of inequality and social exclusion. In that regard it has followed the agenda mapped out by the Commission on Social Justice:

> The first and most important task for government is to set in place the opportunities for children and adults to learn to their personal best. By investing in skills, we raise people's capacity to add value to the economy, to take charge of their own lives, and to contribute to their families and communities . . . A good education is the most effective way to overcome inequalities of birth and status, to enable people to create and seize new opportunities, and to promote social improvement and mobility.[6]

Education was therefore identified as a key to achieving the desired social and economic goals based around the idea of social justice.

New Labour's school reforms have come in three separate waves, starting with the abolition of assisted places, under the Education (Schools) Act 1997,[7] but more particularly with the School Standards and Framework Act 1998, which among other things created new categories of schools, set a limit on infants' class sizes, introduced provision for education action zones covering areas of social deprivation, reformed the systems of school admissions and school exclusions (although it did not alter their fundamentals) and created new powers of local or central intervention in respect of schools causing concern. It was followed by the Education Act 2002, which covered similar ground but also replaced the legislative framework on the school curriculum and introduced new provisions for schools to acquire autonomy. The Education Act 2005, mostly concerned with inspections of education, has supplemented the general push towards ensuring higher standards of education. The third wave will arrive with the enactment of the Education and Inspections Bill 2006, based around the White Paper, *Higher Standards, Better Schools for All*.[8] The Bill, discussed more fully below, makes wide-ranging provision, including measures on discipline and to make the system more responsive to parents, plus the further extension of school autonomy. The extent of regulation of education today marks one of the most dramatic differences from the Butler era. It exemplifies what Wade has described as 'legislative omnipotence'[9] and what Loughlin calls the 'instrumentalization of law'[10] in the way that the law becomes a tool of regulatory (often economic) control in areas of social welfare, where resource-sensitivity is most acute. It has established a territory in which, as is discussed elsewhere in this book, individual

---

[6] Commission of Social Justice, *Social Justice. Strategies for National Renewal* (London, Vintage, 1994) 120.

[7] Noted in Chap 1.

[8] DfES, *Higher Standards, Better Schools for All*, Cm 6677 (London, TSO, 2006).

[9] HWR Wade, *Constititutional Fundamentals* (London, Stevens, 1980) 22.

[10] M Loughlin, *Public Law and Political Theory* (Oxford, OUP, 1992) 258–9.

and group rights may struggle to gain ground, and even where they appear to do so, as in the case of choice of school, they too may be instrumentalised as a facet of governance.[11]

THE SCHOOLS SYSTEM INHERITED BY NEW LABOUR

The state's growing responsibility for education was a common trend throughout the nineteenth century across Europe and the United States, even though there were differences in the social, economic, political and ideological forces that lay behind it.[12] In England, Forster's Elementary Education Act 1870 began the process by providing for the establishment of school boards in areas where elementary schools were needed to supplement existing, mostly church or charitable, provision. Finance came from local rates and government grants. Free places could be awarded, but in general parents had to find around one third of the cost of their child's education.[13] The boards were able to exercise powers to enforce school attendance, which became compulsory for all 5–12-year-olds from 1880 (under local by-laws). The state schools were run side by side with denominational schools. It was not until after the Education Act 1902, when school boards became integrated into local education authorities (LEAs), that provision was made for secondary and technical education. The 1902 Act also extended state funding to denominational schools, which became eligible for government grants to meet current expenditure. Under the Education Act 1918, all fees for attending elementary schools were abolished and the school leaving age was raised to 14 (where it remained until after the Education Act 1944).

Throughout the inter-war years of the twentieth century, most children attended elementary school until the school leaving age (then 14). Through an examination at the age of 11, some children were selected to attend LEA secondary schools. Free places were available, although just over one half of pupils attending them were fee payers.[14] Other academically bright children went to independent grammar schools or public schools, at their parents' expense. However, only one fifth of all children were in formal education beyond the age of 14.[15] The Education Act 1944 provided for compulsory education between the ages of 5 and 15 (inclusive) (although it empowered the raising of the school leaving age at a later date) and for publicly provided education to be available free to all up to the age of 18. LEAs were also placed under a duty, which

---

[11] See Chap 5.

[12] C Glenn and J De Groof, *Finding the Right Balance. Freedom, Autonomy and Accountability in Education Vol. II* (Utrecht, Lemma, 2002) 28–49, contains a very useful historical overview. The authors note (at 28) that 'Churches in Europe and the United States played the dominant role in the provision of education until late in the 18th century—and in many areas for a hundred years more'.

[13] N Timmins, *The Five Giants. A Biography of the Welfare State* (London, Harper Collins, 1995) 69.

[14] Ibid, 72–3.

[15] D Bell, 'Change and Continuity: Reflections on the Butler Act', Speech to Commemorate the 60th Anniversary of the 1944 Education Act: House of Commons, 21 Apr 2004.

continues today under the Education Act 1996, to ensure that there are in their area 'sufficient' schools for primary and secondary education, that is, schools 'sufficient in number, character and equipment to afford for all pupils opportunities for education, offering such variety . . . as may be desirable in view of their different ages, ability and aptitudes, and of the different period for which they may be expected to remain at school . . .'[16]

What was so significant about the 1944 Act was that it was built around the principle of universalism. It was also broadly egalitarian, in that education was to be available free of charge. But by permitting selection, normally at the age of 11, with the more academically able children being placed at grammar schools, and by tolerating the private sector, it maintained the broad class divisions that dominated British society. It also established the basic idea that education, while a national service, should be locally controlled and administered. Indeed, while the increasing centralisation of governmental power over the education system during the 1980s and 1990s enabled ministers to exercise firm controls over many areas of provision,[17] the position was very different under the 1944 Act. The Secretary of State's role was, by modern standards, a fairly limited one. Under section 1(1) the Minister was placed under a general duty to promote education and institutions devoted to it and to secure execution of the national policy 'for providing a varied and comprehensive educational service in every area'.

Viewing the 1944 Act as a whole, it is clear that the legislators believed in the 'importance of diffusing power over educational decision-making so as to prevent unwarranted concentration of control over such a vital service'.[18] Actual provision of schooling was to be the responsibility of LEAs,[19] guided by national policy objectives—for example, through the use of government circulars and administrative memoranda.[20] Ministerial influence grew in the 1960s, particularly when the Labour Government under Wilson attempted to cajole LEAs into abolishing selection[21] and introduced inner city Education Priority Areas, with

---

[16] Education Act 1944, s 8. See now the Education Act 1996, s 14.

[17] For a detailed account see N Harris, *Law and Education: Regulation, Consumerism and the Education System* (London, Sweet and Maxwell, 1993), ch 2. See also S Ranson, 'From 1944 to 1988: Education, Citizenship and Democracy' in M Flude and M Hammer (eds), *The Education Reform Act 1988: Its Origins and Its Implications* (Basingstoke, Falmer, 1990) 1.

[18] Ibid (Ranson), 3.

[19] County councils or county borough councils: Education Act 1944, s 6.

[20] In *R v Inner London Education Authority ex parte Bradby*, 30 Jan 1988 (Lexis), Woolf J emphasised that ministerial circulars had no statutory authority and 'are no more than guidance from the minister as to a course which, in general, he suggests the education authority should follow'. See further *R v London Borough of Islington ex parte Rixon* [1997] ELR 66; Sedley J, referring to the guidance in Circular 1/93 covering students with learning difficulties, said (at 82F) that 'this circular must conscientiously be taken into account by Islington's education department in coming to its decision about [J]'. It is common practice today to place LEAs and schools under a statutory duty to have regard to the Secretary of State's guidance. See, eg, Education Act 1996, s 403(1B), inserted by the Learning and Skills Act 2000, s 148(4), placing head teachers and governing bodies under a duty to have regard to the Secretary of State's guidance on sex education.

[21] Department of Education and Science Circular 10/65, followed by Circular 10/66, which stated that capital grants would be withheld if they were for building projects that were not consistent with the comprehensivisation policy. See further N Harris, *Law and Education: Regulation, Consumerism and the Education System* (London, Sweet and Maxwell, 1993), ch 2.

additional staff and funding levels for areas of particular deprivation.[22] But local government remained in control. The secular curriculum was guided by LEAs, apart from in voluntary aided schools, where it was under the control of the school's governing body.[23] Essentially LEAs were the providers of most schooling and further education (at 'county colleges').[24]

The statutory system of education was to be organised into 'three progressive stages'—primary, secondary and further education[25]—a structure that continues to this day. Also surviving is LEAs' duty to ensure sufficient schools, noted above, and a general duty 'so far as their powers extend, to contribute towards the spiritual, moral, mental and physical development of the community by securing that efficient education throughout those stages shall be available to meet the needs of the population of their area'.[26] In ensuring a sufficiency of schools LEAs had to have regard to the need to ensure provision of 'special educational treatment' for 'pupils who suffer from any disability of mind or body', not merely those considered 'mentally defective' or epileptic, as in the past.[27] (This was later amended by the Education Act 1981 to: having regard to the need to ensure 'special educational provision for those with special educational needs'.) It also laid down a duty for LEAs to identify all such children.[28] Over subsequent years the courts confirmed that LEAs had a 'broad discretion' as regards the most appropriate means of ensuring suitable schools provision in their area;[29] that the 'sufficient schools' duty was not an absolute duty, so that the availability of resources and other factors could legitimately affects its discharge;[30] and that in fulfilling their duty LEAs had to act consistently with their non-discrimination duties under the Sex Discrimination Act 1975, so that neither sex should have greater access than the other to a place at a single-sex school.[31] Although the Secretary of State was given default powers—which also continue—to enable him or her to intervene where LEAs or governing bodies are 'acting or proposing to act unreasonably' with respect to the exercise of a power or performance of a duty under the Act or are in default of any statutory education duty imposed on

---

[22] P Daniel and J Ivatts, *Children and Social Policy* (Basingstoke, Macmillan, 1998) 173. They had previously been recommended by the Plowden Committee: Central Advisory Council for Education (England) (chair Lady Plowden), *Children and their Primary Schools* (London, HMSO, 1967), I, paras 151–154 and 174.

[23] EA 1944, s 23.

[24] Ibid, ss 41–43.

[25] Ibid, s 7.

[26] Ibid. See now the Education Act 1996, s 13.

[27] EA 1944, s 8(2).

[28] Ibid, ss 33 and 34.

[29] *Secretary of State for Education and Science v Tameside Metropolitan Borough Council* [1976] 3 All ER 665, per Lord Diplock at 695B; *Equal Opportunities Commission v Birmingham City Council* [1989] 1 All ER 769, per Lord Goff at 775C.

[30] *Meade v Haringey London Borough Council* [1979] 2 All ER 1016; *R v Inner London Education Authority ex parte Ali and Murshid* [1990] 2 Admin LR 822, where Woolf J referred to the duty in s 8 as a 'target duty'.

[31] *R v Secretary of State for Education and Science ex parte Keating* (1985) 84 LGR 469; *Equal Opportunities Commission v Birmingham City Council* [1989] 1 All ER 769; *R v Secretary of State for Education and Science ex parte Malik* [1992] COD 31; *R v Birmingham City Council ex parte Equal Opportunities Commission (No 2)* [1994] ELR 282 (CA); *R v Northamptonshire County Council and the Secretary of State for Education ex parte K* [1994] ELR 397. See further p 9 above and p 147 below.

them,[32] these powers were (and still are) rarely invoked.[33] The courts were also, in general, very reluctant to intervene where the Secretary of State decided, as a matter of judgement, not to exercise one or other of the powers in an individual case.[34] Even during the period from 1979 when centralisation of power was well under way, the Department of Education and Science (now the Department for Education and Skills) expressed reluctance to be too interfering over matters that Parliament had entrusted to local decision-makers, resisting calls for stronger powers from the House of Commons Select Committee which had concluded that the existing default powers were difficult to enforce.[35]

So, under the arrangements set in place under the 1944 Act, LEAs were responsible for local planning of educational provision, with little interference. The 'sufficient' schools duty meant that they had to manage the overall organisation of schooling, including the establishment, alteration or closure of schools under statutory powers, as demanded by economic circumstances or demographic changes. Some schools, notably the voluntary aided schools (mostly Roman Catholic), remained semi-autonomous, and their governing bodies had separate powers to initiate school changes, although formal approval from the Secretary of State was often needed.[36]

The equal place of denominational schools within the state system as a result of the Education Act 1944 was one of its most significant features. As we saw in Chapter 1, there are over 7,000 such schools today. Butler believed in the goal of education for all and, to this end, found a way of integrating into the state sector many of the schools run by the Church of England and the Catholic Church, a number of which were in dire financial straits and finding it difficult to maintain their buildings and meet operational costs. In 1939, the churches were running half the schools in England and Wales, although they were providing schooling for less than one third of the total school population.[37] The 1944 Act offered most of these church schools a choice between 'voluntary controlled' and 'voluntary aided' status. The former meant that the school would retain its

---

[32] EA 1944, ss 68 and 99; see now EA 1996, ss 496 and 497. On s 68, see *Secretary of State for Education and Science v Tameside Metropolitan Borough Council* [1977] AC 1014 (HL). On s 99, see *Meade v Haringey London Borough Council* [1979] 2 All ER 1016 at 1024, per Denning MR; see also *Watt v Kesteven County Council* [1955] 1 All ER 473 (CA); *Bradbury v London Borough of Enfield* [1967] 3 All ER 434; *R v Inner London Education Authority ex parte Ali and Murshid* [1990] 2 Admin LR 822. For analysis, see Harris, n 21 above, 33–7 and N Harris, 'Education by Right? Breach of the Duty to Ensure "Sufficient Schools"' (1990) 53 *MLR* 525.

[33] See N Harris, *Law and Education: Regulation, Consumerism and the Education System* (London, Sweet and Maxwell, 1993), ch 2.

[34] *Bradbury v London Borough of Enfield* [1967] 3 All ER 434, per Diplock LJ at 440; *Secretary of State for Education and Science v Tameside Metropolitan Borough Council* [1976] 3 All ER 665, per Lord Diplock at 695 and Lord Wilberforce at 681–2. In *R v Secretary of State for Education and Science ex parte Chance*, 26 July 1982 (unreported), Woolf J found that the Secretary of State had, when asked to intervene in a case where the LEA was alleged to have failed in its duty to make provision for a child with dyslexia, failed to take proper account of the relevant legislation and said it was a case where the court could intervene.

[35] House of Commons Education, Science and the Arts Select Committee, *Second Report 1981–82. The Secondary School Curriculum and Examinations*, HC 116-1 (London, HMSO, 1982), part 9; Department of Education and Science, *Initial Observations on the Second Report from the Education, Science and the Arts Committee Session 1981–82*, Cmnd 8551 (London, HMSO, 1982).

[36] See N Harris, *The Law relating to Schools* (Croydon, Tolley, 1995), ch 2.

[37] N Timmins, *The Five Giants: A Biography of the Welfare State* (London, Harper Collins, 1995) 79.

religious character but would be funded entirely by the LEA, which would have control over staff appointments and would generally follow a locally agreed syllabus for religious education.[38] Aided status, on the other hand, would give the school's foundation body (its founders or their successors) much more control over staff appointments and the content of religious education, plus majority membership in the school's governing body, known as a 'board of managers' in primary schools or a 'board of governors' in secondary schools, both known today as the 'governing body'. Aided status suited the Catholic Church, which wanted to retain control of its own schools. However, it meant that the school's foundation body would need to find some of the funding: the LEA would meet the school's operational costs, but the foundation body would have to cover 50 per cent of the capital costs: this was later reduced in stages to 15 per cent, and it currently stands at 10 per cent.[39] While aimed primarily at the Catholic sector, aided status was also chosen by some of the Church of England schools. However, the Church of England's main concern was that lack of funding put the future of its schools in jeopardy. Controlled status maximised financial support and was adopted by most. A small number of denominational schools were in a third category, 'special agreement' schools, which had similar status to aided schools but were funded under an agreement with the LEA: this category has since been abolished and these schools were designated as aided schools under the School Standards and Framework Act 1998.

The majority of schools, which were non-denominational and mainstream, were classed as 'county' schools under the 1944 Act. They were under the control of the LEA, which funded them in full. Today these schools are 'community' schools.[40] Special schools, catering for pupils with various forms of learning difficulty, also operated and had a higher profile after the Education Act 1981 imposed duties on LEAs to identify, and make provision for, pupils with special educational needs. Most special schools within the state sector are now classed as 'community special schools' under the 1998 Act, but an increasing proportion of pupils with special educational needs are educated in mainstream schools.[41] Schools were also identified by academic ethos and pupil selection methods. Secondary schools which selected pupils wholly or partly on the basis of their academic ability were generally classed as 'grammar' schools, while children who failed the examination (the 11-plus) attended 'secondary modern' schools.[42] Butler envisaged a 'gradual melding' of the two categories, and he later was critical of Labour's obsession with comprehensivisation of

---

[38] The position today is that in most categories of school the LEA is, for legal purposes, the employer of staff (Education Act 2002, s 35; see also *Green v Victoria Board School*, Employment Appeal Tribunal, 18 Mar 2003). But since the Education (No 2) Act 1986 the school's governing body has been responsible for making appointments and decisions on dismissals, although curiously the LEA is the respondent to any employment tribunal applicaiton.

[39] SSFA 1998, Sched 3, para 5, as amended.

[40] SSFA 1998, s 20.

[41] See Chap 6.

[42] It had been envisaged that in addition to these two types there would be 'technical' schools, but despite ministerial encouragement for them they proved unviable. See P Sharp and J Dunford, *The Education System in England and Wales* (Harlow, Longman, 1989) 21.

secondary schools,[43] which led to government attempts during the 1960s and 1970s to abolish academic selection of pupils at the secondary level. Legislation to that effect (the Education Act 1976) was never brought into force, however, and was later repealed by the Conservatives.[44] Although most state secondary schools became non-selective 'comprehensive' schools, grammar schools survived in six LEA areas and there are still 164 such schools today.

The Conservative Government elected in 1979 railed against the uniformity of the comprehensive school system that had developed incrementally during the previous two decades and the increasing political interference in children's education by left-leaning local councils and teachers. The Conservatives' education reforms sought to wrest control of schools from LEAs, reducing LEA representation, guaranteeing parental representation on school governing bodies and placing governors in charge of their schools and their curriculum policies, human resources and finances. Indeed, there was an ideological assault on LEAs, which were condemned as profligate with public finances, inefficient, hidebound with restrictive practices and doctrinaire in their approach to education.[45] It led to a range of measures intended, at first, to reduce the role of LEAs to a largely strategic one (and in the case of the left-dominated Inner London Education Authority, involving its complete abolition[46]). Moreover, starting with the Education Act 1980, the Conservatives aimed to realise their ideological commitment to marketise education and introduce competition and parental choice. They wanted to place schools under the control of governing bodies with increased elected parental representation. The Education (No 2) Act 1986 produced changes to school government, devolving power and responsibility to re-constituted school governing bodies, which were to operate under more regulated decision-making procedures.[47] That Act also made governing bodies responsible for the secular curriculum in their schools, although schools' freedom in this area was soon rendered somewhat theoretical by the establishment of the mandatory National Curriculum under Part I of the Education Reform Act 1988.[48]

The 1988 Act was a major landmark in education reform. Of particular importance was the establishment of grant-maintained (GM) schools and the

---

[43] P Cosgrave, *RA Butler An English Life* (London, Quartet, 1981) 81. Furthermore, when Minister of Education during the war, Butler had actually had on his reform agenda the integration of private or independent schools into the state sector.

[44] By the Education Act 1979.

[45] See G Whitty and I Menter, 'Lessons of Thatcherism—Education Policy in England and Wales 1979–88' (1989) 16 *Journal of Law and Society* 42; L Bash and D Coulby, *The Education Reform Act. Competition and Control* (London, Cassell, 1989).

[46] Education Reform Act 1988, s 162ff. See C Jones, 'The Break-up of the Inner London Education Authority' in L Bash and D Coulby, *Education Reform Act: Competition and Control* (London, Cassell, 1989) 85; N Harris, *Law and Education: Regulation, Consumerism and the Education System* (London, Sweet and Maxwell, 1993) 39–42. Feintuck refers to the abolition of the Authority as a 'political victory' for the Thatcher government: M Feintuck, *Accountability and Choice in Schooling* (Milton Keynes, Open University Press, 1994) 23.

[47] See, eg, the Education (School Government) Regulations 1989 (SI 1989/1503) (no longer in force) and DES Circular 7/87. Later, governing bodies were accorded corporate status in order to protect individual governors from incurring personal liability: Education Act 1993, s 238.

[48] See Chapter 7.

creation of city technology colleges (part-funded by private sector sponsorship), which marked the beginning of a process towards increasing diversity within the schools system, but also its fragmentation. GM schools served a number of the Government's objectives, since they not only gave greater diversity to the system, but also introduced more competition and choice and, because they were outside the LEA-maintained sector altogether, weakened LEA control of education. They also transferred some power to parents, since the process for the acquisition of GM status included a parental ballot.[49] GM schools were funded by the Department for Education, but later, following the Education Act 1993, via a separate body, the Funding Agency for Schools. Although their funding allocations were based on the amount they would have received had they been part of the LEA sector, they received an additional element to reflect the reduction of LEA services input. They also benefited from generous capital allowances. For example, in 1993–4 they received 15 per cent of the total capital investment for schools in England even though they constituted only 4 per cent of the schools.[50] From the perspective of LEAs, the presence of GM schools outside their control made it more difficult for the 'sufficient' schools duty to be performed and could hinder school places planning.[51] Here was a whole cadre of schools that were completely outside LEA control, but were instead subject to the executive authority of the Secretary of State.[52] The acquisition of GM status, or 'opting out' as it became known, represented a significant assault on the central–local government partnership provided for by the 1944 Act. The implications for LEAs became even more stark following the introduction of the Funding Agency for Schools (above). The Agency handled an executive responsibility and allocated funds to GM schools. Its members were appointed by the Secretary of State. The 1993 Act provided that once 10 per cent of the pupils attending schools in the LEA's area were registered at a GM school, the LEA's 'sufficient' schools duty would be shared between the LEA and the Agency. Once that figure reached 75 per cent (referred to as the 'exit point' by the 1992 White Paper[53]) the Agency would assume sole responsibility.[54] Primary or secondary school sectors were treated independently, so it was possible for an LEA to lose control of one sector or both. Meredith argues that a vital LEA role was thereby surrendered to 'a body with no democratic foundation, with little sensitivity to local needs and accountable only to the Secretary of State'.[55]

There was fierce opposition to GM schools from the Labour Party, local government and teaching unions, based on perceptions that the schools' position

---

[49] See N Harris, n 46 above, 122–7. The procedure for the acquisition of GM status involved a ballot of parents following two resolutions in favour by the governing body; if the ballot went in favour the matter was referred to the Secretary of State for final decision: 47–58.

[50] Cited in P Daniel and J Ivetts, *Children and Social Policy* (Basingstoke, Macmillan, 1998) 186.

[51] See Harris, n 46 above, 54–7.

[52] See M Flude and M Hammer, 'Opting for an Uncertain Future: Grant-Maintained Schools' in M Flude and M Hammer (eds), *The Education Reform Act 1988: Its Origins and its Implications* (London, Falmer, 1990) 51.

[53] Department for Education, *Choice and Diversity*, Cm 2021 (London, HMSO, 1992), para 4.5.

[54] S 12.

[55] P Meredith, 'The Fall and Rise of Local Education Authorities' (1998) XX *Liverpool Law Review* 41 at 46.

was privileged and by virtue of the risk they posed to local authority control. Yet GM status had less of an impact than had been expected. By November 1992 there were just 340 GM schools,[56] and attempts to breathe new life into the policy via the 1993 Act, which streamlined the acquisition procedure, permitted smaller primary schools to apply and authorised joint applications by schools, only partially succeeded. By July 1994, there were 930 GM schools but the 10 per cent control threshold was reached for primary schools in only three out of the 109 LEAs in England, although for secondary schools it was reached in 45 LEAs. In only one LEA (Brent) was the 75 per cent 'exit point' reached.[57] Just 8.4 per cent of state school pupils (2 per cent of primary school pupils and 17.6 per cent of secondary school pupils) in England attended GM schools.[58] The number of GM schools slowly increased, so that by 1997 the 75 per cent exit point had been reached for secondary schools in four LEAs, while the 10 per cent threshold was reached in respect of primary schools in eight LEAs and for secondary schools in a total of 57 LEAs.[59] Around 1,000 schools had GM status immediately prior to its abolition under the School Standards and Framework Act 1998.[60] These schools are now once again part of the LEA sector and most are 'foundation' schools, a new category introduced by the 1998 Act, which, while retaining some autonomy, is part of the LEA sector.[61] But the ideal of the autonomous and self-governing school has survived and there are currently attempts to revive it through independent trust schools under the Education and Inspections Bill 2006.[62]

Accompanying the introduction of GM schools was, as noted above, the creation of a new form of school, the city technology college (CTC) (which could also be established as a 'city college for the technology of the arts'). The colleges were public–private hybrids, established with the aid of private sector sponsorships by proprietors under an agreement with the Secretary of State, but also receiving substantial amounts of public money. From the outset they were categorised under statute as independent schools, but have nonetheless been subject to a certain degree of control by the Secretary of State.[63] To belong to this category the school had to cater for pupils of 'different abilities' of the age of 11 or older (this age limit has since been revoked[64]). By 1997 there were 15 of these colleges. Throughout, these institutions have been exempt from the statutory requirements concerning the National Curriculum and religious education and worship applicable to mainstream state schools, although their funding agreement with central government has provided for minimum curriculum

[56] HC Debs, Vol. 213, Col. 494w, 6 Nov 1992.
[57] HC Debs, Vol. 246, Col. 451, 11 July 1994.
[58] Ibid, Cols 451–453.
[59] Department for Education, *GM School Statistics* (London, DfE, 1997).
[60] Hansard, HL Debs, Vol. 312, Col. 1608, 19 May 1998.
[61] School Standards and Framework Act 1998, Sched 2. Schools that were previously voluntarily aided or special agreement schools had a choice as to whether to be classed as 'aided' or 'foundation'.
[62] Note that the term 'trust' school is not used in the Bill. See below.
[63] Education Reform Act 1988, s 105 (see now EA 1996, s 482, as amended by the EA 2002, s 65); see also *R v Governors of John Bacon School ex parte Inner London Education Authority* (1990) 88 LGR 648; and *R v Governors of Haberdashers' Aske's Hatcham College Trust ex parte T* [1995] ELR 350.
[64] By the 2002 Act s 65.

requirements consistent with a school's statutory duty to offer a broad curriculum. Their autonomy includes the regulation of their own admission procedures. After the Learning and Skills Act 2000 these colleges could be known as academies, a name which, since the Education Act 2002, is in any event now attached to all these institutions, whose numbers are set to expand greatly (see below). CTCs or academies, together with the 'assisted places' scheme, which, as noted in Chapter 1, provided parents with means-tested assistance with school fees and incidental expenses to enable their children to attend participating independent schools, are seen as representing the partial privatisation of education through state assistance towards what is essentially private provision. However, as noted below, public–private partnership has been very much part of the Labour government's policy post-1997.

LEA-maintained schools also gained greater autonomy through the devolution of school budgets to governing bodies, under the Local Management of Schools (LMS) initiative,[65] a process of devolved financial management that has continued to this day (although the LMS name has been dropped). As funding allocations are firmly linked to pupil numbers, there has always been an incentive for schools to attract the maximum number of pupils. With parents enjoying a right to express a preference for a school and an appeal right over admissions decisions,[66] the intention was that a market for schooling would operate and that the forces of competition would drive improvements in standards. To support parental choice and marketplace accountability, LEAs and schools were placed under a duty to provide information to parents about schools, local education policies, and pupil success rates in public examinations.[67]

For teachers, seen as the third partners (with LEAs and the Secretary of State) in meeting the goals of the 1944 Act, and who in 1967 were still said to enjoy 'the responsibility and spur of freedom',[68] there was a significant undermining of professional autonomy as a result of the introduction of the National Curriculum, preceded by unprecedented requirements regarding sex education and political content.[69] By the time Labour came to power in 1997, the teaching profession in England and Wales was in a state of near crisis. Its autonomy had been seriously weakened; the introduction of competition within a quasi-market for schooling, combined with increased accountability to parents through the publication of pupil results and inspection reports (compiled for the most part by Ofsted inspectors[70]) and the planned introduction of school performance

---

[65] R Wallace, 'The Act and Local Authorities' in M Flude and M Hammer (eds), *The Education Reform Act 1988: Its Origins and Its Implications* (Basingstoke, Falmer, 1990) 225 at 238.

[66] See Chap 5.

[67] Eg ERA 1988 s 22. See N Harris, *Law and Education: Regulation, Consumerism and the Education System* (London, Sweet and Maxwell, 1993), ch 5.

[68] Central Advisory Council for Education (England) (chair: Lady Plowden), *Children and their Primary Schools* (London, HMSO, 1967), i, para 876.

[69] Education (No2) Act 1986, ss 44 and 46. See Chap 7.

[70] Under arrangements within the Education (Schools) Act 1992. See further N Harris, 'Quality Control and Accountability to the Consumer' in T Brighouse and B Moon (eds), *School Inspection* (London, Pitman, 1995) 46.

targets[71] had maximised pressures to succeed; and pay and career progression difficulties hindered the recruitment and retention of staff. The fact that the determination of teachers' pay and conditions by order made by the Secretary of State, albeit on the advice of a review body and after consultation with interested parties including the unions, had largely replaced national negotiations with the teachers' associations, had added to the sense of disempowerment and subjugation.[72] Although teachers were represented on the Teacher Training Agency that was established under the Education Act 1994 as an executive agency to co-ordinate teacher training and qualification as a teacher and to 'promote teaching as a career',[73] the Agency had little power and the Secretary of State had powers to issue binding directions to it.[74]

For LEAs, the period from 1979–97 was one of 'challenge and reductionism'.[75] They retained responsibility for special educational provision, education welfare, the enforcement of school attendance, provision of school transport, alternative provision for those unable to attend school due to illness or exclusion, and the administration of various forms of financial support, such as school uniform grants and discretionary awards for young people in further education.[76] They also remained the employers of most staff working in schools, even though their control over staff appointments, promotions, discipline and dismissal had been transferred to school governing bodies.[77] But the role of LEAs was much diminished overall and key areas of responsibility were lost.[78] Ranson sees the Education Act 1993 as particularly significant in terms of policy shift, in the sense that while the introduction, under the Education Reform Act 1988, of greater autonomy for schools and reduced LEA control could at least be rationalised as enabling authorities to 'concentrate on overall strategy, support to schools and

[71] Education Act 1997, s 19. See DfEE Circular 11/98, *Target-setting in Schools* (London, DfEE, 1998).

[72] See the Teachers' Pay and Conditions Act 1987, replaced by the School Teachers' Pay and Conditions Act 1991. Teachers' pay and conditions were determined under an annual *School Teachers' Pay and Conditions Document*, which was given effect to by order. The Secretary of State was advised by an Interim Advisory Committee under the 1987 and by the School Teachers' Review Body, whose members were appointed by the Prime Minister, under the 1991 Act. The Education Act 2002 (Sched 21 and s 130) has repealed the 1991 Act, but the School Teachers' Review Body continues, although its members are now to be appointed by the Secretary of State rather than the PM: Education Act 2002, s 119 and Sched 11. The functions and consultation duty of the Review Body and the power of the Secretary of State to prescribe the pay scales and conditions of teachers are as before: ibid, ss 120–122.

[73] EA 1994, s 1(2)(b).

[74] Ibid.

[75] S Whitbourn with K Mitchell and R Morris, *What is the LEA For? An Analayis of the Functions and Roles of the Local Education Authority* (Slough, Education Management Information Exchange/National Foundation for Educational Research, 2000) 2.

[76] Paid under the Education Act 1962.

[77] See N Harris, *The Law relating to Schools* (2nd edn, Croydon, Tolley, 1995), ch 5.

[78] Within further and higher education, parallel power transfers occurred. The Education Reform Act 1988 removed polytechnics from LEA control, putting each one under its own higher education corporation, and gave them a central funding body, the Polytechnic and Colleges Funding Council. The Further and Higher Education Act 1992 placed financial control over the sector and overall responsibility for securing sufficient provision for further education with a Further Education Funding Councils for England and Wales and gave each college a degree of autonomy (as a 'further education corporation'). For background see Secretary of State for Education, *Higher Education: Meeting the Challenge* (London, HMSO, 1987); Idem, *Education and Training for the 21st Century: The Challenge to Colleges*, Cm 1536 (London, HMSO, 1991), ii; Idem, *Higher Education: A New Framework*, Cm 1541 (London, HMSO, 1991).

assuring the quality of their performance', the 1993 Act seemed to be questioning 'the very idea of a local system of education . . . and with it the role of the LEA'.[79] Indeed, central powers were introduced under the 1993 Act, enabling the Secretary of State to direct LEAs to reduce 'excessive' provision, such as by ordering them to publish proposals for schools reorganisation or closures or, if the LEAs failed to do so, bringing forward proposals of her own. The Secretary of State rather than the LEA was the judge of whether local provision was excessive. The aim was to remove over-capacity from schools (there being some 1.5 million surplus places across England and Wales) at a time of falling rolls, and thereby achieve a more efficient use of resources.[80] The effect was to weaken still further LEAs' planning function. Another reform of particularly symbolic importance was the repeal of parts of the 1944 Act that had required LEAs to establish an education committee and had empowered an authority to authorise the committee to exercise on the authority's behalf any of its functions relating to education.[81] According to Simon and Chitty, this reform 'to all intents and purposes implies the end of the local *education* authority' and would destroy a crucial element of the 1944 Act's scheme of administration.[82] Moreover, the 1993 Act also reformulated the Secretary of State's duty to promote education, previously section 1 of the 1944 Act, by omitting the reference to the execution of national policy by local authorities.[83] Although the Government could claim that that was because, unlike the previous duty, the new duty was intended to apply to *all* levels of education, including higher education,[84] which was not the LEA's responsibility, it was seen by some as effectively signifying or presaging the end of the LEA. Ranson, for example, argues that it challenged the notion of local democracy that the 1944 Act structure represented.[85]

The final Conservative statute on education before Labour took office, the Education Act 1997,[86] was something of a compromise. Provisions that would have paved the way for extension of selection were among several contentious areas that were jettisoned by ministers in order to ensure the Bill's smooth passage as time began to run out prior to the general election. The 1997 Act contained arrangements for the inspection of LEAs, at the instigation of either the Secretary of State or the Chief Inspector of Schools. It included no specific sanctions for LEAs found to be under-performing in relation to any of their educational functions, but further emphasised the strict control under which LEAs operated. In one of their residual areas of responsibility, however, LEAs' role was marginally increased: they were placed under a duty to prepare a statement setting out their arrangements in connection with children with behavioural

---

[79] S Ranson, 'Local Democracy for the Learning Society' in National Commission on Education, *Briefings* (London Heinemann, 1993), 267 at 271–2.

[80] HL Debs, Vol 545, Col 1031, per Baroness Blatch, Minister of State.

[81] Education Act 1944, s 6(2) and First Sched, Part II, repealed by the Education Act 1993, s 296.

[82] B Simon and C Chitty, *SOS—Save Our Schools* (London, Lawrence and Wishart, 1992) 149–50 (original emphasis).

[83] EA 1993, s 1.

[84] HL Debs, Vol. 544, Col. 1374, per Baroness Blatch, Minister of State.

[85] S Ranson, n 79 above, at 272 and 275.

[86] EA 1997, ss 38–41.

difficulties.[87] Nonetheless, as Meredith says, the overall effect of the Conservatives' reforms was that LEAs' 'functions as a whole, and the strategic planning function in particular, had reduced greatly in significance'.[88] In all sectors of education, including further and higher education, central control was now firmly established. Institutions had gained autonomy from LEAs, but at a considerable cost due to the strict regulatory regimes that had been imposed upon them. Some individual rights among parents had also been recognised, as noted in Chapter 2 and as will be discussed in detail in later chapters. They were extremely important in specific areas, such as special educational needs and provision. But as a source of accountability on the part of providers, their *overall* impact was relatively limited compared to the top-down controls set in place over this period.

EDUCATION REFORM POST-1997

The First Administration, 1997–2001

In its 1997 schools White Paper, published shortly after the general election that returned Labour to power after 18 years, the new Government said it had placed education 'at the heart of government' and had ranked it its 'number one priority'.[89] This might have been rhetoric, but it was undeniable that the Blair government was prepared to commit additional resources to underscore its policy goals. The White Paper contained a pledge that 'over the lifetime of this Government we will increase the proportion of national income spent on education as we decrease it on meeting the bills of past social and economic failure'.[90] The Government intended to make 'a £19 billion investment over three years to tackle the problems in our schools and equip our children to play a full part in society when they grow up'.[91] The Government's central message was that there was a need to improve educational standards for all children. It announced national targets for literacy and numeracy among 11-year-olds and a commitment to tackle the under-achievement among children from the ethnic minority backgrounds with the poorest record of academic attainment.[92] This was part of a wider goal of increasing social inclusion, reflected in the tabling of amendments when the School standards and Framework Bill was before

---

[87] EA 1997, s 9, inserting s 527A into the EA 1996 (since repealed—see now Children Act 2004, s 17).

[88] P Meredith, 'The Fall and Rise of Local Education Authorities' (1998) XX *Liverpool Law Review* 41 at 46.

[89] Department for Education and Employment, *Excellence in Schools*, Cm 3681 (London, TSO, 1997), ch 1, para 15. See also, Welsh Office, *Building Excellent School Together*, Cm 3701 (TSO, 1997).

[90] *Excellence in Schools*, n 89 above, ch 1, para 15.

[91] Secretary of State for Social Security, *Opportunity for All. Tackling Poverty and Social Exclusion*, Cm 4445 (London, TSO, 1999) 45.

[92] DfEE n 89 above, ch 4, para 2. The targets were that 80 per cent of 11-year-olds would reach the required levels in English and 75 per cent the required level in mathematics, compared with less than 60 per cent who were achieving those levels in these subjects: ibid, ch 2, para 21.

Parliament to incorporate Social Exclusion Unit recommendations on ways of tackling truancy and reducing levels of pupil exclusion, noted in Chapter 1.[93] This commitment was reinforced in 1999 in the Government's report *Opportunity for All*, which cited education as 'the most important route into work, and out of poverty and social exclusion'.[94]

The School Standards and Framework Act (SSFA) 1998, which was the first major piece of education legislation on schools ever enacted under a Labour Government in the UK, had as its central purpose the raising of standards of education for all children of school age. But it in fact covered a very wide range of important education matters and, despite the White Paper's claim that 'standards matter more than structures' and that 'the preoccupation with school structure has absorbed a great deal of energy to little effect',[95] it did in fact make some important structural changes to the education system. For example, it dissolved the Funding Agency for Schools and established a new categorisation of schools, including the abolition of grant-maintained (GM) status, with GM schools being placed in a new category—foundation schools—unless they had been voluntary aided or special agreement schools before they acquired GM status, in which case they became voluntary aided schools.[96] Nonetheless, it could be argued that by downplaying the importance of 'structures' the Government was in fact attempting to justify its overall unwillingness to replace or reform many of key parts of the structure set in place between 1979 and 1997, such as devolved budgetary and managerial control to school governing bodies (indeed, the Government wanted to increase the proportion of LEAs' schools budgets devolved to governing bodies, previously around 90 per cent[97]) and the quasi-market for school places based on the exercise of parental choice. The school inspection system under Ofsted and controls over failing schools were also retained (although the basic statutory framework under the School Inspections Act 1996 was later repealed and replaced by Part 1 of the Education Act 2005[98]), while the National Curriculum also continued, although was incrementally reformed.[99] For the most part, the system set in place under the changes made by the SSFA 1998 is still in operation.

One of the significant features of the 1998 Act was the way it halted, and to some extent reversed, the decline in the role of LEAs. The abolition of GM status

[93] Social Exclusion Unit, *Truancy and School Exclusion: Report by the Social Exclusion Unit*, Cm 3957 (London, TSO, 1998).

[94] Secretary of State for Social Security, *Opportunity for All. Tackling Poverty and Social Exclusion*, Cm 4445 (London, TSO, 1999) 45.

[95] Department for Education and Employment, *Excellence in Schools*, Cm 3681 (London, TSO, 1997), ch 1, para 17.

[96] SSFA 1998, Sched 2 para 3. The main difference between foundation and voluntary aided (VA) schools is that the latter have a majority of governors appointed by the religious foundation. In foundation schools (whether religious or not) the foundation governors are in the minority. Also, VA schools normally have to meet 10 per cent of their capital costs themselves; foundation schools do not. On school government, see further below.

[97] Department for Education and Employment, *Excellence in Schools*, Cm 3681 (London, TSO, 1997), ch 7, para 21. See also Department for Education and Employment, *Fair Funding: Improving Delegation to Schools* (London, Department for Education and Employment, 1998).

[98] Amendments are also made by this Act with regard to the inspection of independent schools.

[99] See Chap 7.

and the dissolution of the Funding Agency for Schools have already been mentioned. As a consequence of these reforms there was no longer a threat to LEAs' overall strategic role in respect of schools provision, although the introduction of an office of 'adjudicator' to whom objections about school changes or admissions policies could be taken showed that their freedom over planning was not being completely restored.[100] LEAs were also placed under increased regulation. The Act gave them a duty to prepare, and seek the Secretary of State's approval for, an education development plan for their area, setting out proposals for 'raising the standards of education' for children, at the LEA's own schools or elsewhere, and 'improving the performance' of schools.[101] This emphasis on standards was also reflected in LEAs' new general duty under the Act to exercise their functions 'with a view to promoting high standards of education',[102] which parallels the duty on school governing bodies to 'promote high standards of educational achievement' at their school.[103]

It was noted above that under the Education Act 1997 a new system for the inspection of LEAs was instituted. There were no enforcement measures or sanctions under the Act in respect of failure by an LEA, although the general default powers originating from the 1944 Act[104] and consolidated into the 1996 Act[105] were available to the Secretary of State. The SSFA 1998 introduced a new default power, exercisable where an LEA fails to carry out any of its functions adequately or at all. Under it, the Secretary of State can give specific directions to an officer of the LEA and appoint a person (or persons) external to the LEA to carry out any of the LEA's functions.[106] A minor change was also made to the structure of LEAs, ostensibly to make them more accountable to parents: on education committees there are to be one or more parent governors, or, where expedient, representatives of parents of registered pupils, elected to serve on the committee or a sub-committee.[107] The Government argued that 'parents . . . and their children are the consumers of the education service and in principle we should allow parents to have a voting right'.[108] However, while the voice of the parent (but not the child) may be heard, the representation is somewhat token-istic and, in any event, the devolution of many key education responsibilities to

---

[100] See Chap 5.

[101] SSFA 1998, ss 6 and 7. See further Department for Education and Employment, *Excellence in Schools*, Cm 3681 (London, TSO, 1997), ch 3, paras 21–24.

[102] SSFA 1998, s 5, adding s 13A to the Education Act 1996. This duty is to be replicated in the replacement s 13A to be introduced under the Education and Inspections Bill 2006, cl 1, but 'promoting the fulfilment by every child . . . of his educational potential' will be added.

[103] EA 2002, s 21(2).

[104] EA 1944, ss 68 and 99.

[105] EA 1996, ss 496 and 497.

[106] EA 1996, ss 497A and 497B, added by s 8 of the SSFA 1998. Note also new s 497AA, added by the EA 2002, s 61 (below), under which an LEA one or more of whose schools has serious weaknesses or is failing can be required to enter into a contract or arrangement to be provided with services of an advisory nature.

[107] SSFA 1998, s 9, amending s 499 of the EA 1996. See further the Education (Parent Governor Representattives) Regulations 1999 (SI 1999/1949), revoked and replaced by the Parent Governor Representatives (England) Regulations 2001 (SI 2001/478).

[108] HC Standing Committee A, 29 Jan 1998, Col 219, per Mr Stephen Byers MP, Minister for School Standards.

schools and the increasing centralisation of power over recent decades have left education committees with a much restricted role. The Local Government Act 2000 has made further changes, making provision for overview and scrutiny committees, which have to have elected parental representation in addition to representation of certain religious or foundation bodies.[109]

A new statutory framework for LEAs' role in managing school places was also established by the 1998 Act. LEAs were placed under a new duty to prepare a school organisation plan, explaining, inter alia, how the authority would meet the educational needs of the population of its area, including special educational needs.[110] The LEA had to publish the plan and submit it and any objections made to it to a school organisation committee (a body which will be abolished under the Education and Inspections Bill, as noted below) established by the LEA.[111] The committee was not, however, obliged to hold an oral hearing to hear from objectors.[112] If the committee was unable to agree a plan it had to refer the matter to the 'adjudicator'.[113] Furthermore, the LEA had a power to refer the plan to the adjudicator if the school organisation committee failed to vote on it. The adjudicator, whose jurisdiction in respect of school admission arrangements is discussed in Chapter 5, is appointed by the Secretary of State and falls within the Council on Tribunals' supervisory jurisdiction,[114] although there is no requirement for him or her to have legal qualifications. The office of adjudicator is new in this field. The adjudicators began their work in 1999. A Chief Adjudicator (the first was Sir Peter Newsom, replaced in 2002 by Professor Philip Hunter) and 16 other adjudicators were appointed.[115]

While a central element of the Government's programme was the 'New Deal for Schools', under which more support staff would be provided and bids could be made for funds to improve the condition of school buildings and enhance technological facilities in them,[116] the powers of intervention in respect of under-performing schools were also tightened. New powers were introduced to enable the LEA intervene in any school where the standard of performance among pupils was unacceptably low, where management at the school had broken down to such an extent that educational standards were being, or were likely to be, prejudiced, or where the safety of pupils or staff at the school

---

[109] Local Government Act 2000, s 21 and the Parent Governor Representatives (England) Regulations 2001 (SI 2001/478).

[110] SSFA 1998, s 26; the Education (School Organisation Plans) (England) Regulations 1999 (SI 1999/701), as amended; the Education (School Organisation Plans) (Wales) Regulations 2003 (SI 2003/1732) (W 190).

[111] SSFA 1998, s 24 and Sched 4. The committee is to include representation of the LEA, religious bodies with educational responsibility (such as diocesan boards) and school governing bodies: see further the Education (School Organisation Committees) (England) Regulations 1999 (SI 1999/700).

[112] *R (WB and KA) v Leeds School Organisation Committee* [2003] ELR 67.

[113] SSFA 1998, ss 25, 26 (now repealed) and 27 and Sched 5. See Department for Education and Employment, *School Organisation and Admissions Adjudicator—A Note by the DfEE* (London, Department for Education and Employment, 1998). See p 262 below.

[114] Tribunals and Inquiries Act 1992, Sched 1, para 15(f), inserted by the SSFA 1998, Sched 5, para 10(2).

[115] Of the 16, 9 were reappointed on fixed-term contracts of varying lengths from Apr 2003.

[116] See, eg, DfEE, *New Deal for Schools (NDS): Schemes Beginning in 1998–99* (London, DfEE, 1997).

was under threat.[117] Additional governors could be appointed or the school's right to a delegated budget could be suspended, following the issue of warning notices and other procedural steps. The powers of intervention were also available where a school was found by inspectors to have 'serious weaknesses'[118] (a classification since replaced by that of 'requiring significant improvement'[119]), as well as where the school had failed its inspection and been found to require 'special measures', meaning that it was categorised as 'failing', a concept that has since been re-defined.[120] The Secretary of State was also given powers—to appoint additional governors or to direct the closure of the school (although it could be re-opened under new management under the Fresh Start initiative)—in respect of failing schools, presumably because he or she might sometimes disagree with the action (or lack of it) planned or taken by the LEA.[121] Separate powers were later introduced under the Learning and Skills Act 2000 which could lead to the closure of an inadequate sixth form.[122]

The Government also saw the 1998 Act as part of an overall strategy for reducing social exclusion. One of the initiatives it launched was education action zones (EAZs). The zones reflect the government's 'partnership' approach to public services provision, but as such represent a further loss of LEA control. The intention has been to establish such zones, comprising two or more schools, in 'areas with a mix of underperforming schools and the highest levels of disadvantage'.[123] The Secretary of State has been given a wide discretion to establish an EAZ where it is considered 'expedient to do so with a view to improving standards in the provision of education at maintained schools'.[124] In effect, there is a bidding process for the establishment of a zone. The first 25 zones were established in September 1998 and January 1999; a second round of 47 zones commenced in September 2000.[125] A zone may be established for three years initially, with the possibility of an extension for a further two years.[126] Most of the initial zones were granted an extension.[127] The intention of the DfES is that once an EAZ has operated for five years it should be transferred into an 'Excellence Cluster' or become an action zone within the Excellence in Cities programme (below). Typically, a zone covers two or three secondary schools and

---

[117] SSFA 1998, ss 14 and 15(1)–(3).

[118] Ibid, ss 14 and 15(4)–(5). A school has 'serious weaknesses' if 'although giving its pupils in general an acceptable standard of education, it has significant weaknesses in one or more areas of its activities': School Inspections Act 1996, s 16A, inserted by the 2002 Act, s 54. See also the 1998 Act, s 15(5).

[119] SSFA 1998, s 14(1)(b) and (3), as amended by the EA 2005, s 14(2).

[120] SSFA 1998, ss 14 and 15(6). See now the Education Act 2005, s 44(1), which says that a school requires special measures where not only is it 'failing to give its pupils an acceptable standard of education' but also 'the persons responsible for leading, managing or governing the school are not demonstrating the capacity to secure the necessary improvement in the school'.

[121] SSFA 1998, ss 18 and 19 (which has been amended by the EA 2005, s 45).

[122] Learning and Skills Act 2000, s 113 and Sched 7.

[123] Department for Education and Employment, *Excellence in Schools*, Cm 3681 (London, TSO, 1997), ch 4, para 7.

[124] SSFA 1998, s 10(1).

[125] Ofsted, *Excellence in Cities and Education Action Zones: Management and Impact* HMI 1399 (London, Ofsted, 2003), para 13.

[126] SSFA 1998, s 10(2).

[127] Ofsted, n 125 above, para 13.

their feeder primary schools. Under an amendment made by the Education Act 2002, it may include not only maintained schools, but also nursery schools, pupil referral units[128] and independent schools.[129] Each EAZ is under the overall management of an 'education action forum' typically comprising representatives of schools, the LEA, parents and the business and social communities.[130] Leadership of the forum is often undertaken by local business people.[131] The forum's main object is prescribed as 'the improvement of standards of education at each of the participating schools',[132] although its remit has been extended by the Education Act 2002 to 'carry on any other activities which it considers will promote the provision of, or access to, education whether in a participating school or otherwise', provided the Secretary of State consents.[133] This reflected the Government's growing confidence in the role of EAZs, which is also evidenced by the freedom for the structure of individual EAZs to evolve under new powers for forums to add or remove a school from a zone (albeit, again, with the consent of the Secretary of State).[134] Governing bodies within an EAZ are empowered to delegate any of their powers—for example, over school admissions—to a forum.[135]

The Government has viewed the EAZ initiative as enabling educational problems in socially deprived areas to be targeted more effectively and as a key element in its drive towards achieving the national targets for literacy and numeracy announced in the 1997 White Paper. Many of the schools within EAZs are ones which were found by inspectors to have serious weaknesses or require special measures.[136] The contribution of EAZs to improved levels of attainment and participation among children and young people from areas of social disadvantage and under-achievement is bolstered by giving them a high priority for central government funding for a range of initiatives such as those concerned with the improvement of literacy and numeracy levels, the provision of homework centres and out of school facilities, and subject specialisation in areas such as technology, languages, sports or the arts. In addition, the intention is that schools within EAZs will benefit from the funding allocations made to the zones

---

[128] These are schools for young people who require special arrangements due to their exclusion from school, illness or other reason: Education Act 1996, s 19(2) and Sched 1, as amended.

[129] SSFA 1998, s 10(1A), inserted by the Education Act 2002, Sched 15, para 2(2).

[130] The 1998 Act stipulated that the membership of a forum had to include one representative of each of the governing bodies of the schools concerned, plus one or two persons appointed by the Secretary of State: SSFA 1998, s 11(3). The other members would have been prescribed by the order constituting the forum and the EAZ. Amendments made by the Education Act 2002, Sched 15, inserting s 11A into the 1998 Act, give the governing bodies of schools participating in the zones or the Secretary of State the option of not appointing a member (or, in the case of the latter, one or two members) to the forum. The proceedings of a forum are governed by the Education Action Forum (Proceedings) Regulations 1998 (SI 1998/1964), as amended.

[131] Ofsted, *Education Action Zones: Commentary on the First Six Zone Inspections* (London, Ofsted, 2001), para 13.

[132] SSFA 1998, s 12(1).

[133] SSFA s 12(1A), inserted by the EA 2002, Sched 15, para 7.

[134] SSFA 1998, ss 11B and 11C, inserted by the Education Act 2002, Sched 15, para 5.

[135] SSFA 1998, s 12(2). See further HC Standing Committee A, Cols 239 and 243, 3 Feb 1998, per Mr Stephen Byers MP, Minister for School Standards.

[136] Ofsted, n 131 above, para 7.

of up to £1,000,000, of which up to £750,000 would come from the public sector and £250,000 from private sector sponsorship.[137] In two of the first six zones that were inspected by 2001 the target for private sector sponsorship was not in fact reached.[138]

Within EAZ schools there is flexibility in both the curriculum and the pay and conditions of service of teaching staff. [139] For example, there can be departure from the National Curriculum and staff can be expected to work non-standard hours such as weekends or during school holidays. Within the first year of the establishment of the initial 25 zones, some 13 had introduced flexibility into the National Curriculum.[140] EAZs also run a range of non-traditional activities within their schools, aimed at promoting inclusion, including artistic projects, breakfast clubs and mentoring and counselling schemes.[141] These separate arrangements and the additional funding promised for EAZs were factors in the concerns expressed in response to the White Paper that the zones could be divisive as a result of their schools being likely to have superior facilities and provision to many schools outside them.[142] The promise of higher salaries for teachers working in zones has also been potentially divisive, but could be justified with reference to the greater teacher recruitment difficulties in low-achieving urban schools.

The problems of educational under-achievement and social exclusion, which are distributed unevenly across the social divides, were noted in Chapter 1. The EAZ initiative has been seen as a flagship government policy for tackling these problems. When considering its impact it is necessary also to take account of the complementary Excellence in Cities (EiCs) programme, launched in 1999. This also operates on a national basis and in 2003–4 the annual funding allocation for the EiC programme was £350 million.[143] Included in the first phase of the EiC programme were 25 LEAs and 438 secondary schools; in the next two phases there were a total of 33 LEAs and over 600 secondary schools. The programme has been extended to include some primary schools and post-16 provision as well.[144] Specific features of the EiC programme are the employment of learning mentors, provision for gifted and talented pupils and the creation of a learning support unit on a school's site or in the neighbourhood. The aims of the EiC programme are similar to those of the EAZ programme: 'to break the spiral of poor attendance, poor behaviour and high exclusion rates among the most disaffected and vulnerable pupils, by offering them personal and academic

---

[137] HL Debs, Vol 589, Col 1558, 19 May 1998, per Baroness Blackstone. In their two-year extension period the zones receive an annual grant of £500,000 plus £1 for each £1 of private sector sponsorship, up to £250,000: Ofsted, n 131 above, para 19.

[138] Ibid, para 19.

[139] SSFA 1998, s 13.

[140] Secretary of State for Social Security, *Opportunity for All. Tackling Poverty and Social Exclusion*, Cm 4445 (London, TSO, 1999) 51.

[141] Ofsted, *Excellence in Cities and Education Action Zones: Management and Impact*, HMI 1399 (London, Ofsted, 2003), para 50.

[142] Department for Education and Employment, *Summary of Main Points Arising from the Responses to School Consultations* (London, DfEE, 1997) (published Dec 1997).

[143] See Ofsted, n 141 above, para 15.

[144] Ibid, para 15.

support they needed to make the best of their opportunities in school'.[145] It also aims to raise overall levels of attainment, increase diversity of provision, and strengthen partnerships in education, especially between LEAs and schools.[146] The LEA is seen as a 'significant member of the partnership but is not automatically in a controlling position'.[147] Ofsted has found that EiCs have largely succeeded in improving partnerships between LEAs and schools.[148]

As regards the impact of these programmes on levels of attainment among the socially excluded, an Ofsted report in 2001, covering the first six inspections of EAZs, concluded that in general the EAZ programme had led to improvements in numeracy and literacy in primary schools, but that in secondary schools the gap at Key Stages 3 and 4 between national and EAZ averages for progress was not closing overall.[149] It was also reported that 'there are few instances of significant zone-wide improvements in pupils' attendance'.[150] A subsequent Ofsted survey, published in 2003, revealed that, viewed as a whole, the EiC programmes had brought about overall improvements in attainment that were above those achieved nationally, at Key Stages 3 (ages 11–14) and 4 (ages 15–16).[151] Within EAZs the picture was more mixed.[152] Moreover, school attendance had not improved in EAZ schools and school exclusions had not declined relative to levels in other schools.[153] The average school attendance rate in EAZ secondary schools was found to be 88 per cent, which meant that 'in a secondary school of 1,000, on average 120 pupils are absent each day'.[154] As there is a strong correlation between poor school attendance and low achievement,[155] this has been a particular cause for concern.

Another initiative to improve educational standards was a reduction in class sizes in infants' classes (ages 5–7) in primary schools, to be funded by the resources (£140 million in England and £4.5 million in Wales) made available as a consequence of the phasing out of the assisted places scheme under the Education (Schools) Act 1997. Under section 1 of the SSFA 1998 the Secretary of State is give a power to make regulations imposing a limit (amendable by order) of 30 pupils for infants' classes in maintained schools. The Government gave a commitment in the 1997 White Paper that by the end of the Parliament there would be no 5, 6 or 7-year-olds taught in classes larger than that.[156] The new limit came into effect in the 2001–2 school year. LEAs were able to apply for

[145] Ibid, para 19.
[146] Ibid, paras 27 and 28.
[147] Ibid, para 29.
[148] Ibid, para 30.
[149] Ofsted, *Education Action Zones: Commentary on the First Six Zone Inspections* (London, Ofsted, 2001), para 38.
[150] Ibid, para 39.
[151] Ofsted, n 141 above.
[152] Ibid, paras 51–53 and 219.
[153] Ibid, para 71.
[154] Ibid, para 220.
[155] Ibid.
[156] Department for Education and Employment, n 89 above, ch 2, para 16; see also HC, Standing Committee A, Col 65, 22 Jan 1998, per Ms Estelle Morris MP, Under-Secretary of State.

grants to meet expenditure incurred in complying with the limit.[157] LEAs had to prepare plans concerning implementation but the Government stipulated that they should not diminish parental preference. However, a Coopers and Lybrand report for the Local Government Association doubted whether this was achievable without significant extra resources to pay for more classrooms or space in popular schools. [158] The impact on parental choice of reduced class size limits is discussed further in Chapter 5. Notwithstanding the introduction of the new class size limit, the Government's failure to make progress in addressing the disparity between state and private school class sizes for the over 7s and, more especially, secondary school pupils is seen by Maitles as a major failure to tackle underlying structural inequalities in the education system.[159]

The theme of improved standards and attainment levels was carried through into nursery education.[160] The contribution that nursery education can make to the fulfilment of the requirements of Article 29 of the UNCRC concerning the development of the child's personality, talents and mental abilities to their fullest potential has increasingly found recognition under post-1997 government initiatives. Prior to the 1998 Act LEAs had a power to establish nursery schools[161] and the Secretary of State had a power to provide grants to nursery education providers.[162] The previous Conservative Government used this power to establish a 'nursery voucher' scheme, which was under-resourced and soon discontinued.[163] The 1998 Act implemented a proposal in the 1997 White Paper that LEAs should set up in their area an 'early years forum', referred to in the Act as an 'early years development partnership', representing providers, parents, employers and others.[164] LEAs were placed under a duty to ensure that nursery education provision was 'sufficient' in their area and to prepare an early years development plan.[165] At that time only one in three children aged 3 was receiving a publicly funded nursery education and the Government wanted to increase that proportion.[166] It was announced in the 2001 Green Paper that two thirds of 3-year-olds would have free nursery places by March 2002 and that all who wanted a place would have one by September 2004.[167] The 1998 Act amended the School Inspections Act 1996 to empower the Chief Inspector of Schools to

---

[157] SSFA 1998, ss 2 and 3 and the Education (Infant Class Sizes) Grant Regulations 1999 (SI 1999/14).

[158] See S Thornton, 'Class size cannot limit choice, ministers warn', *Times Educational Supplement*, 12 June 1998, available at www.tes.co.uk/search/story/?story_id=301407.

[159] H Maitles, 'Children and Education: Inequalities in Our Schools' in B Goldson, M Lavalette and J McKechnie (eds), *Children, Welfare and the State* (London, Sage, 2002) 73.

[160] SSFA 1998, ss 117–124.

[161] Education Act 1996, s 17. Nursery schools are defined as schools used 'wholly or mainly' for the purpose of educating children aged 2 or over but under 5 years: ibid, s 6(1) (as amended).

[162] Nursery Education and Grant-Maintained Schools Act 1996, ss 1–3 (now repealed).

[163] See Chap 5 at pp 248–9.

[164] SSFA 1998, s 119; DfEE, *Excellence in Schools* Cm 3681 (London, TSO, 1997), ch 2, paras 5 and 6.

[165] SSFA 1998, ss 118 and 120.

[166] HC Standing Committee A, Col 743, 3 Mar 1998, per Ms Estelle Morris MP, Under-Secretary of State.

[167] Department for Education and Employment, *Schools: Building on Success*, Cm 5050 (London, TSO, 2001) 18.

publish reports of nursery inspections and to tighten up the inspection of nursery education.[168]

The changes to the structure of education made by the 1998 Act were completed by the re-categorisation of schools and the abolition of GM status, both of which were noted above, and by changes to the composition of school governing bodies,[169] including slightly increased parental representation: for example, a community secondary school with 600 or more pupils had to have six parent governors out of a total of 20 governors, compared with five out of 19 under the previous legislation. LEAs were given representation on the governing bodies of foundation schools which, when GM schools previously, had no LEA governors. Further substantial reforms to school governing bodies were made by the Education Act 2002 (see below). Comprehensive changes were also made to the law governing admission to schools and selection of pupils, as discussed in Chapter 5. A new framework for discipline in schools, including exclusion from schools, was also introduced, of which perhaps the most significant elements were the increased independence of appeal panels hearing appeals against permanent exclusion and the duty on those with responsibility for decisions on exclusion to have regard to DfES guidance.[170] At a time when the number of permanent exclusions in England had reached an annual total of 12,655 cases in 1996–7, the highest since national monitoring was first instituted in the early 1990s, the guidance was seen as important in trying to rein in and prevent exclusion, which had damaging effects and was experienced disproportionately by some minority ethnic groups, and boys in particular.[171]

Although the 1998 Act was concerned with the quality of educational provision, it in fact made only a limited number of changes to the law governing the content of school education itself. It did not alter the structure of the National Curriculum (described in Chapter 7), although it effected some improvements to educational opportunities for older pupils. In particular, it extended the powers to provide pupils at Key Stage 4 (broadly ages 14–16) with work experience and enabled arrangements to be made for this age group to undertake some or all of their secondary education in a further education institution.[172] Work-related learning is seen as a means to help to motivate young people who, by the age of 14, have become 'disaffected with the schools system and a traditional curriculum'.[173] The intention is that while gaining experience of the world of work pupils will be able to follow a programme towards vocational qualifications,[174] an aim that, as discussed in Chapter 7, has been consolidated under the 2002 Act.

---

[168] SSFA 1998, ss134 and 135 and Sched 28.

[169] SSFA 1998, Sched 9.

[170] SSFA 1998, ss 64–68 and Sched 18.

[171] As noted in Chap 1.

[172] SSFA 1998, ss 112 and 113.

[173] Department for Education and Employment, *Excellence in Schools*, Cm 3681 (London, TSO, 1997), ch 6, para 39.

[174] HC Debs, Vol 308, Col 666, 22 Dec 1997, per Mr David Blunkett MP, Secretary of State for Education and Employment.

Looking back at the reforms instituted under the 1998 Act, it is clear that the Government considered it necessary to institute a wide range of regulatory measures in order to drive up improvements in standards and levels of attainment. They ranged from compelling LEAs and schools to plan for improvement through to various processes for holding schools and LEAs to account if targets went unmet or if standards, including standards of pupil behaviour, were unreasonably low. New powers, for example, were available by which the Secretary of State could instigate a takeover or closure of a school. In targeting the inner cities for greater support via a range of initiatives, the Labour Government could be said to have recognised that the schools located in such areas tend to be the worst casualties of the market system, under-achieving and under-funded, while offering a poor choice to parents who want a good education for their children. There was also a growing realisation that education failures have wider social consequences, that the importance of improving education stems from a need to tackle a range of social problems.

From the perspective of schools and the country's 400,000 teachers,[175] however, the scale and speed of reform and the growing pressure to succeed presented an enormous challenge at a time of demoralisation. The Chief Inspector of Schools in England stated in 1997 that an estimated 13,000 teachers and head teachers were unsatisfactory. The 1997 White Paper pulled no punches in this regard: 'because teachers play such a key role, they must be held accountable for their success in sustaining and raising the achievement of their pupils. We will be prepared to act where the performance of teachers or heads falls below acceptable standards'.[176] The spectre of liability for educational malpractice also appeared as a result of the High Court's decision in *Phelps* later that year.[177] The Government considered there to be a need to modernise the teaching profession, to equip it better for the challenges that lay ahead. The first stage involved the establishment, under the Teaching and Higher Education Act (THEA) 1998,[178] of a General Teaching Council (GTC) in England and Wales (one for each jurisdiction), intended as a representative body equivalent to the Law Society or the General Medical Council.[179] As Blair and Whalley comment, however, the GTC has less autonomy than these professional bodies, as its constitution and role are to some extent controlled by the Secretary of State.[180] The functions of the GTC are to advise the Secretary of State and others on teaching standards and teacher recruitment, maintain a register of qualified teachers, and issue and keep under review a Code of Practice laying down standards of

[175] Department for Education and Employment, Press Notice 206/98, *Teachers in Service (January 1998)*, 27 Apr 1998.
[176] Department for Education and Employment, *Excellence in Schools*, Cm 3681 (London, TSO, 1997), ch 5, para 4.
[177] *Phelps v London Borough of Hillingdon* [1998] ELR 38 (decided 23 Sept 1997). See further p 324.
[178] Ss 1–15 and Scheds 1 and 2 and the General Teaching Council for England (Constitution) Regulations 1999 (SI 1999/1726) (as amended) and the Same (Wales) Regulations 1999 (SI 1999/1619).
[179] Department for Education and Employment, *Excellence in Schools*, Cm 3681 (London, TSO, 1997), ch 5, para 35.
[180] A Blair and G Whalley, 'An Assessment of the Present Role of the General Teaching Council for England' (2003) 4 *Education Law* 148 at 149.

professional conduct and practice expected of teachers.[181] Teachers form a majority of the members of the GTC, but employers and parents are also represented. The GTC was expected, somewhat over-optimistically, to 'help to restore the morale of the teaching profession'.[182] The THEA 1998 also introduced a power for the Secretary of State to require head teachers to hold a 'professional headship qualification'.[183]

There followed a consultation document, *Teachers: Meeting the Challenge of Change*,[184] heralded by the education press as 'the most significant event since the 1988 Education Reform Act.'[185] The aim of further reform was to improve training and support, as had been indicated in the White Paper, but also, more significantly, to change the career structure of the teaching profession in England and Wales. There would be greater rewards, in terms of career advancement and higher pay, but in return for high levels of performance. Some 5,000 'advanced skills' teachers could be placed on a new 'leadership' grade, with enhanced pay. Teachers would have to participate in new appraisal arrangements, involving an annual assessment of their performance against agreed objectives. Talented trainee teachers could be placed on a fast track for career progression. Experience in other countries where incentive and reward schemes have been introduced, such as Sweden and parts of the United States, has not been altogether positive, as there is evidence that they have proved divisive and their operation has been highly stressful and burdensome for principals in conducting the evaluations and making recommendations.[186] Fear of similar consequences in England and Wales was expressed by teachers' leaders in response to the proposals in the consultation paper.[187] All of these proposals have nonetheless been implemented, mostly by statutory instrument.[188] Further changes to the legal structure governing the teaching profession have been made by the 2002 Act (below).

The THEA 1998 also made changes to the system of student support that clearly have a bearing on access and inclusion in relation to higher education. These are discussed in Chapter 4. Sandwiched between the 1998 legislation and the Education Act 2002 (below) is the Learning and Skills Act 2000, which placed

---

[181] Teaching and Higher Education Act 1998, ss 2–7 and the General Teaching Council for England (Additional Functions) Order 2000 (SI 2000/2175) (as amended) and Sames (Wales) Order 2000 (SI 2000/1941) (as amended).

[182] Department for Education and Employment, *Excellence in Schools*, Cm 3681 (London, TSO, 1997), ch 5, para 36.

[183] THEA 1998, s 18, amending the ERA 1988, s 218. See further n 276 below.

[184] Department for Education and Employment, *Teachers: Meeting the Challenge of Change* (London, DfEE, 1998).

[185] Editorial, *The Times Educational Supplement*, 4 Dec 1998, 14.

[186] K Riley, 'And the winner is...', *Guardian Education*, 8 Dec 1998, 4.

[187] 'Frosty on the fast track and anxious about appraisal', *The Times Educational Supplement*, 4 Dec 1998, 4.

[188] Eg, The Education (School Teacher Appraisal) (England) Regulations 2001 (SI 2001/2855) and (Wales) Regulations 2001 (SI 2001/1394 (W.137)) (made under the Education (No 2) Act 1986, s 49, as amended); the Education (Headteachers' Qualifications) (England) Regulations 2003 (SI 2003/3111), made under the Education Act 2002, s 135, which now applies in place of s 218 of the Education Reform Act 1988, as amended by the Teaching and Higher Education Act 1998. Allowances for advanced skills teachers were first prescribed in the Education (School Teachers' Pay and Conditions) (No.3) Order 2001 (SI 2001/1284).

responsibility for post-16 education in the hands of the Learning and Skills Council (LSC) and empowered it to fund sixth form provision via grants to LEAs.[189] It also gave the LSC the power to initiate changes to sixth form provision, including closure of sixth forms, where the provision was found by the inspection process to be 'inadequate'.[190] The LSC was placed under a duty to have regard to the needs of persons with learning difficulties and to have due regard to the need to promote equality of opportunity 'between persons of different racial groups . . . between men and women, and . . . between persons who are disabled and persons who are not'.[191] As noted in Chapter 4, colleges themselves are under wide-ranging duties with regard to ensuring equality of access to provision.

Labour's Second Administration 2001–2005

As we have seen, the 1997–2001 administration placed an emphasis on school standards and social inclusion. Seen against a background of two decades of enormous structural reforms to the way education was organised and controlled, Labour's reforms were relatively modest even though quite diverse. Even selective admission arrangements were not abolished; existing grammar schools could continue as such so long as parents wanted them to.[192] The Labour Government now wanted to liberate parts of the education system from some of the intense controls and regulation that had built up over the years, while maintaining an emphasis on its avowed goals of improved pupil attainment levels and greater social inclusion.[193] Yet it is somewhat ironic that the greater institutional freedom that has been introduced on a selective basis has in fact been accompanied by an even tighter regulatory framework than existed before. Regulation has also been employed to introduce greater diversity into the system, by broadening the range and character of institutions providing education and, as discussed in Chapter 7, introducing greater flexibility within the school curriculum. The aim has been to ensure that 'schools—individually and as a broader family locally and nationally—cater significantly better for the diverse requirements and aspirations of today's young people'.[194]

One of the interesting aims behind the 2002 Act was the modernisation of education law via the creation of new central powers to make changes to the law via secondary legislation.[195] Traditionally, as we have seen, primary legislation has been the principal tool for wholesale reform, despite the extensive use of

---

[189] Learning and Skills Act 2000, s 36.

[190] Ibid, s 113 and Sched 7. A school is defined as having inadequate sixth form provision if it is 'failing or likely to fail to give pupils over compulsory school-age an acceptable standard of education, or . . . the school has significant weaknesses in one or more areas of its activities for pupils over compulsory school age': ibid, Sched 7, para 1(2).

[191] Ibid, ss 41 and 42.

[192] SSFA 1998, ss 104–109.

[193] See Department for Education and Skills, *Schools: Achieving Success*, Cm 5230 (London, TSO, 2001) and Welsh Assembly, *The Learning Country (Y wlad sy'n Dysgu)* (Cardiff, National Assembly for Wales, 2001).

[194] DfES, n 193 above, para 1.5.

[195] See ibid, ch 9.

delegated legislation. Ministers regarded the lengthy legislative process for statutes as inconvenient for a government in a hurry to 'transform the knowledge and skills of its population' so that it can 'prosper in the 21st Century'.[196] The Government's assertion that education law 'is a highly complex area, where a great deal of detail is set out in primary legislation, restricting the ability of the education system to innovate and to respond to innovation'[197] may be true. Nonetheless, the use of delegated legislative powers raises standard concerns about the 'democratic deficit' arising from the fact that 'Parliament's scrutiny of secondary legislation is second rate',[198] whilst ministers' powers and opportunities for central government interference and control are increased. In practice, little has in fact changed. The Education Act 2005 (see below) has 128 sections and 19 Schedules. The Education and Inspections Bill 2006 is even longer.

School government was one of the principal areas of education law chosen for modernisation through this shift from primary to secondary legislation.[199] Over the years the law on school government has become increasingly complex as a consequence of the close attention given to providing a strict procedural and organisation framework for decision-making over a growing range of areas of responsibility. The constitution of governing bodies and arrangements for the appointment or election of governors are now prescribed by regulations.[200] As under the previous law, regulations are to specify the terms of reference for governing bodies, LEAs and head teachers.[201] The 2002 Act itself contains only a basic framework, providing that the general responsibility for the running of a school is to be under the governing body's direction.[202] Two other areas where the shift to secondary legislation has occurred are the control of school premises[203] and the employment of staff at a school.[204] These changes have not reduced legal complexity. Indeed, it has increased by virtue of measures to encourage greater collaboration and mutual support between schools. The Act enables governing bodies of two or more schools to form or join a federation of schools under a single governing body.[205] A federation is to be treated as a single school for some purposes, although not school admissions (so that parents are still able to select an individual school as their preference for admission). Regulations which deal with most aspects of the establishment, constitution and

---

[196] Ibid, para 1.2.

[197] Ibid, para 9.4.

[198] P Tudor, 'Secondary Legislation: Second Class or Crucial?' (2000) 21 *Statute Law Review* 149 at 150–1, who comments that 'at the same time as the quantity and importance of secondary legislation has increased,the parliamentary time devoted to debating it has decreased' (150).

[199] Part 3, replacing the SSFA 1998, ss 36–44 and Scheds 9–11. See further, Department for Education and Skills, *The Way Forward—A Modernised Framework for School Governance* (London, DFEE, 2001).

[200] The School Governance (Constitution) (England) Regulations 2003 (SI 2003/348). Sched 1 to the 2002 Act itself deals with incorporation of governing bodies.

[201] EA 2002, ss 22 and 23. All maintained schools must have an instrument of government setting out the constitution and other matters: ibid, s 20.

[202] Ibid, s 21.

[203] Via regulations to be made under s 31.

[204] EA 2002, ss 35, 36, 39 and 40; The School Staffing (England) Regulations 2003 (SI 2003/1963), as amended by the School Staffing (England) (Amendment) Regulations 2003 (SI 2003/2725).

[205] Ibid, ss 24 and 25. Part 5 of the Act amends existing law on the establishment of schools to enable schools to be established as 'federated' schools under a single governing body: s 74.

dissolution of a federation prescribe the maximum number of schools which can comprise a federation as five.[206] A less integrationist form of collaboration between schools is also provided for, involving the discharge of any of their respective governing bodies' functions via joint committees.[207]

The 2002 Act nonetheless seeks to free some schools from some of the burden of regulation. This occurs through its provision for new legal frameworks intended to facilitate innovation by schools and LEAs, amongst others, with a view to the 'raising of the educational standards achieved by children in England'.[208] Innovation within the terms of this part of the Act must be with the approval of the Secretary of State, who must have regard to the need for a balanced and broadly based school curriculum and consider the likely effect of the project on the children who may be affected by it.[209] One of the most far-reaching provisions is a new power, limited in its effect to four years, for the Secretary of State to make an order exempting a school from 'any requirement imposed by education legislation' or to relax or modify the effect of such legislation for up to three years, extendable by one further such period.[210] To benefit from such an order a school must, inter alia, meet prescribed criteria relating to the performance of the school, the quality of leadership or the quality of its management.[211] In the order, any curriculum or pay and conditions legislative measure can be designated as attracting exemption or modification.[212] The exemption or modification may be categorised by regulations as discretionary or as of right. If the latter, the Secretary of State must grant the order. The aim of this exemption power is 'to facilitate experimental pilot projects in the education system',[213] but its implications are enormous. Here is a power whose premise seems to be that close regulation is needed for some schools but not the favoured few, on which a degree of freedom may be conferred as a reward for achievement: so-called 'earned autonomy'. The idea is that schools that are deemed to be good can be trusted with the freedom to manage parts of the curriculum or determine pay or conditions without central direction. Yet surely the justification for the regulation from which these schools are now able to secure exemption is precisely that it is necessary in order to maintain standards in schools. Some less successful schools might well argue that, on that basis, they might in fact do better if they too had more freedom.

The emphasis on increasing flexibility and freedom is also evident in the

---

[206] The Federation of Schools (Community Schools, Community Special Schools, Voluntary Controlled Schools and Maintained Nursery Schools) (England) Regulations 2003 (SI 2003/1965).

[207] EA 2002, s 26. Detailed provision is made in the School Governance (Collaboration) (England) Regulations 2003 (SI 2003/1962).

[208] EA 2002, s 1(1). 'Qualifying bodies' here are LEAs, school governing bodies, education action forums (that is, bodies that run education action zones: above) or the proprietors of approved independent (private) special needs schools: ibid, s 1(3).

[209] EA 2002, s 1(2).

[210] Ibid, s 2.

[211] Ibid, s 6(1).

[212] Ibid, s 7.

[213] Ibid, ss 2–4. See also the discussion of the Education Bill 2001 in N Harris, 'Regulating School Education for Social Inclusion' in C Russo (ed), *U.S. Yearbook of Education Law 2002* (Dayton, Ohio, Education Law Association, 2002), 307.

provisions making it easier for community groups, including religious groups, to apply for the establishment of a school funded by the LEA. A new procedure is introduced for LEAs to publish a notice inviting proposals for the establishment of a new, additional, secondary school: in other words one that is not replacing existing provision.[214] This is, in part, intended to overcome one of the principal barriers to the establishment of voluntary aided schools by religious bodies where there is no shortage of school places in the locality.[215] Furthermore, the Secretary of State is given a power to direct the LEA to exercise either this new power to invite proposals or its existing powers to establish or change provision, where the Secretary of State is of the opinion that primary or secondary education provision in an area is, or is likely to become, insufficient.[216] The Learning and Skills Council for England is also given a right to make proposals for the establishment, alteration or closure of sixth forms,[217] while community school governing bodies may publish proposals for prescribed alterations to schools,[218] which is intended to enable increases in pupil numbers or sixth form provision to be accommodated.

One of the features of the 1980s legislation affecting schools was the strengthened autonomy and increased responsibility of school governing bodies and the conferment of corporate status on them, noted above. The corporate model suited the entrepreneurial spirit that schools were encouraged to adopt by, for example, seeking private sector sponsorship and embarking upon marketing strategies to aid their competitiveness. It also seems to suit the New Labour ideas for schools and LEAs to work in innovative ways in partnerships with each other, with independent schools (see below) and with the business sector. The 2002 Act develops this further by empowering governing bodies to form or jointly operate companies for certain purposes, such as the provision of services to other schools, whether directly or by acting as an agent for a third party provider.[219] The Secretary of State may also now form or participate in the forming of companies 'for purposes connected with any functions of his relating to education'.[220]

With regard to the important matter of the finance, devolved funding to individual schools, first introduced under the Education Reform Act 1988 (above), continues. The basic framework under the 2002 Act is that there is the 'LEA budget' (covering the authority's central functions), the 'schools budget' (total expenditure by the LEA on pupils) and the 'individual schools budget' (the part of the schools budget that is to be placed under the control of individual

---

[214] Ibid, s 70.

[215] Voluntary aided status was denied to the Islamia Primary School in Brent on that basis in 1990: see *R v Secretary of State for Education and Science ex parte Yusuf Islam* [1994] ELR 111.

[216] EA 2002, s 71. Changes have also been made to the statutory procedures for consideration of proposals on the establishment, alteration or discontinuance of schools: ibid, s 75 and Sched 10.

[217] Ibid, s 72 and Sched 9, inserting Learning and Skills Act 2000, s 113A and Sched 7A.

[218] EA 2002, s 73, amending the SSFA 1998, s 28.

[219] EA 2002, ss 11–13 and the School Companies Regulations 2002 (SI 2002/2978) (as amended by the School Companies (Amendment) Regulations 2003 (SI 2003/2049)) and the School Companies (Private Finance Initiative Companies) Regulations 2002 (SI 2002/3177) made under s 12.

[220] EA 2002, s 13(1).

schools).[221] The size of the schools budget is dependent on a range of factors specified in the LEA's approved financial delegation scheme, including the number of schools, the location and design of the buildings, the numbers, ages and special needs of the pupils, and so on. Much of the detailed provision on finance is to be set out in regulations, but that does not represent a change on the previous position; financial arrangements always need to be revised frequently and the law has always provided for that flexibility.[222] One significant change is that the Secretary of State now has a power to set a minimum schools budget for the LEA where the amount set for a particular year is inadequate.[223] This power was exercised for the first time in 2003, in respect of the school budgets proposed in Croydon and Westminster.[224] The Government has also aimed to increase still further the proportion of the schools budget that is delegated to individual schools.[225] A target of 87 per cent delegation was set for 2002, although it was reported that 33 LEAs did not meet it.[226] Allocations to authorities already take account of levels of deprivation (such as the proportion of pupils on free school meals or areas where vandalism generates extra costs), but the Government has also sought to ensure that more is allocated to LEAs 'where significant deprivation adds to the challenge of achieving high standards.'[227] The DfES has also been encouraging LEAs to delegate more, if not all, of their special educational needs budget to schools, mostly comprising the amount used to meet the requirements as to provision specified in statements of special educational needs.[228] The Government has also proposed three-year rather than annual budgets for schools. Provision for this has been made by the Education Act 2005, which replaces the 'financial year' for which each school should be allocated a budget share with the 'funding period'.[229] In the light of this, it will be important that the Audit Commission's recommendation that local authorities should have more robust, accurate and up-to-date information about the state of school budgets is properly implemented.[230] The process by which each LEA takes account of the views of schools concerning the allocations made to them under the schools budget has been formalised by the 2002 Act through the required establishment, by LEAs, of a 'schools forum' in their areas.[231] The forum is a

---

[221] A new s 45A is added to the SSFA 1998 by s 41 of the 2002 Act (first effective in the financial year from 1 Apr 2003).

[222] Among the provisions that have made are the LEA Budget, Schools Budget and Individual Schools Budget (England) Regulations 2003 (SI 2003/3170) and the Financing of Maintained Schools (England) (No 2) Regulations 2003 (SI 2003/3247), both as amended, the Financing of Maintained Schools (England) Regulations 2004 (SI 2004/3130) and the School Finance (England) Regulations 2006 (SI 2006/468), which apply to financial years 2006 and 2007.

[223] The LEA will have 14 days in which to state its objections to the determination: new ss 45B and 45C of the SSFA 1998, inserted by the 2002 Act, s 42.

[224] See A Ruff, 'Newsline' (2003) 4 *Education Law* 75.

[225] It rose from 79 per cent to 84 per cent between 1997 and 2001: Department for Education and Employment, *Schools: Building on Success*, Cm 5050 (Norwich: TSO, 2001), para 6.5.

[226] A Ruff, 'Newsline' (2002) 3 *Education Law* 141.

[227] N 225 above, para 6.13.

[228] See Chap 6.

[229] EA 2005, Sched 16, amending SSFA 1998 s 45 and other provisions.

[230] Audit Commission, *Education Funding: the Impact and Effectiveness of Measures to Stabilise School Funding* (London, TSO, 2004).

[231] S 43, inserting a new s 47A into the SSFA 1998.

representative body of head teachers and governing bodies of schools maintained by the LEA and any other bodies the authority determines in accordance with regulations.[232]

The 2002 Act has also built on the Government's social inclusion agenda that, as noted above, was reflected in parts of the 1998 Act governing matters such as education action zones. In particular, the 2002 Act has brought education and childcare provision closer together, thereby aiding lone parents and others for whom pre- or post-school childcare may present barriers to employment. The Government's 1998 Green Paper, *Meeting the Childcare Challenge*,[233] pointed to the inadequate and uneven provision of childcare facilities across the country and emphasised that many schools 'are ideally placed to provide and develop suitable and accessible premises for out of school childcare'.[234] Facilities for childcare have expanded fairly rapidly since the launch of both the National Childcare Strategy in 1997[235] and the Government's Sure Start scheme to enable parents to work or study while their children are cared for.[236] The rationale for schools' involvement in childcare is regarded as lying not merely in helping to ameliorate shortages of provision, however, but also in the inter-relatedness of childcare and education: 'there is no sensible distinction between good early education and care: both enhance children's social and intellectual development in a safe and caring environment'.[237] Moreover, ministers have pointed to the perceived benefits of breakfast clubs and after-school arrangements in areas of social and educational disadvantage, including those served by EAZs. Homework clubs and summer literacy and numeracy schools, which are seen as having similar educational and social benefits, are part of this new emphasis on provision out of school hours. Ofsted has adjudged the bulk of such provision to be satisfactory or good.[238]

The Care Standards Act 2000 brought childcare provision under the education inspection system managed by Ofsted. The 2002 Act has continued the process of

---

[232] The Schools Forums (England) Regulations 2002 (SI 2002/2114) have been made.

[233] Secretary of State for Education and Employment, Secretary of State for Social Security and Minister for Women, *Meeting the Childcare Challenge*, Cm 3959 (London, TSO, 1998).

[234] Ibid, para 5.10.

[235] By 2001 nearly 400,000 additional childcare places were created: Secretary of State for Social Security, *Opportunity for All. The Annual Report for 2001* (London, Department for Work and Pensions, 2001), paras 18–20, table 2.1, available at www.dwp.gov.uk/publications/. By Mar 2003 that total had reached 700,000: Secretary of State for Work and Pensions, *Opportunity for All. Fifth Annual Report 2003*, Cm 5956 (London, TSO, 2003), para 231. By Mar 2004 the total number of places created since 1997 had reached 1,006,000: DfES Press Notice, 23 June 2004.

[236] See Secretary of State for Work and Pensions, *Opportunity for All. Fifth Annual Report 2003*, Cm 5956 (London, TSO, 2003), paras 37, 38 and 232. As at June 2004 there were 524 Sure Start programmes (covering some 400,000 children living in disadvantaged areas): DfES Prtess Notice, 23 June 2004. There are also Early Excellence Centres set up to develop models of good practice in this field.

[237] Secretary of State for Education and Employment, Secretary of State for Social Security and Minister for Women, *Meeting the Childcare Challenge*, Cm 3959 (London, TSO, 1998), para 1.4. See also Scottish Executive, *Regulation of Early Education and Childcare: The Way Ahead* (Edinburgh: Scottish Executive, 1999).

[238] Ofsted, *The Annual Report of Her Majesty's Chief Inspector of Schools 1999–2000* (London, TSO, 2001), paras 26, 67, 68.

integration.[239] The Secretary of State now has a power to give, or make arrangements for giving, financial assistance to any person for specified purposes, which include the provision of education or educational services or the provision of childcare or services related to it.[240] Moreover, the 2002 Act recognises the broader role that schools might potentially play within local communities—as 'extended' schools—by widening school governing bodies' powers to run childcare and other services, either directly or with partners or via outside organisations, on school premises.[241] The Government announced in March 2003 that sufficient funding would be made available for at least one 'extended' school, providing a full range of community services, to be established in each LEA by 2006. Schools are now able to provide any facilities or services to further any charitable purpose for the benefit of their pupils or their families or people who live or work in the locality.[242] The assumption is that the meeting of childcare needs would further a charitable purpose. Governing bodies may charge for this childcare provision provided it does not take the form of curricular provision, in respect of which there are long-standing prohibitions on charging.[243] It is possible that, as the Government's hope is that childcare for 3 and 4-year-olds will be combined with education,[244] that restriction could prove a little problematic. It is envisaged that a good deal of pre-school education in deprived areas will take place in Sure Start children's centres, which offer integrated provision including childcare, health, family services and welfare to work support; the 2004 Budget statement announced that there will be 1,700 centres by 2008. According to the Government, each children's centre will provide 'good quality early education combined with full day care provision (minimum 10 hours a day, 5 days a week, 48 weeks a year)'.[245] LEAs have been placed under a new duty to review annually the sufficiency of childcare provision in their area.[246] The 'early years development and childcare partnerships', renamed from 'early years development partnerships' established under the SSFA 1998, have a duty to assist LEAs with this.[247] LEAs must also establish and maintain an information service for the public on childcare provision and related services[248] and include the provision or promotion of childcare in their early years development plan.[249] They have also been given the power to grant financial assistance to nursery

[239] EA 2002, s 152 and Sched 13.

[240] EA 2002, ss 14-17.

[241] EA 2002, Part 2.

[242] EA 2002, s 27. The power cannot be used for a purpose inconsistent with restrictions imposed by the school's constituting instrument of government or the LEA's financial delegation scheme or if it will interfere to a significant extent with the performance of various other duties: s 28.

[243] See Part 6, Ch 3, of the Education Act 1996.

[244] House of Commons, Standing Committee G, Education Bill, Col. 264, 8 Jan 2002.

[245] DfES Press Notice, 23 June 2004.

[246] EA 2002 s 149 inserts new s 118A into the SSFA 1998. It has replaced the previous duty on local authorities (usually undertaken by social services departments) under the Children Act 1989 s 19(1) and (2) (now repealed) to carry out periodic reviews of childcare.

[247] EA 2002, s 150(1), amending s 119 of the 1998 Act.

[248] EA 2002, s 149(1), inserting s 118A into the 1998 Act.

[249] EA 2002, s 150(2), amending s 120 of the 1998 Act.

education providers.[250] By 2003 part-time education was available to all 4-year-olds, and 88 per cent of 3-year-olds, in England.[251]

The 2002 Act also promotes the 'academy' model, which is one of the more controversial areas of policy on secondary education. The Learning and Skills Act 2000 extended the idea of city technology colleges and city colleges for the technology of the arts established by independent proprietors under an agreement with the Secretary of State, by creating a new category of public–private hybrid, the 'city academy', specialising in modern foreign languages, visual or performing or media arts, sport or another prescribed subject. The 2002 Act has brought all these types of institution together under the name 'Academy', with greater flexibility in terms of the specialisms that may be offered.[252] The Government seems to see these quasi-independent institutions lying outside LEA control, of which there are just 27 at present, as making a positive contribution to raising educational standards and injecting valuable additional resources into the education system. It has plans for up to 200 academies to be established or in preparation by 2010. But opponents regard the colleges' superior facilities and quasi-independent status as making them elitist and there is reported to be some Cabinet disapproval;[253] and, according to a survey by ICM, only 6 per cent of head teachers support such expansion.[254] Academies certainly are expensive: they cost on average £4 million more to set up than other similar-sized secondary schools, although the National Audit Office says that it is too soon to judge their cost effectiveness.[255] There is further discussion of academies in Chapters 5 and 7.

The range of measures introduced under the SSFA 1998 in respect of failing schools and those with serious weaknesses, now known as schools 'requiring significant improvement', were noted above. The 2002 Act made changes designed to facilitate earlier intervention in relation to such schools.[256] As noted above, the 'special measures' that may be taken in respect of a school that is failing are the appointment of additional governors, the suspension of the school's budgetary control and the closure of the school.[257] The first two of these measures may be exercised by LEAs, and the first and the third may be exercised by the Secretary of State. Under an amendment made by the 2002 Act, the Secretary of State could use his powers if Her Majesty's Chief Inspector of Schools stated that the school required special measures or requires significant

[250] EA 2002, s 153. See also s 155, which brings into operation Sched 14, amending Sched 26 to the SSFA 1998 governing inspections of nursery education.

[251] Secretary of State for Work and Pensions, *Opportunity for All. Fifth Annual Report 2003*, Cm 5956 (London, TSO, 2003), paras 38 and 231.

[252] EA 2002, Part 5. Institutions already established when the 2002 Act came into force had the choice of retaining their designation, as 'city technology college' and so on.

[253] H Rumbelow and T Baldwin, 'More city academies despite Cabinet row', *The Times*, 28 June 2004, 2.

[254] R Smithers *et al*, 'Headteachers raise doubts on academies', *The Guardian* 13 Sept 2005, 11.

[255] Comptroller and Auditor General, *Department for Education and Skills. Improving Poorly Performing Schools in England*, HC 679, Session 2005–06 (London, TSO, 2006), Summary, para 20 and Report, para 2.47.

[256] EA 2002, ss 54 and 55. Collectively they are known now as schools 'causing concern'.

[257] SSFA 1998, ss 14–19.

improvement.[258] Previously the power applied only to schools requiring special measures. However, the previous position was restored, in relation to the closure of a school, by the EA 2005,[259] which also makes changes to the inspection process itself and extends the range of matters concerning education on which the Chief Inspector should report to the Secretary of State, including how far the education provided by schools 'meets the needs of the range of pupils' attending them.[260] In 2002–3, 160 schools in England were placed under special measures (up from 129 the previous year); 163 schools were found to have serious weaknesses (down from 201 the previous year); and five schools were re-opened under the Fresh Start initiative.[261] Looking at the total number of schools in 2005 actually under special measures (242) or classed as having serious weaknesses (286) or under-achieving (49), together with those considered to be low- or under-achieving (980), there are 1,577 schools that, according to the National Audit Office (NAO), were providing an 'unsatisfactory education' to an estimated 980,000 pupils (or 13 per cent of the total school population in England).[262] The NAO report points to the factors that contribute to poor performance and highlights ways in which it might be improved, placing a strong emphasis on good leadership and governor and community support.

One way of improving schools that has been identified by the Government is to put them under the control of a specially appointed board in place of the school's governing body. It is a drastic step, as the governing body is intended to bring an element of local democratic decision-making into schools through parental and community representation (but see below). Under the Education Act 1993, a failing school could be placed under the control of an 'education association', a board of around five or six people combining a range of relevant skills and experience to manage the school for a period of around six months with a view to securing its improvement (or, if that was not possible, its closure).[263] The power was used only once and was revoked by the SSFA 1998. The system established by the 2002 Act similarly involves replacement of the school's governors. There is a new power by which the governing body of a school that is a failing, has serious weaknesses or has formally been warned may consist of at least two 'interim executive members'.[264] When the school has

---

[258] SSFA 1998, ss 18 and 19, as amended by the 2002 Act, s 56. HMCI is under a duty to notify the Secretary of State and send the inspector's report to the LEA where the inspector has concluded that a school requires significant improvement or the taking of special measures: EA 2005, ss 13 and 14, replacing School Inspections Act 1996, s 16A, inserted by the 2002 Act, s 54.

[259] EA 2005, s 45, amending the SSFA 1998, s 19.

[260] EA 2005, s 2(1) and more generally Part 1.

[261] Her Majesty's Chief Inspector of Schools in England, *Annual Report 2002–03* (London, Ofsted, 2004).

[262] Comptroller and Auditor General, *Department for Education and Skills. Improving Poorly Perfoprming Schools in England*, HC 679, Session 2005–06 (London, TSO, 2006), para 1.5. Note that since Sept 2005 the two categories of 'serious weaknesses' and 'underachieving' have been combined into 'needing significant improvement'.

[263] Education Act 1993, ss 218–228. See further N Harris, 'Too Bad? The Closure of Hackney Downs School under section 225 of the Education Act 1993' (1996) 8 *Education & the Law* 109.

[264] SSFA 1998, s 19A, inserted by the 2002 Act, s 59. This power is exercisable by or with the consent of the Secretary of State: SSFA 1998, ss 16A and 18A, inserted by the 2002 Act, ss 57 and 58. The constitution of the governing body with interim executive members is prescribed by the 1998 Act, new Sched 1A, inserted by the 2002 Act, Sched 6.

improved sufficiently it will once again have a standard governing body, following a period of at least six months where there is to be a 'shadowing governing body'.[265]

Turning to LEAs, the introduction of a regime for their inspection and for enforcement under the Education Act 1997 was noted earlier. The powers of inspection have been widened by the 2002 Act to include premises where children are being educated otherwise than at school, apart from a private residence.[266] Powers granted by the SSFA 1998 whereby the Secretary of State may issue a direction to an LEA which is failing to perform, adequately or at all, any function relating to the provision of education[267] and which may, for example, specify a person outside the LEA to perform a function in which the authority is failing, have been extended by the 2002 Act.[268] The powers, under which several authorities—for example, Islington, Hackney, Southwark and Waltham Forest—have had a number of their key functions compulsorily contracted out to private management companies, now cover all educational functions, including early years education. Moreover, directions may now be repeated. LEAs may also now be directed by the Secretary of State to contract with an outside body to obtain services of an advisory nature where they have been unable to eliminate the deficiencies in a school which required special measures or had serious weaknesses.[269] LEAs are also being given a role, under the EA 2005, in setting targets for the performance of pupils in schools maintained by them and in respect of children being looked after by the LEA.[270] As noted in Chapters 1 and 4, the latter are a group whose educational under-achievement is a subject of considerable concern.

Teachers are also among those with responsibility for educational provision who have been caught by measures to regulate and raise standards. Various changes made by the 2002 Act to the legislative framework governing entry to the teaching profession and the pay and conditions of teachers have been implemented.[271] They build on the Government's previous reforms aimed at 'modernising' the profession which were introduced from 1998–9. The 2002 Act sets out a framework, supplemented greatly by regulations,[272] for teacher appraisal,[273] qualified teacher status and registration,[274] and requirements on

---

[265] School Governance (Transition from an Interim Executive Board) (England) Regulations 2004 (SI 2004/530).

[266] 2002 Act, s 180, substituting Education Act 1997, s 40.

[267] S 8, inserting Education Act 1996, s 497A.

[268] EA 1996, s 497AA, inserted by the EA 2002, s 61; EA 1996, ss 497A and 497B, as amended by the EA 2002 Act, ss 60 and 62.

[269] 2002 Act, s 63. The body contracted to give advice will have powers of entry, inspection, and so on, and the governing body must co-operate with it: s 64.

[270] EA 2005, s 102.

[271] EA 2002, Part 8.

[272] See the Education Act 2002 (School Teachers) (Consequential Amendments, etc) (England) Regulations 2003 (SI 2003/2039); the Education (School Teachers' Qualifications) (England) Regulations 2003 (SI 2003/1662); and the Education (Health Standards) (England) Regulations 2003 (SI 2003/3139).

[273] 2002 Act, s 131.

[274] Ibid, s 132-135.

health and fitness.[275] Specified qualifications for head teachers are also prescribed.[276] Under regulations, only a person who is registered (under the Teaching and Higher Education Act 1998) as a qualified teacher may carry out prescribed work in a school, including planning and preparing lessons and courses for pupils, delivering lessons and assessing and reporting on pupils' development, progress and attainment.[277] The Secretary of State's previous power to make a direction prohibiting or restricting particular individuals from providing education or from managing an independent school is replicated, with amendments.[278] At the time of writing there are plans to tighten up this area further following revelations that some individuals on the register of sex offenders have been given permission to work in schools.[279] The general position on pay and conditions remains as before: these matters are determined centrally by the Secretary of State, under secondary legislation, based on the recommendations of a School Teachers' Review Body, whose members are now to be appointed by the Secretary of State rather than the Prime Minister.[280]

The 2002 Act has also made a number of important changes to the law governing school admissions, as discussed in Chapter 5, and exclusion from school. In relation to the latter, the changes are principally ones of form rather than substance. In particular, this area of the law has been included in the 'modernisation' changes, so that much of it is now in secondary legislation.[281] Even the maximum length of a period or periods of fixed term exclusion (set at 45 school days in total per school year) is no longer in an Act of Parliament. The Act has also amended the legal framework governing the school curriculum and introduced a new and much tighter regulatory framework for independent

[275] Ibid, s 141.

[276] See the Education (Head Teachers' Qualifications) (England) Regulations 2003 (SI 2003/3111) (heads will not need to have the qualification, or to have started a course, before 2009; acting heads will not need to satisfy these requirements anyhow).

[277] The Education (Specified Work and Registration) (England) Regulations 2003 (SI 2003/1663), reg 6. 'Delivering' includes delivery via distance learning or computer aided techniques.

[278] EA 2002, s 142. A direction by the Secretary of State may be given only if the person is on a list kept under s 1 of the Protection of Children Act 1999 (List 99), or the person is unsuitable to work with children, or on the grounds of the person's misconduct or health, or (in the case of management of an independent school) on the ground of the person's professional misconduct. A person who is subject to a direction may appeal (s 144) to a tribunal established under the 1999 Act. If the person acts in contravention of the direction or is subject to an order under the Criminal Justice and Court Services Act 2000 ss 28 and 29 disqualifying him or her from working with children, such a school could be removed from the register of independent schools: 2002 Act, s 169.

[279] See the Safeguarding Vulnerable Groups Bill (HL Bill 79).

[280] As noted above, p 99. EA 2002, ss 119–127 and Sched 11. The School Teachers' Pay and Conditions Act 1991 is repealed by the 2002 Act, Sched 21 and s 130. The Education (School Teachers' Prescribed Qualifications, etc) Order 2003 (SI 2003/1709) specifies the qualifications needed for qualified teacher status for the purposes of these provisions. The Secretary of State can exclude teachers in an education action zone from an order: s 128. This reflects the previous position. Adjustments to the teachers' pay spine are effected by s 147.

[281] EA 2002, s 52; the Education (Pupil Exclusions and Appeals) (Maintained Schools) (England) Regulations 2002 (SI 2002/3178) came into force on 20 Jan 2003. Amendments have been made by the Education (Pupil Exclusions) (Miscellaneous Amendments) (England) Regulations 2004 (SI 2004/402). The Education (Pupil Exclusions and Appeals) (Pupil Referral Units) (England) Regulations 2002 (SI 2002/3179) also came into force on 20 Jan 2003. The previous law was in SSFA 1998, ss 64–68 and Sched 18. See also p 113 above.

schools,[282] including prescribed standards on the quality of education, pupil welfare and other matters.[283] Both areas are discussed in Chapter 7. In addition, LEAs and governing bodies of schools and colleges are now placed under a general duty to promote the welfare of pupils or students in the exercise of their respective functions.[284] The Act has also introduced the new duties on consultation with pupils noted in Chapter 2.[285]

Highly relevant to the Government's aim of maximising participation in education, including widened access, the 2002 Act has also introduced a new system of educational allowances, as outlined in Chapter 4, to encourage young people to continue in full-time education beyond the age of 16 (when they cease to be of compulsory school age),[286] at a time when 13 per cent of 18-year-olds and 7 per cent of 16-year-olds are not in education, training or employment.[287] While support for students in higher education is now the subject of separate reforms that are being phased in under the Higher Education Act 2004, discussed in Chapter 4, the 2002 Act has given the Secretary of State a new power to pay off a person's student loans under the (pre-September 2006 admission) student support scheme.[288]

Whose Empowerment? Some Conclusions on Labour's pre-2006 Reforms

The above discussion has concentrated on changes to the institutional structure built around legislative reforms of considerable range and intensity. These have sought to bring about highly significant changes to schools and their role. The system has become more diverse, with a wide range of different institutions operating partly under discrete legal regimes, including academies, schools in education action zones and foundation schools. There has been a considerable increase in legislative complexity. The scope of the statutory scheme of education has been broadened through, for example, new powers and duties in the area of early years education. Generally, while schools have been given scope for 'earned autonomy' and for some relaxation of regulation, the mechanisms for the accountability of schools have been tightened, with new powers of intervention. This has contributed to a changing and uncertain role for LEAs which, despite an

---

[282] The definition of independent school is changed. In addition to including schools which are not maintained by an LEA and which provide full-time education for five or pupils of compulsory school age, the definition covers non-maintained schools where at least one pupil of that age has a statement of special educational needs (or is a 'looked after' child under s of the 22 Children Act 1989): 2002 Act, s 172, substituting Education Act 1996, s 463.

[283] EA 2002, s 157. See the Education (Independent School Standards) (England) Regulations 2003 (SI 2003/1910), which came into force on 1 Sept 2003.

[284] EA 2002, s 175.

[285] Ibid, s 176. See pp 58–60 above.

[286] Ibid, ss 181–185. See Secretary of State for Work and Pensions, *Opportunity for All. Fifth Annual Report 2003*, Cm 5956 (London, TSO, 2003) 62 and Department for Education and Skills, *Education Maintenance Allowance—an Introduction* (London, DfES, 2003).

[287] Cited in J Flaherty, J Veit-Wilson and P Dornan, *Poverty: the Facts* (London, CPAG, 2004) 154.

[288] EA 2002, s 186.

increase in the range of their powers and responsibilities, has resulted in their involvement in schools becoming more distant. Perhaps the most fundamental change, however, has been in making education central to two broad policy goals—those of reducing social exclusion and its social costs and of ensuring that long-term economic interests are served by the more effective skilling of the young workers of the future. Both demand an institutional framework that is capable of maximising levels of attainment among the widest range of young people, including those whose backgrounds and individual circumstances present significant barriers to personal achievement, as highlighted in Chapter 1. This has required an emphasis to be placed on improving standards of provision, for which measures such as capping infant class sizes and reform of the teaching profession are among the numerous initiatives taken, along with the curricular reforms which are among the matters discussed in Chapter 7. But it also demands the widening of inclusion and effective participation; and some of the principal ways in which this has been done are assessed in later chapters, particularly Chapter 4 which discusses access to education.

Some further conclusions about the changes to the education system are drawn at the end of the chapter, following discussion of the next phase of education reform that is promised by the October 2005 White Paper and the Education Bill 2006. As the discussion below indicates, one of the themes of these planned developments is that of ensuring 'empowerment' of parents and of 'real and effective parental engagement'.[289] The question whether the capacity for *individual* parents to exert some influence over their own child's education has increased is discussed in various specific contexts such as choice of school, special educational provision and sex education in later chapters. But as regards the *collective* influence of parents, it is clear from the reforms instituted under the Conservative governments and continued under the Labour Party that parental involvement has been built into the institutional framework concerning the governance of education as well as some of the decision-making processes affecting local schools.[290]

Participation in the community as a school governor was specifically referred to in *The Citizen's Charter*[291] and continues to fall within Labour's communitarian ideal that is based around the idea of balancing the rights and reciprocal obligations of citizens, particularly within local community settings.[292] We saw earlier how parent governors, who are elected by other parents, became mandatory under the Education Act 1980 and how the size of parental representation increased subsequently. In view of the increasing autonomy and responsibilities of school governing bodies, including financial management, the potential for the parental voice to exert a significant influence over schools was

---

[289] The Labour Party, *Britain Forward not Back* (London, The Labour Party, 2005) 34.

[290] This includes parental rights to consultation and to raise objections to school changes, such as closures and amalgamations (SSFA 1998, Ch II, Part II), and admission arrangements (see Chap 5), which must be considered.

[291] HM Government, *The Citizen's Charter*, Cm 1599 (London, HMSO, 1991), foreword.

[292] H Dean, *Welfare Rights and Social Policy* (Harlow, Prentice Hall, 2002) 197–9.

greatly enhanced. It was also noted that parents had voting rights in relation to grant-maintained status for a school under the Conservatives and have been given such rights in relation to grammar school status under Labour. But the latter is the only matter on which parents may collectively exercise a direct vote. The SSFA 1998 gave parents rights of representation on local authority education committees[293] and the EA 2002 has provided for their membership of admission forums.[294] However, as noted in Chapter 2, children have been largely excluded from rights of participation, although we saw that under the EA 2002 there is a duty on schools to consult with pupils over various policy matters and, under the EA 2005, on school inspectors to have regard to any views expressed by pupils.[295]

The evidence suggests that parents have gained little collective power through the various rights of representation. In some instances, for example, parent members constitute a small minority of the relevant bodies' membership. Moreover, several of the bodies of which the parents are members have very little power, and their influence is likely to be marginal. Both of these factors are applicable to admission forums introduced under the 2002 Act. Although there must be between one and three parent governors within the forum, there is a total of eight categories of member, and in any event the forum merely has an advisory role. Furthermore, while parent governor representation (two to five members) on local authority education overview and scrutiny committees implies a degree of empowerment, especially since they have voting rights, a survey of a random sample of authorities' committees by the author revealed that none had more than three such members nor did they comprise more than 23 per cent of the total membership: see table 3.

Of course, this representation has at least ensured that the parent governor perspective may be aired. On the other hand, there is some force in the argument that these forms of representation are not intended to empower consumer or

Table 3: Parent governor representation on five English local authority education and scrutiny committees (2005)

Local education authority	Total membership of committee	Parent governor members (% of total)
Birmingham	18	2 (12.5)
Durham	30	3 (10)
Greenwich	14	2 (14.3)
Lewisham	13	3 (23)
Trafford	15	3 (20)

[293] SSFA 1998, s 9.
[294] SSFA 1998, s 85A; Education (Admission Forums) (England) Regulations 2002 (SI 2002/2900).
[295] EA 2002, s 176; EA 2005, s 7.

client groups. As Bessant, talking about opportunities for young people's public participation, comments, 'participation is confined to specific issues that do not challenge the political power of policy makers on significant issues'.[296] It could therefore be argued that their true purpose is simply to add legitimacy to the decision-making processes. Young argues that when ordinary citizens enter such public spheres of decision-making they tend to face a form of exclusion, which she terms 'internal exclusion', because others who exert a more powerful position tend ignore or dismiss their arguments or concerns, which in turn limits the citizen's capacity to influence decisions.[297] In theory, the parental interest is significantly promoted through the inclusion of parent governors on school governing bodies, which must comprise nine to 20 members, of whom, in most schools, parent governors must comprise at least one third of the total membership.[298] The other categories of governor are: staff governor, LEA governor, community governor, foundation governor, partnership governor and sponsor governor.[299] Overall, of 350,000 school governor places in England, 90,000 are for parent governors, although there was a vacancy rate for parent governors of 11 per cent (about average across the different categories of governor) in 2003.[300] However, there is evidence that the focus within school government work on improvements to school performance and the management of finances limits the opportunity for parent governors to have an impact on the direction of the school. Instead, as the IPPR has found, parents tend to be 'co-opted into using managerial skills, such as accounting'.[301] In relation to many school policy and resource matters, therefore, they are likely to be marginalised by other, often professional, voices.[302] An example identified by researchers is the policy of a school for charging (for example, in relation to school trips).[303] This lack of effective participation has also been found to occur among the lay membership of education action forums and on boards of NHS primary care groups.[304]

The House of Commons Education and Employment Select Committee

---

[296] J Bessant, 'Youth Participation: A New Mode of Government' (2004) 24 *Policy Studies* 87 at 98.

[297] I Young, *Inclusion and Democracy* (Oxford, OUP, 2002) 55.

[298] School Governance (Constitution) (England) Regulations 2003 (SI 2003/348), regs 12-15. The exception is voluntary aided schools: they are required to have at least one parent governor: ibid, reg 16.

[299] See ibid as to their representation. Community schools, eg, have parent, staff, community and LEA governors but may also appoint sponsor governors (persons who have given substantial resources or services to the school). Foundation governors, in the case of schools with a religious character, are persons 'appointed for the purpose of securing that that character is preserved and developed': ibid, reg 9. They are required (along with other such as staff and parent governors) in voluntary aided and voluntary controlled schools, along with foundation schools apart from those which are not under a foundation (religious body), which are to have partnership governors instead.

[300] S Bird, *Do the Right Thing. How Governors can Contribute to Community Cohesion and Accountability* (London, DfES, 2003) 11.

[301] J Hallgarten, *Parents Exist OK? Issues for Parent–School Relationships* (London, IPPR, 2000) 96.

[302] Ibid. See also R Deem, K Brehony and S Heath, *Active Citizenship and the Governing of Schools* (Buckingham, Open University Press, 1995).

[303] KJ Brehony and R Deem, 'Charging for Free Education: an Exploration of a Debate in School Governing Bodies' (1990) 5 *Journal of Education Policy* 333.

[304] S Power *et al*, 'Paving a "Third Way"? A Policy Trajectory Analysis of Education Action Zones' (2004) 19 *Research Papers in Education* 461; S Pickard and K Smith, 'A "Third Way" for Lay Involvement: What Evidence So Far' (2001) 4 *Health Expectations* 170.

stated that governing bodies play an important role 'in ensuring a direct line of accountability from the school to its local community'.[305] Representative school governing bodies which are closely engaged with local communities are now seen as having an important role to play in community cohesion. This had led to strong encouragement to LEAs to assist in overcoming the various barriers to participation in school government that appear to be particularly marked in the case of minority ethnic communities, leading to their under-representation in many areas,[306] a situation that is mirrored in the further education sector.[307] According to one report, women are well represented on school governing bodies, at 54 per cent of all governors, but under-represented among chairs (37 per cent) and vice-chairs (41 per cent).[308] Research has also revealed that disabled people, people on low incomes, unemployed people, young people and lone parents are under-represented.[309] Disabled people, for example, not only face physical barriers but also have concerns about the financial implications of participation: transport costs or the cost of support workers are often not covered within governors' expenses and there are also fears (often ungrounded) that service as a governor might affect entitlement to social security benefits.[310] Moreover, recruitment of governors is particularly problematic in inner city schools, special schools and areas of social deprivation,[311] a problem that the Select Committee described as 'serious . . . not least because it is these schools that often are faced by the most serious challenges, and may need more than other schools the support of effective governing bodies'. [312] The Committee found that in some areas language barriers could be a 'significant disincentive' to the recruitment from minority ethnic communities.[313] One study of participation in school government for the DfES concluded that 'a culture of involvement within education for people from black and other minority ethnic groups needs to be established'.[314] The Government has, however, been working with governor associations to improve recruitment in general, and from minority ethnic communities in particular. This is important, since, as noted in Chapter 2, the practical enjoyment of participation rights as social rights tends to be significantly hindered by entrenched social inequalities.[315]

---

[305] *Fifth Report, Sessions 1998–99, The Role of School Governing Bodies* (London, TSO, 1999), i, para 10.
[306] Bird, n 300 above, 12.
[307] A Foster, *Realising the Potential. A Review of the Future Role of Further Education Colleges* (London, DfES, 2005) 22.
[308] Bird, n 300 above, 16. This report expresses alarm that many authorities were unable to supply data, indicating that they did not monitor minority ethnic recruitment onto governing bodies.
[309] A Ellis, *Barriers to Participation for Under-represented Groups in School Governance*, RR500 (London, DfES, 2003).
[310] Ibid, 39–40.
[311] H Scanlon, P Early and J Evans, *Improving the Effectiveness of School Governing Bodies* (London, DfEE, 1999).
[312] Fifth Report, n 305 above, para 43.
[313] Ibid, para 45.
[314] Ellis, n 309 above, 39.
[315] See C Stychin, 'Consumption, Capitalism and the Citizen: Sexual and Equality Rights Discourse in the European Union' in J Shaw (ed), *Social Law and Policy in an Evolving European Union* (Oxford, Hart, 2000) 258.

School governing bodies are seen as a bridge between schools and local communities. Indeed, their community role is reinforced by their powers under the 2002 Act to provide community facilities (provided the purpose is charitable) for pupils, families or others in the local area.[316] Even though parent governors are representatives rather than delegates, they ought to be able to communicate the views of other parents on issues of particular importance, as part of what the Education and Employment Select Committee (above) identified as a necessary two-way process of communication between the school and its local community. However, such communication has always been less effective than it might be,[317] and the IPPR report concluded that '[p]arents need new access routes to decision-making'.[318] Exemplifying some of the problems has been the annual meeting between governors and parents that was first introduced under the Education (No 2) Act 1986, as the forum in which an annual report by the governing body, which this Act also required, could be discussed.[319] These duties, which were subsequently re-enacted with amendments in the 2002 Act, have however been abolished in England under the 2005 Act.[320] The Select Committee had recommended as along ago as 1999 that the annual meeting requirement should end, on the basis that the meetings were 'poorly attended at best, and contribute little to the effective governance of the school'.[321] The Committee considered that parents who attended such a meeting might form the view that governing bodies were 'irrelevant'.[322] The Select Committee favoured retention of the report as a means by which governing bodies would be obliged to account to parents, but the 2005 Act has substituted a requirement to maintain and publish a 'school profile'.[323] The intention is that these profiles will be posted on school websites; provision has been made for the piloting of this under the wide-ranging power to exempt from or modify the application of statutory requirements introduced under the 2002 Act.[324] It will enable the profiles to be routinely updated, but, with the abolition of the meetings, there will no longer be the opportunity for parents collectively to confront the governors about matters of particular concern, although they will at least have a guaranteed opportunity to voice concerns to school inspectors when the school is inspected.[325] The Government's plans to introduce a general statutory duty for governing bodies to have regard to the views of parents (see below) is perhaps an acknowledgement of the deficiencies in respect of governing bodies' proper engagement with parents, something which is now considered to be a school

---

[316] EA 2002, ss 27–29.

[317] M Golbey, 'Parent Governorship in the New Order' in F Macleod (ed), *Parents and Schools: The Contemporary Challenge* (London, Falmer, 1989) 143.

[318] J Hallgarten, *Parents Exist OK? Issues for Parent-School Relationships* (London, IPPR, 2000) 96.

[319] Education (No 2) Act 1986, ss 30 and 31.

[320] EA 2005, s 103, which confines these duties to Wales.

[321] Fifth Report, n 305 above, para 66.

[322] Ibid.

[323] EA 2005, s 104, inserting s 30A into the EA 2002.

[324] EA 2002, s 2(1); New Relationship with Schools (Governors' Annual Report) Order 2004 (SI 2004/2683) and (No.2) Order 2004 (SI 2004/2810).

[325] EA 2005, s 7.

standards issue and is included among factors to which Ofsted inspections will give attention.[326]

School governing bodies have ultimate responsibility for the conduct of the school and for standards within them. They must 'exercise their functions with a view to fulfilling a largely strategic role in the running of the school', setting aims and objectives for the school and devising policies and targets for achieving them.[327] They now play a central role within the provision of school education, one that has been consolidated under the New Labour reforms. Indeed, they will be critical to the success of the Government's policy of according schools yet further autonomy and independence (see below). Despite the responsibilities that rest with governing bodies, the Select Committee reached the conclusion that 'properly managed, the workload of governors is not too burdensome'.[328] It is assumed that head teachers will lead a management team within the school and the governing body, whose members must be provided with training (and expenses, although not remuneration),[329] will provide a support role even if the legal responsibility ultimately rests with them. This partnership generally functions well but, as the National Audit Office discovered when examining schools' financial management, sometimes governing bodies fail to adopt the 'critical friend' role that is contemplated by the prescribed terms of reference and provide too little oversight of the head teacher's management.[330]

THE WHITE PAPER 2005 AND THE EDUCATION AND INSPECTIONS BILL 2006[331]

In the White Paper which followed the general election in 2005 the Secretary of State for Education and Skills described various improvements in pupil attainment and school standards that she claimed had resulted from the first two phases of education reform under the post-1997 Labour Government. She said that '[t]he first phase launched in 1997 addressed the acute problems of the educational system we inherited' and concentrated on 'getting the basics right and restoring the morale and pride of teachers', while 'the second phase . . . focussed on building a system of strong confident schools able to sustain the

---

[326] DfES, *Higher Standards, Better Schools for All*, Cm 6677 (London, TSO, 2005), para 5.18.

[327] EA 2002, s 21; the Education (School Government) (Terms of Reference) (England) Regulations 2000 (SI 2000/2122), reg 4(1)–(3).

[328] Fifth Report, n 305 above, para 55.

[329] EA 2002, s 22; the Education (Governors' Allowances) (England) Regulations 2003 (SI 2003/523), made under the 2002 Act, s 19(3)(f).

[330] EA 2002, s 21(3)(a); the Education (School Government) (Terms of Reference) (England) Regulations 2000 (SI 2000/2122), reg 4(5) of which provides that the governing body 'shall act as "critical friend" to the head teacher, that is to say, they shall support the head teacher in the performance of his functions and give him constructive criticism'. See also the Education (School Government) (Terms of Reference) (Wales) Regulations 2000 (SI 2000/3027), as amended.

[331] All clause number references here relate to the version of the Bill as first published on 28 Feb 2006, which received its First Reading on 14 Mar 2006 and Second Reading on 21 Mar 2006.

improvement in standards that was underway'.[332] The acquisition of specialist school status by many secondary schools[333] is seen as indicative of this 'powerful sense of [schools'] own ethos and mission'[334] that is said to be strengthening them. Measured in terms of pupils' assessment results and the numbers of failing schools, there is evidence of improvement consequent on the reforms. For example, the proportion of pupils gaining five or more A*–C grades in GCSE in 2004–5 was nearly 10 per cent higher than in 1997 and there were 112 schools where less than 25 per cent of pupils achieved five or more A*–Cs, compared with 616 in 1997.[335] Of course, there remain quite wide disparities between schools. As noted in Chapter 1, there is still considerable pupil under-achievement among schools with above average numbers of pupils in receipt of free school meals. The White Paper, however, highlights the progress made within disadvantaged areas, stating that '[p]erformance in inner cities and in our more deprived communities has improved more quickly than the national average'.[336] However, the Government acknowledges that this is partly due to the support targeted on those areas, such as through the EiCs programme.[337] Indeed, the various improvements across the schools system to which the Government can point have been achieved at considerable additional public expense: as noted in Chapter 1, annual expenditure on education has risen from £35 billion in 1997–8 to £51 billion in 2004–5; and, in real terms, expenditure per pupil has increased by 29 per cent over this period.[338] The increases are partly are due to additional resources directed towards schools facing extra burdens due to social deprivation among their pupils. Just over 10 per cent of the dedicated schools grant, £2.8bn in 2006–7, is distributed in response to deprivation, contributing between 5 and 22 per cent to individual local authorities' schools funding.[339]

The achievements heralded by the Government might prompt the question why yet further reforms are needed. According to the White Paper, the reforms to date have merely laid the basis for the next phase of reform, the goal of which is 'no less than to transform our schools system by turning it from one focused on the success of institutions into one which is shaped and driven by the success and aspirations of parents and pupils'.[340] This seems to contain an odd distinction, because surely the success of institutions to which the Government refers is based in large part on pupils' success. The rationale for reform is to raise standards for all, especially the least advantaged, involve parents more fully in their children's

---

[332] DfES, *Higher Standards, Better Schools for All,* Cm 6677 (London, TSO, 2005), paras 1.1 and 1.2.

[333] See Chap 5.

[334] DfES, *Higher Standards, Better Schools for All,* Cm 6677 (London, TSO, 2005), para 1.2.

[335] DfES, *National Statistics. GCSE and Equivalent Results and Associated Value Added Measures for Young People in England, 2004/05 (Revised)* (London, DfES, 2006).

[336] DfES, n 334 above, para 1.7.

[337] Ibid. See above pp 107–8.

[338] DfEE, n 334 above, para 1.4.

[339] Secretary of State for Education and Skills, *The Government's Response to the House of Commons Education and Skills Committee Report: The Schools White Paper: Higher Standards, Better Schools for All,* Cm 6747 (London, TSO, 2006) 19. See further HM Treasury/DfES, *Child Poverty: Fair Funding for Schools. A Review of the Ways in which Local Authorities Fund Schools to Meet the Costs Arising from Social Deprivation among their Pupils* (London, DfES/Treasury, 2005).

[340] DfES, n 334 above, para 1.16.

education, match provision with the needs of each and every child, and 'ensure we have schools that parents are pleased to choose between'.[341] Yet it is unclear why 'this requires schools to have the freedom to tailor the way they manage themselves, and the teaching and support they offer, to the talents of individual pupils and their parents' and why, in respect of the goal of establishing 'a more diverse set of providers',[342] which Le Grand has argued is 'the only effective way of increasing contestability and driving up productivity' within public services such as education,[343] there is not already sufficient diversity in the system to allow parents to select the school that they believe will meet their child's needs and aspirations. The Government is, however, on firmer ground in its case for improving the opportunities for those from deprived backgrounds. Despite claiming that school performance in the inner cities has progressed well overall, it acknowledges that pupils from deprived backgrounds 'have not improved as much as others—the attainment gap for pupils has not narrowed'.[344] But it is still not clear why diversity of school providers holds the key to breaking cycles of under-achievement and deprivation that the Government says it is committed to tackling.

The idea that what is needed is 'schools working with parents, children and local communities to drive reform'[345] reflects a form of communitarian idealism. It is part of the general notion of empowerment that pervades many of the reforms, which contemplate a localised system shaped by parental involvement. The Government would claim that communitarian ideals are also served by its proposed self-governing trust schools (occupying a similar place within the system to GM schools in the past), with their own distinct ethos and values. Such a view would not, however, be as sustainable in relation to the possibility of schools expanding in response to parental demand and of new schools being proposed by parents on various grounds, including to meet 'a lack of faith provision' or 'to tackle entrenched inequalities',[346] which despite their appeal to notions of citizenship are partly attuned to consumerist ideals. Indeed, that is probably also true of the chapter in the White Paper entitled 'Parents Driving Improvement', which stresses the benefits of parental engagement for schools' effectiveness. Among the proposed reforms[347] now included in the Bill are a power for Ofsted to investigate parental complaints about a school once they have progressed through the local complaints procedure[348] and a new general duty on school governing bodies to have regard to the views of parents.[349] However, while representing an element of democratic citizen participation in

---

[341] Ibid, para 1.18.

[342] Ibid, para 1.19.

[343] J Le Grand, 'The Blair Legacy: Choice and Competition in Public Services', Transcript of Public Lecture, LSE, 21 Feb 2006, available at www.lse.ac.uk/collections/LSEPublicLecturesandEvents/.

[344] DfES, *Higher Standards, Better Schools for All*, Cm 6677 (London, TSO, 2005), para 1.24.

[345] Ibid, para 2.7.

[346] Ibid, part 2 and paras 2.32.

[347] DfES, *Higher Standards, Better Schools for All*, Cm 6677 (London, TSO, 2005), part 5.

[348] See Education and Inspections Bill 2006, cl 145, inserting EA 2005, ss 11A–11C. The condition that other complaints procedures available to the parent may have to be exhausted first may be imposed by regulations.

[349] Proposed new s 21(6) EA 2002, inserted by cl 35 of the Bill.

education, any element of empowerment inherent in this seems overshadowed by instrumentalism of the kind seen in the past in the attempt to establish a quasi-market in schooling, as discussed in Chapter 5.

Whitty has argued that community education forums and bodies of that kind represent a potential means by which the prerogative of the state and that of the market can be counterbalanced and citizen rights in education asserted.[350] One of the ways in which the White Paper envisages parents' participation being facilitated is via 'parent councils' which would be mandatory in those new trust schools (see below) which have fewer elected parent governors because the trust appoints a majority of the governing body.[351] They would also be encouraged in other schools. The parent councils would provide 'a forum for parents to express their views and influence the running of their school' and would be 'relatively informal and engage people who may not have the confidence or desire to be a parent governor'.[352] The Bill prescribes their purpose as 'to advise the governing body on matters relating to the conduct of the school and the exercise by the governing body of their powers [to provide community facilities etc]'.[353] The constitution of parent councils is to be determined by regulations. The Government has also proposed that governing bodies which want to apply for independent 'trust' status for their schools will have to consult with parents.[354] In fact, under the Bill, such a change would be classed as a 'prescribed alteration' to a school for which proposals will have to be published for consultation and on which objections may be raised; and, subject to provision in regulations, the LEA would be able to refer the matter to the adjudicator.[355] Although parents are not being given a power of veto over the decision, the local authority could refer the proposal to the schools adjudicator if, for example, it considered that the view of the majority of parents was not properly being taken into account or that trust status would be detrimental to standards at the school.[356] As noted in Chapter 2, the Bill would also place LEAs under a new duty to consider and respond to representations from parents about the way that the authority is fulfilling its 'sufficient schools' duty under section 14 of the EA 1996.[357]

While all these opportunities for parental participation do imply a degree of collective empowerment, there is no transfer of decision-making power per se towards parents collectively. Moreover, there are many other proposals that indicate that parental participation is being encouraged as a means of governance, as noted in Chapter 2, in order to reinforce the principle of parental responsibility for their children's education. For example, there is a proposal to update and re-launch the home–school agreement initiative that was set in place

---

[350] G Whitty, *Making Sense of Education Policy* (London, Paul Chapman, 2005) 91.

[351] DfES, *Higher Standards, Better Schools for All*, Cm 6677 (London, TSO, 2005), Part 5. These matters will be covered by new ss 23A SSFA 1998 and 23A EA 2002, inserted by the Education and Inspections Bill (as first published), cll 31 and 32.

[352] DfES, above n 351, para 5.20.

[353] Proposed new s 23A(3) of the EA 2002, inserted by cl 32 of the Bill.

[354] Education and Inspections Bill 2006, cll 18–20. Trust status is discussed below at pp 134–6.

[355] Ibid, cll 17, 19 and 21.

[356] Ibid, cl 21 and regs to be made.

[357] See above, p 91. The new duty, in EA 1996 s 14A, is to be introduced via cl 3 of the Bill.

under the 1998 Act but which, as the Government euphemistically acknowledges, was not exploited to its full potential by schools.[358] Indeed, parent contracts and the imposition of parenting orders under the Anti-social Behaviour Act 2003, which are currently able to be used in cases of truancy and permanent exclusion from school, will be extended under the Education and Inspections Bill to include cases where the pupil is responsible for serious misbehaviour.[359] This is one of several reforms to school discipline, such as a more explicit right for teachers to discipline pupils,[360] that are the least contentious areas of proposed reform. It is also proposed in the Bill that parents will have responsibility for ensuring that their child is not found in a public place in school hours during the first five days of the child's exclusion from school.[361]

The self-governing or independent 'trust' school outside local authority control has proved to be perhaps the most contentious of the proposed reforms.[362] Such a school would become a foundation school, but different from other such schools in that its foundation would be a trust under a charity,[363] with the freedom to set its own admission arrangements.[364] The governing body of any primary or secondary school would be able to create its own trust, or link with an existing trust.[365] A trust could be formed by local groups of parents, but also by universities and independent schools, while some state schools might 'form their own "bespoke" trusts'.[366] It seems that there could, however, be difficulties in finding external organisations interested in establishing trusts.[367] Concern has also been expressed about whether unsuitable bodies might set up trusts in order to gain influence over a school, although the Secretary of State has given an assurance that 'there will be very strong safeguards to prevent the acquisition of inappropriate trusts' through regulation by the Charity

---

[358] DfES, *Higher Standards, Better Schools for All*, Cm 6677 (London, TSO, 2005), para 5.14. Home–school agreements are provided for by the SSFA 1998, ss 110–111. School are required to have them, but a parent cannot be compelled to sign up to one, nor can a child's admission to a school be conditional upon the parent's signature. As noted in Chapter 2 at p 51 above, in some circumstances a child may be invited to sign an agreement: see s 110(5).

[359] Cls 84–86 (as per the Bill as first published), amending Anti-social behaviour Act 2003, ss 19–21 and inserting new ss 22A into it. Parenting orders are made by the magistrates' court, normally where a parent has defaulted on a voluntary parenting contract between the parent and the LEA or school governing body: Anti-social Behaviour Act 2003, ss 19–21. The order is made under the Crime and Disorder Act 1998, s 8, as amended. See also the Education (Parenting Orders) (England) Regulations 2004 (SI 2004/182). Under the terms of the contract or order the parent would be expected to attend a parenting programme which could include counselling or guidance sessions. Parental participation in parenting programmes has been found to help to improve parents' confidence in coping with their misbehaving children: Youth Justice Board for England and Wales, *Positive Parenting—the National Evaluation of the Youth Justice Board's Parenting Programme* (London, Youth Justice Board, 2002) 49–51.

[360] DfES, *Higher Standards, Better Schools for All*, Cm 6677 (London, TSO, 2005), para 7.8; Education and Inspections Bill 2006, Part 7, Ch 1.

[361] Ibid, cl 90.

[362] DfES, n 360 above, paras 2.7–2.28.

[363] Proposed new s 23A of the SSFA 1998, inserted by cl 31 of the Bill.

[364] But subject to the same statutory limitations as other schools: see Chap 5.

[365] Education and Inspections Bill 2006, cl 20, read with cll 18 and 19.

[366] DfES, n 360 above, para 2.19.

[367] House of Commons Education and Skills Committee, First Report of Session 2005–06, *The Schools White Paper: 'Higher Standards, Better Schools for All'*, HC 633–I (London, TSO, 2006), para 54.

Commission and by the local authority, which will fund them.[368] In any event, the rationale for external involvement is brought into question by the lack of evidence that it brings about improvements to schools: '[n]o causal link has been demonstrated between external partners and the success of a school, or between the independence of a school from local authority control and its success'.[369] To some, the introduction of these schools could restore to the education system an elitism that the GM sector once represented, even though there is no explicit proposal to privilege them via extra capital funding,[370] nor to permit the selective status that some GM schools enjoyed.

The trust schools, like GM schools before them, 'will employ their own staff, control their own assets and set their own admissions arrangements'.[371] They may acquire some freedom over the curriculum and teachers' pay and conditions, although, as the Education and Skills Select Committee has noted, there are already similar opportunities for other schools to do so under the arrangements introduced under the Education Act 2002.[372] The White Paper, in fact, sends out some contradictory messages with regard to this freedom. On the one hand, it seeks to downplay it by stressing (under the heading 'Safeguards') that in trust schools '[t]he National Curriculum, the assessment regime and the usual provisions on teachers' pay will apply, except where the Trust has agreed flexibilities'.[373] Yet this section of the White Paper begins by arguing that 'every school needs to be free to develop a distinctive ethos and to shape its curriculum, organisation and use of resources. These decisions cannot be prescribed uniformly.'[374] The idea here is that through the involvement of outside organisations schools would be able to develop a stronger leadership and a distinctive ethos which, through widening diversity, will enhance parental choice.[375] Yet the White Paper also envisages the possibility that *groups* of trust schools could be formed 'to operate with a common ethos and a shared identity',[376] which to some extent undermines the prospects of a widening of diversity and choice, although the House of Commons Education and Skills Committee saw advantages to this collaborative model.[377] The White Paper proposed a 'Schools Commissioner' to advise those interested in seeking trust status for a school, but with a remit that would extend to advising independent schools that want to join the state sector. He or she will be 'a high level [DfES] official' and so the Education and Inspections Bill makes no mention of this office.[378]

---

[368] HC Debs, Education and Inspections Bill, Second Reading, Vol 443, Col 164, 15 Mar 2006 (Ruth Kelly).

[369] House of Commons Education and Skills Committee, n 367 above, para 50.

[370] The Secretary of State confirmed that '[t]rust schools will be funded on exactly the same basis as any other local authority maintained school': HC Debs, Education and Inspections Bill, Second Reading, Vol 443, Col 1464, 15 Mar 2006 (Ruth Kelly).

[371] Above n 358, para 2.16.

[372] EA 2002, s 2 (above). House of Commons Education and Skills Committee, n 367 above, para 47.

[373] DfES, *Higher Standards, Better Schools for All*, Cm 6677 (London, TSO, 2005), para 2.26.

[374] Ibid, para 2.7.

[375] See DfES, *What Trust Schools Offer* (London, DfES, 2006) 1.

[376] DfES, n 373 above, para 2.17.

[377] House of Commons Education and Skills Committee, n 367 above, para 63.

[378] Ibid, Mins of Ev, Q47, 2 Nov 2005 (Ruth Kelly); DfES, n 373 above, para 2.17.

The most controversial aspect of the proposals on trust schools concerns their right to set their own admission arrangements.[379] It has given rise to fears that a school with trust status might operate academic selection. This concern is somewhat exaggerated, given that, as discussed in Chapter 5, the SSFA 1998 only permits selection on the grounds of general academic ability in grammar schools, or schools which were authorised to use it at the start of the 1997–8 academic year and have continued to use it since, or where it is permitted for the banding of pupils (which involves admissions that are broadly representative of the range of abilities).[380] The Education and Inspections Bill consolidates and re-states these restrictions on selection by ability.[381] The Secretary of State has also indicated that the policy of permitting successful schools to expand will not apply to schools that select pupils on the basis of their academic ability.[382] Selection on the basis of children's aptitude for particular subjects will continue to be permitted, but, as at present, only in respect of an aptitude for a prescribed subject; not more than 10 per cent of the intake can be selected in this way.[383] Opponents focused on the fact that at present the admissions code of practice, which merely reflects these statutory restrictions, is only something to which regard must be had by admission authorities, rather than having statutory force.[384] The Government has responded to that concern, which threatened to be one of the major objections in a possible backbench revolt, by providing for admission authorities to have to a duty 'to act in accordance with' the code[385] and that the local admission forum[386] would have powers of objection where this was not done.[387] Although the White Paper stresses that selection by aptitude 'is entirely different from an 11-plus system that divides children into different schools on the basis of academic ability' and that '[t]here will be no return to the 11-plus',[388] opponents of the trust schools are concerned lest these schools use their control over admissions to practise covert selection by manipulation of the aptitude rule. A further concern is that trust schools may not be placed under the obligation that rests with other schools concerning the admission of pupils with special educational needs;[389] that seems unlikely, but the Select Committee has recommended that trust schools should be expressly covered by this duty.[390]

A further cause of opposition to the reforms from the Government's own benches is the reduced role that is contemplated for local authorities in relation

[379] Ibid, para 2.9.

[380] SSFA 1998, ss 99–101. See Chap 5.

[381] Education and Inspections Bill 2006, cl 36.

[382] HC Debs, Education and Inspections Bill, Second Reading, Vol 443, Col 1472, 15 Mar 2006 (Ruth Kelly).

[383] SSFA 1998, s 102.

[384] SSFA 1998, s 84(3); DfES, *School Admissions Code of Practice*, DfES/0031/2003 (London, DfES, 2003).

[385] Education and Inspections Bill 2006, cl 37, amending the SSFA 1998, s 84.

[386] See p 260 below.

[387] Education and Inspections Bill 2006, cll 38 and 42, amending SSFA 1998, ss 89 and 90. See also P Wintour, 'Blair's school concessions win over leading rebels', *The Guardian*, 7 Feb 2006, 2.

[388] DfES, *Higher Standards, Better Schools for All*, Cm 6677 (London, TSO, 2005), para 3.21.

[389] See Chap 6.

[390] House of Commons Education and Skills Committee, n 367 above, para 75.

to educational provision. Local authorities will have a role in 'commissioning rather than providing education' and as 'champions of pupils and parents'.[391] The name LEA may be dropped via statutory amendment made by statutory instrument, in order to reinforce the integration of education and other children's services that the Children Act 2004 set in motion.[392] The role of local authorities in relation to education will be a strategic one. The White Paper even went so far as to propose that LEAs would not be able to establish new community schools themselves, but while the Bill places an emphasis on LEA invitations for proposals from others wishing to establish a new school,[393] which could include groups of parents, one of the Government's concessions to opponents from within its own ranks is to enable the LEA/local authority to apply to the Secretary of State if it wishes to set up a new community or community special school.[394] In some cases it will do this only for the purpose of competing with the aforementioned invitees.[395] The Government's intention is that the competition should be referred to the adjudicator, with a view to ensuring that it is genuinely open. In judging whether the local authority's proposal should succeed the adjudicator would 'take into account the track record of the local authority in terms of educational performance, the degree of diversity in the schools system and parental preference'.[396] Part of local authorities' role under the post-Bill system will be the development of a plan as to the number of schools that are needed in the area and where they should be located, as is the case at present, but they will also have a new duty to 'promote choice, diversity and fair access'[397] (the Bill separates this out into 'securing diversity in the provision of schools' and 'increasing opportunities for parental choice'[398]). It was proposed that local authorities' plans would be scrutinised by the proposed Schools Commissioner (above) who would be able to challenge them.[399] The Commissioner will exercise functions on behalf of the Secretary of State. Even if the independence of the Schools Commissioner were increased, as the House of Commons Education and Skills Committee recommended,[400] this would represent a most serious interference with local government's authority over planning of schooling, as far-reaching in its implications as the role of the Funding Agency for Schools in the past.

School organisation committees, first established under the SSFA 1998 as

---

[391] DfES, n 388 above, 103 and para 9.20.

[392] Ibid, paras 9.5 and 9.6. Education and Inspections Bill, cl 147.

[393] Education and Inspections Bill 2006, cll 7 and 8 and Sched 2.

[394] Ibid, cl 9 and Sched 2. They may also propose to set up a maintained nursery school or a school for people above compulsory school age: ibid, cl 10.

[395] Ibid, cl 7.

[396] Secretary of State for Education and Skills, *The Government's Response to the House of Commons Education and Skills Committee Report: The Schools White Paper: Higher Standards, Better Schools for All*, Cm 6747 (London, TSO, 2006) 22.

[397] DfES, *Higher Standards, Better Schools for All*, Cm 6677 (London, TSO, 2005), para 9.7.

[398] EA 1996, s 14(3A), to be inserted by the Education and Inspections Bill 2006, cl 2.

[399] N 397 above, para 9.11.

[400] House of Commons Education and Skills Committee, First Report of Session 2005–06, *The Schools White Paper: 'Higher Standards, Better Schools for All'*, HC 633–I (London, TSO, 2006), i, para 65.

noted above, will be abolished.[401] In future, local authorities will decide whether proposals for new schools or changes to schools are needed, although in some cases, such as where the authority itself has published the proposals, the matter will have to be referred to the adjudicator; objections to all proposals will also lie to the adjudicator. [402] The Government argues that as school organisation committees represent existing schools and providers in an area, there is currently a 'bias in favour of the status quo'.[403] Local authorities' role as 'champions of pupils and parents' (above) will involve not only playing a more active role in ensuring school standards are met, by more 'radical action' and referral to Ofsted in the case of underperforming schools, but also providing more choice and information to families. These modest extensions of their role do not, however, detract from the broad direction of policy towards local authorities. The reduction in their overall control of local schooling represents a further weakening of the connection between citizenry and local government that is central to local democratic accountability in respect of a key service in which all have an interest, whether direct or indirect. The proposed attempt to make the schools system more responsive to parents will not counter this democratic deficit.

CONCLUSION

Change has become a constant in educational policy in England and Wales over the past quarter of a century, and one of the consequences (and causes) has been a proliferation of complex and wide-ranging legislative measures. Each of the major policy-laden statutes—the Education Reform Act 1988, the Education Act 1993, the School Standards and Framework Act 1998 and the Education Act 2002—has made significant changes to the schools system. The overall effect of all these measures is a significant 'layering' of education statute law. Most of the benefits of codification that occurred in 1996 have been undone. The complexity is compounded by the continuing conferment and employment of delegated legislative powers, resulting in an annual total of over 100 statutory instruments on education, a process that is likely to intensify if the Government makes a more determined effort to carry through its plan to 'modernise' education law and make it more amenable to reform in response to changing needs by enabling future changes to be made via secondary rather than primary legislation.

It is difficult to draw general conclusions from the past 60 years of education reform in England and Wales, and especially the past 25 years of rapid change. The most obvious conclusion is that, as noted in Chapter 1, education became highly politicised and has remained so, even if the policy divisions along strict doctrinaire party lines have become increasingly less distinct. Looking back to the

---

[401] Education and Inspections Bill 2006, cl 27, repealing SSFA 1998, s 24 and Sched 4.
[402] Education and Inspections Bill 2006, Sched 2, part 2.
[403] DfES, *Higher Standards, Better Schools for All*, Cm 6677 (London, TSO, 2005), para 9.12.

late 1970s, few, if any, would have predicted that a Labour government would be willing to permit the private sector to run some LEAs and for independent schools to enter into collaborative arrangements with the state sector. One of the most striking features of this period of reform is the amount of common ground between the Conservatives' and post-1997 Labour Government's policies. Both parties have promoted or supported more parental involvement and choice in education; an emphasis on raising standards and regulation to maintain the process through inspection, auditing and resource targeting; increased diversity and specialisation within the schools system; a curriculum that is largely centrally controlled; a substantial degree of managerial and financial autonomy for schools, under the control of their governing body rather than the LEA; and the subjugation and reform of the teaching profession. Both sets of governments have been responsible for a massive growth in regulation and bureaucracy.

In comparing today's schools system with that which emerged from the Education Act 1944, how far have things changed? In some respects there has been a complete transformation. Central government now directs education in a way that is very far removed from the distant oversight of town halls and schools that prevailed for over three decades. Although head teachers and senior staff manage their schools on a day-to-day basis, school governing bodies have since 1986 borne the legal responsibility for much of what goes on there. Schools have become much more autonomous over many areas of decision-making, largely independent from the LEA over matters such as finance, staffing and pupil discipline, but their activities are still tightly constrained by central regulation, despite the prospects of 'earned autonomy' that the Education Act 2002 offers for some, and of independent trust status that the Education and Inspections Bill may well, in due course, offer for many more. The relationship between parents and the education system has also changed, through increasing formalisation of their status as 'partners' in the provision of education for their child and through the consumer-orientated rights concerned with the exercise of choice over admissions or special educational provision, access to published information about schools and their performance, rights of appeal over admission, special educational needs and exclusion decisions, and representation on school governing bodies. Even children are finally being accorded some independent rights in the context of education, as we saw in Chapter 2. Accountability on the part of schools, teachers and LEAs has greatly increased. Overall, therefore, perhaps the more significant change has been in the nature and character of the relationships between the various interests in education than in the institutional framework per se, although it is clear that these two aspects are inextricably linked.

Institutionally, some aspects are essentially preserved. The organisation of schooling, now governed by a very elaborate legal framework, is still a local matter and the basic role of LEAs over it has continued, even though they are no longer responsible for maintaining all schools in their area (in particular, schools that have foundation status or are city colleges or academies) and must engage a range of committees and partnerships in decision-making processes. LEAs retain responsibility for enforcing school attendance and for catering for the needs of pupils unable to attend school.[404] State primary and secondary schools still provide free education[405] and are still divided into non-denominational and denominational categories, although the broader range and larger contingent of schools within the state sector catering for minority faiths, including Muslim and Sikh schools, is an important new feature. Selection of pupils by ability at the age of 11 to attend grammar schools largely ended by the mid-1970s (although remains in respect of over 150 schools); most secondary schools today are comprehensives, catering for the full ability range, although specialisation among secondary schools has increased significantly, and with it the possibility of selecting up to 10 per cent of pupils on the basis of their aptitude for the particular school's specialist subject(s). The independent schools sector survives, although is now more closely regulated. Its legitimacy has been reinforced through Government overtures towards it to share its expertise and 'partner' state schools in some areas. Much has changed within the classroom, of course (as we shall see in Chapter 7). Indeed, the social, economic and legal contexts of teaching have changed; for example, the profile of the pupil population obviously reflects wider demographic changes. The gender mix of the teaching profession is also changing; there are fears that shortages of male teachers in primary schools will deprive male pupils of role models and have negative effects on their education, although that notion is contested.[406]

As we saw in Chapter 1, greater social diversity and the demand for equality of opportunity and social inclusion have become more influential factors in the development of education policy. Since 1997, the most significant changes to the schools system have been the reforms designed to promote higher levels of attainment and reduced social exclusion. Initiatives noted in this chapter have included education action zones or the modernisation of the teaching profession. Most of the key changes targeted on particular kinds of disadvantage, such as disability, have occurred in areas which are the subject of the following chapters in this book.

---

[404] See Chap 4.

[405] Ibid.

[406] M Mills, W Martino and B Lingard, 'Attracting, Recruiting and Retaining Male Teachers: Policy Issues in the Male Teacher Debate' (2004) 25 *British Journal of Sociology of Education* 355.

4

Equality of Access to Education

INTRODUCTION

THIS CHAPTER DEVELOPS one of the themes outlined in Chapter 1, that of access to education including the issue of equality of access. The level of priority accorded to the realisation of the principle of equal access is clearly affected by political and economic considerations. Yet no reasonable person would demur from the views about equality expressed by Chief Justice Warren in the landmark decision in *Brown v Board of Education of Topeka*:

> Today education is perhaps the most important function of the state. Compulsory school attendance laws and the great expenditure for education both demonstrate our recognition of the importance of education to our democratic society. It is required in the performance of most basic public responsibilities . . . It is the very foundation of good. Today it is a principal instrument in awakening the child to cultural values, in preparing him for later professional training, and in helping him to adjust normally to his environment. In these days, it is doubtful that any child may reasonably be expected to succeed in life if he is denied the opportunity of an education. Such an opportunity, where the state has undertaken to provide it, is a right which must be available to all on equal terms.[1]

As long ago as 1967 the Plowden report made the point that 'there should be equality of opportunity for all, but . . . children in some districts will only get the same opportunity as those who live elsewhere if they have unequally generous treatment'.[2] The report advocated 'positive discrimination' in the allocation of resources in favour of primary schools in deprived areas in order to provide a 'compensating environment' for the deprived home circumstances that many experienced in the inner cities.[3] It noted that provision was already made for

---

[1] 347 US 483 (1954).

[2] Central Advisory Council for Education (England) (chair: Lady Plowden), *Children and their Primary Schools* (London, HMSO, 1967), para 152.

[3] Ibid, para 151.

children from such backgrounds to receive free school meals[4] and said that there was also a need for their 'intellectual nourishment'.[5] As noted in Chapter 1, and as the Plowden report recognised, underlying social and economic inequalities mean that in order to maximise equality of access and opportunity in relation to education, specially targeted policies and provision may be needed.

In the past, recognition of the principle of equal access to education appears to have been predicated upon the belief that the role of the state was merely to ensure that there was universal provision. As we have seen, the Universal Declaration on Human Rights (1948) proclaims that '[e]veryone has the right to education'[6] and the ECHR provides that '[n]o-one shall be denied the right to education'.[7] It was accepted that education should, at least at elementary level, be available free of charge, but no obligation was placed upon the state to 'compensate' for the social and economic factors that hindered equality of access. The state was barred from practising discrimination that might hinder or prevent the enjoyment of the right to education, and the effect of Article 14 ECHR in this regard was discussed in Chapter 2. But we also saw how, in the *Douglas* case, the Court of Appeal held that financial support to enable people to attend a higher education course was not sufficiently linked to the right to education under the ECHR: it was 'a facilitator of education but . . . one stage removed from the education itself', and the regulations limiting support to the under 55s made it 'more difficult for a student [aged 59]to avail himself of his Art 2 rights but they are not so closely related as to prevent him from doing so'.[8] Scott Baker LJ in that case also reiterated the established principle under the Strasbourg jurisprudence, notably the ECtHR's decision in *Belgian Linguistics*[9] (also discussed in Chapter 2), that the right to education under the ECHR 'is the right to avail oneself of such education as the State provides, that is to participate in the facilities existing at a given time'.[10] In an earlier case that predated implementation of the Human Rights Act 1998, *O'Connor v Chief Adjudication Officer and Secretary of State for Social Security*,[11] the Court of Appeal applied that principle when a student challenged the denial of income support (which happened because he was classed as a full-time student on a course even though he was repeating the year by not attending university and was not entitled to student support). It was held that the state was not obliged to subsidise the student in the exercise of his right to avail himself of education provided by the state.

However, for the human rights position to be that the state's duty is little more than to provide educational facilities and do nothing more to facilitate access to

---

[4] Education Act 1944, s 49. There was also provision of free school milk for all primary school pupils, but this was ended by the Education (Milk) Act 1971, earning the minister responsible for this policy, Margaret Thatcher, the nickname 'milk snatcher'. The current law on free school meals is outlined below.

[5] Central Advisory Council for Education, n 2 above, para 152.

[6] Art 26(1).

[7] Art 2 of Prot 1.

[8] *R (Douglas) v North Tyneside Metropolitan Borough Council and the Secretary of State for Education and Skills* [2004] ELR 117 (CA), at para [57] per Scott Baker LJ

[9] *Belgian Linguistics (No 2)*, 1 EHRR 252 (1979–80), 289–90.

[10] Ibid, para [55].

[11] [1999] ELR 209.

them seems absurd. The notion of universal provision surely implies its practical availability and that its denial, other than on sound academic grounds, must be prevented if at all possible. While, as we have seen, it is for the state to make policy decisions about the allocation of resources, a situation that helps to prevent the right to education from being absolute, one would assume that a guarantee of support for access is necessarily implied. If there is no such guarantee, then the right to education becomes somewhat meaningless.

In relation to the compulsory stage of education, the practical reality is that the child's right to education is underpinned by a positive obligation on the state to enforce school attendance (or a suitable alternative to it). We saw in Chapter 2 that several international instruments, such as the UNCRC, require primary education to be compulsory,[12] but in any event the law in England and Wales has included this principle for over 100 years and indeed has been amended of late to include a more strict range of enforcement measures and sanctions for non-compliance,[13] although in 2004–5 the rate of *unauthorised* absence was at the highest level for nine years.[14] The Education and Inspections Bill will strengthen LEAs' duties by requiring them to establish the identity of children in their area who are not registered at school or receiving suitable education elsewhere (as might be the case with some of those from Traveller communities: see below).[15] Nonetheless, one of the exceptions to the school attendance duty[16] is where the child does not live within walking distance of his or her school and

---

[12] See, in particular, the UNCRC, Art 28(1)(a).

[13] These include: (i) targets for schools: School Standards and Framework Act 1998, s 63, as amended by the Education Act 2002, s 53; the Education (School Attendance Targets) Regulations 2005 (SI 2005/58); (ii) a power to return a child to school or to designated premises where found in a public place during school hours (Crime and Disorder Act 1998, s 16), thereby reinforcing the effectiveness of truancy sweeps/patrols; (iii) a new separate non-attendance offence where a parent 'knows that his child is failing to attend regularly at the school and fails without reasonable justification to cause him to do so' (EA 1996 s 444(1A), introduced under the Criminal Justice and Court Services Act 2000; where reasonable justification is argued, it does not mean that the burden of proof lies with the defendant to show the offence was not committed: *R (P) v Liverpool City Magistrates* [2006] EWHC Admin 887); (iv) a new attendance duty once alternative arrangements for a child are put in place (Education Act 1996, s 444ZA), introduced by the Education Act 2005, s 116; (v) the use of parenting contracts and imposition of parenting orders in truancy cases (Anti-social Behaviour Act 2003, ss 19 and 20 and see DfES, *Guidance on Education-Related Parenting Contracts, Parenting Orders and Penalty Notices* (London, DfES, 2004))—as noted earlier (p 134 above) their use, which may also occur in cases where pupils are permanently excluded from school, is to be extended to cases of serious misbehaviour by pupils, under the Education and Inspections Bill 2006, cll 84 and 85; and (vi) new powers to issue penalty notices (Education Act 1996, ss 444A and 444B, inserted by the Anti-social Behaviour Act 2003; the Education (Penalty Notices) (England) Regulations 2004 (SI 2004/181) (£50 or £100 penalty); see DfES, above). The effectiveness of these measures is assessed in N Harris, 'Making Parents Pay: the Legal Enforcement of School Attendance in England' in D Glendenning and W Binchy (eds), *Litigation Against Schools: Implications for School Mangement* (Dublin, First Law, 2006) 202–21.

[14] DfES, *Pupil Absence in Schools in England 2004/05* (Provisional), SFR 40/2005 (London, DfES, 2005).

[15] Education and Inspections Bill 2006 (as first published), cl 4, inserting EA 1996 s 436A.

[16] As noted in Chap 2, the parent's duty is first and foremost to ensure that their child, if of compulsory school age, receives 'efficient full time education suitable—(a) to his age, ability and aptitude, and (b) to any special educational needs he may have, either by regular attendance at school or otherwise': EA 1996, s 7. If the child is registered at a school, the parent commits an offence under EA 1996, s 444, if the child fails to attend regularly. The exceptions to this are contained in s 444(3) and (4): see n 17 below.

the LEA has failed to make suitable arrangements for transport of the child to school or for him or her to attend a school nearer home.[17] This duty will be amended under the Education and Inspections Bill 2006 to place within the scope of this exception children in respect of whom LEAs are under new duties to make travel arrangements or those who are covered by the new duties on school travel schemes.[18] These and the existing duties on LEAs to provide free school transport to some children,[19] are discussed below.

These arrangements illustrate how, despite the absence of firm guarantees of access under the ECHR, state welfare provision in England and Wales includes important measures that are necessary in order to support access. Indeed, there is a long tradition in England and Wales of financial support to facilitate access to education. For example, under the Education Act 1944, the minister had a power to make regulations

> empowering [LEAs], for the purpose of enabling pupils take advantage without hardship to themselves or their parents of any educational facilities available to them—
>
> (a) to defray such expenses of children attending [state] schools as may be necessary to enable them to take part in any school activities . . .
>
> (c) to grant scholarships, exhibitions, bursaries and other allowances in respect of pupils over compulsory school age . . .[20]

But the impact of poverty and social exclusion on access to education is not ignored in international treaty obligations. In particular, the European Social Charter, in its revised form from 3 May 1996, provides that:

> With a view to ensuring the effective exercise of the right to protection against poverty and social exclusion, the Parties undertake:
>
> a. to take measures within the framework of an overall and co-ordinated approach to promote the effective access to persons who live or risk living in a situation of social exclusion or poverty, as well as their families, to, in particular, employment, housing, training, education, culture and social and medical assistance;
>
> b. to review these measures with a view to their adaptation if necessary.[21]

---

[17] EA 1996, s 444(4); see below. The other exceptions are that the child is absent with leave (see further *Bromley London Borough Council v C* [2006] EWHC Admin 1110); the child was prevented from attending by 'sickness or unavoidable cause' (it must be a cause affecting the child) (see *Jenkins v Howells* [1949] 2 KB 218, *Jarman v Mid-Glamorgan Education Authority, The Times*, 11 Feb 1985—'the words "unavoidable cause" . . . should in no way be equated with "reasonable grounds"' (per May LJ); *Bath and North-East Somerset District Council v Warman* [1999] ELR 81; *R v Leeds Magistrates Court and Others* [2005] EWHC 1479); or it is a day set aside for religious observance by the religious body to which the parent belongs.

[18] Education and Inspections Bill 2006 (as first published), cll 64–67.

[19] Education Act 1996, ss 509 (as amended) and 509AA–509AC.

[20] Education Act 1944, s 81(a) and (c) and the Scholarships and Other Benefits Regulations 1977 (SI 1977/1443). See now Education Act 1996, s 518.

[21] Art 30 (headed 'The right to protection against poverty and social exclusion').

The Explanatory Report on the revised Charter indicates that financial support for those who cannot help themselves by their own means may be implied in this provision.[22] Thus developments in the UK such as the extension of financial support for those continuing in education from the age of 16 by the introduction of education maintenance allowances[23] may be seen as consistent with the social protection referred to in the Charter. It is arguable that because Article 30 imposes positive obligations on states, measures to ensure effective access to education might even include taking steps to minimise the risk of exclusion from school.

Access to education, whether in the exercise of a right or consequential on the fulfilment of a parental responsibility, is affected not only by poverty but a range of other social and cultural factors, as noted in earlier chapters. English law provides formal guarantees of equality of access through its anti-discrimination legislation, discussed below. But equal access also demands the adoption of specific policies, often targeted, to reduce social and economic barriers. As we saw in Chapter 1, access to education is seen as having important social benefits in terms of increasing opportunities for self-sufficiency and attainment and reducing dependence on the state; but it is also contingent upon some amelioration of the inequalities and disadvantages that create the need for targeted support for access in the first place. Questions nonetheless arise as to how far education policies should go in seeking to redress social inequalities. Some have argued that affirmative action in relation to university admission policies, whereby (for example) qualifications obtained by persons from less advantaged educational backgrounds are assigned greater value than those obtained by other applicants, represents a form of 'social engineering'. This argument has arisen recently in the context of debates surrounding the establishment of the Office for Fair Access (OFFA) and other measures aimed at widening participation in higher education contained in the Higher Education Act 2004, plus access to financial support (see below).

But the question that needs to be addressed is why should education be considered different from other areas of social policy, such as winter fuel payments or free bus rides for pensioners, that aim to tackle structural inequalities that affect access to services? Is perhaps the difficulty that some find in accepting redistributive ideology influenced by fears that, because education is central to the intellectual and cultural development of the individual and to the values of the whole nation, there is a risk that such policies might do more harm than good overall? Or might it in some cases be less altruistic in nature, concerned merely with the protection of self-interest?

The last of these seems likely to have featured in the grossly discriminatory policies that were opposed in the *Brown* case itself.[24] Challenges were brought by black children from Kansas, South Carolina, Virginia and Delaware against the

---

[22] Council of Europe, *Social Protection in the European Social Charter* (Strasbourg, Council of Europe, 1999), App V, para 116.

[23] The weekly award is £10, £20 or £30 depending on household income of up to £30,000. See pp 223–4 below.

[24] N 1 above.

decision by the public authorities to deny them admission to schools which were attended by white pupils, on the basis of district or state laws permitting racial segregation. The claimants argued that segregated public (state) schools were not equal and could not be rendered equal, so that their Constitutional right to the equal protection of the law under the Fourteenth Amendment had been denied. The Supreme Court considered whether, where facilities and other tangible factors were equal, the children from this racial minority group were denied equal opportunities. Chief Justice Warren, giving the Court's unanimous decision, answered that question in the affirmative. He said that '[t]o separate them from others of similar age and qualifications solely because of their race generates a feeling of inferiority as to their status in the community that may affect their hearts and minds in a way unlikely ever to be undone' and would affect their educational development and motivation to learn. He concluded, '[s]eparate educational facilities are inherently unequal'. Viewed today, the situation that the Supreme Court was considering made this an extreme case, although the recent suggestion by Trevor Phillips, chairman of the Commission for Racial Equality, that there might be a case for tackling under-achievement by African Caribbean boys by teaching them separately from others for some of the time, in order to 'break through the wall of attitude that surrounds black boys' and inhibits their attainment,[25] raises similar concerns. It has been argued that Phillips' proposal runs the risk of stigmatising the children and young people concerned.[26] Either way, the crucial point about the *Brown* judgment is that it confirmed the overriding importance of equality of access to education to the public good, a principle that transcends all others in this context.[27]

In fact, the balancing of arguments and interests is more closely weighted in cases concerning affirmative action. This has also been a live issue in the United States and, in the light of the reforms relating to university recruitment, in the UK. In relation to areas of education where opportunities are necessarily limited and places are competitively sought, it is sometimes the case that, in order to widen opportunity, and promote greater social equality, overall, access will have to be denied unequally. This issue is discussed below.

This chapter proceeds to examine equality of access in three separate contexts. First, it discusses the effects of anti-discrimination law, including the case for positive discrimination. Secondly, it assesses specific measures directed towards or affecting discrete groups facing particular barriers to full access. Finally, it reviews arrangements for financial support for persons in further or higher education.

---

[25] BBC TV's *Inside Out* programme, 7 Mar 2005, and reported in A Blair and D Charter, 'Segregation could help black pupils, says race chief', *The Times*, 7 Mar 2005, 1 and 6.

[26] Ibid, citing the views expressed by Simon Woolley, co-ordinator of Operation Black Vote.

[27] On the wider impact of *Brown* within the US, see MJ Klarman, *From Jim Crown to Civil Rights* (New York, OUP USA, 2004).

ANTI-DISCRIMINATION LAW

Article 14 of the ECHR, which requires states to ensure that the enjoyment of the Convention rights occurs without discrimination 'on any ground such as sex, race, colour, language, religion, political or other opinion, national or social origin, association with a national minority, property, birth or other status', was discussed in Chapter 2. We saw that, read together with Article 2 of Protocol 1, Article 14 gives rise to a principle of equality of access to education provided by a state, but that discrimination or differential treatment which can be shown by the state to have a reasonable and objective justification, and which is proportionate, may be sanctioned. *Karus v Italy*[28](higher university fees paid by a German national in Italy) and *Angelini v Sweden*[29] (refusal to excuse atheists from attending Christian-based religious knowledge classes), both of which were discussed in Chapter 2, provide examples of discriminatory policies that were held to be justified under the ECHR. The Human Rights Act 1998 has obviously given the Convention a critical importance to any assessment of the law's protection against discrimination in England and Wales, as the *Douglas* case, noted above, illustrates, although to date Article 14 appears not to have been successfully invoked in a domestic education case in England and Wales.[30] Article 14 is also relevant to the issue, discussed below, of whether positive discrimination in connection with access to higher education is legitimate.

Domestic anti-discrimination law will continue to be extremely important in respect of both protection for the individual against discrimination affecting access to education and the promotion of the principle of equality of access.

Sex, Race and Religion

Both the Sex Discrimination Act (SDA) 1975 and the Race Relations Act (RRA) 1976 contained from the outset measures outlawing discrimination[31] in the context of education. Almost all of the sex discrimination cases have arisen in the context of the provision of single-sex schools. A series of decisions during the 1980s and 1990s confirm that it is normally contrary to the SDA 1975 for there to be unequal numbers of local single-sex places as between boys and girls.[32]

---

[28] App no 29043/95, 20 May 1998 (Commission of Human Rights).

[29] (1988) 10 EHRR CD 123.

[30] See further the discussion of school admission and choice in Chap 5.

[31] Namely direct or indirect discrimination or victimisation on the grounds of (1975 Act) sex or marital status or gender reassignment or (1976), colour, race, ethnic or national origins or nationality. See SDA 1975, s 1, as substituted by the Sex Discrimination (Indirect Discrimination and Burden of Proof) Regulations 2001 (SI 2001/2660), and s 4; and RRA 1976, ss 1 and 2.

[32] *R v Secretary of State for Education and Science ex parte Keating* (1985) 84 LGR 469; *Equal Opportunities Commission v Birmingham City Council* [1989] 1 All ER 769; *R v Secretary of State for Education and Science ex parte Malik* [1992] COD 31; *R v Birmingham City Council ex parte Equal Opportunities Commission (No 2)* [1994] ELR 282 (CA). In *R v Northamptonshire County Council and the Secretary of State for Education ex parte K* [1994] ELR 397 it was held that the closure of the only boys' school in the area was justified because, although s 23 of the 1975 Act required the LEA to

Discrimination by the 'responsible body'[33] is unlawful in relation to: decisions on admission to the establishment, including the terms on which admission is offered; the way in which access is afforded to benefits, facilities or services, or denial of access to them; and excluding a person from the establishment or subjecting them to any other detriment.[34] In the case of the SDA 1975, the Act includes exemptions that permit the obvious discrimination in admissions to single-sex establishments or where a school is changing from single sex; and mixed schools where the school admits boarders of only one sex. It also disapplies the relevant provisions in the case of further or higher education courses in physical education or where the education is provided outside Great Britain.[35] In the case of the RRA 1976, discrimination is permitted if it occurs through action 'in the performance of an express obligation' in a statute or statutory instrument.[36] Both Acts also make it unlawful for an LEA to practise sex or race discrimination in the exercise of any of its functions[37] (a proscription that, subject to certain exceptions, also covers discrimination on the ground of religion or belief under the relevant provisions of the Equality Act 2006, when in force[38]) or for it to fail to 'secure that facilities for education provided by it, and any ancillary benefits or facilities, are provided without [sex or race] discrimination'.[39] Amendments to the RRA 1976 by order, which came into force in July 2003, have extended both the former and the non-discrimination duties (above) relating to admission, access to benefits, etc, and exclusion. They now also apply to the application of a provision, criterion or practice to a person (the person in question) which is or would be applied equally to another person who is not of the same race, ethnicity or national origins as the person in question, but which would put persons of the same race, etc, as the person in question at a disadvantage compared to other persons. If the provision, criterion or practice that is applied actually puts the person in question at such disadvantage and cannot be shown to be 'a proportionate means of achieving a legitimate aim' then its application is unlawful discrimination.[40] It is also unlawful race

---

ensure that there was no discrimination arising from its performance of its duty to ensure sufficient schools in its area (under s 8 of the Education Act 1944—now s 14 of the 1996 Act), the fact that the school's pupil numbers had fallen so low that it had ceased to be viable meant that the authority would not be able to fulfil its sufficient schools duty. See p 9 above and N Harris, *Law Relating to Schools* (2nd edn, Croydon, Tolley, 1995) 22–5.

[33] The LEA or the governing body of the school (depending upon which has the responsibility for the function in question) or the proprietor of an independent school or a special school; and the governing body of a university or other further or higher education institution: SDA 1975, s 22; RRA 1976, s 17.

[34] SDA 1975, s 22; RRA 1975, s 17.

[35] SDA 1975, ss 26–28.

[36] See *Hampson v Department for Education and Science* [1991] 1 AC 171, per Lord Lowry at 180.

[37] SDA 1975, s 23; RRA 1976, s 18. Note also the non-discrimination duties on the Teacher Training Agency and the Further and Higher Education Funding Councils: RRA 1976, ss 18A, 18D.

[38] Equality Act 2006, s 51(1) and (2). For the meaning of 'religion or belief', see below, p 163.

[39] SDA 1975, s 25; RRA 1976, s 19.

[40] RRA 1976, s 1(1A) and (1B), inserted by the Race Relations Act 1976 (Amendment) Regulations 2003 (SI 2003/1626), reg 3.

discrimination to subject a person who applies for admission to an educational establishment (or who is a pupil there) to harassment.[41]

These provisions have been augmented by important new duties introduced under the Race Relations Amendment Act 2000 and regulations pursuant thereto. The amendments to the RRA 1976 made by the Amendment Act were phased in between April 2001 and May 2002. The 2000 Act was in large part a response to the findings of Lord Macpherson's Inquiry[42] into the police investigation of the death of Stephen Lawrence concerning institutional racism within public authorities and other organisations.[43] The Macpherson report referred to the important role that education can play in addressing racism, and recommended that this should be backed up with a formal duty on the part of LEAs and schools and that Ofsted inspections should monitor anti-racist strategies. The 2000 Act has made it unlawful for public authorities,[44] in carrying out any of their functions, to do any act which constitutes race discrimination,[45] and there are also duties concerning the promotion of equal opportunities and racial harmony, discussed below. Under the Equality Act 2006, parallel provisions will be introduced in respect of sex discrimination or sexual harassment and religious discrimination.[46] As the basic definition of 'public authority' is broadly the same as that under the Human Rights Act 1998,[47] the recent guidance given

---

[41] RRA 1976, ss 3A and 17(2) of the 1976 Act, inserted by the Race Relations Act 1976 (Amendment) Regulations 2003 (SI 2003/1626), regs 5 and 18. The Teacher Training Agency and the Further and Higher Education Funding Councils are also governed by anti-harassment duties: ibid, reg 19, amending the RRA 1976, ss 18, 18A and 18D.

[42] Sir William Macpherson, *The Stephen Lawrence Inquiry: Report*, Cm 4262–I (London, TSO, 1999).

[43] See Home Office, *Race Relations (Amendment) Act 2000, New Laws for a Successful Multi-Racial Britain, Proposals for Implementation* (London, Home Office, 2001).

[44] Defined in almost the same way as under the Human Rights Act 1998, s 6. It therefore includes 'any person certain of whose functions are functions of a public nature' (RRA 1976 s 19B(2)(a)) but not in respect of a particular act that is private (ibid, s 19B(4)). See further n 47 below.

[45] RRA 1976, s 19B(1).

[46] Equality Act 2006, ss 52, 83 and 84 (see below); s 83 introduces new s 21A into the SDA 1975. Note also the duty not to 'operate a practice which would be likely to result in unlawful discrimination if applied to persons of any religion or belief': ibid, s 53(1).

[47] But note the slightly different wording in the proposed SDA 1975 (proposed s 21A(2)) definition and in the context of the new religious discrimination provision: '"public authority" includes any person who has functions of a public nature' (the discrimination that is proscribed relates to the carrying out, by the authorities, of a 'function', defined for this purpose as a 'function of public nature'): Equality Act 2006, ss 52(2) and 83. In the Human Rights Act 1998, the definition is in s 6(3)–(6). See further D Oliver, 'Functions of a Public Nature under the Human Rights Act' [2004] *Public Law* 329 and the useful references cited in n 1 thereof. The position of private schools and the question whether they carry out acts of a public nature so as to fall within the scope of the s 6(1) duty to act compatibly with a Convention right is discussed in Chap 7. Universities are considered to be public authorities, at least in relation to the majority of their educational functions: see A Bradley, 'Scope for Review: The Convention Right to Education and the Human Rights Act 1998' [1999] *European Human Rights Law Review* 395 at 409; K Kerrigan and P Plowden, 'Human Rights and Higher Education' (2002) 3 *Education Law* 16 at 16–20; D Feldman, *Civil Liberties and Human Rights in England and Wales* (2nd edn, Oxford, Oxford University Press, 2002) 97. Feldman points out that while universities receive substantial public funding they do engage in commercial activities, which could be private acts. In the context of EC public procurement directives (Council Directives 92/50/EEC ([1992] OJ L/209/1); 93/36/EEC ([1993] OJ L/199/1) and 93/37/EEC ([1993] OJ L/199/54), a university is a 'contracting authority' as a body 'governed by public law' if at least half of its income in a budgetary year came from payments by public authorities for which the university gave no consideration: Case C-380/98 *R v HM Treasury, ex p University of Cambridge* [2000] ECR I–8035.

by the courts on its meaning under the 1998 Act in the context of education is relevant.[48] In the Court of Appeal, Sedley LJ said it was 'manifest that the LEA is such a body'.[49] Referring to the guidance given by the House of Lords in *Aston Cantlow* (where a parochial church council, which received no public funding and was not accountable to the general public, was held not to be a public authority),[50] Sedley LJ said that the governing body of a school was 'incorporated by statute' and had obligations for running the school, giving him no reservations about holding it too to be a public authority.[51] Likewise, Baroness Hale of Richmond, in the House of Lords, confirmed that the school in the case (which was a maintained school) was a public authority for the purposes of the 1998 Act.[52] In the case of head teachers, the amenability of their actions (as opposed to those of the governing body) to judicial review has been doubted in the past.[53] However, so far as the head teacher's status under the 1998 Act is concerned, Sedley LJ said there was 'no institutional sense in which his functions are private or sectional' and those functions were publicly funded and were 'directed by statute to the purposes of an institution designed to serve the community and for which the larger responsibility rests on both central and local government'.[54] The fact that the head teacher held no formal office and was not a local government employee did not offset the essentially public role she performed. Despite feeling a 'visceral unease' about holding the head teacher to be a public authority for the purposes of the Human Rights Act, he felt that on balance it was the correct conclusion.[55]

The question whether academies and city technology colleges (CTCs) might be public authorities despite being public–private hybrids and classed as independent schools under education law has yet to receive judicial consideration. CTCs have, however, been held to be amenable to judicial review.[56] Furthermore, given that in *Aston Cantlow* the House of Lords indicated that a public authority for the purposes of the Human Rights Act would be a body in

---

[48] *A v The Head Teacher and Governors of Lord Grey School* [2004] EWHC Civ 382; [2004] ELR 169; *Ali v Headteacher and Governors of Lord Grey School* [2006] UKHL 14; [2006] 2 WLR 690.

[49] *Lord Grey School*, above n 48, para 36.

[50] *Aston Cantlow and Wilmocote with Billsey Parochial Church Council v Wallbank and Another* [2003] UKHL 37; [2003] 3 WLR 283. Lord Nicholls considered (at para 12) that such factors as whether the body was publicly funded, exercised statutory powers, performed a function in place of central or local government or even provided a public service would be relevant in determining the issue.

[51] Ibid, para 38.

[52] *Ali v Headteacher and Governors of Lord Grey School* [2006] UKHL 14; [2006] 2 WLR 690, at para 79 (UKHL).

[53] See, in particular, *R v Head Teacher and Independent Appeal Committee of Dunraven School ex parte B* [2000] ELR 156 (QBD) and (CA), per Nigel Fleming QC (sitting in the QBD as a deputy High Court judge) at 173 B–C.

[54] Ibid.

[55] Ibid.

[56] *R v Governor of Haberdashers' Aske's Hatcham College Trust ex parte T* [1995] ELR 350. Otherwise, independent schools would probably be classed as public authorities only in the very limited circumstances when they exercised public functions. On that basis, they were held to be amenable to judicial review when administering the assisted places scheme, but not when excluding a pupil from school: *R v Cobham Hall School ex p S* [1998] ELR 389; *R v Muntham House School ex p R* [2000] ELR 287; *R v Fernhill Manor School ex p A* [1994] ELR 67.

respect of whose actions the UK's responsibility under the ECHR would be engaged, and that in *Costello-Roberts v UK*[57] the European Court of Human Rights held that the UK was responsible for discipline in independent schools by virtue of its responsibility for the education of all children under Article 2 of Protocol 1 to the Convention, it seems likely that CTCs/academies would also be classed as public authorities. As Quane argues:

> If a private body is involved in the discharge of the United Kingdom's obligations under the Convention (for example, the right to education) then *Costello-Roberts* suggests that it engages the responsibility of the State and, on the basis of *Aston Cantlow*, can be classified as a functional public authority bound by the HRA.[58]

This question has also come up for consideration in the context of the proposals for independent 'trust' schools, discussed in Chapter 3. The Government's view is that these schools would be no different from maintained schools, which are classed as public authorities; and that the fact that CTCs/academies exercise functions of a public nature by providing education at public expense (which was part of the basis for their amenability to judicial review[59]) means they must also be public authorities.[60] This view is probably correct, notwithstanding doubts expressed by the Joint Committee on Human Rights.[61]

The Equality Act 2006 provides that public authorities will have a duty, when carrying out their functions, to have due regard to the need to eliminate unlawful discrimination and harassment and to promote equality of opportunity between men and women.[62] When in force this duty will complement the existing duty of local authorities under section 71(1) of the RRA 1976 to make appropriate arrangements with a view to securing that their functions are carried out with due regard to the need to eliminate unlawful racial discrimination and to promote equality of opportunity and good relations between people from different racial groups.[63] This RRA duty has been extended by the 2000 Act to governing bodies of LEA-maintained educational establishments, institutions of further and/or higher education, and other prescribed bodies.[64] A subsequent order has added a range of other education bodies, including city academies (now simply known as academies), city technology colleges or city colleges for the technology of the arts, the General Teaching Councils, the Learning and Skills

---

[57] [1994] ELR 1; (1995) 19 EHRR 112.

[58] H Quane, 'The Strasbourg Jurisprudence and the Meaning of a "Public Authority" under the Human Rights Act' [2006] *Public Law* 106, at p.112.

[59] *R v Governor of Haberdashers' Aske's Hatcham College Trust ex parte T* [1995] ELR 350.

[60] HL Debs, Col WA 46, 31 Jan 2006, per Lord Adonis, Under-Secretary of State for Education and Skills.

[61] Joint Committee on Human Rights, Ninth Report of Session 2005–06, *Schools White Paper*, HL 113, HC 887 (London, TSO, 2006), para 24.

[62] Equality Act 2006, s 84, inserting new s 76A into the SDA 1975. 'Public authority' is defined in the same way as for the purposes of the new non-discrimination duty in proposed s 21A of the SDA 1975 (above).

[63] RRA 1976, s 71.

[64] Ibid, s 71(1) and Sched 1A, as substituted by the Race Relations (Amendment) Act 2000, s 2 and Sched 1 respectively.

Council, and the Higher Education Funding Councils for England and for Wales, to the list of prescribed bodies.[65] This duty clearly applies to a wide range of potential functions but arguably has a particular relevance to recruitment and admission to institutions, particularly in view of the traditional under-representation of students from some ethnic minority groups in further and higher education, generally and in relation to particular institutions.[66] The Commission for Racial Equality (CRE) is given a power to issue codes of practice on the performance of these duties.[67] The CRE (and the Equal Opportunities Commission and the Disability Rights Commission) will be replaced by a Commission for Equality and Human Rights under measures set out in the Equality Act 2006,[68] but their codes will have continuing effect unless or until revoked.[69] The current CRE code on the promotion of race equality was published in 2002.[70] Its application is intended across a range of functions and especially in the areas of admission policies and the exercise of discipline, particularly exclusion.[71] For example, the code highlights a possible scenario where a secondary school's admission policy includes preference for admission to those attending particular feeder schools. Those feeder schools happen to have a high proportion of white pupils, thereby giving rise to a potentially disproportionate impact on black pupils. A local primary school with more black pupils is not a feeder school. The code suggests[72] that this situation would give rise to unlawful indirect discrimination under the 1976 Act unless justification could be shown for the policy on other than racial grounds (as in fact happened in relation to an admissions policy in Bradford[73]). Although a failure to observe the code does not, in itself, render a person or institution liable to proceedings, it falls to be taken into account by a court in deciding questions arising under proceedings under the RRA 1976.[74] The CRE has also issued non-statutory guides for public authorities, schools and further and higher education institutions.[75]

The amended 1976 Act also empowers the Secretary of State by order to impose such duties as he or she considers appropriate for the purpose of ensuring the better performance by the relevant bodies of their section 71 duty.[76]

---

[65] RRA 1976, Sched 1A, as amended by the Race Relations Act 1976 (General Statutory Duty) Order 2001 (SI 2001/3457). Note also the Learning and Skills Act 2001, s 14, which provides that in exercising its functions the Learning and Skills Council for England must have due regard to the need to promote equality of opportunity between persons of different racial groups, between men and women, and between people who are disabled and those who are not.

[66] See Chap 1 at p 28.

[67] RRA 1976, s 71C(1).

[68] See Equality Act 2006, s 36.

[69] Equality Act 2006, s 42.

[70] See Commission for Racial Equality, *Code of Practice on the Duty to Promote Race Equality* (London, Commission for Racial Equality, 2002).

[71] A Dorn, 'Race Equality in Schools: New Law and New Code' (2002) 3 *Education Law* 146.

[72] Commission for Racial Equality, n 70 above, 5–6.

[73] *R v City of Bradford Metropolitan Council ex parte Sikander Ali* [1994] ELR 299. See Chap 5, at p 269 below.

[74] RRA 1976, s 71C(11).

[75] Commission for Racial Equality, *A Guide for Public Authorities* (London, CRE, 2002); Idem, *A Guide for Schools* (London, CRE, 2002); Idem, *A Guide for Institutions of Further and Higher Education* (London, CRE, 2002).

[76] Ibid, s 71(2).

This power has been used, in the case of education, to impose a duty on governing bodies of maintained schools, CTCs/academies, and further and higher education institutions to have a race equality policy and monitor and assess its impact on pupils or students, staff and (in the case of schools and CTCs/academics) parents.[77] In relation to further and higher education institutions, the duty includes monitoring, by reference to different racial groups, the admission and progress of students.[78] Institutions are required to take reasonable steps to publish annually the results of their monitoring under this provision.[79] LEAs, the funding councils and the Learning and Skills Council each have a duty to publish a scheme, known as a 'race equality scheme', showing how they intend to carry out their section 71 duties.[80]

Whereas complaints of race discrimination by individuals affected can be taken to a designated county court, as is also the case for equivalent complaints under the SDA 1975,[81] a complaint of breach of the general duty (under RRA 1976 section 19) not to discriminate in relation to facilities provided for education is enforceable only by complaint to the Secretary of State for Education under section 496 or 497 of the Education Act 1996.[82] This appears to occur very rarely: a Parliamentary answer indicates that in 1999–2000 there were no such cases.[83] The Secretary of State route is also the only one for enforcing the parallel non-discrimination duty under the SDA 1975.[84] For breach of the general duty under section 71(1) (or of the parallel duty under s 76A of the SDA 1975, when introduced), enforcement is via judicial application by the complainant or the CRE (or the new CEHR when it replaces it), whereas for breach of the specific duties, such as having a race equality policy, the enforcement procedure involves the issuing of a compliance notice by the CRE.[85] The compliance notice requires the duty to be carried out. It also requires that information on the steps taken, or being taken, to comply should be provided to the CRE within the prescribed time limit. If neither is done the CRE may take the matter to a county court. The Government has explained that the aim behind the new duties under the 2000 Act has been not to achieve a particular outcome for an individual but rather to bring about general improvements from which the individual will derive benefit. As a consequence, it has left it to the CRE to bring complaints. However, it 'expects . . . that the CRE will use its powers only if a partnership approach fails to work'.[86]

---

[77] Race Relations Act 1976 (Statutory Duties) Order 2001 (SI 2001 No 3458), Art 3 and Sched 2. Pupil attainment levels are among the matters to be mentioned.

[78] It also includes the recruitment and career progress of staff. In addition, Art 4 provides for LEAs and others to carry out various duties concerned with the ethnic monitoring of staff.

[79] Ibid, Art 3(5).

[80] Ibid, Art 2.

[81] SDA 1975, ss 62 and 66. The Equal Opportunities Commission can also conduct a formal investigation: SDA 1975, s 60.

[82] See Chap 3.

[83] House of Commons, Col 180W, Written Answers, 3 May 2000, Jacqui Smith MP.

[84] SDA 1975, s 25(4).

[85] RRA 1976, ss 71D and 71E. This notice procedure will also apply to the general duty when the Equality Act 2006 s 32 is in force, with enforcement in the High Court.

[86] Home Office, *Race Relations (Amendment) Act 2000. New Laws for a Successful Multi-Racial Britain. Proposals for Implemetation* (London, Home Office, 2001), para 5.11.

The fact that race discrimination cases have been relatively rare in relation to access to education may be partly attributable to the efforts made at a local level, often directed by LEAs and reinforced by CRE guidance,[87] to adopt equal opportunities policies, combined with efforts to promote greater racial awareness. But it does not mean that discrimination has not occurred. Many commentators regard the over-representation of black children of African Caribbean origin among excluded pupils, noted in Chapter 1, as providing evidence of discrimination arising from factors such as racial/cultural stereotyping or a misreading by white teachers of some black pupils' behaviour, as well as simple racial bias.[88] Parsons re-iterates a widely advanced belief that school staff 'need to look even more closely at the conflict situations that arise with ethnic minority children to see if, in their responses to them, they are sufficiently racially aware and culturally sensitive to the lives of these young people and their families'.[89] Proof of discrimination can also be difficult for its victims to establish even where it is systemic.

Race discrimination can take insidious forms. Take, for example, the exercise of choice. As discussed in Chapter 5, recognition of parental rights of choice over school selection can lead to forms of segregation through 'white flight', as in the case of the Dewsbury parents in 1988, or as a result of the Asian parents in some areas gravitating towards particular schools, leading to schools with a high proportion of Asian pupils, while the *Cleveland* case indicated that the mandatory nature of the duty to comply with parental preference where a community school has places may serve to reinforce this process.[90] While segregation of pupils on the basis of race or ethnicity is a form of unlawful discrimination, the law does not prevent de facto segregation from occurring through parental choice. In effect, therefore, LEAs and schools are unable to avoid reinforcement of the discriminatory behaviour of some parents. For many parents, however, this is not simply an issue of choice but an issue of access to a social institution that safeguards their cultural integrity. The effects of choice on social segregation is considered further in Chapter 5.

Although race discrimination cases have been surprisingly rare, the well-known decision of the House of Lords in *Mandla v Dowell Lee*[91] still stands out. The primary importance of the judgment arises from its consideration of the definition of an ethnic group,[92] holding that Sikhs (and Jews) fall within the definition; but the case also illustrates how unlawful indirect discrimination can arise from the imposition of school rules that run contrary to the cultural values and traditions of particular minorities. The school was found to have acted unlawfully (in the form of indirect race discrimination) by refusing to allow a

---

[87] See, eg, CRE, *Code of Practice for the Elimination of Discrimination in Education* (London, CRE, 1989) and idem, *Learning for All. Standards for Racial Equality in Schools* (London, CRE, 2000).

[88] J Bourne, L Bridges and C Searle, *Outcast England: How Schools Exclude Black Children* (London, Institute of Race Relations, 1994); M Blair and J Bourne, *Making the Difference: Teaching and Learning Strategies in Successful Multiethnic Schools* (London, DfEE, 1998).

[89] C Parsons, *Education, Exclusion and Citizenship* (London, Routledge, 1999) 47.

[90] *R v Cleveland County Council ex parte the Commission for Racial Equality* [1994] ELR 44 (CA).

[91] [1983] 2 AC 548.

[92] See S Fredman, *Discrimination Law* (Oxford, Oxford University Press, 2002) 70–72.

Sikh boy to school wearing the turban which its rules prohibited with the aim of ensuring racial harmony and the creation of an egalitarian culture by eliminating marks of difference and diversity. Similar issues have arisen over the years concerning the dress worn to school by Muslim girls, notably the hijab (headscarf), shalwar kameeze (covering of head and shoulders) or jilbab (full length tunic with head covering).[93] The fact that Muslims have not been regarded as an ethnic group under the RRA 1976[94] has hindered the pursuit of complaints, although an alternative basis for a challenge might be that a school rule discriminates against pupils of, say, Pakistani origin where most of the pupils of such origin are Muslim.[95] In any event, matters will change when the relevant provisions in Part 2 of the Equality Act 2006 are brought into force. As things stand at present, the ECHR and Human Rights Act 1998 would, on the face of it, appear to render a ban on such forms of dress potentially unlawful, either as discrimination for the purposes of the right to education[96] or an interference with freedom of religion.[97] But the decision of the High Court, Court of Appeal and House of Lords in *R (Shabina Begum) v Head Teacher and Governors of Denbigh High School*[98] has shown the matter not to be straightforward. Although seemingly not fought on discrimination grounds, the case is included here to facilitate comparison with developments in other jurisdictions and with the decision in *Mandla v Dowell Lee* (above).

In *Begum*, a community school, Denbigh High, whose pupils came from 21 ethnic groups and 79 percent of whose pupils categorised themselves as Muslim, refused permission for a Muslim girl, Shabina Begum (SB), to wear the jilbab because it conflicted with the school's dress code. The dress code had been drawn up in consultation with local Muslim representatives and permitted the wearing of the shalwar kameeze. SB wore the shalwar kameeze to school from 2000 to 2002. Due to a change in her beliefs she subsequently considered it necessary to wear the jilbab. There were other schools in England that permitted the wearing of the jilbab, but Denbigh High believed that to permit it would cause divisions

---

[93] S Poulter, *Asian Traditions and English Law* (Stoke on Trent, Trentham and Runnymede Trust, 1990) 177; See N Harris, *Law and Education: Regulations, Consumerism and the Education System* (London, Sweet and Maxwell, 1993) 231; and note the decision by one school in Luton to ban the hijab, being the only school in England and Wales to do so: G Owen, 'Religious fury erupts over school headscarf ban', *The Times*, 28 Jan 2004.

[94] *J-H Walker v Hussain* [1996] IRLR 11 (EAT). Other groups held to have been excluded include Jehovah's Witnesses (*Lovell and Badge v Norwich City College of Further and Higher Education* (1999) 39 EOR Discrimination Case Law Digest 4); and Rastafarians (*Crown Suppliers (Property Services Agency) v Dawkins* [1993] ICR 517).

[95] S Fredman, *Discrimination Law* (Oxford, Oxford University Press, 2002) 72.

[96] ECHR Art 14 read together with Art 2 of Prot 1. Poulter argues that exclusion of a school pupil for wearing the headscarf would amount to violation of the right to education without religious discrimination: S Poulter, 'Muslim Headscarves in School: Contrasting Legal Approaches in England and France' (1997) 17 *Oxford Journal of Legal Studies* 43, at 69–70. Poulter highlights the case of the school in Altrincham which attempted to ban Muslim headscarves, although a compromise was reached between the parties before the matter came to court (also noted in N Harris, *Law and Education: Regulation, Consumerism and the Education System* (London, Sweet and Maxwell, 1993) 231).

[97] ECHR, Art 9.

[98] [2004] EWHC Admin 1389, [2004] ELR 374 (QBD); [2005] EWCA Civ 199, [2005] ELR 198 (CA); [2006] UKHL 15, [2006] 2 WLR 719.

between different pupils, and the school was also worried that some pupils would feel pressured to adopt it. SB did not attend school and claimed that she had, in effect, been excluded from school ('constructive exclusion') and was denied her right to education under Article 2 of Protocol 1 to the ECHR. No complaint of discrimination under Article 14 appears to have been included; certainly it is not referred to in the initial judgment. A further complaint was of breach of her right to freedom of religion, including the right to manifest her beliefs, under Article 9. At first instance Bennett J held that SB had not been excluded from school, but that, even if she had been, 'she was excluded for her refusal to abide by the school uniform policy rather than her religious beliefs as such'.[99] In his view there was no denial of her right to education because the school had been able and willing to accommodate her and that she had the option of transferring to another school where she could wear the jilbab.[100] Noting that SB had selected Denbigh High with knowledge of its school uniform policy, Bennett J said that the school's refusal to change its policy in order to accommodate her changed beliefs did not constitute a breach of Article 9.[101] Of course, she had specifically wanted a place at Denbigh High, but to the judge the important consideration was whether she had the freedom to express her religious beliefs elsewhere. In any event, Bennett J found legal justification for the school's policy in Article 9(2), which states:

> Freedom to manifest one's religion or beliefs shall be subject only to such limitations as are necessary in a democratic society in the interests of public safety, for the protection of public order, health, or morals, or for the protection of the rights and freedoms of others.

Bennett J was unsympathetic to the contention that the ban on the jilbab was justified on health or safety grounds (something which arguably could be invoked more easily in the case of the kirpan (dagger), a religious symbol worn by Sikhs: but see below). But Bennett J found that the restriction was necessary 'for the protection of the rights and freedom of others'. In a conclusion that contains echoes of the argument used to try to justify the turban ban in *Mandla* (above), Bennett J said that the school's policy promoted 'a positive ethos and a sense of communal identity' and that the shalwar kameeze was worn not only by the school's Muslims but also by Hindus and Sikhs, resulting in 'no outward distinction' between female pupils of these respective faiths.[102] Muslim girls were protected from pressure from inside or outside the school to wear the jilbab if they did not want to. Finally, he concluded that the school uniform policy had a legitimate aim and was proportionate.[103] The London Borough of Tower Hamlets, where over one third of the population is Muslim, was reported to have introduced a similar ban on the jilbab in all 16 of its secondary schools shortly

[99] Ibid (QBD), at para 74.
[100] Ibid, at para 103.
[101] Ibid, at para 73.
[102] Ibid, at para 90.
[103] Ibid, at para 91.

after this decision.[104] However, the Court of Appeal held that there had been a breach of the Human Rights Act in that, in instituting the ban, the school authorities had not given proper consideration to all necessary matters such as whether the claimant's right under Article 9 would be or had been interfered with (which, as discussed in Chapter 7, the court in fact considered to be the case) and whether there was justification for interference with the right to manifest one's religion or beliefs for the purposes of Article 9(2), noted above.[105] The Court of Appeal also rejected Bennett J's conclusion that the claimant had not been excluded from school by virtue of the ban.[106] The House of Lords subsequently upheld an appeal by the school.[107] As noted in Chapter 2, three of their Lordships found that there had not been an interference with the right under Article 9(1), but there was a unanimous view that in any event the interference was justified under Article 9(2). The House rejected the procedural approach adopted by the Court of Appeal[108]—Lord Hoffmann said that 'article 9 is concerned with substance, not procedure'[109]—and held that it was the outcome of the school's decision rather than the 'quality of the decision-making process that led to it' that was important.[110] All that mattered was whether in practice the claimant's rights under Article 9 had been violated. The court found the school's action to have been justified under Article 9(2), in that some restrictions on dress were necessary to protect the rights and freedoms of others. The school uniform policy had been carefully drawn up[111] in consultation with 'mainstream Muslim opinion',[112] and had a legitimate aim of striving for religious and ethnic harmony in a balanced way: in the words of Baroness Hale, it was 'a thoughtful and proportionate response to the complexities of the situation'.[113] As noted in Chapter 2, the House of Lords found no violation of Article 2 of Protocol 1, which the court also confirmed does not guarantee the right to attend any particular institution.[114] SB's lack of education was due to the fact that she had effectively withdrawn herself from the school whose policy was legitimate and had failed to secure a place at another school where she could wear the jilbab.

In a similar case to *Begum* in the Netherlands that came before the Equal Treatment Commission (a case not cited in *Begum*) under domestic equal

---

[104] A Taher, 'Stay-at-home protest as schools ban Islamic dress', *Sunday Times*, 7 Nov 2004.

[105] *R (SB) v Head Teacher and Governors of Denbigh High School* [2005] ELR 198; [2005] EWCA Civ 199.

[106] Ibid, paras 24 and 84, per Brooke LJ and Mummery LJ respectively.

[107] *R (Begum) v Head Teacher and Governors of Denbigh High School* [2006] UKHL 15; [2006] 2 WLR 719.

[108] Criticised in T Poole, 'Of Headscarves and Heresies: the *Denbigh High School* Case and Public Authority Decision-making under the Human Rights Act' [2005] *Public Law* 685.

[109] *R (Begum) v Head Teacher and Governors of Denbigh High School* [2006] UKHL 15; [2006] 2 WLR 719, per Lord Hoffmann at para 68.

[110] Ibid, per Lord Bingham of Cornhill at para 31.

[111] Lord Scott of Foscote, eg, said that '[t]he care taken by the school to try and ensure that the shalwar kameeze school uniform was acceptable for female Moslem pupils is impressive': ibid, para 83.

[112] Ibid, per Lord Bingham of Cornhill, at para 33.

[113] Ibid, at para 98.

[114] Ibid, per Lord Hoffmann at para 69, citing the House's judgment, the same day, in *Ali v Headteacher and Governors of Lord Grey School* [2006] UKHL 14; [2006] 2 WLR 690.

treatment legislation and which concerned the wearing of the chador (which covers the face apart from the eyes), the school's pedagogic argument for the ban, namely that it was in the interests of better communication and in preparing students for future employment where good communication was essential, was rejected by the Commission, which noted that several teachers had reported no difficulties in teaching pupils who wore the chador. The Commission found that the ban was not necessary and not objectively justified.[115] In an almost identical Dutch case more recently, however, the Commission reached the opposite conclusion, accepting the school board's arguments concerning communication difficulties.[116] There has also been an important decision of the Canadian Supreme Court in the case of *Multani*,[117] which also resonates with *Begum*. In this case the issue was religious freedom and a ban on the carrying of the kirpan in school by a Sikh pupil. There had been conflicting Canadian judgments on the justification for such a ban.[118] In *Multani* the Supreme Court held that the ban amounted to an infringement of freedom of religion that was not justified under the Canadian Charter.[119] Although the school's ban had been based on rational concerns for safety and a possible ripple effect from permitting a potential weapon to be carried (albeit worn covertly and sealed under outer garments), there was held to be a very low risk from the particular pupil or from anyone else seizing the kirpan to use for violent purposes. Moreover, in the leading judgment (concurred with by four of the other judges) the Court considered that the ban was not only disrespectful to Sikhs but did not take account of 'Canadian values' based on multiculturalism and religious tolerance.[120] Although deciding on the basis of religious freedom rather than discrimination per se,[121] the Court noted that if the ban sent out the message that some religious practices warranted more protection than others that would be wrong, since it would contradict the importance attached by Canadian society to freedom of religion and respect for minorities.

There has also been a case in the US arising in similar circumstances. There, in *Cheema*,[122] the Court of Appeals for the Ninth Circuit upheld an order of the district court imposing on a school district arrangements for accommodating the wearing of the kirpan by pupils that were similar to those in place in the Canadian case. The litigants, Sikh pupils, successfully asserted that the district's

---

[115] Cgb, 6 Sept 2000, decision 2000–63, Rechtspraak onderwijsrecht 2000–2002, 49, cited in B-P Vermeulen and C-W Noorlander, 'The Legal Rights of Students in the Netherlands' in C Russo and J De Groof, *The Legal Rights of Students* (Lanham, Mld, Scarecrow, forthcoming), 000–000 at 000.

[116] Cgb. 20 Mar 2003, decision 2003–40, [2003] Administratierechtelijke Beslissingen 233, cited in ibid.

[117] *Multani v Commission scolaire Marguerite-Bourgeoys and Attorned General of Quebec and World Sikh Organisation of Canada and others* [2003] 2006 SCC 6 (Sup C of Canada).

[118] See AN Khan, 'Canadian Education Authorities' Duty to Make Reasonable Accommodation for Religious Belief' (1997) 9 *Education & the Law* 307 at n 22.

[119] Arts 1 and 2 of the Canadian Charter of Rights and Freedoms.

[120] Ibid, at para 71.

[121] Charron J, giving the leading judgment, stated (at para 80) that in view of the Court's finding that religious freedom had been violated it was not necessary consider the claim of breach of the equality provision (Art 15 of the Canadian Charter).

[122] *Gurdev Kaur Cheema v Thompson and others*, 67 F3d 883 (1995).

prohibition on the wearing of the kirpan in furtherance of its weapons policy violated their right of free exercise of religion contrary to the Religious Freedom Resotration Act of 1993.[123] The district court's order had included various safety measures such as that the kirpan would have a dull blade, be sewn tightly to its sheath and hidden under clothing; and an inspection of it could be made by an authorised official. The Act permits interference with religious freedom where it is in pursuance of a 'compelling governmental interest' and is 'the least restrictive means of furthering that compelling governmental interest'.[124] While there was a compelling interest in ensuring that schools were safe places, the Court of Appeals considered that the school district had not established that a total ban would be the 'least restrictive means' of maintaining safety.

Of course, while the freedom to express one's religion through forms of dress was central to the legal action in *Begum* and these other cases, the key issue before the House of Lords in *Mandla* was one of race discrimination—indeed, neither the House of Lords nor the Court of Appeal[125] in that case referred to the ECHR. If *Mandla* had been brought post-October 2000, when the HRA 1998 came fully into force, similar Article 9 arguments may well have been raised. However, if the matter was before a court today, it would have to be judged in the light of the ECtHR's decision in *Leyla Şahin v Turkey*.[126] In that case, as in *Mandla*, the policy the legality of which was challenged was that of banning religious dress in order to promote the notion of equality and neutrality in relation to state education—in that case, a university education. The applicant, a Muslim, was a student at Istanbul University, at which she enrolled in August 1997. A circular that was issued by the Vice-Chancellor of the university in 1998 banned students with beards or those wearing the Islamic headscarf from lectures, tutorials or courses. The applicant, who had worn a headscarf at the university since joining it, complained that the ban infringed her rights under the ECHR, Articles 8, 9 and 14 and Article 2 of Protocol 1. In its judgment, the Court reviewed the constitutional framework for the secularism in modern Turkey. It found that there was an interference with the applicant's right to manifest her religion for the purposes of Article 9.[127] The Court found, however, that there was a basis under Turkish law for interference with the right and that the applicant would have been aware of the legal threat to the wearing of the headscarf.[128] It acknowledged that the Turkish courts had accepted that if a right to wear religious symbols in universities were recognised it would be inconsistent with the principle of neutrality in state education and could generate conflict between students with differing religious convictions or beliefs. The court found that the ban had pursued the legitimate aim of protecting the rights and freedoms of others,[129] and could be justified under Article 9(2) of the

---

[123] 42 USCA § 2000bb ff.

[124] Ibid, s 3(b).

[125] *Mandla (Sewa Singh) v Dowell Lee* [1983] QB 1 (CA).

[126] App no 44774/98, Judgment (Grand Chamber), 10 Nov 2005 (Chamber judgment, 29 June 2004). See also Chap 2 above, especially pp 75, 76.

[127] Grand Chamber judgment, para 98.

[128] Ibid, para 81.

[129] Ibid, at para 99.

Convention (above), particularly where there was a risk of 'fundamentalist religious movements . . . exerting pressure on students who did not practise their religion or who belonged to another religion'.[130] The Court also noted that the state's 'margin of appreciation' was particularly relevant where the relationship between the state and religion was concerned.[131] The aim of preserving pluralism and secularism in the university was felt to be consistent with the protection of democracy in Turkey. The Grand Chamber agreed with the Chamber that the ban was justified, in that it met the test of being 'necessary in a democratic society' and was proportionate to the legitimate aims pursued.[132] The applicant also argued that there was a violation of Article 14 (discrimination) read together with Article 9, on the basis that the ban discriminated against believers, and of her right to education under Article 2 of Protocol 1. But the Court found that no separate question arose under those provisions and it dismissed her claim. When the alleged breach of Article 2 of Protocol 1 was referred to the Grand Chamber it was held that the right to education was not absolute and might be subject to state-imposed limitations provided they did not destroy its very essence and deprive it of its effectiveness, and provided they were proportionate and did not conflict with other Convention rights, as was considered to be the case here.[133]

The fact that the national context to this ban was considered important means that one cannot be absolutely certain that a similar view would be taken of the equivalent ban on the wearing of religious symbols or dress in France. There, after two decades of debate and controversy over the wearing of the hijab (and especially after the ruling of the Conseil d'Etat in 1989 that this practice was protected by the right to freedom of expression and did not, of itself violate the neutrality of the public (and thus secular) school[134]), the National Assembly passed an Act on 10 February 2004[135] prohibiting the wearing in primary and secondary schools of 'signs or dress by which pupils overtly manifest a religious affiliation'. This resulted by early 2005 in the exclusion of 48 school students for violation of the new law.[136] However, it seems likely that the state's adherence to the principle of secularity in France would result in a similar outcome were a challenge under the ECHR to be brought. So far as the UK is concerned, clearly there are similarities between the issues in *Şahin* and *Begum* and the approach taken by the respective courts in these cases. Of course, in *Begum*, the restriction was not a total ban on religious dress. Moreover, it was a local one. Just as the various courts in *Begum* did not regard the fact that other schools permitted the wearing of the jilbab to cast doubt on the justifiability of the rule at Denbigh

---

[130] Ibid, at para 111.
[131] Ibid, at para 109.
[132] Ibid, paras 115–122 and Chamber judgment (2004), n 126 above, para 114.
[133] Grand Chamber judgment, n 126 above, paras 154–162.
[134] See, especially, S Poulter, 'Muslim Headscarves in School: Contrasting Legal Approaches in England and France' (1997) 17 *Oxford Journal of Legal Studies* 43. See also CL Glenn, 'Hijab and the Limits of Tolerance' in J De Groof and J Fiers (eds), *The Legal Status of Minorities in Education* (Leuven, Uitgeverj Acc, 1996) 127. A similar approach was taken by courts in Germany and Switzerland: M Verlot, 'The Hijab in European Schools. A Case for the Court of a Challenge for the School' in ibid, at 146.
[135] Law no 2004–228, 15 Mar 2004, [2004] JORF 5190.
[136] 'Muslims expelled', *The Times*, 21 Jan 2005, 37.

High, so the Court in Şahin did not consider that the fact that another Turkish university, Bursa, permitted the wearing of the headscarf meant that the ban at Istanbul was unjustified.[137]

One of the arguments raised by the applicant in Şahin was that the ban on religious dress 'obliged students to choose between religion and education'.[138] Certainly, that may well be the implication of this ruling for universities in Turkey (despite the amnesty declared recently by the Turkish Parliament for all students excluded from university since 2000, including women barred for wearing headscarves, although the existing rules on dress are not yet outlawed[139]) and of the *Begum* decision in respect of particular schools in England, at least in relation to some forms of religious expression. They reinforce the conclusion that in a modern, secular state the expression of religious freedom is subject to limitations where access to social institutions such as schools and universities is concerned. An important factor is that these are essentially artificial communities governed by their own internal rules, culture and traditions. The university has, for example, been described as a 'society of structured social spaces'[140] and the description is also apt in relation to schools. The principle of egalitarianism is often considered fundamental to such social organisation. Moreover, there is an assumption that the widest social benefits and least disadvantages, both for members and wider society, derive from a harmonious community, and that where there is religious diversity this is more likely if individual religious expression is subjugated to wider social goals. Yet the argument of the applicant in Şahin, that if the state wanted to promote these aims and reduce tensions between groups it was best not to try to mask pluralism but to promote greater respect between groups, has some cogency. Moreover, empirical research suggests that higher education institutions are places which foster, among students, a sense of 'mutuality' and 'sociality', whereby membership of this community can serve to engender empathy and cohesiveness through the experience of interacting with people from often very different backgrounds.[141] Ahier *et al* argue that, with the Government's policy of expansion of access to higher education, this contribution of university life to social citizenship (a concept discussed in Chapter 2) should be recognised and preserved. In this context, a question that arises from the above discussion of the rights of religious minorities is how those cohesive forces within the university membership can be best served by accommodation of religious difference and freedom of religious expression. A related question is how far the 'code of civility' between students that Ahier *et al* have identified[142] is both able to withstand the divisive forces that

[137] Above n 126 (Grand Chamber), para 112.
[138] Ibid, para 116.
[139] The amnesty resulted in the resignation of the Minister of Culture, but the Minister of Education is reported to be planning to introduce higher education reforms that would reverse the ban on headscarves, a previous attempt in 2004 having failed: D Jones, 'Amnesty for Turks expelled for wearing religious headscarves', *Times Higher Education Supplement*, 4 Mar 2005, 13.
[140] J Ahier, J Beck and R Moore, *Graduate Citizens? Issues of Citizenship and Higher Education* (London, Routledge Falmer, 2003) 159.
[141] Ibid.
[142] Ibid.

are said to flow from certain forms of religious expression and to contribute to tolerance, respect and cohesion. Despite evidence of tension between, or victimisation of, religious groups on some campuses in the UK,[143] the diversity of student bodies is generally unproblematic, and indeed mostly accepted as a positive feature of university life. Evidence of racial or religious tensions within schools has surfaced of late, but its extent is as yet unquantified.

Discrimination on religious grounds in the UK has been proscribed in particular spheres of education, but not yet in relation to schools, although this will change when the relevant provisions of the Equality Act 2006 come into force (see below). Moreover, under the Education and Inspections Bill, the reasonableness (and therefore legality) of any disciplinary penalty imposed by a school on a pupil will in part be judged with reference to whether any religious requirements affecting the particular pupil have been taken into account.[144] Further and higher education are currently covered by equality duties, as a result of the implementation of the EC Council Directive on equal treatment irrespective of racial or ethnic origin[145] and a separate EC Council Directive (the 'framework directive') establishing a general framework for equal treatment in employment and occupation in relation to 'religion or belief, disability, age or sexual orientation',[146] via the Employment Equality (Religion and Belief) Regulations 2003.[147] The regulations on religion and belief, in common with corresponding provisions on sexual orientation which are also in furtherance of the framework directive,[148] impose non-discrimination duties broadly equivalent to those contained in the RRA 1976 not only on employers but also on providers of vocational training[149] and on institutions of further or higher education in relation to students or those who apply for places as students.[150] Harassment is included as unlawful conduct.[151] The regulations refer specifically

---

[143] See, eg, P Weller, A Feldman and K Purdam, *Religious Discrimination in England and Wales* Home Office Research Study 220 (London, Home Office, 2001) 26, which notes that two thirds of Jewish and Sikh organisations and 5 out of 7 black-led churches which were surveyed complained about unfair treatment from the behaviour of other students; and BBC, 'Jewish students suffer "racist abuse"', BBC News Report, 20 Nov 2002, available at www.bbc.co.uk/news.

[144] Education and Inspections Bill 2006, cll 77, 78(6).

[145] Council Directive 2000/43/EC of 29 June, 2000 implementing the principle of equal treatment between persons irrespective of racial or ethnic origin [2000] OJ L/180/22.

[146] Council Directive 2000/78/EC of 27 Nov 2000 ([2000] OJ L/303/16).

[147] SI 2003/1660, as amended by the Employment Equality (Religion or Belief) (Amendment) Regulations 2004 (SI 2004/437). See T Linden, 'The New Employment Equality (Religion and Belief) Regulations 2003' (2003) 4 *Education Law* 217.

[148] The Employment Equality (Sexual Orientation) Regulations 2003 (SI 2003/1661), reg 20. See also the provisions governing age discrimination below.

[149] SI 2003/1660 above n 147, reg 17. Schools and further and higher education establishments are excluded from the scope of this reg.

[150] Ibid, reg 20, which also covers access to training provided by further or higher education institutions, but not in respect of admission to the institutions on a list (in ibid, Sched 1B) as being specifically excepted from the scope of reg 20 by the amendment regulations (SI 2004/437), above n 147. Both regs 17 and 20 also proscribe harassment and both exempt from the non-discrimination duty training for employment covered by the genuine occupational qualification ground on which an employer could refuse employment (see ibid, reg 7). Reg 20 applies to university halls as well.

[151] Harassment is defined for this purpose as 'unwanted conduct which has the purpose or effect of: (a) violating [the victim's] dignity; or (b) creating an intimidating, hostile, degrading, humiliating or offensive environment for [the victim]': SI 2003/1661, reg 5.

to discrimination in respect of a person's 'religion or belief', which is defined simply as 'any religion, religious belief, or similar philosophical belief'.[152] This means that Muslims, Roman Catholics and other religious groups previously excluded from protection would now be covered, although Lord Denning MR's statement in *Mandla* in the Court of Appeal that '[y]ou can discriminate for or against the hippies as much as you like, without being in breach of the law'[153] would probably still be accurate!

There is an exception to the non-discrimination duty under the regulations in respect of access to further or higher education. The exception relates to training that would help fit a person for employment which, by virtue of regulation 7, the employer would be entitled to refuse to offer an applicant, on the basis that being of a particular religion etc is, inter alia, a 'genuine and determining occupational qualification', and it would be proportionate for the employer to apply such a requirement. In relation to the parallel provisions on discrimination on the grounds of sexual orientation, covered by separate regulations,[154] it has been held that the exception is to be narrowly construed: 'for training to come within the exception, it must be training that would only help fit a person for a relevant employment . . . training directed specifically and solely towards an employment to which an occupational requirement can lawfully be applied under reg 7'.[155]

The fact that (apart from via the Human Rights Act 1998) there has been no specific protection under domestic legislation against religious discrimination in schools has flown in the face of the evidence from the Home Office study that informed the above legislation.[156] The research found it to be 'the case for most faith groups that aspects of the education system were second only to the media, and roughly on a par with employment, in the extent to which unfair treatment was indicated by organisations from within [their] tradition'.[157] Moreover, the survey on which the report was based found that unfair treatment was more prevalent in schools than in higher education,[158] which was covered by legislation. The principal problems in schools concerned teacher attitudes, aspects of the secular curriculum,[159] collective worship, dress and religious education (which, for example, failed to recognise or include certain minority

---

[152] SI 2003/1660, above n 147, reg 2(1). Linden says that the definition of 'religion or belief' has been framed to ensure consistency with Art 9 of the ECHR: T Linden, "The New Employment Equality (Religion and Belief) Regulations 2003' (2003) 4 *Education Law* 217, at 220. See further the discussion of the Equality Act 2006 below

[153] *Mandla (Sewa Singh) v Dowell Lee and Another* [1983] QB 1 (CA), at 8–9.

[154] The Employment Equality (Sexual Orientation) Regulations 2003 (SI 2003/1661), reg 20(3).

[155] *R (Amicus) v Secretary of State for Trade and Industry and Others* [2004] EWHC Admin 860, per Richards J at paras 132–134. Sexual orientation, while not officially listed as a prohibited ground of discrimination in Art 14, has been held by the ECtHR and the House of Lords to be covered by this Art (see in particular *Salgueiro Da Silva Mouta v Portugal* (2001) 31 EHRR 47, at para 28, *Fretté v France* (2003) 2 FLR 9, para 32, and *Ghaidan v Godin-Mendoza* [2004] UKHL 30, per Lord Nicholls, at para 9 and Baroness Hale at 136), which would be read (in connection with access to education) together with Art 2 of Prot 1.

[156] P Weller, A Feldman and K Purdam, *Religious Discrimination in England and Wales*, Home Office Research Study 220 (London, Home Office, 2001).

[157] Ibid, 23.

[158] Ibid, 24.

[159] This issue is explored in Chap 7.

faiths present in the school, such as Zoroastrianism). Although higher education had fewer problems, two thirds of Muslim organisations reported 'unfair treatment from the behaviour of staff and students in higher education, and from the policies and practices of universities/colleges'.[160]

The Equality Act 2006 remedies the anomaly concerning schools and religious discrimination and will impose equivalent non-discrimination duties to those concerning sex and race.[161] Thus, when the relevant provisions are in force, it would be unlawful for the responsible body (either the LEA, school governing body or proprietor of a school) to discriminate on the grounds of religion or belief (including the absence of religion or belief) in the context of admission; access to any benefit, facility or service; or exclusion or subjection to any other detriment.[162] However, the Act excludes from the relevant provisions anything done in connection with 'the content of the curriculum' and 'acts of worship or religious observance organised by or on behalf of an educational establishment'.[163] As, leaving aside school admissions and school uniform, these may be the areas that are most likely to give rise to complaints of religious discrimination, these exceptions do weaken the protection afforded by the Act. There is also a general exception to the above non-discrimination duties (but not in relation to exclusion or the subjection of the pupil to any other detriment) in the case of maintained schools that have a religious character and independent schools whose entry in the register of such schools indicates that they have a 'religious ethos'.[164] This would, for example, prevent any challenge to a lower priority being afforded in the admissions process to persons not of the relevant faith. It might also have implications for cases such as *Begum*, if they concern denominational schools, although, given the exceptions, not if the issue falls more properly under exclusion than admission. In the Netherlands, where such cases are already dealt with under the general equality legislation,[165] the exclusion of a Muslim girl from a public-sector school (all such schools are non-denominational) for wearing the hijab would be unlawful under that legislation (and also the principle of state neutrality), but would be permissible if undertaken by a denominational school (such schools are private, but generally state-funded) if based on a coherent and consistent policy. That resonates with the approach taken by the House of Lords in *Mandla* above. The Equal Treatment Commission in the Netherlands, which examines complaints on behalf of individuals or organisations, has ruled that it is lawful for a Roman Catholic School to bar pupils who wear the hijab in view of the school's strict policy in forbidding, on religious grounds, clothing that has non-Christian connotations.[166]

The Equality Act 2006 also provides that an organisation the purpose of which is the teaching of the practice or principles of a religion or a belief can

---

[160] P Weller *et al*, n 156 above, at 26.

[161] Equality Act 2006, s 49.

[162] Ibid, ss 44, 45 and 49. 'Religion' is defined, somewhat tautologically, as 'any religion'; and 'belief' as 'any religious or philosophical belief': s 44(a) and (b).

[163] Ibid, s 50(2).

[164] Ibid, s 50(1).

[165] The *Algemene Wet Gelijke Behandeling* (General Equal Treatment Act).

[166] Cgb, 5 Aug 2003, decision 2003–112, [2003] Administratierechtelijke Beslissingen 375.

impose restrictions on the provision of services or participation in activities undertaken by the organisation, if imposed for a reason concerned with the purposes of the organisation or 'in order to avoid offence on the grounds of religion or belief to members of the organisation'.[167] This does not apply to the provision of facilities or services to students of the institution.[168] It seems to permit religious discrimination in the context of religious teaching outside schools, for example in a place of religion.[169]

Disability

Another significant group at risk of discrimination is disabled children and young people. Unlike race and sex, however, disability is not referred to specifically in Article 14 of the ECHR, which provides for the enjoyment of Convention rights (including the right to education) to be without discrimination on various grounds. However, while these grounds are illustrative rather than exhaustive,[170] there is little doubt that disability is covered.[171] Furthermore, in the equivalent non-discrimination provision in the UNCRC, disability is specifically included[172] and the UNCRC also requires states parties to provide assistance to the disabled child and his or her family, 'designed to ensure that the disabled child has effective access to and receives education, training [and various other prescribed facilities and opportunities]'.[173] In any event, rights of access to education by disabled children and adults are protected by anti-discrimination legislation in England and Wales.

The Special Educational Needs and Disability Act (SENDA) 2001 extended the Disability Discrimination Act (DDA) 1995 to discrimination in relation to access to school education and to further and higher education. It has also amended the law of special educational needs under the Education Act 1996 to strengthen the obligations of LEAs and schools to include pupils with learning difficulties in mainstream education.[174] Although disability and special educational needs are distinct concepts (indeed, under the Education and Inspections Bill 2006, for example, they are separate factors that will have to be taken into account in determining whether any disciplinary penalty imposed by a school on a pupil is reasonable[175]), they are related. For example, a child may have special educational needs, and thus be owed a range of specific obligations, if he or she has a learning difficulty which calls for special educational provision to be made for him/her; a

---

[167] Equality Act 2006, s 59(1), (2).

[168] Ibid, s 59(3).

[169] See ibid. Charities are also exempt from the non-discrimination duty in providing benefits for members of a particular religion or belief: ibid, s 58. That would appear to apply to provision by education charities, but presumably it would not be the intention that schooling provided by schools which were charities would be exempt?

[170] *Rasmussen v Denmark* (1985) 7 EHRR 371, para 34.

[171] *Malone v UK* [1996] EHRLR 440.

[172] UNCRC, Art 2.

[173] Ibid, Art 23.

[174] See Chap 6.

[175] Education and Inspections Bill, cl 78(6).

learning difficulty will take the form of, inter alia, 'a disability which either prevents or hinders him from making use of the educational facilities of a kind generally provided for children of his age in schools within the area of the [LEA]'.[176] Although a child's learning difficulty may also arise from simply having a 'significantly greater difficulty in learning then the majority of children of his age',[177] the fact that the definition of special educational needs is dependent upon having a need for special educational provision means that disability and other causes of special educational need give rise to a form of 'otherness', which could be exclusionary. Nonetheless, the law has incorporated a principle of integration or inclusion (dating back to the Education Act 1981) which, as noted above, has been given a significant advance by the 2001 Act.[178] The Government has argued that '[t]here are strong educational, as well as social and moral, grounds for educating children with SEN, or with disabilities, with their peers'.[179] (In relation to the provision and funding of post-16 education, there is a parallel definition of learning difficulty.[180])

The primary aim of the law of special educational needs is, essentially, to ensure that appropriate educational provision is made for those with learning difficulties, preferably in a mainstream setting. In the case of the DDA 1995, as amended, the aim is a broader one of widening social participation by reducing barriers to inclusion in the institutional setting in which education is provided. The former is directly concerned with matching appropriate educational provision to educational needs of individuals identifiable as having learning difficulties, whereas the latter's concern for access to institutions and facilities is about helping to create an inclusive society for the benefit of all and ensuring greater equality of opportunity in a wide range of social contexts, including the workplace and education, rather than (other than indirectly) about realising the individual's learning potential. Not surprisingly, therefore, there are many differences between the two statutory schemes in respect of the definitions by which those individuals needing the relevant types of support and/or protection are identified and resources expected to be allocated.[181] A person need not have a disability to have special educational needs, as the concept of learning difficulty is disjunctively defined as arising not only from a disability but alternatively, as noted above, from 'a significantly greater difficulty in learning than the majority of children of his age'.[182]

It is estimated that approximately 3 per cent of children have some form of disability,[183] whereas around 18 per cent of children are believed to have special

---

[176] EA 1996, s 312(1) and (2)(b).

[177] EA 1996, s 312(2)(a).

[178] See Education Act 1996, ss 316 and 316A, substituted/introduced by SENDA 2001, s 1. See Chap 6.

[179] Department for Education and Employment, *Meeting Special Educational Needs: A Programme of Action* (London, TSO, 1998), ch 3, para 1. See also Welsh Assembly, *Shaping the Future for Special Education—An Action Programme for Wales* (London, TSO, 1999), ch 3, para 1.

[180] Learning and Skills Act 2000, s 13(5).

[181] A Blair and A Lawson, 'Disability Discrimination Reforms In Education—Could Do Better?' (2003) 15 *Child & Family Law Quarterly* 41.

[182] Education Act 1996, s 312(2)(a). Para (b) of that subs refers to disability. See further Chap 6.

[183] P Daniel and J Ivatts, *Children and Social Policy* (Basingstoke, Macmillan, 1998) 40–1.

educational needs as defined.[184] They represent different constituencies although a significant number of children will belong to both. In the recent case of *R (H) v Chair of the Special Educational Needs Tribunal and R School*[185] a 16-year-old boy's behavioural problems were the subject of a statement of special educational needs. He had Asperger's Syndrome with features of dyspraxia and Attention Hyperactivity Deficit Syndrome (ADHD), but the Special Educational Needs and Disability Tribunal (SENDIST) hearing his complaint of disability discrimination decided as a preliminary issue that he did not have a substantial impairment for the purposes of the DDA 1995. Leveson J considered its conclusions to be flawed and ordered the matter to be reheard by a fresh tribunal. The point here, as the same judge noted in *R (A) v Governing Body of HM Primary School*,[186] is that it is not the degree of a person's physical or mental impairment that defines his or her disability for the purposes of the DDA 1995, but rather its impact on the person's day-to-day activities. The Act applies not only to physical disability but also to 'mental impairment'. In either case there must be a 'substantial and long term adverse effect' (long term being 12 months or more,[187] including recurrences[188]) on the disabled person's ability to carry out 'day-to-day activities',[189] which could include 'memory or ability to concentrate, learn or understand' and 'perception of the risk of physical danger'.[190] The basic approach in determining whether the impairment has a 'substantial' effect is whether the effect is more than 'minor' or 'trivial' and causes a limitation that goes beyond the 'normal differences in ability that may exist among people'.[191] In determining that matter it is necessary to 'concentrate on what the applicant cannot do or can only do with difficulty rather than on things they can do . . . [thereby avoiding] the danger of . . . concluding that as there as so many things that an applicant can do the adverse effect cannot be substantial'.[192] In one case the SENDIST was held to have failed to do this in concluding that a child with features of Asperger's Syndrome, ADHD and dyspraxia did not suffer from a substantial impairment because, inter alia, the evidence of his academic achievements suggested that his condition had

---

[184] DfES, *First Release. Special Educational Needs in England*, Jan 2005 SFR 24/2005 (London, DfES, 2005).

[185] [2004] EWHC Admin 981; [2005] ELR 67.

[186] [2004] EWHC Admin 2165, at para 22.

[187] In particular, it must have lasted for 12 months, or be likely to last for at least 12 months or for the rest of the person's life: DDA 1995, Sched 1 para 2(1).

[188] Disability Rights Commission (DRC), *Disability Discrimination Act 1995: Guidance on Matters to be Taken into Account in Determining Questions Relating to the Definition of Disability* (London, DRC, 2006), available at www.drc.gov.uk, paras C4 and C5. This is revised guidance which came into force on 1 May 2006. It is not legally binding, but under the DDA 1995, s 3(3), a court or tribunal has a duty to take it into account.

[189] DDA 1995, s 1(1) and Sched 1(1).

[190] DDA 1995, Sched 1 para 4. Depression has also been acknowledged as potentially disabling: see *Prison Service v Beart* [2003] ICR 1068. Excluded from the definition are conditions such as voyeurism, a tendency to steal and exhibitionism: Disability Discrimination (Meaning of Disability) Regulations 1996 (SI 1996/1455), reg 4(1).

[191] DRC, *Disability Discrimination Act Guidance on Matters to be Taken into Account in Determining Questions Relating to the Definition of Disability*, available only at www.drc.org.uk/docs/definition_guidance_final.doc, above n 187, paras B1, D16–D20.

[192] *Leonard v Southern Derbyshire Chamber of Commerce* [2001] IRLR 19 (EAT), per Nelson J at para 27. See also *Goodwin v Patent Office* [1999] ICR 302.

no substantial adverse effect.[193] In another case where the tribunal had wrongly refused a complaint on behalf of a child, aged 8, who had been denied automatic progression into year 3 and complained that she was discriminated against on account of her problems with mobility, speech and vision, the court confirmed that in the case of someone suffering from several types of impairment, the question to be decided is whether the impairments individually or collectively affected their activities in a more than minor or trivial way.[194]

In 2004 the Joint Committee on the Draft Discrimination Bill recommended that the list of day-to-day activities should be amended to include the ability to care for oneself, the ability to communicate and interact with others and the capacity to maintain a 'perception of reality'; the Committee felt in particular that greater clarity was needed as regards the coverage of people with mental illness.[195] In view of evidence that depression may not be sustained over a 12-month period but can lead to discrimination, the Committee also recommended a reduced definition of 'long term' in the case of any person with the condition.[196] These changes have not been made. However, the Disability Discrimination Act 2005 has extended the definition of disability in the 1995 Act to include among those deemed to be disabled persons those suffering from cancer, HIV infection or multiple sclerosis.[197] It has also removed the condition that mental illness could not be recognised as 'mental impairment' (and thus potentially a disability) unless the illness was clinically well recognised.[198]

The extension of the definition of disability to include those infected with HIV is of particular importance to education, despite the fact that relatively few children have the infection. HIV-seropositivity is also considered to fall within 'other status' for the purposes of Article 14 ECHR (above).[199] In the UK, as at the end of September 2005, there were 3,383 children and young people aged 19 or under who had been diagnosed with the infection, including around 1,800 aged 5–14.[200] In South Africa, where one in eight of the population is HIV-positive and increasing numbers of school pupils are infected, there is specific legislation preventing testing in relation to admission to a school and the child's withdrawal from school in normal circumstances.[201] The DfES guidance in England is clear that HIV status should be no barrier to mainstream education:

---

[193] *R (Mr and Mrs H) v Chair of the Special Educational Needs Tribunal and R School* [2005] ELR 67 (QBD).

[194] *M v SW School and the Special Educational Needs and Disability Tribunal* [2005] ELR 285 (QBD).

[195] Joint Committee on the Disability Discrimination Bill, *First Report* (London, TSO, 2004), paras 86–88.

[196] Namely, that a person suffering separate periods of depression totalling six months over a two-year period would fulfil that condition: ibid, para 99.

[197] DDA 1995, Sched 1 para 6A, inserted by the Disability Discrimination Act 2005, s 18(3), which also empowers regulations to prescribe particular forms of cancer as outside the definition.

[198] DDA 2005, s 18(2), repealing DDA 1995, Sched 1, para 1(1).

[199] J Simor (ed), *Human Rights Practice* (London, Sweet & Maxwell, 2000), para 14–013.

[200] Health Protection Agency, *AIDS/HIV Quarterly Surveillance Tables. Cumulative UK Data to End September 2005* No.68 05/3 (London, Health Protection Agency, 2005), table 8.

[201] See C Van Wyk, 'HIV/AIDS Policy in South African Schools' in N Harris and P Meredith (eds), *Children, Education and Health. International Perspectives on Law and Policy* (Aldershot, Ashgate, 2005), 183.

Children with HIV or AIDS should be allowed to attend school. HIV infection or AIDS should *not* be a factor taken into account by local education authorities, governing bodies and head teachers in discharging either their various duties concerning school admissions, transfers and attendance, or their powers of exclusion from school.[202]

As noted below, the 1995 Act explicitly proscribes discrimination in the context of most of these situations and covers the others implicitly.

Evidence of the prevalence of disability among university students is available from Higher Education Statistical Agency (HESA) figures. Accordingly to the latest complete statistics, of the 818,445 UK domiciled higher education undergraduate and postgraduate students in UK universities in 2001–02, 38,020 were known to have a disability. That constitutes 4.65 per cent of all students (suggesting that the proportion of children with disabilities, above, is probably a significant under-estimation). Of those disabled students, 1,605 (4.22 per cent) had a disability exclusively related to mental health problems (ie, ignoring those with multiple disabilities).[203] It has also been estimated that around 10 per cent of school pupils have mental health difficulties.[204] Mental health problems are often difficult to detect, and many people with them are often unwilling as a consequence of the stigma attached to mental illness and disability to identify themselves, or be identified, as having them.[205] It is likely, therefore, that the official figures do not provide a complete picture and that they under-represent the prevalence of disability among students. Indeed, it seems that among school pupils only 50 per cent of those with mental health problems are identified by schools.[206]

The DDA 1995 proscribes discrimination by the responsible body[207] that takes the form of unjustified, unfavourable treatment, as compared with the treatment of others, for a reason relating to the person's disability, in admission arrangements or terms of admission to the institution, the provision of education or associated services (schools) or student services (further/higher education) to them, or the student's or pupil's permanent or temporary exclusion.[208] The comparative dimension, as in the 1995 Act's reference to treating someone 'less favourably' than 'others to whom that reason does not or would not apply',[209] is

---

[202] Available at www.teachernet.gov.uk/management/atoz/h/hivandaids/ (original emphasis).

[203] Available at www.hesa.ac.uk/holisdocs/pubinfo/student/disab0102.htm.

[204] Department of Health figures cited in Ofsted, *Annual Report of Her Majesty's Chief Inspector of Schools 2004/05* (London, TSO, 2005), para 257.

[205] J Swain *et al*, *Controversial Issues in a Disabling Society* (Buckingham, Open University Press, 2003) 15.

[206] Ofsted, above n 204, para 257.

[207] Generally the institution's governing body, but in the case of a maintained school it is the LEA or governing body (depending upon which has responsibility for the function that is/was exercised); in the case of a pupil referral unit or maintained nursery school it is the LEA; and in the case of an independent school, it is the proprietor: DDA 1995, as amended, Scheds 4A and 4B.

[208] DDA 1995, ss 28A, 28B, 28R and 28S Regulations may prescribe services which are or are not education or associated services: s 28A(3).

[209] DDA 1995, s 28B(1). See also in the context of admission to school, the reference to placing a disabled person 'at a substantial disadvantage in comparison with persons who are not disabled' in ibid, s 28C(1)(a).

important. It necessitates the identification of an appropriate comparator. In one case,[210] a disabled pupil's education was at home, as a form of alternative provision under section 19 of the Education Act 1996,[211] rather than in school. The education was provided by the visiting teacher service and amounted to less than two hours a week at first, later rising to five hours. It was argued that the arrangements were based on disability discrimination.[212] It was held that comparison should be made not with others being educated by the visiting teacher service but others receiving mainstream education. Furthermore, the judge noted that the question is not whether a person receives treatment that is different from that given to others, but whether it is less favourable; '[e]ducation at home is different from education at school, but it is not necessarily less favourable to the pupil'.[213]

It is clear that the comparator in education cases of this kind is to be determined in the same way as for employment cases, where there is settled case law holding that, for example, where a person is dismissed for not being able to do a job, he or she should be compared with an employee who is able to perform the job.[214] Thus in one case it was held that a disruptive autistic pupil excluded from school for a fixed term should be compared with a non-disabled pupil, but with one who is properly rather than badly behaved.[215] The court was influenced by the example given in the schools code of practice of a pupil with Tourette's syndrome who is banned from school trips because of his/her abusive language. The code states that the comparator should be someone who does not use abusive language.[216] The moral justification for such a position is, of course, that a person's behaviour or inability that is the result of their disability is not something reasonably, or at all, within their control. Indeed, the forms of discrimination that are legally proscribed, including those on race and sex, all involve personal characteristics of that kind.[217] If the law did not operate in that way, it would undermine the fundamental purpose of the law in ensuring that people are not disadvantaged by reason of their disability. It would mean that a person's disability was in effect ignored in deciding how they should be treated. Although schools and LEAs might argue that the law might in some cases make it difficult to avoid the obligation of including children and young people with disabilities that are difficult for these bodies to manage, the Act does permit less favourable treatment that is the result of a permitted form of selection or, more importantly, where 'the reason for it is both material to the circumstances of the

---

[213] *VK v Norfolk County Council and the Special Educational Needs and Disability Tribunal* [2005] ELR 342 (QBD).

[211] Alternative provision for those unable to attend school: see above.

[212] Under DDA 1995, s 28B.

[213] *VK v Norfolk County Council*, above n 210, per Stanley Burnton J at para 47.

[214] *Clark v TDG (Trading as Novocold Limited)* [1999] ICR 951.

[215] *M School v CC, PC and Another* [2004] ELR 89.

[216] DRC, *Disability Discrimination Act 1995 Part 4, Code of Practice for Schools* (London, TSO, 2002) 40, Example 5.10C.

[217] But note that in terms of the comparison to be made in disability cases, the 'DDA does not require the sort of like-for-like comparisons which are involved in the Race Relations and Sex Discrimination Acts': *R (T) v Governing Body of OL Primary School* [2005] EWHC Admin 753, per James Goudie QC at para 6.

particular case and substantial'.[218] The code suggests that it might be possible for the school, in the example of the pupil with Tourette's syndrome, to justify the child's exclusion from the school trip on the basis that the pupil's behaviour might prejudice discipline. On the other hand, it would have to show that reasonable adjustments[219] are not possible.[220]

In *R (T) v Governing Body of OL Primary School*,[221] the SENDIST, dismissing the appeal, had concluded that a school was justified in excluding an 8-year-old girl who had global development delay and associated behavioural difficulties. She had bitten another child on the arm, causing deep bite marks. She had also hit, head butted and kicked other children as well as assaulting a learning support assistant and posing a threat to staff. The tribunal found that the school had tried to make reasonable adjustments, by taking advice and involving outside agencies. The court found the tribunal's decision to be lawful. It also concluded that neither the law nor guidance indicated whether the possibility of reasonable adjustments should be considered before that of justification or after it. The judge in fact supported the approach that involved deciding whether there were material and substantial reasons for the unfavourable treatment first, and going on to consider the question of reasonable adjustments only if there were no such reasons. If there were such reasons then the possibility of making reasonable adjustments might trump them.[222] An example of a case where there were clearly no material and substantial reasons would be that of Lee Buniak, a 6-year-old boy with global developmental delay. His mother was not notified about a school photograph session, resulting in him being the only child omitted from the photograph. Moreover, he was the only child excluded from his class's Christmas play and rehearsals for it. He was left out of many other everyday school activities, including assemblies and singing, and was not provided with the necessary learning support assistance by the school. The SENDIST upheld the complaint of disability discrimination.[223]

The nature of the disadvantage that the DDA 1995 is intended to ameliorate is such that, unlike with the SDA 1975 and RRA 1976, it is necessary for the authorities to deal more specifically with the physical barriers to equality of access. Thus it is also unlawful discrimination if the responsible body fails, to the detriment of the disabled person, to take, in relation to admission arrangements and access to education or services, the required reasonable steps to prevent that person from being 'placed at a substantial disadvantage' in comparison with persons who are not disabled.[224] In *R (D) v Governing Body of Plymouth High School for Girls*,[225] for example, a 10-year-old girl with visual impairment was denied access to a work placement organised by a third party because of her

---

[218] DDA 1995, s 28B(7).
[219] As required in relation to admission or access to education and associated services: s 28C(1).
[220] DRC, above n 216, 40, Example 5.10C, Example 15.5C, 42–43.
[221] [2005] EWHC Admin 753; [2005] ELR 522.
[222] Ibid, per James Goudie QC at para 24.
[223] See T Halpin, 'School excluded disabled boy from play and photo', *The Times*, 15 Dec 2003.
[224] DDA 1995, ss 28B(2), 28C, 28S(2) and 28T.
[225] [2004] ELR 591 (QBD).

parent's failure to disclose medical information. The court held that the school could reasonably have done more to ensure that the information was given, so that the pupil did not lose out. In relation to the taking of a step or failure to do so, there is an excuse where the responsible body did not know and could not reasonably have been expected to know that the person in question was disabled.[226] However, anticipatory action may in any event be required, to ensure that there is compliance when disabilities are presented.[227] Moreover, universities have been encouraged to be 'proactive in encouraging people to disclose a disability'.[228] A person may, however, make a confidentiality request asking for the nature or existence of their disability to be treated as confidential (in the case of a pupil, the request would need to be made by the parent unless the pupil was considered to have sufficient understanding of the nature and effect of the request).[229] If they do so, then, for the purpose of determining whether any step is 'reasonable' for the responsible body to have to take, regard must be had to the extent to which taking it is consistent with compliance with the request.[230]

To fulfil the duty to take reasonable steps, 'reasonable adjustments' to provision may be necessary, as suggested by the relevant codes of practice to which responsible bodies must have regard.[231] The code of practice on post-16 education gives as an example a student with depression whose medication makes it difficult to undertake prescribed work experience in the mornings, for whom alternative arrangement should be made.[232] What is reasonable will obviously vary from one case to the next. School trips may present particular dangers or difficulties for some pupils, and here the 'reasonable adjustments' requirement may be problematic. In *White v Clitheroe Royal Grammar School*,[233] a diabetic pupil claimed unlawful discrimination after his school barred him from a school water sports trip to France because he was diabetic and had suffered a hypoglycaemic attack the previous year while on a skiing trip. The pupil, whose claim was able to proceed under section 19 of the DDA, which covers discrimination in the provision of services, prior to the Act's extension to schools, was awarded £3,000 by Preston County Court. The judge found that no risk assessment taking into account the nature of the holiday and the pupil's medical condition was carried out. If such a situation arose in relation to, for

---

[226] DDA 1995, ss 28B(3) and (4) (see *R(O Comprehensive School) v IE, EE and Rimington* [2006] EWHC Admin 1468, per Crane J at para 41) and 28S(3) and (4).

[227] See Department for Education and Skills, *Finding Out About People's Disabilities* (London, DfES, 2002) 1; DRC, above n 216, paras 5.5 and 5.6. For the legal status of this code, see n 231 below. For a discussion of planning carried out in one LEA, see R Thompson, 'First Year of the Disability Discrimination Act 1995 Part IV in Schools in One Local Education Authority' (2003) 4 *Education Law* 233.

[228] *Disability Discrimination Act 1995 Part 4: Code of Practice for providers of Post 16 education and related services* (London, DRC, 2002), para 4.18. For the legal status of this code, see n 231 below.

[229] DDA 1995, s 28C(7).

[230] ss 28C(5)–(7) and 28T(3)–(5).

[231] The code is made (by the Disability Rights Commission) under DDA 1995, s 53A and the duty to have regard to it is in ss 28C(4) and 28T(2). See Disability Rights Commission, n 228 above and DRC, n 216 above.

[232] DRC, Code of Practice, above n 228, example 5.8D

[233] 6 May 2002, Claim no. BB 002640, Preston County Court.

example, a school sports day it would now be covered by the education provisions of the DDA 1995. What was 'reasonable' would be judged by such factors as the cost and practicality of the action needed. Case law on disability discrimination in employment is also going to be relevant here in defining the scope of some of these duties. [234]

The 1995 Act in fact gives specific examples of reasonable steps for an employer to have to take in compliance with the duty not to place a disabled employee at a substantial disadvantage.[235] They include modifying procedures for testing or assessment, permitting absence during working hours for rehabilitation or treatment, and providing supervision. However, the Act makes it clear that, for the purposes of their duty to prevent substantial disadvantage, schools are not required to remove or alter a physical feature or provide auxiliary aids or services.[236] In *K v Special Educational Needs and Disability Tribunal and Governing Body of a Grammar School*,[237] for example, Mitting J held that assistance in the form of cleaning and changing a pupil who was paraplegic and suffered from faecal incontinence constituted an auxiliary service that the school was not obliged to provide, notwithstanding its inclusion within the boy's statement of special educational needs. The family had argued that the failure to provide this assistance constituted disability discrimination, but the judge held that it amounted to personal care rather than education—it was auxiliary, assisting in the provision of education or associated services. Further and higher education are not protected by this exemption, and there has been a phased implementation of duties. Provision of auxiliary aids or services was not required until the end of August 2003, while removal or alteration of a physical feature has been required since the end of August 2005.[238] It should also be noted that the 2005 Act has placed public authorities under a duty not to discriminate by operating a policy, practice or procedure which makes it impossible or unreasonably difficult for a disabled person to receive a benefit that is conferred by the carrying out of a function by the authority.[239] It will be required to take reasonable steps to change the policy, practice or procedure, etc, and, if necessary, remove any physical barrier.[240]

LEAs have to prepare accessibility strategies for the participation of disabled pupils in the school curriculum and for improving the physical environment to facilitate it. At school level accessibility is the responsibility of school governing bodies of maintained schools and proprietors of independent schools, and they

---

[234] See, eg, *M School v CC, PC and Another* [2004] ELR 89, where, as noted above, it was held that selection of proper comparators where discrimination against a pupil is alleged should be done in the same way as when selecting comparators in discrimination in employment cases (per Silber J at para 45).

[235] DDA 1995, s 6.

[236] Ibid, s 28C(2).

[237] [2006] EWHC Admin 622.

[238] Special Educational Needs and Disability Act 2001 Order 2002 (SI 2002/2217(C71)).

[239] It also arises where it would be 'unreasonably adverse' for a disabled person to experience any detriment to which a person would be put by the authority.

[240] DDA 1995, s 21E.

must prepare an accessibility plan.[241] As under the SDA 1975 and RRA 1976, LEAs also have a residual duty in respect of functions under the Education Acts not to discriminate against a disabled pupil or person seeking admission to a school.[242] The Disability Discrimination Act 2005 has placed public authorities (which would include LEAs, unless specifically excluded by regulations) under a duty not to discriminate against a disabled person in carrying out their functions and a separate general duty to carry out their functions having regard to the need to eliminate unlawful disability discrimination or harassment and to improve opportunities for disabled people where they are not as good as those for other persons.[243] A body can be prescribed as a public authority.[244] The Joint Committee on the Bill argued that examination boards should be covered by the 1995 Act, which has not been the case hitherto.[245] The DDA 2005 gives effect to this recommendation;[246] but as yet the provisions, which include a duty to make adjustments, have not been brought into force.

The DDA's protection against disability discrimination in the context of education aims to tackle the physical or mental barriers to access, which shows that the Act is concerned with the social model of disability because the relevant provisions aim to remove or reduce the barriers to participation in ordinary community life. [247] However, it may not be able to counteract any pre-existing educational disadvantage. In particular, less favourable treatment is justified, in the case of a school, if it is the result of a permitted form of selection or, in the case of a further or higher education institution, if it is of a prescribed kind or is 'necessary in order to maintain—(a) academic standards; or (b) standards of any prescribed kind'.[248] An example of the former, given in the DRC's code of practice, is where a young person with learning difficulties, which may include poor literacy skills, applies to study for A level English and the staff considering the application do not have sufficient evidence that he could sustain the reading and writing necessary in undertaking the course.[249] Otherwise, as noted above, less favourable treatment or a failure to take reasonable steps to prevent substantial disadvantage would be justified 'only if the reason for it is both

---

[241] Ibid, ss 28D and 28E Such a strategy or plan is to cover a prescribed period of 3 years: the Disability Discrimination (Prescribed Periods and Times for Accessibility Strategies and Plans for Schools) (England) Regulations 2002 (SI 2005/3221).

[242] DDA 1995, s 28F.

[243] Ibid, ss 21A–21E and 49A–49F.

[244] Ibid, s 21B(5).

[245] Joint Committee on the Disability Discrimination Bill, *First Report* (London, TSO, 2004), paras 379–386.

[246] DDA 2005, s 15, inserting new ss 31AA–31AF into the DDA 1995.

[247] J Swain *et al*, *Controversial Issues in a Disabling Society* (Buckingham, Open University Press, 2003) 23–5; see also R Rieser, 'Disability Discrimination: the Final Frontier' in M Cole (ed), *Education, Equality and Human Rights* (London, Routledge Falmer, 2000) 118 at 119–21.

[248] Ss 28(6) and 28S(5), (6).

[249] Disability Rights Commission, *Disability Discrimination Act 1995 Part 4: Code of Practice for Providers of Post 16 Education and Related Services* (London, Disability Rights Commission, 2002), Example 6.3A

material to the circumstances of the particular case and substantial';[250] and in considering justification the resources available to the LEA are relevant.[251]

While therefore offering the individual, albeit on a conditional basis,[252] a degree of protection and redress[253] in respect of discrimination in access to an institution or its facilities—including situations where educational disadvantage has resulted—the Act's capacity to widen educational opportunities for disabled people in general can only really be felt over the long term, as structural changes occur as a consequence of the Act's wider influence. Moreover, the exceptions, such as those relating to academic standards and substantial reasons, may limit the protection of the Act in the context of higher education in the case of the most disabled students or students whose disability is most difficult to accommodate.[254] Research published within 12 months of the enactment of the 2001 Act suggested that, despite a lack of additional funding for institutions to develop support structures and strategies for disabled students, positive developments were already occurring, with most institutions having at least one support officer and some further education colleges having as many as 30 staff working with disabled students.[255] It also found that most institutions had a comprehensive policy statement on disability and admission and assessment arrangements that attempted to meet the needs of disabled students. Nonetheless, when students were interviewed the researchers found that significant barriers to access remained. The making of reasonable adjustments was sometimes resisted by staff, concerned about erosion of standards. Although many disabled students received the disabled student allowance (paid under the student support legislation[256]), it was dependent upon the student being classified as disabled, which in itself worked against the principles of equality and inclusion. Another study by a different research team, published a year later, has produced similar results. It questioned disabled people and found that significant progress had been made within post-compulsory education in making education available to disabled students and removing barriers to it, but there was perceived

[250] Ss 28B(7) and 28S(8). But see also ss 28B(8) and 28S(9).

[251] See, eg, *VK v Norfolk County Council and the Special Educational Needs and Disability Tribunal* [2005] ELR 342 (QBD), per Stanley Burnton J at paras 64 and 65.

[252] The UK's approach is less enlightened than that of the US, according to O Konur, 'Creating Enforceable Civil Rights for Disabled Students in Higher Education: an Institutional Theory Perspective' (2000), 15 *Disability & Society* 1041.

[253] In the case of school pupils, complaints of discrimination lie to the Special Educational Needs and Disability Tribunal: DDA 1995, ss 28H, 28I and 28J: ibid, Sched 3 para 9. Claims may be brought by the parent, according to the Special Educational Needs and Disability Tribunal (General Provisions and Disability Claims Procedure) Regulations 2002 (SI 2002 No. 1985). It is unclear whether 16–18-year-olds can bring a claim in their own right, but it would appear that they cannot. In the case of further and higher education, redress is via civil proceedings in county courts: ibid, s 28V. Note also the DRC's enforcement and assistance powers under the DRC Act 1999.

[254] See M Davies, 'The Special Educational Needs and Disability Act 2001—The Implications for Higher Education' (2001) 15 *Education & the Law* 19 at 32.

[255] S Riddell *et al*, *Disabled Students and Multiple Policy Innovations in Higher Education* (ESRC, 2002); T Tinkin *et al*, *Wider Access for Disabled Students?* (ESRC, 2002), available only at www.esrc.org.uk; S Riddell *et al*, 'Disability and the Wider Access Agenda: Supporting Disabled Students in Different Institutional Contexts' (2002) 4(3) *Widening Participation and Lifelong Learning* 13; S Riddell *et al*, *Disabled Students in Higher Education* (London, Routledge, 2005).

[256] For 2005–6, see Education (Student Support) Regulations 2005 (SI 2005/52), regs 14 and 38.

to be a lack of awareness and responsiveness among staff around issues of disability and '[p]hysical access needs were felt to be better catered for than needs for academic support'.[257] More recent research has highlighted specific practices in teaching and assessment that cause difficulties for some disabled students, including problems in hearing lectures or being able to read visual displays or handouts, but also areas of good practice. It also notes that students 'differed in their willingness to seek support for their impairment'.[258] The above evidence suggests that further and higher education are making progress towards meeting their obligations towards disabled students but that both, and the latter in particular, still have some way to go. The recent finding by the House of Commons Education and Skills Committee that awareness of the Disability Discrimination Act 1995 duties in schools is low[259] suggests that further efforts are needed in that sector to provide firmer guidance in order to reinforce the aims of the legislation.

The DDA 2005 is bringing the 1995 Act into line with the RRA 1976, as amended, in making discrimination by public authorities unlawful (although, as it is concerned with disability, it also provides for physical alteration or removal of features that disadvantage those with a disability[260]). It also contains a comparable duty to promote equality: public authorities must have due regard, when carrying out their functions, to the need, inter alia, to eliminate disability discrimination and the harassment of disabled persons that is related to their disabilities; to promote equality of opportunity between disabled persons and others; to promote 'positive attitudes towards disabled persons'; and to 'encourage participation by disabled persons in public life'.[261]

Age

Despite the fact that '[t]he identification of education with the first pase of life is very deep rooted',[262] the basic idea that age should be no barrier to access has operated within education for many years and has been given a strong policy impetus through the Government's emphasis on 'lifelong learning',[263] also reflected in EU proposals for education programmes for the period from 2006 to

---

[257] D Molloy *et al*, *Diversity in Disability*, DWP Research Report 188 (Leeds, Corporate Document Services, 2003) 89.

[258] M Fuller *et al*, 'Incorporating Disabled Students within an Inclusive Higher Education Environment' (2004) 19 *Disability & Society* 455 at 466.

[259] Third Report of Session 2005–06, *Special Education Needs Vol 1*, HC 478–I (London, TSO, 2006), para 108.

[260] DDA 1995, ss 21B–21E, inserted by the DDA 2005, s 2. The non-discrimination duty (in ss 29B and 29C) will be in force from 4 Dec 2006. As with the definition in the Equality Act 2006 (see above p 149), 'public authority' 'includes any person certain of whose functions are functions of a public nature': DDA 1995, s 21B(2).

[261] DDA 1995, ss 49A–49F, inserted by the DDA 2005, s 3. These provisions are in force. 'Public authority' 'has the same definition as that in respect of the above duty': DDA 1995, s 49B.

[262] T Schuller, 'Age Equality in Access to Education' in S Fredman and S Spencer (eds), *Age as an Equality Issue* (Oxford, Hart, 2003), 117 at 124.

[263] See below.

2013.[264] Many people enter further or higher education as what are often referred to as 'mature' students: in 2001, for example, over 20 per cent of first year students on full-time higher education courses in the UK were aged 25 or over.[265] Any law which outlawed age discrimination, such as would occur if a course had a minimum entry age, would have to provide a justification defence, since age may be a legitimate criterion in some circumstances. That is certainly the position under Article 14 of the ECHR, discussed earlier; as we saw, it was considered to be satisfied in *Douglas* in the case of the cut-off age of 55 for student loans.[266] Furthermore, in *Reynolds*, the House of Lords held that the discrimination arising from the age-related rates of personal allowance within income support, which involved a lower rate for persons aged under 25 than for those aged 25 or over, was not rendered unlawful by Article 14 (read together with Article 1 of Protocol 1) because the discriminatory policy had a rational and justifiable purpose and a legitimate aim.[267] Presumably a similar justification would be possible for the introduction of free tuition for 19–25-year-olds taking level 3 qualifications (A level or equivalent) within further education, which aims to 'tackle an area of particular weakness in skills development in this country',[268] although, as with the situation in *Douglas*, there might anyway be a problem in showing that the Convention right to education is engaged.[269] Nonetheless, since age discrimination law is founded on the principle that equality should not be diminished by age, the onus would need to be placed on those who favoured age as a specific criterion. That might be easier to justify in relation to some areas of education than others. For example, at present, many university medical schools operate a policy rule that accords persons above a certain age—such as 50—a lower priority for a place. The typical rationale is that medical training is expensive and, given the intense competition for places, it is logical that younger people with potentially longer service to offer should be admitted in preference to older applicants.

The extent to which such policies might be lawful will be judged, from 1 October 2006, by the Employment Equality (Age) Regulations 2006 which, like some of the above provisions, will also give effect to the EC's framework directive.[270] They will prohibit direct or indirect discrimination, where the

---

[264] European Commission, *A Proposal for a Decision of the European Parliament and of the Council Establishing an Integrated Action Programme in the Field of Lifelong Learning*, Commission Documents 11587/04, COM(2004) 474 final and 11587/04 ADD 1, SEC(2004) 971. See also House of Lords European Union Committee, Social and Consumer Affairs Sub-Committee, *Report on the Proposed European Union Integrated Action Programme for Life-Long Learning*, HL Paper 104–1 (London, TSO, 2005).

[265] Office of National Statistics, *Student Enrolments on Higher Education Courses at Publicly Funded Higher Education Institutions in the United Kingdom for the Academic Year 2001/02*, HESA SFR 56 (2002), table 4, available only at www.hesa.gov.uk.

[266] *R (Douglas) v North Tyneside Metropolitan Borough Council and the Secretary of State for Education and Skills* [2004] ELR 117 (CA).

[267] *R (Carson) v Secretary of State for Work and Pensions; R (Reynolds) v Secretary of State for Work and Pensions* [2005] UKHL 37; [2006] 1 AC 673.

[268] DfES, *Further Education: Raising Skills, Improving Life Chances*, Cm 6768 (London, TSO, 2006), para 3.4.

[269] See Chap 2 at p 75 above.

[270] SI 2006/1031; Council Directive 2000/78/EC of 27 Nov 2000 [2000] (OJ L/303/16).

different treatment accorded on the basis of age, or the different provision, criterion or practice that disadvantages persons of a particular age compared with others, cannot be shown to be 'a proportionate means of achieving a legitimate aim'.[271] Although mostly concerned with employment per se, the regulations will also apply to the treatment of students and would-be students. They contain parallel provisions to the regulations governing religious discrimination (above), in the context of decisions on admission to the institution, including the terms of any admission, access by the student to any benefits, and the exclusion of the student or his or her subjection to any detriment.[272] The employment provisions of the regulations contain an exemption where the required characteristic related to age constitutes a 'genuine occupational qualification'.[273] The education and training provisions, which apply to colleges of further education and universities and other higher education institutions,[274] provide that the age discrimination is not unlawful where it concerns training that would fit a person only for employment which, by virtue of this genuine occupational qualification provision, the employer could lawfully refuse to offer the person in question.[275] The Government appears to believe that there could be a legitimate aim in fixing a maximum entry age where the justification relates to the particular training needed or the period of time between the student's training and his or her retirement, although the position is not entirely clear.[276] If the Government's interpretation is correct, then the kind of age discrimination that some medical schools practise may have escaped proscription. In any event, some arrangements could be permitted under the general proportionality and 'legitimate aim' rule that conditions legality (above). Yet one may hope that the circumstances in which age discrimination would be legitimate might be very limited indeed, notwithstanding the clear focus on vocational education within these provisions, since few would favour any kind of age restrictions in today's 'learning age', particularly given the huge potential social benefits of participation in adult learning.[277] Additional financial support for adult learners may be needed, however, if the object of equal access to education regardless of age is to be realised.[278]

---

[271] Employment Equality (Age) Regulations 2006, reg 3(1). The regulations also proscribe victimisation and harassment: see regs 4 and 6.

[272] Ibid, reg 23(1). Harassment is also covered: ibid, reg 23(2).

[273] Ibid, reg 8.

[274] The scope of the education provisions is designed to reflect the EC case law on the meaning of vocational training for the purposes of the framework directive, in that it has been held to include 'any form of education which prepares for a qualification for a particular profession, trade or employment or which provides the necessary skills for such a profession, trade or employment' : Case C–293/83, *Gravier v City of Liège* [1985] ECR 606. It would include most university education: Case C–24/86, *Blaizot v University of Liège* [1988] ECR 355. See below and see DTI, *Draft Employment Equality (Age) Regulations 2006, Notes on Regulations* (London, DTI, 2006), available at www.dti.gov.uk/er/equality/age.htm.

[275] N 271 above, reg 23(3).

[276] See N Saunders, 'The Age Discrimination Regulations' (2006) 7 *European Law Journal* 132.

[277] These are discussed in Schuller, n 262 above.

[278] Schuller (ibid, 141–2) proposes, to this end, a new allowance for persons aged 55 or over.

Discrimination by Pupils or Students

One final point concerning all of the above legislation concerns the actions of pupils or students themselves. In schools in particular, the behaviour of pupils can include acts of disfavour or bullying that are particularly likely to target vulnerable persons and minorities and might, for example, include racial, sexual or homophobic taunts and insults or harassment.[279] Disabled children have been found to be at greater than average risk of being bullied, usually about their disability.[280] Bullying can have a devastating, long term psychological effect on its child victims. [281] It can certainly affect access to education: its victims are particularly liable to stay away from school.[282]

In a case decided by the British Columbia Court of Appeal brought by a student who had suffered several years of homophobic bullying from fellow students it was successfully argued that the school board acted unlawfully in failing to provide a school environment free from harassment.[283] The board was held to have discriminated against the applicant on the basis of sexual orientation, even though the applicant was not in fact gay. Clearly the DDA 1995 and the RRA 1976 (as amended by the 2000 Act) place schools and further or higher education institutions in England and Wales under duties to take reasonable steps to prevent harassment—and there could also be common law negligence liability for failing to intervene.[284] A school that did not specifically refer to disabled children or ethnic minorities in its anti-bullying policies (as recommended in the DfES guidance[285]) would run the risk of being in breach of the DDA 1995 or the RRA 1976, both as amended. It was thought, in the light of a Court of Appeal decision, that a school could also be in breach of the SDA 1975 where its school pupils committed discriminatory acts towards employees, if it did not take reasonable steps to prevent them.[286] However, the House of Lords disagreed with the appeal court judges.[287]

---

[279] C Oliver and M Candappa, *Tackling Bullying: Listening to the Views of Children and Young People* (London, DfES, 2003).

[280] DfES, *Bullying: Don't Suffer in Silence—an Anti-bullying Strategy for Schools* (London, DfES, 2002), para 24.

[281] See, eg, OFSTED, *Bullying: Effective Action in Secondary Schools*, HMI 465 (London, OFSTED, 2003), para 21 and DA Thompson, 'Bullying and Harassment in and out of School' in P Aggleton, J Hurry and I Warwick, *Young People and Mental Health* (Chichester, John Wiley and Sons, 2000) 197.

[282] Social Exclusion Unit, *Truancy and School Exclusion*, Cm 3957 (London, TSO, 1998), para 1.10.

[283] *Board of School Trustees of School District No. 44 (North Vancouver) v Azmi Jubran and British Columbia Human Rights Tribunal (BC)* [2005] BCJ No 733. The applicant's complaint was brought under the BC Human Rights Code, RSBC 1996, c 210.

[284] See *Bradford-Smart v West Sussex County Council* [2002] ELR 139; *Faulkner v London Borough and Enfield and Lea Valley High School* [2003] ELR 426. See further N Harris, 'Bullying, Mental Health and School Pupils in England' in N Harris and P Meredith (eds), *Children, Education and Health International Perspectives on Law and Policy* (Aldershot, Ashgate, 2005), 31.

[285] DfES, *Bullying: Don't Suffer in Silence—an Anti-bullying Strategy for Schools* (London, DfES, 2002), para 25.

[286] *Pearce v Governing Body of Mayfield School* [2002] ELR 16: insulting and offensive behaviour by pupils towards a lesbian teacher on the ground of her sexuality. See further S Whitbourn, 'The Liability of Schools for the Discriminatory Acts of Pupils' [2002] *Education, Public Law and the Individual* 2.

[287] *Macdonald v Advocate General for Scotland; Pearce v Governing Body of Mayfield School* [2003] UKHL 34, [2003] ICR 937.

Positive Discrimination

The debate surrounding university admissions that was prompted by the concern expressed by the Chancellor of the Exchequer and others (in the wake of the Laura Spence affair[288]) about the under-representation of certain socio-economic and ethnic groups among those entering higher education[289] has included discussion of the need for an element of affirmative action or positive discrimination in favour of certain disadvantaged applicants. For example, a question that has been asked is whether universities should accept lower examination grades from pupils who live in poorer areas or who attend schools that have no tradition of placing pupils in university. It was not suggested that action of this kind should target members of ethnic minorities per se, but it might be an indirect effect of giving preference, all other matters being equal, to those from inner city schools with a weak academic tradition. The real question is how far university admissions should address the issue, identified by the report of the independent Admissions to Higher Education Review commissioned by the DfES and chaired by Professor Stephen Schwartz, that 'equal examination grades do not necessarily represent equal potential'.[290]

As the House of Commons Select Committee that examined access to universities noted, the case for widening participation rests not merely on the social justice argument that all who have the potential to benefit from higher education should have the opportunity to do so, but also on the wider social benefits deriving from 'a more representative social mix in admissions to high status research intensive universities, many of whose graduates go on to occupy positions of power and influence in business, industry, the professions and in politics'.[291] Of course, the fact that only 6 per cent of pupils at secondary school are attending independent schools, while the proportion of the students at Oxford, Cambridge and certain other universities who attended such schools exceeds 50 per cent,[292] on the face of it implies a degree of social injustice. But a whole range of factors lie behind this over-representation, which is mirrored by the over-representation of professional and middle class social groupings among students as a whole. The Select Committee noted the efforts made by staff in such universities to attract and admit pupils from state schools. The Government continues to press the case for widened participation, most recently in its five-year plan for education. Moreover, as discussed below, the Higher Education

---

[288] Laura Spence was a state school applicant for a place at Oxford University who was turned down despite gaining five grade As at A level. Her case was widely reported in the media in 2000. For a critical view of the affair see A Smith, 'The Laura Spence Affair and the Contemporary Political Mind' in S Prickett and P Erskine-Hill (eds), *Education! Education! Education! Managerial Ethics and the Law of Unintended Consequences* (Thorverton, Imprint Academic, 2002), 29.

[289] For background, see House of Commons Select Committee on Education and Employment, Fourth Report, Session 2000–01, *Higher Education: Access*, Report, HC 205 (London, TSO, 2001).

[290] Admissions to Higher Education Steering Group (chair Stephen Schwartz), *Fair Admissions to Higher Education: Recommendations for Good Practtice* (2004), available only at www.admissions-review.org.uk, para 4.2.

[291] N 289 above, paras 73–74.

[292] Ibid, para 79.

Act 2004 has provided for the office of Director of Fair Access to Higher Education (who heads the Office for Fair Access (OFFA)) and for access agreements to ensure that the universities are 'reaching out to young people in schools and colleges which have not traditionally sent students to university'.[293]

The case for differential treatment in the form of positive or reverse discrimination or affirmative action by universities in favour of candidates from disadvantaged backgrounds rests in part on moral arguments concerned with the achievement of what Fredman refers to as 'substantive equality'.[294] The argument is that formal equality or neutrality, which is the dominant feature of UK anti-discrimination law—so that sex or race must, for example, be treated as a neutral factor in selection—ignore the social reality of disadvantage, which calls for an asymmetrical approach to reduce it. But positive discrimination in one group's favour in relation to university admissions would almost always be unlawful under anti-discrimination law (save where permitted under statute, such as entry to all-women colleges), because it involves discrimination against another group that is unlikely to have any legal justification.[295]

A person who loses out as a consequence of a policy of positive discrimination might also argue that the discrimination of which they are a victim violates Article 14 of the ECHR in connection with the exercise of their right to education under Article 2 of Protocol 1 (which, as we have seen, includes a right of access to higher education if the person is capable of benefiting from it). As we saw above, Article 14 prohibits discrimination or differential treatment which has no reasonable and objective justification. Such justification will depend upon the legitimacy of the aim and on whether the means employed are proportionate to it. The onus is on the state authorities to show that justification.[296] In theory, therefore, differential offers in relation to university places could be legitimate for the purposes of Article 14 if there were a reasonable and objective justification. In *Karus v Italy*,[297] for example, the Commission of Human Rights accepted that the policy of foreign nationals paying higher fees than home students had an objective and reasonable justification, namely that home nationals were more likely to remain in Italy after completing their studies and thereby able contribute to the general good of the community.

But can justification for the purposes of Article 14 be found in a policy that aims at redressing a pre-existing situation of inequality? It is unlikely that a quota system for particular social, gender or disability groups would justifiable, because its proportionality would be dubious. (It would also involve unlawful fettering of discretion for public law purposes.) On the other hand, a programme of affirmative action, to encourage participation by particular groups, even to the extent that extra resources were expended in pursuing it, would be capable of

---

[293] Secretary of State for Education and Skills, *Department for Education and Skills: Five Year Strategy for Children and Learners*, Cm 6272 (London, TSO, 2004) 78.

[294] S Fredman, *Discrimination Law* (Oxford, Oxford University Press, 2002) 128.

[295] As also argued by N Saunders, 'Fair Admission to Higher Education: Recommendations for Good Practice' (2004) 5 *Education Law Journal* 255 at 258. See also N Saunders, 'Widening Access to Higher Education—the Limits of Positive Action' (2004) 16 *Education & the Law* 3.

[296] See K Starmer, *European Human Rights Law* (London, LAG, 1999) 687–90.

[297] App no 29043/95, 20 May 1998 (Commission of Human Rights).

justification and would surely not be disproportionate. A university which made differential offers on the basis of critieria other than applicants' academic record (including predicted A2 grades) would be likely to meet the test of justifiability if those criteria were aimed at assessing the individual's potential. Indeed, it is arguable that if the university has a reason to doubt the accuracy of A2 grades as a predictor of degree performance and retention it has a positive public *obligation* to draw on wider objective criteria; and it has been suggested that if standard entry requirements unjustifiably discriminate against some groups more flexible criteria may be necessary.[298] On the other hand, in a case in Northern Ireland, *Anderson and O'Doherty*,[299] it was argued that a grammar school's admission criteria providing for priority on the basis of, inter alia, receipt of an award or certificate for any one of a number of extra-curricular activities, including sport, chess, dance, drama, debating and photography, discriminated unfairly against children from poorer backgrounds for the purposes of Article 14 on the basis that they were less likely than others to be able to fulfil this criterion. On the facts, the court did not consider that the policy discriminated on the basis of socio-economic status, so the question of justification was not tested.

   Would an admissions policy be capable of legal justification if its overall aim was the secondary one of widening the social mix in the university in order to achieve greater substantive equality or 'social justice' and more role models to encourage the participation of others? Mountfield suggests that school admission policies might fall foul of Article 14 (with Article 2 of Protocol 1) if they 'discriminate on some impermissible ground, such as, for example, class'.[300] As Lundy points out, class/socio-economic status is not referred to specifically in Article 14, but there is a catch-all phrase at the end, 'or other status'.[301] In *Anderson and O'Doherty*, it was argued—and not specifically rejected by the court—that 'or other status' could include socio-economic status. It does seem likely that university admission policies that involve positive discrimination on the basis of, say, postcode or school background (both of which tend to reflect social class distinctions), would be caught by Article 14.[302] Nonetheless, it has been argued that school catchment areas, that often do reflect and reinforce social segregation (see Chapter 5), although not deliberately, would be likely to withstand an Article 14 challenge if rational.[303] The question of rationality is

---

[298] See T Birtwistle, 'University Student Admissions—a Simple Matter of Contract' (2003) 4 *Education Law* 25, at 32.

[299] *In re an application for judicial review by Anderson and O'Doherty* [2001] NICA 48.

[300] H Mountfield, 'The Implications of the Human Rights Act 1998 for the Law of Education' (2000) 1 *Education Law* 146, at 156.

[301] L Lundy, 'Human Rights and Equality Litigation in Northern Ireland's Schools' (2004) 5 *Education Law* 82, at 85.

[302] That view has apparently been articulated in an unpublished report commissioned by the Headmaster's and Headmistresses' Conference and the Girls' School Association, prepared by Professor Alan Smithers: see T Halpin, 'State-schools bias "could breach human rights"', *The Times*, 7 Oct 2005, 2.

[303] S Fredman, *Discrimination Law* (Oxford, Oxford University Press, 2002) 156. See further the discussion of *R v Bradford Metropolitan Borough Council ex parte Sikander Ali* [1994] ELR 299 in Chap 5 at p 269 below.

important: it has, for example, been argued by Smithers that positive discrimination on the basis of school type is not rational. School type is:

only one of a number of factors having a bearing on participation and performance in higher education . . . [including] father's occupation, gender, ethnicity, postcode and even month of birth . . . [I]solating just one factor is of questionable general effect and making it the basis of a deliberate bias in university entry would make admissions less fair than they are now.[304]

Could, however, the justification for a policy that discriminates on the basis of class or socio-economic status lie, as it did in *Karus*, in its secondary social benefit? As the payment of grants or other support to poorer students but not to others, in order to facilitate access to education, would probably be justified as aiming to redress an existing inequality, it would seem inappropriate to treat admission per se any differently. It should, however, be stressed that in the light of *Douglas* (above), it might be necessary to link the Article 14 claim to the right to possessions in Article 1 of Protocol 1 rather than to the right to education.[305]

The issue of positive discrimination in education has arisen in several important US decisions, including two decisions by the US Supreme Court in 2003.[306] At issue has been the constitutionality of positive discrimination in the face of the Equal Protection Clause of the Fourteenth Amendment, which provides: '[n]o state shall . . . deny to any person within its jurisdiction the equal protection of the law'. In *Regents of the University of California v Bakke* in 1978,[307] the Supreme Court found that, despite the principle of equal treatment on the basis of factors such as race, justification for racial classifications was possible on the basis of overriding statutory purpose. It reiterated, however, the established principle that a government practice or statute that restricted a fundamental right or which contained 'suspect classifications' was to be subjected to 'strict scrutiny'. The complainant, who was white, was twice rejected for a place at the university's medical college despite having a higher points score than some minority ethnic candidates who were admitted. The medical college ran two streams for admission, a general one and a special one, aimed at members of

---

[304] A Smithers, *University Admissions. School Effect and HE Achievement* (Buckingham, University of Buckingham, 2004), para 36. See also HEFCE, *Schooling Effects on Higher Education Achievement* Issues Paper 2003/32 (Bristol, HEFCE, 2003), which seems to show dangers in generalisations about the effect of school type. Cf Admissions to Higher Education Steering Group (chair Stephen Schwartz), *Fair Admissions to Higher Education: Recommendations for Good Practtice* (2004), available only at www.admissions-review.org.uk, para B.7, which accepted the evidence of a 'school effect' on attainment.

[305] In the past, the domestic courts and Strasbourg judges did not fully accept that non-contributory means-tested benefits such as income support, as opposed to contributory benefits, could count as possessions for the purposes of Art 1 of Prot 1, although *R (Waite) v Hammersmith and Fulham LBC and the Secretary of State for Work and Pensions* [2003] HLR 24 (CA), appeared to signify a change of approach. The position now seems to have been resolved in favour of recognising both types as possessions: *Stec and Others v UK*, App nos 67531/01 and 65900/01, Grand Chamber Decision (Admissibility), 6 July 2005.

[306] See RD Mawdsley and CJ Russo, 'The US Supreme Court and Affirmative Action: "Social Experiments on Other People's Children" Gone Awry?' (2004) 5 *Education Law* 25.

[307] 438 US 265 (1978).

minority groups and the economically or educationally disadvantaged. Under the special admissions programme, candidates were ranked against each other and names were put forward to the general admissions committee. They were not ranked against candidates who applied under the general stream. The complainant claimed that the special admissions programme was unlawful. The Court found for him, although four of the nine justices considered that the purpose of achieving greater diversity within the medical profession, amongst whose numbers ethnic minorities were chronically under-represented, was sufficiently important to justify the remedial use of race. A fifth, Powell J, found that this aim could justify positive discrimination on the basis of race in some circumstances, but that this particular admissions programme went too far by foreclosing consideration of an applicant such as the complainant and was unconstitutional.[308]

Powell J's view in *Bakke* was wholeheartedly rejected by the US Court of Appeals for the Fifth Circuit in *Hopwood v State of Texas et al.*[309] Here, a law school gave preference to black and Mexican American applicants by setting a lower entry score threshold in order to meet a goal of admitting a class consisting of 10 per cent Mexican Americans and 5 per cent blacks, being proportions roughly comparable to the percentages of those races graduating from Texas colleges. Among other disparities, the school had separate waiting lists for minorities and others; the former was used to infill minority numbers. The district court had held that 'obtaining the educational benefits that flow from a racially and ethnically diverse student body remains a sufficiently compelling interest to support the use of racial classifications' and that the use of racial classification could be justified as a remedy for the 'present effects at the law school of past discrimination in both the University of Texas system and the Texas educational system as a whole'. The Court of Appeals was, however, unable to accept these arguments. It said that there had been 'no indication from the Supreme Court, other than Justice Powell's lonely opinion in *Bakke*, that the state's interest in diversity constitutes a compelling justification for governmental race-based discrimination'.[310] The Court considered that the use of race as a factor in determining admissions in order to increase diversity 'contradicts, rather than furthers, the aims of equal protection' and, by treating minorities as a group rather than as individuals, could 'promote improper racial stereotypes, thus fuelling racial hostility'.[311] The court also noted that diversity could 'take many forms'[312] and that the selection of race as a factor to make the student body more diverse was 'no more rational on its own terms than would be choices based upon the physical size or blood type of applicants'.[313] While other factors, such as (American) football prowess, the ability to play the cello, the applicant's home state and even 'factors such as whether an applicant's parents attended

---

[308] Ibid, at 313–4.
[309] 78 F 3d 932(1996) (US CA, 5th Cir).
[310] At para 28.
[311] Ibid.
[312] Ibid, para 31.
[313] Ibid, para 28.

college or the applicant's economic and social background' could be taken into account by universities, consideration of race was, on the basis of the authorities, unconstitutional.[314]

Regardless of whether this approach was strictly correct in law, it failed to reflect the fact that race remains a defining characteristic for social purposes and is associated with deeply entrenched social disadvantage. As Fredman says, 'it is based on an explicit rejection of the ways in which race (or gender) affect a person's life experience, opportunities, and perspectives'.[315] In *Grutter v Bollinger*,[316] however, the Supreme Court endorsed the policy of the University of Michigan law school which, with a view to enrolling a critical mass (but not a fixed percentage or number) of minority students, was furthering what it considered to be a 'compelling interest in securing the educational benefits of a diverse student body'. The law school's policy of admitting minority ethnic students with lower entry scores more readily than others was held to be justified by the majority on the basis that the admissions criteria were narrowly tailored towards the goal of diversity. The law school's admissions programme was found by the majority to be 'flexible enough to assure that each applicant is evaluated as an individual and not in a way that makes an applicant's race or ethnicity the defining feature of his or her application'.[317] On the same day, in *Gratz v Bollinger*,[318] the Supreme Court held that the system operated by the university's College of Literature, Science and the Arts of allocating a prescribed number of points to applicants of a particular race or ethnicity was insufficiently narrowly tailored to the diversity goal. The system allocated 20 points to an applicant from an 'underrepresented minority' group, as defined by the university and, as such, was not based on 'individualised consideration'.[319] The court pointed out that '[e]ven if [a white student's] extraordinary artistic talent rivalled that of Monet or Picasso, the applicant would receive, at most, five points' whereas any member of a relevant ethnic minority would automatically be credited with 20 points.[320]

These Supreme Court decisions therefore confirm that a quota system would be unconstitutional, but that a process that enables race to be a factor in prioritising admissions would be legitimate if properly focused, although the element of uncertainty created by *Grutter*, which failed to lay down definitive guidance, has attracted the criticism that students have become 'social experiments in the hands of jurists and educators'.[321] The Schwartz report has nevertheless accepted the basic case for efforts to be made by institutions in the UK to recruit a diverse student body, although it is careful to stress that it is not recommending a specific bias for or against any particular group or particular background, but rather the need for a holistic assessment of individual potential and merit,

---

[314] Ibid, paras 28–30.
[315] S Fredman, *Discrimination Law* (Oxford, Oxford University Press, 2002) 157.
[316] 539 US 306 (2003).
[317] Ibid, Opinion (O'Connor J), III B.
[318] 539 US 244 (2003).
[319] Ibid, at 11B of the court's opinion.
[320] Ibid.
[321] Mawdsley and Russo, above n 306, at 35, drawing on dissenting judge Thomas's reference to 'social experiments on other people's children' in *Grutter* at 2361–2362.

looking at a range of contextual factors.[322] But in the real world of university admissions decision-makers will need some kind of policy framework to facilitate the processes involved. The inherent dangers in constructing such a framework are evident from the US experience, although the Schwartz report also presents a cogent argument for transparency in admissions.[323]

University admissions are discussed further below in the context of access regulation under the Higher Education Act 2004.

ACCESS TO SCHOOLING

Minimum provision

Most children are entitled to attend a school, the exception being those who require alternative provision due to 'illness, exclusion from school or some other cause' (eg bullying),[324] although even they are entitled, if of compulsory school age, to suitable educational provision.[325] The provision of schools in England and Wales is a responsibility of LEAs but, as we saw in Chapter 3, they are not under an *absolute* duty to ensure that their area has sufficient schools. Moreover, the provision of quite small amounts of weekly provision for those out of school under the duty to make alternative provision may be sufficient in particular circumstances.[326] However, in furtherance of their general duty to ensure that there are sufficient schools LEAs must do their utmost to ensure that the necesssary amount of educational provision is available;[327] moreover, alternative provision made for an individual child must be sufficient to be consistent with the statutory duty to ensure that the child or young person receives a suitable education.[328] The courts have not accepted that a private law right to education exists, at least in relation to the public sector of education.[329] Nonetheless, by accepting a child into school, the state assumes a public law responsibility to educate him or her to a particular level, as determined by the statutory requirements for the basic curriculum, the National Curriculum and

[322] Admissions to Higher Education Steering Group (chair Stephen Schwartz), *Fair Admissions to Higher Education: Recommendations for Good Practtice* (2004), available only at www.admissions-review.org.uk, paras C4–C6.

[323] Ibid, paras D5–D8.

[324] See *R (G by his father and litigation friend RG) v Westminster City Council* [2004] ELR 135 (CA).

[325] Education Act 1996, s 19(1), as amended by the Education Act 1997, s 47. As regards 'suitable', see s 19(6) and *R v East Sussex County Council ex p T* [1998] ELR 251 (HL).

[326] Ibid. See below.

[327] *Meade v Haringey LBC* [1979] 2 All ER 1016 (CA); *R v Inner London Education Authority ex parte Ali and Murshid* [1990] 2 Admin LR 822 (QBD); EA 1996, s 14.

[328] *R v East Sussex County Council ex parte T* [1998] ELR 251 (HL); see pp 42–3 above.

[329] *R (B) v Head Teacher of Alperton Community School and Others; R v Head Teacher of Wembley High School and Others ex p T; R v Governing Body of Cardinal Newman High School and Others ex p C* [2001] ELR 359, at para 43. A private law right would of course arise in relation to access to education provided under a contract with a private school: see, eg, *Mount v Oldham Corporation* [1973] 1 QB 309.

the delivery of special educational provision for those with special educational needs.[330]

There must be a minimum threshold of provision necessary to meet the child's right to education. As noted above and in Chapter 2, international law sets various norms in this regard—for example, that primary education should be compulsory and free and education should be available on the basis of equality of opportunity[331]—including the aims to which it should be directed.[332] Moreover, while the first sentence of Article 2 of Protocol 1 to the ECHR merely proscribes the denial of anyone's right to education, this may mean more than that there is to be merely a right of access to educational institutions, because it is implied that a minimum level of provision must be made (see below). This is separate from the question of choice of institution, where the second sentence of the Article, calling for respect for parental religious or philosophical convictions, may come into play.[333]

Claims relating to a simple denial of access to education are not as unlikely as might be supposed. They have arisen in the context of school exclusion (see below) and, linked to an Article 14 discrimination claim, in connection with a denial of student support (*Douglas*, above).[334] Another example arose out of the Holy Cross School affair in Northern Ireland. During September–November 2001 children and their parents who walked along the Ardoyne Road in Belfast to Holy Cross primary school for girls, a Roman Catholic school, were subjected to intimidation and attacks from members of the local community and loyalists. The parents' complaint was that the police had failed to enforce the criminal law and secure their safe passage to school. Among the arguments on which the application, which was brought by one child, E, was based, was that her right under Article 2 of Protocol 1 was violated. Kerr LCJ held, however, that the efforts made by the parents and the principal and other staff at the school to ensure that the school remained open and that the children could attend, in the face of serious threats, meant that 'the right of the applicant's child and other children to an education was assured'.[335] There was evidence that some children were quite badly distressed by the intimidation of the mob, so it is perhaps surprising that its impact on their enjoyment of the right to education was not considered in the court's judgment. It could be argued that a failure by the state to take reasonable steps to deal with bullying at school could, in view of its potential psychological effects such as school phobia, amount to a failure to protect the right to education. By analogy, the distress many of the Holy Cross children suffered in the course of trying to exercise their right to education called for proper steps to be taken by the state—in this case through the agency of the

---

[330] See Chaps 6 and 7.
[331] UNCRC, Art 28.
[332] See especially, Art 29 of the UNCRC.
[333] See Chap 2.
[334] *R (Douglas) v North Tyneside Metropolitan Borough Council and the Secretary of State for Education and Skills* [2004] ELR 117 (CA). See p 142 above
[335] *In re the application of E* [2004] NIQB 35, at para 51.

police. In the event, Kerr LCJ did not consider that the policing in the Ardoyne Road was legally flawed.

We also saw in Chapter 2 that, for the purposes of the ECHR, Article 2 of Protocol 1, 'the Contracting Parties do not recognise such a right to education as would require them to establish at their own expense, or to subsidise, education of any particular type or at any particular level'.[336] In all other respects, the state is competent to determine the minimum level of provision. For example, in *Kjeldsen* the European Court of Human Rights held:

> the setting and planning of the curriculum fall in principle within the competence of the Contracting State. This mainly involves questions of expediency on which it is not for the Court to rule and whose solution may legitimately vary according to the country and the era.[337]

In England and Wales, the prescription of a basic curriculum and a National Curriculum has established a framework of required provision. Moreover, there are regulations made by the Secretary of State and the National Assembly for Wales requiring the school year to consist of 380 sessions, with each school day to comprise two sessions separated by a break in the middle of the day, save in exceptional circumstances, and for nursery classes normally to comprise a minimum of three hours of 'suitable activities'.[338] This is linked to teachers' statutory conditions of service which impose a requirement to teach for 190 days of the year.[339] A power under the Education Act 2002 to vary statutory requirements in respect of any one or more identified schools has been used to reduce the number of school sessions in a school year in primary, secondary and special schools in Yeovil from 380 to 378 in 2003–4 and 376 in 2004–5.[340] Apart from in the case of nursery education, the length of the school day is not prescribed. Power to determine the times of school sessions rests with the governing body of a school; in the case of a foundation, voluntary aided or foundation special school, the governors also fix the dates of school terms and holidays, but in other schools this is a matter for the LEA.[341]

In any event, parents have a statutory duty to ensure that their children receive 'efficient full-time education . . . at school or otherwise',[342] and LEAs must ensure

---

[336] *Belgian Linguistics (No 2)* (1979–80) 1 EHRR 252, para 3.

[337] *Kjeldsen, Busk Madsen and Pedersen v Denmark*, 1 EHRR 711 (1976), at para 53. See also *Valsamis v Greece*, Case No 74/1995/580/666 (1996) 24 EHRR 294; [1998] ELR 430, also discussed in Chap 2.

[338] Education Act 1996, s 551; the Education (School Day and School Year) (England) Regulations 1999 (SI 1999/3181), as amended; the Education (School Day and School Year) (Wales) Regulations 2003 (SI 2003/3231 (W311)). 'School day' is defined as 'any day on which at that school there is a school session': Education Act 1996, s 379(1).

[339] Department for Education and Skills, *School Teachers' Pay & Conditions Document 2006 and Guidance on School Teachers' Pay and Conditions* (London, TSO, 2006).

[340] Education Act 2002, s 2(1) and the Yeovil Schools (School Day and School Year Regulations) Order 2004 (SI 2004/1191), varying the application of the School Day etc Regulations (above), to substitute 378 for the number of sessions in 2003–4 and 376 in 2004–5.

[341] Education Act 2002, s 32. Regulations make provision as regards changes: Change of School Session Times (England) Regulations 1999 (SI 1999/2733), which remain in force.

[342] Education Act 1996, s 7.

that 'efficient primary, secondary and further education are available to meet the needs of the population of their area'.[343] Neither 'efficient' nor 'full-time' is defined for this purpose. In relation to the duty on LEAs to make arrangements for suitable education (meaning 'efficient education suitable to [the child's] age, ability and aptitude'), full-time or part-time, for children of compulsory school age who are ill or have been excluded from school, the House of Lords has confirmed that 'the decision as to what constitutes "suitable" or "efficient" is a matter for the LEA'.[344]

The extent to which children are guaranteed a minimum level of suitable educational provision, qualitatively and quantitatively, can best be considered by looking at the nature of this particular duty, under the Education Act 1996, section 19. Under section 19(1):

> Each local education authority shall make arrangements for the provision of suitable education at school or otherwise than at school for those children of compulsory school age who, by reason of illness, exclusion from school or otherwise, may not for any period receive suitable education unless such arrangements are made for them.[345]

The Education and Inspections Bill 2006 will clarify that (save for exceptions, to be prescribed) this duty will apply, inter alia, where a child permanently excluded on discipline grounds has not subsequently been admitted to a school other than a pupil referral unit (PRU) or has been excluded for a fixed period from a PRU.[346] In construing the section 19(1) duty, the courts have stressed its strictness, notably in *ex p T*, where the House of Lords held that an LEA was unable to justify in law a reduction in a child's hours of home tuition from five hours to three hours per week on the ground of financial constraints, and *R (M) v Worces-tershire County Council*,[347] where Collins J held that weekly arrangements for the education of a 15-year-old with behavioural problems comprising 2.5 days plus one hour of mentoring was not suitable provision and rejected the LEA's claim that it was acceptable as merely a stop-gap arrangement until a suitable placement became available. Nevertheless, the courts have also avoided a rigid approach and have accepted that LEAs can legitimately set in place 'suitable' provision for excluded pupils that is not full-time. In one case the court was unsympathetic to the argument that the placement of an excluded pupil at a PRU at which he would be provided education amounting to less than 50 per cent of typical school provision breached the obligation to ensure 'suitable' education. The evidence suggested that it was an effective unit where pupils made progress and behaviour was good; and it provided a 'stepping stone back to mainstream

---

[343] Ibid, s 13.
[344] *R v East Sussex County Council ex parte T* [1998] ELR 251 at 256B, per Lord Browne-Wilkinson.
[345] Education Act 1996, s 19, as amended. The duty becomes a power in relation to those over compulsory school age: s 19(4).
[346] Education and Inspections Bill 2006 (as first published), cl 88, inserting subs (3A) into EA 1996, s 19.
[347] [2005] ELR 48.

school education'.[348] In another case[349] an excluded child, aged 12, received 10 hours per week of home educational provision and claimed, inter alia, a breach of section 19. Newman J refused to consider the suitability of the child's education, saying that while the child's prolonged exclusion from mainstream schooling gave cause for concern it would be wrong for the court to assess the suitability of the provision made for him on the basis of the evidence available to it, and implied that it was a matter for the authorities to determine.[350]

Nonetheless, as Sedley LJ confirmed in the Court of Appeal in *Ali*,[351] the effect of section 19 is that 'it is the LEA's obligation to ensure that no child falls out of the education system, even if excluded from school';[352] or, as Lord Bingham of Cornhill put it in the House of Lords in that case (where the nature of the LEA's duty was not in fact a significant issue at that stage), it was 'plainly intended that every child of compulsory school age should receive appropriate education in one way if not another, and that the responsibility rests in the last resort with the LEA'.[353] In the Court of Appeal, Sedley LJ said that the content of the duty was amplified:

—by the provision of subs (5) that any such child continues to be a pupil for all statutory purposes;

—by the provision of subs (6) that 'suitable education' means efficient education suitable to the child's age, ability and aptitude;

—by Circular 11/99,[354] which requires LEAs to ensure that temporarily excluded pupils are reintegrated where possible and educated meanwhile; and

—by Circular 10/99,[355] which reminds LEAs that the obligations to provide for the education of permanently excluded pupils reverts to them.[356]

---

[348] *R (S) v Head Teacher of C High School and Others* [2002] ELR 73.at para 49.

[349] *R (B) v Head Teacher of Alperton Community School and Others; R v Head Teacher of Wembley High School and Others ex p T; R v Governing Body of Cardinal Newman High School and Others ex p C* [2001] ELR 359.

[350] Ibid, at para 69.

[351] *A v The Head Teacher and Governors of Lord Grey School* [2004] ELR 169.

[352] Ibid, at para 6.

[353] *Ali v Headteacher and Governors of Lord Grey School* [2006] UKHL 14; [2006] 2 WLR 690, at para 16 (UKHL).

[354] Department for Education and Employment, Circular 11/99, *Social Inclusion: The LEA Role in Pupil Support* (London, Department for Education and Employment, 1999).

[355] Department for Education and Employment, Circular 10/99 *Social Inclusion: Pupil Support* (London, Department for Education and Employment, 1999). See now Department for Education and Skills, *Advice and Guidance to Schools and Local Authorities on Managing Behaviour and Attendance: Responsibility for Educating Pupils out of School and Re-integrating Them into School* (London, Department for Education and Skills, 2005), available at www.dfes.gov.uk/ behaviourandattendance/guidance/IBAGuidance. LEAs have a duty to have regard to the guidance on exclusion: see below.

[356] N 351 above, at para 6.

The relevant provision in Circular 11/99[357] in fact applied to permanently excluded pupils as well. It stressed the expectation that LEAs should make arrangements for an excluded child's full-time education (whether at a PRU or elsewhere[358]) within 15 school days of a permanent exclusion; it was in response to the huge amount of evidence that provision for excluded pupils has often been as little as a few hours per week.[359] Ofsted appears to be keeping under review LEA provision in respect of children out of school and has found improvements, but also some risk of children out of school still being lost in the system.[360] The official guidance, which LEAs are required by law to take into account,[361] was updated in 2005 but still requires alternative provision to made by the sixteenth day of the child's exclusion;[362] but the 2005 White Paper proposes a reduction to the sixth day.[363] It also proposes that during those first five days when the child is unlikely to be receiving formal schooling of any kind the parent is to be expected to take responsibility for their child by, for example, ensuring that he or she is 'supervised doing schoolwork at home or, for example, at a relative's house'.[364] There must, however, be doubts as to the practicability of this since it may well involve a parent having to arrange to take holiday entitlement at short notice or to forgo employment altogether. The House of Commons Education and Skills Select Committee has stated that it is 'not . . . realistic to expect parents in low paid or insecure employment to take time off work in these circumstances without the risk of losing their job'.[365] The Education and Inspections Bill 2006 would in fact limit the parent's responsibility, during the first five school days of the child's exclusion (which, in the case of a child excluded in the morning, would run from the afternoon of that day), to ensuring that the child 'is not present in a public place at any time during school hours'.[366] The parent would commit an offence, punishable on summary conviction by a fine of up to level 3, if he or she failed in that duty.[367] However, a penalty notice could be issued first, by an officer of the LEA, a police officer or a head teacher or other authorised

[357] Department for Education and Employment Circular 11/99, *Social Inclusion: The LEA Role in Pupil Support* (London, Department for Education and Employment, 1999), para 5.1.

[358] According to DfES figures, around 50 per cent of excluded pupils are educated in PRUs: DfES, Press Notice, 24 Jan 2002.

[359] See N Harris and K Eden with A Blair, *Challenges to School Exclusion* (London, RoutledgeFalmer, 2000), ch 4.

[360] Ofsted, *Out of School: A Survey of the Educational Support and Provision for Pupils Not in School* (London, Ofsted, 2004).

[361] The Education (Pupil Exclusions and Appeals) (Maintained Schools) (England) Regulations 2002 (SI 2002/3178), reg 7(2).

[362] Department for Education and Skills, *Advice and Guidance to Schools and Local Authorities on Managing Behaviour and Attendance: Responsibility for Educating Pupils out of School and Re-integrating Them into School* (London, Department for Education and Skills, 2005), available at www.dfes.gov.uk/behaviourandattendance/guidance/IBAGuidance.

[363] DfES, *Higher Standards, Better Schools for All*, Cm 6677 (London, TSO, 2006).

[364] Ibid, para 7.13.

[365] House of Commons Education and Skills Committee, First Report of Session 2005–6, *The Schools White Paper: 'Higher Standards, Better Schools for All'*, Vol. 1, HC 633-I (London, TSO, 2006), para 29.

[366] Education and Inspections Bill 2006 (as first published), cl 90.

[367] Ibid.

member of staff. The parent would not be convicted of the offence if he or she paid the relevant penalty.[368]

The principal issue in the *Ali* case, the background to which was the claimant's suspected involvement in an incident of arson at school leading to his exclusion while a criminal investigation was carried out by the police, was whether the boy was entitled to damages under section 8 of the Human Rights Act 1998 in respect of his exclusion from school. It was alleged that the exclusion gave rise to a breach of his right under Article 2 of Protocol 1 to the ECHR. This issue was approached quite differently as between the Court of Appeal and House of Lords in this case.[369] In the Court of Appeal, Sedley LJ (with whom the other law lords concurred) said that the starting point was whether the exclusion was unlawful under domestic law. The period following the decision to exclude comprised six identifiable phases. In the fourth phase, starting from the time that the total number of days of temporary exclusion experienced by the boy had exceeded the statutory limit (45 days in aggregate), his exclusion was unlawful because he had neither been permanently excluded (indeed no grounds existed for his permanent exclusion) nor readmitted to school. Sedley LJ said that if there had been no breach of domestic law then a human rights challenge was sustainable only if the law itself was incompatible with the Convention. If domestic law had been breached, then the relevant question was whether a Convention right had been denied, which would be the case where:

> breach of the domestic law has resulted in the pupil's being unable to avail himself of the means of education which currently exists in England and Wales—not, for example, by being temporarily unable to reach the school premises for want of transport, but by being shut out for a significant or an indefinite period from access to such education as the law provides for him.[370]

In the circumstances, even thought the school was offering to provide him with homework, his right to education was denied during the fourth phase.[371] The arrangement for the provision of homework 'may go to the damages for this phase of exclusion, but it does not affect liability'.[372] It may conveniently be noted here that school governing bodies, or proprietors of academies or CTCs, may in fact face a new statutory duty under the Education and Inspections Bill 2006 to make arrangements for the provision of 'suitable full-time education' for a pupil who is excluded for a fixed period on disciplinary grounds.[373] Regard will have to be had to DfES guidance on the matter,[374] but it seems unlikely that the mere provision of homework will suffice for this purpose.

---

[368] Ibid, cl 92.
[369] *A v Head Teacher and Governors of Lord Grey School* [2004] ELR 169 (CA); *Ali v Headteacher and Governors of Lord Grey School* [2006] UKHL 14; [2006] 2 WLR 690.
[370] Ibid (CA), at para 45.
[371] Ibid, para 60 and 61.
[372] Ibid, para 61.
[373] Education and Inspections Bill (as first published), cl 87.
[374] Ibid, cl 87(4).

In the House of Lords, only Baroness Hale of Richmond adopted similar reasoning to that of Sedley LJ. While, for reasons discussed below, the other judges were not convinced that the right to education under Article 2 of Protocol 1 had been denied to the claimant, her Ladyship held that the school had 'effectively excluded a pupil when it had no good reason to do so and without affording him any of the procedural protection afforded by the established system'.[375] Referring to the possibility that the claimant could attend a PRU she opined that 'that sort of fall back is no substitute for ordinary access to the full national curriculum as a pupil at an ordinary school'.[376] Although, on one reading, an implication of Baroness Hale's remarks might be that by virtue of attending such a unit, a young person is being denied his or her right of access to education, a proper reading would be that she was referring to the suitability of the proposed arrangements out of school for someone in the claimant's position, although it is not clear why the kind of provision that would actually be made at the unit for the claimant would indeed have been unsatisfactory. Baroness Hale concluded that the claimant 'had a right not to be denied the education which the established system had provided for him'; and she was not convinced that if the matter were before the ECtHR it would regard the fall-back provision as a proper justification for the school's action, at least in the period from when it removed his name from the school roll despite receiving notification from the police that no criminal prosecution would be brought against the boy.[377] Baroness Hale nonetheless rejected the idea that damages should be awarded. She considered a declaration that the school had acted in a way that was incompatible with his right to education would be the appropriate outcome.[378]

Several of the other judges questioned whether the claimant had been excluded at all, since 'exclude' for the purposes of exclusion from school was defined in the legislation as 'exclude on disciplinary grounds'.[379] Lord Scott argued that the claimant's 'enforced absence' was a 'management decision' of the same kind as one to send home a pupil with an infectious disease, rather than being a disciplinary exclusion.[380] Accordingly, the school was not prevented by the 'statutory straitjacket' on exclusion from removing him temporarily from school.[381] In his Lordship's view the school had acted responsibly in the circumstances, including its decision to remove the boy's name from the roll after the parents had failed to respond to letters or attend a meeting. Lord Hoffmann too did not consider that the claimant had been excluded on disciplinary grounds, 'except in the broad sense that it was thought necessary to exclude him while an allegation of a disciplinary offence was being investigated'.[382] His

---

[375] *Ali v Headteacher and Governors of Lord Grey School* [2006] UKHL 14; [2006] 2 WLR 690, at para 81 (UKHL).
[376] Ibid, para 81.
[377] Ibid.
[378] Ibid, para 83.
[379] SSFA 1998, s 64(4). See now EA 2002, s 52(10).
[380] *Ali v Headteacher and Governors of Lord Grey School* [2006] UKHL 14; [2006] 2 WLR 690, at paras 68 and 69.
[381] Ibid, para 69.
[382] Ibid, para 37.

Lordship did not think that a 'precautionary exclusion' of the kind that had occurred fitted into the statutory code on exclusion from school,[383] although it might fall within the scope of the school's statutory power to require a pupil to attend another place to receive curricular instruction or training.[384] Lord Bingham of Cornhill highlighted a gap in the legislation in cases where the school had exceeded the maximum aggregate period of fixed term exclusion but, for good reason, did not want either to re-admit the child or to permanently exclude him or her.[385]

The question whether the claimant had been denied his right to education was answered negatively by the majority. Lord Bingham considered that alternative arrangements were made available (the parents in fact chose not to take up the offer of a PRU place) and the LEA had found another school place for the child as soon as was feasible in the circumstances. His Lordship noted that the right to education under the ECHR was, in comparison with most of the other Convention guarantees, a weak one: it did not guarantee education of a particular kind or quality, nor (in contradistinction to the view taken by Sedley LJ) did it offer a guarantee of compliance with domestic law by the relevant authority.[386] Lord Hoffmann similarly noted that the Strasbourg case law, which was discussed in Chapter 2, did not acknowledge a right to attend any particular form of institution, nor had it been concerned with procedures, but 'only with results: was the applicant denied the basic minimum of education available under the domestic system?'[387] This is perhaps a sad reflection of the courts' general unwillingness to extend the reach of Article 2 of Protocol 1 and to take the opportunity that was open to it to give a view as to what should be considered the bare minimum in the national context. In Lord Hoffmann's view, the availability of alternative provision at the PRU meant the claimant was not denied the right to education and the Strasbourg court would not concern itself with the question whether provision there rather than at the school would have been in accordance with domestic law.[388] Lord Hoffmann concluded that, as it had not been shown that there was a systemic failure to ensure minimum provision, there was no breach of the Convention right, so the question of which public authority bore the primary responsibility for the education of the child did not fall for conclusive determination.[389] All of the judicial reasoning in this case appears broadly consistent with the Strasbourg jurisprudence and, as such, provides a further illustration of the limitations to the Convention right to education, as discussed in Chapter 2. It also shows that in the sixth year following the implementation of the Human Rights Act 1998, the courts still consider themselves unable to develop the boundaries of this

---

[383] Ibid, para 40. Cf Baroness Hale of Richmond at para 74.
[384] Ibid, para 41, referring to the power in the EA 2002, s 29(3).
[385] Ibid, para 23.
[386] Ibid, paras 24 and 25.
[387] Ibid, para 57.
[388] Ibid, para 58.
[389] Ibid, para 61.

particular right further in the national context. Only Baroness Hale hinted at a more progressive approach.

A further issue on access to education that arises from school exclusion concerns the situation where a pupil is reinstated by an appeal panel. It might be assumed that he or she would be fully reintegrated within the school, attending classes as before. However, that was not what happened in *Re L*.[390] Here the House of Lords upheld (by majority) a decision by a head teacher (who was motivated by the threat of industrial action by teaching unions opposed to the boy's reinstatement) to educate separately from other pupils, and with no face-to-face teaching, a pupil whose reinstatement following permanent exclusion had been ordered by an independent appeal panel. The court held that in the management of a pupil's behaviour, access to education can be restricted. This power extended to the case of a pupil who was reinstated just as much as to that of a pupil who had not been excluded. Human rights arguments concerning the right to education were not pursued, the matter being decided on the meaning of 'reinstatement', the majority not finding the arrangements that were put in place to be inconsistent with the meaning of the word or the purpose of the provision. In his dissenting judgment (with which Lord Hoffmann concurred), however, Lord Bingham held that if a pupil is reinstated he must 'be put back in substantially the same position as he was before he was excluded', and that holding mere restoration of a formal relationship (by being placed back on the school register) to be sufficient was 'to take an unrealistic and realistic view of a practical educational situation'.[391]

The reintegration of pupils excluded for a *fixed term* would become the subject of a new statutory duty under the Education and Inspections Bill 2006; regulations could require the head teacher to request a parent of a temporarily excluded pupil to attend a reintegration interview at the school whose purpose would be to assist the pupil's reintegration after exclusion and to promote improvement in his or her behaviour.[392] Given the possibility that among those *permanently* excluded pupils who are reinstated following a successful appeal will be some whose absence from school due to exclusion will be of a relatively similar length to those temporarily excluded, this new duty ought perhaps to have been extended to them as well.

Access to Schooling Without Cost

It was noted in Chapter 2 that under the UNCRC the state's obligation to ensure the child's right to education includes a requirement that education be available free to all, at least at the stage of primary education.[393] All state school education in the UK is available free of charge, but access is not without financial cost to the

---

[390] *Re L (A Minor by His Father and Litigation Friend)* [2003] ELR 309.
[391] Ibid, paras 19 and 20.
[392] Education and Inspections Bill (as first published), cl 89.
[393] UNCRC, Art 28(1)(a).

parent. The law explicitly prohibits a charge being made for admission to a maintained school[394] or for educational provision made there or, if it is made outside school, provision under a syllabus for a public examination for which the child is being prepared by the school or under the National Curriculum or statutory religious education.[395] Moreover, neither a parent of a pupil nor the pupil him/herself may normally be required to pay for, or to supply, any materials, books, instruments or other equipment for use in respect of any education for which no charge may be made or in connection with a syllabus for a prescribed public examination for which the pupil has been prepared by the school.[396] Schools often request 'contributions' from parents towards the cost of, for example, some educational visits. The law permits requests for voluntary contributions 'for the benefit of the school or any school activities', but it must be clear from the terms in which the request is made 'that there no obligation to make a contribution' and that 'registered pupils at the school will not be treated differently according to whether or not their parents have made any contribution in response to the request or invitation'.[397]

In theory, therefore, there is a legal guarantee of free school education to the age of 18 (including any education provided to those aged 2 or over in a nursery school or nursery class in a school[398]). There is also a right to free school meals if the pupil or his/her parents are in receipt of income support or income-based jobseeker's allowance. Indeed, in the face of evidence that low income families found it 'questionable whether those who move into work can stand the withdrawal of free school meals',[399] the Government has extended this right to those who are in receipt of tax credits under the Tax Credits Act 2002 and those

---

[394] A 'maintained school' here is any school maintained by an LEA: Education Act 1996, s 449, as substituted by the SSFA 1998, Sched 30, para 119. 'School' is defined in the 1996 Act, s 4(1), as including an institution providing primary education. 'Primary education' is defined in s 2(1) of the 1996 Act (as substituted by the Education Act 2002, s 156(2)) as, inter alia, education suitable for those aged 2 and under compulsory school age (essentially 5). *Therefore*, the ban on charging applies to children in nursery classes in schools or in nursery schools (defined as being schools wholly or mainly for 2–5-year-olds: 1996 Act, s 6(1), as amended by the Education Act 2002, s 156(1)).

[395] Education Act 1996, ss 450 and 451. An exception to the ban on charging applies in respect of music tuition to an individual pupil or in groups of up to 4 pupils unless for public examination for which the pupil or pupils is/are being prepared by the school or in pursuance of national curriculum or statutorily-required RE: ibid., s 451(1)–(3). There are special provisions covering educational provision partly inside and outside school hours, where pupils fail to meet examination syllabus requirements or where pupils are on school trips: see ibid, ss 453, 455, 456. Schools are required to have charging and remission of charging policies: ibid, s 457, which also provides that in some instances remission of board and lodging charges for those on a residential trip must occur if the child's parents are in receipt of particular social security benefits or tax credits.

[396] Ibid, s 454(1). The exception to this rule relates to 'any materials for use for the purposes of the production, in the course of the provision of education for the pupil at the school, of any article incorporating those materials, where the parent has indicated before that requirement is made that he wishes the article to be owned by him or the pupil': ibid, s 454(2).

[397] Education Act 1996, s 460.

[398] See ibid.

[399] W McMahon and T March, *Filling the Gap. Free School Meals, Nutrition and Poverty* (London, Child Poverty Action Group, 1999) 20, a conclusion based on H Parker (ed), *Low Cost but Acceptable* (London, Policy Press, 1998).

entitled to asylum support.[400] The right to free school meals is not, however, always exercised; 1.2 million children are currently eligible for them but the take up is just under one million.[401] A major factor is the stigma of claiming them.[402] The cost of school meals to those parents who would have to pay for them has risen significantly since the Education Act 1980 permitted LEAs to make a reasonable charge for them.[403]

These rights go only so far in limiting the financial barriers to access to schooling. A study for the Child Poverty Action Group (CPAG) found that '[d]espite having a "free" school system in the UK, the costs associated with education are a key problem facing parents living on a low income'.[404] These include costs in connection with school uniform or other clothing and optional extras such as music lessons and school trips. A research study published by the DfES at the end of 2004 found that the average amount spent by parents on costs associated with sending their child to a state school for 12 months (in 2003) was £736.22, with secondary schooling being more expensive than sending a child to primary school.[405] School uniform costs alone represented an average of £157.50 and the PE kit £78.47.[406] These are significant amounts for many families. In the CPAG study it was found that a substantial number, albeit a minority, of parents found these expenses difficult or prohibitive. This was especially the case where lone parents and those who had more than one child at the school were concerned.[407] They also felt pressured to respond to requests for a contribution, even though such contributions were voluntary. The contributions that parents are therefore finding they have to make to their child's 'free' education are in fact an international phenomenon. The World Bank has noted in relation to Europe and Central Asia as a whole that 'supplementary payments at school level have now become common'.[408]

The House of Commons Work and Pensions Committee said in its *Child*

---

[400] Education Act 1996, ss 512(3) and 512ZB (substituted and added by the Education Act 2002, s 201); and the Education (Free School Lunches) (Prescribed Tax Credits) (England) Order 2003 (SI 200/383) and Same (Wales) Order 2003 (SI 2003/879 (W110)).

[401] House of Commons Work and Pensions Committee, First Report, Session 2003–04, *Child Poverty in the UK*, HC 85–I (London, TSO, 2004), i, para 100.

[402] See T Smith and M Noble, *Education Divides. Poverty and Schooling in the 1990s* (London, Child Poverty Action Group, 1995) 106–11; P Storey and R Chamberlain, *Improving Take-up of Free School Meals* (London, Child Poverty Action Group and Department for Education and Employment, 2001); Child Poverty Action Group, Memorandum, Ev 180 in House of Commons Work and Pensions Committee, First Report, Session 2003–04, *Child Poverty in the UK*, HC 85–II (London, TSO, 2004), ii, EV 180.

[403] T Smith and M Noble, *Education Divides. Poverty and Schooling in the 1990s* (London, Child Poverty Action Group, 1995) 100–1. For evidence of wide regional variations, see W McMahon and T March, *Filling the Gap. Free School Meals, Nutrition and Poverty* (London, Child Poverty Action Group, 1999), ch 7.

[404] E Tanner *et al*, *The Costs of Education. A Local Study* (London, Child Poverty Action Group, 2003) 1. For a useful historical summary, see also A Riley, 'The Role of School Meals in Tackling Child Poverty' in C Hurley and A Riley, *Recipe for Change* (London, Child Poverty Action Group, 2004) 13.

[405] T Brunwin *et al*, *The Cost of Schooling*, Reseach Report RR588 (London, DfES, 2004) 136.

[406] Ibid, 141 and 142.

[407] Tanner *et al*, n 404 above.

[408] N Vandycke, *Access to Education for the Poor In Europe and Central Asia. Preliminary Evidence and Policy Implications* (Washington, DC, World Bank, 2001) 13.

Poverty report that there was 'compelling evidence that children experience further exclusion through the financial costs of participation in school life, which further reduce family finances'.[409] LEAs have powers to provide clothing for pupils, including those attending independent schools,[410] in addition to their general power to pay expenses to enable children to take part in school activities.[411] The *Child Poverty* report notes that the availability of school clothing grants has declined since 1990 and that not all LEAs provide them—indeed only a minority provide them to primary *and* secondary school pupils. Support for school uniform costs under the Social Fund within the social security system is available only in the form of a budgeting loan, eligibility for which is restricted to persons who have a current entitlement to income support or income-based jobseeker's allowance that has subsisted for at least 26 weeks.[412] While not going as far as Citizens' Advice in recommending that grants should be mandatory,[413] the *Child Poverty* report recommends a national strategy of school clothing grants backed by adequate resources.[414]

One particular expense arising in the context of access to school, other than as a boarding pupil, concerns daily travel. Indeed, there is a link in this context between transport and social exclusion. The Social Exclusion Unit has said that difficulties with regard to transport 'can prevent people from participation in learning or restrict their choice . . . Transport is therefore an integral part of the drive to increase participation and achievement in education.'[415] The *2002 Families and Children Study* revealed that nearly one third of children in Great Britain face a journey to school of over two miles: 21 per cent of children travel three miles or more to school and a further 8 per cent travel two to three miles.[416] The distance travelled is, not surprisingly, greater among those attending secondary schools than those at primary school. Only 15 per cent of 5–10-year-olds travel more than two miles to school, compared to 36 per cent of 11–15-year-olds and 59 per cent of 16–18-year-olds.[417] As regards the mode of transport, among those pupils who travel three miles or more, 30 per cent use a school bus, 28 per cent use a public bus, 32 per cent travel by car and 5 per cent use the train. Those who travel two to three miles are as likely as those travelling

---

[409] House of Commons Work and Pensions Committee, First Report, Session 2003–04, *Child Poverty in the UK*, HC 85–I (London, TSO, 2004), para 95.

[410] Education Act 1996, ss 510 and 511.

[411] Ibid, s 518.

[412] Social Fund Directions, direction 8(1). For a critical evaluation of the conditions surrounding, and amounts available under, this scheme, see R Thompson, 'A Critique of the New Budgeting Loans Scheme' (2000) 7 *Journal of Social Security Law* 35. See also T Buck, *The Social Fund: Law, Policy and Practice* (2nd edn, London, Sweet & Maxwell, 2000). Directions 23 and 29 exclude eligibility for community care grants or crisis loans in the case of 'distinctive school uniform'.

[413] See K Lane, 'School Uniform: Financial Assistance as a Statutory Obligation' (2001) 2 *Education Law* 213.

[414] House of Commons Work and Pensions Committee, First Report, Session 2003–04, *Child Poverty in the UK*, HC 85–I (London, TSO, 2004), para 98.

[415] Social Exclusion Unit, *Making the Connections: Final Report on Transport and Social Exclusion* (London, TSO, 2003) 103.

[416] M Barnes *et al*, *Families and Children in Britain. Findings from the 2002 Families and Children Study (FACS)*, DWP Research Report 206 (Leeds, Corporare Document Services, 2004), table 4.2.

[417] Ibid.

further to use a public bus but are more likely to journey by car than by school bus.[418] Overall, 2 per cent of 5–10-year-olds, 15 per cent of 11–15-year-olds and 39 per cent of 16–18-year-olds use public transport.[419] Separate Department of Transport figures indicate that, in 2002, 23 per cent of 11–16-year-olds used the local bus to travel to school.[420] There are costs associated with such travel, especially where the child is accompanied to school by an adult, although this is the case with only a minority of secondary school children.[421] However, LEAs have a duty to make arrangements for the provision of free 'transport and otherwise, as they consider necessary, or as the Secretary of State may direct', to facilitate school attendance or, in the absence of such arrangements, to pay reasonable travel expenses.[422] The duty applies only to those who are not of sixth-form age, but LEAs must now co-ordinate transport provision and policies for post-16 attendance and, in connection with that role, prepare a 'transport policy statement' stating the arrangements considered necessary for facilitating attendance for education and training at schools, further education institutions and elsewhere, including arrangements for persons with disabilities.[423] LEAs also have a power to provide travel assistance to enable children to receive nursery education otherwise than at school.[424] Altogether, some 700,000 pupils in England, approximately 10 per cent of all pupils (but a higher proportion in rural areas), currently receive free home to school transport on a daily basis; in Wales, 200,000 (or 20 per cent of) pupils receive it.[425] The total cost of school transport in England stood at £662 million in 2002–3.[426] Around half this total goes on transport provision for pupils with special educational needs (SEN), or 70 per cent if one includes the children with SEN who attend mainstream schools.[427] LEAs are under an obligation to meet the costs of transport requirements specified in a child's statement of SEN.[428]

In March 2004 the Government published for consultation a draft School Transport Bill, intended to enable pilot 'school travel schemes' to be introduced in some LEAs with a view to reducing the proportion of children being driven to school by car each day, which causes traffic congestion and reduces physical exercise.[429] The draft Bill would have enabled charges to be made by LEAs for

---

[418] Ibid, table 4.4.

[419] Ibid, table 4.3.

[420] Department for Transport, *National Travel Survey 2002. Transport Statistics Bulletin* (London, Department for Transport, 2004), table 6.1.

[421] Some 85 per cent of 5–10-year-olds, 24 per cent of 11–15-year-olds and 17 per cent of 16–18-year-olds are usually accompanied to school by an adult: ibid, table 4.5.

[422] Education Act 1996, s 509.

[423] Ibid, ss 509AA–509AC, inserted by the Education Act 2002, Sched 19, paras 3–5.

[424] Ibid, s 509A.

[425] House of Commons Education and Skills Committee, Third Report, Session 2003–04, *Draft School Transport Bill Report*, HC 509 (London, TSO, 2004), para 19.

[426] Ibid, para 10.

[427] Ibid, paras 10 and 14.

[428] But 'transport should only be recorded in the statement in Part 6 [non-educational provision] in exceptional cases where the child has particular transport needs': DfES, *Special Educational Needs Code of Practice* (London, DfES, 2001), para 8.89.

[429] Department for Education and Skills and Welsh Office, *School Travel Schemes—Draft Bill and Prospectus* (London, DfES/Welsh Office, 2004).

transport provided other than to 'protected children', defined as those eligible to free school meals and milk.[430] This legislation was not pursued, although in the 2005 White Paper the idea was revived through proposals to introduce pilot transport projects, aimed not only at environmental benefits but also at the link between 'better transport and fair admissions'; they could involve 'a charging regime for better off parents'.[431] Moreover, in the light of evidence showing that pupils in receipt of free school meals are more likely than other pupils to be attending a school within two miles of their home and less likely to be attending one that is at least three miles away, the Government acknowledged that parental concern about the cost of transport may be hindering choice of school for some.[432] It therefore proposed to introduce legislation to ensure that children from families in receipt of free school meals or the maximum rate of working tax credit would be entitled to free transport to any of three suitable schools within a six-mile radius of their homes. In addition, local authorities would be placed under a duty to consider home-to-school travel as part of a new general duty to promote 'choice, diversity and fair access'.[433] The Education and Inspections Bill 2006 now provides a broad framework for most of these proposed developments.[434] LEAs will be placed under a duty to prepare a 'sustainable modes of travel strategy' covering the school transport needs for their area, related to the physical well-being of users and the environmental well-being of the area.[435] They will also have to ensure that there are in place suitable arrangements for home to school travel, provided free of charge, to facilitate school attendance for an 'eligible child' (replacing the term 'protected child' adopted earlier) in their area, where existing arrangements provided free of charge made by other persons for such a child are not suitable.[436] They will have a power, but not a duty, to make school travel arrangements in respect of a child who is not an 'eligible child'.[437] Eligible children will include those covered by the current eligibility criteria and children with special educational needs, or who are disabled or have mobility problems. They will also include, subject to certain conditions, children from low income families (defined with reference to entitlement to free school meals or milk for the child or to working tax credit at the maximum rate): they must be children who, in the case of those aged 8–10, live more than two miles from their school or, in the case of those aged 11 or over, live more than two but less than six miles from their school (provided that in either case the school is a state school or academy or an independent school

---

[430] The House of Commons Education and Skills Select Committee wanted a more sophisticated test of entitlement, for example based on working tax credit eligibility: above n 425 at para 46.

[431] HM Government, *Higher Standards, Better Schools for All*, Cm 6677 (London, TSO, 2005), para 3.17.

[432] Ibid, para 3.13.

[433] Ibid, paras 3.18 and 9.7.

[434] Education and Inspections Bill 2006 (as first published), Part 6. In relation to the functions covered by the provisions in the next two footnotes, LEAs will have to have regard to guidance by the Secretary of State: ibid, cl 65, inserting s 508E into the EA 1996.

[435] Ibid, cl 63, inserting s 508A into the EA 1996.

[436] Ibid, cl 64, inserting s 508B into the EA 1996.

[437] Ibid, inserting s 508C into the EA 1996.

approved to take children with special educational needs).[438] The travel arrangements that are required within school travel schemes that LEAs have a discretion to make[439] will have to include arrangements specifically aimed at such 'eligible children'.[440]

Although the strength of LEAs' current duty as regards transport arrangements appears to be cut down by an element of discretion within the law at present, there is an important interrelationship between this duty and the law on school attendance. As noted above, one of the statutory permitted excuses from the offence committed when a child fails to attend school regularly is that the school is not within walking distance of the child's home and no suitable arrangements have been made by the LEA for his transport to and from school, or for him/her to board at a school or to enable him or her to attend a school nearer his or her home.[441] 'Walking distance' is defined, with regard to a child aged under 8 as 3.218688 km (two miles), and for an older child as 4.828032 km (three miles).[442] The effect of this statutory excuse, read with the transport duty, is therefore that the LEA must make arrangements for transport for children not living within walking distance of school, save where it has made boarding provision or 'suitable arrangements' for a child to attend a nearer school.[443] In a recent judgment,[444] Collins J confirmed that if the parents had that school non-attendance excuse it would be necessary for the LEA to conclude that free transport should be provided. In that case it was agreed that the nearer school to the child's home in Wales was an English-medium school, whereas the school he attended was Welsh-medium. Collins J confirmed that 'suitable arrangements' could not be made if the school was unsuitable; here it was considered unsuitable in educational terms. The suitability of a placement at a nearer school is a matter for the LEA (often via a school transport panel), and the court's role in reviewing that decision is to decide whether the LEA's decision was 'lawfully reached, which in most cases will require no more than a consideration of the rationality of its conclusion'.[445]

In *R v Carmarthenshire CC ex p White*,[446] for example, the parents of a girl who was attending a school where she was bullied and felt stressed withdrew the child and had her admitted to another school, further from her home. The LEA's refusal to meet the cost of transport to her new school was based on the fact that,

---

[438] Ibid, Sched 8, inserting Sched 35B into the EA 1996.

[439] Ibid, cl 65 and Sched 9, inserting, respectively, s 508E and Sched 35C into the EA 1996.

[440] Ibid.

[441] EA 1996, s 444. As noted above, this will be extended under the Education and Inspections Bill 2006, cl 69 (amending s 444) to include cases where LEAs have failed to comply with their new duties to ensure transport for certain children.

[442] Ibid. s 444(5). This distance is to be measured by the 'nearest available route'; see further *Rogers v Essex CC* [1985] 1 WLR 700 and *R v Devon CC ex p George* [1989] AC 573 (a route does not cease to be available merely because a child cannot travel it unaccompanied without risk of danger).

[443] As regards the meaning of 'suitable arrangements', see *Re S (Minors)* [1995] ELR 98 (CA); *Re C (A Minor)* [1994] ELR 273 (CA); *R v Kent CC ex p C* [1998] ELR 108 (QBD); *R v Vale of Glamorgan CC ex p J* [2001] ELR 223 (QBD); *R (on the application of T) v Leeds City Council* [2002] ELR 91 (QBD).

[444] *R (Jones) v Ceredigion County Council* [2004] ELR 506.

[445] *R v Kent County Council ex parte C* [1998] ELR 108 (QBD), at 14B–C, per McCullough J.

[446] [2001] ELR 172.

in its view, the nearer school was suitable and that it was reasonable for her to attend it. There was a suggestion that the child's stress was induced by the parent's irrational dislike of the previous school. In confirming that the suitability of the arrangements was a matter for the LEA rationally to assess, taking account of the stress caused by alternative arrangements, the court rejected the application by the parents. The LEA had been concerned with the ability of the child to receive an effective education at that school. The parents had also argued that ECHR Article 2 of Protocol 1 was violated, on the basis that the girl could not benefit from her education (and thus from her education right) unless she was free from psychiatric problems and stress. Tomlinson J simply said that the Article was concerned with 'effective education' and that 'the Convention is at one with English jurisprudence, so far as concerns this issue'.[447] The LEA's decision had been 'within the bounds of reasonable decision-making'.[448] A similar conclusion was reached in a subsequent case[449] involving a child whose white mother and African Caribbean father moved him away from a primary school where he had been subject to racist bullying at school. The new primary school had a higher proportion of ethnic minority pupils and the parents said it was essential for psychological reasons that he should attend such a school. They sought transport costs from the LEA and applied for judicial review of the LEA's refusal. The boy was about to transfer to secondary school at this stage, but the same issue arose in connection with the secondary school preferred by the parents and the two nearer schools the LEA said were suitable. Elias J held that the LEA's decision had been reasonable as there was no evidence to support the contention that the only suitable school for the boy would be a multi-racial one; in any event, the environment at secondary school would be different from that at primary school and it could not be assumed that the problems the boy had experienced would be replicated.

The child's age and the nature of the route, or any reasonable alternative routes, are among the matters that the LEA must take into account in considering whether to make transport arrangements for a particular individual.[450] Unlike in the law on school transport in Denmark, there is no statutory requirement that the route be safe nor a definition of what constitutes a safe route.[451] The LEA must also 'have regard to' any wish of the parent for the child to be provided with education at a school where the religious education corresponds with the religion or denomination to which the child's parent adheres.[452] In a case in which Orthodox Jewish parents living in Leeds failed in their claim for the transport costs of sending their children to the nearest Jewish school, in Manchester,

---

[447] Ibid, paras 54 and 55.
[448] Ibid, para 55.
[449] *R v Vale of Glamorgan County Council ex parte J* [2001] ELR 223 (QBD).
[450] Education Act 1996, s 509(4)(a).
[451] House of Commons Transport Committee, Eighth Report, Session 2003–04, *School Transport*, HC 580 (London, TSO, 2004), para 16.
[452] EA 1996, s 509(4)(b).

Turner J held that 'have regard to' in this context was 'not to be equated with "comply with"'.[453]

Although many of the disputes over school transport costs are concerned with the question of parental choice, they do concern questions of access to suitable education. Where a child has been bullied or racially abused, as in some of these cases, the parents and the child are likely to be highly sensitised to the potential dangers of an unsuitable school placement. Ultimately, though, it is the LEA's view of this matter rather than the parents' that seems likely to prevail, on the basis of the LEA's capacity to take an objective view, subject to the test of rationality. While human rights law has not yet been fully tested in this context, the law on the provision of transport at least seems broadly consistent with Article 2 of Protocol 1 to the ECHR, although the statutory requirement to have regard to parents' religious preferences would obviously need to be read with the addition of philosophical convictions. Indeed, the House of Commons Education and Skills Committee, citing the case of an atheist from Lancashire who wanted his child to attend a non-denominational school rather than a nearer denominational school, has recently recommended that 'in order to reduce the potential for discriminatory practices, and to clarify the legal situation under the Human Rights Act, guidance to LEAs must make clear that where transport arrangement exist to support parents' denominational preferences, they must also cater for strongly held philosophical preferences'.[454] Of course, in the light of *Douglas* decision, noted above,[455] a court might now take the restrictive view that, like financial support, transport is 'one step removed' from education and outside the scope of Article 2 of Protocol 1 altogether.

Indeed, an argument to that effect was recently accepted in another case brought by several Orthodox Jewish parents living in Leeds who, as in the case noted above, challenged the education authority's refusal to fund transport to Manchester where the nearest Jewish school was located.[456] The LEA contended that the Article was concerned with access to educational institutions that the state makes available and merely required account to be taken of religious convictions, which the authority had done. Wilkie J found that the Article was not engaged, but he said that even if it had been the authority would have been able to rely on the UK's reservation, which meant that the duty to respect religious convictions could be denied if it gave rise to unreasonable public expenditure. The parents' argument that, although the cost per child would be high, the overall cost was de minimis set against the overall transport budget, and so could not amount to unreasonable public expenditure, was rejected. The court also rejected claims based on Article 9 (freedom to manifest one's religion), on the ground that the children in question were not prevented from attending a

---

[453] *R (T) v Leeds City Council* [2002] ELR 91 at 97E–F. See also *R (R and Others) v Leeds City Council/Education Leeds* [2006] ELR 25; [2005] EWHC Admin 2495, per Wilkie J at para 11.

[454] House of Commons Education and Skills Committee, Third Report, Session 2003–04, *Draft School Transport Bill Report*, HC 509 (London, TSO, 2004), para 66.

[455] *R (Douglas) v North Tyneside Metropolitan Borough Council and the Secretary of State for Education and Skills* [2004] ELR 117 (CA); see p 142 above.

[456] *R (R and Others) v Leeds City Council/Education Leeds* [2005] EWHC Admin 2495; [2006] ELR 25.

Jewish school notwithstanding the lack of funding. An Article 8 (right to respect for private or family life) claim was also rejected on the same basis. This decision offers further discouragement to those who might consider the Human Rights Act 1998 to support claims for transport provision, but, as we saw in Chapter 2, where resources are at issue these rights lose their potency.

Groups Facing Particular Problems in Relation to Access to Schooling

A wide range of groups face particular barriers to access to education. Among them are children in care, pregnant young people or teenage mothers and those in custody. Children within groups who lead a nomadic or unsettled way of life, whether for cultural reasons or because they have arrived in the UK from another country, hoping to remain, are also at risk of missing out on effective educational provision. Gypsies/Travellers and asylum seekers are particularly likely to have reduced access to education, a cause and a consequence of their wider social exclusion. They are also groups that are particularly vulnerable to racism and are also socially and economic vulnerable as a result of their often physical as well as political isolation. The educational and general social inclusion of their children has been highlighted by the UN Committee on the Rights of the Child.[457] Their position and that of other groups facing problems in relation to access to schooling are discussed below.

Children and young people in care

As the Social Exclusion Unit has noted, those in care suffer a wide range of problems arising from a disrupted home life, the psychological effects of abuse and deleterious peer influences.[458] Access to education and school attendance are adversely affected, and this in turn hinders their attainment levels, which tend to be well below average. For example, only 7.5 per cent get five GCSEs grades A*–C compared with an average of 53 per cent in the population as whole.[459] It was estimated in 2003 that only 1 per cent of care leavers went on to university, compared with over one third of the population as a whole.[460] The Government set a target to increase to 15 per cent (double the rate in 2001–2) the proportion of children in care who obtain five GCSEs at grades A*-C and for 11-year-olds to achieve at least 60 per cent of the level of attainment among their peers, targets to be met by 2006.[461] Nevertheless, the charity NCH subsequently called for a range

---

[457] UN Committee on the Rights of the Child, *Concluding Observations: United Kingdom of Great Britain and Northern Ireland*, CRC/C/15/Add.188, 9 Oct 2002 (Geneva, United Nations, 2002).

[458] Social Exclusion Unit, *A Better Education for Children in Care* (London, Social Exclusion Unit, 2003).

[459] House of Commons Education and Skills Committee, Fourth Report, Session 2003–04, *Secondary Education: School Admissions, Vol. 1, Report*, HC 58–1 (London, TSO, 2004), para 65, citing evidence from the Minister for Children, the Rt Hon Margaret Hodge MP.

[460] Cited in NCH, *Close the Gap for Children in Care* (London, NCH, 2005) 5.

[461] Social Exclusion Unit, *A Better Education for Children in Care* (London, Social Exclusion Unit, 2003) 2.

of measures to close the gap between the achievements of those in care and others, including more resources for local authorities, stricter duties on schools and more effective targets for the education of children and young people in care.[462] The arrangements for local authorities and agencies concerned with education and social care, including schools and children's trusts, to work together, as articulated in the Green Paper *Every Child Matters* and provided with a framework in the Children Act 2004, are particularly aimed at ensuring the necessary holistic response to the problems faced by this group.[463]

People in juvenile detention/youth custody

For young people in juvenile detention/youth custody, access to education can be particularly problematic. Their position has been highlighted by the UN's Special Rapporteur on the Right to Education[464] and by the UN Committee on the Rights of the Child, which expressed concern that they 'do not have a statutory right to education, that their education is not the responsibility of the departments responsible for education, and that they do not have support for special education needs'.[465] The Committee recommended that they should be given an 'equal statutory right to education'.[466] This has not happened, but under a Prison Service Order introduced in July 2002[467] the *National Specification for Learning and Skills for Young People on a Detention and Training Order* has been introduced, one of the aims of which is to ensure that at least 90 per cent of young offenders are in suitable full-time education, training and employment during and at the end of their sentence. By the end of 2005, 75 per cent of young offenders were in full-time education, and although this is below the official target level it does represent an increase from the 2002 figure of 64 per cent.[468] The specification currently provides for 30 hours per week of learning, skills and development work, plus a programme of enrichment activities. Provision is

---

[462] NCH, n 460 above. See further Chap 5 pp 270–1 on the new measures to ensure that children in care are given priority under school admissions policies, the aim being to ensure that they do not always end up in the least successful or 'sink' schools.

[463] DfES, *Every Child Matters* (Green Paper) Cm 5680 (London, TSO, 2003). See further, DfES, *Every Child Matters: Change for Children in Schools* (London, DfES, 2004). Children's trusts are a form of partnership between different agencies, including local authorities and health authorities, although not including schools. They are not separate legal entities, nor are they specifically required under the Children Act 2004. However, they are being formed as a means of meeting of the co-operation duties set out in that Act. It was expected that most areas in England would have one by 2006 and the rest are expected to have them by 2008.

[464] UN Commission on Human Rights, *Report submitted by Katarina Tomaševski, Special Rapporteur on the Right to Education, Addendum. Mission to the United Kingdom 18–22 October 1999*, E/CN4/2000/6/Add 2 (Geneva, Centre for Human Rights, Geneva, 2000), available at www.unhcr.ch/Huridcoda, paras 55–59, noting that at that time their entitlement was only 15 hours of education per week.

[465] UN Committee on the Rights of the Child, *Concluding Observations: United Kingdom of Great Britain and Northern Ireland*, CRC/C/15/Add.188, 9 Oct 2002 (Geneva, United Nations, 2002), para 47.

[466] Ibid, para 48(d).

[467] Prison Service Order (PSO) 4950.

[468] DfES/Home Office/Department for Work and Pensions, *Reducing Re-offending through Skills and Employment*, Cm 6702 (London, DfES, 2005), para 83.

managed through the Youth Justice Board which enters into a 'service level agreement' with each institution. Given the low level of prior attainment of many juvenile offenders, significant numbers of whom have learning difficulties, combined with the reduced recidivism that is associated with receipt of education, this provision, which includes co-ordinators for special educational needs and literacy and numeracy, is vitally important, and the House of Commons Education and Skills Committee has recommended that a similar regime is introduced for offenders aged 18 or over.[469] In December 2005 the Government published a Green Paper which proposes a more comprehensive provision of training and education for offenders, including a 'campus' approach, involving new centres of excellence linked with a range of providers including colleges of further education.[470] The Green Paper also gives specific attention to provision for offenders aged 16–17, whose 'learning journey' while in custody is discussed; there will be a new targets regime for young offenders in custody and the community, 'with performance indicators to support an approach based on progression and "distance travelled"'.[471] Modification of the curriculum, in line with the reforms to the 14–19 curriculum more generally (see Chapter 7) is also planned.

Pregnant girls and teenage mothers

Another category of persons requiring special attention is pregnant girls and young mothers. Teenage pregnancy is discussed in Chapter 7 in the context of sex education. It is noted there that around 7,500 under-16-year-olds were recorded as pregnant in 2004; and among the under 18s as a whole it was 41,700.[472] Abortion rates vary according to age of parent, but more than half of pregnant girls under 16 have an abortion, as do just under half those age under 18.[473] In 2004, live births to girls and young women aged 19 or under reached their highest annual total since 2000.[474] Numbers of live births in 2004 to those aged under 18 are shown in table 4. It is also clear that 'a significant number of young women conceive more than once in their teens'.[475]

The DfES guidance on the education of pregnant school pupils or teenage mothers is premised on the belief that these young people should be educated within a school if possible. The guidance warns against the perception that the

---

[469] House of Commons Education and Skills Committee, Seventh Report, Session 2004–05, *Prison Education*, HC 114-I (London, TSO, 2005), para 104. The Government replied that it was considering the matter: HM Government, *Government Response to the House of Commons Education and Skills Committee Report—Prison Education*, Cm 6562 (London, TSO, 2005), para 13. The Forum on Prisoner Education has criticised what it sees as the inadequate progress made by the Government over these matters: Briefing Paper No 22, *House of Commons—Education and Skills Committee, Prison Education Report, One Year On* (Forum on Prisoner Education, 2006), available at www.fpe.org.uk/filestore/bp22.pdf.

[470] DfES/Home Office/Department for Work and Pensions, *Reducing Re-offending through Skills and Employment*, Cm 6702 (London, DfES, 2005).

[471] Ibid, para 85.

[472] *Health Statistics Quarterly 29, Spring 2006* (2006), October table 4.1.

[473] *Health Statistics Quarterly 26* (2004), October table B.

[474] *Health Statistics Quarterly 29*, n 472 above, table 3.1.

[475] Social Exclusion Unit, *Teenage Pregnancy*, Cm 4342 (London, TSO, 1999) 12.

Table 4: Live Births to Child, England and Wales (2004)[a]

Age of parent	Number of live births
11	1
12	1
13	24
14	183
15	1,013
16	3,633
17	8,823

[a]National Statistics, Series FM1 no 33 *Birth Statistics* (London, Office for National Statistics, 2005), table 3.2.

presence of pregnant girls in school will encourage others to become pregnant. It stresses that a pupil should not be excluded from school by reason of her pregnancy or parenthood (indeed, that would be likely to constitute unlawful sex discrimination). The expectation is that the school would only exceptionally not be a suitable environment for the girl's education and that efforts should be made to ensure that the girl continues to be educated to the full extent for as long as possible, with provision of work for completion at home where health reasons preclude attendance.[476] Research has, however, shown that where the girl was already disaffected or disengaged from school education, as evidenced by a poor attendance rate, alternative settings for her education while pregnant or post-natally are likely to be more appropriate.[477] The researchers found that fewer than half of pregnant school pupils were attending school regularly during the period in which conception occurred. Alternative settings could, for example, be a special unit or a pupil referral unit, both before and after the birth. Such arrangements would, of course, be covered by the statutory duty under section 19 of the Education Act 1996, which requires such alternative provision to be 'suitable', as discussed above. The researchers found that specialist provision for pregnant young women was more likely to ensure that they continued their education after birth and after the age of 16. They also found that those pupils who had had a positive experience of schooling and had been regular attenders with a good academic record prior to conception were more likely to be well supported by the school and to maintain their record of attendance and achievement thereafter. For young mothers, the importance of appropriate childcare in order to ensure proper access to education is stressed both by the researchers and in the DfES guidance.

[476] DfES, *Guidance on the Education of School Age Pupils*, DfES 0629/2001 (London, DfES, 2001), available at www.dfes.gov.uk/schoolageparents/.

[477] N Dawson and A Hosie, *The Education of Pregnant Young Women and Mothers in England* (London, DfES, 2005), available at www.dfes.gov.uk/research/data/uploadfiles/RW40.pdf.

Migrants and immigrants

In the 'Children and Migration' survey, Stalford found that educational factors were important considerations in migration decisions by EU Member State families.[478] Within the EU, Article 12 of Regulation 1612/68[479] guarantees equal access to education (at all levels) for children of migrant workers:

> The children of a national of a Member State who is or has been employed in the territory of another Member State shall be admitted to that State's general educational, apprenticeship and vocational training courses under the same conditions as the nationals of that State, if such children are residing in its territory.
>
> Member States shall encourage all efforts to enable such children to attend these courses under the best possible conditions.

As Hervey explains, the underlying assumption here is that 'the needs of the migrant child can be met by simple access to the education system of the host state, in the sense of the same provision for migrant children as for nationals'.[480] Thus it is somewhat narrowly focused on equality of access per se rather than on integration.[481] Notwithstanding this limitation in the purpose of the provision, its effect appears to have been extended a little by virtue of the Advocate General's Opinion in *Baumbast and R v Secretary of State for the Home Department*, which indicates that the child's right under Article 12 will continue and they will be able to remain in the country to take advantage of it even after the parent's right to remain is threatened because their work has finished; indeed, in such circumstances the parent will be able to remain if necessary to ensure that the child is able to exercise that right.[482] However, that position has been undermined somewhat by the decision in *Ali v Secretary State for the Home Department*,[483] where the Court of Appeal held that a child, who was a Dutch citizen, did not have a right of residence in the UK under the EC Treaty, Article 18 (right to free movement and residence for EU citizens) merely because he was in receipt of primary education, nor did his Somali father have a derivative unfettered right of residence. In any event, differences in states' education provision, including curricula and qualifications (whose transferability to the host state can be problematic, thereby hindering progression to other levels of education), compromise the benefits of the Article 12 right.[484]

---

[478] H Stalford, 'Transferability of Educational Skills and Qualifications in the European Union: The Case of EU Migrant Children' in J Shaw (ed), *Social Law and Policy in an Evolving European Union* (Oxford, Hart, 2000) 243 at 246.

[479] [1968] OJ Spec Ed 475. See also, in the wider international context, the International Convention on the Protection of the Rights of All Migrant Workers and Members of their Families, Art 30; the UK has not ratified this Convention.

[480] T Hervey, *European Social Law and Policy* (London, Longman, 1998) 118.

[481] See also L Ackers and H Stalford, *A Community for Children? Children, Citizenship and Internal Migration in the EU* (Aldershot, Ashgate, 2004) 210.

[482] Case C–413/99, Opinion of Geelhoed AG; see also the judgment of the ECJ, [2002] ECR I–7091.

[483] [2006] EWCA Civ 484.

[484] Ackers and Stalford have found that this is especially the case at primary and secondary school levels: Ackers and Stalford, n 481 above, 217.

Education is more firmly within EU competence following the Amsterdam Treaty that resulted in Article 149 (ex 126) EC Treaty, requiring the Community to 'contribute to the development of quality education' via co-operation between Members States and, if necessary, via support and supplementation of their action, while 'fully respecting the responsibility of the Member States for the content of teaching and the organisation of education systems'. It extends to areas, such as pre-school and school education, that were not regarded as vocational education covered by Article 128 EEC.[485] Various soft law developments have occurred, including the introduction of exchange and mobility programmes such as SOCRATES,[486] consistent with the aims of Community action spelled out in Article 149. Nonetheless, 'concrete provision for EU migrant children continues to be framed within the context of their parents' rights as workers'.[487] They are derivative rights, as illustrated by the case of *Echternach and Moritz v Netherlands Minister for Education and Science*.[488] German parents worked in the Netherlands and their child was educated there from the age of 5. When the boy was at technical college he and his parents returned to Germany. However, the boy wanted to continue his studies in the Netherlands because his Dutch diplomas were not recognised in Germany. The European Court of Justice (ECJ) held that, as there was no co-ordination of qualifications and the young person had no choice but to return to the country where his schooling took place, he had a right of access to education in the Netherlands under the Regulation and, because his education in the host country was continuous, he did not lose it.[489] The Court also confirmed that the right applied to all forms of education, whether vocational or technical, including university courses.[490] The Court also held that the Regulation 1612/68 Article 12 right referred not only to admission but also to 'general measures intended to facilitate educational attendance' and that the right under that Article was given practical effect via the right to enjoy 'the same social and tax advantages as national workers' under Article 7(2), so that there should be equal access to an education grant to cover the costs of students' education and maintenance as that enjoyed by host nationals.[491] This line of reasoning was adopted subsequently in *Casagrande v Landeshauptstadt München*,[492] where a child of an Italian working in Germany claimed an education grant from the authorities in Munich, but was denied it because

---

[485] T Hervey, *European Social Law and Policy* (London, Longman, 1998) 114.

[486] See ibid, 115. For a review of these programmes, see House of Lords European Union Committee, Social and Consumer Affairs Sub-Committee, *Report on the Proposed European Union Integrated Action Programme for Life-Long Learning*, HL Paper 104–1 (London, TSO, 2005).

[487] Hervey, n 485 above, 252. In the COMENIUS programme, Action 2 is targeted at the children of migrants and is concerned with 'promoting intercultural education to prepare schoolchildren for life in a society of ever-increasing cultural and linguistic diversity'. As noted in Chap 2, Stalford discusses problems over the transferability of academic and vocational qualifications.

[488] Cases 389, 390/87 [1989] ECR 723.

[489] At paras 21–23.

[490] Ibid, paras 28–30.

[491] Ibid, paras 33–36.

[492] Case 9/74 [1974] ECR 773.

German law restricted the grant to German nationals, stateless persons and persons granted asylum.

There are many other migrants and members of immigrant communities whose access to education is hindered by language difficulties and cultural barriers and who may lack a great deal of formal education themselves. In the EU context, Directive 77/486 promotes the teaching to migrants of the official language of the host state as well as the mother tongue and culture of the family of origin.[493] Yet Ackers and Stalford have found the Directive to be fulfilled by Members States in only a 'half-hearted fashion' and concluded that national provision tends to be focused rather more on non-EU nationals whose linguistic needs are seen as greater, perhaps because of a perception that children of EU migrants tend to have a more affluent background.[494] Within the UK, these problems have been addressed via various initiatives over a number of years, although mother tongue teaching has not had a great deal of attention within them[495] (notwithstanding that languages such as Arabic, Bengali, Urdu, Gujerati and Chinese have been included as approved modern languages which schools can offer as part of the National Curriculum[496]).

Perhaps the best known domestic provision has been 'section 11 funding',[497] now incorporated into and superseded by Ethnic Minority and Travellers Achievement Grant (EMAG),[498] which provides grants to LEAs, although they in turn devolve much of it to schools. Originally, section 11 funding was targeted on local authorities which, in the Home Secretary's opinion, needed to make special provision because of the presence within their area of 'substantial numbers of immigrants from the Commonwealth whose language or customs differ from those of the community'.[499] However, after 1993 the term 'immigrants from the Commonwealth' was replaced by 'persons belonging to ethnic minorities' and the phrase 'the rest of' was inserted after 'those of'. The funding has also become available to city technology colleges and academies and to governing bodies of further education institutions.[500] The grant later became payable under the Education Standards Fund, first introduced in 1999, for '[m]easures to provide equality of educational opportunity for all minority ethnic groups, including in

---

[493] On the link between education and culture, especially in the EU context, see C Wallace and J Shaw, 'Education, Multiculturalism and the Charter of Fundamental Rights of the European Union' in TK Hervey and J Kenner (eds), *Economic and Social Rights under the EU Charter of Fundamental Rights—A Legal Perspective* (Oxford, Hart, 2003) 223.

[494] Ackers and Stalford, above n 481, 260.

[495] While DES Circular 5/81 called on LEAs to 'explore ways in which mother tongue teaching might be provided, whether during or outside school hours', it has generally been the case that it has been left to migrant communities themselves to make their own arrangements: see Chap 7. Ackers and Stalford comment that throughout the EU, mother tongue teaching is not seen as a priority for the educational development of children of migrants: Ackers and Stalford, above n 481, 250.

[496] Education (National Curriculum) (Modern Foreign Languages) Order 2004 (SI 2004/256); see pp 376–7 and 382 below. As regards minority linguistic rights, see Chap 7 at pp 422ff.

[497] Under the Local Government Act 1966, s 11.

[498] The DfES uses this acronyn and its website still refers to the grant by its previous name of Ethnic Minority Achievement Grant.

[499] Local Government Act 1966, s 11.

[500] Education Reform Act 1988, s 211; Education Act 1996, s 490.

particular measures to assist pupils for whom English is an additional language and measures to raise standards of achievement for those minority ethnic groups who are at particular risk of under-achieving'.[501] The Government allocated £155 million to the grant in 2003–4 and £162 million in 2004–5. LEAs are expected to prepare action plans and set targets for improved attainment among ethnic minority children. A research study covering 1998–2000 found that EMAGs were making a positive contribution to raising attainment levels although there was considerable variation across different LEAs.[502]

Persons seeking asylum

As we have seen, immigrants, especially those with poor English, are the subject of special funding arrangements aimed at providing additional support for their effective inclusion in the education system. There is an assumption that immigrants, including those granted asylum, will have access to mainstream schooling and, to facilitate this, there has been flexibility within the National Curriculum since it was first introduced, in the form of statutory provision for temporary exception to be granted in respect of individual pupils.[503] The exceptions are intended to benefit, inter alios, those who need a concentrated period of English language tuition.[504] The education of asylum seekers is, however, beset with problems which in part stem from the current government's policy towards this group, including the dispersal policy.[505] An even greater threat would be posed by the legislative measures aimed at curbing abuse of the right to claim asylum, which pave the way for asylum seekers to reside in reception centres or 'accommodation centres' while their claims are assessed.[506]

In 2002, there were 84,130 applications for asylum, 42 per cent of which succeeded (including those decided on appeal), but the numbers have fallen steadily since then and there were 33,960 in 2004, with 25 per cent of applications (including appealed decisions) succeeding.[507] When dependants are included, the

---

[501] The Education Standards Fund (England) Regulations 2002 (SI 2002/510), Sched 1 para 3(b)(i)—in force until 1 Apr 2004. The statutory provisions under which these regulations were made have been replaced by the Education Act 2002, ss 14–18. These provisions confer very wide powers indeed on the Secretary of State to provide financial assistance for the provision of education on any conditions he or she wishes to impose.

[502] L Tikly *et al*, *Ethnic Minority Achievement Grant: Analaysis of LEA Action Plans*, DfES Research Report No. 371 (London, DfES, 2002).

[503] Education Act 2002, ss 93 and 114; the Education (National Curriculum) (Temporary Exceptions for Individual Pupils) Regulations 1989 (SI 1989/1181); the Education (National Curriculum) (Temporary Exceptions for Individual Pupils) (Wales) Regulations 1989 (SI 1989/1815).

[504] See Department for Education and Science, Circular 15/89, *The National Curriculum: Exceptions for Individual Pupils*, which referred to the equivalent provision made in the Education Reform Act 1988, s 19.

[505] See below.

[506] See Home Office, *Secure Borders, Safe Haven: Integration with Diversity in Modern Britain*, Cm 5387 (London, TSO, 2002). See below.

[507] National Statistics, *Asylum Statistics United Kingdom 2002* (London, Office of National Statistics, 2003), available at www.statistics.gov.uk, fig 1; National Statistics, *Asylum Statistics United Kingdom 2004* (London, Office of National Statistics, 2005), para 44. The figures include, in addition to the numbers granted asylum per se, those granted humanitarian protection or discretionary leave.

total numbers seeking asylum were 103,080 in 2002 and 40,625 in 2004.[508] Of the 19,000 dependants in 2002 and 6,600 in 2004, the majority (80 per cent in 2002 and 90 per cent in 2004) were aged 20 or under, and most of them were aged 15 or under.[509] A number of children arrived in the UK unaccompanied: the applications included 6,200 in 2002, and 2,990 in 2004, made by unaccompanied people aged 17 or under.[510] Therefore, there have been large numbers of children of UK school age seeking asylum (over 20,000 in 2002 and nearly 10,000 in 2004), usually, but by no means exclusively, as part of asylum seeker families. The Government acknowledges that it has a responsibility for the education of such children. The DfES website says that it is 'Government policy that children from asylum seeking and refugee backgrounds are given the same opportunities as all other children to access education'. It refers to the LEA's statutory duty to ensure that education is available for all children of compulsory school age in their area, suitable to their age, ability and aptitude and to any special educational needs they may have.[511] As the DfES acknowledges, asylum seeker children are within the scope of that duty (and therefore schools receive funding for asylum seeker children as part of their share of formula-based funding). Children of parents who are in receipt of asylum support[512] are also entitled to free school meals, as noted above. It is also the case, as the Joint Committee on Human Rights has noted, that asylum seeker children are no different from any other children in the UK in being protected by Article 2 of Protocol 1 to the ECHR from a denial of their right to education.[513] In the Netherlands, education law interprets this as requiring that children of asylum seekers or illegal immigrants have a right to be admitted to primary or secondary education.[514] Anti-discrimination rights are also relevant. By virtue of Article 14, the Protocol 1 Article 2 right is to be enjoyed on the basis of freedom from discrimination. In *Holub v Holub*[515] a Polish couple who had been denied asylum had claimed that an enforced return to Poland would damage their 14-year-old daughter's educational progress which had been excellent in the UK. They said that on her return she would need to resume her education where she had left it at the age of 8 and would not catch up. They argued that her right to education under the Convention would therefore be denied.[516] The Court of Appeal held that the Secretary of State had to consider the educational implications of any asylum decision, but was not

[508] Ibid (2003), para 13, (2005), para 2.

[509] Ibid (2003), para 15, (2005), para 20.

[510] Ibid (2003), para 9, (2005), Table 2.3.

[511] Education Act 1996, ss 13 and 14. But note that in the definition of special educational needs it is provided that a child is not to be taken to have such needs merely because the language or languages in which he is or will be taught is or are different from any language spoken at home: ibid, s 312.

[512] Paid under the Nationality, Immigration and Asylum Act 2002, s 55. See further R Thomas, 'Asylum Seeker Support' (2003) 10(4) *Journal of Social Security Law* 163.

[513] Joint Committee on Human Rights, Seventeenth Report, Session 2001–02, *The Nationality, Immigration and Asylum Bill* (London, TSO, 2002), paras 53 and 54.

[514] BP Vermeulen and CW Noorlander, 'The Educational Rights of Students in the Netherlands' in C Russo and J De Groof, *The Legal Rights of Students* (Lanham, Md, Rowman and Littlefield, forthcoming), 129–45 at 131.

[515] [2001] ELR 401 (CA).

[516] *Holub and Holub v Secretary of State for the Home Department* [2001] ELR 401.

obliged to take a view on whether the Convention right under Article 2 of Protocol 1 was infringed. The court regarded Poland as having a well-developed education system, and the fact that the girl would receive a better education in the UK did not count. The court stated that there is a right to a 'minimum standard' of education, but did not define what that meant.[517]

Since 2000, a dispersal policy has operated, in order to reduce the pressure on local authorities in the South East of England, involving the accommodation of asylum seekers in locations mostly in Northern England, the Midlands and Scotland. A recent Cambridge University study found evidence that, even though asylum seekers have a legal right of access to education, its enjoyment has been compromised by this policy.[518] The study, covering 58 LEAs, found that many authorities were given insufficient notice about the arrival of asylum seekers and refugees, and there was therefore a perception that 'the educational needs of asylum-seeker and refugee children have tended to be marginalised or ignored'.[519] Some families were dispersed to areas where schools had no available places or had inadequate resources to meet the additional educational needs (such as language problems) of the children or where schools had little experience of children with these kinds of difficulties or of non-white children generally. Despite these difficulties, a report by Ofsted has painted quite a positive picture of the role played by schools in the integration of asylum-seeker pupils: in a survey of 37 schools in England, almost all of these pupils had made satisfactory or good progress, despite the initial language barriers in some cases.[520] However, the report stressed that schools should 'ensure that all staff are up to date with their knowledge and understanding of the linguistic, educational and cultural needs of the asylum-seeker pupils'.[521] Evidence from Wales also suggests that LEAs and schools have responded positively to the challenge of including asylum-seeker and refugee children, although educational arrangements require modification and the schools' task has often been hindered by their having been provided with incorrect or limited background information on the children.[522] The Cambridge study highlights the right given to schools to exclude asylum-seeker or refugee pupils from their published examination results where the children have been in the UK for less than two years, which it says might encourage schools to accept and welcome these pupils without fear of prejudicing the school's record of achievement. However, the report also identifies negative implications, in particular that schools might 'take away the message that they have limited responsibility towards these children and that they are not entitled to the same opportunity as other pupils'.[523] Although the

---

[517] Ibid, para 25, referring to the right to an 'effective' education.

[518] M Arnot and H Pinson, *The Education of Asylum Seeker and Refugee Children* (Cambridge, University of Cambridge, 2005).

[519] Ibid, 16.

[520] Office for Standards in Education, *The Education of Asylum-Seeker Pupils*, HMI 453 (London, Ofsted, 2003).

[521] Ibid, para 9.

[522] A Reakes and R Powell, *The Education of Asylum Seekers in Wales: Implications for LEAs and Schools* (Slough, NFER, 2004).

[523] Arnot and Pinson, above n 518, 19–20.

DfES guidance stresses the importance of maximising the educational achievements of asylum-seeker and refugee children,[524] the Cambridge study found that many schools were not aware of the guidance.[525]

As yet, the Government's policy that asylum seekers' education should generally be provided within the proposed accommodation centres rather than in LEA schools, incorporated within highly controversial provisions in the Nationality, Immigration and Asylum Act 2002 and outlined below, has not yet been implemented. Several attempts were made to thwart the policy when the Bill was before Parliament. For example, in the House of Commons Standing Committee, Karen Buck MP opined that the interaction between asylum-seeker and other children was important: 'The socialisation, confidence building and engagement that would come from being located in a community setting rather than an accommodation centre are critical'.[526] The Government, however, argued that educating asylum-seeker children in a separate environment might be important because those who had had 'traumatic experiences might benefit from specialist provision and concentrated help when they arrive in this country' and that special arrangements already existed for school phobics and others to be educated outside the mainstream.[527] The Government also considered that integration was inappropriate and would be unnecessarily disruptive to schools, when some children would be excluded from the country after perhaps three months. In fact, the Government's expectation was that children would not normally remain in an accommodation centre for more than *six* months, with a possibility of a further three months in certain cases.[528]

Opposition to the proposal was reinforced by the Joint Committee on Human Rights, which said that the proposals gave rise to 'troubling echoes of historical educational regimes in some other countries where children were educated separately on the basis of race or colour, under the now discredited pretence that the separate provision was equal'.[529] The Committee might well have had in mind the 'separate but equal' principle that underlay segregation in schooling that the US Supreme Court declared unconstitutional in *Brown* (above), as well as the Apartheid system in South Africa. In the Committee's view, separate educational arrangements on the basis of nationality or ethnicity tended to increase social and educational inequality and give rise to a potential breach of Article 14 ECHR,

---

[524] DfES, *Aiming High: Guidance on Supporting the Education of Asylum Seeking and Refugee Children* (DfES/0287/2004) (London, DfES, 2004); see also DfES, *Educating Asylum-seeking and Refugee Children: Guidance on the Education of Aslyum-Seeking and Refugee Children* (London, DfES, 2002).

[525] Arnot and Pinson, n 518 above, 18.

[526] House of Commons Standing Committee E, Nationality, Immigration and Asylum Bill, Col 141, 9 May 2002.

[527] Ibid, cols 143 and 144, per David Lammy MP.

[528] See DfES 'teachernet' website, www.teachernet.gov.uk, accessed 23 July 2004, 'A to Z of School Leadership—Refugee and asylum seekers' children'.

[529] Joint Committee on Human Rights, Seventeenth Report, Session 2001–02, *The Nationality, Immigration and Asylum Bill* (London, TSO, 2002), para 62.

read with Article 2 of Protocol 1, unless there was legitimate aim to which separation was 'proportionate and rationally related'.[530]

In the House of Lords, a Report stage amendment to remove the relevant clauses was carried by one vote, after an intense debate,[531] although the provisions were later restored. Doubt was expressed by peers concerning the Government's claims that education in accommodation centres would be best for the children of asylum applicants, that the education provided would be equal in quality to that made in schools and that integration of such children would be inappropriate. The Bishop of Portsmouth argued that the benefits of mainstream schooling for asylum-seeker children, even for a few months, would outweigh the concerns of disruption to schools and to a child if he or she had to leave.[532] Indeed, Lord Bhatia argued that the way to deal with those concerns was to provide adequate resources to support schools and teachers in educating these children.[533] To another opponent of the policy, Baroness Kennedy of The Shaws, the relevant provision in the Bill was 'a disgrace' and 'source of shame', and it would mean that 'children in our schools will lose out in learning lessons of tolerance and in the transmission of the values that we think matter'.[534] The Government's defence,[535] which included arguments that the Bill would enable any of the children who had special educational needs to be educated in schools, educational provision in accommodation centres would be inspected by Ofsted, and provision would be year-round, thus preventing those who arrived in the UK during the summer holiday period from being deprived of provision until September, seemed rather weak.

The Government's defeat was later overturned and the relevant provisions of the Nationality, Immigration and Asylum Act 2002 Act empower the Secretary of State to arrange for the provision of education and training to residents of accommodation centres[536] and put a resident of an accommodation centre that provides education outside the remit of the LEA's general educational duty.[537] The Act further provides that a child who is a resident of an accommodation centre that provides education may not be admitted to a maintained school or a maintained nursery school unless the school is either a community special school or foundation special school and is named in a child's statement of special educational needs.[538] As Dorn has argued, the policy 'is in stark contrast to previous policies on [school] admissions . . . which stated in no uncertain terms that the immigration or nationality status of parents could not be a ground for refusing their children admission to schools, and did not qualify parental

---

[530] Ibid, para 62. As Dorn explains, the proposal would also be inconsistent with the non-discrimination duty in the RRA 1976 but for the statutory exception in s 41 of that Act, permitting race etc discrimination if done under other statutory powers: A Dorn, 'Race Equality in Schools: New law and New Code' (2002) 3(3) *Education Law* 146, at 150.

[531] HL Debs, cols 325ff, 9 Oct 2002.

[532] Ibid, col. 328.

[533] Ibid, col. 339.

[534] Ibid, col. 343.

[535] Ibid, col 345ff, per Baroness Ashton of Upholland.

[536] Nationality, Immigration and Asylum Act 2002, s 29(1)(f).

[537] Ibid, s 36(1), referring to the duty in the EA 1996, s 13.

[538] Nationality, Immigration and Asylum Act 2002, s 36(2)–(4) and (10).

rights . . . regarding choice of school'.[539] LEAs' and schools' basic duties towards children with special educational needs are not excluded by the Act, but various education duties are excluded in the case of children resident in an accommodation centre that provides education, including parents' rights to express a preference as to the school to be named in a statement and the LEA's duty to educate a child with special educational needs in a mainstream school.[540] Children with special educational needs will have to be educated in an accommodation centre unless that would not be compatible with their receiving the special educational provision they need, the provision of efficient education for other children in the centre (but only if there was no action that could reasonably be taken to avoid the problem) or the efficient use of resources.[541] Those who provide education in a centre may, however, apply to the LEA for the area for it to make provision for the child 'on the grounds that his special circumstances call for provision that can only or best be arranged by the authority'.[542] The LEA is given a discretion, rather than a duty, to make such provision,[543] and if it exercises it a school must (provided the LEA consults with the school) comply with a requirement by the LEA that it admit the child, unless that would conflict with the statutory class size limit.[544] Although an accommodation centre will not be classed as a school for the purposes of education law, it will be subject to school inspections under the School Inspections Act 1996.[545]

These provisions are of considerable symbolic importance, indicating that part of the price considered acceptable for the limitation of asylum abuse is the educational segregation of many children who, through no fault of their own, are caught up in the asylum-seeking process away from their country of birth and early upbringing and who would have enjoyed integration in the past. But despite the understandable controversy over these provisions, their practical effect could be quite limited overall. The DfES website had noted that even when the two proposed trial accommodation centres were opened, 'the vast majority of children of asylum seekers will continue to be educated in mainstream schools'. In any event, the Government's abolition of plans for these centres means that the educational arrangements in the 2002 Act seem certain to be shelved permanently.

The case of *Holub v Holub*,[546] discussed above, illustrates how the risk or certainty of a lower standard of education on return to one's country of origin is highly unlikely to provide a basis upon which to found a successful claim of asylum. Could a more potent claim could be based upon a breach of Article 8 (right to respect for private and family life), particularly where a child has special

---

[539] A Dorn, 'Race Equality in Schools: New Law and New Code' (2002) 3(3) *Education Law* 146, at 150.

[540] Nationality, Immigration and Asylum Act 2002, s 36(5) and (10).

[541] Ibid, s 36(7) and (8).

[542] Ibid, s 37(1) and (3).

[543] Ibid, s 37(2).

[544] Ibid, s 37(2), (4) and (6) (consultation must be in accordance with regulations made by the Secretary of State). A separate consultation duty over admission is specified in s 37(7).

[545] Ibid, s 36(9).

[546] [2001] ELR 401 (CA). See above pp 212–3.

educational needs due to disablement? In *R (Razgar) v Secretary of State for the Home Department*, Lord Bingham, in the leading judgment, explained that a court reviewing an asylum decision should ask itself essentially the same questions that an adjudicator should ask:

> (1) Will the proposed removal be an interference with the exercise of the applicant's right to respect for his private or . . . family life? (2) If so, will such interference have consequences of such gravity as to as potentially to engage the operation of Article 8? (3) If so, is such interference in accordance with the law? (4) If so, is such interference necessary in a democratic society in the interests of national security, public safety or the economic well-being of the country, for the prevention of disorder or crime, for the protection of health or morals, or for the protection of the rights and freedoms of others? (5) If so, is such interference proportionate to the legitimate public end sought to be achieved.[547]

He focused on point (5), which required 'the striking of a fair balance between the rights of the individual and the interests of the community which is inherent in the whole of the Convention', and said that at that stage 'careful assessment' was needed of the 'severity and consequences of the interference'.[548] He expressed the view that in the case of decisions taken pursuant to lawful immigration control there would be only a 'small minority of exceptional cases' where the proportionality defence would not stand up to scrutiny.[549]

This jurisprudence was cited by Carnwath LJ giving the Court of Appeal's judgment in *Dbies and Others v Secretary of State for the Home Department*,[550] a case which arose out of an adjudicator's decision to refuse asylum to a Lebanese woman and her two young sons, one of whom (T) had cerebral palsy and was attending a school in Hounslow with specialist support for children with physical disabilities. The adjudicator found that the medical facilities in the Lebanon would be adequate, but he noted that the level of educational support would not be comparable. Nevertheless, he concluded that there was an education system in the Lebanon that 'may not be as sophisticated' as that in the UK, but was not such as to render the decision to return the family there disproportionate for the purposes of Article 8. The Immigration Appeal Tribunal (IAT) concluded that there was no basis for finding the adjudicator's decision wrong in law or on the facts. The Court of Appeal, noting that fresh evidence before the IAT that was not strictly admissible, to the effect that T would not have access to suitable educational facilities and would face a negative attitude towards his physical disabilities, made the matter 'distressing', but nonetheless found no fault in the decision for the purposes of Article 8. Although it was 'a harsh result that [T] is likely to be deprived of the higher standard of educational support which he can expect in this country . . . that on the authorities does not constitute an

---

[547] [2004] UKHL 227; [2004] 3 WLR 58; at para 17.
[548] Ibid, para 20.
[549] Ibid. See also *Huang and Others v Secretary of State* [2005] EWCA Civ 105, where a similar view of the balance to be struck was taken by Laws LJ (at para 56).
[550] [2005] EQCA Civ 584.

exceptional case, sufficient to override immigration control'.[551] This decision shows that it is going to be difficult to overcome the defence that a decision not to grant asylum is, notwithstanding its effect on education, proportionate to a legitimate aim. As in other circumstances in which Article 8 is invoked in asylum claims,[552] the courts have set a very high legal hurdle over which applicants must jump if they which to succeed.

Gypsies and Travellers

Gypsies (Roma) as a whole comprise an ethnic group,[553] whereas travellers are drawn from a range of other groups such as Irish and Scottish nomadic people and so-called New Age Travellers.[554] Indeed, there are also occupational travellers such as circus and fairground people: an EC Council Resolution in 1989 called for Member States to introduce various measures, including flexible arrangements, to improve access to schooling for their children.[555] Gypsies/Roma are recognised by the UK as a minority for the purposes of the Framework Convention for the Protection of Minorities[556] and by the EC and Council of Europe as a group in need of special protection and measures to improve their social situation.[557] They have a distinct national origin, having left India around the tenth century and spread across Europe. Their history is one of suffering repression and a denial of citizenship in both de facto and de jure senses.[558] Various official sources point to there being around 30–40,000 Gypsies in the UK living in caravans, with a slightly smaller number living in houses.[559] An Ofsted report in 1996 estimated the total number of 'Gypsy Travellers' (including Irish Travellers) at 70,000; there were also 10,500 fairground or show-people, 2,000 circus people, 6,500 'New Travellers' and 500 bargees/boat dwellers.[560] But Ofsted believed these figures to under-represent the true total; in Ofsted's estimation,

---

[551] At para 26.

[552] *Anufrijeva and anor v Southwark London Borough Council; R (N) v Secretary of State for the Home Department; R (M) v Secretary of State for the Home Department* [2003] EWCA Civ 1406.

[553] They are recognised as such for the purposes of the Race Relations Act 1976: *Commission for Racial Equality v Dutton* [1989] QB 783; [1989] 1 All ER 306 (CA).

[554] See C Clarke, 'Race, Ethnicity and Social Security: the Experience of Gypsies and Travellers in the United Kingdom' (1999) 6 *Journal of Social Security Law* 186.

[555] Resolution of the Council and the Ministers of Education Meeting Within the Council of 22 May 1989 on School Provision for Children of Occupational Travellers (89/C 153/01). See also COM(96) 494 final, reporting on the implementation of these measures.

[556] Under Art 4(1) of the Convention, the Parties 'undertake to guarantee to persons belonging to national minorities the right of equality before the law and of equal protection of the law. In this respect, any discrimination based on belonging to a national minority shall be prohibited'. Art 4(2) requires states parties to 'adopt, where necessary, adequate measures in order to promote, in all areas of economic, social, political and cultural life, full and effective equality between persons belonging to a national minority and those belonging to the majority. In this respect, they shall take due account of the specific conditions of the persons belonging to national minorities'. As regards cultural preservation, see Art 5, discussed in Chap 7.

[557] See the range of instruments listed by the ECtHR in its judgment in *Chapman v United Kingdom* (2001) 33 EHRR 399.

[558] A useful potted history and range of sources can be found in S Poulter, *Ethnicity, Law and Human Rights* (Oxford, Clarendon Press, 1998), ch 5.

[559] Ibid, 148.

[560] Ofsted, *The Education of Travelling Children* (London, Ofsted, 1996), para 37.

there were 50,000 children aged 0–16 across these groups.[561] Other estimates have put the Gypsy and Traveller population as a whole in the UK at up to 300,000.[562]

Despite various initiatives to ensure that Gypsy and Traveller children have access to education, they have traditionally been, and remain, poor school attenders, at greater risk of exclusion from school and likely to be weak educational achievers. The Plowden report described Gypsy children as

> probably the most deprived children in the country. Most of them do not go to school, and the potential abilities of those who do are stunted. They tend to be excluded by their way of life and their lack of education from entering normal occupations and confined to others that compel continuing travelling.[563]

The UN Committee on the Rights of the Child has identified Gypsy/Roma children as a socially vulnerable group and called for measures to reduce both their segregation in education and their exclusion from school.[564] The barriers, cultural and linguistic, to educational access by Gypsies/Roma are common to many parts of Europe. In Portugal, for example, the enforcement of their attendance at school 'faces the ancestral customs of gypsy nomadism and that many times there are no registers for their children'.[565] In some countries Roma are segregated for school education, and this has led to several legal challenges, based primarily around issues of discrimination, most notably in relation to Bulgaria[566] and the Czech Republic.[567] In the case of the latter, the European Court of Human Rights has recently rejected a complaint based on ECHR Article 14 read together with A2P1 that the disproportionate placement of Roma children in special schools, which the Court described as 'worrying', evidenced a form of institutionalised racism that resulted in discrimination against the applicant children.[568] The Court found that the parents had failed to take action in response to information that their child had been placed in a special school, or in some cases had asked for a special school placement, whilst some of the

---

[561] Ibid, para 45.

[562] R Morris and L Clements, *At What Cost? The Economics of Gypsy and Traveller Encampments* (Bristol, The Policy Press, 2002); H Crawley, *Moving Forward: The Provision of Accommodation for Travellers and Gypsies* (London, IPPR, 2004).

[563] Central Advisory Council for Education (England) (chair: Lady Plowden), *Children and their Primary Schools, Report* (London, HMSO, 1967), i, para 155. See also ii, App 12. See also S Cemlyn and C Clark, 'The Social Exclusion of Gypsy and Traveller Children' in G Preston (ed), *At Greatest Risk. The Children Mostly Likely to be Poor* (London, CPAG, 2005) 150.

[564] UN Committee on the Rights of the Child, *Concluding Observations: United Kingdom of Great Britain and Northern Ireland*, CRC/C/15/Add.188, 9 Oct 2002 (Geneva, United Nations, 2002), paras 47 and 51.

[565] AP Barbas Homem, 'Right to Education and Minorities: Portuguese Report' in J De Groof and J Fiers (eds), *The Legal Status of Minorities in Education* (Leuven, Uitgeverj Acc, 1996), 273.

[566] See www.errc.org/cikk.php?cikk=1319 (European Roma Rights Centre (ERRC) website).

[567] The case of *DH and Others v The Czech Republic* (below) was supported by ERRC and alleged that school selection procedures frequently discriminated against the Roma. The European Court of Human Rights unanimously declared admissible the applicants' main complaint of racial discrimination in the enjoyment of the right to education (ECHR Art 14, read together with Art 2 of Prot 1, discussed above): www.errc.org/cikk.php?cikk=2248&archiv=1 (11 Jan 2006).

[568] *DH and Others v The Czech Republic*, App no 57325/00, Judgment, 7 Feb 2006, para 52.

parents had successfully requested an ordinary school placement. The Court held that while the Roma parents may 'have lacked information about the national education system or found themselves in a climate of mistrust', the evidence did not show that the placements in a special school were the result of racial prejudice.[569]

The first time that specific provision for those who lead a nomadic lifestyle was recognised in education law in England and Wales appears to have been in the Education Reform Act 1988. It empowered the making of central government grants in respect of provision of education for, inter alios, a person who 'by reason of his way of life (or, in the case of a child, his parent's way of life) . . . either has no fixed abode or leaves his main abode to live elsewhere for a significant period of the year'.[570] This provision continues in the Education Act 1996.[571] Travellers were defined by the Department for Education as 'Gypsy and other Travellers whether living on official long or short stay sites or unofficial sites, and circus, fairground and bargee families'.[572] Also included were Travellers who had settled in housing in the previous two years.[573] Displaced persons covered by the grants, which could cover such matters as school uniform and transport, included refugees or similarly displaced persons living in special camps or discrete accommodation, but did not include homeless persons per se. The generic term 'Traveller' continues to be employed by the Government and official agencies.

The impact of these grants was assessed in a report by Ofsted in 1996.[574] It found that over 3,000 schools had Gypsy and Traveller children whose education was supported by a grant. Reflecting on progress made over the previous decade or more, the report found that there were improvements in registration, attendance and achievement among these children, and also better relationships between education authorities and Gypsy and Traveller communities. The report noted, however, that the good start achieved by many of the children at Key Stage 1 (ages 5–7) was not maintained through to age 14, making continuous progression through the National Curriculum 'at best a distant aspiration'.[575] The nomadic lifestyle continued to create 'practical difficulties for access to schools', while there were in any event 'still many Gypsy and New Traveller families who harbour both anxiety and resistance towards education'.[576] By 1999 some 120 LEAs were receiving grants for the education of Gypsies and Travellers.[577] Reviewing progress that year, Ofsted found that despite the considerable efforts made by schools and LEAs (especially the Traveller Education Services), Gypsy

---

[569] Ibid.

[570] Education Reform Act 1988, s 210.

[571] EA 1996, s 488. See also the Education (Grants) (Travellers and Displaced Persons) Regulations 1993 (SI 1993/569) (as amended), which have continuing effect.

[572] Department for Education, Circular 11/92, *Education Reform Act 1988: Specific Grant for the Education of Travellers and of Displaced Persons* (London, Department for Education, 1992), para 11.

[573] Ibid.

[574] Ofsted, *The Education of Travelling Children* (London, Ofsted, 1996).

[575] Ibid, para 98.

[576] Ibid, para 99.

[577] HM Government, *Second Report to the UN Committee on the Rights of the Child by the United Kingdom* (London, TSO, 1999), para 9.49.1.

and Traveller children continued to lag well behind other groups; this was particularly marked as they entered the secondary stage, where a majority were in fact officially classified as having special educational needs.[578] By year 9 (ages 13–14) many, especially boys, had opted out of education and very few went on to achieve success at GCSE or beyond. Similar concerns were raised in another report two years later.[579]

The most recent report by Ofsted, in 2003, based on a survey of 11 LEAs, suggests that progress in securing improved access to education among what were referred to by the generic term Traveller children (the grants became known as Traveller Achievement Grants, until April 2003) has been very slow.[580] One of the problems has been a lack of co-ordination between different departments within local authorities, with the response to unauthorised or temporary encampments being at odds with published council policies on inclusion and racial equality under the Race Relations Amendment Act 2000.[581] Participation rates at the secondary stage remain poor: on average, only 60 per cent of Traveller children were registered at school at Key Stages 3 and 4 (ages 11–16) and by Key Stage 4 alone it was as low as 47 per cent, rates that were comparable with data for other regions.[582] Moreover, the evidence suggested that nationally some 12,000 Traveller pupils were not registered at school (compared with 10,000 in 1996). The report concludes that 'a very significant number of Traveller children, mainly at Key Stages 3 and 4, lack education', although attendance rates in primary schools have improved.[583] A separate study of 44 pupils found that the participation rate was higher among those who were living in settled encampments or housing,[584] thus emphasising the importance of local authority site provision in supporting access to education.

The Ofsted report also found that an increasing number of Traveller children are being educated at home, mostly at the secondary stage, often under the (somewhat distant) supervision of LEA Traveller Education Services. LEA staff expressed a number of concerns about the quality of home education, the books and other resources available to support it and the achievements and progress of pupils.[585] Home education, while necessary for some children due to their physical or mental health problems, is of variable quality and is outside the framework of Ofsted inspection (local authorities monitor it as part of their enforcement of the parental duty to ensure a child receives an efficient full-time education suitable to the child's age, ability and aptitude[586]). The fact that home education is growing among Traveller peoples is therefore a worrying sign, and

---

[578] Ofsted, *Raising the Attainment of Ethnic Minority Pupils* (London, Ofsted, 1999), paras 36–38.

[579] Ofsted, *Managing Support for the Attainment of Pupils from Minority Ethnic Groups* (London, Ofsted, 2001).

[580] Ofsted, *Provision and Support for Traveller Pupils*, HMI 455 (London, Ofsted, 2003).

[581] Ibid, para 15.

[582] Ibid, para 18.

[583] Ibid, para 19.

[584] C Derrington and S Kendall, *Gypsy Traveller Students in Secondary Schools: Culture, Identity and Achievement* (Stoke on Trent, Trentham Books, 2004).

[585] Ofsted, above n 580, paras 27 and 28.

[586] Education Act 1996, s 7. See further AJ Petrie, 'Home Education and the Law' (1998) 10 *Education & the Law* 123.

perhaps a reaction by Traveller parents to the problems that formal education, based on the National Curriculum and its systematic testing of pupils, causes for those whose attendance is irregular. Either way, the report's conclusion that 'Traveller pupils are still the group most at risk in the education system. They are the one minority ethnic group which is too often "out of sight and out of mind"'[587] reflects a disappointing lack of real progress in securing effective access to education for Traveller children.[588]

It is tempting to suggest that the statutory framework should be tightened up to place LEAs under specific obligations as regards the education of Traveller children. That might, however, be seen as unreasonably singling out one group for specific attention, which could be construed as unlawfully discriminatory even if their situation were especially precarious. Another approach would be to apply the existing framework more effectively. Both such strategies would have to face up to the cultural barriers that make this group particularly difficult to include in the education system and, indeed, in wider society, because that very inclusion poses a clear threat to the autonomy and cultural traditions of Traveller (especially Gypsy) communities.[589] Poulter argues powerfully that Gypsies should be 'guaranteed the right to maintain their identity as a distinctive ethnic minority and to enjoy their own culture'.[590] The resistance of Traveller children's educational problems to the many policy efforts that have been made to improve their access to education[591] and the additional financial support provision now made via 'Vulnerable Children Grants'[592] suggest that only significant changes to the education system itself, to provide a less rigid framework for their education, are likely to make a substantial difference.

ACCESS TO FURTHER AND HIGHER EDUCATION

Not least because it is accepted that tertiary education falls within the scope of the right to education under Article 2 of Protocol 1 to the ECHR,[593] it is appropriate to conclude this chapter with discussion of access to further and

[587] Above n 264, para 54.
[588] See alsoU Kilkelly *et al*, *Children's Rights in Northern Ireland* (Belfast, Queen's University Belfast, 2004) 138.
[589] C Moore, 'Group Rights for Nomadic Minorities: Ireland's Traveller Community' (2004) 8 *International Journal of Human Rights* 175.
[590] S Poulter, *Ethnicity, Law and Human Rights* (Oxford, Clarendon Press, 1998) 194.
[591] Including Department for Education and Skills, *Aiming High: Raising the Achievement of Gypsy Traveller Pupils—A Guide to Good Practice*, DfES/0443/2003 (London, DfES, 2003); and Scottish Executive *et al*, *Inclusive Educational Approaches for Gypsies and Travellers* (Edinburgh, Scottish Executive, 2003).
[592] These grants subsumed Traveller Achievement Grants in Apr 2003 and aim to support the attendance and integration (or reintegration) into school of 'vulnerable children' and to provide them with educational and pastoral support: see DfES, *Vulnerable Children Grant—Guidance for the Financial Year 2004–05* (London, DfES, 2004).
[593] See pp 67–8 above.

higher education. The Labour Government has made access to lifelong learning and to higher education central to its education policy.[594] In the further education sector, and in relation to sixth form education in school, the Government has recently established as a primary long term aim '[t]he idea of leaving education at 16 a thing of the past—virtually every 16–19 year-old engaged in education or training'.[595] A recent report by the Social Exclusion Unit notes that 'Turkey and Mexico are the only OECD countries with fewer 18-year-olds enrolled in education than the UK'.[596]

Further Education[597]

Financial support is one of the key elements in maximising the take-up of educational opportunities among those aged 16 or over.[598] Today there is a complex and evolving legislative framework for financial support. The process of reform began with the Teaching and Higher Education Act 1998,[599] which abolished from September 1999 the discretionary power of LEAs under the Education Act 1962 to make awards for post-16 study, which by then were being paid to decreasing numbers of further education students; indeed, some LEAs made hardly any awards.[600] In anticipation of this reform, the Government introduced an amendment to the School Standards and Framework Bill to empower LEAs to continue to offer financial support for further education students, under the terms of regulations, although LEAs were under no obligation to make this provision.[601] In 1999, however, and at a cost of £100 million, the Government piloted for three years a new scheme of education maintenance allowances for those aged 16–18, amounting to up to £30 per week, dependent upon a means test,[602] and subject to signature of an education maintenance learning agreement covering such matters as attendance.[603] The aim

---

[594] See Department for Education and Employment, *Higher Education in the 21ˢᵗ Century* (London, Department for Education and Employment, 1997); Idem, *The Learning Age: A New Renaissance for a New Britain*, Cm 3790 (London, TSO, 1998).

[595] Secretary of State for Education and Skills, *Department for Education and Skills: Five Year Strategy for Children and Learners*, Cm 6272 (London, TSO, 2004) 70.

[596] Social Exclusion Unit, *Transitions: Young Adults with Complex Needs* (London, Office of the Deputy Prime Minister, 2005), para 2.9.

[597] Further education is defined in the EA 1996, s 2(3), as full-time and part-time education for persons over compulsory school age which is not secondary education (essentially, education in a school) or higher education.

[598] See, eg, H Kennedy QC (Chair), *Learning Work: Widening Participation in Further Education* (London, Further Education Funding Council, 1997).

[599] S 44.

[600] A Herbert and C Callender, *The Funding Lottery: Student Support in Further Education* (London, Policy Studies Institute, 1997). Further statistical evidence of the decline of discretionary awards is set out in N Harris *et al*, *Social Security Law in Context* (Oxford, Oxford University Press, 2000) 354–5.

[601] Education Act 1996, s 518, as substituted by the School Standards and Framework Act 1998, s 129. The Local Education Authority (Post-Compulsory Education Awards) Regulations 1999 (SI 1999/229) and (Wales) Regulations 2002 (SI 2002/1856 (W180)) were made under this power.

[602] The weekly award is £10, £20 or £30 depending on household income of up to £30,000.

[603] Education Act 1996, s 518; the Education Maintenance Allowance (Pilot Areas) Regulations 1999 (SI 1999/2168). For details of the 2005/06 scheme, see DfES, EMA Guidance for Schools and Colleges, 2005/06 (London, DfES, 2005), available at http://www.dfes.gov.uk/financialhelp/ema

of the pilot scheme, which operated in 15 areas, was to encourage young people to stay on in education beyond compulsory school age.[604] The Government says that there has been an increase in the full-time education participation rate of 3.8 per cent in year 12 as a result of the pilots, which does not seem to be all that marked, but it includes 'a particularly strong impact for young people from the lowest socio-economic groups, and for boys'.[605] The figure of 3.8 per cent is in fact the average across all 16-year-olds: the research for the DfES study which produced these results in fact showed an increase of nearly 6 per cent in the participation rate among young people eligible for an allowance.[606] From September 2004 the scheme was extended nationally under the framework established under the Education Act 2002. The 2002 Act provides for the allowance to be paid by the Secretary of State (or the National Assembly for Wales), but there are separate powers to transfer functions to the LSC or an LEA.[607] A further important change, under the Child Benefit Act 2005 and pursuant regulations (which came into force in April 2006), designed to encourage and facilitate participation in education or training post 16,[608] has been an extension of child benefit for persons engaged in such education or training full-time until their twentieth birthday (one year greater than the previous age limit) where they started their full-time education before the age of 19, although on the down side the changes also appear to mean that persons aged 16 who continue in home education which started before that age will no longer qualify.[609] Aside from child benefit (and related dependency elements to parents' benefits and tax credits), the general policy thrust in the area of social security

(4 Jan 2006). From Apr 2006, in 8 pilot areas, support in the form of an 'activity allowance' has been provided to 16–17-year-olds who are not in learning or employment, on the condition that they take specific steps to move into education or training. They will have to enter into an 'activity agreement' to this end: HM Treasury *et al*, *Supporting Young People to Achieve: the Government's Response to the Consultation* (London, HM Treasury, Mar 2005), available at www.hm-treasury.gov.uk, para 2.15. See also HM Treasury, *Budget 2005, Investing for our Future*, HC 372 (London, TSO, 2005), available at www.hm-treasury.gov.uk, paras 5.29–5.32. The Chancellor of the Exchequer has argued that the allowance should also be used to reward those participating in community work: Speech by the Rt Hon Gordon Brown MP, Chancellor of the Exchequer, at the Fabian Society New Year Conference, London, 14 Jan 2006, available at www.hm-treasury.gov.uk/newsroom_and_speeches/press/2006/press_03_06.cfm.

[604] The pilot schemes were revoked by SI 2004/1006 with effect from 31 Aug 2004.

[605] Secretary of State for Education and Skills, *Department for Education and Skills: Five Year Strategy for Children and Learners*, Cm 6272 (London, TSO, 2004), ch 6, para 44.

[606] S Middleton *et al*, *Evaulation of the Educational Maintenance Allowance Pilots: Young People Aged 16–19 Years. Final Report of the Quantitative Evaluation*, DfES Research Report RR678 (London, DfES, 2005).

[607] Education Act 2002, ss 181–185.

[608] See HM Treasury *et al*, *Supporting Young People to Achieve: Towards a New Deal for Skills* (London, HM Treasury, 2004); and HM Treasury *et al*, *Supporting Young People to Achieve: the Government's Response to the Consultation* (London, HM Treasury, Mar 2005), available at www.hm-treasury.gov.uk.

[609] See Child Benefit Act 2005, s 1(2), inserting replacement s 142 into the Social Security Contributions and Benefits Act 1992; Child Benefit (General) Regulations 2006 (SI 2006/223). If home education were to be approved by HMRC for the purposes of the regulations it might, however, meet the prescribed education condition: see reg 3. See further N Wikeley, 'The Child Benefit Act 2005: One Small Step Towards a More Radical Future for Child Benefit?' (2005) 12(3) *Journal of Social Security Law* 132.

over the past 20 years has been to take out of entitlement under the benefit system young people engaged in education, although it is still the case that part-time students and others in particular categories of need may in some circumstances be entitled to support in their own right.[610] Furthermore, those on income-related welfare benefits will generally receive full remission of course fees, but the Government wants such entitlement to be focused on particular courses such as those leading to level 2 (or 3) qualifications, and has announced that an individual's entitlement 'will be time limited . . . and not open ended, in order to provide the greatest incentive for progression . . .'[611]

A system of 'learner support funds' (at first called access funds) has also been introduced. Learner support funds are paid to colleges and other education providers to enable them to offer financial help to students whose access to education might otherwise be limited by lack of funds. This support is provided on a discretionary basis, but providers are restricted by the terms and conditions under which the grants are provided to them.[612] Funds are allocated by the Learning and Skills Council (LSC) and currently cover hardship/general costs, childcare and residential/lodging funds. They are currently paid to around one in 12 of the most disadvantaged young people in further education.[613] The LSC's priorities ensure that, for example, students who receive jobseeker's allowance and certain other benefits or support will be a high priority for support, on the basis of financial need. In 2003–4 some 200,000 learners received support via these funds.[614] The Government proposes to tie this support in the future to its objectives under its skills strategy which aims to strengthen the UK economy by remedying the so-called 'skills deficit' through 'a new Skills Alliance where every employer, employee and citizens plays their part'.[615] There will be entitlement to 'free learning' for those with few or no qualifications who are aiming for level 2 qualifications (GCSE or equivalent).[616] For adults, this will come from the new Adult Learning Grant, which is currently being piloted in 10 regions at a cost of £2 million and is due to come into operation nationally in 2005–6.[617] It will be paid at the rate of £30 per week. The grant, which is means tested, will also be available to those aged 30 or below who are seeking to obtain their first level 3 qualification (eg, A level or A2 qualification). According to the further education White Paper, the grant is particularly useful for people in their early twenties studying for their first level 3 qualifications while living at home. It will form a

---

[610] This is a very complex area and cannot be analysed here. See N Harris, *Social Security for Young People* (Aldershot, Avebury, 1989) and N Harris *et al*, *Social Security Law in Context* (Oxford, Oxford University Press, 2000), ch 11.

[611] DfES, *Further Education: Raising Skills, Improving Life Chances*, Cm 6768 (London, TSO, 2006), para 6.27.

[612] See, eg, Learning and Skills Council/Department for Education and Skills, *FE Learner Support Funds 2003/04 Terms and Conditions* (Coventry, Learning and Skills Council, 2003).

[613] Ibid, para 5.

[614] Learning and Skills Council, *Investing in Skills: Taking Forward the Skills Strategy* (Coventry, Learning and Skills Council, 2004), para 4.5.

[615] Department for Education and Skills, *21st Century Skills: Realising Our Potential—Individuals, Employers, Nation* Cm 5810 (London, TSO, 2003), para 1.4.

[616] Ibid, para 4.32.

[617] Learning and Skills Council, n 614 above, para 4.5.

'valuable complement' to the planned introduction of entitlement to free tuition for those aged 19–25 undertaking such study (for two A levels or equivalent, including Access to Higher Education programmes) from 2007–8, which was announced in the 2006 Budget; at present free tuition is guaranteed to all those aged under 19 only. [618] A system of loans has also been discussed.[619] There is also an Ethnic Minority Student Achievement Grant, paid by the LSC, that parallels the arrangements made in the schools sector to raise achievement levels among ethnic groups that are under-achieving relative to others.[620]

One scheme has, however, been scrapped. With a view to encouraging more people to undertake education and training and to increase the number of providers, the Learning and Skills Act 2000 made provision for grants to be paid to or in respect of individuals undergoing education or training and holding a 'qualifying account' (a learning account) or in certain other circumstances.[621] The scheme enabled some private sector bodies to run training programmes funded via the amounts notionally credited to the individual learning accounts. However, the scheme was terminated in England in December 2001 following evidence of abuse of the system by certain private sector education and training providers, which led to fraud investigations in some cases.[622] However, the idea of learner accounts has recently been revived as a means by which adult learners will 'purchase' their learning or receive free tuition under the new scheme for 19–25-year-olds noted above. The Government claims that 'giving learners greater choice and control over their learning energises people and gives them a real sense of empowerment'; and the idea is that they will have an account number and card and that their account will hold 'virtual funds' which can be used to pay for learning provided by any provider which is sponsored by the Learning and Skills Council.[623] The Government asserts that illicit exploitation will be prevented under the new scheme by firmer quality assurance measures.[624]

One of the criticisms of the support arrangements as a whole has been that they are complex, insufficiently flexible and fail to make adequate provision for those in part-time education. The Government is committed to a single system of support for 16–19-year-olds and has commissioned research to examine the arrangements made elsewhere.[625] In a review in the late 1990s the Further Education Support Advisory Group was impressed by the fully integrated system of support for young people in full-time education beyond the age of 16 in

---

[618] DfES, *Further Education: Raising Skills, Improving Life Chances*, Cm 6768 (London, TSO, 2006), paras 3.4 and 6.21.

[619] Learning and Skills Council, n 614 above, paras 4.16–4.18.

[620] See Learning and Skills Council, *Moving Forward—the Learning and Skills Council's Annual Equality and Diversity Report 2002–2003* (Coventry, Learning and Skills Council, 2004) 23.

[621] Learning and Skills Act 2000, ss 104–108; Individual Learning Accounts (England) Regulations 2000 (SI 2000/2146) and Individual Learning Accounts (Wales) Regulations 2000 (SI 2000/3384).

[622] In Wales, see the Individual Learning Accounts (Wales) Regulations 2003 (SI 2003/918).

[623] DfES, *Further Education: Raising Skills, Improving Life Chances*, Cm 6768 (London, TSO, 2006), paras 3.7–3.10.

[624] Ibid, para 3.10.

[625] See further HM Treasury *et al* (2004), above n 608.

Australia.[626] The LSC has recently acknowledged that there is a need for a more coherent framework that is 'easy to understand for the learner'.[627] It remains to be seen whether the Government can deliver one. A review of the Australian youth allowance commissioned by the Department for Work and Pensions concludes, inter alia, that the adoption of a similar system of unified support here, which would be complex in itself, would raise a number of difficult questions, such as: the appropriate level of support; whether and to what extent parental income should be taken into account; how benefit sanctions should be used to ensure activity by the young person; and whether the responsibility, that goes with independent entitlement, to inform the agencies of changes in circumstances might lead to overpayments for which recovery might be needed.[628] It must also be appreciated that the main barrier to participation in education beyond the age of 16 is in fact low educational attainment before that age. A House of Commons Select Committee said a few years ago that:

> any attempt to improve participation rates in post-compulsory learning will depend heavily on improving levels of achievement in primary and secondary school, and particularly on reducing the 'long tail' of under-achievers which has for many years bedevilled the education system.[629]

It also cited entrenched attitudinal and cultural barriers to learning as highly significant factors.[630]

Higher Education[631]

Turning to higher education, the Government seems to have accepted that its original target of having 50 per cent of all young people going into higher education by 2010 may not be achieved. It now anticipates that participation will be increased 'towards' that figure by then.[632] The rate is currently 44 per cent, just one per cent higher than in 2003.[633] The Government nonetheless appears to remain committed to expansion of participation, especially (as noted above)

---

[626] The AUSTUDY scheme, which was replaced by the Common Youth Allowance scheme. See The Further Education Support Advisory Group, *New Arrangements for Effective Support in Further Education* (London, Department for Education and Employment, 1998).

[627] Learning and Skills Council, *Investing in Skills: Taking Forward the Skills Strategy* (Coventry, Learning and Skills Council, 2004) para 4.7.e.

[628] D Finn and N Branosky, *Financial Support for 16 to 19 Year Olds. A Review of the Literature and Evidence on the Australian Youth Allowance*, DWP Research Report 215 (Leeds, Corporate Document Services, 2004).

[629] House of Commons Education and Employment Committee, Eight Report, Session 1998–99, *Access for All? A Survey of Post-16 Participation, Vol. I—Report and Proceedings*, HC 57–I (London, TSO, 1999), para 46.

[630] Ibid, para 47.

[631] Higher education is defined with reference to first or higher degree courses and courses leading to various professional diplomas and qualifications, such as the Certificate in Education: Education Reform Act 1988, ss 120 and 235(1) and Sched 6; EA 1996, s 579(1).

[632] HM Treasury *et al* (2004), above n 608, 89.

[633] Department for Education and Skills, *The Future of Higher Education*, Cm 5735 (London, TSO, 2003), para 5.7. The rate is expected to dip in 2006 when new fees are introduced.

among those groups traditionally under-represented among entrants to university or college, who include persons from families with no history of university entry[634] and those from areas of the least advantage.[635] It wants to expand foundation degree programmes and 'second chance' routes into higher education. But it also wants to provide for 'fair access' to higher education, part of its goal of making education 'a force for opportunity and social justice, not for the entrenchment of privilege'.[636] The 2003 higher education White Paper proposed an independent 'access regulator',[637] who would supervise access arrangements which institutions wishing to change the new variable fees would have to have in place, setting out their method of safeguarding access and establishing targets. It was proposed that the regulator would have the power to withdraw approval for institutions' variable fees, or to impose financial penalties, if the agreement was not fulfilled. Subsequently, the Government opted for an Office for Fair Access (OFFA) instead,[638] but still with the role of approving access agreements, to which financial strings will be attached. Access agreements were recently criticised by the House of Commons Select Committee on Education and Skills as appearing to be 'driven by political considerations rather than having a practical purpose'.[639] The Committee recommended that the Government should not proceed with OFFA but should leave responsibility for monitoring universities' access with the Higher Education Funding Council for England (HEFCE).[640] The Government also proposed an increase from 5 per cent to 20 per cent in the additional funding per student via the so-called 'postcode premium' for students from areas where few participate in higher education,[641] but the House of Commons Education Committee was critical of the fact that the extra allocation would come from a redistribution of the resources allocated for teaching.[642]

The Government has been confronted by a huge amount of accumulated evidence concerning the deterrent effects of the costs of participation in higher education in the form of fees, maintenance costs and lack of income. The

---

[634] The class divide across the UK higher education system has been shown to have widened since the mid-1990s by virtue of a greater percentage increase in the participation rate among those from higher income groups than among those from lower income families: P Hill, 'Class gap widens under Blair', *The Times Higher Education Supplement*, 2 July 2004, 1, reporting research by the Institute of Education and LSE.

[635] Data for the period 1994–2000 show that young people living in the highest quintile of neighbourhoods in terms of social advantage were 5–6 times more likely to enter higher education than those in the lowest quintile: HEFCE, *Young Participation in Higher Education*, HEFCE 2005/03 (Bristol, HEFCE, 2005), available at www.hefce.ac.uk/pubs/hefce/2005/05–03/, 10–11. By 2000 young women were 18 per cent more likely to enter HE than young men: ibid, 11. See also L Bibbings, 'Widening Participation in Higher Education' (2006) 33 *Journal of Law and Society* 74, at 76–80.

[636] Above n 633, at 67.

[637] Ibid, paras 6.29–6.31.

[638] See Department for Education and Skills, *Widening Participation in Higher Education* (London, DfES, 2003). Note that OFFA's remit does not include tutition fees for part-time courses or for international (non-EU) or postgraduate students.

[639] House of Commons Select Committee on Education and Skills, Fifth Report, Session 2002–03, *Reform of Higher Education* (London, TSO, 2003), para 140.

[640] Ibid.

[641] Ibid, paras 6.24–6.25.

[642] Fifth Report, Session 2002–03, *Reform of Higher Education* (London, TSO, 2003), para 135.

evidence includes the detailed findings and trenchant observations in the report of the National Committee of Inquiry into Higher Education (the Dearing Committee) in 1997,[643] when Labour came into office. Yet the evidence is not unequivocal. For example, HEFCE report, in relation to the period 1994–2000, that despite the replacement of grants with loans and the introduction of tuition fees, '[n]o evidence is found that this had any material effects on participation . . . there is no evidence that young people changed their decisions on whether to enter HE, when to enter HE or where to study to avoid the introduction of tuition fees'.[644] The Secretary of State was given a power under the Education Act 2002 to make regulations enabling him to clear or reduce outstanding student loan debts or the amount of repayments, but its effect seems intended to be quite limited.[645] The political arguments continued to rage around the issue of student debt; the incompatibility of expanding student numbers with the under-funding of higher education; the disadvantaged position of students at English universities compared to their Welsh and especially Scottish counterparts following the introduction of prescribed fees under the Teaching and Higher Education Act 1998; and the alleged 'elitism' inherent in certain universities' admission policies.

These issues were debated with considerable intensity in Parliament during the passage of the Higher Education Act 2004. The Act has abolished the system of fees which has been in place since the Teaching and Higher Education Act 1998 and which in 2004–5 required a fee of £1,130 to be paid by home students studying in English universities. In its place is means tested liability to fees (up to £3,000 per home or EU student for undergraduate courses),[646] to be repaid from earnings after graduation. It appears that, in fact, a majority of institutions will charge the maximum fee for most of their courses and that, rather than competing with each other on price for applicants, they are more likely to rely on scholarships and bursaries.[647] The Education Select Committee (see above) considered that the repayment threshold for student fees, set at £15,000 in the White Paper, was too low. The Government has since agreed that liability to repay will not start until the student's earnings reach £18,000 per annum. Repayment debts will be extinguished if not paid off within 25 years. The Government bowed to backbench concern about the possibility of increases in the maximum fee of £3,000 by agreeing to concessions in the Bill when it was before Parliament,

---

[643] National Committee of Inquiry into Higher Education, *Report of the National Committee* (London, Department for Education and Employment, 1997).

[644] HEFCE, *Young Participation in Higher Education*, HEFCE 2005/03 (Bristol, HEFCE, 2005), available at www.hefce.ac.uk/pubs/hefce/2005/05–03/, 10.

[645] EA 2002, s 186. According to the Bill's Explanatory Note, '[i]t provides the basis for the Government to implement plans to pay off loans for newly qualified teachers in shortage subjects in maintained schools or the FE sector'. See the Education (Teacher Student Loans) (Repayment etc) Regulations 2003 (SI 2003/1917).

[646] Differential fees for home based and other EU nationals for university courses were declared unlawful under EC law by Case 293/83, *Gravier v Ville de Liège* [1985] ECR 593 and Case 24/86, *Blaizot and Others v University of Liège and Others* [1988] ECR 379. The latter confirmed that almost all university courses were vocational for the purposes of the EEC Treaty Art 128 (see now EC Treaty Art 150).

[647] See P Hill, 'Perks on offer to lure students', *The Times Higher Education Supplement*, 23 Apr 2004, 1 and 3.

so that not only would the affirmation of both Houses be needed for any increase but the fee would be capped at that level for at least two Parliaments. The Act provides that the higher amount cannot be set unless the Secretary of State is satisfied that the increase is no greater than is required to maintain the value of the amount in real terms;[648] and otherwise each House of Parliament must pass its resolution to increase the maximum fee, after 1 January 2010.[649] An independent review of the variable fees system is to take place in 2009. The Government agreed to an amendment carried in the House of Lords to enable students taking a gap year in 2005 to be exempt from the new system provided their offer of a place, conditional or not, was received before 1 August 2005.[650] Despite concerns that those on courses of four or more years' duration could face an even bigger cumulative debt than the estimated £20,000 or much more that some groups have suggested will arise for those on three-year courses and which could operate as a significant deterrent,[651] the Government refused to limit variable fees liability to the first three years of these longer courses.

In addition to the possibility of being awarded one of the bursaries or scholarships that individual universities may be offering in support of their plans for widening access for students from disadvantaged backgrounds (see below), the poorest students may also qualify for a statutory maintenance grant (of around £1,500 per annum). Such grants, which will be paid under the Education (Student Support) Regulations, are being reintroduced for the first time since their abolition in 1991 under the Education (Student Loans) Act 1990. Maximum loans for maintenance, also covered by the regulations, are being increased and, like fees, will be repayable from future earnings. Access to maintenance support under the regulations has been held by the ECJ in *R (Bidar) v London Borough of Ealing and the Secretary of State for Education and Skills* to fall within the scope of Articles 12 and 18 of the EC Treaty (covering, respectively, freedom from discrimination on the grounds of nationality and freedom of movement).[652] By virtue of the conditions set out in the regulations then in force the claimant had to be ordinarily resident in the UK as at the first day of their course, and to have been so for a three-year period preceding that date. Moreover, throughout that three-year period their residence must not have been wholly or mainly for the purposes of receiving full-time education.[653] The ECJ held that the residence condition was justifiable in showing attachment to the UK, but that not permitting residence for education to count for that purpose was not justifiable.

---

[648] Higher Education Act 2004, ss 24 and 26 and the Student Fees (Inflation Index) Regulations 2006 (SI 2006/507).

[649] Higher Education Act 2004, s 26.

[650] Higher Education Act 2004, s 25(2). The Act also exempts persons whose entry onto a course due to start on or after 1 Sept 2006 was delayed because of an appeal against his examination grades which was successful: s 25(3).

[651] See, eg, A Lipsett, 'Top-ups blamed for wane in demand', *The Times Higher Education Supplement*, 16 Dec 2005, reporting an average 5 per cent fall in applications for September 2006, compared with the previous year; H Rumbelow, 'Fees deter 70,000 students', *The Times*, 14 Aug 2004, reporting on research conducted for The Children's Mutual.

[652] Case C–209/03 [2005] ELR 404; [2005] ECR I–2119.

[653] Education (Student Support) Regulations 2001 (SI 2001/951), Sched 1, para 4.

Accordingly, the regulations were amended[654] so that EU nationals or their children who have lived in the UK or Islands for three years (apart from temporary absences) from the relevant date can qualify for support. The Government has estimated that around 6,000 full-time EU students studying in English institutions could be eligible for maintenance support in 2006–7 as a result of the amendments necessitated by the ECJ ruling,[655] although a minor restriction has since been introduced whereby a person whose residence during those three years was wholly or mainly for the purposes of receiving full-time education must, immediately before then, have been resident in the EEA.[656] Leaving aside this latest, minor, change, the total potential cost of this maintenance has been estimated at £10 million in grants and £40 million in repayable loans.[657] Eligibility to student support has now been widened still further (for example, to include family members of economically inactive EC nationals),[658] and amendments extending equal treatment with nationals of the UK have also occurred to the regulations on fees and discretionary awards,[659] in the light of the 2004 EC Directive on free movement and residence for EU citizens and members of their families.[660]

The 'access regulator' of the White Paper has become the 'Director of Fair Access to Higher Education' in the 2004 Act, to be appointed by the Secretary of State.[661] The Director must perform his or her functions in 'such a way as to promote and safeguard fair access to higher education' (the term 'fair access' is, unsurprisingly, not defined); but he or she must protect academic freedom, in particular in relation to the content of courses and the criteria for admission to them and their application in individual cases.[662] Institutions' plans setting out proposed fees for courses and provisions relating to equality of opportunity (as required by regulations[663]), including measures to attract people from members of groups traditionally under-represented in higher education and for financial

---

[654] Education (Student Support) Regulations 2005 (SI 2005/52), Sched 2 para 9, as amended by the Education (Student Support) (Amendment) Regulations 2005 (SI 2005/1341) and Same (No 2) Regulations 2005 (SI 2005/2084). See now the Education (Student Support) Regulations 2006 (SI 2006/119), Sched 1, part 2, as substituted by the Education (Student Support) (Amendment) Regulations 2006 (SI 2006/955).

[655] HC Written Answers, Col 356W, 14 June 2005, per Mr Bill Rammell MP (Minister for Higher Education).

[656] Amendment made by the (No 2) Regulations (n 654 above).

[657] A Blair, 'Bill for EU students will hit £50m a year', *The Times*, 10 Aug 2005, 12.

[658] See the Education (Student Support) (Amendment) Regulations 2006 (SI 2006/955).

[659] The Education (Fees and Awards) (Amendment) Regulations 2006 (SI 2006/483), amending the Education (Fees and Awards) Regulations 1997 (SI 1997/1972), as previously amended; Education (Student Loans) Regulations 1998 (SI 1998/211), as further amended by the Education (Student Loans) (Amendment) (England and Wales) Regulations 2006 (SI 2006/929).

[660] Directive 2004/38/EC of the European Parliament and of the Council of 29 Apr 2004 (OJ L/158/77)—see in particular Art 24, on equal treatment.

[661] Higher Education Act 2004, s 31. Sir Martin Harris, retired Vice Chancellor of the University of Manchester, was appointed.

[662] Ibid, s 32.

[663] The Student Fees (Approved Plans) (England) Regulations 2004 (SI 2004/2473). There is also a guidance note. For a detailed review of the approval criteria and enforcement procedures, see D Palfreyman, 'Does OFFA have teeth?' (2004) 16 *Education & the Law* 249.

assistance to students, need to be approved by the Director.[664] Financial support to the institution (either from HEFCE or the Teacher Training Agency) must be made conditional on the compliance by the institution's governing body with the approved plan, including any qualifying fees set out in it.[665] The governing body is not to be regarded as having failed to comply with the approved plan if it has 'taken all reasonable steps to comply'.[666] The sanctions for failure to comply may be 'specified financial requirements' or a refusal to approve a new plan on the expiry of the existing one.[667] Institutions will therefore avoid financial penalties if they are taking reasonable steps to widen access under their plans. This seems fair, given the powerful academic arguments for maintaining rigorous entry requirements, albeit with a commitment to ensure that the applicants' potential to succeed on a course is judged with reference to a broad range of factors and not exclusively examination grades. Moreover, as the House of Commons Select Committee which examined access to higher education a couple of years ago observed in relation to the factors which result in the under-representation of some socio-economic groups among those admitted to university, 'only some of these causes are amenable to direct intervention by higher education institutions'.[668] For example, the Committee cited HEFCE's view that the prospects for widened participation could be transformed if schools could persuade more pupils from poor backgrounds to stay on in school beyond the age of 16.[669] In any event, HEFCE will continue to provide additional support to institutions through the Widening Participation allocation (based on entrants' postcodes and other factors). The legality of affirmative action in admission procedures was discussed earlier.[670]

The Government has vowed not to set national targets for improved access across social groupings, believing that they 'may do more harm than good'.[671] Perhaps the real reason is that such targets may have to be very modest if they are to be achievable. Evidence compiled by the Association of University Teachers has revealed that the proportion of undergraduates from 'working-class' backgrounds rose between 1997–8 and 2003–4 from 25 per cent to just 28.8 per cent over that period, despite a massive increase in the amount of central government funds expended on widening participation.[672] However, it remains to be seen whether greater progress can be made under the framework set in place under the 2004 Act.

---

[664] Higher Education Act 2004, ss 33 and 34.

[665] Ibid, ss 23 and 24; the Student Fees (Qualifying Courses and Persons) Regulations 2006 (SI 2006/482).

[666] Ibid, s 37(2).

[667] Ibid, s 37(1).

[668] House of Commons Select Committee on Education and Employment, Fourth Report, Session 2000–01, *Higher Education: Access*, Report, HC 205 (London, TSO, 2001), para 16.

[669] Ibid, para 15.

[670] See pp 180–6 above.

[671] Alan Johnson (Minister for Higher Education), quoted in P Hill, 'No test for access goal, Johnson says', *The Times Higher Education Supplement*, 16 July 2004, 7.

[672] Reported in C Stothart, 'Access drive has failed to bride class divide', *The Times Higher Education Supplement*, 17 Mar 2006, 10, which notes an increase in such funding from £22m per annum to £364m per annum over this period.

CONCLUSION

This chapter's exploration of access to education has revealed that the law provides an extensive framework to support free and equal access to the provision which it is the duty of the state to make available to all children and young people. The terms 'free' and 'equal' are, however, not absolute but relativistic in this context. As we have seen, there are financial costs associated with accessing education, not merely further and higher education but also schooling that is statutorily required to be provided free. So far as equal access is concerned, formal legal guarantees have been extended, with the aim of ensuring that barriers due to factors such as disability and religion are to some extent reduced. However, the law is still tending to have difficulty in reconciling the sometimes conflicting aims of respecting individual rights and meeting collective needs.

It is clear that because the state's commitment in both financial and political terms to combating the effects of wider social and economic inequality and circumstances cannot be unlimited, full and equal access to education cannot in reality be fully guaranteed. Those entering the education system or moving to a new stage within it carry with them the advantages and disadvantages from their prior educational experience, home upbringing and material circumstances. These factors, which have a direct bearing on equality of opportunity, are difficult to compensate for or eradicate. Of course, within the limits set by legal, political and economic constraints, affirmative action and targeted support have made important inroads into unequal access to education. Moreover, while a degree of cynicism continues to be expressed at the quest for continually increasing rates of participation in further and higher education, the assumption that education is a lifelong experience is beginning to register in the public conscience, although it still has some way to go to becoming a cultural norm. Across a wide range of areas, recent government policies and legislative reforms have supported more effective access to education and begun to improve equality of opportunity. All of this progress has nonetheless thrown into even sharper relief the continuing, entrenched problems experienced by certain groups, such as the children of immigrant, asylum-seeker and Gypsy and Traveller families, whose access to education remains extremely uneven.

Access to education is considered to be, and is to a large extent respected as, a basic human right, as we have seen in previous chapters. But in modern democratic countries there has come to be an expectation that beyond the basic right of access is the right to a degree of choice. Greater equality of access means greater choice, since the competitive disadvantages flowing from factors such as low income are reduced while the barriers that limit choice on the supply side (such as a disabled person accessing the standard school curriculum in a non-specialist setting) are increased. The *Begum* case was not merely about equal access to education irrespective of race or religion; it was also about the right to make individual choices about what to wear and where to receive schooling. The next two chapters explore the impact of choice in two important spheres, school admission and special educational needs. They consider, inter alia, the extent to which the accommodation of rights of choice is integral to rights of access to education and whether choice ultimately promotes or hinders social inclusion and social cohesion.

5

Choice of School and its Effects

INTRODUCTION

THIS CHAPTER AND the next one consider the opportunities that the law affords for the realisation of parental choice of school in two important contexts: school admission for children in general and school placement for pupils with special educational needs. This chapter assesses the impact of over 20 years of parental choice and, in particular, considers whether the individualism promoted by legal rights and co-relative duties associated with choice has give rise to a social dis-benefit, in the general admissions context, by increasing social divisions and segregation, and/or whether, through the underlying message of universalism, it has contributed to a widening of citizenship and social participation that may be a key to greater equality. In relation to special educational needs,[1] and more particularly the education of pupils for whom a statement of such needs is maintained by their LEA (some 237,000 children in 2006[2]), the issue under consideration in Chapter 6 is the wider effect that the opportunities for parents to influence the nature and extent of the provision made (and especially the school placement) have on the education system, in terms both of the distribution of resources and the inclusion of those with learning difficulties in mainstream schools.

Parental choice in education, the principle of which is reinforced by a general statutory duty on the Secretary of State to exercise his or her powers with a view to 'encouraging diversity and increasing opportunities for choice',[3] a duty that the Education and Inspections Bill 2006 would similarly impose on LEAs,[4] is most closely associated with school admission. This is partly because, as Brighouse explains, choice of school became 'the leading idea of education reform'[5] and was given a prominent place in the reform of the education system during the 1980s

---

[1] For the legal definition of 'special educational needs' see EA 1996, s 312, below p 325.

[2] DfES, *Special Educational Needs in England* (London, DfES, 2006), Table 1a.

[3] EA 1996, s 11(2). Also to be encouraged by the Secretary of State are improving standards.

[4] Education and Inspections Bill (as first published), cl 2, inserting s 14(3A) into the EA 1996. LEAs will also be under a duty to promote high standards: the Bill, cl 1, inserting s 13A into the EA 1996.

[5] H Brighouse, *School Choice and Social Justice* (Oxford, Oxford University Press, 2000) 19.

and early 1990s—in particular, the creation of a market for schooling within the state system.[6] It is also because the continuing diversity and disparity in academic attainment levels among schools has, in the minds of parents, highlighted the fundamental importance of choice of school for their child's educational opportunities and thus future career prospects. The growing utilisation of appeal rights when choice is denied (from 10,000 appeals lodged in 1983, to 39,600 in 1993, 91,400 in 2002/03, although declining to 85,990 in 2003/04[7]) exemplifies the weight attached to it. Indeed, according to a 2004 poll by YouGov, 76 per cent of parents with children in state schools considered it important or fairly important that they have greater school choice.[8]

In relation to the placement of a child with special educational needs, the issues surrounding parental choice and the effects of the policy are somewhat different from those concerning school admission in general. Whilst a consumerist element is common to the exercise of choice in both contexts, and the respective policy aims include a common objective of achieving a more even balance between education providers' and users' interests than would otherwise be the case, there has been no expectation or conscious wish on the part of policy-makers to harness parental choice relating to special educational needs for the wider political purpose of establishing a (specialist) market for education in that field. Through a range of Acts, notably the Education Acts 1981 and 1993 (the latter consolidated into the Education Act 1996), the policy of parental choice in the field of special educational needs has in most respects merely built on key recommendations in the Warnock Report in 1978, namely that the education system should pay heed to parental knowledge about their child's needs and respect parental wishes regarding the child's education.[9] At the same time, adherence to parental wishes has had to be balanced against one of Warnock's other key recommendations concerning the principle of 'integration' (more commonly referred to today as 'inclusion')—that pupils with special educational needs should, as far as possible, be educated alongside other children in mainstream schools.

The duty to adhere to parental choice over school admissions in general or over a special educational needs school placement is subject to conditions which refer, inter alia, to 'efficient education' and 'the efficient use of resources'.[10] As we shall see, conditions of this kind ensure that there can be no guarantee of choice. We also saw in Chapter 2 that the Human Rights Act 1998 has made little or no difference to the realisation of choice in education: the parental right in the second sentence of Article 2 of Protocol 1 concerns matters that

---

[6] See p 244ff below.

[7] Council on Tribunals *Annual Report* for 1982–3 (London, HMSO, 1983) and 1992–93 (London, HMSO, 1993); DfES, *Admission Appeals for Maintained Primary and Secondary Schools in England 2002/03*, SFR 19/2004 (London, DfES, 2004), available at http://www.dfes.gov.uk/rsgateway/DB/SFR/, table 1; and Idem, *Schools and Pupils in England, January 2005 (Final)* (London, DfES, 2005), table 10.

[8] Cited in J Le Grand, 'The Blair Legacy: Choice and Competition in Public Services', Transcript of Public Lecture, LSE, 21 Feb 2006, available at www.lse.ac.uk/collections/LSEPublicLecturesandEvents/.

[9] HM Warnock (chair), *Special Educational Needs. Report of the Enquiry into the Education of Handicapped Children and Young People* (London, HMSO, 1978).

[10] SSFA 1998, s 86(3)(a); EA 1996, Sched 27, para 3.

are resource-sensitive, almost rendering the UK's reservation concerning the 'avoidance of unreasonable expenditure' unnecessary. The rights of the individual are conditioned by the state's overriding responsibility to manage the education system in a way that serves economic and other collectivist goals. Nonetheless, the underlying assumption, and the 'default' position, is that individual preference will generally be acceded to and the evidence shows that the majority of placements or school admissions do, in fact, accord with parental wishes.

School admission or placement decisions can have important social consequences, not merely for the relevant families but also for wider society. Of particular concern to this book is the risk of social segregation through the operation of school choice. Yet it is necessary to assess whether those consequences flow primarily from the positive exercise of parental choice, or rather the passive acceptance of the choices made by administrators. One might reasonably assume that parents who are competent and determined enough will take preparatory action, such as moving into a school catchment area, in order to have priority status within a school admissions policy. On the face of it, their acceptance of an offered place will appear passive, but in reality they have taken positive action to ensure that their choice is guaranteed. Such a strategy favours middle-class or better-off families, thereby creating the potential for social division by serving to drive up still higher the house prices within catchment areas for schools favoured by such parents, as the Education and Skills Select Committee found.[11] Thus the choices made by individual parents may have a wider, and often long term, social impact, as discussed below. Government proposals to reform the schools system, published in October 2005 and contained in the Education and Inspections Bill 2006, include reforms on school choice which could in fact have an impact on the current advantages enjoyed by middle class families in the school admissions process.

THE DUTY TO HAVE REGARD TO PARENTS' WISHES

The legal framework that was established under the Education Act 1944 only weakly incorporated the principle of parental choice. Section 76 placed a duty upon the Secretary of State and LEAs to 'have regard to the general principle . . . that children are to be educated in accordance with the wishes of their parents'.[12] This duty continues and is today found in the Education Act 1996, section 9. The fact that the duty is subject to the condition that adherence to parental wishes must be 'compatible with the provision of efficient instruction and training and the avoidance of public expenditure'[13] has limited its potential value as a means of guaranteeing choice for the individual. A Ministry of Education circular

[11] House of Commons Education and Skills Committee, Fourth Report, Session 2003–04, *Secondary Education: School Admissions*, HC 58–1 (London, TSO, 2004), para 98. See below.
[12] Education Act 1944, s 76.
[13] Ibid, now s 9 of the EA 1996.

published in 1946, although entitled *Choice of Schools*, made it clear that the Ministry's view was that the section 'does not confer on the parent complete freedom of choice'.[14] As shown below, the courts subsequently regarded the principle in the section as but one of a number of factors to which the LEA might have regard (both in its policies and in practice) in exercising its functions concerning the provision of school places.[15] It was, and remains, a duty which the courts have consistently over a period of 50 years regarded as imposing little more than a procedural requirement to consider expressions of parental preference, leaving the state authorities free to make policy choices in accordance with their discretionary powers.[16]

What the duty did recognise, however, is that parents have a moral claim to some measure of influence over their children's education. In particular, it seems to have been accepted that, while this duty did not confer freedom of choice, it did require LEAs to pay particular regard to parents' preference for a place for their child at either a denominational school, founded by a religious body, or a non-denominational school.[17] Moreover, the 1953 edition of the Ministry of Education's circular (which was not withdrawn until 1981) referred also to parental preference for single-sex or mixed schooling.[18] However, that did not mean that LEAs had to make that choice available to parents in their area. Indeed, in a case in Blackburn in 1972, a Muslim father who kept his daughter away from school because he was concerned that a mixed school might have a bad moral influence on her, felt compelled to do so by the absence of any single-sex secondary schools in the town. He was fined £5 for breach of his duty to ensure his child's efficient full-time education.[19]

With regard to denominational schooling in particular, the general principle of adherence to parental wishes needs to be viewed in the context of the schools framework as a whole, as established by the 1944 Act. The Act provided for a dual system of religious and secular schools. As noted in Chapter 3, RA Butler, the Minister of Education and architect of the Act, sought to include within the state sector schools run by the Church of England and the Catholic Church. He regarded this as important to his broader policy goal of education for all. At this time many of these schools were struggling to maintain their buildings and meet operating costs,[20] so state support was critical to their long term future. Parents were also given the right, which continues to the present, to withdraw their child from religious education or collective worship at school.[21] Thus, the core purpose of such rights of parental choice as existed under the 1944 Act appears to have

---

[14] Ministry of Education, Circular No 83, *Choice of School* (London, Ministry of Education, 1946).

[15] *Watt v Kesteven County Council* [1955] 1 QB 408; *Cumings v Birkenhead Corporattion* [1972] Ch 12.

[16] In the context of special educational needs see p 345ff below.

[17] See Ministry of Education, Circular No 83, *Choice of School* (London, Ministry of Education, 1946).

[18] Ministry of Education, *Choice of School* (London, Ministry of Education, 1953).

[19] *Daily Mail*, 3 Nov 1972, cited in GR Barrell and JA Partington, *Teachers and the Law* (6th edn, London, Methuen, 1985) 31.

[20] See N Timmins, *The Five Giants—A Biography of the Welfare State* (London, Harper Collins, 1995), chs 4 and 5.

[21] EA 1944, s 25(4).

been religious freedom, as further exemplified by the stipulation that it could not be a condition of a child's admission to a (non-denominational) county school or a (denominational) voluntary school 'that he shall attend or abstain from attending any Sunday school or place of religious worship'.[22]

The centrality of religious freedom to the 1944 Act's concept of choice is further reinforced by the circumstances surrounding the leading attempts to enforce the 'wishes of their parents' duty in the courts, although in no case did the court consider the religious preference of the parent to be determinative. In a case reported in 1955, *Watt v Kesteven County Council*,[23] the LEA did not maintain a grammar school in its area but funded places at an independent school. A Roman Catholic man did not want his two sons to attend the independent school. He preferred that they should attend a Roman Catholic boarding school, at the LEA's expense, but the LEA denied his request. Denning LJ, in the Court of Appeal, said that the matter did not depend upon the religious views of the parent but was essentially about whether the LEA had an obligation to accede to parental choice. In his view, the 1944 Act required the LEA to ensure there were schools available for all the children in the area, which it was doing, and that while it was to have regard to parents' wishes, under section 76, that was only a:

> general principle [which] leaves it open to the county council to have regard to other things as well, and also to make exceptions to the general principle if it thinks fit to do so. It cannot therefore be said that a county council is at fault simply because it does not see fit to comply with the parent's wishes.[24]

Denominational schooling was also the backcloth to another important case concerning the section 76 duty, in the early 1970s. In *Cumings v Birkenhead Corporation*[25] the LEA sent a circular to parents of primary school pupils stating that, in the next round of school admissions, children attending Roman Catholic primary schools would be considered only for places at Roman Catholic secondary schools and their parents could not select a county school. The LEA's rationale was that county and Church of England secondary schools would have sufficient places only for pupils attending non-Roman Catholic primary schools. Provision was, however, made for consideration of exceptional circumstances in individual cases. The parents of pupils who were allocated a place at a Roman Catholic secondary school and were refused a place at a non-Roman Catholic school challenged the legality of the policy. In the High Court (at which stage there were three applicants), Ungoed-Thomas J could find no unreasonableness or irrationality in the admissions policy, although he acknowledged that it would have been preferable that the LEA should have given all parents a choice between all schools without restriction, so that, for example, the wishes of parents of Roman Catholic children attending non-Roman Catholic primary schools might

[22] Ibid, s 25(3).
[23] [1955] 1 QB 408.
[24] Ibid, at 424.
[25] [1972] Ch 12; [1971] 2 All ER 881.

better have been complied with. The parents argued that the restriction based on whether the child had attended a Roman Catholic or non-Roman Catholic school was contrary to public policy on religion in education, as it involved 'involuntary segregation' or involuntary 'educational apartheid' on religious grounds contrary to the 'great principle that religion is totally voluntary' embodied in the 1944 Act.[26] In response the judge noted that parents still had a right under the Act to withdraw their children from religious education or worship and that no objection based on religion had been made to policy.

In the Court of Appeal, in an appeal brought by only one of the original applicants, it was argued that this segregation of pupils was unlawful for failing to take account of parental wishes for the purposes of section 76 and that the LEA had unlawfully fettered its discretion. In the leading judgment, Lord Denning MR reiterated his views on the scope of section 76 as previously articulated in *Watt* (above) and said that the LEA was entitled to have regard 'not only to the wishes of the parents of one particular child, but also the wishes of parents of other children and of other groups of children'.[27] He said that in this case the LEA was having regard to the wishes of the *generality* of parents who sent their children to Roman Catholic primary schools or other schools. Although he did not say so explicitly, Lord Denning seemed to believe that the admissions policy was consistent with parental wishes, although not necessarily with those of every single parent, which in his view was not required. He also rejected the argument that there was a fettering of discretion, because there could be exceptions in individual cases. He considered that the expressed rationale for the policy indicated that the LEA had made a 'sound administrative policy decision' in the circumstances.[28] (A similar view was taken of an almost identical admissions policy operating in Lancashire in the early 1990s, which was unsuccessfully challenged under *Wednesbury* unreasonableness.[29])

As the admissions policy was considered acceptable to the generality of parents, the court's decision had the effect of adding legitimacy to a piece of local decision-making by a democratically elected council exercising a discretion conferred by Parliament, even though the policy had the effect of segregating pupils by religion. The suggestion by Denning MR that section 76 had a collec-tivist as well as individualist orientation represented a divergence from the view

---

[26] That principle was, at that time, in the EA 1944, s 25(3).

[27] [1972] Ch 12; [1971] 2 All ER 881, at 884H.

[28] Ibid, at 885H–J.

[29] *R v Lancashire CC ex parte F* [1995] ELR 33. As Kennedy LJ explained, the rationale for the policy, which limited choice of county secondary school for those Roman Catholics attending Roman Catholic primary schools, unless they had a sibling at the county school or there were exceptional special reasons of a medical, social or welfare nature for admission, was:

'If too many Roman Catholic children from Roman Catholic primary schools express a preference to go to county schools and those preferences are considered in the same way as all other preferences, then the [LEA] will be left with a number of children who cannot be given places, as they should be, in the areas in which they live . . .' (at 41C–D).

The *Wednesbury* test required that the courts ask whether the policy was one which was 'unrea-sonable' in the sense that it was one which 'no sensible authority acting with due appreciation of its responsibilities would have decided to adopt': per Lord Diplock in *Secretary of State for Education and Science v Tameside Metropolitan Borough Council* [1977] AC 1014 at 1064.

expressed five years earlier by Goff J in *Wood v Ealing LBC*,[30] where a group of parents had opposed plans by the LEA, acting in furtherance of central government policy of comprehensivation, to end selective admission to local secondary schools. They had contended, inter alia, that the LEA had disregarded section 76 by failing to have regard to their wishes. Goff J accepted a construction put forward by counsel that section 76 could not mean that pupils generally had to be educated in accordance with the wishes of parents as a body or group and that all that the section 76 duty implied was that 'an individual pupil should be educated in accordance with the wishes of that individual pupil's individual parent'.[31] Goff J said that 'it would be wholly impractical if section 76 meant parents in general, since they would almost certainly not agree in most, if not all, cases and would be, moreover, a constantly fluctuating body'.[32] He accepted that the section 76 duty could be applied to the LEA's section 8 duty (the duty to ensure that there were available in their area 'sufficient' schools offering an appropriate 'variety of instruction'). However, he considered that the former related to matters such as the curriculum and whether it included religious education or whether a school was co-educational or single sex 'and not the size of the school or its conditions of entry'.[33]

The fact that the duty in section 76 (or now section 9 of the 1996 Act) is conferred on the Secretary of State as well as LEAs does in fact suggest that it was intended to have a collectivist orientation. The Secretary of State, acting via the DfES, has no direct involvement in decisions on provision for individual children, except in so far as he or she may give directions to an LEA or school under his or her statutory powers following a complaint made to him or her.[34] Even though, in 1944, LEAs had a more direct involvement in the operation of individual schools than they do today, section 76 still seems to be concerned with LEAs' responsibility for the organisation of schooling and for general policy on schools in their area.

When this issue came before the House of Lords in *Harvey v Strathclyde Regional Council* in 1989, however, Lord Keith, giving the court's judgment, indicated that there might be a question mark over the applicability of section 28(1) of the Education (Scotland) Act 1980 (the equivalent of section 76 in England and Wales) to a decision relating to the discontinuance of a school (a decision which clearly affected the interests of parents in general), in view of the separate statutory provision for consultation and objection to proposals.[35] The court was nevertheless prepared to proceed on the basis that the parental wishes duty was applicable, particularly as neither party had raised the issue in the proceedings. At first instance in this case the court had held that the decision by the education authority to close three of its six non-denominational secondary schools in Paisley (a decision necessitated by surplus capacity in schools due to

---

[30] [1967] Ch 364.
[31] Ibid, at 373A–B.
[32] Ibid, at 373B–C.
[33] Ibid, at 384A–B.
[34] Education Act 1996, ss 496 and 497.
[35] 1989 SLT 612, at 615.

falling school rolls) was contrary to the wishes of the overwhelming majority of parents in the area, who favoured the retention of four schools. It held that the authority's decision had led to the prima facie inference that the authority had not had regard to the principle in section 28(1) and that, on the facts, the authority had not been able to displace that inference. On appeal, this idea that the divergence between the parents' wishes and the authority's decision gave rise to a rebuttable presumption of a failure to engage with the section 28(1) duty was rejected by the First Division judges. On appeal to the House of Lords the parents argued that the general principle in section 28 should be treated as a 'primary consideration' of the education authority in the discharge of its functions under the Act. Lord Keith of Kinkel said, however, that an applicant seeking to mount a challenge under section 28(1) had to show that 'the respondents paid no regard at all to the general principle embodied in section 28(1), or paid to it a degree of regard lesser than any reasonable education authority would have paid'.[36] The court found no evidence of such a degree of disregard.

On the whole, however, section 76/section 9 has been relied on more or less exclusively to support claims by *individuals*, despite its clear limitations as a means to ensure guarantees of choice. It was, for example, raised by the applicant in *R v London Borough of Lambeth ex p G*.[37] He was a student who claimed that he suffered an unlawful denial of choice due to his LEA's refusal to provide him with a grant to enable him to take an A level course in a neighbouring borough. The authority's refusal was based on its policy not to provide such an award for attendance at a college or school that was outside the LEA's area if there was an equivalent course at an institution within its area. As the LEA did not establish any financial justification for its policy, Potts J said that it was in breach of the principle in section 76 (and also the 'enhanced principle of parental choice' in section 6 of the Education Act 1980).[38]

Over the past decade, almost all of the attempts to enforce the obligations of LEAs under section 9 have occurred in cases where the parents of a pupil with special educational needs (that is a pupil who has 'a learning difficulty which calls for special educational provision to be made for him'[39]) have sought a funded placement for their child in a particular school. The cases are discussed in the next chapter, but it will be seen that the courts have not really altered their position that section 9 makes parental wishes 'important' but 'not decisive'.[40] Thus while parental wishes and preferences have to be taken into account, such rights as exist by virtue of this general statutory duty have been of extremely limited potential in ensuring choice of educational provision. Indeed, the comment by the Plowden report in 1967 that, in practice, the freedom of choice

---

[36] Ibid, at 615.

[37] [1994] ELR 207.

[38] Ibid, at 218D. See below.

[39] Education Act 1996, s 312(1). For discussion of the terms 'learning difficulty' and 'special educational provision', see Chap 6.

[40] *A v Birmingham City Council* [2004] EWHC Admin 156; [2004] ELR 563, at para 24, per Sir Richard Tucker.

section 76 conferred was 'often nominal'[41] has been shown to, if anything, over-exaggerate its importance. Moreover, as the cases on special educational needs discussed in the next chapter show, the Human Rights Act 1998 has merely shown the ECHR to be enshrining a similar balance of interests to that which the general statutory duty reflects.

Since the early 1980s, however, the politics of education have shifted in favour of parental rights, as we saw in Chapter 3. While some parental demands might still warrant reference to the general duty in section 9, the scope of parental choice is determined primarily with reference to the parental preference and appeal provisions within school admissions law, which commenced with the Education Act 1980,[42] or with the right of parents (noted above) to specify a maintained school placement to be included in a child's statement of special educational needs, which was first introduced under the Education Act 1993.[43] This chapter now examines the first of these areas. As noted above, the issue of choice in relation to special educational needs is covered in Chapter 6.

LEGISLATING FOR CHOICE IN RELATION TO SCHOOL ADMISSION

Policy Background

LEAs held control over admissions to county schools under the Education Act 1944 as an implicit element of their duty to ensure there were 'sufficient' schools.[44] In the case of voluntary (denominational) schools, admissions were generally determined by school governing bodies. There was no statutory framework specifically for the allocation of school places to any of these schools beyond the general duty to ensure that children were educated in accordance with the wishes of their parents under section 76, discussed above. However, by virtue of duties imposed by the Education Act 1980, discussed below, parents gained the right to information about schools, to express a preference for a school and, subject to conditions, to have their choice met.[45] The Act also provided for a right of appeal to an education appeal committee.[46] Whether the 1980 Act precipitated a cultural shift or merely underlined the trend towards greater consumerism that was already under way is, however, open to debate. Certainly there was a growing demand for recognition of consumer rights in general during the 1960s and 1970s and, in relation to services provided by the state, a focus on both the procedural rights and substantive rights of individual

---

[41] B Plowden (chair), *Children and their Primary Schools. A Report of the Central Advisory Council for Education (England)* (London, HMSO, 1967), para 120.
[42] Education Act 1980, ss 6 and 7.
[43] Education Act 1993, Sched 10, para 3—now the EA 1996, Sched 27, para 3.
[44] Education Act 1944, s 8.
[45] Education Act 1980, s 6.
[46] Ibid, s 7.

recipients of welfare provision. Moreover, in education circles, the benefits of parent participation in the education system, for example as school governors, and through individual parents communicating their knowledge of the child's needs and expressing choices, were increasingly being recognised.

In 1967, the Plowden report on primary schools recommended that 'parents should be allowed to choose their children's primary school whenever this is possible' and they should be 'given booklets prepared by schools to inform them in their choice'.[47] Significantly, the report was conscious of the relationship between social class and the realisation of choice: 'choice is more often exercised by middle class parents'.[48] According to the report, the rationale for extending choice was that parents 'are more likely to support a school they have freely chosen, and to give it the loyalty which is so essential if their children are to do the same'.[49] The exercise of choice would also give an indication to the LEA, where a school proved an unpopular choice, 'to find out why and make it better'.[50]

Further moves to introduce more active parental participation in education occurred during the 1970s, when an impetus for change was generated by a combination of concern about educational standards (highlighted in the so-called 'Great Debate' sparked by James Callaghan's speech in Ruskin College in 1976) and the growth in consumer pressure in general: Maclure refers to the 'rising tide of consumerism which encouraged the idea of more direct participation by parents' during this period.[51] In 1977 a Committee of Enquiry report argued that parents should have equal representation on school governing bodies with each of three other groups: teachers and other staff; LEA members; and members of the local community.[52] In the same year, a DES circular encouraged LEAs to make information about schools available to parents.[53] Subsequently the Warnock report[54] called for the parents of a child with special educational needs to have an input into the decision-making processes concerning their child's assessment and educational provision, plus a right of appeal. Therefore, by the time that parent participation was enshrined in law under the Education Act 1980 (in relation to choice of school, access to information and service as a parent governor[55]) and the Education Act 1981 (covering the education of children with special educational needs), it had already to some extent gained cultural acceptance as having value to the schools system.

---

[47] Plowden (chair), n 41 above, para 130.
[48] Ibid, para 120.
[49] Ibid.
[50] Ibid.
[51] S Maclure, *Education Re-formed* (3rd edn, London, Hodder & Stoughton, 1992) 139. See also A Richardson, *Participation* (London, Routledge & Kegan Paul, 1983); N Beattie, *Professional* Parents (London, Falmer, 1985); and J Sallis, *Schools, Parents and Governors: A New Approach to Accountability* (London, Routledge, 1988).
[52] Taylor Committee, *A New Partnership for Our Schools* (London, HMSO, 1977).
[53] DES Circular 15/77 *Information for Parents* (London, DES, 1977).
[54] HM Warnock (chair), *Special Educational Needs. Report of the Enquiry into the Education of Handicapped Children and Young People* (London, HMSO, 1978).
[55] The Act required all schools to have two parent governors.

Brighouse explains that school choice has the potential to meet the 'ideological commitment to the market of the libertarian right'.[56] The ideology of the free market has an economic justification that the proponents of school choice see as bringing practical benefits. The Conservative governments of the 1980s were committed to freeing schools from the power of LEAs and creating a competitive market type system for education services. The assumption that parental choice can effect a form of marketplace accountability for poor standards is something on which the school choice policies that followed in the 1980s substantially rested. The 'New Right' Conservative approach involved utilising consumer choice as part of the mechanism for allocating central government resources most efficiently. The idea was that schools would compete for pupils and the best schools would attract the most pupils—at a time when school rolls were falling in some areas—and would be rewarded by the allocation of resources tied to pupil numbers. Weak, under-performing schools would be unpopular, thereby losing market share and funding. LEAs would cease to be able to prop them up. Schools would therefore have a clear incentive to do better. This consequence of the exercise of choice had been recognised by Lady Plowden, although her committee had envisaged LEAs being in control of schools. In the 1991, the Prime Minister, John Major, wrote in the foreword to the Government's *Citizen's Charter* that 'choice, wherever possible between competing suppliers, is the best spur to quality improvement'.[57] To enhance parental choice the Government also promoted greater diversity in the education system—for example, through the assisted places scheme, established under the 1980 Act, to fund places for pupils at participating independent schools; and, more particularly, the introduction of grant-maintained schools and city technology colleges in the late 1980s.[58]

The assisted places scheme was a very much watered-down version of the voucher concept that had attracted support from right-leaning think tanks such as the Institute of Economic Affairs in the 1960s and 1970s.[59] It was originally the idea of Milton Friedman in the US.[60] Although Friedman saw the provision of vouchers as a means by which the state could support parents and their children, and thereby ensure the wider social benefits that accrue from education, he presupposed that the state's role in educational provision itself might be limited and might focus primarily upon regulation of minimum standards.[61] In practice, vouchers have been used in the US, within states such as Wisconsin and Ohio, for the purpose of enabling public funds to support attendance at private schools, including religious schools, by children and young people from low-income

---

[56] H Brighouse, n 5 above, at 19.

[57] HM Government, *The Citizen's Charter*, Cm 1599 (London, HMSO, 1991), 4.

[58] See pp 95–8 above.

[59] See, eg, EG West, *Education and the State* (London, Institute of Economic Affairs, 1965).

[60] M Friedman, 'The Role of Government in Education' in RA Solo (ed), *Economics and the Public Interest* (New Brunswick, Rutgers University Press, 1955); M Friedman, *Capitalism and Freedom* (Chicago, IL, University of Chicago Press, 1962).

[61] Ibid, 89. As regards the influence of Friedman (and Hayek) on the views of members of the Conservative Party in relation to state education, see D Lawson, *Education and Politics in the 1990s* (London, Falmer, 1992).

families. Indeed, the Prime Minister referred to one state where they are used, Florida, in the foreword to the 2005 White Paper: while not mentioning vouchers, he held up the state as one that facilitated choice as a means of improving school standards, by enabling parents to select an alternative school where their school had 'failed' in two of the previous four years. It remains a controversial and contentious policy area in the US. Indeed, Moe describes it as being, 'for the past decade (and longer) . . . the most controversial reform in all of American education'.[62] The arguments adhered to by its proponents are redolent of those adopted by the New Right Conservatives in the UK in the 1970s and 1980s in support of both vouchers and the assisted places scheme, namely that they foster greater competition between schools and increase pressure to raise standards. They are also said to increase choice for parents and promote social equity by affording greater opportunities for those from less advantaged backgrounds. US opponents to vouchers have similar objections to those raised by opponents of the assisted places scheme in England and Wales, seeing them as potentially harming 'the low-income and at-risk students they are intended to help by diverting funds from government schools',[63] which themselves would be 'wreck[ed]' by this deprivation of resources.[64] Furthermore, vouchers are seen as having a tendency to 'undermine cherished values the public school system has long stood for—common schooling, equal opportunity, democratic control—and create a system driven by private interests'.[65] According to Peterson, '[m]ost Republicans, especially social conservatives and libertarians who have read their Milton Friedman, support vouchers in principle', because they support choice, but vouchers are seen as primarily benefiting poor black Americans, who are 'the most faithful of all Democratic voting blocs'; and in any event, vouchers have little appeal to 'well-heeled suburbanites who already have a range of educational choices'.[66] But for Democrats, public support for vouchers would be 'political suicide', not least because of opposition to them among a key Democrat constituency, the teaching profession.[67] For the teaching unions, vouchers are, according to Moe, 'a nightmare in the making', because they would result in more teachers being employed in the private sector where it is more difficult to exercise industrial muscle.[68] Less politically controversial than vouchers, and more acceptable to many in the US, are tax credits for families paying for private education or into private scholarships, which have so far been introduced in six states.[69]

---

[62] TM Moe, 'The Future of School Vouchers' in PE Peterson (ed), *The Future of School Choice* (Stanford, Cal, Hoover Institution Press, 2003) 135 at 136.

[63] RW Garnett, 'Regulatory Strings and Religious Freedom: Requiring Private Schools to Promote Public Values' in PJ Wolf and S Macedo (eds), *Educating Citizens. International Perspectives on Civic Values and School Choice* (Washington, DC, Brookings Institution Press, 2004), 324 at 335.

[64] TM Moe, n 62 above, 137.

[65] Ibid, 137.

[66] PE Peterson, 'After Zelman v Simmons-Harris, What Next?' in Peterson (ed), n 62 above, 1 at 7.

[67] Ibid.

[68] TM Moe, n 62 above, 135 at 138.

[69] See MR West, 'The Future of Tax Credits' in Peterson (ed), n 62 above, 157.

In 2002 the US Supreme Court (by the narrowest majority) held in *Zelman v Simmons-Harris*[70] that the school voucher programme in Cleveland, Ohio, through which scholarships which were publicly funded could be used for attendance at private religious schools, did not violate the Establishment Clause of the US Constitution that prohibits the 'establishment' of religion by the state.[71] The essential point, as articulated by Chief Justice Renquist, was that the choices of individual parents which resulted in funds going to these schools could not in themselves carry with them the '*imprimatur* of government endorsement'. Furthermore, according to the majority, the parents were not being forced to apply for a voucher scholarship and send their children to religious schools, in that they had alternative educational choices open to them. As the Chief Justice put it in another Supreme Court decision, *Locke v Davey*, 'the link between government funds and religious training is broken by the independent and private choice of the recipients'.[72] The *Zelman* decision therefore 'removed a key legal obstacle to the extension of new voucher programs.'[73] But in addition to the political barriers to expansion discussed above, there are the so-called 'Blaine' amendments, originating in the mid-nineteenth century, which prohibit funds raised by the government from taxation for the support of public schools to be placed under the control of a religious sect or allocated to religious sects or denominations, and many states' constitutions incorporate this principle.[74] Notwithstanding the *Zelman* decision, an intermediate appellate court in Florida held recently that Florida's state constitutional prohibition against state provision of indirect benefits to denominational schools meant that it was not legitimate for private schools to receive tax revenue through the voucher programme.[75] The voucher concept is still very much alive in the US although it is considered that

---

[70] 536 US 639(2002). See CJ Russo and RW Mawsdley, 'The Supreme Court upholds vouchers' (2002) 14 *Education & the Law* 275.

[71] First Amendment: 'Congress shall make no law respecting an establishment of religion'.

[72] 540 US 712 (2004), Opinion of the Court, 5.

[73] TM Moe, 'The Future of School Vouchers' in Peterson (ed), n 62 above, 135 at 135.

[74] James G Blaine was Speaker of the House of Representatives. His amendment to the US Constitution marginally failed to attract sufficient votes in the Senate in 1868, but in the ensuing years 15 states made 'Blaine' amendments to their constitutions. Today, some 37 states' constitutions place some restrictions on state aid to religious schools. See LR Cohen and C Boyden Gray, 'The Need for Secular Choice' in Peterson (ed), n 62 above, 87 at 96–105. See also SK Green, 'Seminal or Symbolic' in Peterson (ed), n 62 above, 35 at 48–54.

[75] *Bush v Holmes*, 886 So 2d 340, 193 Educ L Rep 938 (Fla Dist CA 2004). The constitutional provision in question was Art I, §3: '[t]here shall be no law respecting the establishment of religion or prohibiting or penalising the free exercise thereof . . . No revenue of the state or any political subdivision or agency thereof shall ever be taken from the public treasury directly or indirectly in aid of any church, sect, or religious denomination or in aid of any sectarian institution'. The case was subsequently heard in the Florida Supreme Court, which confirmed that the programme ran counter to the state constitution: *Bush v Holmes*, Case No SC04-2323, Sup C Florida, 5 Jan 2006. However, Art IX, § 1 was the determinative factor here. It requires adequate provision to be made by law 'for a uniform, efficient, safe, secure, and high quality system for free public schools that allows students to obtain a high quality education . . .' The voucher programme permitted some children to attend private schools that were not subject to the uniformity requirements (on curricula; and other forms of regulation concerned essentially with quality standards) that applied to public schools. See RW Garnett and CS Pearsall, '*Bush v Holmes*: School Vouchers, Religious Freedom, and State Constitutions' (2005) 17 *Education and the Law* 173.

the battle between conflicting vested interests may slow any expansion that the *Zelman* decision could otherwise precipitate.

In the UK, the long tradition of state involvement and the potential political costs of de-nationalising schools limited the potential for privatisation of education to the extent that the voucher idea contemplated.[76] Moreover, although in the early 1980s both Keith Joseph, then Education Secretary, and the Prime Minister, Margaret Thatcher, were attracted to the idea of vouchers as a means to establish a market within the state system, the Department of Education had practical concerns about it. According to Timmins, the idea was finally killed off in 1983 on the ground that schools could not be expected to operate along commercial lines, when (at that time) they had no history or experience of financial control and budgeting.[77] A further factor, noted by Maclure, was that there was a looming General Election that year and there was no feasible scheme to present to voters.[78] Subsequently, as noted in Chapter 3, the Education Reform Act 1988 did introduce many of the key elements that would have been needed for a voucher system: devolved budgets and financial control to schools, 'open enrolment' (schools admitting pupils up to the full extent of their capacity) and per capita formula funding, based on pupils numbers. But, as Timmins explains, that system did not provide 'the psychologically important piece of paper to spend'.[79] Proponents of vouchers hoped that once the new funding system was established 'it would be simple to go to the next stage and make the *per capita* payment to the parent instead of the school'.[80]

In the 1990s the Government did pilot training vouchers by which a young person could 'purchase' vocational training from a provider up to a set amount (£1,000),[81] which in fact operated via a special training 'credit card' in the mid-1990s.[82] This concept was subsequently adopted via the Connexions card for rewarding participation in post-16 education and has recently been seen in proposals for young people to have an 'opportunity card' by which they can earn credit for good behaviour, educational attainment or voluntary work.[83] However, the only other concrete attempt to introduce vouchers occurred via the Nursery Education and Grant-Maintained Schools Act 1996. The Act provided, inter alia, for a new system of funding of nursery education via grants made to providers, including LEAs and private sector organisations.[84] The level of the grant was to

[76] See R Rose, *Ordinary People in Public Policy—A Behavioural Analysis* (London, Sage, 1989) 21.

[77] N Timmins, *The Five Giants—a Biography of the Welfare State* (London, Harper Collins, 1995) 421.

[78] S Maclure, *Education Re-formed* (London, Hodder and Stoughton, 1988) 164.

[79] N Timmins, n 77 above, 422.

[80] S Maclure, n 79 above, 164.

[81] N Timmins, n 77 above, 513.

[82] The Conservative Government had announced a 'training credit' scheme in a White Paper, *Education and Training for the 21st Century,* in May 1991. The aim was that by 1996 all 16- and 17-year-olds not in education would be eligible for training up to the value of £1,000 from competing National Vocational Qualification suppliers. The Government, it seems, was so committed to and confident about the training credit scheme that it did not wait for the results of evaluation studies which were being carried out in selected areas. The scheme operated under the title 'Futures'.

[83] DfES, *Youth Matters*, Cm 6629 (London, TSO, 2005), paras 103–117.

[84] Nursery Education and Grant-Maintained Schools Act 1996, s 1. See Department for Education and Employment, *Nursery Education Scheme: The Next Steps* (London, DfEE, 1996).

be determined with reference to the level of demand, measured with reference to the presentation of vouchers by parents. The vouchers themselves were not to have face value and were not to be a means of exchange. Parents would apply to a new agency for a voucher. Once they received it they could present the voucher to the provider who would return it to the agency. Assuming it was bona fide the agency would pass it to the Department for Education and Employment for payment of the relevant amount of grant.[85] As the Secretary of State indicated, the voucher was little more than 'an administrative tool for determining the grants to be paid to the providers chosen by parents'.[86] In the event, the voucher scheme proved impracticable due its complexity, administrative costs and the shortage of providers. It was soon abandoned.

The basic law on choice of school in England and Wales did not radically alter after 1980, although artificially low admission limits for individual schools were removed as a consequence of the introduction of 'open enrolment' under the ERA 1988. Parents of children with statements of special educational needs also acquired a basic right to express a preference for a school under the Education Act 1993, as noted above. Nonetheless, the apparent popularity of a basic right of choice and thus its political potency led to continuing efforts to promote it, including the publication of two editions of the Government's *Parent's Charter* (in 1991 and 1994). The extension of opportunities for the exercise of choice by parents was, for example, at the heart of the case for introducing greater diversity into the schools system, not merely through grant-maintained schools and city technology colleges (noted above) but also through the establishment of more specialist schools.[87] Of more symbolic significance than substantive importance was that the Secretary of State was also given a new statutory duty under the Education Act 1993 to exercise his or her powers in the field of education with a view to, inter alia 'improving standards, encouraging diversity and increasing opportunities for choice'.[88] The conjunction of these three elements of standards, diversity and choice was designed to reflect the Government's linkage of improvements in standards to the operation of parental choice in a quasi-market for schooling.

By 1996 the Conservative Government was still pushing for increased diversity in the schools system. A draft Department for Education circular published that year also proposed that schools could decide to select up to 15 per cent of pupils on the basis of their aptitude for a particular subject or subjects or on the basis of their general ability, without requiring formal approval for this as giving rise to a 'significant change in character' of the school.[89] Their final Education Bill prior to the Conservatives' electoral defeat in 1997 aimed to make it easier for selection

---

[85] HC Debs, Vol 270, Col 30, 22 Jan 1996, per Mrs Gillian Shephard MP.

[86] Ibid.

[87] See Department for Education, *Choice and Diversity; A New Framework for Schools*, Cm 2021 (London, HMSO, 1992).

[88] EA 1993, s.2; now consolidated in the EA 1996, s 11(2).

[89] Such changes to schools were governed by the EA 1980, ss 12 and 13 and the EA 1993, s 96. The official limit was set at the time at 10 per cent. See P Meredith, 'The Legality of Selection' (1996) 8 *Education and the Law* 7.

to be reintroduced into school admissions and sought an increase in the number of grant-maintained schools. These aspects of the Bill were in fact lost as the Government was forced to jettison them in order to ensure that the Bill as a whole, which also contained changes on school discipline, LEA inspection and a range of other matters, survived the fierce opposition to it and passed into law before the imminent general election. Had they been re-elected to office in 1997, the Conservatives would also have had an electoral commitment to extend the assisted places scheme, give grant-maintained schools more freedom to expand, and 'help schools to become grammar schools in every major town where parents want that choice'.[90] There was no commitment to extend individual choice of school in general, however, indicating that, despite its vote-winning potential, this was a commitment that was in practice undeliverable.

Choice was largely absent from the rhetoric surrounding the Labour Party's commitment to raise standards and increase opportunities for all following its accession to power in 1997. Its 1997 White Paper *Excellence in Schools* proclaimed the Government's wish that 'as many parents as possible . . . be able to send their children to their preferred school', but it did not promise to extend choice, acknowledging that 'where demand exceeds supply and one school is more popular than another, some parents will be disappointed'.[91] This perhaps represented a tacit acknowledgement of the Conservatives' legislation's inability to guarantee choice. Either way, reform of the basic legal structure on school choice was not on the Labour Party's agenda. Instead, the new Labour Government concentrated on improving the administration of admissions. Thus the School Standards and Framework Act 1998 requires admissions authorities to have regard to a code of practice on admissions (although, as discussed below, this is to be replaced with a duty to act 'in accordance with' the code) and, together with the Education Act 2002, introduced a more consultation-based process of establishing local admissions policies, with representative admission forums to provide advice[92] and adjudicators to resolve disputes over admissions arrangements.[93] Schemes for the co-ordination of admissions in an area, to be made by the LEA (or, in the event of default, by the Secretary of State) were also provided for[94] to ensure greater efficiency.[95] Also designed to smooth the admission process are regulations providing for admission decisions by all the

---

[90] The Conservative Party, *You Can Only be Sure with the Conservatives. The Conservative Manifesto 1997* (London, Conservative Centra Office, 1997) 24.

[91] Department for Education and Employment, *Excellence in Schools,* Cm 3681 (London, Stationery Office, 1997), ch 7, para 28.

[92] SSFA s 85A, added by the EA 2002, s 46; and the Education (Admission Forums) (England) Regulations 2002 (SI 2002/2900). See p 260 below.

[93] SSFA 1998, s 25.

[94] Via the 1998 Act new ss 89B and 89C, introduced by s 48 of the 2002 Act. Academies are not covered directly, but are required to participate in co-ordination schemes by the terms of their funding agreements. The existing city technology colleges are only encouraged to participate.

[95] LEAs may be required to take 'prescribed action' to secure the adoption of a scheme by themselves and by each of the governing bodies which is an admissions authority for a maintained school in the area: SSFA 1998, s 89B(1).

admissions authorities in the LEA's area to be issued to parents on a single day in each year (1 March has been prescribed as that day).[96]

The Labour Government has also promoted increased diversity within the schools system, ostensibly on the ground that the system will thereby become better able to meet the wide-ranging educational needs of an intellectually and socially diverse population of children and young people. It has consistently supported a degree of specialisation within schools and has retained the Conservatives' policy of permitting, in schools granted approval to do so, the selection of a proportion of the school's annual intake of pupils on the basis of their aptitude. The idea of extending selection on the basis of general academic ability was rejected:[97] the SSFA 1998 provides that a school admissions scheme may not make provision for selection by ability[98] unless the school is designated as a grammar school[99] or selection falls within the permitted arrangements provided for under the Act, namely (i) where, at the beginning of the school year 1997–8 selection by ability or aptitude operated at the school (up to 50 per cent of a school's pupils could be selected in this way) and the proportion of selective admissions has not altered and no significant change has been made to the basis of selection; or (ii) children are banded to ensure the representation of the range of ability levels among applicants for admission;[100] or (iii) there is selection on the basis of aptitude for prescribed subjects.[101] An expansion of banding is seen by the current government as one of the ways to widen choice and access.[102] This is because it would reduce the exclusionary impact of catchment areas in middle class areas, which is discussed below,[103] by ensuring that schools would probably

---

[96] See the Education (Co-ordination of Admission Arrangements) (Primary Schools) (England) Regulations 2002 (SI 2002/2903), as amended by Same (Amendment) Regulations 2003 (SI 2003/2751) and Same 2005 (SI 2005/2) and the Education (Co-ordination of Admission Arrangements) (Secondary Schools) (England) Regulations 2002 (SI 2002/2904) as amended by Same (Amendment) Regulations 2004 (SI 2004/1516).

[97] DfES, *Excellence in Schools*, Cm 3681 (London, TSO, 1997), ch 7, para 33.

[98] Ability is defined as 'general ability or ability in any particular subject or subjects': SFFA 1998, s 99(5)(b).

[99] Under SSFA 1998, s 104.

[100] The principle of 'fair banding' has been adopted: see DfES, *School Admissions Code of Practice*, DfES/0031/2003 (London; DfES, 2003), paras 3.26–3.30 and App A, paras A66–A69. According to the 2005 White Paper, since 2000 13 maintained schools and 8 academies have adopted banding: HM Government, *Higher Standards, Better Schools for All*, Cm 6677 (London, TSO, 2005), para 3.23.

[101] SSFA 1998, s 99. When the clause that became this section was being debated in Standing Committeee, 'aptitude' was defined by the Minister of Education, Mr S Byers, as 'the natural talent and interest that a child has in a specific subject—in other words the potential to develop a skill or talent', whereas 'ability' was reflected in what the child had 'already achieved': Official Report, Standing Committee A, col. 649, 24 Feb 1998. Subjects have been prescribed for the purposes of s 99 by the Education (Aptitude for Particular Subjects) Regulations 1999 (SI 1999/258): modern foreign languages, performing or visual arts (including music), physical education or sport, design and technology and information technology. Proposed amendment regs will indicate that from 2007–8 aptitude may be for either one *or* more than one modern language, performing art, etc: The (Draft) Education (Aptitude for Particular Subjects) (England) (Amendment) Regulations 2005. At the time of writing, these amendments to the 1999 Regs have yet to be made, possibly delaying implementation of the changes.

[102] HM Government, *Higher Standards, Better Schools for All*, Cm 6677 (London, TSO, 2005), paras 3.23 and 3.24. And see below.

[103] See below pp 298–9.

need to attract more pupils from outlying poorer areas. The Education and Inspections Bill 2006 would broaden the range of reference groups for banding, so that the admission arrangements could enable the representativeness of the pupils admitted to be determined with reference to the level of ability across not merely applicants for admission to the school in question, as at present, but: all those seeking admission to that school *and* one or more others; all children in that age group living in the LEA's area; and all such children in England as a whole.[104] So far as selection by aptitude for particular subjects is concerned, the 1998 Act sets a limit on the proportion of the pupil intake that, in any particular year, can be selected on that basis: it must not exceed 10 per cent.[105] This reflects the previous limit imposed in practice by the Department for Education and Employment,[106] although, as noted above, the Conservatives had had plans to increase it. The only state schools to select primarily on the basis of overall academic ability (although religion is also an important factor in many of them) are the surviving grammar schools.

Selection remains controversial because of its association with social division and inequality; we saw in Chapter 1 the wide disparities in average attainment levels across different ethnic and social groups; and, in Chapter 3, we saw the Government's efforts to assuage fears that the introduction of 'trust' status for schools, which would then be responsible for their own admissions, could lead to increased selection of pupils, by proposing a requirement that admission authorities should act in accordance with the admissions code of practice, which bars selection by academic ability in all circumstances save where permitted under primary legislation (below). The case against selection is that it creates a two tier system of education that reinforces social division and hinders social mobility and integration. There are, however, continuing efforts to justify the acceptability of at least some element of selection, for example based on aptitude, with reference to standards and the benefits of 'personalisation' (involving a schools system that is capable of meeting 'individual needs' through a diversity of providers).[107] As a gesture towards traditionalist Labour Party sensibilities, the SSFA 1998 enables each of the remaining 164 grammar schools (which are located in only one fifth of LEAs) to lose their selective status if and when a local community ballot votes for the end of selection.[108] Such a ballot would be triggered by a request by 20 per cent of eligible parents and it could cover one or more grammar schools in the area.[109] Since the introduction of this legislation

---

[104] Education and Inspections Bill 2006, cl 43, amending SSFA 1998, s 101. Area based banding is seen as having several advantages over school based banding, such as removing any vested interest a particular school may have in the outcome of the banding and reducing school segregation: see H Pennell *et al, Secondary School Admissions in London* (London, LSE Centre for Educational Research, 2006), 10.

[105] Ibid, s 102.

[106] DES Circulars 6/93 and 6/96.

[107] See DfES, *Five Year Strategy for Children and Learners,* Cm 6272 (London, TSO, 2004); DfES, *Higher Standards, Better Schools for All,* Cm 6677 (London, TSO, 2005), ch 4.

[108] The one vote to date occurred in Ripon. The voters rejected the ending of selection in relation to the town's grammar school.

[109] SSFA 1998, ss 105–107; the Education (Grammar School Ballots) Regulations 1998 (SI 1998/2876).

there has been only one ballot, in North Yorkshire, which was not in favour of change. Labour's five-year strategy for education, published in 2004, indicated that, although selection by ability 'denies parents the right to choose', it will not be abolished, although its expansion will not be permitted.[110] This position was reiterated in the 2005 White Paper[111] and the Education and Inspections Bill aims to re-state the current restrictions on selective admissions more clearly.[112]

An expansion of the number of specialist secondary schools, that is, schools whose curriculum and facilities are focussed on one or two approved specialist subject areas (there are currently 10 such subject areas[113]), was envisaged by the 2001 White Paper: it stated that there would be 1,000 of them by 2003 and at least 1,500 by 2005.[114] In fact, by early 2005 there were 2,174 specialist schools, representing 69 per cent of all secondary schools in England.[115] The evidence is that specialist schools are proving relatively successful in areas such as pupil attainment and teaching quality, but need to do more to counter pupil disaffection and increase the range of vocational courses they offer.[116] The Government's ultimate aim is that all secondary schools should eventually become specialist (see below). To be eligible for specialist status a school must currently raise £50,000 in private sponsorship (less in the case of schools with fewer than 500 pupils on roll, and there is a fund to help schools which are unsuccessful in securing sponsorship) and submit a four-year school and community development plan showing how they will increase provision, raise standards, encourage take-up in their specialist subject(s) and share good practice, expertise and resources with other schools and community groups. The schools that succeed with their application can look forward to a capital grant of £100,000 (in 2004–5) to enhance their specialist facilities and an extra £129 in recurrent funding per pupil. It was announced in January 2005 that Microsoft would be donating £1.5 million to support 100 schools applying for specialist status.[117] Specialist status does not, however, in itself give these schools the power to select their pupils. The current guidance to schools confirms that 'designation as a specialist school is not a statutory process and does not result in any change in admissions criteria.'[118] Specialist schools are in no different a position to other schools, in that they too may select up to 10 per cent of their pupils on the basis of their subject aptitude.[119] However, the list of approved subjects for selective

---

[110] Department for Education and Skills, *Department for Education and Skills: Five Year Strategy for Teachers and Learners*, Cm 6272 (London, TSO, 2004).

[111] HM Government, *Higher Standards, Better Schools for All*, Cm 6677 (London, TSO, 2005), para 3.21.

[112] Education and Inspections Bill 2006, cl 36.

[113] Arts; Business & Enterprise; Engineering; Humanities; Languages; Maths and Computing; Music; Science; Sport; and Technology.

[114] DfES, *Schools: Achieving Success* (London, DfES, 2001), para 5.31.

[115] DfES Press Notice 2005/0008, 26 Jan 2005.

[116] Ofsted, *Specialist Schools: a Second Evaluation* (London, Ofsted, 2005).

[117] DfES Press Notice 2005/0008, 26 Jan 2005.

[118] DfES, *Specialist Schools Programme Application Guidance* (London, DfES, 2004), para 11.

[119] SSFA 1998, s 102.

admission by aptitude excludes several of those for which a school can be granted specialist status.[120]

Labour's five-year strategy for education[121] argues that a key to improve parental choice at the secondary stage is to give greater independence to schools to develop a specialist focus and individual ethos. It contemplates 'a new generation of independent specialist schools serving their students and communities with significantly extended freedom, diversity and capacity'.[122] The expectation is that specialist status will become synonymous with achievement and raised standards. 'Independent specialist schools' will be developed 'in place of the traditional comprehensive'.[123] Following on from an expressed intention to make specialist provision at the secondary stage universal,[124] the strategy documents says that by 2008 'every community should have one or more specialist schools, offering choice and excellence to parents and children alike'.[125] The White Paper published in October 2005 stated that there were 2,300 specialist schools and proclaimed that within two years there would be a 'fully specialist school system', and that, '[p]articularly in urban areas, this will offer greater choice so that parents can choose a school that suits their child's strengths and interests'.[126] These plans are additional to those for the establishment, by 2010, of 200 'academies' (promoted and managed by independent sponsors), an extension of the city technology college/city academy public–private concept discussed in Chapter 3.[127] At present there are only 27 open.[128]

The Government has also expressed positive support for denominational or 'faith' schools within the state sector. As we saw in Chapter 1, approximately one third of all state schools are denominational. Such schools are able to discriminate on religious grounds in their admissions policies, by prioritising members of the particular faith which they represent. There is no doubt that religious segregation does occur by virtue of the strong, continuing presence of such schools within the state system.[129]

The policies set out in the five-year strategy indicate that the principle of choice is to remain an important feature of Labour's education policy. For example, greater partnership in provision between schools and colleges will, it is claimed, lead to more choice both pre- and post-16.[130] Successful and popular schools will be given opportunities (and capital funding) to expand, although the

---

[120] In particular, Business & Enterprise; Engineering; and Humanities.

[121] Department for Education and Skills, *Department for Education and Skills: Five Year Strategy for Teachers and Learners*, Cm 6272 (London, TSO, 2004).

[122] Ibid, ch 4, para 8.

[123] Ibid, ch 4, para 3.

[124] See DfES, *A New Specialist System: Transforming Secondary Education* (London, DfES, 2003).

[125] Ibid, para 16.

[126] HM Government, *Higher Standards, Better Schools for All*, Cm 6677 (London, TSO, 2005), para 3.6.

[127] See pp 96–7 and 120 above.

[128] HM Government, *Higher Standards, Better Schools for All*, Cm 6677 (London, TSO, 2005), para 2.30.

[129] See 'The Impact and Effects of Choice of School', below p 295ff.

[130] Department for Education and Skills, *Department for Education and Skills: Five Year Strategy for Teachers and Learners*, Cm 6272 (London, TSO, 2004), ch 1, para 36.

2005 White Paper adopts a cautious tone, arguing that '[e]xpansion will not be the answer for every good school'; merger with another school might be a better option in some cases.[131] The White Paper refers to an 'easy route to expansion'[132] rather than a 'fast-track' procedure that was proposed in the five-year strategy, which also said that the Government will 'mandate competitions for new schools which will enable parents' groups and others to promote schools.'[133] The idea that parents would have an easy route for initiating the establishment of a new state school was fleshed out in the 2005 White Paper's proposal for parents to be given the right to request a new primary or secondary school.[134] The mechanisms provided for in the Education and Inspections Bill include the right of any parent to make representations about the exercise by the LEA of its duty to ensure that there are sufficient schools in the area, to which the LEA must give consideration and furnish a response,[135] and the duty on LEAs, outlined in Chapter 3, to invite proposals for the establishment of a new school.[136] The suggested grounds on which such new school provision might be sought include a desire to 'improve standards of local education' or 'to promote innovative teaching methods'.[137] Why such laudable aims should require the establishment of new schools as opposed to changes to existing schools is not clear, although the two are not mutually exclusive. The other possible bases for new schools that are referred to are the need to remedy a lack of faith provision or to 'tackle entrenched inequalities'.[138] The identification and realisation of such objectives would traditionally have been left to LEAs' strategic judgement. Therefore it would have been unrealistic for the proposals to suggest that parents should have the final say on the matter. Accordingly, the local authorities will decide whether the new school is needed; and if an authority rejects the parents' proposals the matter will be able to be referred to the schools adjudicator for a determination.[139]

These ideas for the collective empowerment of parents are not directly concerned with individual choice of school. The Labour Party's avowed belief in 'parents choosing schools not schools choosing parents'[140] could, however, be construed as having both a collectivist and an individualist focus. The idea is that a system that is partly shaped by parents collectively also gives rise to greater individual choice for each parent. The Liberal Democrats, however, have accused Labour of presenting parents with 'the illusion of more choice over the education

---

[131] HM Government, *Higher Standards, Better Schools for All*, Cm 6677 (London, TSO, 2005), para 2.45.

[132] Ibid, para 2.43.

[133] Department for Education and Skills, *Department for Education and Skills: Five Year Strategy for Teachers and Learners*, Cm 6272 (London, TSO, 2004), Executive Summary. See also ibid, ch 4, paras 25–27.

[134] HM Government, *Higher Standards, Better Schools for All*, Cm 6677 (London, TSO, 2005), paras 2.31 and 2.32.

[135] Education and Inspections Bill 2006, cl 3, inserting new s 14A into the EA 1996, referring to the duty in EA 1996, s 14.

[136] Ibid, cl 7. See above p 137.

[137] N 134 above, para 2.32.

[138] Ibid.

[139] Ibid, para 2.33. Education and Inspections Bill 2006, Sched 2, part 2.

[140] The Labour Party, *Schools—Forward not Back* (London, The Labour Party, 2005), introduction by Tony Blair and Ruth Kelly.

of their children'.[141] Certainly, there is no undertaking to confer significantly enhanced rights of choice in relation to the securing of a place at particular primary or secondary school. When Labour's manifesto talked of giving 'all parents the choice of a good secondary school'[142] it meant that its commitment towards improvements in all or most schools would result in parents who want the best education for their child having more schools from which to make their choice: 'we want every parent to be able to choose a good school, in which the great majority of 16-year-olds achieve five or more good GCSEs (or equivalent) . . . We will make school choice more effective.'[143]

It has been argued that permitting schools to expand in response to parental choice, a process that would be assisted by making admissions decisions up to twelve months earlier than at present (for example, in the January in the calendar year before the year in which the September admission will occur), could, as a former minister, Stephen Byers, put it, 'revolutionise our schools system' and mean that 'school choice puts levers of power in the hands of parents'.[144] Indeed, the idea of citizen empowerment has been strongly articulated by Labour across a range of social policy areas and was the overarching theme in Tony Blair's 'Reforming the welfare state' speech in October 2004. Here the Prime Minister spoke of an inverted state/citizens relationship, 'with the citizen not at the bottom of the pyramid taking what is handed down; but at the top of it with power in their hands to get the service they want'.[145] Putting the individual citizen first connoted greater 'flexibility and adaptability' in services such as education, welfare and health in order to meet each individual's needs. Labour's education manifesto subsequently argued that '[t]he education system at every level must be driven by the needs and preferences of pupils and their parents'.[146] The idea of expanding schools and the opportunity to establish new schools, in order to enhance choice, are entirely consonant with this vision, as is the broader principle of parents being enabled to shape the system in order meet their aspirations as regards the choice of 'personalised' provision for their child.[147] Whether all, or even a majority, of individuals can be expected to have the competence, capacity or desire to demand the particular form of service they require may, however, be open to question. Nonetheless, the Prime Minister envisages a society in which social mobility is easier and working-class families could acquire 'middle-class aspirations'. These ideas are consistent with the 'Third Way' approach which, in the context of school choice, means a middle course between a free market, which a voucher-type system would have underscored, and a locally managed and unresponsive system beset with political and bureaucratic obstacles to change.

---

[141] Liberal Democrats, 'Education and Skills News: Children should be at the heart of the education agenda—Willis', 3 Mar 2005, available at www.libdems.org.uk/education.

[142] N 140 above.

[143] Ibid, 4.

[144] Cited in P Webster, 'Bad schools face closure in plan for more choice', *The Times,* 8 Feb 2005.

[145] At Beveridge Hall, University of London.

[146] N 140 above, 4.

[147] See HM Government, *Higher Standards, Better Schools for All*, Cm 6677 (London, TSO, 2005), part 4.

The Conservatives' 2005 general election manifesto proposals for extending choice in education also envisaged the expansion of popular schools and provision for new schools to open in response to parental demand, but their model of empowerment was much more firmly rooted in the market-orientated model of the 1980s. Indeed it even proposed a quasi-voucher scheme whereby parents would be able to 'take the money that the taxpayer spends on their child's education to any school—whether State or independent—that can offer a good education as long as no charge is made to parents'.[148] Under-performing schools would be expected to strive to improve in a more competitive environment, and failing schools would be taken over by more effective new management.[149] But it is hard to see how an under-performing but improving school would benefit greatly from the exercise of market choice by parents, and there is no certainty that new schools established in response to parental demand would be better than those which they would replace or supplement.

There is an assumption, on which both the major parties' policies have been predicated, that an increase in the supply of 'good' places will ensure that a greater number of parents' school choices would be met. On that basis, there is perceived to be no need for the law to offer any firmer guarantees than at present. Yet this assumption rests on another, false, one: that 'good' schools will be equally 'good' and will have equal appeal to parents. Choice is a relativistic concept, since it rests on the idea of ranking or prioritising from the options available. Over-subscription for places at the most popular schools will continue; it is difficult to see how expansion will do more than modestly ameliorate the competition for places, while there are also legitimate concerns about the effect of expansion in the size of a school through additional pupil numbers, in terms of its potential impact on other schools which might suffer from reduced demand.[150] But the practicability of expanding schools in the way that is envisaged is, in any event, yet to be properly tested. So if choice was genuinely to be widened there needed to be a commitment, previously lacking, to re-examine the legal basis on which choice might be denied in individual cases, otherwise the combined effects of admissions policies and the statutory grounds for refusing admission would continue to restrict it. Proposals for supporting parents in exercising choice, through the provision of further information and advice, and for removing barriers to choice caused by transport costs and catchment areas, were set out in the 2005 White Paper and are considered below. In order to assess their potential impact it is necessary to examine the current law governing decisions on school admission, which the White Paper proposals (and the Education and Inspections Bill 2006) would not alter all that significantly in any event. The chapter will then consider the wider social effects of school choice. In relation to the collective effects of the admissions decisions made under the law

---

[148] The Conservative Party, *Right to Choose, Education Issue*, available at www.conservatives.com, 36.

[149] Ibid, 36–7.

[150] House of Commons Education and Skills Committee, First Report, Session 2005–06, *The Schools White Paper: 'Higher Standards, Better Schools for All'*, HC 633–I (London, TSO, 2006), para 99.

on school choice, an important question is how far social divisions are reinforced by the way that school places are allocated to parents.

SCHOOL ADMISSION DECISIONS AND THE LAW

Introduction

Parents were first given the statutory right to express a preference for a particular school under the Education Act 1980.[151] Over the ensuing years, the law has been amended, most recently by the Education Act 2002, but its essential elements providing the basis on which choice may be granted or denied are relatively unchanged. As noted above, the 1980 Act also introduced a right for parents to appeal against a school admission decision.[152] This has also continued and, as noted above, parents have had recourse to it in ever increasing numbers. While, for the most part, the appeal panels must reach decisions on the same legislative basis as the admissions authorities that made the original decision,[153] the decision-making process is more complex at the appeal stage because in most cases there are many appellants chasing a very small number of possible places at an over-subscribed school. The panels, criticised in the past by the Council on Tribunals and others for their poor standards of adjudication, including a number of procedural shortcomings,[154] have a difficult task despite the publication of an appeals code of practice, to which they are statutorily required to have regard in exercising their functions,[155] and regulations governing some basic aspects of procedure (for example, the right of the appellant to attend and make representations and the duty of the appeal panel to give written reasons for the decision).[156] The constitution of the panels is outlined below.

The law on admissions is now very complex and despite the simple presumption in favour of the granting of a parent's preference,[157] an admission decision will necessarily be based upon a range of factors in addition to the expressed preference. First, the admissions policy for the school or area will determine which applicants will have priority; the most important factors will generally include residence in a defined catchment area[158] or, in the case of a

---

[151] EA 1980, s 6.

[152] EA 1980, s 7.

[153] A major exception is cases concerning admissions to primary school year groups governed by the statutory class size limits: see below.

[154] For a detailed review, see N Harris, 'The Developing Role and Structure of the Education Appeal System' in M Partington and M Harris (eds), *Administrative Justice in the 21st Century* (Oxford, Hart, 1999) 296.

[155] SSFA 1998, s 84(3). DfES, *School Admission Appeals Code of Practice*, DfES/0030/2003 (London, DfES, 2003). As noted below, the law is being amended to require admission authorities and others to act 'in accordance with' the code, made under s 84.

[156] Education (Admission Appeal Arrangements) (England) Regulations 2002 (SI 2002/2899), in particular Sched 2.

[157] Currently in SSFA 1998, s 86(2)—originally in the EA 1980, s 6(2).

[158] See p 271 below.

denominational school, religious affiliation. Secondly, there will be the statutory grounds for denying admission, of which the most important was and continues to be that 'compliance with the preference would prejudice the provision of efficient education or the efficient use of resources'.[159] Thirdly, there is the guidance contained in the admissions code of practice, [160] to which at present regard must be had by LEAs and other admission authorities,[161] although in the face of concern by some Labour MPs that schools acquiring the new trust status might use their freedom over admission arrangements to introduce some forms of selection, that is set to change (via the Education and Inspections Bill 2006) to a duty to act 'in accordance with' the code. The code, for example, proscribes selection other than in the limited circumstances where it is permitted by statute.[162] The fourth factor will be the individual circumstances of appellants. At the appeal stage there is also the appeals code of practice, noted above, to be taken into account, along with the parent's preference and the admissions policy, plus the statutory grounds for denying preference.[163] Since the introduction of class size limits for 5, 6 and 7-year-olds under the SSFA 1998,[164] appeals concerning admission to a primary school subject to the class size limit are decided under different statutory criteria from those in other cases.[165] The admission and appeal processes are also subject to anti-discrimination law, as discussed in Chapter 4. Furthermore, a large body of case law has developed surrounding the key admissions provisions, which are currently contained in the SSFA 1998, as amended by the EA 2002. Moreover, over the past few years, the Human Rights Act 1998 has also resulted in admissions policies and decisions being subjected to juridical analysis with reference to the ECHR, which, as we saw in Chapter 2, contains several provisions of particular relevance to parental choice.

The law on admissions has been problematic in a number of respects, despite the various reforms to improve the administration of the admissions and the evidence from a research study, commissioned by the DfES, which found high levels of satisfaction about the admissions process,[166] although these findings were questioned by the House of Commons Education and Skills Select Committee. The Committee, which investigated secondary school admissions, commented in 2004 that '[f]ar from being an empowering strategy the school admissions process, founded on parental preference, can be a time-consuming cause of much distress in the lives of many families'.[167] As discussed below, at the end of this process many parents (although a minority) will not secure the school

---

[159] Ibid, s 86(3)(a).
[160] The *School Admissions Code of Practice*, DfES/0031/2003 (London, DfES, 2003).
[161] SSFA 1998, s 84(3).
[162] See pp 293–5 below.
[163] See the Education (Admission Appeals Arrangements) (England) Regulations 2002 (SI 2002/2899), reg 6.
[164] S 1: the limit is set at 30 pupils.
[165] See pp 289–92 below.
[166] Previously in the SSFA 1998 Sched 24, para 12 and now replicated in the Education (Admission Appeals Arrangements) (England) Regulations 2002 (SI 2002/2899), reg 6(2).
[167] Fourth Report, Session 2003–04, *Secondary Education: School Admissions*, HC 58–1 (London, TSO, 2004), i, Summary.

of their choice. One of the critical issues here is that successful navigation of the school admissions process may be contingent upon social and class background, and this in turn raises questions whether the presumption of equal access to schooling of choice within the state sector is realisable.[168]

Admission Authorities and Admission Arrangements

The arrangements for school admissions in any area are the responsibility of the admissions authority, that is, in the case of community or voluntary controlled schools, the LEA or (only by arrangement) the school's governing body; or in the case of foundation or voluntary aided schools, the governing body.[169] If the proposed arrangements under which some schools would be able to acquire 'trust' status become law, those schools would also be responsible for their own admission arrangements.[170] As part of the move to ensure a more effective system of admissions within a particular area, the Education Act 2002 introduced a duty for LEAs to establish an 'admission forum' for its area, with up to five LEA representatives, up to three representatives of each of the different categories of schools, up to three parent governors and up to three local community members. The forum's role includes giving advice to the LEA on its statutory admissions functions, and advising other admission authorities.[171] Its role is to be extended to include the preparation and publication of reports on matters, to be prescribed, concerning school admissions in the area.[172] Another significant feature of the system remodelled by the 2002 Act has been the new arrangements for co-ordination of admission arrangements across an area. This has been introduced with a view to preventing the chaos that can ensue when the various admission authorities make separate decisions which could result in some parents receiving more than one suitable offer (with the result that the rejected places have to be reallocated later), whilst other parents receive none and face a period of uncertainty, not knowing where their child may be placed. As noted above, under the new system, 1 March each year has been prescribed as the day on which all parents are to be informed of admission decisions.

The admission authority must determine the admission arrangements following consultation.[173] The arrangements must include the number of pupils in each relevant age group that are intended to be admitted to the school for the year in question.[174] This admission number is significant, because (other than in certain boarding schools) any admission of a pupil that is not in excess of that

---

[168] The arrangements for advice and other support for parents in the admissions process are discussed below.

[169] SSFA 1998, s 88. See further the SSFA 1998, Sched 2. As regards these school categories, see Chap 3.

[170] See p 136 above. As regards academies, see below.

[171] SSFA 1998, s 85A, inserted by the EA 2002, s 46; see also the Education (Admission Forums) (England) Regulations 2002 (SI 2002/2900).

[172] Education and Inspections Bill 2006, cl 38, inserting subss (1A)–(1C) into the SSFA 1998, s 85A

[173] SSFA 1998, s 89; and the Education (Determination of Admission Arrangements) Regulations 1999 (SI 1999/126) and same (Wales) Regulations 2006 (SI 2006/174) (W25).

[174] Ibid, s 89A (inserted by the EA 2002, s 47).

number will not be taken to give rise to prejudice to either efficient education or the efficient use of resources, of a kind that would provide a ground for denying parental preference as regards admission to the school.[175] This is therefore the latest version of the 'open enrolment' principle, noted above, that was first introduced into admissions law by the Education Reform Act 1988.[176]

The role of the adjudicator

Since 1999, objections to the admission arrangements for any particular year have had to be referred to an adjudicator.[177] While objections can be made by parents or by the governing bodies of schools affected, a majority are in fact brought by LEAs and concern treatment of particular groups of children or the order of preference set by the admissions criteria.[178] However, under the Education and Inspections Bill 2006 the admission forum will also be given a right to raise such objections.[179] In the case of admissions criteria relating to 'a person's religion, religious denomination or religious practice', the adjudicator will have to refer the matter to the Secretary of State for determination.[180] This happened in 2004 when objections were made in respect of the over-subscription criteria adopted by the London Oratory School. Under the criteria, the first priority was related to the child and his parents being practising Catholics; the second criterion was their commitment to the Catholic Church, the life of the parish, 'the ethos and expectations' of the school, and their Catholic education. The objections to the over-subscription criteria were referred by the adjudicator to the Secretary of State, who deleted the reference to 'the ethos and expectations of the school'. A legal challenge, discussed below, was brought against the adjudicator's separate ruling on the interview with parents and child that formed part of the admissions process.[181] Under the SSFA 1998, the adjudicator's or Secretary of State's decision with regard to the admission arrangements will be binding.[182] Moreover, once a decision has been made on objections to admission arrangements for a school in respect of a particular year, no objection raising substantially the same concerns can be referred to them for the next school year.[183]

---

[175] Ibid, s 86(5)–(5B) as substituted by the EA 2002, s 47. The admission authority may not set the admission number below a prescribed figure (s 93 and Sched 93).

[176] ERA 1988, s 26(9). See pp 148, 149 above and 286 below.

[177] SSFA 1998, s 90. A Chief Adjudicator was appointed—Sir Peter Newsam was the first incumbent; his successor since 2002 has been Professor Philip Hunter. See the Education (Objections to Admission Arrangements) Regulations 1999 (SI 1999/125), as amended.

[178] See, eg, Chief Adjudicator, *Annual Report September 2004 to August 2005* (Darlington, Office of Schools Adjudicator, 2005), Annex 2. The objections of two thirds of the objectors were partially or wholly upheld: ibid.

[179] Education and Inspections Bill, cl 38, amending SSFA 1998, s 90.

[180] SSFA 1998, s 90(3)(b) and SI 1999/125, above n 177, reg 7(1).

[181] *Governing Body of The London Oratory School; Adams; Goodliffe; and Lindsay v The Schools Adjudicator* [2005] ELR 162.

[182] SSFA 1998, s 90.

[183] See the Education (Objections to Admission Arrangements) Regulations 1999 (SI 1999/125), as amended, reg 9(1). Following the *London Oratory School* case (n 181 above), Jackson J had quashed a decision of the adjudicator relating to the school year 2005–6 and had refused to remit the matter to

Adjudicators are appointed by the Secretary of State.[184] There is no requirement for them to have legal qualifications, but their activities are under the supervision of the Council on Tribunals which, while noting that the adjudicator will be involved in very controversial issues, has to date not reported any significant problems. Nonetheless, there have been legal challenges to adjudicator decisions, as discussed below, a reflection of the unwillingness of LEAs and schools in some cases to accept the adjudicator's ruling over admission arrangements that they have been drawn up by those with a detailed local knowledge. Indeed, in *R v The Schools Adjudicator ex p Metropolitan Borough of Wirral* Latham J acknowledged that it was important for the adjudicator to have been mindful of the LEA's concern to develop admissions arrangements that are designed to meet 'local needs and requirements'.[185]

Perhaps the most controversial aspect of the adjudicators' powers is that, in addition to rejecting or approving (in whole or in part) the admission arrangements, they also have the power to modify them, even in ways not suggested by objectors. This power is to be clarified by amendments to be made by the Education and Inspections Bill, which would enable the adjudicator, when deciding whether or not to uphold any objection, to consider whether it is appropriate for changes to be made to the admission arrangements irrespective of whether or not he or she would be required to do so for the purposes of determining the objection.[186]

In exercising their jurisdiction, one of the matters to which adjudicators have given particular attention is the social impact of admission policies. In that respect, it is important to note that the adjudicator also had powers in respect of an LEA's school organisation plan.[187] This was a plan dealing, inter alia, with how the authority intended to exercise its functions 'with a view to securing the provision of primary and secondary education that will meet the needs of the population of their area',[188] including how it would remedy any excess or insufficiency of places for primary or secondary education in the schools it maintained.[189] Following an important amendment in 2003, the plan had to

the adjudicator on the ground that it would be unreasonable if the adjudicator then forced the school to change its admission arrangements so near to Sept 2005 (a view upheld by Laws LJ in a permission hearing in the CA in that case). It was subsequently held that there had been no 'decision' by the adjudicator for the purposes of that regulation, with the result that fresh objections to the same school's interviewing procedures could be raised in respect of 2006–7 admissions: *The Governing Body of the London Oratory School v Schools Adjudicator and (1) the Secretary of State for Education and Skills and (2) the Governing Body of Peterborough Primary School* [2005] EWHC Admin 1842; [2005] ELR 484, per Crane J. Note that Laws LJ's judgment (which is not publicly available in its entirety) is cited by Crane J at para 14.

[184] Under s 25 of the SSFA 1998.
[185] [2000] ELR 620, at para 35.
[186] Education and Inspections Bill 2006, inserting subss (5A)–(5C) into SSFA 1998, s 90.
[187] If the school organisation committee for the area could not unanimously agree the plan or failed to vote on it within a prescribed period it had to be referred to the adjudicator, who could modify it or substitute his or her own plan: the Education (School Organisation Plans) (England) Regulations 1999 (SI 1999/701). These plans have been abolished—below.
[188] SSFA 1998, s 26(2)(a).
[189] The Education (School Organisation Plans) (England) Regulations 1999 (SI 1999/701), reg 3, as amended. Children and young people's plans have replaced them: see p 59 n 167 above.

indicate how, in seeking to meet the needs of the local population, it would ensure 'greater community cohesion'.[190] As the adjudicator surely needed to take account of the plan in considering admissions arrangements, the combined effect of these provisions has been that adjudicators may have had a significant impact on local access to school education and the capacity of the system to offer and uphold parental choice.

A particular concern in matters that have come before adjudicators seems to have been the impact of selection. To date, it has been a feature of most of the admission arrangements the adjudication of which has resulted in legal challenges. However, the adjudicator's jurisdiction does not extend to the question whether a grammar school should select *any* of its pupils on the basis of their ability,[191] as that is covered by separate statutory procedures (as noted above). Nevertheless, it does extend to decisions about changes on partial selection which do not constitute a 'prescribed alteration'.[192]

In the first of the challenges, *R v Downes ex p Wandsworth LBC*,[193] the adjudicator had decided to reduce the proportion of pupils who could be selected for admission on ability grounds to three secondary schools in Wandsworth. He decided that the admission arrangements were not in the best interests of local children and ordered that the proportion be cut from 50 per cent to 25 per cent in relation to two of the schools and from 32 per cent to 25 per cent in relation to the other. Objections were brought by a local junior school, which wanted partial selection to be replaced by a different admission system, and by the parents of children attending one of the primary schools, who preferred the previous admission arrangements. The court held that the school had no right to have its objections considered by the adjudicator, because they related to the principle of partial selection itself. But it was not clear that the adjudicator had considered whether the change to the selection arrangements might be so fundamental as to bring about a significant change in the character of the school. If such a change had occurred, then, by virtue of section 103 of the SSFA 1998, the adjudicator would have had no jurisdiction.[194] A similar challenge occurred in *R (Watford Grammar School for Boys and Watford Grammar School for Girls) v Adjudicator for Schools*,[195] when two selective schools in Watford objected to the adjudicator's decision to cut from 35 per cent to 25 per cent the proportion of pupils selected by ability or aptitude (for music). The decision had been taken because the combined effect of the ability and aptitude tests plus giving priority on the basis of having a sibling already at the school meant that only four places were available for other pupils who lived close to the school. The adjudicator's ruling would have freed up another 14 places. Collins J, while regarding the problem of

---

[190] Ibid.

[191] The Education (Objections to Admission Arrangements) Regulations 1999 (SI 1999/125), as amended, reg 2(2).

[192] As per SSFA 1998, s 28.

[193] [2000] ELR 425. For the view of Wandsworth's Principal Solicitor on the case, see T Lewis Brooke, 'The Future of Partial Selection: Issues raised by R v Downes ex parte Wandsworth London Borough Council' (2000) 1 *Education Law* 159.

[194] Ibid, per Sullivan J at 432D.

[195] [2004] ELR 40.

the disadvantage to local children under the arrangements as a legitimate consideration, nevertheless held that the adjudicator had been wrong not to consider other ways of achieving the desired result, such as a modification of the sibling policy.

The factual background to a further case in which the adjudicator was found to have acted unlawfully, the second involving Wandsworth, *R (Wandsworth London Borough Council) v The Schools Adjudicator,*[196] underlines the traditional objection to a schools system in which selection, even partial selection, is permitted, namely that non-selective schools in the area suffer and educational inequality is reinforced. The adjudicator received parental objections to admission arrangements that permitted partial selection by three schools in the borough. The parents' concern was that partial selection by these schools worked against the interests of most parents and children in the area of another school, in Battersea, because that school had surplus places and had recently been placed in 'special measures' by Ofsted (which meant that it was classed as failing). Essentially, the objectors argued that there was an uneven spread of pupils by ability across the borough's schools. The adjudicator accepted that the school in Battersea did suffer from a significantly unbalanced intake so far as academic ability and social disadvantage were concerned, but he did not regard the system of partial selection as a sufficient and primary cause of unfairness towards parents in the area. He considered that the three schools with partial selection should be allowed to retain it, although one of the schools was required to make a reduction from 33 per cent to 30 per cent in the proportion to be selected. The LEA challenged that reduction. Goldring J held that a reduction in the selective intake was not justified because it would not correct the overall unfairness across the schools of which the objectors had complained.

The adjudicator has, however, successfully defended two challenges to decisions concerning the admissions arrangements involving schools in the Wirral, where the LEA's admission arrangements involved maintaining a mix of grammar and all-ability secondary schools. For admissions in 2000–1 the adjudicator overturned the arrangements. In *R v The Schools Adjudicator ex p Metropolitan Borough of Wirral,*[197] the LEA challenged this decision, arguing that the admission arrangements had been intended to assist parents who wanted a place at one of the authority's grammar schools but who, if their child did not perform well enough in tests, ran the risk of being a low priority for a place at a preferred all-ability school. The arrangements had therefore enabled these parents to have two first choices: a grammar school and an all-ability school. The adjudicator's decision had been in response to the objection made by the head teacher of an all-ability school, who had argued that these parents had an unfair advantage over the others who simply selected an all-ability school. The adjudicator agreed and imposed different arrangements, under which all parents simply expressed an order of preference. Latham J ruled that the adjudicator had acted lawfully; he had tried to produce a fair system overall. Subsequently, in *R on*

---

[196] [2004] ELR 274.
[197] [2000] ELR 620.

application of Metropolitan Borough of Wirral v Chief Schools Adjudicator,[198] which concerned the arrangements for 2001–2, the LEA proposed that selection tests for its grammar schools should precede the expression by parents of their preference for the LEA's schools as a whole. The idea was when parents first expressed their preference they would have a better idea whether their child would secure a grammar school place. Otherwise, they might waste their first preference and thus have less chance of a place at a preferred all-ability school. Objections made to the adjudicator stated that the new system enabled some parents to have an alternative first preference. The adjudicator felt that the system was lawful but unfair. He considered that first preferences should be expressed before the grammar school selection process began. He reasoned that parents who consistently maintained a preference for a particular school should have priority over those whose preference for that school was contingent upon their child qualifying or not qualifying for admission to another school (ie, a grammar school). Again the challenge failed. Ouseley J held that the adjudicator had acted within his jurisdiction, had not acted irrationally and had taken account of relevant considerations.

Admissions criteria

A key feature of all admission arrangements is the criteria by which applications are prioritised. Admissions authorities are free to apply any reasonable criteria they wish, but this is subject to the principle established by case law that there should be some scope for the exercise of discretion in exceptional cases.[199] Moreover, the admission arrangements must be consistent with anti-discrimination law, which refers specifically to admission to schools, plus the duty to promote race equality.[200] As noted above, admission authorities are also subject to the duty to have regard to the admissions code of practice made by the Secretary of State,[201] a duty which is to be replaced under the Education and Inspections Bill by one to act 'in accordance with' the code.[202] Indeed, its proposed new description as a 'code for school admissions' rather than a 'code of practice' signifies the Government's wish to tighten up on the application of the code, as does the redefining of the permitted content from simply 'may include guidelines setting out aims . . .' to 'may *impose requirements*, and may include guidelines setting out aims . . .'[203] The application of the code is also to be tightened by the right of admission forums, which themselves will now be required to act in accordance with it,[204] to object to the adjudicator where an

---

[198] [2001] ELR 574.

[199] Eg, *Cumings v Birkenhead Corporation* [1972] Ch 12, per Denning MR at 38.

[200] Sex Discrimination Act 1975, s 22; Race Relations Act 1975, ss 17, 71(1) and Sched 1A, as substituted by the Race Relations (Amendment) Act 2000; Equality Act 2006, s 49; Disability Discrimination Act 1995, s 28A. See Chap 4.

[201] SSFA 1998, s 84. See p 269 below.

[202] Education and Inspections Bill 2006, cl 37, amending SSFA 1998, s 84.

[203] Ibid, amending SSFA 1998, s 84(1) and (2), emphasis added.

[204] Education and Inspections Bill, cl 37, amending SSFA 1998, s 84. For the forum's role, see p 260 above.

admission authority is believed to have failed to comply with its corresponding duty.[205] It should be noted that city technology colleges have not been covered by the code of practice and have been free to determine their own admission arrangements. Academies, on the other hand, while also outside the scope of the statutory duty on governing bodies to have regard to the provisions of the code, are in effect bound by the code through a clause in their funding arrangements. The agreement between the academy company and the Secretary of State (that is, the agreement by which the academy's proprietor undertakes to conduct a school and the Secretary of State agrees to provide funding in return, provided specified conditions and requirements are fulfilled[206]) will 'require the Academy's admissions policy and arrangements to be consistent with admissions law and the Codes of Practice'.[207]

The compatibility of admissions arrangements with the European Convention on Human Rights will also need to be considered. Indeed, it has been raised in two cases where the effect of an admissions policy was that sibling connection—that is, that the applicant for a school place already has a child who is a pupil at the school in question—was an insufficiently weighty factor under the admissions criteria to prevent the separation of siblings. A sibling connection priority has been held to be a legitimate policy provision in itself,[208] but if the admissions policy gives sibling connection a lower priority than residence in a catchment area, which itself is another legitimate and commonly used criterion,[209] it could well result in the separation of siblings where the school is over-subscribed. It has been argued that the separation of siblings might represent an unjustifiable interference with private and family life for the purposes of Article 8 of the ECHR. In *R (O) v St James RC Primary School Appeal Panel*, however, Newman J accepted, without deciding, that while Article 8 rights could be at issue in admissions decisions (particularly in the case of admission to a religious school), the Article conferred 'no absolute right to have a child admitted to a school already attended by a sibling'. [210] However, a more recent comment, by Collins J in *R (K) v London Borough of Newham*,[211] implies that the courts might in future consider such claims to be more weighty. Collins J said that:

> The desirability of enabling children to attend the same school as siblings is already recognised and most . . . perhaps all, admissions policies have that as a very important criterion. That is now rendered the more necessary because of the provisions of Article 8 of the Convention.[212]

---

[205] Ibid, cll 38 and 42, amending SSFA 1998, ss 89 and 90.

[206] See EA 1996, s 482, as substituted by the EA 2002, s 65.

[207] DfES, *School Admissions Code of Practice Draft 2005* (London, DfES, 2005), para 1.1, n 2.

[208] *R (L) v The IAP of St Edward's College* [2001] ELR 542, per Morison J at para 34. See also *R v Greenwich London Borough Council ex parte the Governors of the John Ball Primary School* (1990) 154 LGR 678 (CA).

[209] Ibid; *R v Rotherham MBC ex p Clark* [1998] ELR 152 (QBD and CA).

[210] [2001] ELR 469, at para 36.

[211] [2002] ELR 390.

[212] Ibid, at para 39.

Admissions arrangements must also be consistent with Article 2 of Protocol 1 (A2P1) of the Convention, discussed in Chapter 2, which provides that there must be no denial of the right to education, and that respect must be paid to parents' religious and philosophical convictions as regards the teaching of their child. This means that any religious or philosophical basis for the parents' choice must be taken into account within the decision-making process, not least in view of the positive action required of the state to ensure compliance with this Article.[213] Thus, in one case it was held to be wrong to infer a parent's preference for single-sex schooling for their child rather than to provide an opportunity for the parent to express their (religious) reasons for their choice.[214] For the purposes of the Sex Discrimination Act 1975, single-sex schools are entitled to deny admission on the grounds of sex,[215] but many of these schools are also denominational and parents seeking admission to them on religious grounds face a particular barrier if their child, while of the relevant sex, does not have the required religious affiliation. In *Choudhury and Another v Governors of Bishop Challoner Roman Catholic Comprehensive School*,[216] the House of Lords upheld a single-sex Roman Catholic school's policy of giving priority to Roman Catholics where the school was over-subscribed, which had resulted in a Muslim girl and a Hindu girl being refused a place. Lord Browne-Wilkinson considered the policy to be rational and to provide a legitimate basis on which a school of that denomination could prioritise applicants. Often the admissions criteria for such schools will aim to take account of the applicant's *commitment* to his or her religion. The Local Government Ombudsmen have indicated that this is often based on 'regular worship' or 'regular attendance' at a church, but have argued that such criteria are too imprecise and should be more specific, referring for example to 'weekly worship' or attendance at church fortnightly.[217] Such commitment has, in the past, often been ascertained via an interview, which has proved a controversial practice the legality of which has been called into question, particularly since the code of practice sought to ban the practice for admissions from September 2005 onwards.[218]

Given that, as we saw in Chapter 2, the right in A2P1 does not guarantee a right to any particular form of schooling, it is not clear whether Article 14 (no discrimination in the enjoyment of a Convention right) could be sufficiently engaged with regard to a *Bishop Challoner* type policy. Even if it could, the policy might well satisfy the tests of legitimate purpose and proportionality applicable to Article 14 cases. A similar difficulty would face anyone seeking to impugn the kinds of policies challenged in *Cumings v Birkenhead Corporation*[219] and the case

---

[213] *Valsamis v Greece*, Case No 74/1995/580/666 (1996) 24 EHRR 294; [1998] ELR 430.

[214] *R (K) v London Borough of Newham* [2002] EWHC Admin 405; [2002] ELR 390, per Collins J.

[215] SDA 1975, s 26.

[216] [1992] 3 All ER 277.

[217] Local Government Ombudsmen, *Special Report. School Admissions and Appeals* (London, Commission for Local Administration in England, 2003), part A, para 9.

[218] DfES, *School Admissions Code of Practice*, DfES 0031/2003 (London, DfES, 2003), para 3.16. See *Governing Body of The London Oratory School; Adams; Goodliffe; and Lindsay v The Schools Adjudicator* [2005] ELR 162. See pp 306–9 below.

[219] Above n 25.

arising out of admission policies in parts of Lancashire,[220] where the secondary schools admissions policy was that, where non-denominational secondary schools were over-subscribed, pupils at Roman Catholic primary schools would be considered a lower priority than other children for a place at these non-Roman Catholic schools (see below).

Another admissions criterion that has been upheld by the UK courts but the impact of which has led it to be called into question under the Human Rights Act 1998 concerns home–school distance. Both the Court of Appeal[221] and the House of Lords[222] have treated proximity as a lawful criterion. But in *School Admission Appeals Panel for the London Borough of Hounslow v The Mayor and Burgesses of the London Borough of Hounslow*[223] it was argued that an admissions policy that gave applicants living in priority admission areas that were in proximity to the school a higher priority than those living elsewhere but who had a sibling already on the roll was incompatible with Articles 8 and 14 and A2P1. However, Maurice Kay J held that in the light of the case law the policy did not offend any of these Articles.[224] When the matter came before the Court of Appeal, the principal human rights argument was that the discrimination against applicants not living in the priority admissions areas was not proportionate to the LEA's objective in determining priority for admission. May LJ acknowledged that where a school was over-subscribed there would necessarily be discrimination against some children. However, there was a question whether the discrimination had an objective justification for the purposes of Article 14. His Lordship did not think that it did:

> Some children will have stronger cases than others for admission. A child with an elder brother or sister in a school may well have a strong case wherever they live; but so may a child who lives close to the school. Neither child's case is by definition stronger than the other child's case. Neither child's relevant Convention rights are by definition infringed, nor is it by definition objectively unfair, if either of them fails to gain admission . . . [LEAs] have to make practical admission decisions which are objectively fair and by a process which is fair.[225]

Thus while the parent would need to establish that the decision not to admit the child was 'perverse',[226] the LEA would need only to show that its decision was

---

[220] *R v Lancashire CC ex parte F* [1995] ELR 33.

[221] In *R v Greenwich London Borough Council ex parte the Governors of the John Ball Primary School* (1990) 154 LGR 678 (CA).

[222] In *Choudhury and Another v Governors of Bishop Challoner Roman Catholic Comprehensive School* [1992] 3 All ER 277, p 267 above.

[223] [2002] EWCA Civ 900, [2002] ELR 602 (CA).

[224] *The Queen on the Application of the Mayor and Burgesses of the London Borough of Hounslow v The School Admission Appeals Panel for the London Borough of Hounslow* [2002] EWHC Admin 313, [2002] ELR 402, at para [81].

[225] Ibid, para [62].

[226] This was because the admission decision concerned admission to a primary school infant class and the appeal decision was covered by the special statutory rules concerning such appeals. As noted below (pp 289–93), they state that the panel may uphold an appeal only if, inter alia, the decision not to admit the child 'was not one which a reasonable admission authority would make in the circumstances of the case': Education (Admission Appeal Arrangements) (England) Regulations 2002

'objectively fair'.[227] The Court of Appeal nonetheless implicitly accepted the view of Stanley Burton J in an earlier decision, *South Gloucestershire*,[228] that for an admissions policy to accord priority on the basis of residence could be potentially discriminatory under Article 14 read together with A2P1.

That viewpoint might be particularly relevant to admission areas that have become segregated for demographic reasons, as in Bradford. In the mid-1990s the admissions policy for secondary schools in Bradford was based on catchment areas which were reviewed each year and, if necessary, altered in the light of the demand for places at particular schools, taking account also of the extent of community–school links in particular areas. It was possible for an area of the city not to be within any catchment area. That was the case with regard to Manningham, an area with a high proportion of Asian residents. In *R v Bradford Metropolitan Borough Council ex parte Sikander Ali*[229] the court found that Bradford's policy had a rational basis. It was also considered not to give rise to race discrimination, on the ground that whites and Asians in Manningham were equally disadvantaged. Similarly, in *R v Lancashire County Council ex p F*,[230] referred to above, Kennedy LJ explained that, bearing in mind that it would be difficult for a non-Roman Catholic to secure a place in a Roman Catholic secondary school, an admissions policy that gave Roman Catholics equal priority with non-Roman Catholics for places at non-denominational secondary schools could result in some non-Roman Catholics being left without a school place. The court held that although, on the face of it, the policy was discriminatory, there was a rational basis for it and it could not be said that it was so unreasonable a policy that the court should interfere. It is unlikely that an Article 14 argument in such cases would be any more likely to succeed today, give the rather strict test for interference that has been laid down. Leaving aside human rights arguments, the legality of most admissions policies will continue to depend upon the rationality test.[231]

As noted earlier, guidance on admissions criteria is set out in the *School Admissions Code of Practice*.[232] In the past, admission policies that were inconsistent with the official guidance were not necessarily unlawful. In the *Lancashire* case noted above,[233] for example, the LEA's policy was upheld notwithstanding the view expressed in the guidance in force at the time that 'the Secretary of State does not believe that it is reasonable for non-denominational schools to distinguish between applicants on the basis of their faith or

---

(SI 2002/2899), reg 6(2)(a) (and previously in the SSFA 1998, Sched 24, para 12(a)). The CA in this case held that that gave rise to a basic test of perversity, namely whether it was perverse, in the light of the admission arrangements, to admit the particular child.

[227] N 224 above, para [63]. The court also considered whether human rights arguments could legitimately be considered by an appeal panel as a public authority for HRA purposes.

[228] *R on the Application of South Gloucestershire Local Education Authority v The South Gloucestershire Schools Appeal Panel* [2001] EWHC Admin 732, [2002] ELR 309.

[229] [1994] ELR 299.

[230] N 220 above.

[231] *Cumings v Birkenhead Corporation* [1972] Ch 12; [1971] 2 All ER 881; *Choudhury* n 222 above.

[232] DfES/0031/2003 (London, DfES, 2003).

[233] *R v Lancashire CC ex p F* [1995] ELR 33.

denominational background'.[234] The circumstances in which a departure from the guidance might be countenanced judicially are likely to be somewhat more restricted, as the guidance is now contained in a code of practice to which regard must be had by admission authorities.[235] However, in one recent case Jackson J held that in requiring regard to be had to the code of practice the legislation did 'not connote slavish obedience or deference on every occasion'.[236] The House of Commons Select Committee rejected the idea of converting the code into a set of mandatory rules as impracticable, while at the same time recommending that the code should be enforceable and that sanctions should apply when it is 'breached'.[237] As noted above, the concern that the admissions code should be made mandatory has arisen from the perceived danger that schools that become responsible for their own admissions, such as the new 'trust' schools proposed in the 2005 White Paper, may use their autonomy to select some pupils by academic ability.[238] The Education and Inspections Bill 2006 will not give the code statutory force but, as noted above, will place admission authorities under a duty to act 'in accordance with' its provisions,[239] which is virtually the same thing.

The code of practice does not express any preference for particular admission criteria, merely indicating that '[c]ommonly used and acceptable criteria include sibling links, distances from the school, ease of access by public transport, medical or social grounds . . . catchment areas, transfer from named feeder primary schools and whether the child is in public care'.[240] Proposals for a revised code were circulated in 2005, although a new code has yet to be introduced, presumably because of the impending changes to the law under the Education and Inspections Bill. The 2005 draft revised code includes a list of 'commonly used and acceptable over-subscription criteria'.[241] Like the current version of the code it identifies children in local authority care or accommodation ('looked after' children) as requiring 'top priority' in over-subscription criteria.[242] This is because of the disadvantage faced by these children, whose suitable placement is a matter of great importance, not least in the light of the duty on local authorities under the Children Act 2004 to promote the educational achievement of a child looked after by them.[243] The House of Commons Education and Skills Select Committee concluded that the recommendation in the code of practice

---

[234] DfE, Circular 6/93, *Admissions to Maintained Schools* (London, DfE, 1993), para 21.

[235] SSFA 1998 s 84.

[236] *Governing Body of the London Oratory School; Adams; Goodliffe; and Lindsay v The Schools Adjudicator* [2004] EWHC Admin 3014; [2005] ELR 162, at para 40.

[237] House of Commons Education and Skills Committee, First Report, Session 2005–06, *The Schools White Paper: 'Higher Standards, Better Schools for All'*, Vol. 1, HC 633–I (London, TSO, 2006), paras 96, 113 and 127. Cf H Pennell *et al*, *Secondary School Admissions in London* (London, LSE Centre for Educational Research, 2006), which recommends (at 24) underpinning the code with regulations setting out 'a "menu" of acceptable types of [admission] criteria'.

[238] Ibid, para 116.

[239] Cl 37(4), to amend SSFA 1998, s 84(3).

[240] DfES, *School Admissions Code of Practice* DfES/0031/2003, para 3.5. The legitimacy of catchment areas was confirmed in *Greenwich*, n 208 above.

[241] DfES, *School Admissions Code of Practice Draft 2005* (London, DfES, 2005), Annex B.

[242] Ibid and DfES, *School Admissions Code of Practice*, DfES/0031/2003 (London, DfES, 2003), para 3.14.

[243] Children Act 2004, s 52, amending Children Act 1989, s 22.

concerning children in public care should be replaced by a statutory duty.[244] This has now occurred, via an amendment made by the Education Act 2005: admission authorities may be required to include in their admission arrangements prescribed provision relating to children who are looked after by a local authority,[245] including 'provision for securing that . . . such children are to be offered admission in preference to other children'.[246] The children's charity NCH has, however, argued that that priority will have effect only in the normal admissions round, which relates to the beginning of each school year. NCH says that, accordingly, the changes will not make a significant difference because most children in care will need to enter school at different times—'care placements do not respect the school year'—and thus 'there is a risk that many children in care will continue to be consigned to the less popular and less successful schools'.[247] The House of Commons Education and Skills Select Committee has now recommended that the position of children with special educational needs also needs to be monitored, particularly in the light of the proposed establishment of trust schools that are able to determine their own admission arrangements. The Committee is proposing that all schools should be given a duty to operate equitable admission policies for such children across the local authority's area.[248] In addition, Pennell *et al* and the House of Commons Education and Skills Committee have separately recommended that admissions criteria should state that priority will be given to children for whom there is a statement of special educational needs.[249] The argument is that this could help to prevent parents of such children from being deterred from seeking their child's admission to a particular school.

A survey has shown that some 86 per cent of secondary school admission policies give high priority to those living close to the school and 60 per cent to those residing in a catchment area.[250] Although another common criterion is having a sibling already at the school (96 per cent of policies), home address is probably the most important factor determining admission.[251] It certainly causes wider effects, as discussed below. The code of practice further stresses that the

[244] House of Commons Education and Skills Committee, Fourth Report, Session 2003–04, *Secondary Education: School Admissions, Report*, HC 58–1 (London, TSO, 2004), para 72.

[245] This means 'looked after' for the purposes of the Children Act 1989, s 22, namely in the local authority's care or provided with accommodation by the local authority under its social services function.

[246] SSFA 1998, s 89(1A), inserted by Education Act 2005, s 106; and the Education (Admission of Looked After Children) (England) Regulations 2006 (SI 2006/128). A new clause (inserting ss 97A and 97B, SSFA 1998) added to the Education and Inspections Bill in Standing Committee in the House of Commons on 9 May 2006 would empower local authorities to give a direction to a school to admit a specific 'looked after' child.

[247] NCH, *Close the Gap for Children in Care* (London, NCH, 2005) 7.

[248] House of Commons Education and Skills Committee, First Report, Session 2005–06, *The Schools White Paper: 'Higher Standards, Better Schools for All'*, HC 633–I (London, TSO, 2006), para 87.

[249] Pennell *et al*, n 237 above, 24; House of Commons Education and Skills Committee, Third Report, Session 2005–06, *Special Education Needs*, HC 478–I (London, TSO, 2006), para 193.

[250] House of Commons Education and Skills Committee, Fourth Report, Session 2003–04, *Secondary Education: School Admissions, Report* HC 58–1 (London, TSO, 2004), para 56, citing research by Professor Anne West at LSE.

[251] Ibid.

criteria should be clear, fair and objective, stating the order in which they should be applied (and how 'tie-break decisions' would be made), and that admissions authorities have 'a fairly wide discretion in deciding what these over-subscription criteria should be', provided they are lawful and recognise the importance of children receiving an efficient and suitable education.[252] The code also draws attention to the fact that it cannot be a condition of admitting a child to a school that his or her parent signs a home–school agreement.[253]

Facilitating the exercise of preference

Authorities are under a duty to publish their admission arrangements not later than six weeks before the date by which parents must express a preference.[254] LEAs must publish a composite prospectus showing, inter alia, all schools' names, addresses and their religious affiliations (if any), together with a summary of the admissions policy; the information must reveal the number of school places available and the number of applications made to the school in the previous school year.[255] Parents will also have access to information on school perform-ance, such as the proportion of pupils gaining particular grades in GCSE examinations and rates of unauthorised absence.[256] The data aim to facilitate the evaluation of schools.[257] This information continues to excite controversy, since it is considered unfair to judge schools by raw output measures without taking account of input factors, such as the abilities among the pupils when admitted to the school, and wider social factors, such as the neighbourhood and the educational backgrounds of pupils' parents. There have, however, been efforts in recent years to ensure that the data reflect the 'added value' of the education provided by the school (as judged by the progress made by pupils).[258] There is no requirement that school performance information be set out in 'league tables', as press presentations of it tend to do. Bearing in mind that approximately 1.5 million children are admitted to maintained primary or secondary schools each year, these data hold considerable interest for many parents in exercising their

---

[252] DfES, *School Admissions Code of Practice*, DfES/0031/2003 (London, DfES, 2003), paras A49–A51.

[253] Ibid, para A52. See SSFA 1998, s 111(4).

[254] SSFA 1998, s 92. In *R v Stockton-on-Tees Borough Council and Another, ex p W* [2000] ELR 93 (CA), the court did not consider that the failure of the published admissions arrangements to mention provision made for parents moving into the area later gave rise to unfairness. That provision was a matter that the LEA was entitled to deal with on an ad hoc basis.

[255] Education (School Information) (England) Regulations 2002 (SI 2002/2897), as amended by the Same (Amendment) Regulations 2005 (SI 2005/2152).

[256] Education (School Performance Information) (England) Regulations 2001 (SI 2001 No 3446) (as amended).

[257] DfES, *Schools: Building on Success*, Cm 5050 (London, DfES, 2001), para 6.39.

[258] After the 1980 Act, which required the publication of information (s 8 and the Education (School Information) Regulations 1981 (SI 1981/630)), information on school examination results was not required to be published on a comparative basis, but the Education Reform Act later required it to be comparative and led to the annual league tables of schools based primarily on pupils' examination results, compiled by the press from official statistics which individual schools were required to release and LEAs were under a statutory duty to make available to parents: see N Harris, *Law and Education: Regulation, Consumerism and the Education System* (London, Sweet and Maxwell, 1993) 162–6.

rights to express a school preference. In fact, according to a DfES survey, fewer than 50 per cent of parents select their first preference school on the basis of the school's academic results. Factors such as travel convenience, the resources available to the school, the school's facilities, pupil behaviour and their child's wish to join the same school as their friends were found to be influential.[259]

The range of available information on schools clearly enhances the exercise of choice, but at the same time it increases the pressure on parents to make the best choice for their child. The House of Commons Education and Skills Select Committee found that surrounding the operation of the admissions system is 'an environment of, sometimes frenzied, competition between parents for places in the most popular schools'.[260] It concluded that 'the school admissions process, founded on parental preference, can be a time-consuming cause of much distress in the lives of many families'.[261] An example of the desperate lengths to which parents may go to secure a place at the school of their choice is the reported attempt by one parent to have her daughter adopted by the girl's aunt, whose own daughter already had a place at the school in question, which gave priority to siblings.[262] The Local Government Ombudsmen have referred to the problem of parents making a false residence claim and have recommended warnings to parents and better checks by authorities.[263]

As it places an onus on parents to select a school for their child, there is a real risk that the school admissions process will underscore the existing relative disadvantage experienced by particular social or ethnic groups. Research has, for example, shown that parents' capacity as school choosers is closely linked to their social class.[264] The *Code of Practice* tacitly acknowledges the barriers for particular groups in its recommendation that common admission criteria such as sibling links should be properly explained 'because different ethnic groups may understand terms to have different meanings'.[265] However, it does not fully address this inequality. The proposal in the 2005 White Paper for independent 'choice advisers' is arguably a step in the right direction. The White Paper acknowledges the unequal capacity of parents to understand the system and make properly informed choices, and proposes 'a network of choice advisers—people based in the community who can offer independent, unbiased advice and raise the interest, expectations and aspirations of those who may not previously have felt that they had any real choice'.[266] Disadvantaged areas and parents, 'those who are currently least well equipped to make effective choices', are to be targeted by this initiative, which aims to cover every local authority area

---

[259] J Flatley *et al*, *Parents' Experiences of the Process of Choosing a Secondary School*, Research Report 278 (London, DfES, 2001), Part 5.

[260] n 250 above, para 144.

[261] Ibid, Summary.

[262] O Wright, 'Parents want aunt to adopt girl for place at school', *The Times*, 30 Apr 2002.

[263] Local Government Ombudsmen, *Special Report. School Admissions and Appeals* (London, Commission for Local Administration in England, 2003), part B, paras 5 and 6.

[264] S Gewirtz *et al*, *Markets, Choice and Equity in Education* (Buckingham, Open University Press, 1995).

[265] DfES, *School Admissions Code of Practice*, DfES/0031/2003 (London, DfES, 2003), para 3.6.

[266] HM Government, *Higher Standards, Better Schools for All*, Cm 6677 (London, TSO, 2005), para 3.12.

by 2008.[267] Such is the complexity of admissions systems that this will be a job requiring considerable expertise. The statutory basis for this system of advice provision is provided by the Education and Inspections Bill, which aims to place LEAs under a duty to provide parents with 'advice and assistance . . . in connection with the preferences expressed or to be expressed by them'.[268]

Another means by which the White Paper has proposed to make the admissions system fairer is to remove some of the travel barriers to choice of school. Those from low income families would be entitled to free transport to any three suitable secondary schools within a two to six mile radius of their home.[269] As noted in Chapter 4, current legislation requires LEAs to provide free transport to anyone whose nearest suitable school is more than two miles (in the case of children under 8) or three miles from their home. The new provision would therefore lift an economic restriction on choice for low income families. According to the White Paper, those on free school meals are less likely than other pupils to be travelling three miles or more to and from school.[270]

The Statutory Grounds for Denying Choice of School

Background

The Education Act 1980 permitted parents to express to the relevant school admission authority a preference for a state ('maintained') school for their child. It set out grounds on which preference could be denied and enabled parents to appeal to an appeal committee the decision of which was binding on the authority.[271] The principal ground used for denying preference was that the admission of the child to the school would not be compatible with 'efficient education or the efficient use of resources'.[272] The prejudice to efficiency ground thereby provided a rationing tool for admissions authorities. It could be used by an LEA in conjunction with a cap on its schools' admission numbers, a device which enabled the LEA to distribute pupil numbers more evenly around its schools and thereby help to ensure the viability of schools with falling rolls where there were social reasons for maintaining them in particular neighbourhoods. A local policy of that kind would limit places at popular schools and preserve pupil numbers at less popular schools whose rolls would otherwise have fallen further, making them unviable, but whose closure would be unpopular with the local community. The Education Reform Act 1988 did not remove the efficiency ground itself, but rather the ability of LEAs to use it in that way. It provided that the ground could not be applied until the total number of pupils to be admitted had reached the 'standard number', which reflected the physical capacity of the

---

[267] Ibid, paras 3.11 and 3.12.
[268] Education and Inspections Bill 2006, cl 39, inserting s 86(1A) into the SSFA 1998.
[269] DfES, *Higher Standards, Better Schools for All*, Cm 6677 (London, TSO, 2005), para 3.15.
[270] Ibid, para 3.14.
[271] Education Act 1980, ss 6 and 7.
[272] Ibid, s 6(3)(a). See now the School Standards and Framework Act 1998, s 86 (3)(a).

school.[273] The law has since been reformulated so that the efficiency ground cannot now be applied where the number of pupils being admitted in a year is below the number fixed by the admissions authority for that year as part of the admission arrangements.[274] Another important development of lasting significance in the late 1980s was a landmark ruling by the Court of Appeal in *Greenwich*, discussed below, which confirmed the basic principle that parents living outside the LEA's boundaries should not, simply by virtue of that fact, be denied equal preference with those living inside the authority's boundaries for a place at one of the authority's schools.[275] With most LEAs operating catchment areas, which enable priority for a place at a school to be determined primarily by address, the result of these legal developments was that schools could admit pupils until they were physically full, but parental choice could still be frustrated as a result of the location of their home and the fact that parents living outside the LEA's area altogether could have as legitimate a claim for a place at a school as those who lived within the LEA's area but outside the school's catchment area.[276] Parental choice was also affected by the statutory limit on infant class sizes (set at 30 pupils, subject to a few exceptions) introduced by the SSFA 1998 (see below).[277] Whitty argues that this limit has a more marked impact upon advantaged groups, since they are more likely to be in larger classes,[278] presumably because they tend to be in over-subscribed schools.

Aside from the efficiency ground, the only two other statutory grounds applied to particular categories of school. First, in the case of some types of denominational school that had entered into arrangements with the LEA 'for preserving the character of the school', admission could be denied where it would be incompatible with those arrangements.[279] This ground has since been repealed, but even where such arrangements were not made, religion was, and still is, regarded as a rational admissions criterion to determine priority as between different categories of applicant to denominational schools, as noted above.[280] Secondly, if entry to the preferred school was by selection with reference to a child's ability or aptitude, admission could be refused where it would not be compatible with the selection arrangements.[281] This ground continues to apply, and under amendments made by the Education Act 2002, admission to a school sixth form may also be denied on ability and aptitude grounds, assuming these

---

[273] ERA 1988, ss 26(9) and 27.

[274] Ibid, s 89 (read together with new s 89A, inserted by the 2002 Act, added by s 47); see also the Education (Determination of Admission Arrangements) Regulations 1999 (SI 1999/126). However, exception is made in relation to schools providing boarding accommodation.

[275] *Greenwich*, n 208 above.

[276] See *R v Wiltshire County Council ex p Razazan* [1997] ELR 370 (CA).

[277] SSFA 1998, s 1. See also the Education (Infant Class Sizes) (England Regulations 1998 (SI 1998/1973) and Same (Wales) Regulations 1998 (SI 1998/1943). The exceptions to the limit include pupils admitted outside the normal admissions round who have statements of special educational needs or who have moved into the area and no other school is available within reasonable distance.

[278] G Whitty, *Making Sense of Education Policy* (London, Paul Chapman, 2005) 122.

[279] EA 1980, s 6(3)(b); EA 1996, ss 411(3)(b) and 413. The schools in question were 'voluntary aided' or 'special agreement' (see p 94 above) and were mostly Roman Catholic schools.

[280] *Choudhury and Another v Governors of Bishop Challoner Roman Catholic Comprehensive School* [1992] 3 All ER 277.

[281] EA 1980, s 6(3)(c).

are the basic criteria for admission.[282] It has become fairly common for pupils to change school for sixth form education, either because the pupil's school covers only ages 11–16 or because an alternative school is perceived to have a better academic record, a wider range of option choices or better facilities. The amendment therefore ensures that there are firm legal grounds for denying admission to young people regarded as unsuited to the kind of sixth form education a particular school provides. The right of appeal has been extended to cover a refusal to admit a pupil into a school's sixth form.[283]

Two further developments should be mentioned. First, the SSFA 1998 replicated provisions, first enacted in the Education Act 1997, dis-applying the duty to grant parental preference and the right of appeal in the case of a child who has been permanently excluded from two or more schools. In relation to a particular child, the dis-application runs for two years, starting from the date of the most recent exclusion of the child.[284] Secondly, an amendment made by the EA 2002 enables parents to be given a right to select more than one school in the admission process where there is a co-ordinated admissions scheme in the area.[285] However, there is no obligation to offer a place at any particular chosen school if, under a co-ordination scheme, the child has been offered a place at another school for which the parents expressed a preference.[286] This means that if a parent selects, say, a Roman Catholic School and a (non-denominational) community school, it is likely that he or she will not be offered a place at the community school if a place is offered at the Roman Catholic school, depending on the terms of the scheme itself. The draft revised code of practice on appeals indicated that the parent would have a right of appeal in respect of each of the schools for which he or she had expressed a preference.[287]

The law governing parental choice over school admission operates slightly differently at the initial decision and appeal stages. What follows is an attempt to summarise the position, but it should be borne in mind that the issues arising from the case law are very complex.

Arrangements for parents to express a preference

As already explained, the law does not provide parents with a specific right of choice. Rather, the LEA must make arrangements for enabling a parent 'to express a preference as to the school at which he wishes education to be provided for his child' and to give reasons for his or her preference.[288] There is no specific requirement to ensure that children are involved in this process, notwithstanding: the House of Commons Education and Skills Committee's view that they should be;[289] evidence that moving to secondary school is regarded by children as an

---

[282] SSFA 1998, s 86(3A) and (3B), inserted by the 2002 Act, Sched 4.
[283] SSFA 1998, s 94, as amended by the 2002 Act, s 51 and Sched 4.
[284] Ibid, ss 87 and 94; previously in the EA 1997, ss 11 and 12. See pp 282–5 below.
[285] SSFA 1998, ss 89B and 89C, inserted by the EA 2002, s 48.
[286] Ibid, s 86(2A), added by 2002 Act, Sched 4.
[287] DfES, *School Admission Appeals Code of Practice Draft 2005* (London, DfES, 2005), para A20.
[288] SSFA 1998, s 86(1).
[289] House of Commons Education and Skills Committee, Fourth Report, Session 2003–04, *Secondary Education: School Admissions*, HC 58–1 (London, TSO, 2004), paras 118–120. Accordingly,

important step towards independence;[290] and the state's duty under Article 12 of the UNCRC to enable a child to express his or her view freely on matters affecting him or her and for those views to be taken into account in the light of the child's age and understanding. The evidence suggests that parents do tend to involve their children in school choice decisions, particularly for secondary school admission; but children's participation is invited only after the parents have decided independently on the type of school they want for their child and narrowed the choice down to a few alternatives, with the result that the children 'feel more empowered than they actually are'.[291]

These provisions connote positive action by the parent, as was made clear by the Court of Appeal in striking down the practice employed in Rotherham.[292] There, the LEA allocated school places primarily on the basis of residence in a zone. At the start of the admissions round each year the LEA notified the relevant parents of the school allocated to them on the basis of their residence and told them that they should complete a form (on which they could select another school) if they did not want the place offered. Both the High Court and the Court of Appeal held that the LEA's system did not enable the parents to express a preference, and thus it was in breach of the legislation. Morritt LJ said that the legislation presupposed that the expression of preference was a positive act. He said that 'silence is not indicative of a preference for it is equally consistent with indifference'.[293]

The *Rotherham* decision was applied subsequently in a case involving the London Borough of Newham,[294] whose published school admissions policy provided for six categories of preference. They included having a younger sibling already at the school; attending a linked primary school; and, in descending order of priority, placing the school as first, second or third choice. Within each category, first priority was given to those with a sibling already at the school, then those whose parents stated a preference for single-sex education, and finally those living closest to the school. The form indicated that preference for a single-sex school was determined by the LEA 'by looking at the type of school you have applied for as your first preference'. The claimant parent stated on the form that a particular school was his first, second and third choice. No space was provided on the form for reasons to be given. When the child failed to secure a place at the

---

children are also not able to bring an admission appeal in their own right or to apply for judicial review in this context: see *R v London Borough of Richmond ex p JC* [2001] ELR 21 (CA), per Kennedy LJ at para 31; and *R (B) v Head Teacher of Alperton Community School and Others; R v Head Teacher of Wembley High School and Others ex p T; R v Governing Body of Cardinal Newman High School and Others ex p C* [2001] ELR 359. The codes of practice make no mention of the child in these situations either.

[290] I Butler *et al*, *Children's Involvement in Family Decision-making* (York, Joseph Rowtree Foundation, 2005).

[291] S Gorard, 'Three Steps to "Heaven"? The Family and School Choice' (1996) 48 *Educational Review* 237 at 248.

[292] *R v Rotherham Metropolitan Borough Council ex Clark and others* [1998] ELR 152 (QBD and CA).

[293] At 181D.

[294] *R (K) v London Borough of Newham* [2002] ELR 390.

school her parent appealed. At the hearing the parent stated that the child had friends going to the school and had two cousins there already, and that he did not want to send the child to a mixed school, for religious reasons. The appeal failed. But Collins J quashed the decision of the appeal panel. A2P1 of the ECHR, which refers to the parent's right to ensure that their child is taught in accordance with their religious or philosophical convictions, required positive action on the part of the LEA, initially, and then the appeal panel on appeal, to 'give weight to such conviction' and to ensure that there was 'a means of identifying religious conviction'.[295] He also said that the admission policy failed to enable the weight attached by the parent to the importance of single-sex education to be indicated.[296] The claimant was a devout Muslim who, Collins J noted, was concerned that his daughter should not mix with boys or young men after the age of 11 when at school, because it would be contrary to his religious convictions. Collins J was concerned that a religious preference for single-sex education should be properly taken into account for the purposes of the Article. Collins J's comment that 'it may that it is unusual that religious conviction should play a part in a decision whether a single-sex or mixed school should be chosen' seems somewhat wide of the mark, particularly given the number of Muslim and other families which are likely to hold similar views to those of the claimant and the existence of a House of Lords' decision on school admission based around such a preference.[297] But he did at least acknowledge that there could be others in the same position as the claimant.[298]

The duty to comply with parental preference

As discussed above, the law contains a presumption in favour of the granting of parental preference. Unless either of the statutory exceptions applies, the LEA and governing body of the school, if it is a 'maintained school' (most state schools are, but academies and city technology colleges are not[299]), must comply with the preference.[300]

The introduction of co-ordinated admission schemes in some areas has necessitated a qualification to this basic duty to comply with parental preference,

---

[295] Ibid, at paras 38–39.

[296] Ibid, at para 41.

[297] *Choudhury and Another v Governors of Bishop Challoner Roman Catholic Comprehensive School* [1992] 3 All ER 277.

[298] N 294 above, at para 29.

[299] They are classed as 'independent' (ie, non-maintained) schools by EA 1996, s 482, as amended. But note the effect of the funding agreement between the Secretary of State and the academy company as to admissions policy and practice to mirror the requirements of admissions law, noted above at p 166.

[300] SSFA 1998, s 86(2). Where, however, a place has been allocated in error it will be difficult to prevent its withdrawal, notwithstanding any legitimate expectation which has arisen, as in two cases, one involving an offer which was made to the parent by mistake and the other where the LEA's correspondence was ambiguous and the parent mistakenly believed that an offer of a place had been made: *R v Beatrix Potter School ex K* [1997] ELR 468; *R v Birmingham City Council ex p L* [2000] ELR 543. On the other hand, if the application was fraudulent or intentionally misleading, the code of practice advises that the school place may be withdrawn: DfES, *School Admissions Code of Practice*, DfES/0031/2003 (London, DfES, 2003), para 7.26.

however. Under such a scheme, parents can express a preference for more than one school and might qualify for a place at each one of them; in such a case, the duty to comply with parental preference does not apply in relation to every school,[301] since otherwise it would work against the purpose of a co-ordinated scheme, as discussed above. Instead, the terms of the scheme itself will decide at which one of the schools a place will be granted (for example, it may be the school which the parent ranked as the higher priority).[302]

The nature of the duty to grant parental preference was considered by the Court of Appeal in the important and well-publicised case of *R v Cleveland County Council ex p Commission for Racial Equality*.[303] A mother requested that her child be transferred from a primary school which had a high proportion of pupils of Pakistani origin to one 'where there will be the majority white children not Pakistani'. She explained to the court that her motive was not racist but was rather borne out of her perception that 'the Asian girls did not speak good English and did not mix with the white children' and that her daughter was being taught songs in a Pakistani language 'when in my view she had to read, write and speak her own language first'. The LEA felt obliged to grant the mother's request, on the basis of its statutory duty to comply with parental preference.[304] The Commission for Racial Equality asked the court to quash the decision, on the ground that the duty was qualified or overridden by the separate statutory duty on the LEA, in carrying out its functions, not to do any act that constituted racial discrimination.[305] The Court of Appeal concluded that there was no conflict between the two duties, and that the former duty, which was mandatory, was not qualified by the latter duty, because the Race Relations Act 1976 permitted race discrimination 'in the performance of an express obligation' under a statute.[306] Notwithstanding the court's acknowledgement that the mother was not racially motivated, the decision clearly confirmed that LEAs are powerless to prevent individual parental choice from indirectly leading to ethnic segregation across schools.[307]

Enforcement of the duty to comply with parental preference would be via complaint to the Secretary of State, who, as noted in Chapter 3, has a power to issue directions to an authority that is acting unreasonably or in default of its duty.[308] This power was used in one case where the school's decision not to admit a child to the school was based on the child's parent's conduct; the father was being sued for assault by the head teacher and others and the governing body

---

[301] SSFA 1986, s 86(6).

[302] DfES, *School Admissions Code of Practice*, DfES/0031/2003 (London, DfES, 2003), para 7.1.

[303] [1994] ELR 44 (CA).

[304] At the time, it was in the Education Act 1980, s 6(2).

[305] Race Relations Act 1976, s 18(1). It would not have been covered by the separate duty not to discriminate in relation to a decision to admit a child to a school, since that applies only to refusals to admit or the terms of admission: ibid, s 17. See p 148 above.

[306] Ibid, s 41(1)(a), referred to by Parker LJ at 51H. The court also rejected an argument that the LEA's decision amounted to unlawful segregation contrary to the 1976 Act: ibid, at 53B–C.

[307] See 'The Impact and Effects of Choice of School', p 295ff below.

[308] Education Act 1996, ss 496 and 497.

feared industrial action by staff if the child were admitted. The Secretary of State initially declared the governing body to be in breach of its statutory duty to admit the child,[309] and directed it to admit him; but in June 1997, following the general election, and by which time the LEA had found a place for the child elsewhere, the new Secretary of State (David Blunkett) revoked the direction. The court held that the Secretary of State had acted lawfully and that, although the governors were in breach of their duty, the court had a discretion whether to grant judicial review and felt that the circumstances justified its refusal to grant relief.[310]

The duty to comply with parental preference also extends beyond the area of the LEA: '[t]he duty in subs.(2) [of section 86] . . . shall apply also in relation to—(a) any application for admission to a maintained school of a child who is not in the area of the authority maintaining the school . . .' It was the Government's expressed intention at the time that this provision was first introduced that parents should be able to select from a wide area, in the interests of parental choice. In *Greenwich*,[311] noted above, the Court of Appeal confirmed that, taking account of the wording of the statute,[312] it was not lawful for the LEA to discriminate in favour of its own residents as against applicants living outside its area. Greenwich had reversed its previous policy of accommodating those who had been attending primary schools in neighbouring Lewisham in its secondary schools. This meant that many Lewisham residents would not be able exercise any preference in respect of secondary schools in Greenwich. In the Court of Appeal (upholding the Divisional Court's decision), Lloyd LJ said that the legislation intended to ensure that when an LEA decided school admission cases 'all children from within or outside the area rank *pari passu*, that they all come from the starting gate at the same time'.[313] Subsequently, in *R v Bromley LBC ex p C*,[314] it was held that in the light of *Greenwich* it was not even possible for the admissions policy of an LEA, Bromley, to state that its own residents and those living outside the district would have equal priority, if it was subject to the proviso that if the result was that the LEA's own residents' educational needs could not be met (because too many places were taken up by those living outside the LEA's area), they would have priority. Bromley's attempt to avoid the full effect of *Greenwich* was accordingly struck down by the court. Moreover, when *Greenwich* was implemented in Kingston-upon-Thames and there were complaints that competition for places at single-sex schools in Kingston would be so tight that fewer Kingston residents than previously would be able secure this form of education for their child, Watkins LJ confirmed that the LEA's implementation of *Greenwich* was consistent with its statutory obligation, notwithstanding its consequences.[315] Those Kingston parents who missed out

---

[309] As it happens, the school was grant-maintained and the duty to admit was therefore laid down in the articles of government prescribed by statutory instrument.

[310] *R v Secretary of State and Governors of Southlands Community Comprehensive School ex parte K* [1998] ELR 413.

[311] *R v London Borough of Greenwich ex p Governors of John Ball Primary School* (1990) 88 LGR 589 (CA).

[312] Then, s 6(5) of the EA 1980.

[313] At 597.

[314] [1992] 1 FLR 174.

[315] *R v Royal Borough of Kingston upon Thames ex p Kingwell* [1992] 1 FLR 182.

would find that '[p]resumably the education would be available in the area of another education authority'.[316]

Greenwich caused many LEAs to change their admission arrangements and has, to some extent, enhanced parents' rights over choice of school. But it has been particularly problematic for LEAs and other admission authorities, hindering effective planning. The problem has been most acute in London, where there are 'large-scale cross-border flows of children travelling to school in authorities other than those in which they reside' and extra-district applications can result in some parents receiving several offers of a place, whereas other parents may not receive any.[317] In response to these difficulties a Pan-London Co-ordinated Admissions Scheme has been introduced, reportedly with beneficial effects.[318]

One area of uncertainty arising from *Greenwich* is how the duty to ensure parity between in-borough and out-borough applications is affected by catchment areas, which, as we have seen, are commonly used to determined priority. The decision in *Razazan*[319] confirmed that *Greenwich* does not preclude an LEA from denying an extra-district applicant a place at one of its schools on the ground that that person does not live in the school's catchment area (especially when that person will generally have been offered a place at a school in his or her own area by his/her LEA). The Court of Appeal held that the applicant, who lived in Somerset and sought a school place in Wiltshire, was in legal terms in the same position as a Wiltshire resident who lived outside the particular school's catchment area. But it is important that catchment area boundaries are not contiguous with LEA boundaries. In *R v Rotherham Metropolitan Borough Council ex p LT*[320] the applicant lived in Nottinghamshire but wanted a place at a school in a neighbouring authority, Rotherham. But the school was within a catchment area and the applicant did not live in it and was denied a place. The eastern boundary of the catchment area followed the Rotherham LEA boundary. The court held that catchment area boundaries had to be drawn rationally, and suggested that if they had coincided exactly with the LEA boundaries that might be contrary to what Parliament had intended. Here the catchment area was not unlawful merely because it coincided to some extent with the authority boundary.

Under the *Rotherham* judgment[321] the LEA should not apply its admissions criteria—in that case the critical criterion was residence in the catchment area or zone—until it has given the parents a chance to express their preference. Once the parent has expressed a preference for a school, the admission criteria can deny the child a place only if the school is over-subscribed; but in any event choice can

[316] ibid, at 188.

[317] House of Commons Education and Skills Committee, Fourth Report, Session 2003–04, *Secondary Education: School Admissions*, HC 58–1 (London, TSO, 2004), paras 106–107.

[318] H Pennell *et al*, *Secondary School Admissions in London* (London, LSE Centre for Educational Research, 2006), 17–21 and 23.

[319] *R v Wiltshire County Council ex p Razazan* [1997] ELR 370 (CA).

[320] [2000] ELR 76 (CA).

[321] *R v Rotherham Metropolitan Borough Council ex Clark and others* [1998] ELR 152 (QBD and CA).

be denied if one of the statutory exceptions to the duty to comply with parental preference applies. These exceptions are discussed next.

Statutory exceptions to the duty to comply with parental choice of school

Pupils with a record of permanent exclusion

Arguably the most controversial exception to the duty to comply with parental preference[322] is that in SSFA 1998, section 87. This provides that the duty does not apply in respect of a child who has been permanently excluded from two or more schools, provided that the last exclusion occurred within the past two years.[323] What this means in relation to such a child is that only when the most recent exclusion was more than two years ago will the duty to comply with parental preference apply, although the parent will still have the right to express a preference[324] during that period. The section also makes it clear that the length of time elapsing between the periods of exclusion does not matter: therefore, even if a child was excluded six years ago and then again last year, the admission authority will have no duty to comply with parental preference. One of the criticisms of this exception is that it doubly punishes an excluded child and his or her family, especially in view of the fact that the right of appeal is also lost during the period that section 87 applies to the child.[325] Furthermore, if the LEA is the admission authority for a school at which it has allocated a place for a child to which the exception applies, it must make arrangements enabling the governing body to appeal against the decision to admit the child.[326]

The express purpose behind the section 87 exception, first contained in the Conservatives' EA 1997,[327] was to absolve schools where discipline was good from being forced to take a pupil with a bad disciplinary record.[328] Similar reasoning has been applied in Flanders, Belgium, where a pupil excluded in the previous two years may be denied admission and the courts have accepted that the need to protect the rights of other pupils may justify a refusal to accept a pupil who has been excluded for disciplinary reasons.[329] When the exception came before the UK Parliament again in 1998, in the School Standards and Framework Bill, the

---

[322] Under SSFA 1998 s 86(2) above.

[323] A child whose exclusion has been reviewed or has been adjudicated under the appeal arrangements and whose reinstatement would have been ordered had it been practicable is not to be treated as excluded for this purpose: ibid: s 87(4), inserted by the Education Act 2002, Sched 4, para 4.

[324] Under SSFA 1998 s 86(1).

[325] SSFA 1998, s 95(1).

[326] Ibid, s 95(2). The appeal panel is to be as constituted for appeals concerning admission to a community or voluntary controlled school: the Education (Admissions Appeals Arrangements) (England) Regulations 2002 (SI 2002/2899) (see below). Sched 2 to these regulations permits the appeal panel to allow a representative of the LEA, a governor of the school and a representative of the governing body to attend the hearing; it does not mention the parent or child, however.

[327] EA 1997, ss 11 12, inserting ss 411A and 423A into the EA 1996.

[328] HL Debs, Vol 578, Col 14, 10 Feb 1997, per Lord Henley (Minister of State).

[329] See J De Groof, 'Regulating School Choice in Belgium's Flemish Community' in PJ Wolf and S Macedo (eds), *Educating Citizens: International Perspectives on Civic Values and School Choice* (Washington, DC, Brookings Institution Press, 2004) 157 at 175.

minister made it clear that an admission authority was not barred from admitting the child; it was simply not under a duty to do so:

> a school . . . can choose to admit a pupil who has been excluded two, three, four, five or six times. However, if a school deems that it is not in the interests of the child or the school to meet parental preferences in such circumstances, the clause supports its right to make such a judgment.[330]

In the Bill these children were originally referred to as 'disqualifed persons', which, as Monk says, would have denied them both the status of 'pupil' and the specific protection of being classed as 'children' (and thus recognition as future adults and citizens).[331] Despite the abandonment of such terminology, the exception still faces the criticism that it disadvantages those already having the greatest difficulty in coping with the schools system. Only if the child in question has behavioural problems which are such that the child is considered to have special educational needs, and requires a statement to be maintained by the LEA, and the statement names the school preferred by the parent as suitable to meet his needs, may the parents succeed in enforcing their choice (albeit under special educational needs law only).[332]

To some, this treatment of excluded pupils represents a denial of the child's right to education, because alternative educational provision has traditionally been poor.[333] In *Alperton School* it was argued that the right to education in conformity with parental convictions (under the ECHR, A2P1) was denied by the statutory exception in section 87.[334] It was also argued that Article 14 (the non-discrimination provision) was also engaged, because the provision had a disproportionate effect on those most likely to be excluded from school, namely black Caribbean children. It was also argued that the denial of a right of appeal infringed Article 6 (right to a fair hearing in the determination of civil rights), an argument which failed on the basis that the case law was considered not to support the classification of the right to education as a civil right for that purpose.[335] Newman J rejected the A2P1 argument (which therefore defeated the Article 14 claim) on the ground that section 87 did not remove the LEA's obligation to ensure the provision of education for the relevant child,[336] it simply removed the obligation to comply with parental preference. Moreover, the

---

[330] Official Report, Standing Committee A, Col 549, 19 Feb 1998, per Estelle Morris, Minister of State.

[331] D Monk, 'Failing Children. Responding to Young People with "Behavioural Difficulties"' in M King (ed), *Moral Agendas for Children's Welfare* (London, Routledge, 1999) 212 at 218–9.

[332] EA 1996, s 324(5) and Sched 27, para 3. See Chap 6.

[333] C Hamilton, 'Rights of the Child: a Right to Education and a Right in Education' in C Bridge (ed), *Family Law Towards the Millenium. Essays for PM Bromley* (London, Butterworths, 1997) 201. This provision is made under EA 1996, s 19, discussed above, pp 189–90.

[334] *R (B) v Head Teacher of Alperton Community School and Others; R v Head Teacher of Wembley High School and Others ex p T; R v Governing Body of Cardinal Newman High School and Others ex p C* [2001] ELR 359.

[335] See, in particular, *R v London Borough of Richmond ex p JC* [2001] ELR 21 per Kennedy LJ at para 43. See further Chap 2.

[336] EA 1996, s 19, op cit.

removal of that obligation was a consequence and part of the regulation (by the state) of the right of access to education; and, on the facts, the child would be educated.[337] However, it is well known that the education of children who have been excluded from school has in the past often been only part-time,[338] although in recent years the Government's efforts to ensure that better provision is made by LEAs have begun to pay off; for example, according to a recent Ofsted report, five out of six pupil referral units (where many excluded pupils receive provision) were providing a full-time programme.[339]

The rapid reintegration of permanently excluded pupils within school occurs in only about one third of cases.[340] LEAs do have a power[341] to direct that a child be admitted to a particular school for which the LEA is not the admission authority where the child has been refused admission to 'each school' in the area and/or where he or she has been permanently excluded from 'each school', and the school that refused or excluded is 'a reasonable distance from his home and provides suitable education'. The direction must specify a maintained school that is a reasonable distance from the child's home and from which the child is not permanently excluded. Normally the school in the direction must be in the LEA's area; the exception is where the governing body of the school to be named has petitioned the Secretary of State, who then has a power to determine the school to be named in the direction.[342] The child must be admitted to the school named in the direction.[343]

In one case[344] the parents challenged the LEA's refusal to exercise this power in support of the admission of their child, who was of above average ability, to a named selective school which had rejected him because his verbal reasoning test score was not high enough. The LEA offered the child a place at an alternative school, which was non-selective but the nearest to his home. The court held that the LEA's discretionary power to direct admission did not apply because 'each school' under the provision in question meant 'every school'.[345] Munby J accepted that the effect of the provision was therefore that the exercise of the power would be limited to 'only a few, perhaps a very few cases'.[346] However, that was consistent with the minister's expectation, at the time that the power was first introduced, that the power would not be used at all frequently because it was 'rare for a pupil to be excluded from or refused admission to all suitable schools in the area'.[347] That expectation appears to have been realised.

Aside from pupils who have had two or more exclusions and who fall within the section 87 exception, admission cannot be denied simply on the ground of a

---

[337] N 334 above, at para 62.
[338] See, eg, C Hayden and S Dunne, *Outside, Looking In. Children's and Families' Experiences of Exclusion from School* (London, The Children's Society, 2001).
[339] Ofsted, *The Annual Report of Her Majesty's Chief Inspector of Schools* (London, TSO, 2005) 45.
[340] Social Exclusion Unit, *Truancy and School Exclusion*, Cm 3957 (London, TSO, 1998), para 2.21.
[341] SSFA 1998, ss 96 and 97.
[342] Ibid, s 97(3), (5).
[343] Ibid, ss 96(5) and 97(4) (the latter as substituted by the EA 2002, Sched 4, para 11).
[344] *R (B) v Hertfordshire County Council* [2005] ELR 17 (QBD).
[345] Ibid, para 11.
[346] Ibid, para 16.
[347] HL Debates, Vol 544, Col 1538, per Baroness Blatch, Minister of State.

child's poor disciplinary record. This presents a risk for under-subscribed schools that they will admit a disproportionate number of such children.[348] In any event, both the *School Admissions Code of Practice* published in 2003 and the draft revised code issued in 2005 encourage local discussion of ways to ensure a more even share of pupils with a history of challenging behaviour. Under the latter document, admission forums would be expected to agree 'protocols for the admission of hard to place children', which by September 2007 should cover excluded children.[349] A wider dispersal of unruly pupils is more equitable in terms of evening out the burden of managing challenging behaviour placed on schools and in theory making it easier for schools to devote attention to the pupils concerned and to recruit new staff. However, it may well be the case that the schools which have fewer such children will be less tolerant of their mis-behaviour and will more readily exercise their power to exclude those who misbehave badly. A school from which a pupil has been permanently excluded cannot be directed to re-admit the child, but, on an appeal by the parents, an independent appeal panel may consider that the exclusion was not reasonable and that reinstatement of the child is in the interests of all concerned. Under-subscribed schools with larger numbers of difficult pupils may not only be rather more practised in coping with them but also under pressure to keep them in order to maintain pupil numbers.

'Efficient education or the efficient use of resources'
The most important of the statutory grounds on which parental choice of school may be denied is that compliance with the parent's preference 'would prejudice the provision of efficient education or the efficient use of resources' (the efficiency ground).[350] The wording of this ground has not changed since legislation was first enacted in 1980. This ground seeks to strike an appropriate balance between, on the one hand, individual rights to freedom of choice and, on the other, the demands of 'efficiency' in furtherance of wider social and economic goals. It acknowledges the reality of inelasticity in the supply of places at different schools, a problem that the Government's plans to facilitate the expansion of popular schools will go only a limited way towards remedying. On the other hand, against a background to the EA 1980 in which some LEAs were regarded by the Conservative Government as hindering choice on ideological grounds, such as the quest for greater equality, the efficiency ground was designed to ensure that only overriding logistical or financial factors could stand in the way of meeting parental wishes. The extent to which individual rights could 'trump' the power of LEAs to act in the collective community interest in managing school admissions was, however, unclear.[351]

Certainly they appeared to be given the upper hand when the Education

---

[348] As noted in Ofsted, *School Place Planning. The Influence of School Place Planning on School Standards and Social Inclusion*, HMI 587 (London, Ofsted, 2003), para 51.

[349] DfES, *School Admissions Code of Practice Draft 2005* (London, DfES, 2005), para 7.5.

[350] SSFA 1998, s 86(3)(a).

[351] Cf J Tweedie, 'Rights in Social Programmes: the Case of Parental Choice of School' [1986] *Public Law* 407.

Reform Act 1988 introduced the principle of 'open enrolment', noted above, that the Conservatives had promised during the 1987 General Election campaign. By sweeping away the power of LEAs to set artificially low admissions limits for individual schools, so that the authorities could not apply the efficiency ground in relation to a school unless and until it had admitted pupils up to the 'standard number' (since replaced by the admission limit) applicable to it,[352] parental rights to choice appeared to be strengthened, while LEAs' role in school place planning was undermined.[353] Indeed, by 1990, research showed that some LEAs were operating 'an enforced catchment-area system in order to cope with the more stringent arrangements and the necessary planning of the published intake limits'.[354] There were also concerns that this apparent extension of individual choice, combined with the simultaneous introduction of local financial management to foster greater competition between schools, would result in greater racial stratification and segregation (for example, '[p]arents will be free to prefer all-white schools to those where there is a racial mix') and inequality.[355] In fact, while rights of choice have indeed resulted in ethnic segregation in some parts of the country (see below), the efficiency ground has limited choice and resulted in many parents having to compete for a limited number of places at popular schools.

The efficiency ground has also been affected by the limit to infant class sizes introduced under the SSFA 1998.[356] Prejudice to efficient education or efficient use of resources 'may . . . be taken to arise by reason of measures required to be taken in order to ensure compliance with the duty [to limit infant class sizes to 30 pupils]'.[357] What this means is that prejudice for the purpose of the efficiency ground will arise if an admission would result in the school exceeding the class size limit. It was argued in one case that the limiting effect that the maximum class size has on parental choice could, in a case where the mother and child had health problems, impact upon their lives in a way that constituted an unjustifiable interference with private or family life for the purposes of Article 8 of the ECHR.[358] The court found no evidence of such an interference, but in any event considered that a class size limit was justified within the terms of Article 8(2): 'The rights of other children are entitled to protection. Putting a limit on class

---

[352] Education Reform Act 1988, ss 26–32. See further N Harris, *Law and Education: Regulation, Consumerism and the Education System* (London, Sweet and Maxwell, 1993), ch 5.

[353] P Meredith, 'Educational Reform' (1989) 52 *MLR* 215; P Meredith, *Government, Schools and the Law* (London, Routledge, 1992). The law now in effect states that there will be no prejudice to efficiency if the total number of pupils admitted for the year group does not exceed the admissions total set by the admission authority for the year in question: SSFA 1998, s 86(5), as substituted by the EA 2002, s 47. Exception is made for schools providing boarding accommodation (SSFA 1998, s 86(5A) and (5B), as substituted).

[354] A Stillman, 'Legislating for Choice' in M Flude and M Hammer, *The Education Reform Act 1988. Its Origins and Implications* (Basingstoke, Falmer, 1990) 87 at 104.

[355] D Coulby, 'The Ideological Contradictions of Educational Reform' in L Bash and D Coulby, *The Education Reform Act. Competition and Control* (London, Casell, 1989) 110 at 113 and 115.

[356] SSFA 1998, s 1.

[357] SSFA 1998, s 86(4).

[358] *R v London Borough of Richmond ex p JC* [2001] ELR 21.

sizes seems to me to be within that which is necessary within a democratic society'.[359]

(a) Admissions other than to infant classes subject to the class size limit

In relation to admissions *not* affected by the class size limit, prejudice to efficient education/use of resources as a consequence of the admission of the child in question must be established by the admission authority.[360] In *Choudhury,* Lord Browne-Wilkinson said that 'when a school is over-subscribed it necessarily follows that "compliance with the preference of" *all* applicants would prejudice proper education at the school through over-crowding'.[361] But, by using the singular, 'preference', the Act appears to connote prejudice arising from each application. However, Lord Browne-Wilkinson's approach has been adopted in the guidance relating to cases where the school is over-subscribed by more than one, which is likely to result in multiple appeals. Here the appeal panel would have to decide whether the admission of *all* the children would cause prejudice. If it decided that it would not, then all children would have to be admitted.[362] The position where some but not all of the children could be admitted without causing prejudice is discussed below.

Once it considers the school to be full and it wishes to deny a child admission, the admission authority will normally be relying on the efficiency ground. All parents who are informed that their child will not be admitted to a school, other than those covered by the two-plus (section 87) exclusions ground, above, have the right of appeal to an appeal panel constituted under the 2002 Act and relevant regulations.[363] A two-stage test for the application of the efficiency ground, articulated by Forbes J in *R v South Glamorgan Appeals Committee ex parte Evans*[364] two decades ago and subsequently approved by Woolf LJ in the *Croydon* case,[365] continues to form the basis for the operation of this critical area of admissions law at the appeal stage (although, as the Council on Tribunals has pointed out, there is also a preliminary matter which the panel should decide: whether the admissions criteria have been properly applied).[366]

---

[359] Ibid, per Ward LJ at para 87.

[360] In *R v Commissioner for Local Administration ex Croydon London Borough Council* [1989] 1 All ER 1033. See p 288 below.

[361] *Choudhury and Another v Governors of Bishop Challoner Roman Catholic Comprehensive School* [1992] 3 All ER 277, at 285 (original emphasis).

[362] DfES, *School Admissions Code of Practice* (London, DfES, 2003), para 4.71; see also DfES, *Draft School Admission Appeals Code of Practice* (London, DfES, 2005), para 5.34.

[363] SSFA 1998, s 94, as amended by s 50 of the EA 2002. See the Education (Admission Appeal Arrangements) (England) Regulations 2002 (SI 2002/2899). The panel must have 3 of 5 members. The regs provide for a blend of educational experience and lay (in the sense of not having personal experience in educational management or the provision of education in a school) membership. The panels are appointed by the LEA or, in the case of foundation and voluntary aided schools, the governing body. In some cases LEAs and governing bodies may enter into joint arrangements.

[364] 10 May 1984, CO/197/84, Lexis-Nexis.

[365] *R v Commissioner for Local Administration ex Croydon London Borough Council* [1989] 1 All ER 1033.

[366] Council on Tribunals, *School Admission and Exclusion Appeal Panels—Special Report,* Cm 5788 (London, TSO, 2003), para 2.32. The Council reports an 'apparent lack of understanding of the two stage process' among some panel members, highlighting the need for appropriate training: ibid, paras 2.33 and 2.34.

Under the *Evans* test, at the first stage, the appeal panel must decide whether the admission of one child prejudices the provision of efficient education or the efficient resources at the school. It is clear that it will not be enough for the admission authority to show that the school's admission limit has been reached; the appeal panel should make an independent assessment of whether the child's admission would cause prejudice in the circumstances.[367] Nonetheless, the onus of proof in relation to the existence of prejudice has been held to lie with the admission authority at this stage.[368] In *R v Sheffield City Council ex p N*[369] the LEA claimed that a school could admit no more than 230 pupils. The applicant was ninth on the waiting list. He claimed that the school could admit 240, ie eight classes of 30. The LEA wanted to preserve some flexibility to accommodate any additional pupils who might arrive outside the normal admissions round, taking account of the need for balance in terms of ethnicity, gender and educational reasons. Burton J considered that that satisfied the onus on the LEA to show prejudice.

The second stage, referred to in the *Code of Practice* as the 'balancing stage', is the more problematic. It involves a determination whether the prejudice is sufficient to outweigh the 'parental factors', that is, the particular arguments or circumstances put forward in support of the parent's case. This balancing exercise can be very difficult, since there may be compelling reasons for the parent's choice, while the admission authority will be concerned to avoid overcrowding at the school. The House of Commons Select Committee on Education and Skills noted that 'appeals occur when a school is full', so that 'the consequence of a successful appeal is entry to a school that is already deemed to be full'.[370] Indeed, the Committee 'heard evidence of very significant numbers of children being admitted under these circumstances . . . causing schools to have to make short term arrangements to accommodate and support these additional children'.[371]

In 1989, in the *Croydon* case, Woolf LJ held that the onus of proof at this balancing stage does not lie with either party.[372] However, in a subsequent decision in a case involving Essex County Council which is typical of the kind dealt with by appeal panels, Collins J said that at this stage each appellant before the appeal panel 'had the burden of satisfying the committee that notwithstanding that there would be a prejudice to efficient education, the child in question should be admitted because there were special circumstances relating to that child'.[373] Here the admission limit had been set at 240; but as a result of the LEA's policy that all children living with the school's catchment area should be

---

[367] *R v Appeal Committee of Brighouse School ex G; same ex p. B* [1997] ELR 39, per Sedley J. See also DfES, *School Admissions Code of Practice* (London, DfES, 2003), para 4.61; and DfES, *Draft School Admission Appeals Code of Practice* (London, DfES, 2005), para 5.34.

[368] *R v Commissioner for Local Administration ex Croydon London Borough Council* [1989] 1 All ER 1033.

[369] [2000] ELR 85.

[370] House of Commons Education and Skills Committee, Fourth Report, Session 2003–04, *Secondary Education: School Admissions, Vol. 1*, HC 58–1 (London, TSO, 2004), para 163.

[371] Ibid.

[372] Woolf LJ considered it to be inappropriate to think of it in terms of an onus on one party or the other: n 368 above, at 1041.

[373] *R v Essex County Council ex Jacobs* [1997] ELR 190, at 197H.

guaranteed a place at the school, 257 places had been allocated. There were 32 appeals. The appeal panel (referred to as an appeal committee) decided that no additional pupils could be accepted without prejudice to efficient education. The appellant in question was the father of twin children. Neither he nor his ex-wife lived in the catchment area. He argued that the children should be admitted because their elder sister attended the school and he and his ex-wife, with whom the children resided at different times, both lived within one mile of the school. The committee's decision was quashed (and the matter remitted for fresh consideration) on the ground that it did not give sufficient weight to the parental factors. In particular, the fact that the elder sister also had to travel to both parents' addresses 'provided a more powerful reason for the sibling connection to prevail in the circumstances of the case. Certainly, it is something which . . . the committee ought to have taken into account. Unfortunately, . . . it did not.'[374] The committee also thought that it would have been feasible for the elder sister to be moved to the school at which the twins had been allocated a place. The court held that to have been an irrelevant consideration. Similarly, in another case, where there were 42 appeals, the panel's decision was quashed because its application of the prejudice test was not based on true facts; it was not aware that 14 parents who had been offered places at the school had not accepted them.[375]

Particular considerations apply when appeal panels are faced with multiple appeals in respect of a particular over-subscribed school, as in the *Essex* case. In effect, the appellants are competing with each other for a limited number of possible places. The established practice, judicially approved, is for all the appeals to be heard before decisions are reached.[376] The code of practice indicates that the panel must first look at each individual case to determine whether the parental factors outweigh prejudice. If there are two or more cases where prejudice is outweighed and admission of the child is therefore merited, the panel must decide whether the school could cope if all such children were admitted. If the panel feels that it could not, then it should 'compare cases and decide which of them to uphold', a practice which the courts have endorsed.[377] This is a difficult task, particularly when there are significant numbers of appeals.

(b) Admission to infant classes covered by the maximum class size limit
In the case of admissions to primary school classes covered by the statutory maximum class size limits, noted above, there are special rules and the normal two-stage test does not apply. Prejudice of the above kind 'may arise because of measures required to be taken to ensure compliance' with the duty not to exceed the normal class size limit of 30.[378] So the first matter for determination is

---

[374] Ibid, at 202H–203A.

[375] *R (B) v Head Teacher of Alperton Community School and Others; R v Head Teacher of Wembley High School and Others ex parte T; R v The Governing Body of Cardinal Newman High School and Others ex parte C* [2001] ELR 359.

[376] *R v Commissioner for Local Administration ex Croydon London Borough Council* [1989] 1 All ER 1033.

[377] DfES, *School Admissions Appeals Code of Practice* (London, DfES, 2003), paras 4.71–4.72. *R v Education Appeal Committee of Leicestershire County Council ex p Tarmohamed* [1997] ELR 48.

[378] SSFA 1998, s 86(4), as noted at p 286 above.

whether the admission of the child would cause prejudice because of the qualifying measures that would be needed to comply with the class size limit. It is for the LEA to show that the case is one to which 'class size prejudice applies'.[379] In *R (O) v St James RC Primary School Appeal Panel*,[380] for example, Newman J said that unless a school already had the resources, either a sufficient number of teachers or accommodation or both, it was bound to have to take measures to accommodate more than 30 pupils. It could not be assumed that a further teacher, who would have been needed, would have been available. The school had properly reached a decision on the ground that qualifying measures would have to be taken.

If there would be prejudice due to the qualifying measures needed to ensure compliance with the duty on maximum class size, an appeal may be upheld by an appeal panel only if the panel is satisfied

(a)   that the decision was not one which a reasonable admission authority would make in the circumstances of the case; or

(b)   that the child would have been offered a place if the admission arrangements (as published . . .) had been properly implemented.[381]

The onus of proof in relation to these two grounds has been held to rest with the parents.[382] These are very technical grounds for lay appeal panels to apply. Indeed, in one recent case 15 decisions by the appeal panel in Reading were quashed by the court on the application of the LEA because the panel had mis-applied the statutory test.[383]

The appeals code of practice advises that these grounds be considered in reverse order. Thus the panel would need to consider whether or not the published admission arrangements had been correctly applied in the individual child's case (for example, if a sibling connection should have been, but was not, taken into account). The appeal should be upheld only 'where it is clear that the child would have been offered a place if the admission arrangements had been properly implemented'.[384] If the appeal is not upheld on ground (b), then ground (a) will need to be considered. This provides the basis for a *Wednesbury*-type challenge to the reasonableness of the decision not to admit the child, such as (as the 2005 draft put it) 'whether the decision was one no reasonable admission authority would have reached in the circumstances, ie whether the decision was

---

[379] *R v South Gloucestershire Education Appeals Committee ex p Bryant* [2001] ELR 53 (CA), per Buxton LJ at para 8.

[380] [2001] ELR 469.

[381] Previously in the SSFA 1998, Sched 24, para 12 and now in the Education (Admission Appeals Arrangements) (England) Regulations 2002 (SI 2002/2899), reg 6(2).

[382] *R v London Borough of Richmond ex p JC* [2001] ELR 21 (CA), which also held that fresh evidence supporting the parents' case but not presented to the admission authority could not, unless persuasive, be considered by the appeal panel—which in these class size limit cases (but not in others) is not conducting a rehearing.

[383] *R (Reading Borough Council) v Admissions Appeal Panel for Reading Borough Council and 15 Parents* [2006] ELR 186 (QBD).

[384] DfES, *School Admissions Appeals Code of Practice* (London, DfES, 2003), para 4.57; DfES, *School Admissions Appeals Code of Practice Draft 2005* (London, DfES, 2005), para 5.25.

irrational or perverse, in the light of the admission arrangements, to refuse to admit the particular child',[385] although probably not a challenge to the admission arrangements themselves, unless 'self-evidently or intrinsically unlawful'.[386] This basically reflects recent case law.[387] In the *South Gloucestershire* case the court held that the appeal panel had a power not to apply an admission policy it considered to be unlawful or *Wednesbury* unreasonable.[388] Here the appeal panel upheld an appeal by six children who all had siblings at the school in question. The LEA had argued that to accommodate these children, who lived outside the school's area of prime responsibility (in effect a catchment area), would force the LEA to add an extra class to the school in order to comply with the class size limit. The LEA's admission booklet gave second highest priority (after those with special educational needs) to local siblings (children who lived within two miles of the school, or over two miles where the school was the nearest with a place available, or within the school's area of responsibility). The appeal panel considered this policy to be unclear and potentially unfair and perverse. In *Hounslow*, however, the Court of Appeal held that that there was no need for an appeal panel in such a case to adjourn in order that the lawfulness of the admissions policy could be determined via judicial review.[389] Panels could decide whether a policy was perverse, but earlier case law (in particular, *South Gloucestershire*) should not be taken as inviting appeal panels to embark upon wide-ranging enquiries. They should instead simply look at whether there was self-evident unlawfulness. On the facts, the Court of Appeal held, inter alia, that the panel had not taken into account the particular circumstances of the individual child, which it was required to do for the purposes of deciding whether the LEA's decision was perverse. The idea that, for the purposes of ground (a), the reasonableness of the decision should be judged with reference to the position of the LEA or school alone (for example, in having to take qualifying measures) was rejected by Ward LJ in *R v London Borough of Richmond ex p. JC*; he said that the personal circumstances of the child were relevant to the rationality test in ground (a).[390]

Although unreasonableness (in the sense of perversity) for the purposes of ground (a) has to be judged on an individual case basis, it is possible that there could be more potentially successful appellants than the number of additional pupils who could be admitted without prejudice. In such a case the panel has to

---

[385] DfES, *School Admissions Appeals Code of Practice Draft 2005* (London, DfES, 2005), para 5.29. The panel must not simply consider whether the decision was one that an LEA could not reasonably take, but one that no reasonable authority could have made in the circumstances of the case: *R (Haringey London Borough Council) v School Admission Appeals Panel for Haringey and London Borough Council* [2006] ELR 10, per Stanley Burnton J at paras 14–16.

[386] DfES, *School Admissions Appeals Code of Practice Draft 2005* (London, DfES, 2005), para 5.29.

[387] In particular, the CA's decision in *School Admission Appeals Panel for London Borough. of Hounslow v Mayor and Burgesses of London Borough of Hounslow* [2002] ELR 602, per May LJ at paras 58, 59 and 63. See also *R (Reading Borough Council) v Admissions Appeal Panel for Reading Borough Council and 15 Parents* [2006] ELR 186 (QBD).

[388] *R (South Gloucestershire LEA) v South Gloucestershire Schools Appeal Panel* [2002] ELR 309.

[389] *School Admission Appeals Panel for London Borough. of Hounslow v Mayor and Burgesses of London Borough of Hounslow* [2002] ELR 602.

[390] [2001] ELR 21 at para 79.

move on to follow the two-stage process articulated in *ex p. Evans*, discussed above.[391]

Overall, therefore, this process of decision-making requires fine judgement and logical thinking, but it is by no means straightforward for lay appeal panels, even with legal advice. For parents, particularly those from less advantaged educational backgrounds, the possibility of pressing home an argument in a class size admission case concerning statutory ground (a) or (b) must be rendered extremely difficult. In one of the cases concerning these grounds, where there were five appeals, most of the parents had legal representation, including one who was of Iranian origin and had no family support in the area.[392] The solicitor who acted for several of the appellant parents (presumably there was not considered to be a conflict of interest) presented quite a sophisticated legal argument based on the contention that the Cardiff LEA had erred in allocating places to children who resided within the catchment area without considering whether those living outside might have a more compelling case, and that by failing to consider individual circumstances the LEA's decision was unreasonable. Legal aid is not available for admission appeals, placing those unable to afford legal representation at a disadvantage, although preparation of a written submission might receive Community Legal Services funding. As it happened, the solicitor's argument in the Cardiff case proved of no avail. Richards J confirmed that the LEA had failed to take account of the domestic and other circumstances, which was technically an error of law, and the panel had therefore found the LEA to have acted unreasonably. But the panel had nevertheless considered that even if the LEA had taken account of the individual circumstances it was unlikely to have reached a different conclusion regarding admission. The panel had therefore found against the unreasonableness argument based on ground (a). Richards J in fact held that it had been entitled to do so.

The Council on Tribunals has recommended that 'better information should be provided to parents about the special circumstances of infant class size appeals'.[393] This is not so much in response to the complexity of the provisions, which is a problem for all but particularly for less well educated and skilled parents, as the need to manage effectively parents' expectations of the likelihood of success in these cases, in the face of evidence that 'very few class size appeals are ever likely to succeed', a fact that has apparently led many panel members to regard these cases as a waste of time and to refuse to sit on them.[394] Panel members who do participate in these appeals have been found often to misunderstand how the law is meant to be applied.[395]

---

[391] DfES, *School Admissions Appeals Code of Practice Draft 2005* (London, DfES, 2005), para 5.29.

[392] *R (Khundakji and Salahi) v Admissions Appeal Panel of Cardiff County Council* [2003] EWHC Admin 436, [2003] ELR 495.

[393] Council on Tribunals, *School Admission and Exclusion Appeal Panels Special Report*, Cm 5788 (London, TSO, 2003), para 2.42.

[394] Ibid, para 2.41.

[395] Ibid, para 2.40.

Selection by reference to ability or aptitude

As we have seen, despite the tide of comprehensivisation that swept aside much of selective education in England and Wales in the 1960s and 1970s, selection of pupils by ability remains lawful, within carefully defined parameters. Indeed, as the House of Commons Select Committee on Education and Skills reported in 2004, the Government's education policy, whilst emphasising the goal of greater social inclusion, 'nevethertheless has retained formal selection by academic ability in many parts of England . . . and has extended the total numbers of pupils selected by introducing the concept of selection by aptitude'.[396] To recap on the position outlined earlier, the selection of pupils by ability by the remaining 164 grammar schools is sanctioned, as it is in schools covered by arrangements already in place in the year 1997–8, ie, prior to the SSFA 1998; in schools selecting on the basis of aptitude for a particular subject or subjects (but only up to 10 per cent of pupils may be selected on that basis); and in schools where selection is based on 'banding', which involves admission arrangements which aim to achieve an entry who are representative of all levels of ability, with no level of ability being substantially over- or under-represented.[397] Partial selection by ability or aptitude under pre-existing arrangements is also permitted.[398] Some of the schools operating partial selection describe themselves as 'bilateral schools' because they have a 'grammar' stream and a separate comprehensive stream. As we saw earlier, a number of the challenges to the schools adjudicator's decisions have concerned partial selection. The House of Commons Select Committee says that it found no evidence to suggest that partial selection actually contributes to the improvement of educational standards and it has recommended its abolition.[399]

The social effects and implications of selective education are discussed below. Here we are concerned only with legal position and, in particular, how parental choice can be denied through the application of selection criteria. The basic rule is that the duty to comply with parental preference[400] does not apply if the admission arrangements:

(i)   are wholly based on selection by reference to ability or aptitude, and
(ii) are so based with a view to admitting only pupils with high ability or with aptitude,

and compliance with the preference would be incompatible with those arrangements.[401]

The 1998 Act permits additional criteria to be used where the admission

---

[396] House of Commons Education and Skills Committee, Fourth Report, Session 2003–04, *Secondary Education: School Admissions, Vol. 1*, HC 58–1 (London, TSO, 2004), para 186.

[397] SSFA 1998, ss 99–103, as variously amended. As noted above, these restrictions are restated in the Education and School Inspections Bill 2006.

[398] SSFA 1998, s 100.

[399] House of Commons Education and Skills Committee, Fourth Report, Session 2003–04, *Secondary Education: School Admissions, Vol. 1*, HC 58–1 (London, TSO, 2004), para 204.

[400] Under SSFA 1998, s 86(2), above.

[401] Ibid, s 86(3)(c).

arrangements provide for all pupils to be selected by ability or aptitude but there are more pupils who are of the requisite aptitude or ability that there are places at the school.[402] This reflects an important judgment in 1993 by Schiemann J, holding that admissions arrangements under which applicants were selected, first, on the basis of ability and, secondly (if there were too many able applicants for the places available), home to school proximity were lawful.[403]

West *et al* have argued that 'it does not appear to be feasible to differentiate between "ability" and "aptitude"'.[404] Certainly, the distinction that is intended between ability and aptitude for the purposes of school admission remains unclear, as the House of Commons Education and Skills Select Committee concluded in 2003.[405] However, oral evidence presented to the Select Committee in 2004 by the Chief Schools Adjudicator suggested that aptitude should be defined as the propensity to develop an ability. That is indeed how it was explained by the schools minister when the legislation was before Parliament in 1998: '[a]bility is what a child has already achieved. Aptitude is the natural talent and interest that a child has in a specific subject—in other words, the potential to develop a skill or talent'.[406] In its review of secondary school admissions the Education and Skills Select Committee was critical of selection by aptitude, finding the testing of aptitude to be an 'unnecessary complication in the schools admission process' and costly in terms of staff time.[407] In the 2005 schools White Paper the Government indicates that the arrangements for partial (10 per cent) selection on the basis for aptitude will continue because they support schools in 'developing a specialist ethos'[408] which, as we have seen, the Government is keen to encourage. However, in its subsequent report on the White Paper the Select Committee states that it has 'not yet been presented with a credible explanation of the distinction between ability and aptitude'.[409] It argues that 'aptitude selection should now be prohibited in regulations'.[410] It is not clear, however, whether this refers to covert forms of selection or those which are governed by the statutorily permitted form of selection noted above. If the latter were to be included, the Act would need to be changed.

Selection by ability or aptitude also occurs in the context of entry to a sixth form (ie years 12 and 13 of schooling). The Education Act 2002 amended the law to clarify that entry to a particular sixth form ('secondary education suitable to

---

[402] Ibid, s 86(9).

[403] *R v Kingston upon Thames Royal London Borough Council ex p Emsden* [1993] 1 FLR 179.

[404] A West *et al*, 'School Admissions: Increasing Equity, Accountability and Transparency' (1999) 46 *British Journal of Educational Studies* 188 at 199.

[405] House of Commons Education and Skills Committee, Fourth Report, Session 2002–03, *Secondary Education: Diversity of Provision*, HC 94 (London, TSO, 2003), para 189.

[406] Official Report, Standing Committee A, The School Standards and Framework Bill, col 649, 24 Feb 1998, per Mr Stephen Byers.

[407] House of Commons Education and Skills Committee, Fourth Report, Session 2002–03, *Secondary Education: Diversity of Provision*, HC 94 (London, TSO), paras 200 and 201.

[408] DfES, *Higher Standards, Better Schools for All*, Cm 6677 (London, TSO, 2005), para 3.20.

[409] House of Commons Education and Skills Committee, First Report, Session 2005–06, *The Schools White Paper: 'Higher Standards, Better Schools for All'*, HC 633–I (London, TSO, 2006), para 129.

[410] Ibid.

the requirements of pupils who are over compulsory school age') can also be denied on the ground that the arrangements for selection 'are wholly based on selection by reference to ability or aptitude and compliance with the preference would be incompatible with selection under those arrangements'.[411] This applies not only to persons wishing to join the school for sixth form education but also those already admitted to the school who wish to continue on into the sixth form.[412] The pressure on schools to maximise pupils' A level grades in order to ensure a good showing in the published league tables encourages the firm application of this ground for denying entry to a sixth form. At the same time, there is evidence that increasingly pupils are prepared to change school at the sixth form stage in order to maximise the prospects of success by choosing a school with a good record of examination results. Some of the extra demand for sixth form entry is also the result of government incentives to increase post-16 participation rates, discussed in Chapter 4, in particular the payment of educational maintenance allowances. Something of a market for sixth form entry is being created in some areas, particularly with the movement from the private sector to state schools at the sixth form stage in order to avoid the cost of private education or the perceived discrimination against pupils attending independent schools practised by some university departments, as well as where a pupil's independent school imposes a strict academic threshold for entry to the sixth form.

Those denied admission to a school as sixth-formers have the same right of appeal as others seeking admission to a school. In addition, appeal arrangements must be made for those already admitted to the school but refused entry to its sixth form.[413] No separate statistics on these appeals have been published thus far.

THE IMPACT AND EFFECTS OF CHOICE OF SCHOOL

It is clear that choice of school within the state system is not, nor has at any point in time been, an absolute right. All that the Education Act 1980 and subsequent legislation established is a procedural right to express a preference. Despite the statutory presumption that a preference should be upheld, the statutory exceptions and local admission policies, such as catchment areas or religious preference, impose severe constraints on the exercise of free choice. As the House of Commons Select Committee on Education and Skills concluded:

---

[411] SSFA 1998, s 86(3A), inserted by the EA 2002, Sched 4 para 3(5).
[412] SSFA 1998, s 86(3B), inserted by the EA 2002, Sched 4 para 3(5).
[413] This is the responsibility of the LEA (in the case of a community or voluntary controlled school) or the governing body (in the case of a foundation or voluntary aided school): SSFA 1998, s 94(1A) and (1B), inserted by the EA 2002, Sched 4, para 8.

[T]he language of choice, as opposed to the right to express a preference, in the context of schools admission is inappropriate. For many parents there is little choice; their options are too often limited to an expression of preference for a single school at which they can reasonably expect to be offered a place.[414]

An Audit Commission survey in the mid-1990s found that around 20 per cent of parents did not secure their genuine first choice of school,[415] and more recent evidence suggests that nothing has changed.[416] Measuring levels of choice is in fact problematic because many parents tailor their choices to reflect their reasonable expectations of securing a place at a good local school, rather than making an ideal choice. Suppose, for example, that the parents live in the catchment area of school A, but could express a preference for what they perceive to be the best school in the locality, school B. They have priority for a place at school A, but suppose that they take a chance and apply for school B. The LEA will allocate the place they would have been guaranteed at school A to another child. If they fail in their bid for a place at school B, they may end up having to settle for school C, which is the least popular and successful school of the three. As the House of Commons Education and Skills Select Committee has noted, parents are placed in the position of having to scrutinise schools' admission criteria carefully and, in making their selection, make a judgement not only about school they prefer, but also about which school is most likely to offer them a place.[417] In view of the way in which the expressed order of preference for different schools carries weight in the admission process, 'parents risk putting forward applications with little chance of success and may not only fail to secure a place at their preferred school but also fail to be placed at any school they deem acceptable'.[418] The Committee implies that social class or background might influence the way that parents behave in the admission process, in terms of their ability to assess the risks inherent in expressing preferences.[419]

As noted earlier, London is described as having had the most severe problems from unco-ordinated admissions.[420] It was particularly affected by the *Greenwich* judgment which, as noted above, confirmed that applicants from outside a particular LEA's area could not, merely on the basis of their residence outside the LEA area, be denied equal admission rights to residents of that area who applied for school places within it.[421] In the capital there is a wide range of schools and different admission areas within close geographical proximity. A new

---

[414] House of Commons Education and Skills Committee, Fourth Report, Session 2003–04, *Secondary Education: School Admissions*, HC 58–1 (London, TSO, 2004), para 141.

[415] *Trading Places* (London, Audit Commission, 1996).

[416] See J Flatley *et al*, *Parents' Experiences of the Process of Choosing a Secondary School*, Research Report 278 (London, DfES, 2001) 15.

[417] House of Commons Education and Skills Committee, Fourth Report, Session 2003–04, *Secondary Education: School Admissions*, HC 58–1 (London, TSO, 2004), paras 121–125.

[418] Ibid, para 124.

[419] Ibid, para 147.

[420] M Haddad (ed), *School Admissions* (London, Social Market Foundation, 2004) 13.

[421] On the effects of *Greenwich*, including litigation challenging attempts by two LEAs to ameliorate its effects on choice among their own residents, see also N Harris, *Law and Education: Regulation, Consumerism and the Education System* (London, Sweet and Maxwell, 1993) 152–3.

co-ordinated system has recently been established for London and its eight bordering LEAs, and, as noted earlier, the evidence to date, from a survey of admission offices operating in the Pan London School Admissions Scheme, suggests that the co-ordination it has introduced has improved admissions administration considerably.[422] A report by the Social Market Foundation in 2004 predicted that it would ameliorate some of the current problems, which include 'parents sitting on multiple offers while others have none', but that, in view of the continuing variation among admission policies operated by different schools and LEAs, would not end confusion among parents.[423] A survey was conducted in 2005 by *The Times* to see whether the introduction of co-ordinated admissions schemes under the EA 2002 had made any difference to the satisfaction of parental choice. The survey covered 112 LEAs and found a wide variation in parents' success rates.[424] The average was 87 per cent, but the success rate was much lower in several parts of London. It was as low as 57 per cent in Southwark and 59 per cent in Westminster; and in eight other London boroughs it varied between approx 65 per cent-75 per cent. These figures do not suggest a significant change in the capacity of the system to satisfy individual choice, particularly in the light of an average success rate of 68 per cent in London in a DFES study in 2001,[425] although there are no pre-co-ordination figures for these authorities to enable a true comparison to be made. They also confirm the pattern, noted by Gorard *et al*, that the rates are higher in rural areas than in metropolitan areas, although for most rural parents choice is very limited anyway.[426] Gorard *et al* are sceptical that, in many areas, the current admission process whereby parents express a preference has made any difference to the level of choice and that the significance may be merely symbolic.[427]

It has been suggested that even a conditional duty to accede to parental preference over choice of school enables individual rights to 'trump' wider social goals such as social integration or equity in entitlement.[428] While predicated upon a somewhat exaggerated view of the potency of rights of choice,[429] there is nonetheless evidence that the individualism expressed through the exercise of consumer choice in this context can give rise to social segregation and inequity. Indeed, individualism is associated with social class divisions, because of its tendency to favour those best placed as a result of their social position to exercise

---

[422] Pennell *et al*, n 318 above.

[423] Haddad, n 420 above, 13.

[424] S Kirkham, S Freeman and T Halpin, 'Distress of 70,000 children who must make do with second best', *The Times*, 5 Mar 2005.

[425] J Flatley *et al*, *Parents' Experiences of the Process of Choosing a Secondary School*, Research Report 278 (London, DfES, 2001).

[426] S Gorard, C Taylor and J Fitz, 'Does School Choice Lead to "Spirals of Decline"?' 17 *Journal of Education Policy* 367.

[427] Ibid.

[428] J Tweedie, 'Rights in Social Programmes: the Case of Parental Choice of School' [1986] *Public Law* 407; G Walford, *Choice and Equity in Education* (London, Cassell, 1994); S Ranson, 'From 1944 to 1988: Education, Citizenship and Democracy' in M Flude and M Hammer (eds), *The Education Reform Act 1988: Its Origins and Implications* (London, Falmer, 1990), 1.

[429] See, eg, M Adler, A Petch and J Tweedie, *Parental Choice and Educational Policy* (Edinburgh, Edinburgh University Press, 1989).

their rights and promote their own interests. In relation to competition for places at popular schools in desirable areas, better-off parents will enjoy an advantage. As the Plowden report observed over 30 years ago,[430] it is middle or professional class parents who assert their rights most forcefully.[431] Indeed, a report by the OECD found a similar picture in other industrialised nations[432] and a study in Sweden has noted a similar effect there.[433] Middle or professional class parents are more likely to possess the necessary cultural capital, and in particular, the knowledge, communication skills, professional contacts and financial resources, to assert their rights effectively and realise their goals with regard to choice. A Social Market Foundation report argues that 'effective school choice has become the preserve of the middle classes, who can afford to buy themselves into the catchment areas of the best schools';[434] the House of Commons Select Committee on Education and Skills found that house prices are often inflated in the catchment areas of the most popular schools. [435]

Some have expressed the clear belief that the overall effect of the market and competition in education is the stratification and segregation of children along social class lines.[436] The Swedish study found some evidence of this effect in urban areas.[437] But the segregation effect of school choice is challenged by the empirical evidence of research by Gorard. He says that even before the introduction of market-driven policies for school places, secondary schools were already socially stratified.[438] Indeed, there is evidence of that from Spain, where there is not an open competitive market in the English sense, but where socio-cultural factors influence school choice and tend to privilege the middle classes, with their greater resources and cultural capital.[439] Less advantaged groups tend to be concentrated in local state schools because they cannot afford to send their children to the best school further away or 'find the complexity of

---

[430] Lady Plowden (chairman), *Children and their Primary Schools, A Report of the Central Advisory Council for Education (England)* (London, HMSO, 1967), para 120.

[431] S Riddell, S Brown and J Duffield, 'Conflicts of Policies and Models—The Case of Specific Learning Difficulties' in S Riddell and S Brown (eds), *Special Educational Needs Policy in the 1990s* (London, Routledge, 1994) 119; and N Harris, *Special Educational Needs and Access to Justice* (Bristol, Jordans, 1997) 76. See also S Gewirtz *et al*, *Markets, Choice and Equity in Education* (Buckingham, Open University Press, 1995); and S Tomlinson, *Education in a Post-Welfare Society* (Buckingham. Open University Press, 2001).

[432] OECD, *School: A Matter of Choice* (Paris: OECD, 1994). See also D Hirsch, 'Policies for School Choice: What can Britain Learn from Abroad' in R Glatter *et al*, *Choice and Diversity in Schooling* (London, Routledge, 1997) 152.

[433] Swedish National Agency for Education, *School Choice and its Effects in Sweden* (Stockholm, Swedish National Agency for Education, 2003) 20.

[434] M Haddad (ed), *School Admissions* (London, Social Market Foundation, 2004) 11.

[435] House of Commons Education and Skills Committee, Fourth Report, Session 2003–04, *Secondary Education: School Admissions*, HC 58–1 (London, TSO, 2004), paras 98 and 99.

[436] Eg J Evans and C Vincent, 'Parental Choice and Special Education' in R Glatter *et al*, n 432 above, 102 at 107.

[437] Swedish National Agency for Education, *School Choice and its Effects in Sweden* (Stockholm, Swedish National Agency for Education, 2003).

[438] S Gorard, 'School Choice Policies: the Experience of England and Wales' in PJ Wolf and S Macedo (eds), *Educating Citizens. International Perspectives on Civic Values and School Choice* (Washington, DC, Brookings Institution Press, 2004) 131.

[439] JL Bernal, 'Parental Choice, Social Class and Market Forces: the Consequences of Privatization of Public Services in Education' (2005) 20 *Journal of Education Policy* 779.

choice too puzzling.[440] In England and Wales, where state education is more dominant and admission policies more elaborate, school choice policies may, according to Gorard, 'change the rules by which segregation takes place, but without markedly increasing or eliminating levels of segregation that are largely shaped by structural factors', namely 'the effects of pre-existing catchment areas and "selection by mortgage"'.[441] Gorard found no evidence that markets for education had increased segregation in terms of being associated with greater concentrations of disadvantaged children in particular schools. A crucial factor here must be the fact that choice is far more limited than government rhetoric, at least under the previous administration, would suggest. The Education and Skills Select Committee found that one form of selection, banding, which, as noted above, involves admitting pupils across the full range of abilities by, for example, establishing percentage quotas for different ability ranges, 'offers an important means of mitigating the effects of social segregation inherent in admissions based predominantly on geography'.[442]

Adler, Petch and Tweedie, researching the impact of the equivalent school choice legislation in Scotland,[443] found that because some parents in areas of multiple deprivation were able to send their children to schools in adjacent areas this left the schools they might otherwise have attended under-enrolled, thereby increasing the segregation of the pupils in those schools.[444] But such a phenomenon is also partly associated with migration of some families from poorer areas, which appears to reduce the effect of social segregation.[445] Jenkins *et al* have concluded that '[m]ost segregation in England is accounted for by the uneven spread of children from different social backgrounds within the state sector'.[446] The way that this can occur over time was well brought out by Davies in an investigation into the contrasting fortunes of two comprehensive schools in Sheffield, Abbeydale Grange, formed from grammar schools, and Silverdale, a former secondary modern school. Middle class families drifted away from Abbeydale Grange as its catchment area covered poorer areas of the city and its intake began to include increasing numbers of children from disadvantaged backgrounds, including ethnic minorities, while Silverdale (which had acquired a sixth form) was considered a 'safer bet' by (white) middle class families and its popularity with them grew, leading to declining numbers at the former school.[447]

---

[440] Ibid, 791.

[441] S Gorard, 'School Choice Policies and Social Integration: the Experience of England and Wales' in S Macedo and P Wolf (eds), *Educating Citizens. International Perspectives on Civic Values and School Choice* (Washington, DC, Brookings Institution Press, 2004) 134, at 143 and 150.

[442] House of Commons Education and Skills Committee, Fourth Report, Session 2003–04, *Secondary Education: School Admissions*, HC 58–1 (London, TSO, 2004), para 194.

[443] The Education (Scotland) Act 1981.

[444] M Adler, A Petch and J Tweedie, *Parental Choice and Educational Policy* (Edinburgh, Edinburgh University Press, 1989), at 215.

[445] L Simpson, 'Statistics of Racial Segregation: Measures, Evidence and Policy' (2004) 41 *Urban Studies* 661.

[446] S Jenkins, J Micklewright and SV Schnepf, *Social Segregation in Secondary Schools: How Does England Compare with Other Counties?*, ISER Working Paper 2006–2 (Colchester, University of Essex, 2006) 19.

[447] N Davies, 'Bias that killed the dream of equality. Schools in crisis part 2: How the system works against the poor', *The Guardian*, 15 Sept 1999.

Gorard concludes that school choice policies per se are not the most significant factor in segregation. As noted above, he argues that structural factors are more influential.[448] These might include factors such as social class but also housing patterns, although those patterns might in themselves be influenced by school admission arrangements. Noden, examining schools in the period from 1994 to 1999, found a steady increase in social segregation across secondary schools, a finding he regards as 'consistent with theories suggesting the dynamics of the educational quasi-market would lead to greater social segregation.'[449] While the evidence from these various studies does not entirely point in the same direction, the dominant conclusion seems to be that the legislation on school choice has probably reinforced social segregation.

As the Sheffield example above implies, school choice is also implicated in segregation in terms of race or ethnicity.[450] Hardy and Vieler-Porter, for example, suggest that rights of choice of school 'encourage and enable racist "white flight" from multiracial schools'.[451] The Netherlands is another country where school choice operates (albeit as an 'unwritten constitutional principle' rather than on a statutory basis, but without the fetter of catchment areas, which have been abolished) and where there is a substantial ethnic minority population in urban areas. There, not only do housing patterns have an influence on the make-up of schools, but so also does 'white flight, and the preference of large numbers of Moroccan and Turkish parents for public [ie, non-denominational] and Islamic schools in their neighbourhood that has led to segregation'.[452] The way that parental choice in England and Wales may be linked to ethnic segregation was highlighted in a report by the House of Commons Office of the Deputy Prime Minister Select Committee into the racial disturbances in the north of England in 2001: '[p]arental choice [of school] can unfortunately increase segregation . . . Some choices are motivated by ignorance and fear of other cultures . . .'[453] Thus, notwithstanding evidence showing that, in terms of place of residence, the actual extent of racial self-segregation as a whole in the UK is overstated and that

[448] S Gorard, 'School Choice Policies and Social Integration: The Experience of England and Wales', Memorandum to the Select Committee on Education and Skills, in House of Commons Education and Skills Committee, Fourth Report, Session 2003–04, *Secondary Education: School Admissions*, Vol. 2, HC 58–2 (London, TSO, 2004).

[449] P Noden, 'Rediscovering the Impact of Marketisation: Dimensions of Social Segregation in England's Secondary Schools, 1994–99' (2001) 21 *British Journal of Sociology of Education* 371, at 383.

[450] See, eg the Swedish study: Swedish National Agency for Education, *School Choice and its Effects in Sweden* (Stockholm, Swedish National Agency for Education, 2003). David observes that parental choice has been 'seen to take precedence over promoting racial or religious harmony': ME David, *Parents, Gender and Education Reform* (Cambridge, Polity, 1993) 135.

[451] J Hardy and C Vieler-Porter, 'Race, Schooling and The 1988 Education Reform Act' in M Flude and M Hammer (eds), *The Education Reform Act 1988. Its Origins and Implications* (London, Falmer, 1990) 173 at 178.

[452] B Vermeulen, 'Regulating School Choice to Promote Civic Values: Constituional and Political Issues in the Netherlands' in PJ Wolf and S Macedo (eds), *Educating Citizens. International Perspectives on Civic Values and School Choice* (Washington, DC, Brookings Institution Press, 2004) 31 at 58.

[453] Office of the Deputy Prime Minister Housing, Planning, Local Government and the Regions Committee, *Sixth Report, Session 2003–04, Social Cohesion*, Vol. 1, HC 45–I (London, TSO, 2004), para 55.

self-segregation is a 'myth',[454] there remains a clear view that school choice does reinforce separation along ethnic/cultural lines.

One of the starkest examples of 'white flight' was the highly publicised action by a group of 25 or so white parents in Dewsbury in 1988. They refused to send their children to the school allocated by the LEA because it had a high proportion of Asian children. Instead, arrangements were made for the children to be taught by a retired teacher in a room above a public house, before places were eventually found for them at other schools.[455] A few years after that, a white woman in Cleveland applied to her LEA to request her daughter's transfer to a different school, one that had a smaller proportion of Asian children, where the child would be less exposed to Pakistani culture. The LEA's decision to accede to the request was held by the Court of Appeal not to be contrary to the Race Relations Act 1976,[456] on the ground that the duty (then under section 6 of the Education Act 1980) to comply with parental preference when, as was the case here, the preferred school had available places, was mandatory.[457]

More recently, evidence has emerged of the racial polarity and segregation in schools resulting from the exercise of school choice in parts of the country, such as Oldham, Bradford and Calderdale, with large Asian populations. Ofsted reported in 2003 that in one authority in the north of England there was 'de facto segregation—out of 9 secondary schools only two or three could claim a real mix of pupils of different ethnic backgrounds within their intake . . . an increasing trend for parents of Asian heritage to send their children to independent Muslim faith schools, so entrenching . . . segregation'.[458] The authority's decision to press for such schools to receive voluntary aided status in order to become part of the LEA sector would not alter this ethnic segregation. Another report notes that some schools in such areas have an almost 100 per cent ethnic minority (such as Bangladeshi) intake.[459] This kind of effect has been widely observed in the United States, even though a policy of deliberate segregation has been unlawful since the Supreme Court ruled it unconstitutional in *Brown v Board of Education of Topeka*[460] 50 years ago.[461] In England and Wales, however, there is no such

[454] L Simpson, 'Statistics of Racial Segregation: Measures, Evidence and Policy' (2004) 41 *Urban Studies* 661 at 677.

[455] A Bradney, 'The Dewsbury Affair and the Education Reform Act 1988' (1989) 1 *Education and the Law* 51.

[456] In particular, s 18, which, in effect, proscribes racial discrimination by LEAs in the exercise of their functions under education legislation (apart from functions already covered by s 17 of this Act).

[457] As a result, s 41 of the 1976 Act, which provides exception to the non-discrimination duty where the act is carried out in furtherance of a statutory duty, applied: *R v Cleveland County Council ex parte the Commission for Racial Equality* [1994] ELR 44 (CA). See p 279 above and N Harris, 'Educational Choice in a Multi-cultural Society' [1992] *Public Law* 505. The court did not consider the mother to have been motivated by racism.

[458] Ofsted, *School Place Planning. The Influence of School Place Planning on School Standards and Social Inclusion*, HMI 587 (London, Ofsted, 2003) 23.

[459] Office of the Deputy Prime Minister Housing, Planning, Local Government and the Regions Committee, Sixth Report, Session 2003–04, *Social Cohesion*, Vol. 1, HC 45–I (London, TSO, 2004), paras 50 and 51, citing two schools with 100 per cent Bangladeshi intake and another that was '96 per cent Asian'. See also Community Cohesion Team (Chair T Cantle), *Community Cohesion. A Report of the Independent Review Team* (London, Home Office, 2001), para 4.9.

[460] 347 US 483 (1954).

[461] See pp 145–6 above.

modern history of segregating school pupils on racial or ethnic lines. Moreover, segregation in the form of a policy involving dispersal along ethnic minority lines would clearly be unlawful under the Race Relations Act 1976.[462] Racial quotas that might be needed for a dispersal policy would also fall foul of the ECHR.[463] In any event, there is evidence that parental choice has indirectly resulted in ethnic segregation across urban areas through the division of school populations on the basis of race or religion, which has been described as contributing to the erosion of the comprehensive school as a 'common school' that brings together all children of local communities regardless of social background.[464] Philips, citing figures showing that on average a white child in the US attends a school that is 78 per cent white, while on average a black child attends a school that is 57 per cent black, has expressed concern that schools in England might be 'heading for USA-style semi-voluntary segregation in the mainstream system', a cause of inequality of opportunity because schools attended by black children tend to offer a much poorer standard of education.[465]

In fact, in the US, measures to combat segregation were the subject of important litigation. In the 1960s the Supreme Court was on several occasions critical of the slow pace at which racial de-segregation of schools was occurring in the post-*Brown* era.[466] Measures adopted by many school boards included freedom of choice plans. In one of these cases, *Green v County School Board*, there were two county schools, one catering for black children and the other for white children. After a freedom of choice plan had been in operation for three years no white child had been sent to the black school, which approximately 85 per cent of black children still attended. The court disapproved of the freedom of choice plan.[467] Several other rulings stated that boards were under an explicit duty to bring dual school systems to an end and to desegregate without delay.[468] In *Swann v Charlotte-Mecklenburg Board of Education*,[469] the district was responsible for 100 schools the ethnic profile of whose pupil population was 71 per cent white and 29 per cent black. School admissions were mostly based around geographical zones, but school populations were largely segregated by race. Judge Macmillan approved a plan under which children would be bussed with a view to all schools reflecting the 71:29 ratio in the school population as far as possible. The district officials objected to aspects of the plan approved by the judge,

---

[462] See Commission for Racial Equality, *Secondary School Allocations in Reading—Report of a Formal Investigation* (London, CRE, 1983). See further Chap 4.

[463] A point made by BP Vermeulen and CW Noorlander, 'The Educational Rights of Students in the Netherlands' in C Russo and J De Groof, *The Legal Rights of Students* (Lanham, Md, Rowman and Littlefield, forthcoming) 129 at 141.

[464] T Haydn, 'The Strange Death of the Comprehensive School in England and Wales, 1965–2002' (2004) 19 *Research Papers in Education* 415 at 423.

[465] T Phillips, 'After 7/7: Sleepwalking to Segregation' speech at the Manchester Council for Community Relations, 22 Sept 2005, available at www.cre.gov.uk (accessed 23 Sept 2005).

[466] In particular, the implementation decision, generally known as '*Brown II*': *Brown v Board of Education*, 349 US 294 (1955).

[467] *Green v County School Bd*, 319 US 430 (1968); *Raney v Board of Education*, 391 US 443 (1968); and *Monroe v Board of Commissioners*, 391 US 450 (1968).

[468] See, in particular, *Alexander v Holmes Board of Education*, 396 US 19 (1969).

[469] 402 US 1 (1971).

including the numbers of children to be bussed and the cost of additional buses. The Supreme Court upheld the plan, noting that there was no equality 'in a system that has been deliberately constructed and maintained to enforce racial discrimination'.[470] However, the court held that if a particular school area was racially unitary it was not necessary for the racial mix to reflect that of the district as a whole and that, in any event, it was not forbidden for a few schools to be uniracial or virtually uniracial. The effect of *Swann* was 'the erasure of traditional attendance zones and the modification of the concept of the neighborhood school'.[471] In the subsequent case of *Keyes v School Dist. No.1, Denver, Colorado*, for example, where the complaint was that there was segregation in one part of the school system in Denver, to which the defence was that even if such segregation had occurred it did not mean that the entire school system was a dual one, the court acknowledged that there was no deliberately constructed dual system, but held that the policies, such as attendance zones, in some areas which had the effect of concentrating minorities there in particular schools 'may have a reciprocal effect on the racial composition of residential neighbourhoods within a metropolitan area, thereby causing further racial concentration within the schools'.[472] The court said that the arrangements in one part of a school district could only rarely be viewed in isolation. The board's policy in one area of Denver had knowingly created segregation, and thus the burden fell on the board to show that it had not intentionally ('purposefully') created a segregated system in the district.[473]

The litigation on segregation in the US continued,[474] but by the mid-1970s the Supreme Court was adopting a less interventionist stand in relation to desegregation. An example was the decision in *Dayton Board of Education v Brinkman*,[475] where the court accepted that, while there was de facto segregation, the school board had had no intention to segregate and there was therefore no compelling reason for the court to order it to desegregate. The court did not regard de facto segregation, as evidenced by the existence of predominantly black and predominantly white schools, as unconstitutional. In a number of lower level decisions in the US the courts have confirmed that there is no duty on school boards to correct racial imbalances in school intakes that have resulted from the interaction of housing patterns and school zones.[476] In one case, a court had ordered the relocation of many poor families in Yonkers to correct an imbalance caused by housing patterns, but this was overturned by an appellate court.[477] Running somewhat against the trend of judicial non-intervention is *Sheff v O'Neill*, where

[470] per Burger CJ.

[471] RS Vacca and HC Hudgins Jr, *The Legacy of the Burger Court and the School 1969–1986* (Topeka, Kan, NOLPE, 1991) 80.

[472] 413 US 189, per Brennan J.

[473] See also *Columbus Board of Education v Penick*, 443 US 449 (1979).

[474] See CJ Russo and CT Johnson, 'Brown v Board of Education at 50: Why Desegregation, Not Integration?' (2004) 5 *Education Law Journal* 224.

[475] 433 US 406 (1977).

[476] See generally CJ Russo, *Reutter's The Law of Public Education* (5th edn, New York, Foundation Press, 2004) 934.

[477] *US v Yonkers Board of Education*, 30 F Supp 2d 650 (SDNY, 1998).

the Supreme Court of Connecticut ordered the school board to desegregate regardless of the reasons for which segregation had occurred.[478]

Russo and Johnson report that the situation in the US as far as racial segregation among school pupils is concerned is that 'many locations . . . act as if *Brown* had never been decided, since judicial indifference, beginning with the Supreme Court, has sent out the unmistakeable signal that desegregation is no longer a priority'.[479] Many of the heavily segregated minority schools are in deprived areas and 'court-ordered desegregation did not prevent the continued residential isolation between white and non-white people . . . The bottom line is that schools remain largely segregated, highly unequal, and are becoming more so'.[480] If Philips is correct that parts of the schools system in England are drifting towards segregation along racial/ethnic lines, a phenomenon attributed to both school admission arrangements (particularly catchment areas) and the exercise of parental choice, it is likely that the courts will be no more able or willing to prevent it than the courts in the US have been in respect of segregation there. Nevertheless, Philips argues that there is a need for some form of intervention to prevent schools becoming mono-ethnic or mono-cultural, although not through the introduction of quotas,[481] nor through bussing, which he describes as a 'failed solution'.[482] He raises as possibilities the introduction of funding incentives to encourage a greater diversity of pupil intake; or that the Commission for Racial Equality, in monitoring local authorities' race equality schemes, should check whether school catchment areas are constructed in a way that encourages greater integration. Although there is evidence of a limited reduction, of late, in segregation in one of the worst affected areas, Oldham,[483] it is difficult to see how it can be reduced to a more significant extent without intervention of this kind.

Much of the segregation across the schools system in England and Wales is in fact religious, by virtue of parents' ability to select a denominational school. Although only a minority do so, there are still around 7,000 denominational schools, representing around one in three of all state schools.[484] A majority of denominational schools in the state sector have voluntary aided status;[485] as such, they constitute the admission authority for their school. As we have seen, these schools are free to give priority of admission to those from the religion in question.[486] Their admissions policies are therefore bound to result in

---

[478] 678 A 2d 1267 (Conn, 1996), cited in Russo and Johnson, n 474 above, at 232.

[479] N 474 above, at 231.

[480] Ibid, 232.

[481] That would run into legal difficulties anyway, as noted at pp 181 and 302 above.

[482] T Phillips, 'After 7/7: Sleepwalking to Segregation', speech at the Manchester Council for Community Relations, 22 Sept 2005, available at www.cre.gov.uk (accessed 23 Sept 2005).

[483] Institute of Community Cohesion, *Challenging Local Communities to Change Oldham* (Oldham and Coventry, Oldham MBC/Coventry University, 2006), 40, reporting that over the past few years the pupils in each of 6 primary schools have become less ethnically diverse, but in 14 secondary schools they have become more so.

[484] See p 6 above.

[485] Ibid.

[486] Eg, *Choudhury and Another v Governors of Bishop Challoner Roman Catholic Comprehensive School* [1992] 3 All ER 277; p 267 above.

segregation, although, in a recent survey of admissions in London, 46 per cent of voluntary aided schools were making specific mention of other faiths or another world faith in their admission criteria.[487] It might well be seen as irrational for them not to give priority to members of the faith in question. Nonetheless, the Government has said that such schools should be 'inclusive, and [we] welcome the recommendation that Church of England Schools should serve the whole community, not confining admission to Anglicans'.[488] At the same time, it rejected the idea of compulsion to admit those of another or no faith and especially of a quota of such children, although has since modified its position.[489] In Northern Ireland, there continues to be segregation along religious lines among the overwhelming majority of schools, with the overwhelming majority of Protestant children attending controlled schools and the vast majority of Roman Catholic children attending voluntary schools.[490] Only approximately 5 per cent of children attend integrated schools, which are required to have a balance in the representation of each of the two major religious communities of no worse than 30:70, with a similar balance in relation to the religious affiliations of teachers.[491] In effect there are 'two distinct education systems'.[492] No significant attempt has been made to alter the position, in part because it seems to be what most people want,[493] although a major barrier to reform at present seems to be that a superfluity of school places in the system renders the introduction of new integrated schools inefficient in economic terms.[494] So, instead, the emphasis seems to be on 'separate but equal' provision: Lundy explains that the state has been 'anxious to ensure that those attending each system are receiving an equally good education', because it has recognised that the education system has a pivotal role to play in helping to ensure political stability.[495]

It is clear that if faith schools exist, parents must have the right of selecting them, particularly where they form part of the state-funded system of education (as we saw in Chapter 3, even voluntary aided schools receive most of their funding from the state). However, concerns about the way in which faith schools accentuate social segregation have led to calls for their abolition or that of the right to give preference in admission along religious lines. For example, the chair

---

[487] Pennell *et al*, n 318 above, at 7.

[488] Department for Education and Skills, *Schools: Achieving Success* Cm5230 (London, TSO, 2001), para 5.31.

[489] House of Commons Education and Skills Committee, Session 2001–02, Minutes of Evidence, 14 Nov 2001, HC 304–iii (London, TSO, 2002) QQ 228–230. See p 317 below.

[490] L Lundy, 'Education Law under Devolution: the Case of Northern Ireland' (2000) 1 *Education Law Journal* 81. Lundy considers the potential impact of the Northern Ireland Act 1998, s 75, which provides, inter alia, that public authorities must promote equality of opportunity among persons of different religious belief.

[491] O Boycott, '"What message is this sending?"', *The Guardian (Education)*, 28 Mar 2006, 5.

[492] L Lundy, 'From Act to Order: The Metamorphosis of Education Legislation' (1998) XXI *Liverpool Law Rev* 63 at 91.

[493] Even among 16-year-olds, only 48 per cent (but only 38 per cent of those from the Catholic community) were found to favour mixed-religion schools in a survey by researchers at Queen's University Belfast: P Devine and D Schubotz, 'Us and Them?' (ARK Research Update, 2004), available only at www.ark.ac.uk.

[494] See O Boycott, n 491 above.

[495] L Lundy, n 492 above, at 91.

of the Education Select Committee, Barry Sheerman, was quoted as saying recently: '[d]o we want a ghettoised education system? . . . Schools place a crucial role in integrating different communities and the growth of faith schools poses a real threat to this . . .'[496] Similarly, one of the teaching unions has recently voted in favour of ending state funding for faith schools by 2020, in order to promote integration.[497] It has been observed in the Netherlands, where, as noted above, a similar pattern of segregation to that in the UK has emerged, that Islamic schools attract children of parents who tend to be less well integrated into mainstream Dutch society.[498] Also of concern to some[499] is the effect of religious preference in limiting parental choice for those who do not have, or cannot demonstrate, a particular religious affiliation.[500] As we have seen, the way in which religious preference works in practice is that schools end up selecting the pupils. The Social Market Foundation has argued that faith schools should continue but should not be allowed to operate a religious preference. Their view is that '[p]arents choosing schools on grounds of religion is deemed acceptable—and there is a liberal argument the parents should be able to choose a religious education for their children if they so desire—whereas schools choosing parents on religious grounds is not'.[501] However, notwithstanding the wider mix that exists in some denominational schools and the Government's encouragement to faith schools to admit those of other faiths, it would be unworkable to remove any religious criterion from admission arrangements without threatening to undermine the character and indeed the purpose of these schools.

One controversial issue relating to the admissions process in denominational schools has been interviewing. Denominational schools generally want to ascertain the parents' and child's religious commitment and their sympathy with the ethos and ideals of the school, factors that may be incorporated within the admission criteria. Such was the case with regard to the London Oratory School, where the governors decided to retain an interview system in order properly to assess the applicant parents' and their child's 'catholicity, practice and commitment and whether the aims, attitudes, values and expectations of the parents and the boy are in harmony with those of the school'. Objectors asserted that retention of the interview was in conflict with the DfES's *School Admissions Code of Practice*, and the adjudicator agreed. The *School Admissions Code of Practice* stated that 'for the admissions round leading to September 2005 intakes

---

[496] M Taylor, 'Two thirds oppose state aided faith schools', *The Guardian*, 23 Aug 2005, 1.

[497] A Blair, 'Teachers demand end to state cash for faith schools', *The Times*, 12 Apr 2006, 28. The union concerned is the Association of Teachers and Lecturers.

[498] AB Dijkstra, J Dronkers, and S Karsten, 'Private Schools as Public Provision for Education: School Choice and Market Forces in the Netherlands' in PJ Wolf and S Macedo (eds), *Educating Citizens. International Perspectives on Civic Values and School Choice* (Washington, DC, Brookings Institution Press, 2004), 67–90, at 72.

[499] See, eg, F Millar, 'What's the big secret on school choice?', *The Guardian, Education Guardian*, 20 Sept 2005, 4.

[500] Beckett comments that it is often the case that, in order to secure a place in a good denominational school, 'ordinarily truthful people, as their child reaches the age of 11, get religion all of a sudden. You see them hanging round the local church or synagogue, pathetically trying to look as though they've been there every week of their lives': F Beckett, 'We should abolish faith schools—they breed tolerance and isolation', *The Guardian, Guardian Education*, 14 Oct 2003, 5.

[501] M Haddad (ed), *School Admissions* (London, Social Market Foundation, 2004) 25.

and subsequent admissions, no parents or children should be interviewed as any part of the application or admission process', apart from in relation to a boarding school.[502] In the case of the London Oratory, the governors opted to retain the interview process, notwithstanding the code's advice, on the basis that without it 'the school could not properly and fairly test its admission criteria in respect of religious practice' and that parents were felt to have a 'right . . . to an opportunity to represent at interview how they meet the admission criteria and their commitment to their faith, the Church, Catholic education and the ethos of the school'.[503]

Three parents and the school governors of a primary school brought a legal challenge to the adjudicator's ruling, on various grounds.[504] Jackson J said that the statute merely required regard to be had to the guidance and that it was 'perfectly possible to have regard to a provision but not follow that provision in a particular situation'.[505] Moreover, the adjudicator had failed to take account of the arguments put forward by the school. The adjudicator had also criticised the use of questions about the Ten Commandments or the Scriptures, which she found to test knowledge that went beyond catholicity, but the court found that view to be *Wednesbury* unreasonable.[506] The court also rejected the adjudicator's objection to the interview guidance notes. The three parent complainants argued that the removal of the interviewing process made it more difficult for appropriate candidates to secure places at the school, therefore infringing the rights of Catholic families, and that existing pupils would suffer because the ethos of the school would change as pupils with a lesser commitment to the Catholic faith were admitted to it. The legal basis to this complaint centred upon the ECHR, A2P1.[507] Jackson J held that the parents did have a right to secure education for their children at schools which conformed to the Catholic faith (a view that is perhaps questionable in the light of the Strasbourg jurisprudence[508] but was not fully assessed by the judge), but that that did not mean they had a right to be educated at the London Oratory School specifically. He also rejected the argument that the right under the Article was infringed by any change brought about by differences in the school's intake, since the school 'would remain a Catholic school'.[509] Nonetheless, as noted above, the adjudicator's decision to end the school's use of interviews failed. The London Oratory is, however, the only day school in England that is openly using interviews for the purposes of selection, and the objectors have now asked the Secretary of State for Education and Skills to use her powers to direct the governors to discontinue the

---

[502] DfES, *School Admissions Code of Practice*, DfES/0031/2005 (London, DfES, 2003).

[503] Taken from the governors' minutes, as cited in Jackson J's judgment in *Governing Body of The London Oratory School; Adams; Goodliffe; and Lindsay v The Schools Adjudicator* [2005] ELR 162, at para 22.

[504] Ibid.

[505] Ibid, at para 40.

[506] Ibid, at para 52.

[507] Providing, inter alia, for respect for the right to education on the basis of parents' religious convictions. See p 67 above.

[508] See, in particular, the discussion of the *Belgian Linguistics* case in Chap 2.

[509] N 503 at para 59.

practice.[510] It has been argued that documentary evidence of faith commitment, such as a letter from a member of the clergy, could easily be obtained and used instead.[511] The fact that interviewing is discouraged by the code of practice but there is no legal ban on it was regretted by the House of Commons Select Committee.[512] It contends that interviewing by schools 'is the easiest way that a school can make sure it chooses "people like us"'.[513] It wants regulations to ban interviewing and, indeed, 'other proxies for academic selection' and calls for the entire admissions process to be anonymised.[514] The Government has rejected the latter proposal, primarily because of the costs in adapting local authority and school IT systems and because it would present difficulties where admission policies used sibling criteria.[515] However, a ban on interviewing parents or children for the purposes of admission is being introduced, via the Education and Inspections Bill 2006.[516]

The concern about interviewing procedure such as that by the London Oratory School is thus that attributes not directly related to a person's catholicity may be taken into account. There may be covert selection, for example on the basis of social class or academic ability, a problem that can also arise from the standard scrutiny of parents' written reasons for admission.[517] Specifically referred to by the adjudicator in the case of the London Oratory were the communication or reasoning skills of parents or guardians or the child him/herself. This form of 'covert selection' is likely in schools operating their own admission policy, such as voluntary aided schools.[518] The fear is that the system may be biased in favour of more articulate or intelligent applicants when the school's admission criteria do not provide for selection on that basis. As the House of Commons Select Committee on Education and Skills has stated, the rationale for preventing interviews is that the interview process enables 'judgements to be made about the child's prior attainment as well as the family's social class, educational and professional background and level of support for their child's schooling'.[519] The result is 'a form of selection on grounds of attainment'. [520] The Committee cited evidence that the academic gap between secondary schools with a high proportion of pupils from economically

---

[510] L Lightfoot, 'New row over selection at Blair children's school', *Daily Telegraph*, 19 Oct 2005, 5.

[511] Ibid.

[512] N 442 above, para 89.

[513] House of Commons Education and Skills Committee, First Report, Session 2005–06, *The Schools White Paper: 'Higher Standards, Better Schools for All'*, HC 633–I (London, TSO, 2006), para 127.

[514] Ibid, paras 96, 113 and 127.

[515] Secretary of State for Education and Skills, *The Government's Response to the House of Commons Education and Skills Committee Report: The Schools White Paper: Higher Standards, Better Schools for All*, Cm 6747 (London, TSO, 2006) 18.

[516] Cl 40, inserting new s 88A into the SSFA 1998.

[517] A West et al, 'School Admissions: Increasing Equity, Accountability and Transparency' (1999) 46 *British Journal of Educational Studies* 188, at 193–4 and 197; Pennell et al, n 318 above, 22.

[518] A West and H Pennell, 'Changing Admissions Policies and Practices in Inner London' in R Glatter et al, *Choice and Diversity in Schooling* (London, Routledge, 1997) 186.

[519] House of Commons Education and Skills Committee, Fourth Report, Session 2003–04, *Secondary Education: School Admissions*, HC 58–1 (London, TSO, 2004), para 87.

[520] Ibid.

disadvantaged backgrounds in year 7 (the year into which most pupils are admitted, aged 11) and other schools widens as children get older. The Sutton Trust has argued that the fact that 85 per cent of the top comprehensives (in terms of pupils' attainment of A*–C grades at GCSE) are in postcode areas with higher proportions of children receiving free school meals than is the case among the schools' pupils may be attributable to forms of selection employed by schools, such as interviewing prospective parents and pupils.[521]

The Select Committee also highlighted the fact that the code of practice does not apply to the specialist city technology colleges (CTCs), which use 'structured discussions' in their admissions process. The Committee stated that there was just as great a risk of bias in that process as with interviews. The rationale for the discussions was to ensure that the colleges conform to their funding arrangements by ensuing that among the pupils admitted are a certain number who are most likely to benefit from the education provided by the school. Both CTCs and academies are required to provide education 'for pupils of different abilities' (which is not the same thing as catering for *all* abilities), but are expected to place an emphasis on a particular subject area or on particular subject areas.[522] But, as noted above, academies are required by their funding agreements to follow the code. The Select Committee found that there was no material difference between interviews and structured discussions and that the exclusion of CTCs from the code of practice was inappropriate.[523]

One of the most controversial issues of educational policy in relation to state secondary schools is selection of pupils by ability. There are similar concerns about the socially divisive effects of both selection by ability and selection by aptitude, not least because (as noted above) these two bases for selection are inter-related: for example, the Education and Skills Select Committee reported that it had not 'been made aware of any means by which aptitude can be assessed without reference to ability'.[524] There are long-standing objections both to the principle of selection and its practical effects. The principal concern is that it reinforces social exclusion among those from disadvantaged backgrounds, who will struggle to compete with others for schooling of a kind that better guarantees academic success and thus greater opportunities in life. As we saw in Chapter 1, there is a clear relationship between social class and/or ethnic background and levels of attainment.[525] Selection also increases segregation of pupils and '[i]f children's performance at school depends upon their peers, higher levels of social segregation lead to greater inequality of academic achievement and thence to greater inequality in later-life outcomes'.[526]

---

[521] The Sutton Trust, *Rates of Eligibility for Free School Meals at the Top State Schools* (London, Sutton Trust, 2005), available at www.suttontrust.com/news.asp#a022.

[522] EA 1996, s 482(2), as substituted by the EA 2002, s 65.

[523] Ibid, paras 93–95.

[524] House of Commons Education and Skills Committee, Fourth Report, Session 2002–03, *Secondary Education: Diversity of Provision*, HC 94 (London, TSO, 2003), paras 200 and 201.

[525] See, generally, M Cole (ed), *Education, Equality and Human Rights* (London, Routledge Falmer, 2000).

[526] S Jenkins, J Micklewright and SV, Schnepf, *Social Segregation in Secondary Schools: How Does England Compare with Other Counties?*, ISER Working Paper 2006–2 (Colchester, University of Essex, 2006) 1.

Given the absence of formal selection in relation to most primary school admissions and the limited role it plays in secondary schools, much of the traditional concern about elitism and the reinforcement of social class divisions remains focused on independent schools. There is no indication that any of the major political parties would seek to abolish independent schools, and in any event it would probably run counter to the ECHR to do so.[527] Moreover, social segregation is considered to be driven more by what happens in the state secondary school sector than from the existence of private schools.[528] Selection is considered to increase such segregation by concentrating those from more affluent backgrounds, notwithstanding the argument that grammar schools enhance social mobility for academically able children from poorer families. As we have seen, while the Labour government has no plans to abolish grammar schools it will not permit any new schools to select pupils wholly on the basis of ability or aptitude. The Social Market Foundation has argued that '[t]he immediate removal of grammar schools would encourage flight into the private sector'.[529] If that is true, then retention of a system whereby, as the Government admits, 'schools cherry-pick pupils at the expense of parental choice and other schools',[530] may be the lesser of two evils. The argument that grammar schools can hold the key to social mobility for some children from poorer backgrounds runs into the argument that proportionately fewer children from such backgrounds than others can demonstrate the requisite level of ability when the admissions tests are carried out.

Selective schools, including those in the private sector, remain popular because of their academic record and ethos and their character, particularly the perception that they emphasise 'traditional values'. Despite the post-1997 freeze on new selective state schools, the proportion of the secondary age group attending grammar schools increased from 3.1 per cent to 4.6 per cent between 1983–4 and 2003–4.[531] Their very positive attributes have been acknowledged by the Labour Government; but as expansion of selection would create political and ideological difficulties, it has sought instead to fashion an acceptable alternative in the state sector, the 'independent specialist school', noted above. These schools will be modelled on grammar schools or those in the private sector, but the idea is that they will eschew elitism:

> Independent specialist schools will have all the freedom needed to succeed in the service of their pupils and communities. They will set the highest expectations for their students and teachers, and put in place the means to achieve them. But they will do so within a system of fair admissions and equality of opportunity for all young people and their families. Our conception of independence is of freedom to achieve for all, not a free-for-all in which more state schools are allowed to ban less able children from

---

[527] See p 74 n 274 above.

[528] See Jenkins, Micklewright and Schnepf, n 526 above, 2.

[529] M Haddad (ed), *School Admissions* (London, Social Market Foundation, 2004) 25.

[530] DfES, *Department for Education and Skills: Five Year Strategy for Teachers and Learners*, Cm 6272 (London, TSO, 2004), ch 4, para 21.

[531] House of Commons Education and Skills Committee, Fourth Report, Session 2002–03, *Secondary Education: Diversity of Provision*, HC 94 (London, TSO, 2003), para 208.

applying and turn themselves into elite institutions for the few. Independence, in our policy, will create far more good local schools from which parents can choose; it is not a means for successful schools to start choosing only the brightest children to teach.[532]

As we have seen, the assumption is that most if not all secondary schools will in due course acquire specialist status. Whilst selection is seen as detrimental to parental choice, specialist status will be expected to enhance it. However, although specialist status will not automatically give a right to select pupils on the basis of their aptitude, permission could be sought for up to 10 per cent of the intake to be selected on the basis of aptitude for a prescribed subject area, as noted above. The evidence concerning the first specialist schools is that the presence of those which have partially selective intakes and control their own admissions tends to result in greater social segregation, as the school's ability to attract the most able and socially advantaged pupils is enhanced.[533]

On the other hand, by catering for pupils' specific educational interests, the inclusion of specialist schools in the education system can not only help to ensure that schools more effectively aid the fulfilment by LEAs of their duty to ensure provision which is suitable in the light of children's 'different ages, abilities and aptitudes',[534] but also contribute to the state's potential to deliver on its commitment under the UN Convention on the Rights of the Child to educate each child in a way which develops his or her 'talents and mental and physical abilities to their fullest potential'.[535] A legitimate question to ask, however, is whether children selected on the basis of their aptitude are guaranteed the level of specialist provision that they may need if their particular talents are to be fully realised. Ofsted has reported that in general the overall quality of teaching in specialist schools is better than in non-specialist schools.[536] But only at key stage 4, where most pupils are offered suitable specialist subjects, has there been any real improvement in the years from 2001.[537] Overall, the report indicates that specialist status has helped to generate a positive ethos and raise achievement levels among most pupils. But the report also found that provision for gifted pupils was 'unsatisfactory' in one in five schools and that too few schools—fewer than one in six—had proper strategies to avoid disaffection among pupils.[538] Specialisation always raises concerns about elitism and exclusivity, and some of these findings suggest that further work will be necessary if the schools are to operate in a fully inclusive way.[539]

Specialist schools contribute to the quasi-market for education based on choice and competition and its tendency to cause a hierarchical schools system.

---

[532] N 530 above, para 9.

[533] S Gorard and C Taylor, 'The Composition of Specialist Schools in England: Track Record and Future Prospect' (2001) 21 *School Leadership and Management* 365.

[534] Education Act 1996, s 14(3)(a).

[535] Art 29(1)(a).

[536] Ofsted, *Specialist Schools: a Second Evaluation*, HMI 2362 (London, Ofsted, 2005), table 4.

[537] Ibid, para 21.

[538] Ibid, paras 58 and 60.

[539] Ibid, para 53.

Schools that are academically successful and have few discipline problems will be at the top of the hierarchy, and their popularity will generate additional resources because of the role of pupil numbers in funding allocations.[540] Less popular schools with falling rolls will lose resources.[541] Indeed, one English council, Reading, applied for judicial review to quash appeal decisions in favour of a group of parents because the authority was left with empty school desks elsewhere in the borough.[542] Research in Scotland appears to have shown the emergence of 'a two-tier system of secondary schooling in the big cities', with a 'small number of rump schools located in the most deprived areas' where rolls have fallen.[543] A spiral of decline is said to occur, whereby certain schools gain a reputation as 'sink' schools and the morale of their staff and pupils suffers in consequence, with growing educational underachievement and worsening recruitment and social problems.[544] The existence of a spiral of decline as a result of market forces has, however, been questioned by Gorard *et al*, who found that from 1989 to 1999 schools' pupil numbers more or less across the system were maintained, indeed grew, partly as a result of amalgamations and closures, while (as noted earlier) there was no evidence of certain schools having an increasingly disadvantaged intake of pupils.[545] It has nevertheless been argued that a policy of enabling popular and successful schools to expand, as the Government currently seems keen to introduce, 'may make matters worse for the remaining unpopular schools. Further descent into the spiral of decline may be accelerated, as the school becomes less viable'.[546]

But the greatest concern at present is how the interaction of school admission policies and parental choice makes a contribution to social segregation, whether in terms of social class, ethnicity or religion. Glenn argues that opponents of the notion of choice will find it easier to accept segregation when it is caused by factors such as academic selection as opposed simply to individual parental choices.[547] Indeed, concern over the social divisions reinforced by selective education has been displaced by those over the segregating effects of

---

[540] See T Edwards and G Whitty, 'Marketing Quality: Traditional and Modern Versions of Educational Excellence' in R Glatter *et al*, *Choice and Diversity in Schooling. Perspectives and Prospects* (London, Routledge, 1997) 29; and C Parsons and PJ Welsh, 'Public Sector Policies and Practice, Neo-liberal Consumerism and Freedom of Choice in Secondary Education: a Case Study of One Area in Kent' (2006) 36 *Cambridge Journal of Education* 237.

[541] G Whitty, S Power and D Halpin, *Devolution and Choice in Education: The School, the State and the Market* (Buckingham, Open University Press, 1998).

[542] D Charter, 'We are fighting for the right to a good, local education', *The Times*, 15 Aug 2005. See also *R (Reading Borough Council) v Admissions Appeal Panel for Reading Borough Council and 15 Parents* [2006] ELR 186 (QBD).

[543] M Adler, *An Alternative Approach to Parental Choice* Briefing No13, (London, National Commission on Education, 1993) 3.

[544] B Jordan, *A Theory of Poverty and Social Exclusion* (Cambridge, Polity Press, 1996) 138.

[545] S Gorard, C Taylor and J Fitz, 'Does School Choice Lead to "Spirals of Decline"?' (2002) 17 *Journal of Education Policy* 367.

[546] Ofsted, *School Place Planning. The Influence of School Place Planning on School Standards and Social Inclusion*, HMI 587 (London, Ofsted, 2003), para 56.

[547] C Glenn, 'School Choice as a Question of Design' in P J Wolf and S Macedo (eds), *Educating Citizens. International Perspectives on Civic Values and School Choice* (Washington, DC, Brookings Institution Press, 2004) 339 at 347.

denominational schools,[548] whilst the legitimacy of admissions catchment areas is debated mostly in connection with their effects in limiting choice, and at the same time discriminating in favour of '[m]ore affluent parents [who] are prepared and can afford to transport their children to alternative schools outside their immediate area'.[549] These are factors that the Government says it wants to see ameliorated by the greater use of banding arrangements[550] and through extended transport rights,[551] while at the same time recognising that 'for many schools traditional catchment areas will be the most appropriate option'.[552] Thus while there is a degree of policy emphasis on extending school choice by enhancing the options of the weakest consumers, the segregating effects of school admission systems are unlikely to be greatly diminished.

CONCLUSION

School choice in law began as a means of recognising, at a time when society was less secularised and many people still defined themselves primarily by their religion, that many parents wanted their child's schooling to reinforce their association with a particular religious tradition and faith group. The introduction of a legislative framework for school choice in the early 1980s did not in itself alter the basis on which parents could select or be allocated places in denominational schools. We saw in the cases in Lancashire, for example, that precisely the same system for allocating secondary school places to Roman Catholic primary school children operated there as that introduced in Birkenhead in the early 1970s. What the introduction of a market did, however, do was to raise the stakes for parents in exercising their choices, making denominational schools with good academic and discipline records particularly popular. How else can one explain the huge demand for places at so many Church of England and Roman Catholic schools when church attendances are at an all time low?

The admission process forces parents to exercise their judgement and make a

[548] However, although many of these schools control their own admissions, research cited by the Government has concluded that there is a low correlation between segregation and the percentage of pupils in an area who attend schools which control their own admissions: Secretary of State for Education and Skills, *The Government's Response to the House of Commons Education and Skills Committee Report: The Schools White Paper: Higher Standards, Better Schools for All*, Cm 6747 (London, TSO, 2006), Annex B, 25.

[549] Ofsted, n 546 above, para 52.

[550] As noted above, these involve quotas for pupils of different ability levels to ensure that the intake as a whole is representative of the full range of abilities nationally or locally. The White Paper states the intention to making it easier for schools to introduce banding and suggests that banding could be combined with the use of 'inner and outer catchment areas' which would 'give priority for some places to those living further away from the school': DfES, *Higher Standards, Better Schools for All*, Cm 6677 (London, TSO, 2005), para 3.24.

[551] See p 274 above.

[552] N 408 above, para 3.24.

decision, even if they decide simply to accept the school at which their child is likely to be guaranteed a place under the authority's admissions scheme. Parents have the pressure of knowing that whatever decision they make will have an important bearing on the future social and educational development of their child. A range of statutorily prescribed data on schools and their performance must be made available to them, even though many parents are influenced by wider factors such as the school's local reputation, the impression gained during an open day visit or their child's expressed desire to attend the same school as his or her friends. Against a policy of making the education system more diverse, for example through specialist schools and urban academies, the widening of potential choices makes the decision appear to be of even greater consequence. Some parents will, of course, exercise their choice outside the state system, whether in independent schools or through the education of their children at home. Either way, the message conveyed by the school admissions system, its statutory framework and the Government's policy of diversification of schools is that parents have a moral responsibility to exercise choice over their child's school. It is now regarded as a decision of great importance. As Garnett argues, '[c]hoice in education . . . can . . . be seen as a crucial aspect of parents' responsibility . . . the formation of their children'.[553] Indeed, that mounting sense of responsibility and the risk of making a bad decision appear to have been factors in the growth of home schooling in Canada.[554]

Today, the right to a degree of choice over one's child's school that the Education Act 1980 heralded is so firmly embedded that, in political terms, it is seemingly irremovable. Freedom to choose is a basic libertarian value, yet, as we have seen, for a variety of reasons parents are able to enjoy not so much a right of choice but rather a right to express a preference. It is the right to engage in the process of selection rather than a right to satisfaction of one's preference, even though it appears that parental choice of school in England is high by international standards.[555] The exercise of choice nevertheless represents a form of engagement with the education system that chimes with notions of participatory citizenship and 'empowerment' that, in recent years, government policies have been keen to emphasise. Yet, as noted in Chapter 2, when discussing the enjoyment of social rights, there are dangers in assuming that all groups can avail themselves of the opportunities that rights in education such as those concerned with choice of school seem to offer them. The equity principle that underpins the notion of choice as a universal right is undermined by the very social inequality that it seeks to counter. Those for whom English is a second language, for example, face particular difficulties in articulating their reasons in support of

---

[553] RW Garnett, 'Regulatory Strings and Religious Freedom: Requiring Private Schools to Promote Public Values' in P J Wolf and S Macedo (eds), *Educating Citizens. International Perpsctives on Civic Values and School Choice* (Washington, DC, Brookings Institution Press, 2004) 324 at 325.

[554] J Aurini and S Davies, 'Choice Without Markets: Homeschooling in the Context of Private Education', (2005) 26 *British Journal of Sociology of Education* 461.

[555] See S Jenkins, J Micklewright and SV Schnepf, *Social Segregation in Secondary Schools: How Does England Compare with Other Counties?*, ISER Working Paper 2006–2 (Colchester, University of Essex, 2006).

their parental preference.[556] Moreover, geographical factors and religious affiliation that both continue to play a large role in school admissions privilege some on the basis of class, race or religion. As Evan Harris MP, in speaking to the School Admissions (Prohibition of Religious Discrimination) Bill, his Private Member's Bill, said, 'Why should a child be punished by being prevented from attending a school, which they would otherwise have an opportunity to go to, on the basis of the views or culture of his or her parents? Why should the child be denied fair treatment in school admissions?'[557] The point about choice is that, while all can express their wish for it, in practice some within a culturally, racially and religiously diverse society will have far greater prospects of realising their choice than others. The other problem with choice, as we have seen, is that it reinforces social divisions, with disproportionately more middle class children going to the highest achieving schools (particularly in the case of selective schools) in the more well heeled districts, whilst in some areas a form of ethnic segregation has occurred through school selection influenced by racial considerations. Parental choice also contributes to inequality among schools, as the competitive market for schooling ensures that less popular schools struggle to maintain academic standards.

Could the UK learn lessons from France in the way that choice operates? Of course, there are no denominational schools within the state system there. It is considered that, for pupils, 'the concrete experience of diversity is the best way to learn that other cultures and faiths exist and have value' (although, at the same time, cultural symbols such as forms of religious dress are banned in schools.[558]) Meuret reports that there have been experiments with choice in France, but it has been found that, by virtue of its 'segregating effects', competition harms equality of opportunity.[559] It was therefore decided that parents would not be placed under an obligation to choose, in that they could accept the school allocated, usually on the basis of the *carte scolaire* (catchment area), or seek an exception. Meuret argues that, in making choice 'optional' in this way, there is a 'risk that choice will tend to be exercised mainly by an elite of "skilled choosers" rather than parents as a whole'.[560] There appear to be cultural barriers to the exercise of choice of school in France, as only one in 10 parents currently exercises it. Indeed, Meuert reports that most parents regard the exercise of school choice as embarrassing, hence the notion of 'hidden choice'.[561] He says that some parents choose their schools through their choice of housing or by 'cheating on the *carte scolaire*'.[562]

Inherently, then, rights of choice of school are likely to be enjoyed unequally

---

[556] A West and H Pennell, 'Changing Admissions Policies and Practices in Inner London' in R Glatter *et al, Choice and Diversity in Schooling* (London, Routledge, 1997) 186.

[557] HC Debs, Vol 418, Col 285, 25 Feb 2004.

[558] D Meuret, 'School Choice and its Regulation in France' in PJ Wolf and S Macedo (eds), *Educating Citizens. International Perspectives on Civic Values and School Choice* (Washington, DC, Brookings Institution Press, 2004) 238 at 257.

[559] Ibid, 258.

[560] Ibid.

[561] Ibid, 261.

[562] Ibid, 262.

across society and to create social barriers through the de facto segregation that tends to result from their exercise, and in some cases from a 'strategic withdrawal of the middle classes' from some schools.[563] Given the absence of clear evidence that competition has a marked impact in terms of raising school standards within the state sector,[564] we are left merely with the libertarian argument for choice, which encompasses the right of parents to guide their children's education (for which there is also the utilitarian argument that, because parents know their children best, children's education may more suitable as a result), although, as we have seen, this quickly becomes, in addition, a responsibility in a system based on the universal expression of choice. On the other hand, if admissions systems can be regulated in a way that promotes wider social purposes, such as better integration—for example, by expanding choice so that denominational schools might have to accept members of other faiths or of no faith, or by adopting banding systems so that the intake of all schools is representative of local communities—choice could be a force for greater social cohesion. Indeed, the House of Commons Education Committee has recommended that a duty should be placed upon schools 'to promote social inclusion and community cohesion through all of their institutional policies and procedures, including their admission policies'; and the 2006 Bill now partly effects this.[565]

As noted above, the Select Committee has also recommended that, in relation to secondary school admissions, local authorities should set benchmarks for the numbers of children in receipt of free school meals or whose families are in receipt of tax credits that are admitted in year 7 (age 11) in any year, backed by possible sanctions for those who fail to address the matter.[566] The Government has rejected this proposal, although the local admission forum is to be given a power to report if a school has disproportionately few pupils on free school meals.[567] It might, however, have been a more politically acceptable means to widening intakes than a more directly enforced integration. The Government has also proposed, in the skeleton admissions code shown to the Standing Committee on the Education and Inspections Bill, that admission authorities should 'analyse information about their intakes, and where possible their applicants, to find out whether they attract a wide range of families or whether their school fails to attract all sections of local communities'.[568] However, care would clearly be needed to ensure that any changes to admission arrangements aimed at widening intakes by attracting more members of ethnic or religious minorities do not conflict with anti-discrimination law.[569] Moreover, as noted in

---

[563] G Whitty, *Making Sense of Education Policy* (London, Paul Chapman, 2005) 122.

[564] See S Gorard and C Taylor, 'Market Forces and Standards in Education: a Preliminary Consideration' (2002) 23 *British Journal of Sociology of Education* 5.

[565] House of Commons Education and Skills Committee, First Report, Session 2005–06, *The Schools White Paper: 'Higher Standards, Better Schools for All'*, HC 633–I (London, TSO, 2006), para 85. The amended Bill requires the governors to 'promote community cohesion'.

[566] Ibid, para 141.

[567] P Wintour, 'Blair's school concessions win over leading rebels', *The Guardian*, 7 Feb 2006, 2.

[568] House of Commons, Official Report, Standing Committee E, Education and Inspections Bill, 14th sitting, 2 May 2006, col 608, Mr N Gibb MP. See also D Charter, 'Schools face new rules to balance ethnic mixture', *The Times*, 4 May 2006, 11.

[569] See the discussion of positive discrimination in Chap 4.

Chapter 2, there are strong arguments based around human rights and the preservation of cultural autonomy among particular faith groups that could present difficulties if there were an attempt to enforce wider religious representation among intakes to denominational schools. They are arguments that could have been pressed if the Government had proceeded with its announced plan that local authorities or the Secretary of State should be empowered to prescribe for up to 25% of admissions to new faith schools to be of children from other faiths or no faith (the Church of England having previously announced such a proportion of non-Church of England children in the case of admissions to any of its new schools). But, leaving aside these problems, clearly official acknowledgement that rights of choice currently operate in an exclusionary way is growing. Indeed, shortly before this book went to press the Government published for consultation the new draft code of practice, which aims to ensure an admissions system that is based on the principle of 'equity and fair access', 'where all parents feel they have the same opportunities for the school they want'.[570] In addition to requiring the monitoring of intakes, as per the skeleton code (above), it states that admission policies must be designed so as not to disadvantage particular social groups nor discourage parents from them from applying for a particular school place. Other policies should not undermine the goal of fair access: for example, a school uniform policy that requires a particular uniform that is expensive.[571] The draft says that school places should not be based on sibling connection, although it does not seem to rule this out if, for example, parents might face problems in transporting children, particular younger ones, to different schools.[572] In the admission process, information that identifies the background of families—for example, a parent's occupation or that their first language is not English—should not be sought by admission authorities.[573] A catchment area should 'reflect the diversity of the community served by the school'.[574] The new code is due to come into force in February 2007. It certainly addresses a number of key issues giving rise to unfairness in the current system. Whether or how far it will expand opportunities for choice and reduce social segregation in practice remains to be seen.

[570] DfES, *School Admissions Code Consultation Document* (London, DfES, 2006), paras 1.3, 1.20.
[571] Ibid, para 1.23.
[572] Ibid, para 2.10.
[573] Ibid, para 1.26–1.27.
[574] Ibid, para 2.31.

6

Special Educational Needs: Choice and Inclusion

INTRODUCTION

CHILDREN WITH SPECIAL educational needs are the largest minority group within the school population. At the start of 2005, approximately 18 per cent of children in schools in England had special educational needs, and one in six of these children, or 3 per cent of all pupils, were the subject of a statement of special educational needs (that is, a formal document maintained by the local education authority (LEA) following an assessment of the child, in which the child's needs and the provision required to meet them are recorded).[1] But they are also the most diverse group. Although possession of special educational needs is determined with reference to an overarching legal definition, of having a 'learning difficulty',[2] the causes of problems with learning are multifarious. They derive from physical factors and/or mental incapacity or conditions that also give rise to forms of disability, although, as noted below, disability, which was discussed in Chapter 4, and special educational needs are legally distinct and give rise to discrete sets of rights and responsibilities.

Diversity among pupils also stems from the way in which the incidence of special educational needs varies with gender and ethnicity. So far as gender is concerned, there is a significant disparity. In 2005, three times as many boys as girls had statements; and among pupils with special educational needs but no statement, boys outnumbered girls by a factor of approximately two to one.[3] There are also wide variations in the prevalence of special educational needs across different ethnic groups. In secondary schools in 2005, for example, 52 per cent of Travellers of Irish heritage had special educational needs, including 7.4 per cent who had statements.[4] An above average incidence of special educational

---

[1] DfES, *First Release. Special Educational Needs in England, January 2005* SFR 24/2005 (London, DfES, 2005).

[2] Under EA 1996, s 312: see p 325 below.

[3] DfES, n1 above, table 5.

[4] Ibid, table 8b.

needs was also present in secondary schools among, for example, Gypsy/Roma children (49.6 per cent, and 8.2 per cent statemented) and Black Caribbean children (26.1 per cent, with 2.9 per cent statemented). However, very few children of Chinese origin had special educational needs (9.2 per cent, with 1 per cent statemented) and there was also a below average incidence of them among White British children (16.4 per cent, with 2.4 per cent statemented).[5] All Asian groups were at or around the average. Similar disparaties have also been noted in the United States, where African American children are over-represented among those in special education, a situation to which a cultural gap between mainly white teachers and black pupils is regarded as making a significant contribution.[6] The principal legislation in the US has been amended to require states to adopt policies that seek to avoid over-identification or classification of racial or ethnic groups.[7] In the UK, the relationship between special educational needs and ethnicity has been described in the Audit Commission's latest review of special educational needs as 'complex' and the research evidence on the matter as 'inconclusive'.[8] Nonetheless, it seems likely that the extent of special educational needs among minority ethnic groups in the UK is under-reported. The Audit Commission found that there are difficulties in identifying children with special educational needs among those recently arrived in the UK or who are not fluent in English. Among the causes are the perceived stigma attached to special educational needs in some communities (manifesting in low levels of identified need), and a lack of accessible information for parents in languages other than English.[9]

Special educational needs are also present among all social classes, but the House of Commons Education and Skills Committee has reported 'a strong correlation between social deprivation and [special educational needs]' that, it says, warrants close consideration by the Government.[10] The Committee quotes figures showing that among children of primary and secondary school age, those with statements are twice as likely as other children to have eligibility for free school meals.

The identification of children with special educational needs, and the particular cause or type of their learning difficulty, is considered important not for its own sake, but because appropriate education holds the key to ameliorating some of their inherent disadvantage. The statutory definition of special educational needs, discussed more fully below, is purposive, since the child's learning difficulty must be something that 'calls for special educational provision

   [5] Ibid.

   [6] CJ Russo and C Talbert-Johnson, 'The Over-representation of African American Children in Special Education: the Resegregation of Educational Programming?' (1997) 29 *Education and Urban Society* 136 at 140–1. See also C Talbert-Johnson, 'Why So Many African-American Children in Special Ed?' (1998) 64 *School Business Affairs* 30.

   [7] Individuals With Disabilities in Education Act (IDEA) (revised 2004), 20 USCA §§1412(a)(24), 1418(d)(1)(A), (B).

   [8] Audit Commission, *Special Educational Needs: A Mainstream Issue* (London, Audit Commission, 2002), para 24.

   [9] Ibid.

   [10] House of Commons Education and Skills Committee, Third Report, Session 2005–06, *Special Educational Needs*, HC 478–I (London, TSO, 2006), paras 37 and 38.

to be made for him'.[11] The precise form of provision that is needed will vary from child to child. While the policy, discussed below, of including children with special educational needs within mainstream schools wherever possible, as opposed to educating them separately in special schools (schools specially organised to make special educational provision for pupils with special educational needs),[12] incorporates the idea that they should receive a similar education to that given to the other children alongside whom they will normally be educated, their needs are defined with reference to their requirement for 'special educational provision' to meet them. This provision is defined as 'educational provision which is additional to, or otherwise different from, the educational provision made generally for children of [the particular child's] age in schools maintained by the [LEA]'.[13]

In view of their statutory duties towards children with special educational needs, LEAs will need to allocate specific resources to special educational provision. The allocation per child with special educational needs, particularly one whose needs have been formally assessed and described in a statement maintained by the authority (see below), will tend to be proportionately greater than that in respect of other children. It means that when preferences as regards the form of provision to be made for the child are asserted by parents, questions of need, resources and rights are all in the balance. The field of special educational needs is one in which there is a necessary degree of flexibility as to the educational provision that should be made for each child. LEAs or schools have quite a wide discretion in making the arrangements. Their choices, influenced by policy and resource considerations, are bound to result in frequent conflict with the choices of parents. Notwithstanding the policy emphasis on 'partnership' between parents, schools and LEAs[14] in the context of special educational needs, parents harnessing their rights in an attempt to maximise the educational opportunities of children can represent a threat to LEAs which are attempting to meet their statutory obligations to both the pupil population in general and individual children with specific needs, through the allocation of limited resources. In this sense, the field of special educational needs is of crucial importance, given that the allocation of resources is critical to the realisation of social justice goals such as equity and inclusion. But so far as individual rights are concerned, such as a right to influence the form of provision the child receives and whether his or her interests are best served in a mainstream or specialist setting, it was noted in Chapter 2 that special educational needs is a field where rights are particularly contingent in view of the wider resource and policy issues that come into play and the fact that human rights claims are unlikely to succeed.

Nonetheless, the field of special educational needs is perhaps the most rights-infused area of educational decision-making and provision, and parents

---

[11] Ibid, subs (1).

[12] EA 1996, s 337. The school must be approved by the Secretary of State under ibid s 342.

[13] Ibid, s 312(4).

[14] Despite the planned reform of some local authority education functions, the statutory role of local authorities in relation to special educational needs seems set to continue: DfES, *Higher Standards, Better Schools for All. More Choice for Parents and Pupils*, Cm 6677 (London, DfES, 2005).

often do succeed in overturning decisions by the authorities. The likelihood of their success is governed not merely by the substantive merits of their case, however, but also by their skill, capacity and determination in pursuing a claim or appeal to its conclusion. As with areas that have been examined in Chapter 5, where the legislation provides an element of choice and a procedural framework for the consideration and resolution of claims based on parental preference, the formalities and adversarial nature of dispute resolution in this field presents arguably greater opportunities for more advantaged parents than others to realise their goals.

THE BASIC FRAMEWORK

Introduction

The present legal framework has its origins in the Education Act 1981, which set out the basic definitions noted above and adopted the idea of a formal 'statement' for children with the most significant needs, to be drawn up and maintained by the LEA, recording the child's needs and the provision required to meet them. It also incorporated the principle that the inclusion of children with special educational needs within mainstream settings was highly desirable, for educational, social and psychological reasons. The 1981 Act, which was based around most of the key recommendations of the 1978 Warnock Report,[15] also adopted the basic idea of partnership through parent participation in the decision-making process. Once it was acknowledged that parents should be able to have their say it became necessary to provide a mechanism for resolving conflict and ensuring a degree of accountability. The Warnock Committee recommended that parents should have a right of appeal to the Secretary of State in respect of a decision by the LEA on whether or not the child should be recorded as having a need for special educational provision.[16] The 1981 Act in fact provided two grounds and routes of appeal. First, parents could appeal to the Secretary of State against the decision made after a statutory assessment of the child's needs, as to whether those needs should be formally determined.[17] Secondly, if such a determination of needs occurred, they could appeal to a local education appeal committee (with a right of further appeal to the Secretary of State) against the special educational provision subsequently proposed by the LEA for the statement.[18] Parents' rights of appeal were later significantly extended

---

[15] MH Warnock (chair), *Special Educational Needs. Report of the Committee of Enquiry into the Education of Handicapped Children and Young People*, Cmnd 7212 (London, HMSO, 1978).

[16] Ibid, para 4.74.

[17] EA 1981, s 5. If he or she upheld the appeal, the Secretary of State could merely direct the LEA to reconsider the decision: s 5(6).

[18] ibid, s 8. The committee could either confirm the LEA's decision or remit the matter to the authority, with recommendations, for further consideration. On further appeal, however, the Secretary of State's decision was binding. The Secretary of State had the power either to confirm the decision or to amend the proposed provision or order its cessation.

under the Education Act 1993, which also introduced a new independent tribunal (the Special Educational Needs Tribunal, later renamed the Special Educational Needs and Disability Tribunal (SENDIST)[19]) and a single avenue of appeal. The Act also provided additional participatory rights for parents, as discussed below, including a right to express a preference as regards the school where the child should receive his or her special educational provision.

The 1993 Act was consolidated into the Education Act 1996, part IV, which, as amended (principally by the Special Educational Needs and Disability Act (SENDA) 2001), provides the present legislative basis for special educational needs and provision. There is also a *Special Educational Needs Code of Practice*[20] the provisions of which LEAs, schools and the SENDIST must have regard in exercising their functions.[21] The Act confers a number of rights on parents to have an input into the decisions concerning their child's education. They include a right to express a preference over their child's school placement to be specified in the statement and to appeal to the SENDIST if their choice is denied.[22] Under the current legislative regime, as previously, the statement is a document, maintained by the LEA, containing prescribed information, including details of the LEA's formal assessment of the child and the special educational provision required to meet his or her needs, which would include the name or type of school placement required for the child.[23] The statement, discussed more fully below, is a document the making of which has specific legal consequences, in that the defined educational provision must be made for the child.[24]

Identification and Support

Schools (specifically, governing bodies) have a duty to use their best endeavours to ensure that children with special educational needs receive the special educational provision their needs call for and, where the LEA has informed them that a pupil has special educational needs, to make those needs known to his or her teachers.[25] Furthermore, teachers must in any event be made aware of the importance of identifying and providing for pupils with special educational needs.[26] Intervention to support a child with special educational needs will generally be managed at the school level by the classroom teacher who has noted that there are difficulties, such as a marked lack of progress. The teacher will work in conjunction with the school's special educational needs co-ordinator

---

[19] Under the Special Educational Needs and Disability Act (SENDA) 2001, Sched 8, para 2.

[20] DfES (London, DfES, 2001). It came into operation in January 2002. It replaced the first code, which was introduced in 1994 under the 1993 Act. There is a separate code for Wales: Welsh Assembly Government, *Special Educational Needs Code of Practice for Wales* (Cardiff, National Assembly for Wales, 2004).

[21] EA 1996, s 313(2).

[22] Ibid, ss 326 and Sched 27, para 3.

[23] Ibid, s 324. See also the Education (Special Educational Needs) (England) (Consolidation) Regulations 2001 (SI 2001/2455), part III and Sched 2.

[24] EA 1996, s 324(5).

[25] Ibid, s 317(1).

[26] Ibid.

(SENCO). In the SEN Code this process of intervention is referred to as 'School Action'.[27] The code continues to recommend that strategies to enable the individual child to progress should be recorded within an individual education plan (IEP), which should be reviewed regularly and at least three times a year.[28] The IEP has no specific legal status but represents the means by which the school fulfils its duty to meet the child's needs.[29] In some cases external support, referred to in the code as 'School Action Plus', may also be needed.[30] In recent years, the importance of identifying pupils with problems such as dyslexia and responding appropriately, including, where necessary, referring a pupil to the LEA for a formal assessment, has been strongly reinforced by court judgments that have opened the way for negligence actions based on breach of the duty of care at common law in the performance of ordinary professional duties towards children who may have special educational needs.[31]

In a case where a child without a statement is receiving special educational provision, the governing body of the school has a duty to notify the parents that such provision is being made because it is considered that the child has special educational needs.[32] This duty was introduced by the SENDA 2001, as was that requiring LEAs to arrange for the parents of any child with special educational needs to be provided with advice and information relating to them and that LEAs should publicise their advice and information services.[33]

Definitions and Categories of Special Educational Needs

The Education Act 1944 placed LEAs under a duty to 'ascertain what children in their area require special educational provision' and empowered them to serve a notice on the parent requiring the child to be examined by a medical officer in order to provide the LEA with 'advice as to whether the child is suffering from any disability of mind or body'.[34] The Act also empowered the minister to make regulations defining the categories of pupils who required 'special educational treatment', and 10 categories were subsequently prescribed.[35] They included physical disabilities, such as total or partial deafness or blindness, epilepsy and a

---

[27] DfES, *Special Educational Needs Code of Practice* (London, DfES, 2001), para 5.43.

[28] Ibid, para 4.28.

[29] Education Act 1996, s 317(1). Note that decisions over IEPs carry no appeal rights. For discussion, see L Lundy, 'Stating a Case for the Unstatemented—Children with Special Educational Needs in Mainstream Schools' (1998) 10 *Child & Family Law Quarterly* 39 at 47–9.

[30] DfES, *Special Educational Needs Code of Practice* (London, DfES, 2001), para 5.54.

[31] In particular, *X (Minors) v Bedfordshire County Council; M (A Minor) and Another v Newham London Borough Council and Others; E (A Minor) v Dorset County Council; Christmas v Hampshire County Council; Keating v Bromley London Borough Council* [1995] 2 AC 633; *Phelps v London Borough of Hillingdon; Anderton v London Borough of Bromley; Jarvis v Hampshire County council* [2000] ELR 499; [2000] 3 WLR 776; [2000] 4 All ER 504 (HL). See also *Liennard v Slough Borough Council* [2002] ELR 527 (QBD) and see below.

[32] EA 1996, s 317A, inserted by the Special Educational Needs and Disability Act 2001, s 7.

[33] Ibid, s 332A, inserted by the Special Educational Needs and Disability Act 2001, s 2.

[34] EA 1944, s 34(1).

[35] The Handicapped Pupils and School Health Service Regulations 1945 (SI 1945/1076) and 1959 (SI 1959/365).

general category of physical handicap. There was also a category of 'delicate' children. Mental factors were reflected only in a broad category known as 'educationally sub-normal' and 'maladjusted'. The final category was 'speech defective'. One of the problems of this typology based around the notion of handicap was that it had the potential to exclude many children who needed special forms of educational provision, for example those who were dyslexic.[36] The disability model was also contained in the LEA's duty concerning the placement of the child, which indicated that pupils 'whose disability is serious' should be educated in special schools, where that was practicable.[37] The Warnock Report reflected the view that the medical definitions of special educational needs were stigmatising and inconsistent with a positive approach towards ensuring that appropriate provision that reflected the child's educational needs was set in place. The 1981 Act therefore introduced the much broader (and still central) concept of 'learning difficulty'.

The statutory definition that has been in place since 1981 defines special educational needs with reference to having 'a learning difficulty which calls for special educational provision to be made for [the child]'.[38] A child aged 5 or over has a 'learning difficulty' if he has either 'a significantly greater difficulty in learning than the majority of children his age' or 'a disability which either prevents or hinders him from making use of the educational facilities of a kind generally provided for children of his age in schools within the area of the local education authority'.[39] Thus while many children with special educational needs will have a disability, the two concepts are distinct and are not made inter-dependent by statute, as noted in Chapter 4. Children younger than 5 may also be classed as having a learning difficulty, if they are likely, when they become 5 or over, to fall within the above definition.[40]

The definition of learning difficulty excludes a difficulty arising from the fact that the language in which the child is or will be taught is not the language spoken at any time at home.[41] Over the years, case law has clarified that a child with a condition such as dyslexia[42] or speech difficulties giving rise to a need for speech therapy[43] has special educational needs. On the other hand, the courts have rejected arguments that a child's religion or culture,[44] the domestic circumstances in which

---

[36] V Hannon, 'The Education Act 1981: New Rights and Duties in Special Education' [1981] *Journal of Social Welfare Law* 275, at 277.

[37] EA 1944, s 33(2).

[38] EA 1996, s 312(1).

[39] Ibid, s 312(2).

[40] Ibid.

[41] Ibid, s 312(3).

[42] *R v Hampshire Education Authority ex parte J* (1985) 84 LGR 547. On dyslexia, see D Caskey, 'Dyslexia and the Law of Special Educational Needs in Northern Ireland' (2002) *Education Law Journal* 31.

[43] *R v Lancashire CC ex p CM (A Minor)* [1989] 2 FLR 279 (CA); *X and X v Caerphilly Borough Council and the Special Educational Needs and Disability Tribunal* [2005] ELR 78 (QBD). See also DfES, *Special Educational Needs Code of Practice* (London, DfES, 2001), para 8:49.

[44] *G v London Borough of Barnet and the SENT* [1998] ELR 480; *A v Special Education Needs and Disability Tribunal and London Borough of Barnet* [2004] ELR 293 (QBD).

he or she lives,[45] or a need for constant supervision outside school hours[46] could in themselves constitute or give rise to a special educational need.

Table 5 shows the proportion of maintained school pupils with special educational needs in each of the main categories, who were covered by School Action Plus or a statement of special educational needs at the start of 2005.

In the Audit Commission's survey of LEAs in 2002 significant increases were found in the number of children with autistic spectrum disorders, speech/ communication problems and profound or multiple learning difficulties, whilst the numbers of children with moderate learning difficulties or specific learning difficulties were considered to have fallen slightly.[47] The increase in autism cases is also confirmed by another survey, in which 70 per cent of LEAs reported increases in the number of statements for children with this type of disorder.[48]

Table 5: Pupils with special educational needs in maintained schools by primary type of need (DfES categories) (January 2005)[a]

Primary type of need	School Action Plus %	Statement %
Specific learning difficulty	17.0	8.9
Moderate learning difficulty	30.0	25.9
Severe learning difficulty	1.1	11.6
Profound and multiple learning difficulty	0.1	3.3
Behaviour, emotional and social difficulties	26.2	13.9
Speech, language and communication needs	12.9	10.7
Hearing impairment	1.7	3.0
Visual impairment	0.9	1.8
Multi-sensory impairment	0.1	0.2
Physical disability	2.2	7.2
Autistic spectrum disorder	2.2	11.5
Other difficulty/disability	5.4	2.0

[a]   From data in Department for Education and Skills, *Special Educational Needs in England, January 2005* (London: Department for Education and Skills, 2005), table 9. The percentages shown are the proportion that each category represents of the total number of pupils with special educational needs whose needs are purportedly being addressed via School Action Plus or a statement.

45   *G v Wakefield Metropolitan Borough Council*, 29 Jan 1998 (QBD), unreported.
46   *W v Leeds City Council and the Special Educational Needs and Disability Tribunal* [2005] ELR 459.
47   Audit Commission, *Special Educational Needs: A Mainstream Issue* (London, Audit Commission, 2002), para 16.
48   A Pinney, *Reducing Reliance on Statements: An Investigation into Local Authority Practice and Outcomes*, Research Report RR508 (London, DfES, 2004). For discussion of autism and the rights of autistic children in Canada to the intensive behavioural provision known as the Lovaas therapy, often

Among the various types of learning difficulty the divergence between the rates of statementing and non-statemented School Action Plus provision shown in the table reflects the nature and complexity of the needs of children in each of the categories. Those with a severe learning difficulty or profound or multiple learning difficulties are much more likely than not to be the subject of a statement, whereas the opposite may be true for those with dyslexia, particularly a mild form, or behavioural problems. This disparity also reflects variations in the need for provision in a special school. Very few children whose primary need arises from specific learning difficulty are being educated in a special school, as compared to around two thirds of pupils with a severe learning difficulty. A further point to note is that needs arising from a physical disability are generally identified earlier and 'more reliably' than others.[49]

The idea of a clear and rigid divide between children who do or do not have special educational needs meets the demand for certainty that surrounds the notion of a legal duty, but the House of Commons Education and Skills Committee has found it to be an 'arbitrary distinction that leads to false classifications',[50] and, as Monk argues, the legal construction of a 'special educational need' can contribute to the over-simplification of a complex issue.[51] An example is the case of gifted children, those with exceptional ability who learn far more quickly than other children and for whom standard lessons may therefore be unsuitable. In the past the courts have been equivocal in relation to the question whether giftedness falls within the definition of special educational needs.[52] In recent years 'gifted and talented' pupils have attracted promises of greater government support,[53] in recognition of the fact that they 'have not been well-served by the system in the past'.[54] There is an indication that white pupils are twice as likely as those from minority ethnic backgrounds to be identified as gifted and talented, leading the House of Commons Education and Skills Committee to recommend that the

favoured for inclusion in statements in England and Wales, see S Grover, 'Challenging Statutory Limitations on Children's Education Rights: a Re-examination of the Candian Supreme Court Decision in *Auton*' (2005) 17 *Education & the Law* 43. See also K Syrett, 'Autism—Lovaas Therapy—Human Rights—Canadian and English Approaches' (2005) 27 *Journal of Social Welfare and Family Law* 347. See also M King and D King, 'How the Law Defines the Special Educational Needs of Autistic Children' (2006) 18 *Child & Family Law Quarterly* 23, which provides a critical account, drawing on autopoetic theory, of the law's approach to the labelling of, and provision for, children with autism.

[49] Audit Commission, n 8 above, para 22.

[50] House of Commons Education and Skills Committee, n 10 above, para 34.

[51] D Monk, 'Theorising Education Law and Childhood: Constructing the Ideal Pupil' (2000) 21 *British Journal of Sociology of Education* 355, at 364.

[52] *R v Secretary of State for Education ex p C* [1996] ELR 93; *R v Portsmouth City Council ex p F* [1998] ELR 619.

[53] See DfES, *Higher Standards, Better Schools for All. More Choice for Parents and Pupils*, Cm 6677 (London, DfES, 2005), paras 4.21–4.27.

[54] See Department for Education and Skills, *Department for Education and Skills: Five Year Strategy for Teachers and Learners*, Cm 6272 (London, TSO, 2004), ch 5, para 15. There is now a National Academy for Gifted and Talented Youth, which is 'a centre of excellence advising teachers on the best way to teach gifted young people, and to encourage them to go on to university, offering summer schools and on-line learning for gifted and talented young people so that they can meet and work with other like-minded children and be given extra stretch and challenge': ibid.

Government should take the problem of this disparity seriously in its programme for supporting gifted and talented children, to ensure that its policy guards against 'stereotypes and unintended consequences'.[55]

The DfES continues not to recognise gifted or talented children as having special educational needs. However, the matter received further judicial consideration recently in *S v Special Educational Needs and Disability Tribunal and Oxfordshire County Council*,[56] where it was argued before Elias J that a functional and purposive approach should be adopted in construing the notion of disability for the purposes of the statutory definition of special educational needs, drawing analogy with the House of Lords' approach to the concept of 'family' in *Fitzpatrick v Sterling Housing Association Ltd*.[57] Elias J held that '[e]ven if, which I doubt, it can be said that there has been a change since 1996 in recognizing the needs of the exceptionally able student' the wording of the statute was 'not sufficiently flexible to give effect to any such change'.[58] It was also argued that the effect of Article 2 of Protocol 1 of the ECHR (no-one shall be denied the right to education), read together with Article 14, was such that gifted children should be entitled to equivalent special treatment to that given to others who required special educational provision. Elias J held that Article 2 of Protocol 1 was engaged; there was a need to ensure provision on a non-discriminatory basis; that was not occurring so far as gifted children were concerned; and gifted children could be considered to have a status protected by Article 14. However, he doubted whether gifted children were analogous to slow learners or persons with difficulty in learning for this purpose. There were 'obvious social and economic reasons why it may be thought desirable to use resources to help the less able but not the most able', and while there were cogent arguments for assisting gifted children, they were not the same as those for helping the less able.[59] Justification for the discrimination (the judge hinted at economic considerations) could, if necessary, be established.[60] One way or the other, therefore, while gifted children are accepted as having a need for specialist educational provision the construction of special educational needs precludes their particular difficulties from attracting proper legal recognition.

Assessment and Statementing

Among those pupils who are identified as having special educational needs will be some giving particular concern who may need to be referred to the LEA by the school for possible statutory assessment and statementing. Indeed, the House of Lords has indicated that the head teacher and other staff owe a common law duty

---

[55] House of Commons Education and Skills Committee, First Report, Session 2005–06, *The Schools White Paper:* 'Higher Standards, Better Schools for All', HC 633–I (London, TSO, 2006), para 36.

[56] [2005] ELR 443 (QBD).

[57] [2001] 1 AC 27. This concerned, inter alia, the question, answered in the affirmative, whether a person could succeed to a tenancy on the basis of having been a member of the deceased tenant's 'family' by being his same-sex partner.

[58] At para 26.

[59] Ibid, para 38.

[60] Ibid, para 39.

of care in the performance of their professional role to refer a seriously under-performing pupil to the LEA.[61] The LEA's officers, such as their educational psychologists, may in turn owe a common law duty of care in the exercise of their professional skill and judgment in assessing the child and advising the parent.[62] The LEA has a judgment to make concerning the making of a statement: it is required to make one where, following its formal assessment of the child,[63] it has decided that it is 'necessary' for the LEA to determine the special educational provision which any learning difficulty the child has may call for.[64] According to the *Special Educational Needs Code of Practice*,[65] the basic question for the LEA is whether the school can make the necessary provision for the child from its own resources, albeit with some specialist backup from outside; if not, then a statement will be needed.[66] This framework on statementing continues to leave each authority with considerable discretion, so it is not surprising that the rate of statementing varies widely across LEAs, a variation that has persisted for many years and is explained in part by local policy and cultural traditions within different authorities.[67]

The Government hopes for a reduction in the rate of statementing. It says that it wants 'parents to have confidence that their children's needs will be met effectively in school without feeling that the only way to achieve this is through a statement'.[68] It is claimed that a reduction is achievable by ensuring that schools have the necessary skills and capacities to handle children's learning difficulties without direct outside support. If this is done, 'we would expect only those children with the most severe and complex needs, requiring support from more than one specialist agency, to need the protection a statement provides'.[69] Research has confirmed that reducing statementing can result in a fairer distri-bution of resources, more support for individual children and less paperwork and bureaucracy, although it can also affect the capacity of schools to meet some

---

[61] *X (Minors) v Bedfordshire County Council; M (A Minor) and Another v Newham London Borough Council and Others; E (A Minor) v Dorset County Council; Christmas v Hampshire County Council; Keating v Bromley London Borough Council* [1995] 2 AC 633.

[62] *Phelps v London Borough of Hillingdon; Anderton v Clwyd County Council; G v London Borough of Bromley; Jarvis v Hampshire County Council* [2000] ELR 499; [2000] 3 WLR 776; [2000] 4 All ER 504 (HL); and *Liennard v Slough Borough Council* [2002] ELR 527 (QBD).

[63] Which it must carry out if, having taking account of representations made and evidence submitted, it considers that the child has, or probably has, special educational needs and the LEA considers that it is necessary or probably necessary to determine the special educational provision to meet them: EA 1996, s 323(1)–(3). The parent has a right of appeal to the SENDIST against a refusal to assess under this section: ibid, s 329.

[64] Ibid, s 324(1).

[65] DfES, *Special Educational Needs Code of Practice* (London, DfES, 2001).

[66] Ibid, para 8:2. This will also be an issue where the LEA proposes to terminate a statement: *R (Jane W) v Blaenau Gwent Borough Council* [2004] ELR 152.

[67] House of Commons, Education Science and the Arts Committee, Session 1986/87, *Third Report, Special Educational Needs: Implementation of the Education Act 1981*, HC201–1 (London, HMSO, 1987), para 33; Audit Commission, *Special Educational Needs: A Mainstream Issue* (London, Audit Commission, 2002), para 32.

[68] DfES, *Removing Barriers to Achievement. The Government's Strategy for SEN* (London, DfES, 2004) 3.

[69] Ibid.

children's needs.[70] To Baroness Warnock, chair of the committee on special educational needs in the 1970s, whose 1978 report provided the basis for the Education Act 1981, statementing requires a re-think, in part because statements 'operate so terribly inequitably' as between different children who have 'almost identical disabilities'.[71] Recently, the House of Commons Education and Skills Committee called for a review of the statementing process and the introduction of national guidance to local authorities on when to issue statements.[72]

If the child has special educational needs but there is *no* statement, his or her admission to school will be decided upon via the standard admissions process discussed in Chapter 5: and in any event the law stipulates that the child must be educated in a mainstream school.[73] If there *is* to be a statement, a separate regime will apply (see below), and if a school is named in the statement the child must be admitted to it.[74] In this case the school named may be a maintained mainstream school, an approved independent school[75] or a special school.[76] But there is a statutory presumption, outlined below, in favour of a mainstream placement.

The introduction of the requirements on statements started with the Education Act 1981. Under that Act, parents were entitled to receive a copy of a draft statement and to make representations to the LEA about its contents.[77] The LEA then had a wide discretion to make the statement in its original form, to make it in a modified form, or not to make a statement at all.[78] Although the parent could appeal against the contents of the statement,[79] there was no express right to state a preference for a particular school to be named in the statement, nor was the LEA under any duty (however conditional) to accede to any such preference. Furthermore, the LEA was under a duty to ensure that special educational provision for children with statements was made in a mainstream school, provided that account was taken of the wishes of parents and that a mainstream placement was compatible with the child's receiving the required special education, the provision of efficient education for the children with whom he or she would be educated, and 'the efficient use of resources'.[80] Inclusion also meant that, subject to the same conditions plus its reasonable practicability, the child should engage in school activities 'together with children

---

[70] A Pinney, *Reducing Reliance on Statements: An Investigation into Local Authority Practice and Outcomes* Research Report RR508 (London, DfES, 2004).

[71] Baroness Warnock, Oral Evidence to the House of Commons Education and Skills Committee inquiry into Special Educational Needs, 31 Oct 2005 Q9.

[72] House of Commons Education and Skills Committee, n 10 above, paras 27 and 153.

[73] EA 1996, s 316(2). A 'mainstream school' is a school other than a special school or an independent school; city technology colleges, city colleges for the technology of the arts and academies are not classed as independent schools for this purpose: EA 1996, s 316(4). S 316 is as substituted by the SENDA 2001, s 1.

[74] Ibid, s 324(5)(b).

[75] Ibid, s 347, being a school that is approved as 'suitable for the admission of children for whom statements are maintained'.

[76] If a special school, the school must be approved by the Secretary of State under ibid s 342.

[77] Education Act 1981, s 7(4)–(7).

[78] Ibid, s 7(8).

[79] Ibid, s 8(1).

[80] Ibid, s 2(3).

who do not have special educational needs'.[81] This basic framework continued under the Education Act 1993 with only minor amendments.[82]

The 1993 Act nonetheless made some important changes to this area of the law. An important study by the Audit Commission and Her Majesty's Inspectorate (HMI), published in 1992, had revealed that, a decade on from the implementation of the 1981 Act, LEAs and schools were tending not to pay sufficient attention to parents' views.[83] Although parents had a right of appeal over the contents of a statement, the appeal system (as it then was—prior to the reforms under the 1993 Act that included the creation of the Special Educational Needs Tribunal) involved 'a lengthy process and one which few parents undertake'.[84] The report proposed that parents should be give similar rights to express a preference for a school to those enjoyed by parents of other pupils under the standard admission process, with equivalent rights of appeal. It cited the general policy of extending parental choice and the emphasis placed on it in the Government's *Parent's Charter*.[85] It also argued that the experience in Denmark had shown that giving greater regard to parents' views had 'not evidently resulted in a large number of inappropriate placements'.[86] The report favoured a right for parents to be able to select a maintained special or ordinary school, but, given that the cost of the placement would fall upon the LEA, not an independent school (including one that provided special education), because of the cost.[87] The requirement to adhere to parental preference should, the Audit Commission and HMI concluded, be subject to the same conditions or requirements as those that applied to the inclusion duty (above).[88] Clearly the most significant was bound to be compatibility with 'the efficient use of resources'. As we shall see, it is the cost implications that tends to be the crucial issue in relation to decisions on school placement, as it is with regard to special educational provision as a whole. Resistance by LEAs to parental preference is often born out of a need to limit expenditure. As Beldam LJ noted in *Lane*, where the parents preferred a residential placement for their child at a non-maintained school which provided a 24-hour curriculum:

> It is surely common knowledge that local education authorities have the unenviable task of eking out resources inadequate to meet all the demands upon them and it is obvious that the consequences of making overprovision for one child may mean underprovision for others.[89]

---

[81] Ibid, s 2(7).

[82] Education Act 1993, Part III. One amendment related to the duty to ensure a mainstream placement. Under the 1981 Act account had to be taken of the parents' wishes, but under the 1993 Act, s 160(1), there was to be a mainstream placement 'unless that is incompatible with the wishes of his parent'.

[83] Audit Commission/Her Majesty's Inspectorate of Schools, *Getting in on the Act. Provision for Pupils with Special Educational Needs: the National Picture* (London, HMSO, 1992).

[84] Ibid, para 133.

[85] Ibid.

[86] Ibid, para 135.

[87] Ibid. para 133.

[88] Ibid, para 134.

[89] *Richardson v Solihull Metropolitan Borough Council and the Special Educational Needs Tribunal; White and Another v London Borough of Ealing and the Special Educational Needs Tribunal; Hereford and Worcester County Council v Lane* [1998] ELR 319 (CA), at 334H–335A.

The Court of Appeal concluded in that case that the tribunal, in ordering that the school chosen by the parents should be named in the child's statement of special educational needs, had made an error of law by not taking proper account of the LEAs' need to make an efficient use of the resources available to it.

INCLUSION AND CHOICE

Policy, Presumption and Trends

Inclusion in mainstream education is an important principle that was promoted in the Warnock report in 1978. It is also consistent with the duty of the state under the UN Convention on the Rights of the Child, discussed below, for education and training for a disabled child to be 'conducive to the child's achieving the fullest possible social integration and individual development . . .'[90] Indeed, the same arguments that apply to the inclusion of disabled children within schools that were discussed in Chapter 4 (and see below) apply to children with special educational needs. The EA 1944, which, as noted above, provided for the identification of pupils requiring special educational treatment with reference to their disability, had in fact established a presumption against inclusion, in the case of those whose disability was deemed 'serious', unless their education in a special school was impracticable. In the case of other disabled pupils, it merely permitted their education in 'any school maintained or assisted by the [LEA].'[91] Between 1950 and 1977 the proportion of children attending special schools increased: thus 'the trend was actually towards segregation.'[92] Although the 1981 Act established a firm presumption of inclusion, as noted above, there was pressure against it throughout the period from 1979 to 1997 due to government policy of engendering of market forces and consumer choice within education. Market pressures made schools more antipathetic to the admission of pupils who were likely to contribute much less to academic success.[93] This is still a factor today and was regarded by teachers in one survey as 'perhaps the key issue that the Government in England needed to address if committed to pursuing its policy of greater inclusion,'[94] although an emphasis on pupil progress rather than straight results as performance indicators might ameliorate the problem.

Government policy on special educational needs since 1997 has been dominated by a wish to increase the proportion of pupils with special

---

[90] UNCRC, Art 23(3).

[91] EA 1944, s 33(2).

[92] V Hannon, 'The Education Act 1981: New Rights and Duties in Special Education' (1981) *Journal of Social Welfare Law* 275, at 277.

[93] See, eg, S Riddell and S Brown, 'Special Educational Needs Provision in the United Kingdom—the Policy Context' in S Riddell and S Brown (eds), *Special Educational Needs in the 1990s* (London, Routledge, 1994), 1 at 19.

[94] Audit Commission, *Special Educational Needs: A Mainstream Issue* (London, Audit Commission, 2002), para 122.

educational needs who are being educated in mainstream schools[95] and has been reinforced by legislative changes; and practice standards are proposed.[96] In its 1998 Green Paper the Government argued that '[t]here are strong educational, as well as social and moral, grounds for educating children with special educational needs, or with disabilities, with their peers' and that placement in a mainstream school will lead 'naturally to other forms of inclusion'.[97] In furtherance of the policy, an Inclusion Development Programme has been developed.[98] Tensions arise from the fact that some mainstream school staff feel that they or their schools are not fully able to support children with special educational needs, particularly those with behavioural, emotional or social difficulties (BESD).[99] The Steer report, a report of a practitioners' group on school behaviour and discipline prepared for the DfES in 2005, was clear that further resources needed to be put into assisting schools in meeting the needs of pupils with special educational needs, given the 'close link between poor behaviour and previous failure to deal with a pupil's special needs properly' and the fact that 'pupils identified as having a behavioural, emotional or social difficulty may require a high level of individual support'.[100] The Government claims that additional resources have been provided in recent years and that the spending for each pupil with BESD has increased by £1,070 in real terms since 1997–8, with a further £400 rise expected by 2007–8.[101] But the rate of permanent exclusion among pupils with special educational needs is just over three times the average, with those with or without statements more or less equally likely to be excluded,[102] illustrating the continuing difficulties schools can face in managing the needs of some of these children. On the other hand, inclusion does have potential economic benefits for schools in terms of additional funding, thereby creating

---

[95] See, eg, Department for Education and Employment, *Excellence for all Children: Meeting Special Educational Needs*, Cm 3785 (London, TSO, 1997).

[96] Draft practice standards were published in Oct 2005. The preamble states that the standards 'would not have the force of law but would be a central point of reference for services, designed to improve consistency': DfES, *Draft Standards for SEN Support and Outreach Services* (London, DfES, 2005).

[97] Department for Education and Employment, *Meeeting Special Educational Needs: A Programme of Action* (London, DfEE, 1998), ch 3, paras 1 and 3; Welsh Assembly, *Shaping the Future for Special Education—An Action Programme for Wales* (London, TSO, 1999), ch 3, paras 1 and 3.

[98] Eg, Department for Education and Employment, *SEN and Disability Rights in Education Bill Consultation Document* (London, DfEE, 2000); Department for Education and Skills, *Removing Barriers to Achievement. The Government's Strategy for SEN* (London, DfES, 2004); see also Disability Rights Task Force, *From Exclusion to Inclusion* (London, DfEE/DRTF, 1999). The Inclusion Development Programme, launched in 2004, is initially targeted on autism; behavioural, emotional and social difficulties; speech, language and communication problems, including dyslexia; and moderate learning difficulties.

[99] See Audit Commission, *Special Educational Needs: A Mainstream Issue* (London, Audit Commission, 2002), para 43.

[100] Sir A Steer (Chair), *Learning Behaviour. The Report of the Practitioners' Group on School Behaviour and Discipline* (London, DfES, 2005), para 128.

[101] HC Debs, Vol 444, Col 552W, 23 Mar 2006, per Jacqui Smith MP.

[102] DfES, *Permanent and Fixed Period Exclusions from Schools and Exclusion Appeals in England, 2004–05*, SFR 24/2006 (London, DfES, 2006), available at www.dfes.gov.uk/rsgateway/DB/SFR/, table 10. The rates for fixed term exclusions are broadly comparable with those for permanent exclusions.

incentives for schools to identify and retain pupils with special educational needs.[103] This is especially true of statemented provision; when Hillingdon LEA attempted to cut its special educational needs budget in a way that jeopardised provision set out in children's statements it was held to be acting unlawfully notwithstanding the legitimacy of its case for financial prudence in the face of shortfalls in its overall budget.[104]

For children with statements, the presumption in favour of inclusion in mainstream schools has been strengthened, in that today the only exception to the duty to educate the child in a mainstream school is where it is incompatible with either the wishes of his or her parent or the provision of efficient education for other children.[105] Moreover, the LEA can now rely on this incompatibility ground only if there are no reasonable steps that can be taken to prevent the incompatibility.[106] The Court of Appeal has nonetheless confirmed that if the LEA decides that it should make a mainstream placement it should normally specify the school in the statement, even though the statutory duty is merely to specify the type of school.[107] In the case of non-statemented pupils the position since SENDA 2001 has been that they *must* be educated in mainstream schools.[108] All children with special educational needs may, however, be placed at an independent school or approved special school, if the cost is met other than by the LEA, which in most cases will mean by the parents.[109]

In 1995 approximately 54 per cent of statemented pupils attended maintained mainstream schools, but by 2000 that proportion had reached 61 per cent and currently stands at 60 per cent.[110] Thus the changes wrought by the SENDA 2001 are yet to make their intended impact in terms of increasing the rate of inclusion in mainstream schools. Parental wishes concerning the type of placement are clearly a factor in this. Some parents prefer a special school placement because they consider that their child's needs will be better provided for. In some instances, particularly where a child has significant disabilities and complex needs, they seek an independent school placement, possibly residential, although, as discussed below, there is much less support for such a preference under the legislation. Other parents may prefer a mainstream placement because it reduces the stigma and social segregation brought about by attending a special school, even though the child may be taught separately by specialised staff or in a special

---

[103] See, eg, J Evans and MM Gerber, 'The Changing Governance of Education and its Comparative Impact on Special Education in the United Kingdom and the United States' in MJ Mclaughlin and M Rouse, *Special Education and School Reform in the United States and Britain* (London, Routledge, 2000) 147 at 162.

[104] *R v London Borough of Hillingdon ex p Governing Body of Queensmead School* [1997] ELR 331 (QBD).

[105] EA 1996, s 316(3), as substituted by SENDA 2001, s 1.

[106] Ibid, s 316A(5) and (6).

[107] Ibid, s 324(4)(a); *Richardson v Solihull Metrpolitan Borough Council and the Sepcial Educational Needs Tribunals [Etc]* [1998] ELR 319; *R (MH) v Special Educational Needs and Disability Tribunal and London Borough of Hounslow Borough Council* [2004] ELR 424 (CA).

[108] EA 1996, s 316(2), as substituted.

[109] Ibid, s 316A(1). There are other exceptions to the presumption: eg, when the child attends a special school for the purposes of an assessment of his special educational needs (s 316A(2)).

[110] DfES, *First Release: Special Educational Needs in England; January 2005* SFR 24/2005(London, DfES, 2005) Table 1a.

unit for part of the time and, evidence suggests, is at risk of being excluded from aspects of the mainstream curriculum[111] notwithstanding the statutory principle that children with special educational needs should 'engage in the activities of the school together with children who do not have special educational needs', so far as reasonably practicable and compatible with the child's needs being met and with other children receiving efficient education.[112] As mainstream placements are generally less expensive for LEAs, disputes are more likely to centre on the kind of arrangements made to support the child's learning at the school, which means they will often focus on the specialist teaching arrangements specified in part 4 of the statement. Furthermore, while, as noted above, a mainstream placement must not be incompatible with the wishes of the child's parents,[113] the courts have been reluctant to acknowledge a parental right of veto over such a placement. The reason is that even if parents object to one the LEA has a primary duty to ensure that the child receives a suitable education. The LEA's general duty, in section 9 of the 1996 Act, to have regard to parental wishes is also relevant in this context,[114] but it only establishes a general principle and has proven very difficult to enforce.[115]

Inclusion as an Issue of Human Rights

The European Convention on Human Rights offers little to support a case for inclusion in mainstream education. As noted in Chapter 2, the decision of the Commission of Human Rights in *Simpson v UK*[116] has limited the potential to argue that a particular form of placement that runs contrary to the parent's wishes offends the second sentence of Article 2 of Protocol 1 (A2P1) to the Convention (respect to be paid to the right of the parent for his or her child to be taught in accordance with the parent's religious of philosophical convictions).[117] The LEA's decision to place a boy with dyslexia at a mainstream comprehensive school rather than an independent school offering specialist provision was legitimate as the authorities enjoyed 'a wide measure of discretion . . . as to how to make the best use possible of the resources available to them in the interests of disabled children generally'.[118] The consistent line in the Strasbourg case law, which is to the broad effect that the state authorities are entitled to be

---

[111] Audit Commission, *Special Educational Needs: A Mainstream Issue* (London, Audit Commission, 2002), paras 48 and 62.

[112] EA 1996, s 317(4).

[113] Ibid, s 316(3).

[114] See *L v Hereford and Worcester County Council and Hughes* [2000] ELR 375; *R v London Borough of Brent and Vassie (Chairman of the Special Educational Needs Tribunal) ex p AF* [2000] ELR 550; *L v Worcestershire County Council and Hughes* [2000] ELR 674.

[115] As discussed in Chap 5, and see also the discussion of choice of an independent school below. See also *B v London Borough of Harrow* [2000] ELR 109, per Lord Slynn of Hadley at 116C. See also *S v Metropolitan Borough of Dudley and Another* [2000] ELR 330, per Turner J at 336E–H.

[116] (1989) 64 DR 188.

[117] See pp 67, 71 above.

[118] N 116 above, 7.

resource-driven in their decision-making on education,[119] makes claims for a particular form of provision problematic, not least in view of the high costs that special educational provision can involve. A further factor is that on several occasions in the past the Commission of Human Rights has refused to recognise parental preferences on special educational provision as constituting a philosophical conviction for the purposes of A2P1.[120] In *Graeme*,[121] for example, the mother was opposed to a plan that her son, who had special educational needs, should be sent to a residential boarding school and claimed that there was a breach of A2P1 because, inter alia, her son was not being educated in accordance with her religious and philosophical convictions relating to 'the education of her son with ordinary children' and 'his education in a private, independent school of her choice'. The Commission left open the question whether the parents' disagreement with the LEA over school placement concerned 'deep-founded philosophical convictions rather than a difference of view as to the best way of providing the boy with an education'.[122] The Commission said that even if it did concern philosophical convictions, the child's right to education under the first sentence of the Article was dominant, implying that the most important consideration is that the child is suitably educated. In determining that question, the state is under a duty to ensure that the child's education 'is as far as possible in conformity with the parents' religious and philosophical convictions', but '[i]t does not, however, require the State to provide special facilities to accommodate particular convictions'.[123] The Commission noted, in that regard, the UK's reservation to the second sentence of the Article, namely that the UK accepted this duty 'only so far as it is compatible with the provision of efficient instruction and training and the avoidance of unreasonable expenditure',[124] and the fact that the duty under the Education Act 1981 to educate a child in a mainstream school was subject to conditions as to compatibility with efficient education and the efficient use of resources. The Commission, noting that the principle of inclusion was backed by an increasing body of opinion, nevertheless said that 'this policy cannot apply to all handicapped children'. The Commission reiterated that authorities had 'a wide measure of discretion . . . as to how to make the best use possible of the resources available to them in the interests of disabled children generally', and concluded that while the authorities had to place weight on parental convictions, 'it cannot be said that the second sentence of Article 2 [of Protocol 1] requires the placing of a child with severe development delay in a private school for able children rather than in an available place in a special school for disabled children'.[125]

---

[119] See also *Belgian Linguistics (No 2)* (1979–80) 1 EHRR 252 and the discussion in Chap 2.

[120] *PD and LD v United Kingdom* (1989) 62 DR 292; *Graeme v United Kingdom* (1990) 64. DR 158; *Klerks v Netherlands* (1995) 82 DR 41. See also *W and KL v Sweden* (1983) Application No 14688/83, 45 DR 143, *Simpson v United Kingdom* (1989) 64 DR 188; *Cohen v United Kingdom* (1996) 21 EHRR CD 104.

[121] *Graeme v United Kingdom* (1990) 64 DR 158.

[122] Ibid, 'The Law', Part 1.

[123] Ibid.

[124] See further pp 52 and 67 above.

[125] *Graeme v United Kingdom* (1990) 64 DR 158, 'The Law', Part 1. Cf *Family H v United Kingdom* (1984) 37 DR 105.

For some people, inclusion of children with special educational needs in mainstream schools will represent a moral or ethical issue. Moreover, while both government policy and the domestic legislation now place even greater weight on this principle some professionals and education authorities are, for various reasons, resistant to it, or at least to the idea of extending inclusion. These factors may reinforce the argument that views concerning inclusion could amount to a philosophical conviction, particularly in view of widespread international recognition of its importance. The House of Lords' recent confirmation that a belief in the use of corporal punishment can amount to a religious or philosophical belief[126] surely makes any alternative conclusion on inclusive education less justifiable now, notwithstanding the refusal by Richards J in a 2002 decision, *T v Special Educational Needs Tribunal and Wiltshire County Council*,[127] to accept that a parent's preference in favour of a particular form of special educational provision amounted to such a conviction for the purposes of the Article. The parents wanted their autistic child to receive a home-based specialist programme leading to his integration into mainstream schooling, as opposed to the LEA's plans, upheld by the tribunal, for the boy to be placed at a special educational needs unit. The parents argued that a belief in inclusive education amounted to a philosophical conviction for the purposes of the Convention right and that the tribunal should have interpreted section 9 of the EA 1996 so as to conform with A2P1. Richards J, hearing the appeal on a point of law from the tribunal's decision, said it was too late in such proceedings to raise the human rights arguments, but he in any event rejected them. He said that a belief in inclusive education 'seems to me to fall far short of a philosophical conviction' in favour of the specialist programme.[128] Although it was apparently not determinative, Richards J cited the ruling of Elias J at first instance in the *Williamson* case, where the court had found a belief in favour of the use of corporal punishment at a school to be incapable of amounting to a moral conviction.[129] However, Elias J was subsequently overruled by the majority in the Court of Appeal, whose view was later endorsed by the House of Lords on that point, as noted above.[130] Rix LJ, referring to the Strasbourg jurisprudence that indicated that a 'conviction' denotes a view or views that have reached a certain level of cogency, seriousness, cohesion and importance,[131] said:

---

[126] *R (Williamson) v Secretary of State for Education and Employment and Others* [2005] UKHL 15; [2005] ELR 291; [2005] 2 AC 246. See, eg, Baroness Hale at paras 77 and 78. The ECtHR had two decades earlier confirmed that a belief against the use of corporal punishment could amount to a philosophical conviction: *Campbell and Cosans v UK* (1982) 4 EHRR 293. In the light of that, Black-Branch concluded that a parent's views on a particular form of special educational programme 'seems likely to fall within the scope of a philosophical conviction': J Black-Branch, 'Equality, Non-Discrimination and the Right to Special Education: From International Law to the Human Rights Act' [2000] *European Human Rights Law Review* 297 at 306.

[127] *T v Special Educational Needs Tribunal and Wiltshire County Council* [2002] ELR 704 (QBD).

[128] Ibid, at para [39](iii), per Richards J.

[129] *R (Williamson) v Secretary of State for Education and Employment* [2002] ELR 214; [2002] 1 FLR 493.

[130] *R (Williamson) v Secretary of State for Education and Employment* [2003] ELR 176 (CA); [2005] ELR 291; [2005] 1 AC 246 (HL).

[131] *Campbell and Cosans v UK (No 2)* (1982) 4 EHRR 293 at para 36. See further the discussion in Chap 2.

One may profoundly disagree with the appellants' views, but it seems hard to say that they are not cogent, serious, cohesive and important . . . I cannot see why the belief in favour of the use of corporal punishment in schools as here described does not equally well qualify as a philosophical conviction, and . . . as a religious conviction.[132]

In the House of Lords, Baroness Hale accepted that beliefs in the value or undesirability of corporal punishment would be 'essentially moral beliefs . . . entitled to respect' on the basis that '[a] free and plural society must expect to tolerate all sorts of views which many, even most, find completely unacceptable'.[133] On that basis, it may well be the case that a firm belief in inclusive education, which many in fact hold, may now be recognised as amounting to a philosophical conviction, just as, for example, a religiously-based belief in single-sex education could also fall within the remit of A2P1. But even so, the Strasbourg case law provides the state with ample grounds on which to reject the parents' choice, such as the need to operate policy in the general interest, in addition to those already set by the domestic legislation. In *T*, Richards J noted that even if the parents' preference for inclusive education did amount to a philosophical conviction for the purposes of A2P1, the tribunal had given 'due weight to that preference, to the extent permitted by s 319 of the 1996 Act' (which merely requires the parents to be consulted over an arrangement for special educational provision to be made for a child other than at a school and was 'a permissible legislative choice').[134]

In *Graeme*, above, the mother also argued that the residential placement preferred by the LEA constituted a breach of the right to respect for family life for the purposes of Article 8 of the Convention. The Commission said that the interference was justifiable within the terms of Article 8(2)[135] as it was 'in accordance with the law, or prescribed by law, and necessary in a democratic society for the protection of the rights of others, namely the son's right to a suitable education for his disabilities'.[136] However, in one case in the High Court, a similar complaint was rejected by Sullivan J on the basis that Article 8 was not engaged, because the decision (by the tribunal) that the child should attend a boarding school for those with severe hearing impairment did not compel the child's attendance there, since the parents could make alternative arrangements (although they would have to meet the cost).[137] However, Sullivan J also felt that Article 8(2) would have applied on a similar basis to that identified in *Graeme*. The fact that at the core of parental preference for inclusive education is the desire that children with special educational needs, even quite severe and complex needs, should as far as possible be able to function as social beings within wider society does not mean in itself that exclusion from mainstream schooling necessarily engages Article 8. In one case outside the field of special

---

[132] *Williamson* n 130 above [2003] ELR 176, at paras 150–152.
[133] Ibid, at para 77.
[134] N 127 above, at para 39(iv).
[135] See p 77 above.
[136] N 125 above, 'The Law', Part 1.
[137] *CB v London Borough of Merton and Special Educational Needs Tribunal* [2002] ELR 441.

educational needs where the child had been excluded from mainstream education for disciplinary reasons, the parents argued that the child had a right under Article 8 to develop a personality within the school community and that it was being denied. Newman J refused to recognise the existence of such a right and said that the child was 'not being denied the opportunity to develop his personality in conjunction with others simply because he is not in mainstream school'.[138]

Does the UN Convention on the Rights of the Child (UNCRC) provide a right to inclusive education? Article 23 was referred to above. It recognises the right of the disabled child to a 'full and decent life, in conditions which . . . facilitate the child's active participation in the community' and to assistance 'designed to ensure that the disabled child has effective access to and receives education . . . in a manner conducive to the child's achieving the fullest possible social integration and individual development'. Moreover, as noted in Chapter 2, Article 28(1) of the Convention recognises the child's right to education on the basis of equality of opportunity and provides for secondary education to be 'available and accessible to every child'. Fortin comments that neither of these Articles contains specific references to the disabled child's right to be educated alongside his or her peers in a mainstream school.[139] Saleh, on the other hand, considers that the combined effect of these and other provisions, including Article 6 (the child's right to development), is that inclusive education for disabled children is implicitly recognised as a right of the child.[140] As Kilkelly notes, the UNCRC reflects the increasingly normative status of inclusion internationally.[141] For example, in the United States (a state that is not in fact a signatory to the Convention), states must ensure that each child with a disability (which includes, inter alios, those with autism, specific learning disabilities or developmental delays[142]) must be educated in the 'least restrictive environment', which means being educated alongside other children to the maximum extent possible. Segregation is permitted only where the child's needs cannot be met in a mainstream setting even with the provision of supplementary aids and services.[143] The policy of inclusion has been endorsed by UNESCO in *The Salamanca Statement and Framework for Action on Special Needs Education*, which calls for children with special educational needs to have access to 'regular schools' and for strong governmental support (including funding priority) to be given to inclusive education.[144] In fact, some countries have a poor record as

---

[138] *R (B) v Head Teacher of Alperton Community School and Others; R v Head Teacher of Wembley High School and Others ex p T; R v Governing Body of Cardinal Newman High School and Others ex p C* [2001] ELR 359, para [67].

[139] J Fortin, *Children's Rights and the Developing Law* (2nd edn, London, Lexis Nexis, 2002) 361.

[140] See L Saleh, 'Rights of the Child with Special Needs' in S Hart *et al* (eds), *Children's Rights in Education* (London, Jessica Kingsley, 2001) 119 at 122–3.

[141] U Kilkelly, *The Child and the European Convention on Human Rights* (Aldershot, Ashgate, 1999) 80.

[142] Individuals with Disabilities Education Act (IDEA) 20 USCA § 1401(3).

[143] Ibid, § 1401(5)(A). For a discussion of the relevant US cases, confirming that the 'bottom line is that an inclusionary placement should be the setting of choice', see AG Osborne and CJ Russo, *Special Education and the Law* (3rd edn, Thousand Oaks, Cal, Corwin Press, 2006), ch 2.

[144] (Paris, UNESCO, 1994).

regards the inclusion or integration of children with disabilities into mainstream education, according to reports by the Committee on the Rights of the Child.[145]

Inclusion: the Way Forward

Recently, the House of Commons Education and Skills Committee conducted an inquiry into special educational needs.[146] The issue of inclusion was one of the principal matters reported on by the Committee, which is not surprising in view of its prominence in a paper by Baroness Warnock, published in May 2005,[147] re-visiting the main issues that were the subject of the report of the Committee that she chaired nearly 30 years ago. Baroness Warnock expresses the view that inclusion is not working, at least in secondary schools, and needs to be reconsidered.[148] She expresses concern at the bullying of children with special educational needs in mainstream schools. She argues that children with statements should not be taught in mainstream schools, and that statements should be the passport to special schools, where the provision needed would be made. These views have attracted considerable criticism. In a paper published on the web, for example, Len Barton, Professor of Education at the Institute of Education in London, has argued that Warnock's paper is 'a reflection of naivety, arrogance and ignorance' and downplays the wider importance of special educational needs inclusion as contributing to the challenging of all forms of discrimination and exclusion.[149] In its written submission to the House of Commons Select Committee, the leading voluntary sector organisation supporting parents of children with special educational needs in dispute with their LEA says that 'on the evidence of her 2005 pamphlet Mary Warnock would seem, now, to know little of how the special educational needs system operates'.[150] These criticisms may be valid, but it is important to view Warnock's ideas in the context of the shifting perceptions concerning special educational needs. The Audit Commission noted that 'there are many children for whom the SEN label might no longer be appropriate or necessary, as schools become more adept at responding to the diversity of needs in today's classrooms'.[151] Warnock's proposals focus on those whom she feels cannot fully benefit from their

---

[145] L Lundy, 'Schoolchildren and Health: The Role of International Human Rights Law' in N Harris and P Meredith (eds), *Children, Education and Health. International Perspectives on Law and Policy* (Aldershot, Ashgate, 2005), 3–28. See also J Fortin, *Children's Rights and the Developing Law* (2nd edn, London, Lexis Nexis, 2002) 361.

[146] See House of Commons Education and Skills Committee, *Vol I*, n 10 above, and *Vol 2, Oral and Written Evidence*, HC 478–II and HC 478–III.

[147] M Warnock, *Special Educational Needs: A New Look* (London, Philosophy of Education Society of Great Britain, 2005).

[148] Ibid, 35.

[149] L Barton, *Special Educational Needs: an Alternative Look*, available at www.leeds.ac.uk/disability-studies/archiveuk/barton/Warnock.pdf (3 Nov 2005) 1 and 4.

[150] IPSEA, *Submission to the Education and Skills Select Committee Inquiry into Special Educational Needs* (Woodbridge, IPSEA, 2005), para 3.11.1.

[151] Audit Commission, *Special Educational Needs: A Mainstream Issue* (London, Audit Commission, 2002), para 130.

education if it takes place in a mainstream setting. The challenge will lie in identifying such children more effectively. Meanwhile there are legal presumptions of inclusion within both the Education Act 1996 and the DDA 1995 which reflect the basic principle in the *Brown* case, noted in Chapter 4, that 'separate facilities are inherently unequal'.[152] Warnock may be correct in saying that the policy of inclusion has proved problematic, but the report of the House of Commons Select Committee, published in July 2006, may help to determine whether the policy is worth perservering with in its present form, extending further, or reformulating along the lines suggested by Warnock. However, the Committee's report, while clear that the current system is 'struggling to remain fit for purpose', is somewhat inconclusive on the issue of inclusion, being more concerned to press the Government to clarify its current policy, in which it appears to have backtracked on the idea that placements in special schools must fall, perhaps by a specific rate, and to be contemplating a 'third way' involving a 'flexible continuum of provision'.[153]

CHOICE OF NAMED PLACEMENT

The Right to Express a Preference: Schedule 27 paragraph 3

As human rights arguments are unlikely, in themselves, to secure them any choice over their child's placement, parents must rely on the basic statutory right within Schedule 27 to the 1996 Act. This enables parents to express a preference for a maintained school to be named in the statement, a right which arises when a statement is first proposed, when the LEA decides to amend an existing statement or if the parent simply makes a request for a change of named school.[154] There is a presumption within Schedule 27 paragraph 3 in favour of the upholding of parental preference, provided the expressed preference refers to a specific school. In making his or her choice the parent will have access to a report prepared by the governing body containing 'special needs information' relating to the school.[155] If, when making representations to the LEA after being served with the draft statement or draft amended statement,[156] or when bringing an appeal, the parent is prepared merely to argue for a particular *type* of placement, that issue will need to be considered by the LEA or, in the case of an appeal, the

---

[152] *Brown v Board of Education of Topeka* 347 US 483 (1954). See pp 145–6 above.

[153] House of Commons Education and Skills Committee, n 10 above, paras 63, 64 and 734–785.

[154] EA 1996, Sched 27, paras 3 and 8.

[155] Ibid, s 317(5), as substituted by the EA 2005, Sched 18, para 2. 'Special needs information' is defined (in ibid subss (6) and (6A)) as information to be prescribed plus information as to the arrangements for the admission of disabled (as defined in the DDA 1995: see Chap 4) pupils; the steps taken to prevent disabled pupils from being treated less favourably than other pupils; the facilities provided to assist access to the school by disabled pupils; and the governing body's accessibility plan prepared under its duty in DDA 1995, s 28D (see pp 173–4 above).

[156] EA 1996, Sched 27, paras 2, 2A and 2B.

tribunal.[157] In *Osuala*,[158] for example, the parents of an autistic child wanted a mainstream placement and the tribunal had ordered the LEA to place the child in a school that had sufficient expertise and a special unit catering for the needs of autistic children. In the event the court quashed the decision because the LEA showed that such facilities did not exist in the locality.

The absence of a suitable local specialist placement in *Osuala* is indicative of one of the principal barriers to parental choice of placement. Indeed, parents of autistic children are particularly likely to run into this difficulty, according to the Audit Commission, which noted that parents tend to feel they have 'little choice over which school their child could attend' because either there is no appropriate specialist provision locally or the schools they prefer have 'discouraged them from applying for a place, for example, by suggesting another school might be more suitable'.[159] Non-specialist schools are particularly reluctant to take children with emotional and behavioural difficulties, autistic spectrum disorders, physical difficulties and moderate or severe learning difficulties.[160] Those schools that *are* willing to admit such pupils tend to create a 'magnet effect', which, while beneficial in terms of engendering the development of specialist expertise and provision as the critical mass of children with particular needs grows, could polarise the pattern of provision across schools in the area.[161]

If the parents have expressed a preference for a particular maintained school, the LEA will be under a duty, contained in Schedule 27 paragraph 3(3), to specify that school in the statement, unless one of the statutory exceptions applies. The first ground on which the LEA may deny the preference is that the school is unsuitable for the child's age, ability or aptitude or for his or her special educational needs. The second ground mirrors the school admissions 'efficiency' ground discussed in Chapter 5: that 'the attendance of the child at the school would be incompatible with the provision of efficient education for the children with whom he would be educated or the efficient use of resources'. In its most recent report, the House of Commons Education and Skills Committee states that it regards the qualification relating to the education of other children at the school as putting 'the final discretionary power in the hands of officials and professionals rather than the parents', a position which the Committee in fact supports.[162] Another reason that the efficiency ground is clearly the more problematic for parents is because the additional cost of a placement favoured by a parent can negate his or her choice. In *Wardle-Heron v London Borough of Newham and the SENT*,[163] for example, the court seemed to proceed on the basis that the expression of parental preference itself and the educational advantages of the parents' selected placement had to be weighed against the additional cost. If

---

[157] Ibid, Sched 27, paras 4 and 5; ibid, s 9.

[158] *London Borough of Islington and SENDIST v Osuala* [2005] EWHC Admin 1519.

[159] Audit Commission, *Special Educational Needs: A Mainstream Issue* (London, Audit Commission, 2002), para 42.

[160] Ibid, para 43.

[161] Ibid, para 45.

[162] House of Commons Education and Skills Committee, n 10 above, paras 191 and 194.

[163] [2004] ELR 68 (QBD).

both placements are suitable for the child, the comparative cost will be the decisive factor. As Kay J said in *Surrey County Council v P and P*:

> If the situation was that one alternative would result in significant additional expenditure, then provided both schools were appropriate for the child's special educational needs, the local authority would be entitled to justify sending the child to a school other than that of the parents' choice.[164]

What amounts to 'significant additional expenditure' is uncertain. It is clear that the courts will generally want to leave this to the judgment of the LEA or, on appeal, the tribunal. Indeed, in one case where the tribunal rejected the LEA's preferred placement costing £12,200 per annum and upheld as a reasonable use of public funds the parents' choice of a residential placement which involved an annual cost of £70,000, Jackson J said that, as the High Court is considering an appeal on a point of law only, it 'cannot quash the tribunal's decision on grounds of undue extravagance'.[165] The courts have nevertheless offered some guidance on the matter.[166] In *S v London Borough of Hackney and the SENT*,[167] for example, Collins J said that the tribunal, having found no material qualitative difference between two placements, had been entitled to regard a cost difference of £2,000 per annum between two placements as a significant deciding factor. In another case, the court confirmed that in weighing up the cost of alternative placements, including the transport costs, it is the marginal or additional cost to the authority of each placement that falls to be taken into account: if, for example, the LEA is already paying for a vehicle to take children to a particular school and a further child can be transported at no extra cost, the marginal cost in that case, at least in respect of transport, would be zero.[168] In *R (D) v Davies and Surrey County Council*[169] a cost differential of £20,000 between two placements gave rise to additional expenditure that Maurice Kay J considered to be firmly within the bounds of an inefficient use of resources.

In view of the disparities between different LEAs' special educational needs provision, it may be that in some cases parents will want a particular placement that lies beyond the boundary of their LEA. The question of whose costs are relevant for this purpose has had to be resolved. In *B v London Borough of Harrow and Others*[170] the family lived in the London Borough of Harrow and the child, who was severely disabled, was placed in one of its special schools. The child's mother later argued that the child's needs were not being met and wanted the

---

[164] [1997] ELR 516, at 523C See also *R (RG) v London Borough of Ealing and SENDIST* [2005] EWHC Admin 2335.

[165] *R (Wiltshire County Council) v YM and Special Educational Needs and Disability Tribunal* [2005] EWHC Admin 2521; [2006] ELR 56, at para 21.

[166] See, eg, *Oxfordshire County Council v GB and others* [2002] ELR 8 (CA). For discussion, see N Armstrong and D Wolfe, 'Special Educational Needs: Counting the Cost' [2002] *Legal Action* (January) 23.

[167] [2002] ELR 45.

[168] *R (W) v The Special Educational Needs and Disability Tribunal and the London Borough of Hillingdon* [2005] EWHC Admin 1580; [2005] ELR 599, per Stanley Burnton J.

[169] [2004] ELR 416 (QBD).

[170] [2000] ELR 109.

child to be placed in a school in neighbouring Hillingdon. Harrow refused to support this move, saying that it would make it more difficult for it to manage a co-ordinated response to the girl's needs and would cost too much (an extra £7,000 per annum). The tribunal agreed that a placement at the school in Hillingdon would not be compatible with 'the efficient use of resources'. A question arose as to whose resources fell to be considered for this purpose: the sending authority's (ie, Harrow's) or those of the receiving authority (Hillingdon). The House of Lords held that the relevant resources were those of the sending authority. That enabled account to be taken by the authority which had responsibility for the child (the sending authority) of the additional cost that educating a child outside the borough would generally involve.[171] However, one implication, acknowledged by Lord Slynn of Hadley,[172] is that it could be more difficult for a parent to secure his or her child's placement at a school outside the LEA's area.

The complexity of the law governing school placement and parental choice has increased following amendments made by SENDA 2001. A new provision states that Schedule 27 paragraph 3 is not affected by section 316 which, as noted above, contains the presumption in favour of a mainstream placement.[173] Thus if a parent expresses a preference for a particular maintained special school the LEA has to apply the conditions in Schedule 27 paragraph 3(3) to decide whether parental choice should be met, and in doing so it can ignore the conditional duty under section 316 to ensure a mainstream placement. Thus, as confirmed by the Court of Appeal in *R (MH) v SENDIST and Hounslow*,[174] if the LEA is under a duty under Schedule 27 to adhere to the parents' choice, because neither of the exceptions applies, then that school must be named as the placement, regardless of the section 316 duty. Subsequently a question arose as to whether this judgment applied to a request by a parent for a change of school named in a statement, governed by Schedule 27 paragraph 8, where the same parental preference right and exceptions apply.[175] In *Slough Borough Council and the Special Educational Needs and Disability Tribunal v C*[176] the court answered this question in the negative. The LEA had specified a special school, but the tribunal applied section 316 and found in favour of the parents, who wanted a mainstream school. Richards J held that section 316 did not apply to change of school cases: '[s]ince the *type* of school is not in issue when a determination is made under para 8, there is no reason why s 316 should apply'.[177] Returning to the duty under Schedule 27 paragraph 3(3), if the LEA decides that it is *not* under a duty to accede to the parent's choice because at least one of the two exceptions applies, the LEA's duty under section 316 will apply if or when the authority comes to name a school in the statement.[178]

---

[171] Note that the LEA's duty to admit a child to a school named in the statement applies even where the school is outside the LEA's area: *R v Chair of Governors of A and S School ex T* [2000] ELR 274.

[172] At 116C–D.

[173] EA 1996, s 316A(3).

[174] [2004] ELR 424 (CA).

[175] EA 1996, Sched 27, para 8.

[176] [2004] ELR 546.

[177] Ibid, per Richards J at para 28(vii).

[178] See EA 1996, s 316A(4).

The General Principle that Children Are to Be Educated in Accordance with Their Parents' Wishes

The LEA's duty to adhere to the parents' preference under Schedule 27 paragraph 3(3) applies only where the parent has expressed a preference for a placement in a maintained school, including a state special school. It is clear that, if the parents want an *independent* or *other non-maintained school* to be named in the statement, the Schedule 27 paragraph 3(3) duty will not apply; the House of Commons Education and Skills Committee was critical of the fact that this means that the parents will not be able to select an academy (which is classed as an independent school under statute) under this provision, an inequality that it feels should be removed.[179] But the LEA and tribunal will nevertheless be required to take account of the parents' wishes under section 9 of the Act.[180] As noted in Chapter 5, section 9 requires the LEA and the Secretary of State, in exercising their statutory powers and performing their statutory duties, to 'have regard to the general principle . . . that pupils are to be educated in accordance with the wishes of their parents, so far as that is compatible with the provision of efficient instruction and training and the avoidance of unreasonable public expenditure'.[181] The jurisprudence on section 9 in the context of special educational needs indicates that section 9 'does not require the local education authority to give priority to parental wishes, so long as they are properly considered and taken into account',[182] reflecting the earlier case law on school admission discussed in Chapter 5. As Richards J put it, the established view is that parental wishes, while 'important . . . are not decisive'.[183] Those wishes must, in any event, play against the judgment of the LEA as regards the suitability of the school, for they need not prevail if, for example, the LEA (or, in turn, the tribunal) considers that the school selected by it was markedly more suitable for the child than the parents' choice.[184] As Sullivan J put it in a case where the mother of a 10-year-old boy with dyslexia wanted the LEA to fund a placement for her child at an independent school, parental preference 'will rarely be determinative. In the great majority of cases it will, no doubt, be outweighed by degrees of appropriateness and/or question[s] of cost . . . and convenience'.[185] In one case the court, having judged the tribunal to have properly weighed up the two placement options, considered that the parents' preference for a particular

---

[179] House of Commons Education and Skills Committee, n 10 above, paras 202, 203 and 207. The relevant statutory provision showing the status of academies is EA 1996, s 482.

[180] *C v Buckinghamshire County Council and the Special Educational Needs Tribunal* [1999] ELR 179 (CA).

[181] EA 1996, s 9, previously EA 1944, s 76.

[182] *R v West Sussex County Council ex p S* [1999] ELR 40: per David Pannick QC, sitting as a High Court judge, at 45A–B.

[183] *A v Birmingham City Council* [2004] ELR 563, at para 24, per Sir Richard Tucker.

[184] *C v Buckinghamshire County Council and the Special Educational Needs Tribunal* [1999] ELR 179 (CA) per Sedley LJ.

[185] *B v Gloucestershire County Council and the Special Educational Needs Tribunal* [1998] ELR 539, at 547B–C.

independent school was intrinsically 'of little significance'.[186] Indeed, section 9 seems to come into play only in order to resolve a choice between equal alternatives for meeting the child's needs.[187] It is likely to be the decisive factor only where there is 'parity of cost and parity of facilities'.[188]

Section 9 itself requires account to be taken of the cost of a placement, as the duty to adhere to parental wishes is subject to the condition that the parents' choice does not give rise to 'unreasonable public expenditure', a condition that aims to 'prevent parental choice placing an undue or disproportionate burden on the education budget'.[189] In *S v London Borough of Hackney and the SENT*, Collins J said that 'parental preference will not prevail over unreasonable public expenditure' and that the tribunal had been entitled to conclude that a net cost difference of £2,000 per annum between a private school and maintained school placement was 'significant' and 'meant that the increased public expenditure was unreasonable'.[190] On the other hand, the LEA is under a duty by virtue of section 324 of the 1996 Act to name a school at which the child will receive appropriate provision and, as Jackson J said in a more recent case, that section 'does not permit inappropriate educational provision to be made simply on the grounds of cost'.[191] Once it is established that the provision is appropriate, it becomes a question of determining whether the extra cost of the more expensive independent school placement can be justified. As the Court of Appeal confirmed in the *Oxfordshire* case, the additional cost has to be weighed against the educational benefits of the placement.[192] In *Wardle-Heron v London Borough of Newham and the SENT*, the court seemed to proceed on the basis that the expression of parental preference itself *and* the educational advantages of the parents' selected placement had to be weighed against the additional cost.[193] The question whether 'public expenditure' for this purpose is restricted to expenditure by education authorities is seemingly unresolved: in *HW and W v Bedfordshire County Council*,[194] where the LEA had acknowledged that if the child, who was profoundly disabled, was to be placed in a day school he would also need provision out of school hours from the local authority's social services department, the court decided that it was an issue to be decided 'on another occasion'.[195]

Whatever the parents' preference, the chances of securing an independent or non-maintained school placement are fairly slim. Despite government efforts to

---

[186] *W-R v Solihull Metropolitan Borough Council and Wall* [1999] ELR 528, at 543D–E.

[187] *S and S v Bracknell Forest Borough Council and the Special Educational Needs Tribunal* [1999] ELR 51, per Scott Baker J.

[188] *C v Buckinghamshire County Council and the Special Educational Needs Tribunal* 1999] ELR 179, per Thorpe LJ at 189F–G.

[189] *Oxfordshire County Council v GB and others* [2002] ELR 8 at para [15], per Sedley LJ.

[190] [2002] ELR 45, at paras 40 and 44.

[191] *R (Wiltshire County Council) v YM and SENDIST* [2006] ELR 56, at para 20.

[192] Ibid. See N Armstrong and D Wolfe, 'Special Educational Needs: Counting the Cost' [2002] *Legal Action* (January) 23. See also *R (A) v London Borough of Richmond and the Special Educational Needs and Disabilities Tribunal* [2004] EWHC Admin 1290.

[193] [2004] ELR 68 (QBD), at 16.

[194] [2004] EWHC Admin 560.

[195] Ibid, para 20.

promote inclusion in mainstream education, it is still the case that significant numbers of statemented children are educated in maintained special schools. Placements *outside* the maintained sector are much less common. In January 2005, for example, only 12,670 (5.3 per cent) of the 242,580 statemented pupils were placed in independent or non-maintained special schools, compared to 83,290 statemented pupils (34.3 per cent) who attended maintained special schools.[196]

Although there is no limitation to the subject matter of the parental wishes that fall to be taken into account, the duty in section 9 is in other respects similar to the duty under the second sentence of A2P1 of the ECHR. As noted above, the Article, discussed in depth in Chapter 2, requires the state to respect the right of parents to ensure the teaching of their child in accordance with the parents' religious and philosophical convictions. This is subject to the reservation entered into by the UK that adopts exactly the wording of the conditions attached to section 9 (compatibility with the provision of efficient instruction and training and 'the avoidance of unreasonable public expenditure'). On the basis of the approach adopted by the Strasbourg jurisprudence, and in particular the decisions in *Simpson v UK*[197] and *Belgian Linguistics Case (No 2)*,[198] the state has considerable discretion and is able to take account of the need to manage resources carefully. Against this background, and particularly in the light of the UK's reservation to the Convention, the Human Rights Act 1998 appears not to have advanced the prospects for parental choice of placement in the context of special educational needs and thus far has been little relied upon by parents.[199] However, in one special educational needs placement case the court indicated, hypothetically, that an argument that account should have been taken, for the purposes of the Article, of the parents' preference for a Roman Catholic School placement for their child might have succeeded.[200] Yet it is hard to see how the Article adds anything to section 9. One potential difficulty for a parent relying on Article 2 of Protocol 1 in this context may be in showing that choice of school placement is based on a philosophical conviction, as noted above.

The parents may, of course, seek to exercise choice via other Convention rights, such as those contained in Articles 8 (respect for private and family life) and 9 (freedom of thought, conscience or religion), both of which were discussed in Chapter 2. This happened in *A v Special Education Needs and Disability Tribunal and London Borough of Barnet*,[201] where Jewish parents wanted their disabled child to be educated at a private Jewish day school, but the LEA wanted to place her at a state special school. The tribunal found in favour of the

---

[196] Department for Education and Skills, *Special Educational Needs in England, January 2005* (London, Department for Education and Skills, 2005), table 1a.

[197] N 116 above, 'The Law', para [2].

[198] N 119 above.

[199] See *H v Kent County Council and the Special Educational Needs Tribunal* [2000] ELR 660 and *L v Hereford and Worcester County Council and Hughes* [2000] ELR 375. See pp 335–9 above.

[200] The court said that the point would have to have been raised before the tribunal: *S v London Borough of Hackney and the Special Educational Needs Tribunal* [2001] EWHC Admin 572; [2002] ELR 45.

[201] [2004] ELR 293 (QBD).

authority. The parents argued that the tribunal had failed to take account of the child's cultural and practical need to attend a Jewish school and had thereby breached her rights under Articles 8 and 9. The court, however, held that the tribunal had to consider the child's Jewishness as part of its statutory responsibility under the Education Act 1996, and that as a result the Convention rights 'add nothing'.[202]

DISPUTE RESOLUTION

Riddell et al have explained that the special educational needs system in England and Wales, especially after the Education Act 1993 intensified the legal obligations of LEAs and established the Special Educational Needs Tribunal, is dominated by legal and bureaucratic policy frameworks.[203] There is the application of rules within a bureaucratic framework of decision-making, particularly at LEA level, with the legitimating goal of accuracy and consistency. This is combined with the enforcement of individual rights enshrined in law via an independent appellate framework. While professional judgment (whereby the views and interventions of professionals such as teachers and psychologists dominate the decision-making processes) was the prevailing policy framework in the past,[204] that is no longer the case, despite the continuing element of discretion within the system. Indeed, Riddell *et al* indicate that professional discretion could be viewed as dangerous if it interfered with individual rights. The assertion of rights through the process of challenging a decision, such as by bringing an appeal, could be seen as highlighting the negative consequences of the legal policy framework, particularly the element of consumerism represented by the principle of choice embodied within the law. In particular, given the resources needed to meet children's needs in this field, some view the appeal system as little more than an opportunity for some parents to demand a disproportionate share of limited resources. Evans found that among some LEAs there were concerns that tribunal decisions 'had skewed resource allocation towards one or two cases with the result that there was less availability for the majority'.[205]

The parent (including a foster parent[206]) has a right of appeal against the contents of the statement and must be notified of this right by the LEA when a copy of the statement is served.[207] Many of these appeals will concern the

---

[202] Ibid, at para 41.

[203] S Riddell *et al*, 'Special Educational Needs and Competing Policy Frameworks in England and Scotland' (2000) 15 *Journal of Social Policy* 621, drawing on Mashaw's typology: JL Mashaw, *Bureaucratic Justice: Manging Social Security Disability Claims* (New Haven, Conn, and London, Yale University Press, 1983).

[204] See generally D Armstrong, *Power and Partnership in Education* (London, Routledge, 1995) 20–5.

[205] J Evans, *Getting it Right. LEAs and the Special Educational Needs Tribunal* (Slough, NFER, 1998) 64.

[206] *Fairpo v Humberside County Council* [1997] ELR 12 (QBD).

[207] EA 1996, s 326 and Sched 27, para 6.

particular provision specified in the statement. Among the most problematic questions are the degree of specificity to be employed in the statement[208] and whether particular provision is educational or non-educational. The importance of the latter question arises from the fact that the LEA is under a duty to ensure only that *educational* provision specified in a statement is made, while it has a mere discretion to arrange for non-educational provision.[209] This distinction attracts the criticism that the child with needs arising from a condition such as autism 'has become fragmented, according to which social agency is responsible for which of the child's disabilities'.[210] As a question of law, the problems arising from the uncertain distinction between educational and non-educational have been compounded by the courts' acknowledgment that this often a grey area best left to professional judgment in individual cases. For example, in *London Borough of Bromley v Special Educational Needs Tribunal*,[211] a 12-year-old child had severe physical disabilities and attended an LEA-maintained special school. His parents wanted him to be placed at a specialist independent residential school, at an extra cost to the LEA of £20,000 per annum. The parents argued that the child's needs for physiotherapy, occupational therapy and speech therapy were all educational needs, and that the statement should reflect that fact. The tribunal agreed and held that his needs were not being met and that he should be placed at the school that the parents preferred. The Court of Appeal felt that there was nothing irrational in the tribunal concluding that a need for physiotherapy, occupational therapy and speech therapy might at least in part be an educational need. However, Sedley LJ accepted that there could easily be a difference of opinion on such a matter, and that while the uncertainty was 'less than ideal', it had been 'an intelligible choice on Parliament's part where the alternative is a rigid categorisation productive of far more doubt, dispute and litigation than what I would hold to be the method of Parliament's choice'.[212] So far as the distinction between 'educational' and 'non-educational provision' was concerned, there was:

---

[208] The case law on this is discussed in N Harris, 'Special Educational Needs—the Role of the Courts' (2002) 14 *Child & Family Law Quarterly* 137 at 147–50. See also *R (Wiltshire County Council) v YM and SENDIST* [2006] ELR 56.

[209] Unless the parents have made 'suitable arrangements' the LEA *must* make any specified special *educational* provision and *may* make any *non-educational* provision: EA 1996, s 324(5)(a)(i) and (ii). If the parents make 'suitable arrangements they effectively relieve the local education authority of its duty': *R v Governors of Hasmonean High School ex p N and E* [1994] ELR 343 (CA), at 355D per Glidewell LJ. In *G v London Borough of Barnet and the Special Educational Needs Tribunal* [1998] ELR 480 (QBD), Ognall J said (at 486E) that 'the question of "suitable arrangements" is a question of funding the necessary schooling'. If the parents have not been able to make 'arrangements for funding for a reasonable period of time' the arrangements may not be suitable: *White and Another v London Borough of Ealing and the Special Educational Needs Tribunal; Richardson v Solihull Metropolitan Borough Council; Solihull Metropolitan Borough Council v Finn and the Special Educational Needs Tribunal* [1998] ELR 203, per Dyson J at 225B. Here the parents raised funds for their child, who had cerebral palsy, to attend the Higashi School in Boston (costing approx. £50,000 per annum). Dyson J said (at 225E–F) that 'it would have been unreasonable to decide that suitable arrangements had been made because the parents would be able to finance his schooling by future fund raising'. See also *R v LB Hackney ex GC* [1995] ELR 144 (QBD) and [1996] ELR 142 (CA).

[210] M King and D King, 'How the Law Defines the Special Educational Needs of Autistic Children' (2006) 18 *Child & Family Law Quarterly* 23, at 38.

[211] [1999] ELR 260 (QBD and CA).

[212] Ibid, at 296E.

between the unequivocally educational and the unequivocally non-educational a shared territory of provision which can be intelligibly allocated to either . . . The potentially large intermediate area of provision which is capable of ranking as educational or non-educational is not made the subject of any statutory prescription precisely because it is for the local education authority, and if necessary the [special educational needs tribunal], to exercise a case-by-case judgment which no prescriptive legislation could ever hope to anticipate.[213]

The distinction may be easier to make in some cases than others, particularly where health issues are concerned, as in *City of Bradford Metropolitan Council v A*,[214] where nursing care to enable a severely disabled child to be safe at school was not considered to be 'educational provision'. Assuming that the LEA or tribunal has identified educational provision correctly, the courts are left merely to emphasise the need for joined-up approaches to addressing the needs of the child: 'a child's special educational needs cannot be viewed in isolation . . . A holistic approach is necessary, and inter-agency co-operation is essential'.[215]

Many appeals concern choice of school. For example, of the 134 pupils at one special school in Hampshire, 30 secured their places as a result of bringing an appeal to the tribunal.[216] The 1996 Act provides that the SENDIST, when deciding the appeal, must not order the LEA to specify the name of a school in the statement (either in place of a school already named in the statement or where no school is named in it) unless (i) the parent has expressed a preference for the school under Schedule 27 paragraph 3 or, (ii) in the appeal proceedings, either the parent, the LEA, or both has or have proposed the school.[217] In *Rhondda Cynon Taff CBC v SENT and V*[218] it was held that if the tribunal finds that the school proposed by the LEA is inappropriate, it does not have to give the LEA an opportunity at that stage to suggest another school to be named in its place, because to do so would, inter alia, work against the interests of expedition in resolving disputes and would absolve the LEA of its duty to put forward its case as fully as possible at the outset. If, however, the tribunal does accept evidence from the LEA concerning an alternative placement, it is clear from another judgment[219] that it must ensure that it has sufficient information to evaluate the suitability of the placement and that the parents have a proper opportunity to highlight any weaknesses in it.

In some cases the LEA may, legitimately, decide not to make a statement, despite having carried out an assessment and even issued a draft statement. Given that the statutory test for whether a statement should be made is one of necessity, the statute ultimately leaves this to the discretion of the LEA.[220] If no statement is

---

[213] Ibid at 295G–296A.

[214] [1997] ELR 417 (QBD).

[215] *W v Leeds City Council and the Special Educational Needs Tribunal* [2005] EWCA Civ 988; [2005] ELR 617, per Wall LJ at para 50.

[216] Reported in J Crace, 'Not so much a choice, more a battle of wills', *The Guardian*, 8 Nov 2005, 3.

[217] EA 1996, s 326(4).

[218] [2002] ELR 290 (QBD).

[219] *T v London Borough of Islington and Another* [2002] ELR 426 (QBD).

[220] EA 1996, s 324(1). The LEA will, however, need to have regard to the guidance within the *Special Educational Needs Code of Practice*, n 65 above, as noted above, p 323.

made the child must be placed at a mainstream school, unless the parents have opted to pay for private schooling. The parents could, however, appeal against the refusal to make a statement. If they do, and succeed, the tribunal could order the LEA to make and maintain a statement or remit the matter to the authority for it to decide whether a statement is necessary.[221]

There is evidence from some LEAs that 'parents use the tribunal to circumvent LEA rules on school choice'; this is because the tribunal can direct that a school be named in a statement and, as noted above, the school must admit the child, so that 'in areas where popular schools are over-subscribed, children with statements can have an advantage over children who have to go through the normal application procedure'.[222] However, as we have seen, parental choice of school placement is certainly not guaranteed.

Appeals are heard by the SENDIST, comprising a lawyer as chair sitting with two other members who have knowledge and experience of children with special educational needs.[223] The tribunal now also has jurisdiction over complaints of disability discrimination against pupils under the Disability Discrimination Act 1995,[224] in which case the other members of the tribunal will include persons with knowledge and experience of children with disabilities.[225] While there is not space here for a detailed discussion of the work of the tribunal,[226] particular aspects do require discussion. First, it is important to note that the tribunal continues to play an important role in dispute resolution in this area, notwith-standing efforts to promote mediation.[227] The number of appeals registered with the tribunal each year since it was established in 1994 increased each year until 2003–4, when there was a slight fall from the peak of 3,532 the previous year to 3,354. There was a further fall to 3,215 in 2004–5, but nevertheless, over the past 10 years the number of appeals registered has trebled overall.[228] A separate tribunal was established for Wales in 2003 and in 2003–4 it registered 117 appeals.[229] A high proportion of special educational needs appeals are withdrawn. In 2003–4, this was the case with some 45 per cent of appeals in

[221] EA 1996, s 325.

[222] J Evans, *Getting it Right. LEAs and the Special Educational Needs Tribunal* (Slough, NFER, 1998) 58.

[223] EA 1996, s 333 and the Special Educational Needs Tribunal Regulations 2001 (SI 2000/600).

[224] See Chap 4.

[225] Special Educational Needs and Disability Tribunal (General Provisions and Disability Claims Procedure) Regulations 2002 (SI 2002/1985).

[226] See further N Harris, *Special Educational Needs and Access to Justice* (Bristol, Jordans, 1997); Idem, 'The Developing Role and Structure of the Education Appeals System in England and Wales' in M Harris and M Partington (eds), *Administrative Justice in the 21st Century* (Oxford, Hart, 1999) 296, at 318–24; J Evans, *Getting it Right: LEAs and the Special Educational Needs Tribunal* (Slough, NFER, 1998).

[227] See EA 1996, s 332B, inserted by SENDA 2001, s 3, discussed below.

[228] R Hughes (President), *Special Educational Needs and Disability Tribunal Annual Report 2003–2004* (London, SENDIST, 2004) 6; idem, *Special Educational Needs and Disability Tribunal Annual Report 2004/2005* (London, SENDIST, 2005) 6.

[229] R Ellis Walker, *Special Educational Needs and Disability Tribunal for Wales Annual Report 2003–04* (Llandrindod Wells, Special Educational Needs and Disability Tribunal for Wales, 2004) 4. The Welsh tribunal was established under EA 2002, s 195 and Sched 18. Prior to 1 Sept 2003 appeals in Wales were covered by the main SENDIST jurisdiction.

England, generally because the LEA agreed to meet at least some of the parents' wishes. Decisions that year were issued in 1,200 cases.[230] The SENDA 2001 has in fact made provision for the rapid disposition of unopposed appeals, meaning those where the LEA notifies the tribunal that it will not, or will no longer, oppose the appeal. In such cases the appeal is determined in favour of the appellant and the tribunal is not required to make any order.[231] Appeal against SENDIST decisions lies to the High Court on a point of law.[232]

In 2004–5, some 35.2 per cent of the appeals registered with the tribunal wholly or partly concerned the choice of placement in the statement.[233] In relation to appeals solely concerned with school placement, which is a matter covered by part 4 of the statement, the success rate for parents was 63 per cent, around the average over the past five years.[234] The success rate in appeals which concerned school placement and at least one other aspect of the statement was 93 per cent, although the data do not show how each element was decided; and, according to the two most recent annual reports of the tribunal, the parents will only have achieved 'a small proportion of their objectives'.[235]

The special educational needs of the appellants' children (as we saw in Chapter 2, in these cases parents alone may be appellants) span a wide range, with the largest three groups being those with a 'specific learning difficulty', primarily dyslexia (19.3 per cent); those with autistic spectrum disorder (23.7 per cent); and those with behavioural, emotional or social difficulty (13.7 per cent).[236] The fact that dyslexia is more common among boys than girls[237] is an important factor in the greater incidence of appeals concerning boys,[238] combined with the fact that special educational needs in general appear to be much more prevalent among males, as noted above.

While special educational needs are found across the social spectrum and affect all ethnic groups, one of the issues to have emerged from research on the tribunal is that the experience of parents as regards the accessibility of the appeals

---

[230] Hughes (2004), n 228 above, 7.

[231] EA 1996, s 326A, inserted by the SENDA 2001, s 5. This applies only to appeals under ss 325 (refusal to make a statement), 328 (refusal to carry out an assessment requested by parent), 329A (refusal to carry out review or assessment of child at request of responsible body) or Sched 27, para 8(3) (refusal to comply with a request for a change of school named in statement). Note that a parent may also appeal to the SENDIST against a decision to make, amend or not to amend a statement (s 326); a refusal to carry out an assessment of a child for whom there is no statement (s 329); and a cessation of a statement (Sched 27, para 11).

[232] Tribunals and Inquiries Act 1992, s 11(1) and Sched 1. There were 53 such appeals in 2003–4 and 47 in 2004–5, mostly by parents: R Hughes (President), *Special Educational Needs and Disability Tribunal Annual Report 2004/2005* (London, SENDIST, 2005) 16.

[233] Ibid, 7.

[234] Ibid, 10. Previous annual reports show that it was 71 per cent in 1999–2000, 76 per cent in 2000–1, 67 per cent in 2001–2, 61 per cent in 2002–3 and 66 per cent in 2003–4.

[235] R Hughes (President), *Special Educational Needs and Disability Tribunal Annual Report 2003–2004* (London, SENDIST, 2004) 11; idem, *Special Educational Needs and Disability Tribunal Annual Report 2004/2005* (London, SENDIST, 2005) 10.

[236] Ibid, 8.

[237] J Swain *et al*, *Controversial Issues in a Disabling Society* (Buckingham, Open University Press, 2003) 26.

[238] Trevor Aldridge, former President of SENDIST, reported in N Harris, *Special Educational Needs and Access to Justice* (Bristol, Jordans, 1997) 77–8.

process and their effective participation in it varies across diverse social class and ethnic groups, mirroring the position in relation to the field of special educational needs as a whole.[239] Researchers have, for example, found middle class white parents to have fewer inhibitions, and greater lobbying power, than working class parents in asserting their rights in this field.[240] This has been particularly evident in relation to children with specific learning difficulties, whose parents, in a Scottish study, 'were predominantly middle class, were much more likely to challenge professional judgment than other parents of disabled children' and were seen by the professionals as exerting 'a powerful, many maintained unhealthy, grip on the system, extracting an unfairly large amount of financial support for their particular children to the disadvantage of other groups lacking powerful advocates'.[241] Evans tested the hypothesis that appeals are a 'white middle-class phenomenon' and concluded that there was a 'slight indication that this is the case', but also noted that the appeal rate is in some cases similar across a range of LEAs despite these authorities' diversity in terms of the socio-economic make up of their populations.[242] In a study by the present author, 50 per cent of the randomly selected appellants were from middle class social groups even though a majority of children with special educational needs are from less advantaged backgrounds.[243] Even allowing for the fact that middle class parents are more likely than others to respond to a postal survey, it was reasonable to conclude that middle class parents were over-represented among appellants. Generally the research confirms the view of one special school head teacher that 'tribunals are a complicated process and it's often the dogged, middle-class parents that are prepared to take the process on'.[244]

It was noted above that 18 per cent of pupils at the start of 2005 had special educational needs and 3 per cent had statements, but that there was quite a wide variation in these rates across different ethnic groups, such that children from some ethnic groups are over-represented among those pupils who have special educational needs. Despite the contention that '[n]o direct link between ethnicity and the use of the appeals system can be established',[245] the evidence suggests that

---

[239] Riddell *et al* note that in two local authorities (one in England and one in Scotland) where there were many parents who experienced high levels of social disadvantage and were 'disengaged from the process of assessment and statementing/recording', rather than being empowered they experienced the procedures as, in Foucaldian terms, a 'disciplinary mechanism': S Riddell *et al*, 'Parents, Professionals and Special Educational Needs Policy Frameworks in England and Scotland' (2002) 30 *Policy and Politics* 411 at 424.

[240] See, eg, S Riddell, S Brown and J Duffield, 'Conflicts of Policies and Models. The Case of Specific Learning Difficulties' in S Riddell and S Brown (eds), *Special Educational Needs in the 1990s* (London, Routledge, 1994) 113.

[241] C Lange and S Riddell, 'Special Educational Needs Policy and Choice. Tensions between Policy Development in the US and UK Contexts' in MJ McLaughlin and M Rouse, *Special Education and School Reform in the United States and Britain* (London, Routledge, 2000) 126 at 141; see also J Evans and C Vincent, 'Parental Choice and Special Education' in R Glatter, PA Woods and C Bagley, *Choice and Diversity in Schooling* (London, Routledge, 1997) 102 at 109–10.

[242] J Evans, *Getting it Right: LEAs and the Special Educational Needs Tribunal* (Slough, NFER, 1998) 24.

[243] N Harris, *Special Educational Needs and Access to Justice* (Bristol, Jordans, 1997) 76.

[244] Reported in J Crace, 'Not so much a choice, more a battle of wills', *The Guardian*, 8 Nov 2005, 3.

[245] J Evans, *Getting it Right: LEAs and the Special Educational Needs Tribunal* (Slough, NFER, 1998) 19.

some ethnic minorities are under-represented, proportionately speaking, among those who bring an appeal.[246] For example, of the appellants in 2003–4 2.1 per cent were Black Caribbean and 2.2 per cent were of Pakistani origin.[247] There is now important evidence from a study by Genn, Lever, Gray and Balmer for the DCA examining the impact of ethnicity in the experience of three broad ethnic groups—black (African and Caribbean), South Asian and white—across three tribunals, the SENDIST, Criminal Injuries Compensation Appeals Panels and Appeals Service tribunals.[248] The researchers did not find strong evidence that membership of a minority ethnic group put a person at a significantly greater disadvantage than others in accessing an appeal process, but did find that there were cultural or language barriers for some and a general apprehensiveness among minorities as to how they might be treated within the legal system.[249] The research found no systematic difference in the way tribunals behaved towards the minorities as compared with the white appellants, although the unrepresentativeness of tribunal panels in terms of ethnicity had a negative impact on minorities' perception of fairness.[250] The outcome of SENDIST hearings was broadly the same for all three groups; white appellants had a slightly higher success rate but the researchers found overall that '[e]thnicity did not have a significant impact upon outcome in SENDIST cases'.[251] Appellants' social class was perceived among tribunal judiciary to be a significant factor in the appellants' level of preparedness for tribunal hearings across the three tribunals, but ethnic background per se was not.[252]

Disagreement resolution, as an alternative to an appeal, has increasingly been promoted as a means of ensuring that 'practical educational solutions, acceptable to all the parties, are reached as quickly as possible with minimal disruption to the child's education' and that a long term breakdown in relations between parents and schools or LEAs is prevented and recourse to the tribunal is avoided.[253] Various models were adopted by LEAs during the 1990s, including the involvement of parent partnership officers within the LEA or the establishment by the LEA of a bespoke mediation service, or the commissioning of an independent organisation to provide mediation services. A report by Hall for the Department for Education and Employment concluded that the selection of a particular dispute resolution model, primarily one involving mediation, should be for individual LEAs.[254] That is the approach adopted by the current *Special*

---

[246] N Harris, *Special Educaitonal Needs and Access to Justice* (Bristol, Jordans, 1997) 76.

[247] R Hughes (President), *Special Educational Needs and Disability Tribunal Annual Report 2004–2005* (London, SENDIST, 2005) 15. Note that less than two-thirds of appellants completed the ethnic monitoring form, so these figures have to be viewed with a degree of caution.

[248] H Genn, B Lever, L Gray with N Balmer, *Tribunals for Diverse Users*, DCA Research Series 1/06 (London, DCA, 2006).

[249] Ibid, 109.

[250] Ibid, 171 and 226.

[251] Ibid, 254 and 278.

[252] Iibid, 302.

[253] DfES, *SEN Toolkit* (London, DfES, 2001), 3.10.

[254] J Hall, *Resolving Disputes Between Parents, Schools and LEAs: Some Examples of Best Practice* (London, Department for Education and Employment, 1999) 52.

Educational Needs Code of Practice,[255] the publication of which was subsequent to the creation of a duty for LEAs to make arrangements for the avoidance or resolution of disputes between themselves or governing bodies and parents, including the appointment of independent persons. The Code says that LEAs must operate what it terms 'disgreement resolution services' meeting minimum standards.[256]

Utilisation of these services is encouraged but is ultimately voluntary on the part of parents. This is important, because it is likely to be more difficult to reach compromises in cases where parents are pressurised into participating in a mediation process; but by diverting parents from an appeal it may also be unfair, given the success rate for parents who appeal, noted above. However, it should perhaps be stressed that mediation can occur at any stage in a disagreement, even after an appeal is lodged. Indeed, as we have seen, a high proportion of appeals are withdrawn anyway, generally because a solution has been negotiated. Yet the strong human rights case for access to the courts not to be denied by the use of alternative dispute resolution mechanisms[257] arguably applies equally to access to the SENDIST.

Among the other issues raised by the use of mediation-type procedures is whether they are more conducive to participation by children, which could arguably help to ensure that greater emphasis is placed on the best interests of the child (even though that is not something that is specifically required by legislation).[258] In the United States, where the Individuals with Disabilities in Education Act, while providing for an 'impartial due process hearing' at the request of the parents who are challenging an 'individualized education program' (IEP) drawn up by the school district authorities, also requires independent mediation to be made available in disputes between parents and school authorities over educational provision,[259] children do not attend mediation meetings.[260] This is also the position in England, for the most part, although children may be consulted.[261] As we saw in Chapter 2, limited participation by children in the processes of identifying and determining needs and provision and during the appeal hearing is now provided for under the legislation and is strongly encouraged by the Code of Practice,[262] even though the child cannot bring or be a party to an appeal in his or her own right.[263] This may be

---

[255] DfES, *Special Educational Needs Code of Practice* (London, DfES, 2001), para 2:29.

[256] Ibid, paras 2:24–2:25. See also DfES, *SEN Toolkit* (London, DfES, 2001).

[257] Eg, A Le Sueur, 'How to Resolve Disputes with Public Authorities' [2002] *Public Law* 203.

[258] But is, of course, a principle enshrined in Art 3 of the UNCRC.

[259] IDEA, §§615(e); 1414(d); 1415(f). The Supreme Court has held that at the hearing the burden of proof rests with the parents: *Schaffer v Weast* (04–698), 14 Nov 2005, 546 US 000 (2005). I am grateful to Charles J Russo of the University of Dayton for bringing this decision to my notice.

[260] J Frank, 'The West London Mediation Project' in IS Gersch and A Gersch (eds), *Resolving Disagreement in Special Educational Needs* (Routledge Falmer, 2003) 113 at 118.

[261] J Hall, *Resolving Disputes Between Parents, Schools and LEAs: Some Examples of Best Practice* (London, Department for Education and Employment, 1999) 37.

[262] Eg, when an IEP is being drawn up: see DfES, *Special Educational Needs Code of Practice* (London, DfES, 2001), para 3:7.

[263] As also noted above, p 352; see further *S v Special Educational Needs Tribunal and the City of Westminster* [1996] 1 WLR 382, [1996] ELR 228 (CA); *S and C v Special Educational Needs Tribunal* [1997] ELR 242 (QBD); for a wholly exceptional case, see *R v Special Educational Needs Tribunal ex parte South Glamorgan County Council* [1996] ELR 326.

contrasted with the position in Scotland, where a new framework for supporting those with 'additional support needs' is being introduced.[264] There, young people's independent rights are recognised in that a person aged 16 or over can refer a dispute to the tribunal, although if he or she lacks the necessary capacity to make such a reference the parent would have to act in their place.[265] So far as the mediation process in England is concerned, the Code says nothing specific about the child's involvement but hints at it by saying that '[a]ll participants, including the child, need to feel confident that their views and concerns will receive equal respect'.[266] Clearly the Code could go much further in this regard. In Scotland, similar provision is made concerning mediation; but, unlike in England, mediation is intended to resolve not only disputes between the authorities and parents but also those between the former and young people themselves (ie, those aged 16 or over).[267]

Another concern about mediation is whether it runs into the same problems concerning access that are associated with socio-economic background and ethnicity. Unfortunately there is very little evidence about the effect of social or ethnic background on the utilisation of special educational needs mediation services. In theory, mediation should be easier for persons from disadvantaged backgrounds to use, particularly where, as is meant to happen, parent partnership support is provided. The hiring of professional support, such as lawyers, by parents should not be needed. In some parts of the United States, however, lawyers have become involved on behalf of parents in special education mediation, attending mediation sessions.[268] There is no evidence that this happens in England and Wales, even though lawyers are involved in the early stages of some disputes which later go on to a tribunal, in some cases funded by the Legal Services Commission for advice and preparation work where the client is on a low income.[269] Indeed, Gersch reports that 'in SEN mediation lawyers are specifically excluded from the process', although he wonders how this can be 'reconciled with human rights jurisprudence'.[270] Lawyers can attend a mediation, providing they state that they are present not in their capacity as lawyers, but 'merely to provide support'.[271] Therefore, given the cost of utilising legal services (since legal aid will not be available), where lawyer involvement is permitted persons from more privileged backgrounds would be at an advantage. Indeed,

---

[264] Under the Education (Additional Support for Learning) (Scotland) Act 2004.

[265] Ibid, s 18(2). However, the grounds of appeal in Scotland are slightly different from those in England: see s 18(3), in that they relate to factors such as a decision to, or not to, make or end a 'co-ordinated support plan' for the child or young person; the information contained in a plan; the review of a plan; and delay in preparing a plan.

[266] DfES, *Special Educational Needs Code of Practice* (London, DfES, 2001), para 2:27.

[267] N 264 above, s 15.

[268] P Russell, 'Mediation in Action: Messages from the United States' in IS Gersch and A Gersch (eds), *Resolving Disagreement in Special Educational Needs* (Routledge Falmer, 2003) 15 at 22.

[269] See, generally, DJ Silas, 'Education, Legislation, Litigation: Education Law in Practice' (2005) 6 *Education Law Journal* 240, in which one education law practitioner specialising in special educational needs and disability discrimination cases discusses funding and other issues concerned with professional practice in these related fields.

[270] A Gersch, 'Ethical Issues and Dilemmas' in Gersch and Gersch, n 268 above, 194 at 200.

[271] Ibid.

they would arguably be better able to articulate their views and press their case in mediation in any event. Where lawyers are excluded the principal aim is to prevent unfairness to parents, given the availability of legal services to the LEA.

Lawyers are not, of course, excluded from SENDIST hearings, although the tribunal's guidance for parents stresses that legal representation is not needed, and in any event many parents use voluntary agencies such as the British Dyslexia Association and IPSEA.[272] Nonetheless, in 2003–4 parents were legally represented in 23 per cent of SENDIST hearings (and throughout the appeal process in 17 per cent of cases) and the LEA in 10 per cent; indeed, parents had another type of representative in 22 per cent of cases and were therefore slightly more likely to be represented by a lawyer than a layperson.[273] Again, due to the absence of public legal funding it will generally be better off parents who are able to hire a lawyer to argue their case, although it should be noted that research has indicated that legal representation is not necessarily more effective than lay representation in these cases.[274] The cost of presenting a case, and a reason why having financial resources to support a challenge to the LEA can be advantageous, might also include the fee payable to an educational psychologist or other professional to carry out an independent assessment of the child and prepare a report.[275] These reports can be quite influential in the ultimate decision.[276]

CONCLUSION

The frameworks for special educational needs and school admissions in general are similar in the way that basic procedural and limited substantive rights concerning choice operate. We saw in the previous chapter on school admissions that a broadly individualistic framework, based on the exercise of choice and rights of preference, operates in the field of school admissions. It is essentially a rights-based framework in which parents are encouraged, indeed to some extent compelled, to act in a self-interested way, notwithstanding its moral underpinning by libertarian ideals concerned with personal autonomy and choice. The underlying premise is that agencies such as schools and LEAs cannot be trusted to make the most effective arrangements for all children, nor to guarantee that all provision will be of a high standard. Accordingly, parents are presented with an opportunity to rectify the consequences of unsatisfactory arrangements. This may be represented as a redistribution of power, with the promise of further empowerment in the future. Nonetheless, its benefits are unequally enjoyed

---

[272] Independent Panel for Special Education Advice. For a useful synopsis of the kinds and sources of assistance available to parents for advice and representation, see D Boyle and E Burton, *Making Sense of SEN* (London, New Philanthropy Capital, 2004) 34 and 51.

[273] R Hughes (President), *Special Educational Needs and Disability Tribunal Annual Report 2003–2004* (London, SENDIST, 2004) 16.

[274] N Harris, *Special Educational Needs and Access to Justice* (Bristol, Jordans, 1997) 136–9.

[275] E Andrew, *Representing Parents at the Special Educational Needs Tribunal: An Evaluation of the Work of IPSEA's Free Representation Service* (Marlow, IPSEA, 1996), para 8.7.

[276] N Harris, *Special Educational Needs and Access to Justice* (Bristol, Jordans, 1997) 102.

across society as a whole, thus entrenching inequality of educational opportunity. Moreover, as with mainstream school choice it also, by placing a weight of moral responsibility on parents to take positive action in determining their child's educational future, represents an element of governance and control (or perhaps in Foucauldian terms, discipline).[277] In any event, while a market has not been established within the field of special educational needs, the same element of individualism as in the field of school admissions is evident.

As both areas involve the allocation of limited resources, the outcome of the allocation process will affect not only the position of each individual caught up in it but will also have wider implications. In the case of school admissions, the objection to the operation of a competitive market has always been that schools that are less successful in attracting students will, because of per capita funding, go into a spiral of decline. Some parents have the personal social or financial resources that enable them to avoid such schools, and the result may be yet deeper social segregation. Even though, as we saw in Chapter 5, the evidence of the spiral of decline effect is unclear, the fact remains that school choice policies at present tend to privilege the better off as well as creating inequities between schools, even though initiatives such as Excellence in Cities and the education action zones programme may ameliorate their effects to some extent.[278] In the case of special educational needs, the allocation of resources in individual cases may also have a cumulative effect. For example, the Audit Commission found in 2002 that over the previous few years the amount that LEAs had spent on statemented provision had increased by 10 times more than the overall increase in spending on School Action or School Action Plus provision: and many LEAs reported that there was a '"catch-22 situation" . . . their obligations towards children with statements meant that that they were unable to spend more on children at School Action and School Action Plus; but until they did, demand for statements could be expected to continue to rise'.[279] The wider implications of decisions are also an issue for the tribunal, which, it has been argued, should be required to take account of 'the effect of appeal decisions on other children, from whom resources might be diverted'.[280] While some of the demand for statements comes from schools, it also comes from parents. Those with sufficient cultural capital or determination are more likely to realise their claims of choice over aspects of provision, although the rights that are asserted have inherent limitations due to the resource-dependency of the provision that is sought. If the parents succeed, they may secure arrangements for their children that could restrict the capacity of LEAs to ensure a fair distribution of resources across all pupils. For example, research has shown that LEA officers see middle class professional parents as 'able to "work the system" effectively [and] by winning

[277] See S Riddell *et al*, 'Parents, Professionals and Special Educational Needs Policy Frameworks in England and Scotland' (2002) 30 *Policy and Politics* 411 at 424; N Harris, 'Empowerment and State Education: Rights of Choice and Participation' (2005) 68 MLR 925.

[278] See pp 105–8 above.

[279] Audit Commission, *Special Educational Needs: A Mainstream Issue* (London, Audit Commission, 2002), para 38.

[280] T Aldridge, *Special Educational Needs and Disability Tribunal Annual Report 2002–2003* (London, SENDIST, 2003) 5.

sometimes significant resources for their child . . . interfering with the officers' attempts to distribute limited resources evenly across the entire special education field'.[281] The Audit Commission found that children from disadvantaged backgrounds were relatively less likely to be identified as having special educational needs in the first place, whereas parents 'with the knowledge, resources and confidence to challenge staff in schools and LEAs are more likely to get their child's needs assessed and to secure a more generous package of provision'.[282]

In the process of arguing for additional provision at the tribunal stage, technical skills are now at a premium. As we saw, advocacy is common in this field, and the presentation of independent experts' reports could well form a part of it. Without a specific policy of assisting parents within this process, as happened in the Madison system in Wisconsin in the United States, the surrendering or weakening of professional discretion will not necessarily result in a redistribution of power to parents, nor will it reduce social inequalities.[283] As Lange and Riddell argue, in the field of special educational needs 'professionals still exert great powers in mediating school choice, and parents, often struggling with multiple disadvantages, find it difficult to challenge this control'.[284]

There has been very little research on the impact of choice in the field of special educational needs.[285] One reason that an assessment of its effects is problematic could be that special educational provision is in itself redistributive. While, as Wedell observes, 'the continuum of pupils' SEN merges into the range of diversity of ability identifiable in all pupils',[286] special education attracts a degree of special priority. Overall, special education is allocated greater resources per pupil than general educational provision. While there is a sliding scale of costs in respect of special education, and many of the disputes over choice that call for legal resolution concern the position of the individual child's needs in relation to it, the distribution of resources among pupils with learning difficulties arguably has much less social impact than the targeting of resources on special needs as a whole. A further problem lies in measuring the added value made by special educational provision at a particular level, even though there are increasing attempts within England and Wales and in the United States to do so.[287] As Bowers and Parish observe, '[i]t tends to be easier to define effectiveness

---

[281] J Evans and C Vincent, 'Parental Choice and Special Education' in R Glatter, PA Woods and C Bagley, *Choice and Diversity in Schooling* (London, Routledge, 1997) 102 at 110.

[282] Audit Commission, *Special Educational Needs: A Mainstream Issue* (London, Audit Commission, 2002), para 29.

[283] See J Handler, 'Discretion: Power, Quiesence and Trust' in K Hawkins (ed), *The Uses Of Discretion* (Oxford, Oxford University Press, 1992) 331.

[284] C Lange and S Riddell, 'Special Educational Needs Policy and Choice. Tensions between Policy Development in the US and UK Contexts' in MJ McLaughlin and M Rouse, *Special Education and School Reform in the United States and Britain* (London, Routledge, 2000) 126 at 142.

[285] As noted in ibid.

[286] K Wedell, 'Special Needs Education: The Next 25 Years' in National Commission on Education, *Briefings* (London, Heinemann, 1993) 199 at 210.

[287] T Bowers and T Parrish, 'Funding of Special Education in the United States and England and Wales' in MJ McLaughlin and M Rouse, *Special Education and School Reform in the United States and Britain* (London, Routledge, 2000) 167; DfES, *Removing Barriers to Achievement. The Government's Strategy for SEN* (London, DfES, 2004), s 3.

and efficiency in terms of appropriately targeted and equitable resource allocation than it is to relate them to tangible outcomes for students'.[288]

Of all the diverse causes of educational disadvantage, special educational needs probably has the most established and well developed legal framework to enable problems faced by individual pupils to be addressed, particularly when the specific provisions on disability discrimination, discussed in Chapter 4, are factored in. This is perhaps understandable, given that this group of pupils, or rather the diverse groups classed as having special educational needs (including more than one form of them), are defined with reference to their need for a particular form of education—special educational provision. In that sense, the disabilities or other conditions which these children have are more directly definable as education-related problems than other causes of disadvantage, such as relative poverty or ethnic background. Certainly, as noted earlier, the social and domestic problems experienced by a child are regarded by the courts as not within the definition of special educational needs, notwithstanding their influence on children's capacity to learn. Pupils who have special educational needs come from a range of backgrounds and may have a diversity of problems. For example, at all key stages and across all subjects, pupils with special educational needs who are eligible for free school meals have lower levels of achievement that those who are not.[289] The isolation of special education, with its own statutory regime and matrix of rights and responsibilities, may make sense as a means of ensuring a rational framework for the important educational decisions and resource allocations that need to be made. But it is an artificial separation, both within the field of education itself and in the wider context. Addressing social inequalities and meeting educational and social needs in a coherent fashion are rendered all the more problematic where multiple disadvantage is concerned.

---

[288] Bowers and Parrish, n 287 above, at 179.
[289] DfES, *Removing Barriers to Achievement. The Government's Strategy for SEN* (London, DfES, 2004), para 3.19.

7

Educational Content and Cultural Pluralism

INTRODUCTION

IT WAS NOTED in the course of discussing education rights in Chapter 2 that one of the most important and difficult issues facing modern western states in relation to the role of their education systems lies in reconciling the obligation to respect individual and group rights to religious and cultural freedom and autonomy, with the need, through education, to promote social cohesion to the national benefit at a time of perceived social disharmony. Whilst greater equity in the context of access to education continues to be regarded as a priority consideration for policy, linked to a wider goal of maximising social inclusion, there is less certainty about how to respect the right *not* to be included, or at least not totally so. The ideas, promoted by the present government, of making the education system more responsive to the individual's needs through curricular flexibility and 'personalised learning'[1] (leaving aside the areas of special educational needs and disability, where to some extent the law already requires modification of provision), are directed at ensuring that the individual's talents and potential are more effectively identified and nurtured, rather than with enabling an extension of the range of social or cultural values that state education underpins. Indeed, as we shall see, there are strong moves to reinforce 'common values' through education, such as by providing a universal framework for good behaviour, responsible sexual conduct and citizenship. As we saw in Chapter 2, much of the Strasbourg case law on education has centred on provision in relation to such matters as sex education, special educational needs, the medium of teaching and school parades. In these cases and in those discussed in subsequent chapters, including this one, concerning matters such as school uniform[2] and corporal punishment,[3] there is great potential for conflict between

---

[1] See DfES, *Higher Standards, Better Schools for All*, Cm 6677 (London, TSO, 2005), ch 4, and DfES, *Further Education: Raising Skills, Improving Life Chances*, Cm 6768 (London, TSO, 2006), ch 4.

[2] See pp 55, 79, 80 and 155–7 above and 395–9 below.

[3] Ibid pp 396–9 below.

rights of individual choice, linked often to cultural or religious values, and the collective interests represented by state policies and legislation. The underlying premise in the way that rights are perceived judicially is that the accommodation of individual rights can undermine the democratic state's necessary authority in guiding the education system and managing the available resources in the best way to deliver national educational goals. Only relatively extreme or disproportionate action by the state will give rise to a breach of the ECHR, which is likely to be quite rare in the context of education.

Indeed, individual states have enjoyed almost unhindered freedom in the development and application of their education policies. Yet there will be political constraints and these may well reflect concerns about the way particular group or individual interests are affected by the policies in question. Particularly sensitive in a pluralistic society will be policies and legislation that affect cultural and, in particular, religious interests. Notwithstanding the limitations to the ECHR in this context, the Human Rights Act (HRA) 1998 should cause the state to tread carefully in areas where an impact on minority rights might occur. Indeed, even before the HRA the dominant ideal of multiculturalism generally pushed policy in the direction of protecting minorities' interests (notwithstanding the reforms to collective worship and religious education under the Education Reform Act (ERA) 1988, discussed below). On the other hand, there is an ideology that gives primacy to the collective interest in universal citizen participation and the inculcation of a sense of national identity that is gaining currency and seeks to circumscribe minority rights which undermine it. Ultimately, it is concerned with widening social integration; and education is to the fore in the pursuit of this goal. This chapter will discuss the debates concerning integration and multiculturalism before focussing on core areas of educational content where the accommodation of cultural diversity is most problematic and re-visiting the issue of faith schools.

INTEGRATION, CITIZENSHIP, MULTICULTURALISM AND EDUCATION

The important role of education in the socio-economic advancement of those from disadvantaged backgrounds, particularly where there are multiple disadvantages such as is common among people from particular ethnic minority backgrounds, was highlighted in Chapter 1. It is an uncontroversial role even though there may be debate over the means of fostering better educational achievement and reduced educational inequality. But education's potential to promote social and cultural integration can make some aspects controversial. The education system can bring children from diverse social/cultural backgrounds together within an institutional setting and provide a common education that could give them shared knowledge, experience and core values. Yet, as Lansdown explains, the process of integration can be problematic because it can threaten the distinct culture of a minority community through the invasiveness of the dominant culture, as she says has happened to Albanians in Kosovo and Kurds in Turkey.[4] Hodgson notes that there might be perceived to be an overriding aim of promoting national unity and 'a superficial attraction in a philosophy of assimilation in the educational field with the aim being to improve race relations amongst the next generation by attempting to ensure that its members all have a uniform cultural background'.[5] But he also perceives a risk of severe damage to minorities' religious, cultural or linguistic identities and thus to their chosen way of life and traditions.[6] There is a danger that laws and policies that attempt to downplay, mask or remove the internal differences that charac-terise culturally diverse societies will be viewed as discriminatory and oppressive.[7] For example, while the French state's ban on the wearing of religious dress by school pupils might be consistent with its traditional *laïcité* (loosely, secularity) and was introduced in part at least to advance integration and egalitarianism, in that all groups would be treated the same and no individuals could be ostracised by reason of their wish to adopt culturally distinct dress, it has clearly had a disproportionate impact on particular ethnic or religious groups. That could, it has been argued, have the effect of alienating some members of the communities most affected (in particular, Muslims) and compounding intolerance among school pupils rather than giving a stronger sense of common identity and the notion of mutual respect.[8]

Where separate arrangements based on cultural or ethnic diversity occur within states' education systems, they are often seen as contributing to a wider threat to social cohesion.[9] As Poulter explains, the argument is that members of the various ethnic groups 'identify themselves so strongly with their own distinctive communities (and are so identified by others) that there is little appreciation of the role they can and should be playing in forging and reinforcing a new sense of national identity'.[10] These views are, however, challenged by some minority groups. For example, the assertion that separate schooling necessarily provides for divisiveness in society or that emphasising separate religious or cultural identities prevents an engagement with wider society has been rejected by one group.[11] There is an argument that the threat to social cohesion can be overcome if faith schools ensure that there is coverage of

---

[4] G Lansdown, 'Progress in Implementing the Rights in the Convention' in S Hart *et al, Children's Rights in Education* (London, Jessica Kingsley, 2001) 37 at 47–8.

[5] D Hodgson, *The Human Right to Education* (Aldershot, Ashgate,1999) 113.

[6] Ibid.

[7] T Modood, *Multicultural Politics: Racism, Ethnicity and Muslims in Britain* (Edinburgh, Edinburgh Press, 2005).

[8] See M Idriss, 'Laïcité and the banning of the "hijab" in France' (2005) 25 *Legal Studies* 260 at 284–5.

[9] N Burtonwood, 'Social Cohesion, Autonomy and the Liberal Defence of Faith Schools' (2003) 37 *Journal of Philosophy of Education* 415.

[10] S Poulter, *Ethnicty, Law and Human Rights* (Oxford, Clarendon Press, 1998) 26. Poulter, however, considered himself a cultural pluralist rather than an assimilationist: S Poulter, 'Muslim Headscarves in School: Contrasting Legal Approaches in England and France' (1997) 17 *Oxford Journal of Legal Studies* 43 at 47.

[11] Association of Muslim Social Scientists *et al, Muslims on Education. A Position Paper* (Richmond, Association of Muslim Social Scientists, 2004), paras 4.1.2 and 4.1.5.

other cultures within the school curriculum.[12] Merry argues that as far as separatism is concerned, 'it is not the type of school one attends that matters but the type of curriculum and instruction a school provides, as well as a staff that is committed to teaching respect and tolerance of others regardless of their differences'.[13] Yet not all faith schools have such a commitment to a 'compensatory curriculum' of this kind.[14]

Those who favour cultural pluralism, which received one of its strongest international endorsements under the UNESCO Universal Declaration on Cultural Diversity,[15] argue that the correct response of a liberal democracy to diversity is to accord due respect for different cultures and values such as individual choice and religious tolerance and that the adoption of such a response inculcates a value system that is a force for national unity.[16] Such an approach must be underpinned by a commitment to the principle of equality. Poulter sees 'a common educational system' as important in cultivating such an ethos.[17] Similarly, Lansdown argues that there is a need for the promotion of pluralistic policies 'which allow for the preservation of distinct cultures whilst seeking to create equal opportunities for education for all children'.[18] Yet the way this aim has been realised in Northern Ireland is a system consisting almost entirely of segregated schools (Protestant and Roman Catholic), in which, despite the existence of a proper, evolved, framework for the promotion and protection of human rights, wider social integration is hindered.[19] That may be an extreme example, but both social migration (affecting school admission and the ethnic mix within schools in some areas) and the continuation of and government encouragement for faith schools make it difficult to realise the goal of 'education systems which seek to promote social integration whilst respecting diversity of culture', which Lansdown advances.[20] Another example is the Orthodox Jewish community of Stamford Hill, which was reported to be contemplating relocation to a purpose-built village in Buckinghamshire in which it could live and practise its own way of life and which would eventually have its own shops, schools and community centres.[21] But it is not always the case that minority groups are desirous of separateness. Poulter argues that what they are really seeking is

---

[12] G Short, 'Faith-based Schools and Social Cohesion: Opening up the Debate' (2002) 36 *Journal of Philosophy of Education* 559.

[13] M Merry, 'Cultural Coherence and the Schooling for Identity Maintenance' (2005) 39 *Journal of Philosophy of Education* 477 at 492.

[14] N Burtonwood, 'Social Cohesion, Autonomy and the Liberal Defence of Faith Schools' (2003) *Journal of Philosophy of Education* 415 at 418.

[15] (Paris, UNESCO, 2002), adopted by the 31st Session of the General Conference of UNESCO, Paris, 2 Nov 2001.

[16] See J Raz, *Ethics in the Public Domain. Essays in the Morality of Law and Politics* (Oxford, Clarendon Press, 1994), ch 8 ('Multiculturalism: A Liberal Perspective').

[17] S Poulter, 'Muslim Headscarves in School: Contrasting Legal Approaches in England and France' (1997) 17 *Oxford Journal of Legal Studies* 43 at 47–8.

[18] Lansdown, n 4 above, at 48.

[19] L Lundy, 'Human Rights and Equality Litigation in Northern Ireland's Schools' (2004) 5 *Education Law Journal* 82.

[20] Lansdown, n 4 above, at 48.

[21] J Shamash, 'A proud new Utopia, or just another ghetto?' *The Times*, 16 Apr 2005, 74.

greater recognition from wider society or the state for their cultural values and traditions, as it makes them experience a greater sense of social belonging.[22]

Those who accept that separatism is a necessary means of preserving the rights of minorities in the field of education would acknowledge that there should, at the very least, be some attempt to promote greater unity and commonality. Goldstein argues that there is a need across all schools 'to educate all students both as to the rights and obligations of all citizens in a common civil society as to the appreciation of diversity and the tolerance of other cultural norms, views and ideologies'.[23] Such an approach is, of course, already provided for under various international instruments, and especially in Article 29 of the UNCRC, as noted in Chapter 2. In England, one of the prescribed areas of knowledge for Citizenship within the National Curriculum[24] is 'the diversity of national, regional, religious and ethnic identities in the United Kingdom and the need for mutual respect and understanding' (see below). The Government's second periodic report to the UN Committee on the Rights of the Child referred to the role that the citizenship education can play in 'combating racism and promoting equal opportunities through teaching about fairness, justice, rights and responsibilities and through developing an understanding and appreciation of diversity'.[25] In its concluding observations, the UN Committee welcomed the broad development of citizenship programmes.[26] However, it also highlighted segregated schooling in Northern Ireland and expressed concern that only 4 per cent of schools in the province were integrated.[27] It called upon the UK Government to provide financial support and incentives for the establishment of additional integrated schools in Northern Ireland 'to meet the demand of a significant number of parents'.[28] Research in one integrated school in the province has in fact revealed a 'culture of avoidance' among teachers as regards confrontation of politically or religiously controversial issues and that it has the potential to sustain or intensify psychological boundaries between the different religious groups.[29]

The prospects of increased social, cultural and linguistic diversity among pupils in schools in the UK are growing as a result of the accession of 10 new countries to the European Union on 1 May 2004 and continuing immigration from around the world. The CESCR, referring to the right to education under Art 13 of the ICESCR,[30] says that states must ensure not only the accessibility of

---

[22] S Poulter, *Ethnicity, Law and Human Rights* (Oxford, Clarendon Press, 1998) 26.

[23] S Goldstein, 'Multiculturalism, Parental Choice and Traditional Values: A Comment on Religious Education in Israel' in G Douglas and L Sebba, *Children's Rights and Traditional Values* (Aldershot, Ashgate, 1998) 118 at 132.

[24] See 'The National Curriculum' p 376 et seq below.

[25] UK Government, *Convention on the Rights of the Child. Second Report to the UN Committee on the Rights of the Child by the United Kingdom* 1999 (London, TSO, 1999), para 9.12.8.

[26] UN Committee on the Rights of the Child, *Concluding Observations: United Kingdom of Great Britain and Northern Ireland*, CRC/C/15/Add.188, 9 Oct 2002, para 47.

[27] Ibid.

[28] Ibid, para 48(g).

[29] C Donnelly, 'What Price Harmony? Teachers' Methods of Delivering an Ethos of Tolerance and Respect for Diversity in an Integrated School in Northern Ireland' (2004) 46 *Educational Research* 3.

[30] See Chap 2.

education to all but also its adaptability: 'education has to be flexible so that it can adapt to the needs of changing societies and communities and respond to the needs of students within their diverse social and cultural settings'.[31] A question that arises is not only how far a state's own school curriculum can be adapted to satisfy the needs of all minorities who come to live in another Member State, but also how far that is desirable. Stalford notes that across EU states there are international schools that provide a uniform curriculum (the International Baccalaureat is offered in such schools).[32] While in the host state, migrant workers' children can therefore receive a multicultural education that minimises disruption to their education in the event of their return to their country of origin. The same tension between segregation and integration seems to arise, however. Attendance at such schools can have the effect of 'further marginalizing migrant children', isolating them from the language and culture of the host state and hindering their integration.[33] At the same time, adapting the national curriculum of the host state into a more generic and universal 'European' programme runs the risk of weakening national identity and thus diversity within the EU as a whole.[34] Ackers and Stalford argue that 'maintaining a rich diversity between Member States' education systems is arguably more desirable than achieving uniformity'.[35]

This is indeed the potential effect sought to be avoided by the kind of 'intercultural' approach advocated by the Council of Europe and UNESCO. The latter's recently adopted Convention on the Protection and Promotion of the Diversity of Cultural Expressions states that 'interculturality' 'refers to the existence and equitable interaction of diverse cultures and the possibility of generating shared cultural expressions through dialogue and mutual respect'.[36] Within the context of education, an intercultural approach means that groups such as migrant children and those from minority backgrounds are not educated separately, but enter an inclusive education system which develops educational programmes and strategies that place an emphasis on mutual respect and recognition. This is said to contribute to a 'new culture' in which the original separate cultures 'combine to form something greater than the sum of the parts'.[37] It is argued, however, that an intercultural approach must avoid the false perception that it can bring about 'a state of fusion where all cultures merge into

---

[31] UN Committee on Economic, Social and Cultural Rights, *General Comment 13. The Right to Education (Article 13 of the Covenant)*, E/C12/1999/10. (General Comments), para 6.

[32] H Stalford, 'Transferability of Educational Skills and Qualifications in the European Union: The Case of EU Migrant Children' in J Shaw (ed), *Social Law and Policy in an Evolving European Union* (Oxford, Hart, 2000) 243 at 256. The legislation providing for the right of migrant children to education is outlined in Chap 4, above p 208 et seq.

[33] Ibid and L Ackers and H Stalford, *A Community for Children? Children, Citizenship and Internal Migration in the EU* (Aldershot, Ashgate, 2004) 231–3.

[34] Stalford, n 32 above, 256.

[35] Ackers and Stalford, n 33 above, 223.

[36] UNESCO Convention on the Protection and Promotion of the Diversity of Cultural Expressions, 2005, Art 4. 'Cultural expressions' are defined as 'those expressions that result from the creativity of individuals, groups and societies, and that have cultural content'. Under the Convention, education is given a role in encouraging and promoting understanding of the importance of the protection and promotion of the diversity of cultural expressions: ibid, Art 10(a).

[37] J-M Leclercq, *Facets of interculturality in education* (Strasbourg, Council of Europe, 2003) 71.

harmonious existence or hybridise completely and successfully': interculturality serves to 'build bridges between neighbours, not to eliminate the distance that separates them'.[38] Young's ideas about 'differentiated solidarity' are similar.[39] According to Young, the norms of differentiated solidarity permit minority groups a 'freedom to cluster', but 'oppose actions and structures that exclude and segregate groups or categories of persons'.[40] It 'assumes respect and mutual obligation' but eschews the idea that solidarity demands 'mutual identification and affinity'.[41] Young's thesis is essentially that distance between different peoples is natural and does not undermine norms of solidarity, because there is a connection and inter-dependency between people from different backgrounds or cultures through the causal effects of their daily actions on others. In this regard, Young eschews the idea that policies should have integration as their normative ideal.[42] One of the leading multiculturalists, Parekh, argues that through 'a critically sympathetic dialogue' between cultures each will be enabled to 'appreciate its own strengths and limitations' but also to become conscious of 'what is distinctive to it as well as what it shares in common with them'.[43]

In the UK, the objectives of the intercultural approach were promoted by the Swann Report in 1985, which promoted multiculturalism by encouraging the development of an approach to education that involved inculcating greater awareness among all children of the distinct cultures of those from different racial and ethnic backgrounds, as part of the vision of 'a genuinely pluralist society . . . socially cohesive and culturally diverse'.[44] The rationale for multicultural education was and is that it is necessary to combat the focus traditionally placed by schools on the language, history, religion, customs and traditions of the majority population, at the expense of those of minorities, whose cultural identity is threatened and devalued. Multicultural education could, for example, mean that the curriculum accommodates minority languages, the subject of history includes minorities' history, and religious, social and other studies include minorities' beliefs, arts and preferred way of life.[45]

Yet multiculturalism has in recent years come under attack in debates about Britishness and the need for a common set of values as the core of citizenship. The Government has argued that '[g]reater diversity in our society poses a significant challenge as to how we shape and promote the shared values that underpin citizenship' and has said that '[w]hile respecting and celebrating our differences, citizenship will need to promote wider ownership of these common

---

[38] Ibid, 75.

[39] I Young, *Inclusion and Democracy* (Oxford, OUP, 2000).

[40] Ibid, 221 and 224.

[41] Ibid, 221–2.

[42] Ibid, 219.

[43] B Parekh, 'Barry and the Dangers of Liberalism' in P Kelly (ed), *Multiculturalism Reconsidered* (Cambridge, Policy, 2002) 133 at 141. See also B Parekh, *Rethinking Multiculturalism* (Cambridge, Mass, Harvard University Press, 2000).

[44] Department of Education, *Education for All. Report of the Committee of Inquiry into the Education of Children from Minority Ethnic Groups* (London, HMSO, 1985) 6.

[45] M Sutherland, *Theory of Education* (Harlow, Longman, 1988) 130.

values and a shared sense of belonging'.[46] Recently, this theme was pursued with some vigour by the Chancellor of the Exchequer, Gordon Brown, in a speech to the Fabian Society.[47] Brown argues that 'shared values—not colour, nor unchanging and unchangeable institutions—define what it means to be British in the modern world'. He refers in his speech to three basic values—liberty (for empowerment), responsibility (for a stronger civic society) and fairness (for 'an empowering equality of opportunity for all'). The three make up 'core values of what it is to be British'. Goodhart has observed (although not specifically in response to this speech) that '[i]n the rhetoric of the modern liberal state, the glue of ethnicity ("people who look and talk like us") has been replaced by the glue of values ("people who think and behave like us")'.[48] The kinds of values referred to by Brown are broad and somewhat nebulous. The problem comes when one focuses more specifically on moral and family values, as the discussion of the school curriculum below will explain. As Bainham argues, the notion of shared community values is, at least where the family is concerned, something of an 'illusion';[49] Bainham in fact justifies the case for the accommodation of diverse cultural and religious viewpoints, within limits, partly on the basis of this lack of commonality. But most proponents of multiculturalism also support the promotion of common values. In the Parekh report,[50] for example, it was argued that the rights and cultural identity of minorities should be upheld within a multicultural society based on equality and diversity, but with shared common values. Abbas, who similarly proposes the idea of multiculturalism as 'shared citizenship, allegiance to common values that are universal in nature', argues that it is important that 'ethnic belonging does not impact upon perceived allegiance and loyalty', which is part of the racist response to ethnic diversity.[51] He defends the principle of multiculturalism, but not the way that it operates in Britain, because while it may recognise difference it fails to give ethnic minorities a true sense of belonging through its 'benign egalitarianism'.[52] It has failed to ensure integration and has left some ethnic communities (Abbas refers specifically to Muslims) dependent upon their own communities to 'mobilise what little economic or social development they can achieve'.[53]

Is multiculturalism therefore antithetical to integration and, as such, a hindrance to improved social equality? In principle that should not be the case for, as Kymlicka argues, multiculturalism affects the *means* by which minorities

[46] Secretary of State for Trade and Industry and Secretary of State for Constitutional Affairs, *Fairness for All: A New Commission for Equality and Human Rights*, Cm 6195 (London, TSO, 2004), para 1.10.

[47] Speech by the Rt Hon Gordon Brown MP, Chancellor of the Exchequer, at the Fabian Society New Year Conference, London, 14 Jan 2006, available at www.hm-treasury.gov.uk/newsroom_and_speeches/press/2006/press_03_06.cfm.

[48] D Goodhart, 'Discomfort of strangers', *The Guardian*, 24 Feb 2004, 24–5 (reprint of essay published in Prospect, February 2004).

[49] A Bainham, 'Family Law in a Pluralistic Society' (1995) 22 *Journal of Legal Studies* 234 at 238.

[50] B Parekh, *The Future of Multi Ethnic Britain* (London, Runnymede Trust, 2000).

[51] T Abbas, 'Recent Developments to British Multicultural Theory, Policy and Practice: The Case of British Muslims' (2005) 9 *Citizenship Studies* 152.

[52] Ibid, 156.

[53] Ibid, 160.

integrate into the dominant culture, not whether they integrate.[54] But Trevor Phillips, the Chairman of the Commission for Racial Equality, has argued that it is necessary to reconsider the value of multiculturalism on the grounds that it encourages separatism and undermines a sense of national, British, identity and that that is disadvantageous to the notion of an inclusive, common society. Sir Bernard Crick, chair of the 'Life in the United Kingdom' Advisory Group, whose report in 2003 on the integration of immigrants recommended courses on citizenship for those seeking naturalisation in the UK,[55] has, however, been quoted as saying in response to Phillips that 'Britishness must be part of multiculturalism' and that '[i]ntegration is the co-existence of communities and unimpeded movement between them, it is not assimilation.'[56]

The Crick report itself presents an interesting perspective on the role of education in this context. It recommends 'a comprehensive but flexible Programme of Studies that will lead not only to formal, legal citizenship but also focus at every level on what people need to settle in and begin to be equipped as citizens in the full sense as is now being taught and learnt in our schools'.[57] The report places an emphasis on knowledge and awareness of democratic and political systems and civic institutions (including the police and courts) and respect for 'the laws of the land including Human Rights and Equal Rights legislation' at the core of common citizenship.[58] On the whole it adopts a very narrow perspective towards common values outside democratic ideals of freedom of speech and 'fair play'. It refers to 'the changing role and status of women both in custom and law',[59] but this highlights the report's wider failure to go deeply into the nature of our 'common values'. Is that because the only identifiable common values that are shared are those related to our legal and democratic traditions?[60] Or is it simply that the report is taking a pragmatic but also a practical approach, concentrating on the *core* values, 'common civic values',[61] because that is all that aspiring British nationals can reasonably be expected to absorb? Certainly, the report is careful to eschew any notion of 'assimilation into a common culture so that original identities are lost'.[62] Separation and segregation would be avoided by interaction and engagement in a common culture, in which knowledge and use of the English language (the learning of which is also advocated by the report) would be vital. 'Integration' would thus mean 'not simply mutual respect and tolerance between different

---

[54] W Kymlicka, *Multicultural Citizenship* (Oxford, OUP, 1995) 78.

[55] 'Life in the United Kingdom', Advisory Group (chair Lord Crick), *The New and the Old* (London, Home Office, 2003), ch 3.

[56] Available at http://news.bbc.co.uk/go/pr/fr/-/1/hi/uk/3600791.stm (5 Apr 2004).

[57] N 55 above, para 3.2: the areas to be covered would be (i) British National Institutions in recent historical context; (ii) Britain as a multicultural society; (iii) Knowing the law, (iv) Employment, (v) Sources of help and information and (vi) Everyday needs: ibid, para 3.5.

[58] Ibid, para 2.7.

[59] Ibid, para 3.5.

[60] See further S Poulter, *Ethnicity, Law aand Human Rights* (Oxford, Clarendon Press, 1998) 22.

[61] N 55 above, para 2.6.

[62] Ibid, para 2.8.

groups but continual interaction, engagement and civic participation, whether in social, cultural, educational, professional or legal spheres'.[63]

While not concerned with children per se, the Crick report clearly puts forward an overall approach towards the closer social integration of minorities through education that could have a wider resonance. The report aims to strike a balance between, on the one hand, the rights of minorities to enjoy the freedom to learn and express their own cultural values, and, on the other, the need for wider social stability that may be threatened if common ground between the full range of social, ethnic and religious groups, based on shared cultural and ethical values, cannot be found. Inevitably, though, it does leave itself open to the criticism that its approach to common citizenship education fails properly to take proper account of cultural diversity.[64] David Bell, the then Chief Inspector of Schools in England, has argued that while a common citizenship education can convey an awareness of a common British heritage, it should also ensure that pupils know 'the positives of a diverse community . . . promoting acceptance of different faiths and cultures as well as alternative lifestyles' and learning 'how to say no to racial and religious intolerance'.[65] He says that faith schools have a particular responsibility in this regard: 'I worry that many young people are being educated in faith-based schools, with little appreciation of their wider responsibilities and obligations to British society'. Such fears are grounded in the belief that multiculturalist policies which aim to preserve the cultural integrity and distinctiveness of different groups will in fact promote insularity, because, as Barry says, they 'strengthen the hands of those within each group who wish to impose on its members uniform beliefs and standards of conduct'.[66] Yet some groups resist the dualist argument that more autonomy means less engagement with or integration within society as a whole.[67] Indeed, promoting tolerance and understanding is seen as operating in the other direction as well, through the education system as a whole promoting a greater understanding of Islam and Muslim people. This has been strongly advocated by one of the working groups assembled by the Government in the wake of the terrorist attacks that occurred on London Transport in July 2005.[68] It argues that there is a need for 'securing a faithful reflection of Islam and its civilisation across the entire education system including the National Curriculum, further education, higher education and lifelong learning'.[69]

---

[63] Ibid, para 2.10.

[64] See M Olssen, 'From the Crick Report to the Parekh Report: Multiculturalism, Cultural Difference, and Democracry—the Re-visioning of Citizenship Education' (2004) 25 *British Journal of Sociology of Education* 179.

[65] David Bell, Hansard Society/Ofsted lecture, 17 Jan 2005.

[66] B Barry, *Culture and Equality* (Cambridge, Polity, 2001) 129.

[67] See R Smithers, 'Anger at Muslim schools attack', *The Guardian*, 18 Jan 2005, 1; T Halpin, 'Islamic schools are threat to national identity, says Ofsted', *The Times*, 18 Jan 2005, 11. There is further discussion of citizenship education below.

[68] 'Preventing Extremism Together' Working Groups, Aug–Oct 2005, Report (London, Office of the Deputy Prime Minister, 2005).

[69] Ibid, 31. Seee also Association of Muslim Social Scientists *et al*, *Muslims on Education. A Position Paper* (Richmond, Association of Muslim Social Scientists, 2004). As regards the National Curriculum, see below.

Within the UK, a moderate degree of differentiation within the schools system has been maintained, respecting the rights of minorities to enjoy a degree of separation, such as in faith schools, or, in common with others, to exercise a degree of choice to select local community schools on any basis, including their particular ethnic mix. It has not gone as far as some minority groups might wish, for example in relation to the language used in teaching or complete freedom in the running of independent schools, as later discussion will show. Moreover, among the outstanding questions that need to be resolved—concerning a problematic issue for many western democracies[70]—are those about the role of religion within the education system. For example, while supporting Phillips' call for a stronger national British identity across all communities, Bell argues that difficult questions arise about the statutory requirement that children in state community schools take part in an act of collective worship that is broadly Christian in character.[71] He asks, in particular, whether it really would undermine that strengthening of 'Britishness' to which Phillips refers if children were no longer required to take part in daily worship 'in the Christian tradition which is bound up in our history and heritage?'[72] And might it be better strengthened, and pupils gain a better understanding of Christianity and other religions, if educators were 'more honest about the fact that the majority of people nowadays do not attend church although, intriguingly, observance of other faiths seems to be stronger?'[73] Any reform would be bound to offend some groups' sensibilities or beliefs, just as the present law does. There are no easy solutions for reconciling competing rights and interests, set against the authority of the state, in relation to such aspects of education.

Multiculturalism is discussed further in the context of individual rights, particularly those of minorities, in relation to the school curriculum (below). Human rights clearly have an important bearing on issues such as how far particular groups' or individuals' own value systems should be accommodated within a state education system that aims to provide a framework for universal future citizenship and common values. McGoldrick argues that, as human rights are universal, 'rights to freedom of expression, association, assembly, religion, property, education, use of language and, perhaps most significantly, the right to equality and not to be discriminated against, all have a role in ensuring multicul-turalism and accommodating diversity'. [74] Human rights are applicable to all aspects of education that are delivered to a diverse, pluralistic society, even though they are not given statutory expression within education legislation.[75] There are particular areas of sensitivity, where multiculturalism is most

---

[70] See, eg, C Glenn and J De Groof, *Freedom, Autonomy and Accountability in Education (Vol 2)* (Utrecht, Lemma, 2002); RJ Adbar (ed), *Law and Religion* (Aldershot, Ashgate, 2000).

[71] For a discussion of collective worship see pp 437–41 below.

[72] N 65 above.

[73] Ibid.

[74] D McGoldrick, 'Multiculturalism and its Discontents' (2005) 5 *Human Rights Law Review* 27.

[75] See UN Commission on Human Rights, *Report submitted by Katarina Tomaševski, Special Rapporteur on the right to education, Addendum. Mission to the United Kingdom 18–22 October 1999*, E/CN4/2000/6/Add 2 (Centre for Human Rights, Geneva, 2000), available at www.unhcr.ch/Huridcoda.

problematic, to which they have particular relevance. First, it is necessary to examine the structural framework for the regulation and control of the content of education.

REGULATION AND CONTROL OF SECULAR EDUCATION IN STATE SCHOOLS

The power of the state to control the content of education shifted from local education authorities and teachers to ministers during the 1980s.[76] The Conservative Government's White Paper in 1985 highlighted as a major shortcoming in both primary and secondary education the lack of clear and consistent curriculum policies, including aims and objectives, at school or local authority level.[77] It was seen as a significant cause of the failure of a number of schools to reach high standards. At first the Government was content to maintain the traditional tripartite responsibility for curriculum policy, in which central government had only a broad promotional responsibility for education,[78] whilst LEAs had overall responsibility for the secular curriculum in schools,[79] although they in practice tended to defer to the third party—schools and, in particular, the teachers—over matters of content and broad philosophical approach. Thus the White Paper explained the Government's view that it 'would not be right' for the Secretary of State's policy on 5–16 education 'to amount to a determination of national syllabuses'.[80] Instead, under the subsequent legislation, LEAs were placed under a statutory duty to prepare and maintain a policy on secular provision, giving consideration to the range and balance of the content.[81] But this was also a period in which LEAs' role was being downgraded, although not to the extent that occurred later, and the new powers and responsibilities of school governing bodies included that of specifying a statement of curriculum policy for their school and, under subsequent legislation, a policy on sex education.[82] LEAs lost the power of control that they had enjoyed over the secular instruction in most types of school,[83] while head teachers (or governors of voluntary aided, mostly Roman Catholic, schools and, later, grant-maintained

---

[76] For detailed historical reviews, see P Meredith, *Government, Schools and the Law* (London, Routledge, 1992) and N Harris, *Law and Education: Regulation, Consumerism and the Education System* (London, Sweet and Maxwell).

[77] Department for Education and Science, *Better Schools*, Cmnd 9469 (London, HMSO, 1985), ch 1.

[78] Under the Education Act 1944, s 1.

[79] Ibid, s 23.

[80] Department for Education and Science, n 77 above, para 36.

[81] Education (No2) Act 1986, s 17.

[82] Ibid, s 18(1) and (2); Education Act 1993, s 241(1).

[83] Due to the repeal of s 23 of the 1944 Act by the Education (No 2) Act 1986, Sched 6. This control did not apply in aided schools (mostly Roman Catholic), where it was enjoyed by the governing body: EA 1944, s 23(2).

schools[84]) became responsible for the 'determination and organisation of the secular curriculum'.[85]

The Education (No 2) Act 1986, which introduced the first of these changes, also introduced unprecedented regulation of the content of education in two specific areas. First, in an apparent attempt to prevent political bias and indoctrination in the classroom at a time of growing unease among Conservatives about the policies and practices of left-dominated teachers and local authorities, a duty was placed on LEAs, head teachers and governing bodies to forbid the 'promotion of partisan political views in the teaching of any subject in the school'.[86] They were also required to take reasonable steps to ensure that when 'political issues are brought to the attention of pupils' they should be 'offered a balanced presentation of opposing views'.[87] Given its potential breadth, the term 'political issues' could encompass a wide range of matters, including terrorism and its causes, and immigration. The concern that teachers, schools or LEAs might in some way want to radicalise young children also led to the inclusion of a duty to forbid 'partisan political activities' by junior pupils at school or to make arrangements for such activities off school premises.[88] Whether or not these duties, which are still in force,[89] were and are needed is still unclear. The absence of any evidence in Ofsted reports, including the Chief Inspector's annual reports, of any problem with regard to political bias in teaching and the lack of any other reports mentioning it could prove that the law has worked well; on the other hand it could show that it was not needed in the first place. Recent research into the teaching of environmental issues, which are often controversial, has shown how difficult, if not impossible, teachers tend to find it wholly to realise their belief in a neutral and balanced approach.[90] But, on subjects where young people from different cultural backgrounds may hold polemical views, teachers will be particularly keen to take a neutral stance so as not to exacerbate tensions, increase alienation or cause upset. As regards the forbidding of partisan political activities by junior pupils, there is a potential conflict with Article 15 of the UNCRC, by which states parties 'recognize the rights of the child to freedom of association and to freedom of peaceful assembly'. The Article provides that the only restrictions that may be placed on this right are those imposed by law 'which are necessary in a democratic society in the interests of national security or public safety, public order . . . the protection of public health or morals or the protection of the rights and freedoms of others'. It is not clear that any of the grounds for restricting this right would easily be applied to the ban on partisan political activities. Children are also given the right to freedom of expression by the

---

[84] As regards grant-maintained schools, see pp 95–7 above

[85] Education (No2) Act 1986, s 18(5); and articles of government only, in the case of grant-maintained schools.

[86] Education (No 2) Act 1986, s 44(1).

[87] Ibid, s 45.

[88] Ibid, s 44(1) and (2).

[89] Education Act 1996, s 406.

[90] DRE Cotton, 'Teaching Controversial Environmental Issues: Neutrality and Balance in the Reality of the Classroom' (2006) 48 *Educational Research* 223.

UNCRC,[91] which can be restricted only on similar grounds, and to freedom of thought.[92] There are equivalent rights and restrictions under Article 10 of the ECHR. This provision was invoked when there was censorship by the authorities in Northern Cyprus of school books for primary schools used by Greek Cypriots.[93] The ground of censorship was that the books' content was capable of fostering hostility between the two ethnic communities. The books in question concerned a wide a range of subjects, including the Greek language, English, history, geography, religion, civics, science, mathematics and music. The ECtHR found that school books had been censored or rejected by the authorities 'no matter how innocuous their content'.[94] It was held that there had been excessive censorship and a violation of Article 10. The way that Article 10 has been held to protect pupils from proseltysing by teachers was discussed in Chapter 2. Children are also protected from indoctrination by the right to respect for their parents' religious and philosophical beliefs by Article 2 of Protocol 1 to the Convention, as considered in *Kjeldsen* (below).

The second area in which the 1986 Act sought to control specific content related to sex education. It was not until the Education Act 1993 that sex education became compulsory for pupils of secondary school age (although subject to a parental right of withdrawal).[95] The 1986 Act stated that where a school provided sex education to pupils it should be 'given in such a manner as to encourage those pupils to have due regard to moral considerations and the value of family life'.[96] This value-laden duty is still in force and is discussed below.[97] More controversially, the Government also sought to respond to an apparent moral outrage in some quarters at attempts by some teachers to 'normalise' homosexual relationships. First, its 1987 circular on sex education stated that there was 'no place in any school in any circumstances for teaching which advocates homosexual behaviour, which presents it as the "norm", or which encourages homosexual experimentation by pupils'.[98] While there was no attempt to prevent all references to homosexuality within sex education, the circular advised that the subject should be handled carefully in order to avoid 'deep offence' to those for whom 'homosexual practice is not morally acceptable', such as those of various religious faiths.[99] Subsequently it proposed the notorious 'clause 28', which became section 28 of the Local Government Act 1988.[100] This stated that local authorities must not 'intentionally promote homosexuality or publish material with the intention of promoting homosexuality' nor 'promote the teaching in any maintained school of the acceptability of homosexuality as a

---

[91] UNCRC, Art 13.

[92] Art 14.

[93] *Cyprus v Turkey*, App no 25781/94 (2002) 35 EHRR 731.

[94] Ibid, para 252.

[95] See 'Sex Education—The Development of Compulsory Sex Education and its Moral Framework', pp 403–6 below.

[96] Education (No 2) Act 1986, s 46.

[97] Education Act 1996, s 403.

[98] Department of Education and Science, *Sex Education Act School*, Circular 11/87 (London, DfES, 1987), para 22.

[99] Ibid.

[100] This inserted new s 2A into the Local Government Act 1986.

pretended family relationship'. It will be seen that this duty was placed on local authorities rather than teachers or schools. This provision generated a huge amount of comment (see below) and an active campaign for its repeal, which finally occurred under the Local Government Act 2003.[101]

The Education Reform Act (ERA) 1988 represented a sea change in the way that the school curriculum was determined in England and Wales. The tripartite system of control, which had remained despite the changes under the 1986 Act, was ended. Henceforth central government would dictate the content of the school curriculum and the arrangements for assessing pupils. In the 1985 White Paper the Government had identified certain fundamental principles that should be embedded within the school curriculum: it should be broad; balanced; relevant; and differentiated, so that teaching and content matched pupils' abilities and aptitudes.[102] The ERA provided the opportunity for these principles to be prescribed for the curriculum in all schools, although it covered only maintained (state) schools. Under its provisions the school curriculum was to be 'balanced and broadly based', promoting 'the spiritual, moral, cultural, mental and physical development of pupils at the school and of society'; and it had to prepare pupils for 'the opportunities, responsibilities and experiences of adult life'.[103] This duty survives with one minor amendment ('adult' has been replaced by 'later'); and it now also applies to funded nursery education.[104] This 'whole curriculum' (as it became known) was considered to extend beyond the formal timetable and, as the National Curriculum Council (NCC), the advisory body established under the ERA, explained, it involved the personal and social development of pupils, the development of attitudes and values, and the forging of more effective school–community links.[105] Cross-curricular themes were identified, and these show just how far the framework of regulation was extending, even if the NCC's guidance did not have force of law. It was primarily within this cross-curricular framework that multicultural education was to be developed, although religious education also played a potential role in it, particularly in non-denominational schools. The NCC published guidance on spiritual and moral development of pupils, which emphasised values such as self-discipline, honesty and reliability, and on citizenship.[106]

The ERA 1988 is best known for the creation of the National Curriculum (below), but it also provided for every maintained school to have a 'basic curriculum' comprising religious education and the National Curriculum.[107] Sex education was later added to the basic curriculum for all state secondary schools and for pupils of secondary age attending state special schools.[108] This basic

---

[101] Local Government Act 2003, s 122.

[102] Department for Education and Science, *Better Schools*, Cmnd.9469 (London, HMSO, 1985), para 45.

[103] ERA 1988, s 1(2) and (3).

[104] Education Act 2002, s 78 (England) and 99 (Wales).

[105] National Curriculum Council, *Circular No 6* (York: NCC, 1989), para 6.

[106] National Curriculum Council, *Spiritual and Moral Development* (York, NCC, 1993); National Curriculum Council, *Education for Citizenship* (York, NCC, 1990).

[107] ERA 1988, s 2(1).

[108] Education Act 1993, s 241(1).

curriculum remains within the statutory framework, currently found in Part 6 of the Education Act 2002. However, under that Act central government gained yet further control through a new power for the Secretary of State to change the constituents of the 'basic curriculum' apart from religious education or sex education by order.[109] Previously the basic curriculum could only be changed by Parliament through an amending Act. The detailed framework for religious education and collective worship created by the 1988 Act has, in terms of content, remained largely unaltered.[110]

THE NATIONAL CURRICULUM

Background

In the consultation document which preceded the introduction of the National Curriculum it was argued that a mandatory national system could not be implemented effectively unless it was 'backed by law'.[111] Lest it be considered too dogmatic, it was stressed that the National Curriculum would be analogous to a 'framework not a straightjacket'.[112] However, the fact that greater flexibility had to be introduced in the mid-1990s in response to concerns, confirmed by the Dearing Committee, that the National Curriculum was unduly prescriptive and overly bureaucratic (a problem that arose from the need to record pupils' attainment frequently and in detail in order to provide data by which overall standards could be measured[113]) showed that the straitjacket analogy was not, in fact, inapt. At this time the Secretary of State, Gillian Shephard, talked of 'removing overload, stripping out unnecessary bureaucracy and giving more freedom for teachers to exercise professional judgment'.[114] The basic structure of the National Curriculum did not change, however. It continued to specify the three 'core subjects' of Mathematics, English and Science (plus Welsh in Welsh-medium schools in Wales) and the various 'other foundation subjects': history, geography, technology, music, art, physical education and (for the 11–14 age group only, but subsequently for ages 15–16 also) a prescribed modern language (plus Welsh in non-Welsh speaking schools in Wales).[115] Although the modern languages that were prescribed were all traditional European languages (from Danish through to Spanish), schools were also permitted to offer Russian and a range of middle-eastern and eastern languages, such as Arabic, Punjabi and

---

[109] Education Act 2002, ss 80 and 101.

[110] See 'Religion in State Education', p 429 et seq below.

[111] Department for Education and Science/Welsh Office, *The National Curriculum 5–16—A Consultation Document* (London and Cardiff, DES/Welsh Office, 1987) 5.

[112] Ibid.

[113] R Dearing (chair), *The National Curriculum and its Assessment: Final Report* (London, School Curriculum and Assessment Authority, 1994).

[114] Department for Education, Press Release 277/94 (London, Dept for Education, 1994).

[115] ERA 1988, s 3(1); and the Education (National Curriculum) (Modern Foreign Languages) Order 1989 (SI 1989/825).

Urdu,[116] provided pupils at the school were also given the opportunity to study one of the prescribed European languages. Different attainment targets, programmes of study and assessment arrangements were prescribed via statutory instrument[117] for the National Curriculum subjects at each of the four 'key stages' through which each child passed.[118] The statutory duty to ensure that the National Curriculum was implemented in full was laid upon LEAs, governors and head teachers but not on classroom teachers, whose proposed industrial action due to their opposition to the burden imposed by testing did not therefore conflict with a statutory duty.[119]

For many years there had been deep unease and suspicion about the idea of a centrally dictated curriculum, notwithstanding the adoption of a national (or federal) curriculum in other democratic countries, most notably France, Switzerland and Germany. Traditional resistance to such an idea was born out of an instinctive distrust of central control of educational content in the light of the Nazi and Soviet regimes' approach to education.[120] It was encapsulated in the views of the educationalist, government adviser and sometime editor of the *Times Educational Supplement*, Harold Dent, in 1944: '[w]hat we do not want is lessons laid down by law', as 'stereotyped lessons would mean the end of democratic education'.[121] Consequent on the changes wrought by the ERA 1988, however, we now have one of the most centrally controlled school curricula in the western world, and traditional concerns about central dictation have not disappeared. Indeed, it could be argued that, given the extent of state power over the curriculum, which is barely checked by the standard consultation processes (including referral to the Qualifications and Curriculum Authority (QCA)),[122] it is important that the Government ensures that the curriculum is founded on democratic values, including those values set out in the UNCRC. The law could in fact go much further in importing such values in the way that it prescribes the general requirements (noted above) for a balanced and broadly based curriculum. In addition, it could refer more explicitly to social diversity among pupils and how this is to be addressed within the curriculum. On the other hand, some might view such an approach as potentially too doctrinaire and better left to guidance and teacher training, as at present. A further factor is the democratic safeguard that arises from the fact that, although the detailed content of the National Curriculum is prescribed via Orders made by ministers, the basic framework has been and remains statutory, ensuring Parliamentary scrutiny of

[116] Arabic, Bengali, Chinese (Cantonese or Mandarin), Gujerati, Hebrew (Modern), Hindi, Japanese, Punjabi, Russian, Turkish and Urdu.

[117] Which in turn referred to specific curriculum documents in which the attainment targets, etc, were set out.

[118] ERA 1988, s 2 (as amended by the EA 1993 s 240(1)). The key stages were: 1 (age 5–7); 2 (8–11); 3 (11–14); and 4 (15–16): ibid, s 3.

[119] *The Mayor and Burgesses of the London Borough of Wandsworth v National Association of Schoolmasters/Union of Women Teachers* [1994] ELR 170 (CA).

[120] N Harris, *Law and Education: Regulation, Consumerism and the Education System* (London, Sweet and Maxwell, 1993) 197–200.

[121] HC Dent, *The New Education Bill* (London, University of London Press, 1944) 30.

[122] The QCA is the successor to the School Curriculum and Assessment Authority which had replaced both the NCC and the School Examinations and Assessment Council.

fundamental reforms (although it remains to be seen how far the Legislative and Regulatory Reform Bill which, at the time of writing, is currently before Parliament, might weaken it). Nonetheless, it was argued at the time the National Curriculum was introduced that there was considerable scope for political influence and that right wing politics had strongly influenced the selection of subjects for inclusion.[123] According to Coulby:

> [n]otable absences from the list of national subjects are economics, sociology, social studies and politics. This unsurprising exclusion is in line with the distrust shown by successive Thatcher administrations for the social sciences . . . [which] are seen as dangerously left-wing and their teachers as raving Marxists almost to a person. The consultation document had insisted that the national curriculum would raise standards in the area of education linked to adult life. It is hard to see how responsible, participating democratic citizens can be educated if their curriculum deliberately excludes all issues relating to political, economic and social thinking.[124]

Moreover, Whitty contends that central regulation of the curriculum is concerned not only with standardisation and benchmarks of standards against which parents can exercise choice, but also with 'creating, or recreating, forms of national identity'.[125] It has been argued by David that the content of the National Curriculum was given a specifically 'British' focus, 'valuing only traditional English subjects and knowledge, rather than appreciating the diversity and richness of the varied cultures from which British citizens are now drawn'.[126] To Whitty there has been 'a conscious attempt to position subjects in ways which hark backwards to some imagined past, rather than forwards into new globalised times'.[127] Recently, the Chancellor of the Exchequer has argued for British history to be given even greater prominence in the school curriculum.[128] As we have seen, multicultural education was identified as a cross-curricular theme by the advisory body, rather than being a statutory National Curriculum, or even basic curriculum, requirement.

So there remains the risk that governments with large Parliamentary majorities can impose their doctrinaire view of what children should learn. Moreover, the Secretary of State has a far-reaching power, exercisable via regulations, to dis-apply or apply with modifications the National Curriculum as a whole or particular provisions 'in such cases as may be specified in the

---

[123] See D Graham with D Tytler, *A Lesson for Us All: The Making of the National Curriculum* (London, Routledge, 1993).

[124] D Coulby, 'The National Curriculum' in L Bash and D Coulby (eds), *The Education Reform Act. Competition and Control* (London, Cassell, 1989) 54 at 61–2.

[125] G Whitty, *Making Sense of Education Policy* (London, Paul Chapman, 2005) 102.

[126] ME David, *Parents, Gender and Education Reform* (Cambridge, Polity Press, 1993) 66–7. See also J Hardy and C Vieler-Porter, 'Race, Schooling and the 1988 Education Reform Act' in M Flude and M Hammer (eds), *The Education Reform Act 1988: Its Origins and Implications* (Basingstoke, Falmer, 1990), 173–85.

[127] G Whitty, *Making Sense of Education Policy* (London, Paul Chapman, 2005) 103.

[128] Speech by the Rt Hon Gordon Brown MP, Chancellor of the Exchequer, at the Fabian Society New Year Conference, London, 14 Jan 2006, available at www.hm-treasury.gov.uk/newsroom_and_speeches/press/2006/press_03_06.cfm.

regulations'.[129] However, this power has been used sparingly, and only to make minor adjustments.[130] It should also be stressed that, outside the statutory framework, governments have used various techniques of persuasion or coercion, such as by requiring Ofsted to monitor action taken to secure implementation of national initiatives. An example is Labour's National Literacy Strategy, involving a one hour per week literacy hour in primary schools.[131]

The National Curriculum under Labour Post-1997

While neo-conservativism and New Right thinking dominated the construction of the National Curriculum in the late 1980s,[132] New Labour has since imposed its own thinking in several key changes. It is reflected, first, in the introduction in England of citizenship as a foundation subject[133] and, secondly, in the move in the direction of vocational subjects,[134] notwithstanding the Government's decision not to take the latter further by aligning, indeed combining, vocational and academic qualifications through a unified diploma, as was recommended by the Tomlinson report,[135] although it is planned that by 2013 all young people aged 14 plus will have the choice of pursuing specialist vocational diplomas alongside the National Curriculum.[136] These changes reflect Labour's view that schooling should equip less academic pupils for entry to employment, and thereby help to fill the so-called skills gap,[137] and that it should seek to inculcate greater personal and social responsibility. Although it constitutes only a small part of the curriculum across the final two years of compulsory schooling,[138] citizenship as a subject has the potential to play an important role in providing a framework of knowledge and understanding about legal and political institutions and the rights and responsibilities of citizens, in order to reinforce other values promoted through the school curriculum. Among the areas to be covered are 'the

[129] EA 2002, s 91. The National Assembly has an equivalent power in Wales: ibid, s 112.

[130] See, eg, the Education (National Curriculum) (Exceptions at Key Stage 4) (England) Regulations 2003 (SI 2003/252).

[131] See J O'Leary, 'Heads seek freedom to ignore literacy hour', *The Times*, 26 May 1998, 8. However, this report notes that '[l]awyers specialising in education law have said that the Government would be vulnerable to legal challenge if it tried to enforce the guidelines without enshrining them in legislation'.

[132] See G Whitty, 'The New Right and the National Curriculum' in M Flude and M Hammer (eds), *The Education Reform Act 1988. Its Origins and Implications* (Basingstoke, Falmer, 1990) 21.

[133] Education Act 1996 s 354 as substituted, in relation to England only, by the Foundation Subject (Amendment) (England) Order 2000 (SI 2000/1146). See also the Education (National Curriculum) (Attainment Targets and Programmes of Study in Citizenship) Order 2000 (SI 2000/1603). The introduction of citizenship education under the National Curriculum followed on from the Crick report above.

[134] In part under the Education Act 2002, part 6 (or part 7 in Wales): see below.

[135] DfES, *14–19 Curriculum and Qualifications Reform: Final Report of the Working Group on 14–19 Reform* (London, DfES, 2004).

[136] The first five, from 2008, will cover ICT, engineering, health and social care, creative and media industries, and construction and the built environment. Others, such as manufacturing, health and beauty and sport and leisure will be introduced from 2009 or 2010.

[137] DfES, *14–19 Education and Skills*, Cm 6476 (London, TSO, 2005).

[138] Although elements of it are also expected to be covered in earlier years.

legal and human rights and responsibilities underpinning society, basic aspects of the criminal justice system, and how both relate to young people', and 'the diversity of national, regional, religious and ethnic identities in the United Kingdom and the need for mutual respect and understanding'.[139] The fact that, for the 14–16 age group, citizenship education is expected to provide a critical appreciation of 'different ways of bringing about change at different levels of society' and include school- and community-based activities in which pupils can demonstrate 'personal and group responsibility in their attitudes to themselves and others', is important in showing that co-operation and mutual support represent important social values. The difficulty is in ensuring that all young people feel able to participate effectively in this way and that the subject is presented in a way that does not patronise them. The fact that, according to the annual report for 2004–5 by the Chief Inspector of Schools, the provision of citizenship education is unsatisfactory in a quarter of schools, where 'the place of citizenship in the curriculum is ill-defined and pupils' experiences are shallow',[140] shows there is room for improvement.[141]

The wider potential problem with citizenship education is that it is, by its very nature, value laden. A pupil is to be presented with a model of civic virtue that accords with a particular idea of the kinds of qualities and principles that underpin citizenship. As a consequence, there is a risk of indoctrination (Ofsted has found this to be perceived by teachers themselves[142]) that is in fact anathema not only to teacher ethics but also the ideal of citizenship itself. However, Heater, noting this danger, argues that a teacher is being true to the citizenship ideal by 'responsibly inculcating civic values' and cannot in general be accused of indoctrination.[143] He acknowledges that presenting an unshakeable belief in particular political or social ideologies such as Marxism could amount to indoctrination, but he argues that the main principles of citizenship, such as justice, fairness and freedom, are 'values inseparable from the good life' and are 'universal goods, not subjective propositions'.[144] One can agree with that, but only up to a point. As justice and fairness cannot be presented to school pupils as mere abstract concepts and would need to be considered in various specific social contexts, there is a risk of ideological bias, no matter how unintended. Heater also argues that, provided pupils' citizenship education encourages them to think

---

[139] See www.teachernet.gov.uk/citizenship.

[140] Ofsted, *Annual Report of Her Majesty's Chief Inspector of Schools 2004/05* (London, TSO, 2005), para 62.

[141] A longitudinal study, examining the experience of citizenship education from 2001 to 2009 and taking account of social factors such as gender and ethnicity is currently underway: see, eg, E Cleaver *et al*, *Citizenhip Education Longitudinal Study: Second Cross-Sectional Survey 2004*, DfES Research Report RR626 (London, DfES, 2005), which notes that certain key topics, such as voting and elections, Parliament and governance and the EU, have tended to be ignored in citizenship education. See also K Faulks, 'Education for Citizenship in England's Secondary Schools: a Critique of Current Principle and Practice' (2006) 21 *Journal of Education Policy* 59.

[142] D Bell, HM Chief Inspector of Schools, Hansard Society/Ofsted Lecture, 17 Jan 2005.

[143] D Heater, *Citizenship. The Civic Ideal in World History, Politics and Education* (3rd edn, Manchester, Manchester University Press, 2004) 347.

[144] Ibid.

for themselves, there is safeguard against their indoctrination.[145] There is, of course, the additional safeguard of the statutory proscription of political bias and the requirement to ensure a 'balanced presentation of opposing views' when political issues are considered, in the teaching of any subject, noted above.[146] Moreover, as the European Court of Human Rights said in *Kjeldsen*,[147] when it held that the Danish state was entitled to make sex education compulsory in its schools in the public interest, provided the 'information or knowledge is conveyed in an objective, critical and pluralistic manner', there should not be 'indoctrination that might be considered as not respecting parents' religious and philosophical convictions'.[148] Heater, however, argues that 'there are numerous circumstances in which a balanced sense of citizenship requires an unbalanced programme of teaching', which could include situations where government policies conflict with basic rights, and that, for example, '[t]olerance needs to be accorded particular salience in societies threatened with religious arrogance or prejudice'.[149] This he sees as a matter for the individual judgment of the teacher, acting on the basis of the basic ideals of citizenship. What is also important in this context, and not considered here by Heater, is the framework of rights, freedoms and responsibilities underpinning the provision of education to a child, discussed in detail elsewhere in this book. It includes the teacher's freedom of expression,[150] the child's right to express their views freely on all matters affecting them[151] and to an education that meets the objectives set out in the UNCRC,[152] and the parent's right for their philosophical or religious convictions to be respected in the teaching of their child.[153] The extent to which parents or children have rights over the contents of education is considered below.

Returning to the Labour Government's changes to the curriculum, there has also been an emphasis on ensuring 'a sound beginning for all children's education',[154] and this has led to the introduction of a new 'foundation stage' to the National Curriculum, under the Education Act 2002. The importance of good early years education has been reinforced by recent evidence showing that, even by the age of 5, educational attainment is a 'strong predictor' that a child from a poor background has a chance of 'bucking the trend' towards remaining in disadvantaged circumstances when an adult.[155] Children enter the foundation stage on starting their primary education or, if they are provided with funded

---

[145] Ibid.

[146] EA 1996, s 406.

[147] *Kjeldsen, Busk Madsen and Pedersen v Denmark* (1979–80) 1 EHRR 711.

[148] Ibid, at 731 para 53. See also *Campbell and Cosans v UK* (1982) 4 EHRR 293, and *Valsamis v Greece*, Case No 74/1995/580/666 (1996) 24 EHRR 294; [1998] ELR 430.

[149] D Heater, *Citizenship. The Civic Ideal in World History, Politics and Education* (3rd edn, Manchester, Manchester University Press, 2004) 348.

[150] ECHR, Art 10.

[151] UNCRC, Art 12(1).

[152] UNCRC Arts 28 and 29.

[153] ECHR, Art 2 of Prot 1.

[154] Department for Education and Employment, *Excellence in Schools*, Cm 3681 (London, TSO, 1997) 16, para 3.

[155] J Blanden, *'Bucking the Trend': What Enables Those who are Disadvantaged in Childhood to Succeed in Later Life?* Working Paper No 31 (Leeds, Corporate Document Services, 2006) 26.

nursery education, on their third birthday or such later date as they begin to receive that nursery education.[156] Key stage 1 of the four National Curriculum key stages now begins at the age of 6 rather than at the start of primary school (ages 4/5).[157] The new foundation stage comprises 'areas of learning', and for each of these areas there may be prescribed 'early learning goals', 'educational arrangements' and 'assessment arrangements'.[158] The concept of 'areas of learning' provides a more flexible basis for the curriculum at this stage.[159]

In addition, the 2002 Act has made changes to the foundation subjects at the four key stages. A more technological bent was created by establishing, as separate subjects for key stages 1–3: (i) 'design and technology'; (ii) 'art and design'; and (iii) 'information and communication technology' (ICT).[160] The remaining 'other foundation subjects' at these key stages were, as before: physical education, history, geography, music, and, at key stage 3 only, citizenship and a modern foreign language.[161] However, in primary schools the amount of time devoted to some of the subjects was reduced from 1998 by the Government's numeracy hour and by the literacy hour, noted above.[162] Prior to 2004, there was a long list of prescribed foreign languages that could be offered by schools. In addition to the main European languages such as French, German and Spanish, it included many, but not all, of the languages spoken within particular minority ethnic communities or used within their religion. Under the current law, schools may offer *any* modern foreign language at key stage 3 provided pupils are *also* able study one of more of the official languages of the European Union.[163]

The other foundation subjects at key stage 4 under the 2002 Act were: design and technology; ICT; physical education; citizenship; and a modern foreign language. But at the end of 2003 the Secretary of State exercised her power under the Act to amend the list or to suspend its application.[164] The order effecting this[165] substituted a new section which retained the core subjects for key stage 4 as mathematics, English, and science, but reduced further the list of other foundation subjects to ICT, physical education and citizenship. That meant that a modern foreign language ceased to be compulsory for key stage 4 pupils. But, in

---

[156] EA 2002, s 81.

[157] Ibid, s 82.

[158] Ibid, s 83.

[159] Those prescribed by the 2002 Act, which may be amended by the Secretary of State by order, are 'personal, social and emotional development'; 'communication, language and literacy'; 'mathematical development';'knowledge and understanding of the world'; 'physical development'; and 'creative development'.

[160] EA 2002, s 84.

[161] Ibid. Modern languages are prescribed by Order (ss 84(4), (5)); see the Education (National Curriculum) (Modern Foreign Languages) (England) Order 2004 (SI 2004/260), which has replaced earlier orders.

[162] See D Charter, 'Teachers told to cut subjects and raise literacy', *The Times*, 13 Jan 1998.

[163] SI 2004/260, n 161 above. The list of official languages of the EU was extended on 1 May 2004 to include nine more: Czech, Estonian, Hungarian, Latvian, Lithuanian, Maltese, Polish, Slovak and Slovenian. Irish will be added from 1 Jan 2007.

[164] 2002 Act, s 86.

[165] The Education (Amendment of the Curriculum Requirements for Fourth Key Stage) (England) Order 2003 (SI 2003/2946).

addition, in the interests of greater flexibility and choice, it provided that key stage 4 must also include prescribed 'elements', namely:

(a)   work-related learning;[166] and
(b)   in relation to any pupil who so elects, one subject chosen by the pupil from each of one or more of the four 'entitlement areas':
     —   arts (any of art and design, music, dance, drama and media arts),
     —   design and technology,
     —   humanities (comprising geography and history), and
     —   a modern foreign language.[167]

Pupils may be able to select subjects such as Arabic, Bengali, Modern Hebrew and Urdu as part of their studies at key stage 4 or for advanced (A/AS) level studies in the sixth form.[168] The QCA has encouraged schools to offer courses in community languages such as these,[169] although that will be dependent upon teacher availability. In December 2005 the Government announced measures to encourage a greater take up of all modern language teaching at key stage 4, referring to a benchmark of 50 per cent take up.[170]

The 2002 Act has also provided a new framework to take account of the increasing provision of vocational education at a workplace for part of the time.[171] A central funding body, the Learning and Skills Council, is given powers to fund education or training for 14–16 year olds at the premises of an employer.[172] School pupils can also receive part of their secondary education at a further education institution,[173] which could provide a broader range of choices especially in relation to vocational subjects. However, one area of concern in this context is that course options offered to girls have 'often reinforced sex-stereo-typed vocational options'.[174] Further flexibility in the curriculum at key stages 3

---

[166] Defined in the replacement s 85(10) of the 2002 Act as 'planned activity designed to use the context of work to develop knowledge, skills and understanding useful in work, including learning through the experience of work, learning about work and working practices and learning the skills for work'. Ofsted reported in 2005 that specialist schools had been slow to implement the new vocational courses at key stage 4: Ofsted, *Specialist Schools: a Second Evaluation* (London, Ofsted, 2005), para 27.

[167] The substituted s 85 also requires an LEA, governing body or head teacher to have regard to any guidance relating to work-related learning or the entitlement areas which is issued from time to time by the Qualifications and Curriculum Authority: s 85(9). The Government's intention with regard to modern languages was that all pupils would have the opportunity of choosing this subject, but it would cease to be compulsory for all pupils: see DfES, *Languages for All: Languages for Life* (London, DfES, 2002) 26.

[168] A condition is that they lead to a qualification approved by the Qualifications and Curriculum Authority under the Learning and Skills Act 2000, s 96.

[169] Qualifications and Curriculum Authority, *Modern Foreign Languages in the Key Stage 4 Curriculum* (London, QCA, 2004) 7.

[170] See DfES Press Notice 'Modern Foreign Languages—Ensuring Entitlement At Key Stage 4 is a Reality', 15 Dec 2005, which also outlines the other planned measures to promote language teaching, such as an expansion in the number of foreign languages specialist secondary schools to 400 by 2010.

[171] See, eg, the amended definition of 'secondary education' in s 177 of the Act.

[172] 2002 Act, s 178, amending the Learning and Skills Act 2000, s 5.

[173] EA 1996, s 2(2B) and (6A), inserted by the Learning and Skills Act 2000, s 110, and the EA 2002, s 177.

[174] A Osler and K Vincent, *Girls and Exclusion* (London, Routledge Falmer, 2003) 164.

and 4 is planned 'so that all pupils can benefit from the style and pace of learning that fits in with their aptitudes, interests and learning styles', and there is to be a 'strongly work-focused programme for those 14–16 year olds most at risk of disengagement', which is being be piloted from 2006.[175] The National Association for the Care and Resettlement of Offenders (NACRO) has recommended that a further shift in the National Curriculum towards vocational subjects could reduce dissatisfaction among disaffected pupils and in turn lessen truancy and future offending and anti-social behaviour.[176] As noted above, specialist vocational diplomas are being introduced from 2008. Work-related education is to be more firmly embedded with the key stage 4 curriculum as a result of structural changes to the curriculum requirements for this stage, to be made by the Education and Inspections Bill 2006.[177]

There are, indeed, signs that the notion of a National Curriculum as an essentially 'one size fits all' programme, as perhaps originally envisaged, is not capable of addressing the diverse needs of the wide range of pupils. For example, as we saw in Chapter 1, there has been concern for some years about the under-achievement of particular minority ethnic groups. Anxiety that girls would be disadvantaged by the National Curriculum, particularly in the area of assessment under the standard assessment tasks that occur at the end of certain key stages ('girls . . . may be less likely than boys to function to the best of their ability in such a formal testing situation'),[178] have been displaced by concern to improve attainment levels among boys, who have actually performed less well overall, including in the sciences .[179] As we saw in Chapter 4, a range of policy measures has been taken to raise attainment levels among under-achieving groups. However, the adaptations to the National Curriculum at key stages 3 and 4 are seen as important to provide the flexibility that may help to bring this about, and a review is being undertaken by the QCA.[180] This is focussed on addressing learning problems and ways of raising attainment levels. What is not being considered is the idea of providing a National Curriculum that is tailored to particular cultural or religious preferences, an issue that is considered further below.

[175] HM Government, *Higher Standards, Better Schools for All*, Cm 6677 (London, TSO, 2005), para 7.25. See also ibid, ch 4 and Department for Education and Skills, *14–19 Education and Skills*, Cm 6476 (London, TSO, 2004).

[176] NACRO, *Missing Out: Key Findings from Nacro's Research on Children Missing School* (London, NACRO, 2003).

[177] Education and Inspections Bill 2006, cl 61, which will substiturte a new s 85 and insert a new s 85A (setting out the 'entitlement areas') into the EA 2002.

[178] S Miles and C Middleton, 'Girls' Education in the Balance: The ERA and Inequality' in M Flude and M Hammer (eds), *The Education Reform Act 1988: Its Origins and Implications* (Basingstoke, Falmer, 1990) 187 at 198–9.

[179] Eg, '[g]irls perform as well, or better, than boys in science at every examination from ages 11–18': House of Commons Science and Technology Committee, Third Report, Session 2001–02, *Science Education 14–19*, HC 508–I (London, TSO, 2002), para 50. 'Girls still outperform boys, greatly so in English and slightly in mathematics and science': Ofsted, *The Annual Report of Her Majesty's Chief Inspector of Schools 2003/04* (London, Ofsted, 2005), para 96.

[180] See HM Government, *Higher Standards, Better Schools for All*, Cm 6677 (London, TSO, 2005), ch 4.

The general position is that the prescribed school curriculum is intended to meet the needs of all children. It is, for example, to be the norm for pupils with special educational needs,[181] although a statement of special educational needs[182] may exclude the application of the National Curriculum, or apply it with modifications, in relation to the child or young person in question.[183] Temporary exception to the National Curriculum can also be made for a particular child for a maximum of six months (potentially renewable) by a head teacher.[184] This power is intended to be used where the child's circumstances make the standard curricular framework unsuitable, as in the case of an immigrant child whose first language is not English and who therefore needs extra language provision for a period. Also, the Secretary of State can direct a departure from the National Curriculum in a school, or for some of its pupils, in order to facilitate the carrying out of development work or educational experiments.[185] However, the first potentially significant inroad into the universality of the National Curriculum occurred when education action zones were established, under the School Standards and Framework Act 1998. It was felt that in order to overcome barriers to pupils' progress in the disadvantaged areas served by the zone schools, curricular flexibility was needed, as noted in Chapter 3. Subsequently, all schools have become able to apply for such flexibility under the 'earned autonomy' measures in the Education Act 2002, which empower the Secretary of State to designate via regulations a curriculum provision (or one on teachers' pay and conditions) as attracting exemption, and enable a school which is a 'qualifying school' because of the level of its performance and the quality of its management and leadership to apply for inclusion in an order exempting it from the provision.[186] As the premise behind the National Curriculum was and remains its potential to raise standards of education and pupils' achievements it does seem odd that schools that are deemed to be well run should be able to opt out of it as a 'reward' for their success under its regime. To date, however, no school has been given this curricular autonomy. Even were it to occur, it is certain to involve only a partial exemption. Under proposals set out in the 2005 White Paper, the new 'self governing Trust schools' would also be able to apply for this flexibility,[187] although the fact that the application of the National Curriculum to these schools would be the norm is cited as one of the safeguards in ensuring their proper regulation and public accountability.[188]

Children who attend independent schools are not covered by the National Curriculum at all, since neither it nor the general legal requirements regarding

---

[181] Department for Education and Skills, *Special Educational Needs Code of Practice* (London, DfES, 2001), para 1:5.

[182] See p 319 above.

[183] Education Act 2002, ss 91 and 113.

[184] Ibid, ss 93 and 114; the Education (National Curriculum) (Temporary Exception for Individual Pupils) Regulations 1989 (SI 1989/1181), and the Education (National Curriculum) (Temporary Exception for Individual Pupils) (Wales) Regulations 1999 (SI 1999/1815).

[185] EA 2002, ss 90 and 111.

[186] EA 2002, ss 6–10.

[187] HM Government, *Higher Standards, Better Schools for All*, Cm 6677 (London, TSO, 2005), para 2.16. As regards these schools see Chaps 3 and 5.

[188] Ibid, paras 2.26–2.28.

the basic or whole curriculum apply there. This is not set to change, although the Government intends to make it easier for independent schools to join the state sector as foundation or trust schools[189] (a move that, in the case of religious schools, Ahdar has argued is necessitated by the Human Rights Act 1998[190]). This could be facilitated by removing the traditional condition that the school is needed in order to meet an insufficiency in places in the state sector locally. It has been reported that as many as 100 Muslim schools are likely to apply to join the state sector if and when these reforms are implemented.[191] The Government provided a grant of £100,000 to the Association of Muslim Schools in 2005–6 to enable it to identify generic barriers to joining the state sector and target five schools for preparing their applications.[192] Independent schools that make this transition will become subject to the curriculum requirements applicable to state schools (although that will mean in some cases that they have a right to apply for exemption).[193] This will not necessarily appeal to all religious schools in the independent sector. One head teacher of an independent Muslim school has been quoted as saying that his girls' school did not want to apply to join the state sector because 'We do not want our teaching criteria changed'.[194] In fact, some independent schools already follow a curriculum broadly in line with the National Curriculum; and in any event their curricular provision is now subject to some regulation, and this is discussed below.

Accommodation of Minorities' Wishes

The idea of a National Curriculum with legal force is not consistent with the notion of choice in education. For teachers, it was made clear from the start that, where the new curriculum was concerned, they and schools 'will not be free to pick and choose'.[195] For parents, there have certainly been no equivalent rights of withdrawal under the National Curriculum's statutory framework to those relating to religious education or sex education.[196] The notion of choice in education that became the dominant ideal in the 1980s was associated with school admission rather than the content of education. As Coulby rather bluntly put it, 'parents are free to choose which institution will slavishly teach the Secretary of State's curriculum to their children'.[197] Although the principle that

[189] HM Government, *Higher Standards, Better Schools for All*, Cm 6677 (London, TSO, 2005), para 2.37.

[190] R-J Adhar, *Law and Religion* (Aldershot, Ashgate, 2000) 147–8.

[191] G Hackett, 'State to pay for Muslim schools', *Sunday Times*, 23 Oct 2005, 10.

[192] DfES, *'Working Together': Co-Operation Between Government and Faith Communities Progress Report* (Aug 2005) (London, DfES, 2005), para 3.4.3.

[193] HM Government, *Higher Standards, Better Schools for All*, Cm 6677 (London, TSO, 2005), paras 2.36–2.37.

[194] G Hackett, n 191 above.

[195] Department for Education and Science, *National Curriculum: From Policy to Practice* (London, DES, 1989), para 10.2.

[196] See below: 'Sex Education—The Implications of the Right of Withdrawal', pp 406–10 below and 'Religion in State Education', pp 429 et seq below.

[197] D Coulby, 'The Ideological Contrdictions of Education Reform' in L Bash and D Coulby, *The Education Reform Act. Competition and Control* (London, Cassell, 1989) 110 at 114.

children should be taught according to their parents' wishes was included in the Education Act 1944, section 76, and still has legal effect,[198] it is subject to the proviso that it does not give rise to unreasonable public expenditure and is compatible with efficient education. The authors of a major text on education law in the 1950s considered that this principle of adherence to parental wishes was of 'special significance' as far as the secular curriculum was concerned.[199] Certainly its relevance and application to the curriculum have been confirmed by the courts when considering this section in the context of LEAs' arrangements for schools, as discussed in Chapter 5.[200] But when parental objections were made to the 'standard assessment tasks' (the National Curriculum tests for pupils) in the early 1990s, primarily on the ground that they were too stressful for children, leading to some parents being granted exemption for their children, and in one case in Cardiff the suspension of the tests when the head teacher was concerned about possible breach of the section 76 duty, the Department for Education and Science (as it then was) issued guidance to the effect that this duty was overridden by the statutory duty on schools to implement the National Curriculum.[201] Later guidance on assessment arrangements[202] made clear that only where the child was suffering from a severe emotional problem or in certain other truly exceptional cases would exemption be possible (under the head teacher's power to grant temporary exception[203]).

This parental wishes duty has yet to receive judicial consideration in the specific context of a legal challenge over the curriculum; but, as we saw in Chapter 5, the courts have regarded it in other contexts, particularly choice of school, as providing only a general principle to which regard must be had by the relevant authorities.[204] Moreover, the conditions attached to it clearly limit its potential to guarantee choice. Indeed, adherence to the choices of individual parents over the content of their education in a state school might well prejudice efficient education. That was, in effect, part of the basis for the Secretary of State's refusal to grant Plymouth Brethren children, who are forbidden by their religion to use or be exposed to information technology, exemption from that element of the National Curriculum. It was considered that it would encourage other parents to seek an opt-out and would thereby work against administrative convenience as well as the very idea of a National Curriculum.[205] A further reason was the overriding need to prepare all pupils for the opportunities, responsibilities and experiences of adult life[206] (which is a separate statutory duty, as noted above). Parents' right under the ECHR Article 2 of Protocol 1, as regards the teaching of their children in a manner consistent with their religious and

---

[198] Education Act 1996, s 9.
[199] MM Wells and PS Taylor, *The New Law of Education* (4th edn, London, Butterworths, 1954) 197.
[200] Eg, *Wood v Ealing LBC* [1967] Ch 364. See pp 237–43 above.
[201] Then under the ERA 1988, s 10. See N Harris, *Law and Education: Regulation, Consumerism and the Education System* (London, Sweet and Maxwell, 1993) 222.
[202] DES Circular 14/91 (London, DES, 1991), para 6.
[203] See n 184 above.
[204] See, eg, *Watt v Kesteven County Council* [1955] 1 QB 408.
[205] C Hamilton, *Family, Law and Religion* (London, Sweet and Maxwell, 1995) 323 and 332.
[206] Ibid.

philosophical convictions, was considered by the Government at the time the compulsory National Curriculum was introduced.[207] The Government drew on the principle established in the ECtHR's judgment in *Kjeldsen*,[208] where, as we saw in Chapter 2, it was held that the state was entitled to make sex education compulsory in schools in the public interest, provided the 'information or knowledge is conveyed in an objective, critical and pluralistic manner' and not via 'indoctrination that might be considered as not respecting parents' religious and philosophical convictions'.[209] The Government's case therefore was that, because the National Curriculum would meet these basic criteria and would offer a balanced approach, the overriding of parental wishes was justified in the wider national interest. As the European Court of Human Rights had done, the Government also placed weight on the option available to parents of sending their children to a private school or educating them at home.[210]

The pluralistic approach to teaching is in fact consonant with the idea of multicultural education that gained currency in the 1980s, as noted earlier in the chapter. Sutherland argues that a difficulty with multicultural education is that '[p]rovision for the religious and social beliefs of minority groups within the curriculum is . . . complicated' and can generate dissatisfaction on the part of parents from the majority culture.[211] She says that the teaching of history and other humanities 'should present no great problems if the principles . . . of avoiding parochial or nationalistic interpretations are accepted'.[212] However, the underlying premise to this view is that the curriculum can and should be adapted to avoid offending the sensibilities of all groups. It has been argued in the recent Fabian Society debate on Britishness that this has led, in the case of the history curriculum, to avoidance of aspects of British history that could prove socially divisive. One of the contributors, a member of the Education and Skills Select Committee and a former editor of *History Today*, argued that '[w]hile the school history focus on the "Great Dictators" can convey important moral lessons about citizenship and human rights, teaching a rounded history of the rise and fall of Britain's empire has often been regarded as too tricky, complex or divisive in our multi-ethnic classrooms.'[213] However, Sutherland also argues that if the curriculum is to prepare pupils for living in a multicultural society it has to

---

[207] See ibid, 323.

[208] *Kjeldsen, Busk Madsen and Pedersen v Denmark*, 1 EHRR 711 (1976).

[209] Ibid, at 731, para 53. See p 73 above. See also *Campbell and Cosans v UK* (1982) 4 EHRR 293, and *Valsamis v Greece*, Case No 74/1995/580/666 (1996) 24 EHRR 294; [1998] ELR 430. For an analogous approach to a sex education programme in schools in the US, see *Brown v Hot, Sexy and Safer Productions*, 68 F3d 525 (1st Cir, 1995), 516 US 1159 (1996); and see also *Fields v Palmdale School District*, 427 F3d 1197 (9th Cir, 2005), where the court, considering a case arising out of a survey of pupils by the school that amongst other things covered sexual matters, held that parents do not have a fundamental right over the content of their child's education even with regard to such matters, nor did sexual content within education constitute interference with a right to privacy. The survey also satisfied the test of rationality in that it was in pursuance of a legitimate state interest in advancing education and welfare of pupils.

[210] See C Hamilton, *Family, Law and Religion* (London, Sweet and Maxwell, 1995) 323.

[211] M Sutherland, *Theory of Education* (Harlow, Longman, 1988) 132–3.

[212] Ibid, 132.

[213] G Marsden MP, quoted at www.fabian-society.org.uk/press_office/display.asp?id=511&type=news&cat=24. See further, *The Fabian Review, Britishness Issue*, Dec 2005.

subvert the traditional principle that education should be in line with the wishes of the majority.[214] She sees this as particularly necessary where core beliefs and values are at issue:

> When it is a matter of cultural and social beliefs—e.g. about the freedom of the individual to make certain choices, or about the roles of men and women in society—then the curriculum may have to include both teaching about the principles which are generally accepted by society and indications that some groups within the larger society do not accept those principles. There is a basic incompatibility that cannot be overcome: in multicultural societies, differences of cultural views occur: the curriculum cannot ignore these or offer the impression that all are equally accepted in society outside school.[215]

This idea assumes that choice per se cannot be accommodated and that parents' rights are best protected by measures to ensure a degree of inclusiveness and some recognition of cultural integrity through a pluralistic approach. For example, the education working group which was one of the seven working parties established in 2005 by the Home Office to develop practical proposals aimed at the prevention of extremism and the reduction of disaffection among the Muslim community, has recommended the provision of 'substantive information on Islamic achievements and contributions in and to subjects across the entire National Curriculum'.[216] It is critical of the QCA's 'Respect for all'‐website[217] which, it says, while offering a range of suggestions for including multicultural perspectives in all curriculum subjects, mostly neglects the Islamic dimension. Yet the traditional resistance to the multicultural approach is that, as Merry puts it, 'exposure to cultures different to one's own will lead to a weaker core identity',[218] something that Merry in fact rejects. He argues that the opposite might be true, on the basis that such exposure might 'even enhance one's allegiance to a culturally coherent set of values and norms'.[219] The working group (above) regards an increased coverage of Islam and its contribution to European civilisation as likely to 'enhance self esteem' among Muslim children and help to reduce 'alienation and imbalance that the present lack of such education breeds'.[220] Opponents of multiculturalism might be resistant to the principle of advancing group interests represented in such ideas, particularly if there is a likelihood of other groups asserting similar claims of their own, on the basis that it would detract from their basic idea of common citizenship. However, what those claims are really about is social inclusiveness in the face of exclusion from full citizenship. Kymlicka specifically cites 'changes to the education curriculum

---

[214] N 211 above, 133.

[215] Ibid, 132–3.

[216] 'Preventing Extremism Together' Working Groups, Aug–Oct 2005, Report (London, DfES, 2005), App A, para 1.

[217] www.qca.org.uk/301.html.

[218] MS Merry, 'Cultural Coherence and the Schooling for Identity Maintenance' (2005) 39 *Journal of the Philosophy of Education* 477 at 482.

[219] Ibid, 484.

[220] 'Preventing Extremism Together' Working Groups, Aug–Oct 2005, Report (London, DfES, 2005) 23.

to recognize the history and contribution of minorities' as an example of multiculturalist policy that is 'primarily directed at ensuring the effective exercise of common rights of citizenship' and does not fall within his classification of group differentiated or 'polyethnic' rights that aim to facilitate expressions of cultural particularity, such as the wearing of particular forms of religious dress or, indeed, mother tongue teaching.[221]

If parents from minorities are resistant to a common prescribed curriculum, notwithstanding efforts that have been made to base it on objectivity and pluralism, they may be inclined to remove their children from the state system. The potential areas of objection vary across different cultural groups and also within them (for example, some Muslims might regard particular animal or human representations in artwork as strictly forbidden whereas others might not be so concerned[222]). A study of the statutory arrangements under which parents may bring a complaint about the performance by the governing body of a school (or the LEA) of its statutory curricular responsibilities[223] noted a complaint about alleged sexual innuendo and blasphemous and offensive language in a reading book[224] and another about coverage of Hallowe'en in a primary school.[225] The content of textbooks can also give rise to objections on the basis of cultural sensibilities.[226] There may well be common concerns about aspects of the curriculum across several groups; for example, some religious groups will be opposed to swimming lessons where a girl will be seen in a swimming costume by others,[227] while some Muslims and ultra-Orthodox Jews may take offence over the use of books containing the word 'pig' for teaching children to read.[228] Sex education is another potentially problematic area, but as it lies outside the National Curriculum it is discussed separately below.

In so far as there is any capacity for the accommodation of minorities' wishes, or indeed the wishes of anyone from the majority community, it is clear that it is the parents' rights alone that tend to be considered. As discussed in depth in Chapter 2, the underlying assumption is that while schooling is provided to the child, any influence that is permitted over decisions affecting it is that of the parents alone. As discussed in Chapter 1, one of the difficulties in ensuring that the law acknowledges or responds appropriately to diversity is that of separating children's identities from those of their parents or adults in general, particularly given the importance attached to the interaction between home and school.

---

[221] W Kymlicka, *Multicultural Citizenship* (London, OUP, 1995) 45.

[222] Merry, n 218 above, at 489.

[223] EA 1996, s 409, previously the ERA 1988, s 23. See, further, N Harris, 'Local Complaints Procedures under the Education Reform Act 1988' [1993] *Journal of Social Welfare and Family Law* 19.

[224] G Kemp, *The Turbulent Term of Tyke Tyler* (London, Faber, 1976; Harmondsworth, Puffin, 1977).

[225] N Harris, *Complaints About Schooling. The Role of Section 23 of the Education Reform Act 1988* (London, National Consumer Council, 1992) 91–4 and 101–2.

[226] See C Hamilton, *Family, Law and Religion* (London; Sweet and Maxwell, 1995) 317.

[227] See, eg, the case in the Netherlands: *Hof Den Bosch*, 5 Sept 1989 [1989] *Kort Geding* 394, where a right to refrain from gymnastic lessons on religious grounds was not recognised by the court.

[228] See P Weller, A Feldman and K Purdam, *Religious Discrimination in England and Wales*, Home Office Research Study 220 (London, Home Office, 2001) 23.

Reconciling the potential conflict between minority rights and majority views, as reflected in education policies and practices, is a challenge in itself. Ideally, children's independent rights should be embedded within those policies and practices, but, as we saw in Chapter 2, the various international instruments in which those rights are expressed, particularly the UNCRC, also give cognizance to the role of the family and to the child's cultural identity. The critical question is how far and on what basis the state should override the wishes of the parents in relation to matters that they regard as fundamental to their cultural identity and their community's value system, where the state considers that it is in the child's interests and/or the interests of society as a whole that the child receive a particular form of education and the accompanying knowledge. Liberalism dictates that the state should recognise and uphold the rights, freedoms and choices of individuals and diverse social groups, yet at the same time must aim to prepare children for future life as citizens of the wider society.[229] This means that, as the *Talmud Torah* school judgment below, albeit concerned with an independent school's curriculum, shows,[230] faith schools should not be so narrow in their approach that children are not able to participate in the world beyond their own families and communities. For the state education system it should mean that there should be debate over how much influence parents should be able to enjoy over their children's education, given that there is a 'general public interest in supporting family units in their decisions regarding the upbringing of their children'[231] and a national policy of enforcing parental responsibility over their child's education;[232] over the question whether exemption from particular classes is harmful to the child's interests; and, given that there will be 'certain core values that should be taught' but '[s]chools that teach values will offend some people', the appropriate content of a curriculum that is intended for all.[233]

The US Supreme Court's decision in *Wisconsin v Yoder*[234] is widely cited in this context.[235] Although this case is concerned with the withdrawal of children from schooling altogether, it raises wider issues of how conflict between the state's interest in ensuring universal secular education up to a certain age and the rights

---

[229] See S Macedo, 'Liberal Civic Education and Religious Fundamentalism: The Case of God v John Rawls' (1995) 105 *Ethics* 468; C Glenn and J De Groof, *Finding the Right Balance. Freedom, Autonomy and Accountability in Education* (Utrecht, Lemma, 2002). See also A Bradney, 'Ethnicity, Religion and Sex Education' in N Harris (ed), *Children, Sex Education and the Law* (London, National Children's Bureau, 1996) 87.

[230] *R v Secretary of State for Education and Science ex parte Talmud Torah Machzikei Hadass School Trust* (1985), *The Times*, 12 Apr 1985. Below pp 442–3. The decision is reported in LexisNexis.

[231] L Lundy, 'Family Values in the Classroom? Reconciling Parental Wishes and Children's Rights in State Schools' (2005) 19 *International Journal of Law, Policy and the Family* 346 at 360.

[232] N Harris, 'Empowerment and State Education: Rights of Choice and Participation' (2005) 68 *MLR* 925.

[233] J Spinner-Halev, 'Extending Diversity: Religion in Public and Private Education' in W Kymlicka and W Norman (eds), *Citizenship in Diverse Societies* (London, Oxford University Press, 2000), 68, at 90.

[234] 406 US 205 (1972).

[235] See, eg, S Macedo, 'Liberal Civic Education and Religious Fundamentalism: The Case of God v John Rawls' (1995) 105 *Ethics* 468; J Spinner-Halev, 'Extending Diversity: Religion in Public and Private Education' in W Kymlicka and W Norman (eds), *Citizenship in Diverse Societies* (London, Oxford University Press, 2000), ch 3; A Dagovitz, 'When Choice Does Not Matter: Political Liberalism, Religion and the Faith School Debate' (2004) 38 *Journal of Philosophy of Education* 165.

of minorities who object to the content of that education might be resolved. The case arose out of the refusal by members of the Amish community in Green County, Wisconsin, to continue to send their children to public school (ie, a state funded school) beyond the eighth grade (ages 14–15), even though the school attendance laws required that children attend school until the age of 16. The children were not enrolled at any school and consequently the parents were convicted of an offence and fined. Their Supreme Court challenge was based on the importance of preserving the Amish community and the conflict between the values within post-eighth grade education in schools and those of the Amish community and their religion. In particular, the community was concerned that school education would mean the exposure of their children to worldly influence in conflict with their beliefs. Their society placed an emphasis on learning through doing and a life of 'goodness' rather than on intellectual achievement and competitive success. Burger CJ acknowledged that 'a State's interest in universal education, however highly we rank it, is not totally free from a balancing process when it impinges upon fundamental rights and interests', including parents' interests in the religious upbringing of their children.[236] For a state to be able to justify its policy it was necessary for it to show either that it did not interfere with the free exercise of religion or that there was 'a state interest of sufficient magnitude to override the interest claiming (Constitutional) protection'.[237] Burger CJ explained that only religious beliefs rather than those of a philosophical nature—'secular considerations'—warranted protection in this context. He accepted that the evidence, including 300 years of consistent religious practice, suggested that the Amish people's free exercise of their religious beliefs would be endangered by the compulsory attendance of their children beyond the eighth grade. While agreeing with the state's argument that education was necessary to ensure citizen participation that was essential to the preservation of freedom and independence and to prepare individuals to be self-reliant and self-sufficient, the court concluded that an additional one or two years of high school would in itself do 'little to serve those interests'.[238] Burger CJ noted that the Amish community was a 'highly successful social unit' and its members were 'productive and law-abiding'.[239] As to the argument that without the additional period of schooling any member of the community who later chose to leave it would be ill-equipped for life outside,[240] the court said that was a 'highly speculative' point, since there was little evidence of departure from the community, but that were it to occur the person in question would have other skills, for example related to agriculture, that would prevent them from being a burden on society.[241] Douglas J, in dissent, argued that the right of a child who wanted to remain at school in conflict with the parents' wishes should be upheld,

---

[236] N 234 above, at 214.
[237] Ibid.
[238] Ibid.
[239] Ibid.
[240] As to this, see the argument of S Macedo, 'Liberal Civic Education and Religious Fundamentalism: The Case of God v John Rawls' (1995) 105 *Ethics* 468 at 488.
[241] N 234, at 224.

but the majority refused to consider the point since it was not at issue in the litigation.

While the decision might be seen to have given considerable weight to parents' rights in connection with their children's education, it is important to note the caveats expressed by Burger CJ. First, it seems clear that the court did not consider that mere philosophical objections to the nature of schooling would prevail; only those based on religion would have overriding constitutional protection. Secondly, there was in effect a hierarchy of religions for this purpose. Burger CJ noted the long history and well established traditions and faith-based lifestyle of the Amish community. He emphasised that 'we are not dealing with a way of life and mode of education by a group claiming to have recently discovered some "progressive" or more enlightened process for rearing children for modern life'.[242] Finally, he stressed that, as compared with the school authorities, the courts were 'ill-equipped to determine the "necessity" of discrete aspects of a State's programme of compulsory education' and should approach any questions of exemption on religious grounds 'with great circumspection'.[243]

The *Yoder* decision may no longer be of great practical significance in the United States, since home education is now much more widely accepted,[244] with between 1.7 and 2.2 million children being educated at home in 2002–3.[245] But it is still regarded as raising important issues about when the state should be prepared to yield its sovereignty over a child's education, in the interests of supporting or preserving a minority's way of life. To Freeman, for example, the decision represents 'multiculturalism with a vengeance', preserving the Amish community 'at the expense of civic freedom and individual development and independence of its members'.[246] Macedo argues that accommodations and exemptions in favour of religious minority cultures would be justified only 'where public imperatives are marginal and the burdens on particular groups are very substantial', and it should be accepted that '[l]iberal civic education is bound to have the effect of favoring some ways of life or religious convictions over others'.[247] One of the problems in yielding to the choices of particular faith groups is that singling out any for accommodation, as the Supreme Court did in *Yoder*, gives rise to claims of partiality that are likely to be contested by other groups and individuals; and there is also the slippery-slope argument that was put forward by the minister in resisting opt-outs from the National Curriculum (above). Moreover, if the basis for upholding the cultural autonomy of a group such as the Amish involves forming a judgment on the ethics and lifestyle of

[242] Ibid, at 235.

[243] Ibid.

[244] J Spinner-Halev, 'Extending Diversity: Religion in Public and Private Education' in W Kymlicka and W Norman (eds), *Citizenship in Diverse Societies* (London, Oxford University Press, 2000), ch 3, at 72.

[245] Cited in B Colwell and BSchwartz, 'Tips for Public School Administrators in Monitoring and Working with Homeschool Students' (2006) 41 *ELA Notes* 11.

[246] S Freeman, 'Liberalism and the Accommodation of Group Claims' in P Kelly (ed), *Multicuturalism Reconsidered* (Cambridge, Polity, 2002) 18 at 24.

[247] S Macedo, 'Liberal Civic Education and Religious Fundamentalism: The Case of God v John Rawls' (1995) 105 *Ethics* 468 at 484 and 485.

particular communities, as the Supreme Court did in *Yoder* when it placed weight on the Amish community's productiveness and law-abiding nature, or as to the status of the particular religion, as was also considered, then enormous difficulties would lie, notwithstanding the broader range of beliefs protected under the ECHR, Article 2 of Protocol 1 (and Article 9: see below).

Several of the above arguments were referred to specifically by Judge Kennedy in her Federal Court judgment in a case that is seen as 'emblematic' of the shift from religious liberty and towards greater power of states that occurred in the period after *Yoder*.[248] *Mozert v Hawkins County Board of Education*.[249] Here a mother, described as a 'born again Christian', objected to a reading programme in use in state schools and complained on religious grounds about the 'mental telepathy' that was necessitated by this critical reading scheme and about various passages within the books which she found unacceptable because they touched upon issues such as evolution, 'futuristic supernaturalism' and magic. Initially the school agreed to an alternative programme for the children concerned, who would leave the classroom and use older books in another room or the library. However, the county school board subsequently voted to eliminate any alternative reading programmes. Seven families commenced proceedings and the district court upheld their claim on the ground that their free exercise of their religion had been prejudiced by compulsion to participate in a reading series that offended their beliefs, and the state's 'legitimate and overriding interest in public education' did not excuse it. The court considered that the parents' wishes could be accommodated without disruption to the educational process, by permitting them to opt their children out of the reading programme and providing reading at home. The parents were awarded $50,000 damages. However, the Board of Education successfully appealed the judgment to the Federal Court.

Kennedy J, one of the majority judges, felt that the burden on the parents' free exercise rights resulting from compulsion to engage in the programme was justified by a compelling state interest. In particular, she noted that the Supreme Court in *Bethel School District No.403 v Fraser*[250] (which concerned the question whether a pupil's First Amendment (free speech) right prevented a school from disciplining him for a lewd speech given before the school assembly) had said that public education must prepare pupils for citizenship and self-government. She concluded that '[t]eaching students about complex and controversial social and moral issues is just as essential for preparing public school pupils for citizenship and self-government as inculcating in students the habits and manners of civility' (which was the issue where the Bethel student's behaviour was concerned). She also noted the potential disruption that would be caused by accommodating exemption from a reading programme. Teachers would have to identify potentially offensive material in advance and permit pupils to leave the room when it was discussed. This would also result in 'religious divisiveness' and would 'create a precedent for persons from other religions to request exemptions

---

[248] Anon, '"They Drew A Circle That Shut Me In": The Free Exercise Implications Of *Zelman v Simmons-Harris*' (2004) 117 *Harvard Law Review* 919, at 922.
[249] 827 F2d 1058 (6th Cir, 1987).
[250] 478 US 675 (1986).

from core subjects because of religious objections'. Permitting opt-outs from core courses within a school when materials were found objectionable would 'result in a school system impossible to administer'. Chief Judge Liveley noted that, unlike the situation in *Yoder*, the state's general policy permitted parents to educate their children privately or at home. He also referred to the need for the teaching of values such as tolerance of divergent political and religious views, that had been noted by the Supreme Court in *Fraser*. He said that that was 'a civil tolerance, not a religious one' and as such did not require a person to accept any other religion but merely to acknowledge pluralism. The court did not consider that the reading programme contained any religious or anti-religious messages. Finally, there was the implication that parents might be able to turn any area of the curriculum to which they objected into a matter of religion: '[b]ecause the plaintiffs perceive every teaching that goes beyond the "three Rs" as inculcating religious ideas, they admit that any value-laden reading curriculum that did not affirm the truth of their beliefs would offend their religious convictions'. In this context it may be noted that, as discussed below, when parents in England and Wales were given a statutory right to withdraw their children from sex education in school this right was deliberately not tied to religion, on the basis that a decision to withdraw the child was a sufficient indication of the parents' strength of feeling and the reason was not relevant.

Of course, it might reasonably be assumed that most objections to the secular curriculum in schools will, as in the *Mozert* case, be religiously based. In the UK, at issue may be the right under ECHR Article 9, discussed in Chapter 2, namely the right to 'freedom of thought, conscience and religion' including a person's 'freedom, either alone or in community with others and in public or private, to manifest his religion or belief, in worship, teaching, practice and observance'. It was noted in Chapter 4 how an infringement of this right was alleged to have occurred in *Begum* by virtue of a school uniform policy that prohibited the wearing of the jilbab, a garment that the complainant, a Muslim, had decided to wear after being at her school for two years. The Court of Appeal found that the school authorities had not given proper consideration to all necessary matters involved in deciding the school uniform policy, including in particular whether the claimant's right would be or had been interfered with and whether there was justification for interference with the right to manifest one's religion or beliefs for the purposes of Article 9(2), namely through limitations that 'are prescribed by law and are necessary in a democratic society in the interests of public safety, for the protection of public order, health or morals, or for the protection of the rights and freedoms of others'.[251] As noted in Chapter 4, the House of Lords rejected this procedural approach and in any event found the restriction justifiable under Article 9(2) on the ground of the need to protect the rights and freedom of others and that it was proportionate to that aim. But *Begum* also cast

---

[251] Poole argues that this represents a 'new formalism' in the form of an ex ante procedural test imposed on primary decision-makers of a kind that it was intended might exercise judges in assessing, ex post facto, human rights claims but not administrators: T Poole, 'Of Headscarves and Heresies: the *Denbigh High School* Case and Public Authority Decision-making under the Human Rights Act' [2005] *Public Law* 685 at 690–1 and 694–5.

some light on the types of religious belief that might be protected under the Convention. The Court of Appeal, for example, held that there had been an interference with the girl's freedom to manifest her religion notwithstanding evidence that the mandatory wearing of the jilbab was a minority view within the Muslim faith.[252] Scott Baker LJ confirmed that it was 'not for school authorities to pick and choose between religious beliefs or shades of religious belief'.[253] In the House of Lords, which found that there was no interference with the Article 9 right (see below) and, as noted above, that there was justification for the school uniform policy under Article 9(2), Lord Bingham of Cornhill accepted that '[i]t was not the less a religious belief because her belief may have changed . . . or because it was a belief shared by a small minority of people'.[254] Indeed, it may be noted that in *Hasan and Chaush v Bulgaria* it was held by the ECtHR that 'but for very exceptional cases, the right to freedom of religion as guaranteed under the Convention excludes any discretion on the part of the State to determine whether religious beliefs or the means used to express such beliefs are legitimate'.[255] There is a nice contrast here with *Yoder*, where the nature of the Amish community's religious commitment was in part determinative of the respect accorded to their views. On the face of it, it is clearly relatively easy to invoke Article 9 in support of claims within the field of education, since any form of religious belief would appear to be capable of being advanced by it,[256] provided it is a belief asserted in good faith;[257] and, indeed, freedom of thought and conscience are also protected by the Article.

There is a question as to whether exposure to a particular part of the secular curriculum would, in itself, be capable of interfering with freedom of religion, and also the manifestation of religious belief, for the purposes of the restrictions permitted to be placed upon the right, under Article 9(2). Teaching is certainly included as an explicit example of a manifestation of belief, and the infliction of corporal punishment was also held to be a manifestation in *Williamson*, where teachers at a Christian Fellowship school and parents who believed in the use of corporal punishment as a matter of Christian faith challenged the statutory ban on it as being in conflict with the ECHR.[258] Protection of the manifestation of belief will, of course, be conditional upon the consistency of the belief with basic standards of human dignity, the seriousness (as opposed to triviality) of the

---

[252] *R (SB) v Headteacher and Governors of Denbigh High School* [2005] ELR 198 (CA).

[253] Ibid, at para 93.

[254] *R (Begum) v Headteacher and Governors of Denbigh High School* [2006] UKHL 15; [2006] 2 WLR 719.

[255] App no 30985/96 (2002) 34 EHRR 55, at para 78.

[256] Poole argues that if the ECtHR's statement in *Hasan* 'is to be taken at face value, would it not mean that *any* (sincere) profession that a practice is necessary to meet the requirements of an individual's religion ought to be taken as legitimate for the purposes of Art.9(1)?': T Poole, 'Of Headscarves and Heresies: the *Denbigh High School* Case and Public Authority Decision-making under the Human Rights Act' [2005] *Public Law* 685 at 687, n 12 (original emphasis).

[257] *R (Williamson) v Secretary of State for Education and Employment and Others* [2005] UKHL 15, [2005] ELR 291; [2005] 2 AC 246, per Lord Nicholls at para 22.

[258] *R (Williamson) v Secretary of State for Education and Employment and Others* [2005] UKHL 15, [2005] ELR 291; [2005] 2 AC 246. See, eg, para 35, per Lord Nicholls.

matters with which it is concerned, and its coherence.[259] Should parents seek the removal of their child from a lesson where the education is objectionable on religious grounds, that would probably also involve a manifestation of their belief. Of course, the parents could in any event invoke the protection of Article 2 of Protocol 1 as regards the teaching of their child in accordance with their religious and/or philosophical convictions.[260] But, as discussed above, in the light of the *Kjeldsen* decision[261] it will be very difficult to justify withdrawal on that basis in most cases.[262] However, it is perhaps worth noting that whereas in *Kjeldsen* (and also in *Valsamis v Greece*[263]) the Court placed some weight on the parents' right to have their children educated privately or at home,[264] in *Williamson* Lord Nicholls of Birkenhead supported his conclusion that the statutory ban on corporal punishment interfered materially with the parents' rights under Article 2 of Protocol 1 and Article 9 partly with reference to there being 'no reason to suppose that in general the claimant parents, or other parents with like beliefs, have the personal skills to educate their children at home or the financial means needed to employ home tutors'.[265] In *Begum* Mummery LJ in effect rejected the idea that the claimant could enjoy her religious freedom for the purposes of Article 9 by moving to another school which accepted the wearing of the jilbab. He said that pupils did not have a 'contractual choice', unlike an employee who could change jobs, whereas there was a 'statutory duty to provide education to the pupils'.[266] The House of Lords noted that the Strasbourg jurisprudence made it difficult to establish an interference with the right to manifest a belief where a person had a choice about accepting a role or, as applied to education by Lord Scott of Foscote,[267] in whether to avail oneself of the services provided by a particular public institution, where the practice or observance of their religious belief was compromised and there were other comparable means open to them to practise or observe their religion.[268]

The interference issue in fact split the judges in *Begum*. Baroness Hale considered that the complainant might not have had a freedom of choice as

---

[259] See ibid per Lord Nicholls at para 23 and Baroness Hale at para 76.

[260] As regards the meaning of 'philosophical convictions', which implies beliefs of cogency, seriousness, coherence and importance, see ibid at para 76, per Baroness Hale of Richmond, referring to *Campbell and Cosans v UK* (1982) 4 EHRR 293. See pp 72–4 above.

[261] *Kjeldsen, Busk Madsen and Pedersen v Denmark*, 1 EHRR 711 (1976).

[262] See also *X, Y and Z v Federal Republic of Germany*, App no 9411/81 (1982) 29 DR 224, an admissibility decision in a complaint arising from principled objections to the scientific curriculum in Germany, including mathematics. The reason for inadmissibility was the basis for the parents' convictions and the fact that they had the choice of a schools offering an alternative approaches.

[263] Case No 74/1995/580/666 (1996) 24 EHRR 294; [1998] ELR 430. See Chap 2.

[264] In *Valsamis* the court felt that the parents, who held pacifist beliefs and objected to their children's compulsory participation in school parades that commemorated the outbreak of war between Greece and fascist Italy, could educate their children within the family about matters pertaining to their convictions relating to matters of war and peace.

[265] *R (Williamson) v Secretary of State for Education and Employment and Others* [2005] UKHL 15; [2005] ELR 291; [2005] 2 AC 246, para 41.

[266] *R (SB) v Headteacher and Governors of Denbigh High School* [2005] ELR 198 (CA), at para 84.

[267] *R (Begum) v Headteacher and Governors of Denbigh High School* [2006] UKHL 15; [2006] 2 WLR 719, para 87.

[268] Ibid, per Lord Bingham at para 23 and Lord Hoffmann at paras 52–55. See also the discussion in Chap 2.

regards her school because of her age (she was still under 14 when refused admission while wearing the jilbab and was obviously much younger when starting at the school); and Lord Nicholls of Birkenhead was unsure how easily she could move to another school where she could wear the jilbab (although there were several such schools in the area) and was mindful of potential disruption to her education if she did.[269] These arguments are persuasive because, as discussed in Chapter 5, securing admission to a school of one's choice is not guaranteed and, in any event, it is clear that the child or young person is regarded as having no independent right of choice under the relevant legislative provisions. The issue whether the complainant could have secured a place at another school which permitted the jilbab is unclear, since she had made an application to only one of the three such schools in the area, which was full. In any event, while in the exercise of consumer choice over public services the consumer has the 'exit option' of taking his or her custom elsewhere, there can be formidable human and social costs in doing so.[270] In the case of schooling they may include separation from friends, causing emotional difficulty, which would add to the disruptive effects to education referred to by Lord Nicholls. But the majority judgments concluded that Miss Begum could have moved school in order to fulfil her religious preferences and there was no interference with her right to manifest her belief.[271] Lord Hoffmann even went so far as to say, somewhat harshly, that it 'might not have been entirely convenient for her, particularly when her sister was remaining at Denbigh High, but people sometimes have to suffer some inconvenience for their beliefs'.[272] It is perhaps worth noting in this context that in *Multani*, discussed in Chapter 4, where religious freedom under the Canadian Charter was held by the Supreme Court of Canada to have been denied by a ban on the wearing of the kirpan at school, the fact that the Sikh pupil was unable to attend public (state) school due to this ban was all that mattered; the question of alternative arrangements did not, apparently, require consideration by the court.[273] Linden concluded from the decision in *Williamson* and that of the Court of Appeal in *Begum* that there could be a material interference with Article 9 rights even where a claimant is able to move to another school and thereby end the interference with his or her right. He says that the question will be 'whether the disadvantages of having to leave and find such an alternative are sufficiently serious that the decision of the school . . ., while not rendering manifestation [of belief] "impossible" in all circumstances, nevertheless constitutes a material interference'.[274] Lord Hoffmann in fact lends support to this view when he opines that '"Impossible" might be setting the test

---

[269] Ibid, paras 92–93 and 41 respectively.

[270] R Hambleton and P Hoggett, 'Rethinking Consumerism in Public Services' (1993) 3 *Consumer Policy Review* 103 at 106.

[271] N 267 above, per Lord Bingham of Cornhill at para 25, Lord Hoffmann at paras 50 and 55 and Lord Scott of Foscote at para 89.

[272] Ibid, para 50.

[273] *Multani v Commission scolaire Marguerite-Bourgeoys and Attorned General of Quebec and World Sikh Organisation of Canada and others* [2006] SCC 6 (Sup Ct of Canada).

[274] T Linden, 'School and Human Rights: The *Denbigh High School* Case' (2005) 6 *Education Law Journal* 229 at 233.

rather high', but he concludes that, even so, 'in the present case there is nothing to show that [Miss Begum] would have even found it difficult to go to another school'.[275]

In *Williamson*, the authority of the state to ban corporal punishment by law, in pursuit of a legitimate aim, to meet a pressing social need and without a disproportionate impact on those holding particular beliefs, was held to bring the ban within the scope of Article 9(2) as justifying the interference, particularly since Parliament had instituted it.[276] Analogy could be drawn with the prescribed National Curriculum, because even though decisions as to the precise content of the constituent subjects are delegated to ministers, who in turn are reliant upon departmental and external advisers, there is a statutory requirement on schools to apply it.[277] Moreover, just as Baroness Hale of Richmond in *Williamson* drew support for her position from the protection of the child under various provisions of the UNCRC,[278] so an interference with parental choice over aspects of the secular curriculum could be supported with reference to two of the aims of education in that Convention, namely '[t]he preparation of the child for responsible life in a free society'[279] and the development of respect not only for the child's own cultural identity, language and values, but also 'for the national values of the country in which the child is living'.[280] So the state may be acting in furtherance of a duty, as well as being in pursuit of a legitimate purpose, when it curtails religious freedom in order to meet what Sachs J, in a South African decision concerning the use of corporal punishment in school, referred to in this context as a 'secular purpose':

> [S]chools of necessity function in the public domain so as to prepare their learners for life in the broader society. Just as it is not unduly burdensome to oblige them to accommodate themselves as schools to secular norms regarding health and safety, payment of rates and taxes, planning permissions and fair labour practices, and just as they are obliged to respect national examination standards, so it is not unreasonable to expect them to make suitable adaptations to non-discriminatory laws that impact on their codes of discipline. The parents are not being obliged to make an absolute and strenuous choice between obeying the law of the land or following their conscience. They can do both simultaneously.[281]

Sachs J was mindful of the fact that the Schools Act that effected the ban on corporal punishment did not mean that parents were 'deprived . . . of their

---

[275] *R (Begum) v Headteacher and Governors of Denbigh High School* [2006] UKHL 15; [2006] 2 WLR 719, para 52.

[276] *R (Williamson) v Secretary of State for Education and Employment and Others* [2005] UKHL 15; [2005] ELR 291, per Baroness Hale at para 79. See also Lord Nicholls at paras 49–51.

[277] EA 2002, ss 88 and 109.

[278] In particular, Arts 3(1) (best interests of the child to be a primary consideration), 19(1) (protection of the child from physical or mental violence, etc) and 28(2) (discipline to be consistent with human dignity).

[279] UNCRC, Art 29(1)(d).

[280] UNCRC, Art 29(1)(c).

[281] *Christian Education South Africa v Minister of Education* (Case CCT 4/00) [2001] 1 LRC 441, at para 51.

general right and capacity to bring up their children according to their religious beliefs'.[282] In this case the Constitutional Court rejected the claim that the protection of religious and cultural rights under the constitution meant that there should be exemption from the ban on corporal punishment in schools in favour of Christian parents who favoured the practice on religious grounds.

Of course, the fact that parents in England and Wales have no real right to withdraw their child from aspects of the National Curriculum, even on the basis of sincerely held objection, does not mean that schools should not be sensitive to their wishes and accommodate them where feasible. If a major reason for having a National Curriculum is to ensure equality of opportunity, inclusion and a common cultural framework to provide a grounding for citizenship, this objective would be defeated if parents felt the need simply to take the 'exit' option and educate their child in a private faith school or at home.[283] As Macedo, referring to the initial accommodation of the *Mozert* families' wishes, says, while the families had no constitutional right to be accommodated, 'school administrators who anticipated the withdrawal of these families altogether from the public system may well have had prudential reasons to accommodate them in order to keep the children within the public system'.[284] Withdrawal of objecting parents would reduce diversity in state schools and, as Lundy says, that would be detrimental to schools' role in promoting tolerance and respect for difference.[285] Lundy argues that parents' requests for difference in schooling 'should be accommodated in situations where the outcome does not deny the child an effective education and the decision-making process takes appropriate account of the child's views'.[286] Also relevant would be the practicablity of accommodating parental wishes in terms of cost and the impact of withdrawal on the rights of other children.[287] These would in fact be very limiting factors to the granting of accommodations. Conflict is likely to arise both from permitting withdrawal and denying it, but the balance would seem to be in favour of the former, within reasonable limits. The courts have, as noted above, given some guidance on this matter. It will be tested in future years, as further questions seem certain to arise over the realisation and scope of minority rights and interests within the state education system.

---

[282] Ibid, para 38.

[283] Spinner-Halev argues that 'when it is feasible, religious students ought to be given alternative assignments or texts if they ask for this accommodation . . . [W]hen religious students are are not accommodated, many . . . feel pushed into homogenous parochial schools, where few liberal values are taught': J Spinner-Halev, 'Extending Diversity: Religion in Public and Private Education' in W Kymlicka and W Norman (eds), *Citizenship in Diverse Societies* (London, Oxford University Press, 2000), ch 3, at 69–70.

[284] S Macedo, 'Liberal Civic Education and Religious Fundamentalism: The Case of God v John Rawls' (1995) 105 *Ethics* 468 at 488.

[285] L Lundy, 'Family Values in the Classroom? Reconciling Parental Wishes and Children's Rights in State Schools' (2005) 19 *International Journal of Law, Policy and the Family* 346 at 362.

[286] Ibid, at 364.

[287] Ibid.

SEX EDUCATION

Problems of Sex Education and Rights

The provision of sex education was made a statutory requirement in state schools by the Education Act 1993, but at the same time parents were given an unconditional right to withdraw their children from receipt of the subject,[288] a right that has continued.[289] The right of withdrawal remains controversial, not least as an issue of children's rights.[290] There is also a continuing debate surrounding the nature and content of sex education in schools. Cultural diversity is a significant factor in this. Sex education inevitably demands engagement with issues that are governed by different moral and social codes across diverse cultural groups. Halstead and Rees explain that while the aim of the study of human sexuality within biology or social science 'is for students to come to know more about sex', the aim of sex education is much broader and 'includes encouraging certain kinds of skills, attitudes, dispositions, behaviour and critical reflection on personal experience'.[291] One of the difficulties with sex education is that, whether deliberately or consequentially, it presents school pupils with a range of value perspectives that may be out of step with some of the cultural or religious values of the community to which individual pupils belong. Sex education thereby presents perhaps the greatest risk of conflict between the autonomy of the family over the upbringing of children and the protective and developmental role of the state, a conflict that was discussed in general terms in Chapter 2. While much of the discussion about the content of education at a political level may focus on the idea of shared or common values, as noted earlier, 'the biggest problem facing sex educator today is the sheer diversity of sexual values that exist in our society'.[292] Even within one faith, Christianity, there are divergent views on issues such as contraception and homosexuality. Thus, as Bradney notes, if a school serves a multi-religious and multi-ethnic local community 'there may be widespread differences in what various parents will accept in terms of the delivery and content of sex education'.[293]

This highlights a further problem with sex education, namely that it is seen to bring into play parents' rights rather than those of children, an issue noted in Chapter 2. While children/young people and the state are clearly the principal parties in the matter of sex education, it is the case that when it comes to the content, inherent values and rights associated with its provision, the parents' interest is also recognised and, in a sense, ultimately prevails through the right to withdraw the child from it. The fact that there may be clashes of values as

---

[288] ERA 1988, ss 2 and 17A, as amended or inserted by EA 1993, s 241.

[289] EA 2002, ss 80 and 101; EA 1996, s 405.

[290] See below.

[291] J M Halstead and MJ Reiss, *Values in Sex Education* (London, Routledge Falmer, 2003) 7.

[292] Ibid, 5.

[293] A Bradney, 'Ethnicity, Religion and Sex Education' in N Harris (ed), *Children, Sex Education and the Law: Examining the Issues* (London, National Children's Bureau, 1996) 87 at 97.

between parents and their children on matters such as sex education, as is partic- ularly likely between first and second or third generations within immigrant communities, is ignored. It is also argued that the child's autonomy is ignored. Although sex education is directed at young people and seeks to protect them against health risks and moral danger, it has a wider purpose in trying to influence their behaviour and attitudes in order to ensure conformity to a model of citizenship that, Monk argues, reflects 'adult concerns, anxieties and projections, both progressive and reactionary, for a particular form of social and sexual order'.[294] The parental right of withdrawal cuts across a number of educational rights of the child as well as the broader principle within Article 12 of the UNCRC.[295] It also cuts across the basic requirement that the school curriculum should, inter alia, prepare pupils for the responsibilities and experiences of later life.[296]

Therefore sex education is problematic, first, because it might incorporate values that are not compatible with the sexual and social mores of all religions and cultures within the community. Secondly, it might subordinate the autonomic interests of children and young people to parental concerns or to wider state interests which may not necessarily be compatible with the idea that education should principally be directed towards the best interests of the child.[297] Indeed, its principal mechanism for respecting cultural diversity and family integrity, the parental veto on sex education, enables parental wishes to undermine the attainment of valuable social and educational goals that are of considerable social benefit. These include the health benefits of sex education and the need for all pupils to have insights into aspects of human behaviour across society and not just within their own culture, in order to gain better social understanding and a more rounded citizenship. In one way or another these issues have been considered in debates as the law has developed. The ensuing discussion will therefore centre on the key legal developments and on the official guidance to which governing bodies of schools must have regard in exercising their functions (hereinafter 'the SRE guidance').[298] A crucial issue for sex education as a statutory requirement is, of course, whether it is effective, and this in turn raises questions, addressed later, as to how its effectiveness can be measured and how well it is monitored.

---

[294] D Monk, 'Health and Education: Conflicting Programmes for Sex Education' in E Heinze (ed), *Of Innocence and Autonomy. Children, Sex and Human Rights* (Aldershot, Ashgate, 2000) 179 at 190.

[295] As noted in Chap 2; and see below.

[296] EA 2002, ss 78(1) and 99(1).

[297] Per UNCRC, Art 3.

[298] EA 1996, s 403(1B). The guidance is contained in Department for Education and Employment, *Sex and Relationship Education Guidance* DfEE 0116/2000 (London, DfEE, 2000). The guidance 'must include guidance about any material which may be produced by NHS bodies for the purposes of sex education in schools': EA 1996, s 403(1C).

The Development of Compulsory Sex Education and its Moral Framework

Sex education's broader role in promoting a moral framework for human relations is comparatively recent but nevertheless precedes the introduction of a statutory requirement for its provision. The first national educational initiative for promoting sex education in schools appears to have been a 1943 document published by the Board of Education entitled *Sex Education in Schools and Youth Organisations*. The aims of sex education were in fact guided by public health imperatives, locally determined, until at least the late 1960s.[299] By the 1970s many LEAs had developed sex education policies, although the content of sex education was still determined at school level. Indeed, when the Education Act 1980 introduced school choice rights for parents and schools were placed under a duty to publish information about provision,[300] the regulations fleshing out this duty included a requirement to provide information about the manner and context in which sex education was provided at the school.[301] By the 1980s, sex education provision was under attack—from those on the left, who saw it as inadequate in preparing young people for modern life and risks such as teenage pregnancy and sexual diseases, and from those on the right who, in the face of perceived moral degeneration within society and the scourge of welfare dependency by lone parents, wanted to restore traditional values associated with responsible sexual behaviour and marriage as the foundation for sexual relations. Under the New Right Conservative administration, policy was directed principally around the latter perspective. Then, as it is now, sex education in state schools was 'dominated by political and ideological reaction'.[302]

The 1985 White Paper, *Better Schools*, advocated at the secondary stage of school education 'health and sex education, taught within a moral framework' as 'a necessary preparation for responsible adulthood'.[303] Accordingly, the Education (No 2) Act 1986 introduced a requirement that LEAs and governing bodies should take 'such steps as are reasonable practicable' to ensure that school sex education was 'given in such a manner as to encourage . . . pupils to have due regard to moral considerations and the value of family life'.[304] The Government's guidance left little doubt that what was contemplated was a strict moral code of behaviour: sex education should be 'set within a clear moral framework in which pupils are encouraged to consider the importance of self-restraint, dignity and respect for themselves and others, and helped to recognise the physical, emotional and moral risks of casual and promiscuous behaviour'.[305] Stable married and family life were to be emphasised, although not in a way that might

[299] L Measor *et al, Young People's Views on Sex Education* (London, Routledge Falmer, 2000) 18–19.
[300] See Chap 5.
[301] Education (School Information) Regulations 1981 (SI 1981 No 630), Sched 2.
[302] S Forrest, 'Difficult Loves. Learning about Sexuality and Homophobia in Schools' in M Cole (ed), *Education, Equality and Human Rights* (London, Routledge Falmer, 2000) 99 at 111.
[303] DES, *Better Schools*, Cmnd 9469 (London, HMSO, 1985), para 71.
[304] Education (No2) Act 1986, s 46.
[305] DES, *Sex Education at School*, Circular 11/87 (London, DES, 1987), para 19.

cause upset to children from lone parent families.[306] There was also advice against advocating homosexual behaviour, presenting it as the 'norm' or encouraging homosexual experimentation by pupils,[307] guidance which was subsequently followed by the controversial ban on the promotion of such teaching by local authorities, under the Local Government Act 1988, section 28. The new guidance in 1994[308] omitted these references to homosexuality, but the section 28 ban remained in force until 2003, as noted above. This ban and the continuing stress placed on morality, traditional family values and marriage discouraged coverage of homosexuality.[309]

The guidance also addressed the provision of contraceptive advice, arguing that the *Gillick* decision, which upheld the power of doctors to provide advice on this subject in the absence of parental consent to a girl aged under 16 if she is of sufficient maturity and understanding,[310] had no parallel in schools.[311] Subsequent guidance was less categorical on this point, indeed omitting any specific reference to *Gillick* but indicating that teachers 'are not health professionals, and the legal position of a teacher giving advice [on contraception] has never been tested in the courts'.[312] Yet academic opinion disagreed that teachers lacked legal protection for giving advice responsibly within the framework laid down by *Gillick*.[313] In the current *Sex and Relationship Education* (SRE) guidance it is now acknowledged that staff, including teachers who are appropriately trained, may give advice on contraception to pupils and may discuss this subject in confidence with a pupil aged under 16 provided the pupil is encouraged to talk to their parent about the matter.[314] The ECHR, Article 8 (right to privacy and family life), is unlikely to provide a basis on which to challenge this guidance, given the approach taken by the High Court in *Axon*, where there was a claim arising from the provision of advice and treatment in relation to abortion by medical professionals to girls aged under 16 without parental knowledge or consent.[315] Silber J considered that once the young person reaches *Gillick* competence the parents' Article 8 right to be notified 'does not continue'.[316] The SRE guidance currently omits reference to

---

[306] Ibid.

[307] Ibid, para 22.

[308] Department for Education, *Education Act 1993: Sex Education in Schools*, Circular 5/94 (London, Department for Education, 1994).

[309] L Bibbings, 'Gender, Sexuality and Sex Education' in N Harris (ed), *Children, Sex Education and the Law: Examining the Issues* (London, Sex Education Forum, 1996) 70 at 80.

[310] *Gillick v West Norfolk and Wisbech AHA* [1985] 3 All ER 402 (HL); [2006] 2 WLR 1130.

[311] DES, *Sex Education at School*, Circular 11/87 (London, DES, 1987), para 26.

[312] DfE, *Education Act 1993: Sex Education in Schools*, Circular 5/94 (London, Department of Education, 1994), para 39.

[313] See, A Bainham, 'Sex Education: a Family Lawyer's Perspective' in N Harris (ed), *Children, Sex Education and the Law: Examining the Issues* (London, National Children's Bureau, 1996) 24 at 37–39; J Bridgeman, 'Don't Tell the Children: the Department's Guidance on the Provision of Information about Contraception to Individual Pupils' in N Harris (ibid), 45–69.

[314] DfEE, *Sex and Relationship Education*, DfEE 0116/2000 (London, DfEE, 2000), paras 2.11, 7.10–7.11.

[315] *R (Axon) v Secretary of State for Health and the Family Planning Association* [2006] EWHC Admin 37.

[316] Ibid, para 132. See further 'The Implications of the Right to Withdrawal', pp 406–10 below.

consideration of the child's maturity and understanding in this context and this needs to be rectified.

Although the Government's moral agenda was clearly evident in the sex education provisions, prior to 1994 it was left to individual schools to decide whether to provide sex education, although it became doubtful that schools could ignore it once aspects of human reproduction were included in the National Curriculum attainment targets for science and a statutory requirement to prepare pupils for the responsibilities and experiences of adult life was introduced.[317] The guidance published in 1987 indicated that schools were expected to offer pupils 'at least some education about sexual matters'.[318] Evidence from surveys of young people that schools were the principal source of information about sex reinforced the role of sex education.[319] The imperative to make sex education compulsory in schools subsequently grew as a result of both increasing concern over the scale of teenage pregnancy and the Government's establishment of a target for its reduction. The 1992 health White Paper proposed a target reduction of 50 per cent in under-age pregnancies by 2000 (from 9.5 per 1,000 girls aged 13–15 in 1989 to no more than 4.8).[320] In 1993 the House of Commons Health Select Committee's report, *Maternity Services: Preconception in 1990–91*, highlighted the increasing problem of teenage pregnancy and perinatal mortality and expressed concern that 'health and sex education in schools may not be accorded the priority they require'.[321] There was also evidence that as many as one third of schools in England and Wales did not have a written sex education policy as required by law and that there was widespread confusion in schools about how to provide sex education.[322]

Amendments to the Education Bill that was before Parliament in 1993 proposed to make it compulsory for every secondary school to provide sex education in the secular curriculum, but to omit the study of any sexually transmitted disease from the National Curriculum. Parents were to be given a right to withdraw their children from sex education, but not therefore from a part of the National Curriculum, if they had 'any strong objections on religious grounds' to it.[323] The fact that sex education provision within schools could run counter to religious sensibilities had been recognised by the Government in its 1987 guidance. For example, it had urged schools to take account of possible religious objections when considering whether sex education should be provided at all. Nonetheless, there was a conviction that objections on principle to sex education that were not religiously motivated should also be recognised, a view that is consistent with ECHR Article 2 of Protocol 1, as noted in Chapter 2. The rights of atheists and agnostics should also be recognised in this context, argued

---

[317] Initially under the ERA 1988, s 1(2)(b). See above.
[318] DES, *Sex Education at School*, Circular 11/87 (London, DES, 1987), para 7.
[319] I Allen, *Education in Sex and Personal Relationships* (London, Policy Studies Institute, 1987) 143.
[320] Secretary of State for Health, *The Health of the Nation—A Strategy for Health in England*, Cm 1986 (London, HMSO, 1992) 95.
[321] (London, HMSO, 1993), paras 70–82.
[322] Sex Education Forum, *An Enquiry into Sex Education* (London, Sex Education Forum, 1992).
[323] HL Debs Vol 547, Cols 119–120, 21 June 1993, per Lord Stallard.

Lord Renton.[324] There was also opposition to the right of withdrawal, on the ground that it would deprive children and young people of an important right that should prevail over that of their parents.[325] While these amendments were not carried, they were supported in principle by the Government.

It was noted above that the unconditional right of withdrawal, which was not tied specifically to religious objections, was included in the 1993 Act. As was also noted, the Act also made sex education part of the basic curriculum for pupils of secondary school age. Sex education was defined, although not comprehensively: the Act stated that it 'includes education about—(a) Acquired Immune Deficiency Syndrome and Human Immunodeficiency Virus, and (b) any other sexually transmitted disease'.[326] The Secretary of State's new duty to eliminate sex education from the National Curriculum meant that as 'the basic biological and physical facts of life' would be outside the definition of sex education, no pupil should leave school without such knowledge.[327] The definition was consolidated into the Education Act 1996,[328] but omitted when the requirement for sex education to be included within the basic curriculum within every school was re-enacted in the Education Act 2002.[329] It is not clear why this has occurred and whether it was deliberate, unless perhaps the intention is that individual schools should determine what to cover, following the SRE guidance. It does, however, create potential uncertainty with regard to the matters to which the right of withdrawal might apply, not least because the Secretary of State's duty to ensure that National Curriculum science does not include sex education has also been repealed without re-enactment.

The Implications of the Right of Withdrawal

The Minister argued that the introduction of a right for a parent to withdraw their child from sex education at school was desirable 'to give expression to the right of parents to play an important part in determining how their children should be educated in this particularly sensitive area of the curriculum'.[330] It was felt to be unnecessary to demand reasons for a withdrawal, since the very fact that a withdrawal was made was indication enough of the parent's strength of feeling.[331] As a right conferred exclusively on the parents by domestic statute law,[332] the right of withdrawal raises concerns about the lack of respect for the independent rights of children and young people (withdrawal applies to a pupil regardless of his or her age, so that even pupils aged 16 and over can be

---

[324] Ibid, Col 135.
[325] Eg, Lord Addington, ibid, at Col 128.
[326] EA 1944, s 114(1), as amended by EA 1993, s 241.
[327] HL Debs, Vol 547, Cols 1290–1291, 6 July 1993, per Baroness Blatch.
[328] EA 1996, s 352(3).
[329] EA 2002, ss 80 and 101.
[330] HL Debs, Vol 547, Col 1290, 6 July 1993, per Baroness Blatch.
[331] Ibid, Col 1291.
[332] EA 1996, s 405, which also provides that once a withdrawal has been requested it remains effective unless and until the request is withdrawn.

withdrawn), including the right to be consulted over matters affecting them, 'their views being given due weight in accordance with their age and understanding'.[333] Most young people are opposed to this parental right of withdrawal.[334] In the 20 years post *Gillick* there has been clear recognition that mature adolescents do have legal control over their own bodies, whilst those aged 16 or over are in any event generally competent to give consent to medical treatment.[335] Yet, as discussed in Chapter 2, parental rights still overshadow those of children in the field of education and the parental right of withdrawal epitomises that dominance. Bainham has pointed out that sex education may be considered to be an area in respect of which the state's obligation, under the UNCRC, is to 'respect the responsibilities, rights and duties of parents . . . to provide, in a manner consistent with the evolving capacities of the child, appropriate direction and guidance in the exercise by the child of the rights recognised in the present Convention'.[336] Yet the reference to 'evolving capacities' clearly implies that at the very least the child would have a right to have his or her views on the matter heard and taken into account, as per the right in Article 12 of the Convention. Indeed, it was and remains anomalous that a young person could be denied information about an activity which he or she may lawfully participate in. Moreover, as the Bishop of Guildford pointed out, a 16-year-old could marry but could be denied sex education.[337] An even greater concern has been the potential exposure of children and young people to health risks and, for girls, the risk of pregnancy. The UNCRC refers specifically to the state's duty to take appropriate measures to combat disease and to develop family planning education and services.[338] At the time that the right to withdraw the child was being proposed, various bodies, such as the Sex Education Forum and the British Medical Association, expressed concern that some young people might be left ignorant about sexual matters or receive incomplete information, second hand, from their peers. Given research evidence at that time showing that among young people under the age of 16 between 25 and 35 per cent had had sexual intercourse,[339] the risks were all too evident.

It is reasonable to assume that the withdrawal of most, if not all, children from sex and relationship education is likely to be culturally motivated, probably on the basis of religion.[340] As with the right to withdraw a child from religious

---

[333] UNCRC Art 12.

[334] L Burghes, 'Teenage Sex and Sex Education', *Family Policy Studies Bulletin*, May 1994; L Measor et al, *Young People's Views on Sex Education. Education, Attitudes and Behaviour* (London, Routledge Falmer, 2000) 34.

[335] Family Law Reform Act 1969, s 8.

[336] UNCRC, Art 5. See A Bainham, 'Sex Education: a Family Lawyer's Perspective' in N Harris (ed), *Children, Sex Education and the Law: Examining the Issues* (London, National Children's Bureau, 1996) 24 at 31.

[337] HL Debs Vol 547, Col 1309, 6 July 1993.

[338] UNCRC, Art 24(2)(f).

[339] A Miller, *Young People: Sex Education and Sexual Activity (Report for BBC North-West)* (Liverpool, Liverpool John Moores University, 1994); AM Johnson and others, *Sexual Attitudes and Lifestyles* (Oxford, Blackwell Scientific, 1994).

[340] See Social Exclusion Unit, *Teenage Pregnancy*, Cm 4342 (London, TSO, 1999), para 5.10: '[m]any . . . parents see this right as an important way of ensuring that their children are brought up in accordance with their faith or culture'.

education or collective worship, the law yields to parental autonomy over these matters (but see n 561 below). There is a parallel in this regard with the position of parents who make healthcare decisions concerning their children on a similar basis. Although, as Bridge points out,[341] the courts have yet to adopt a consistent approach to cases where parental wishes conflict with dominant social norms about children's welfare, the broad position is that unless there is a real threat to the child's welfare the courts will not interfere. There is a potential risk to health if the child is not educated about sexual matters, but the assumption is that the parent will cover the subject him/herself or that it will be covered through religious teaching elsewhere. It is not an altogether realistic assumption, however, since there is no guarantee that the child will receive such education or that it will be effective. Ann Blair argues that there may be an underlying premise that the prevalence of early sexual activity will be low among young people from communities whose cultural values are strongly discouraging of sexual activity outside marriage.[342] The balance of welfare in decisions concerning sex education, as with routine health matters, is considered to lie in preserving family integrity on the basis of the parents' cultural values or beliefs, rather than protecting the child from health risks or (temporary) social isolation. Whether that is appropriate is a question that forms part of a much wider philosophical debate partly considered earlier, and to which further attention is given below. There is also one potential risk to all children, regardless of their social or ethnic background, that has been overlooked, although it was highlighted by the NSPCC when the legislation was before Parliament. It is that withdrawal could be used by parents who are subjecting their child to sexual abuse to avoid possible exposure of their activities through discussion of sexual matters in school.[343]

It was argued at the time that the proposed legislation was being debated in Parliament that the child's right to education might be denied by the exercise of the right of withdrawal.[344] As we saw in Chapter 2, however, the various international instruments including the ECHR and the International Covenant on Economic, Social and Cultural Rights do not specify any basic content of 'education', and the UNCRC, while specifying various matters towards which education should be directed, does not mention sex education specifically, and it is only implied in relation to health.[345] The ECHR does not specify the content of education and in effect provides only a right to such education as the state decides should be provided,[346] although, as Lundy argues, the right to education connotes a right to effective education.[347] In *Kjeldsen*[348] the European Court of

[341] C Bridge, 'Religion, Culture and Conviction: the Medical Treatment of Young Children' (1999) 11 *Child & Family Law Quarterly* 1.

[342] A Blair, 'Calculating the Risk of Teenage Pregnancy: Sex Education, Public Health, The Individual and the Law' in N Harris and P Meredith (eds), *Children, Education and Health: International Perspectives on Law and Policy* (Aldershot, Ashgate) 129 at 144.

[343] HL Debs, Vol 547, Col 1295, 6 July 1993.

[344] See HL Debs, Vol 547, Col 1321, 6 July 1993.

[345] UNCRC, Art 24.

[346] See the discussion of *Belgian Linguistics* at pp 70–1 above.

[347] L Lundy, 'Schoolchildren and Health: The Role of International Human Rights Law' in N Harris and P Meredith (eds), *Children, Education and Health. International Perspectives on Law and Policy* (Aldershot, Ashgate, 2005) 1 at 7.

[348] *Kjeldsen, Busk Madsen and Pedersen v Denmark* 1 EHRR 711 (1976). See p 73 above.

Human Rights held that a state's policy of compulsory sex education could override parental convictions in the matter of the teaching of their child, notwithstanding the respect for them that is required under the second sentence of ECHR Article 2 of Protocol 1. But that does not necessarily imply that the child's right to education encompasses a right to sex education. This is primarily a matter within the power and competence of the individual state to determine. Furthermore, the parents' right of withdrawal of their child from compulsory sex education in England and Wales is not necessarily incompatible with the child's right to education under the ECHR. As Fortin says, the *Kjeldsen* decision 'did not assert children's absolute rights to sex education', although on the basis that the Court's decision rested on the fact that Danish sex education was objective, critical and pluralistic, a similar approach to sex education in England and Wales could have justified the omission of a right of withdrawal here.[349] The fact that the right of withdrawal is granted to parents alone, however, does offend against the principle in Article 12 UNCRC, as discussed above.

Article 8 of the ECHR also warrants consideration in this context. Reference has already been made to the health risks or risk of pregnancy arising from unprotected sexual activity. They were a significant factor in the decision in *Axon*, noted above, when the court was considering whether the Government had justification under Article 8(2) for the interference with the parent's Article 8(1) right to privacy and family life, as a result of guidance which permitted girls under 16 to be given advice or treatment in respect of abortion without parental consent or knowledge in certain circumstances. As noted above, the High Court considered the test of *Gillick* competence to be applicable to such cases where Article 8 rights were at issue, on the basis that the parental right or power of control associated with Article 8 was no wider than the right under domestic law. Silber J referred to Lord Scarman's statement in *Gillick* that the right of parents 'exists primarily to enable the parent to discharge his duty of maintenance, protection and education until he reaches such an age as to be able to look after himself and make his own decisions'.[350] Silber J also referred to Strasbourg case law demonstrating that, if there is a conflict between children's and parents' rights under Article 8, the former should be given paramount consideration.[351]

Therefore, there must be a case for arguing, both on the basis of the *Gillick* competence test and by analogy with case law on health advice on sexual matters, that a child of sufficient maturity has a right under Article 8 to decide for him- or herself whether he or she should receive sex education.[352] While that might,

---

[349] J Fortin, *Children's Rights and the Developing Law* (2nd edn, London, LexisNexis, 2003) 190. See also P Meredith, 'Some Shortcomings in the Provision of Sex Education in England' in N Harris and P Meredith (eds), *Children, Education and Health. International Perspectives on Law and Policy* (Aldershot, Ashgate, 2005) 105 at 126.

[350] *Gillick v West Norfolk and Wisbech Area Health Authority* [1986] AC 112, at 185E.

[351] Eg, *Yousef v Netherlands* (2003) 36 EHRR 345, at para 73.

[352] See also discussion of *Re Roddy (a child) (identification: restriction on publication)* [2003] EWHC Fam 2927; [2004] 2 FLR 949 in J Fortin, 'Accommodating Children's Rights in a Post Human Rights Era' (2006) 69 *MLR* 299, especially at 319–21, in which the author explains (at 320) that '[s]plicing the *Gillick* competence test onto article 8 rights suggests that mature teenagers now have complete authority in all matters they fully comprehend'.

under the current arrangements regarding sex education, provide part of the basis for resolving any dispute between parent and child over the matter, it should also be regarded as bringing into question the parental right of withdrawal where pupils of appropriate maturity are concerned. In respect of any argument that to prevent withdrawal would undermine the parent's right to respect for their philosophical or religious convictions as regarding the teaching of their child for the purposes of Article 2 of Protocol 1, it should be understood that, as noted above, the ECtHR in *Kjeldsen*[353] rejected the argument that compulsory sex education necessarily interfered with that right. So far as any interference with the right to private or family life is concerned, the Court has acknowledged that there may be interference with Article 8 rights where education is concerned.[354] In *Kjeldsen* the ground of challenge to compulsory sex education in Denmark based on the parents' Article 8 rights was rejected.[355] In *Axon*, Silber J said:

> if the parents in that case [ie *Kjeldsen*] had no right to control what information their children should receive on these matters, it is not easy to see how and why they could have a sufficient interest under article 8 to override a young person's rights to seek to maintain confidentiality in relation to his or her private medical information on sexual matters.[356]

If the two situations are as analogous as Silber J seems to suggest, then access to information about sexual health through sex education at school should be governed by the same principles as those articulated in *Gillick* and applied in *Axon*. The same can surely be said of access to information about sexual health through sex education at school. As the provision of medical advice is part of the process by which a person is educated about health matters, there is no logical reason why that should be distinguished from education on sexual health provided by schools, particularly given that *Gillick* is considered applicable to teachers giving advice on contraception, as noted above.

In practice, the overwhelming majority of parents support the provision of sex education in schools[357] and the right of withdrawal is not greatly used. The report by the Social Exclusion Unit (SEU) noted in 1999 that around 1 per cent of parents use this right.[358] Ofsted's subsequent review of sex and relationship education, in 2002, indicated that there had been a fall in the numbers withdrawn and that the national rate was only four pupils in every 10,000 (0.04 per cent).

---

[353] *Kjeldsen, Busk Madsen and Pedersen* 1 EHRR 711 (1976).

[354] *Belgian Linguistics (No 2)* (1979–80) 1 EHRR 252, at para 7; *Costello-Roberts v UK* [1994] ELR 1, (1995) 19 EHRR 112, para 36.

[355] *Kjeldsen, Busk Madsen and Pedersen* 1 EHRR 711 (1976).

[356] *R (Axon) v Secretary of State for Health and the Family Planning Association* [2006] EWHC Admin 37; [2006] 2 WLR 1130, at para 128.

[357] NFER, *Parents, Schools and Sex Education* (London, HEA, 1994).

[358] Social Exclusion Unit, *Teenage Pregnancy,* Cm 4342 (London, TSO, 1999), para 5.10.

Cultural Diversity and the Content of Sex Education

Figures from the mid 1990s suggested that around 50 per cent of Muslims and 25 per cent of Sikhs were not supportive of sex education at school.[359] But Ofsted concluded in 2002 that schools were now 'effective in addressing the concerns of parents, communities and religious groups'.[360] This implies that sex education, which in is generally accommodated within a framework of 'personal, social and health education',[361] is adapted to the meet the cultural diversity reflected within school populations and family backgrounds of pupils, although one cannot be sure that all groups are equally content with it. For example, although some religious groups will advocate abstinence from sex among young people, abstinence-based sex education policy has not met with political support in the UK, unlike in the United States where Congress established a programme for it in 1996, had allocated $300 million to it by 2002, and committed $168 million for 2005 alone (although the Bush administration had wanted to spend $270 million).[362] There is no conclusive evidence as to its efficacy, however,[363] and a report by a Congressman in late 2004 on the implementation of the programme found that 11 of the 13 different curricula that were in use contained medically inaccurate or misleading information—for example, that condoms prevent HIV infection in only 70 per cent of acts of heterosexual intercourse in which they are used—that promoted exaggerated fears.[364] An investigation of the US programme by the UK's Sex Education Forum found that most young people in the US considered the abstinence programme to be out of touch with their lives. In the Forum's view, it did not take account of the diversity of young people's family backgrounds or experience and did not meet their needs.[365]

The Government's SRE guidance seeks to adopt a pluralistic approach, although dominated by the very moralistic tone set by the legislative requirement, noted above, that sex education should be 'given in such a manner as to encourage . . . pupils to have due regard to moral considerations and the value of family life',[366] and by the specific requirement that the guidance must be designed to secure that pupils should 'learn the nature of marriage and its importance for family life and the bringing up of children'.[367] The guidance acknowledges that 'there are strong and mutually supportive relationships

[359] Survey figures quoted by the Sex Education Forum, cited in A Blair, 'Calculating the Risk of Teenage Pregnancy: Sex Education, Public Health, The Individual and the Law' in N Harris and P Meredith (eds), *Children, Education and Health: International Perspectives on Law and Policy* (Aldershot, Ashgate, 2005) 129 at 143.

[360] Ofsted, *Sex and Relationships* (London, Ofsted, 2002), para 76.

[361] See Ofsted, *Personal, Social and Health Education in Secondary Schools*, HMI 2311 (London, Ofsted, 2005).

[362] JM Halstead and MJ Reiss, *Values in Sex Education* (London, Routledge Falmer, 2003) 144–5.

[363] Ibid, 145; C Connolly, 'Some Abstinence Programs Mislead Teens, Report Says', *Washington Post*, 2 Dec 2004.

[364] Ibid.

[365] Sex Education Forum, *Just Say No! To Abstinence Education: Lessons Learnt from a Sex Education Study Tour of the United States* (London, Sex Education Forum/National Children's Bureau, 2001).

[366] EA 1996, s 403(1).

[367] Ibid, s 403(1A), inserted by the Learning and Skills Act 2000, s 148(4).

outside marriage' and advises that pupils should learn the significance of stable relationships along with marriage, as 'key building blocks of community and society'.[368] Yet it avoids mention of gay and lesbian partnerships specifically in this context and needs updating to include civil partnership status. Nonetheless, the guidance says that 'there should be no direct promotion of sexual orientation',[369] which can be read either as a replication of previous attempts to proscribe the promotion of homosexual relationships as 'normal'[370] or as a deliberate attempt to stress neutrality as between homosexual and heterosexual relationships. Freeman argues that the UNCRC should be amended to rectify failures such as that in English law on sex education in addressing the needs of gay children.[371] As regards the possible sensitivities of some religious/cultural groups towards issues of sexuality in sex education, the guidance talks about liaising with and reassuring parents but otherwise offers no clear advice on how to deal with a conflict of values in this context.

It would be impossible to align all the values embedded within the official recommendations on the content of sex education with those of all ethnic and religious minority groups. The coverage of some issues of sexuality, such as homosexuality or bisexuality, is likely to prove problematic, given the range of attitudes across different communities towards such subjects and regarding the age or gender groups that should receive information on such matters.[372] The 2000 amendments to the law included a requirement that the Government's guidance should be designed to secure that, where sex education is given to pupils at a school, 'they are protected from teaching and materials which are inappropriate having regard to the age and the religious and cultural background of the pupils concerned'.[373] By using the term 'protected', inappropriate sex education is implicitly portrayed as a threat to cultural and religious values. It is interesting that there is no attempt to identify pupils who may have vulnerabilities due to other personal factors, such as special educational needs arising from, for example, emotional and behavioural difficulties, although this broad group is covered specifically in the guidance,[374] which also distinguishes between

---

[368] Department for Education and Employment, *Sex and Relationship Education Guidance*, DfEE 0116/2000 (London, DfEE, 2000), para 1.21.

[369] Ibid, para 1.30.

[370] Eg, via Local Government Act 1998, s 28, or DES, *Sex Education at School*, Circular 11/87 (London, DES, 1987), para 22.

[371] M Freeman, 'The Future of Children's Rights' (2000) 14 *Children & Society* 277 at 283–4.

[372] See Halstead and Reiss, n 362 above, ch 6; D Archard, *Children, Family and the State* (Aldershot, Ashgate, 2003) 138–9.

[373] EA 1996, s 430(1A)(b), inserted by the Learning and Skills Act 2002, s 148(4). As regards the kinds of matters that might prove objectionable to some groups, see A Bradney, 'Ethnicity, Religion and Sex Education' in N Harris (ed), *Children, Sex Education and the Law: Examining the Issues* (London, National Children's Bureau, 1996) 87 at 92–4. In the early 1990s the Government was preparing to advise schools to 'stream' sex education classes according to pupils' individual maturity and knowledge of sexual matters but was heavily criticised, in particular on the impracticability of ascertaining individuals' degree of knowledge: see 'Unions condemn streaming of sex education', *The Times*, 2 May 1994. The plans were abandoned.

[374] DfEE, *Sex and Relationship Education*, DfEE 0116/2000 (London, DfEE, 2000), paras 1.26–1.29.

pupils in different age groups.[375] So far as cultural or religious background is concerned, despite the references to it in the statutory requirements it receives surprisingly little coverage in the guidance. The two points that are made are, first, that, in some minority communities, children are less able to talk about sex to their families, so schools may be the only source of their sex education.[376] Secondly, it states that sex education policies must be 'both culturally appropriate and inclusive of all children . . . for some children it is not culturally appropriate to address particular issues in a mixed group'.[377] The guidance advocates consultation with parents to find out what is appropriate and acceptable. The Government is not saying that sensitive issues should be avoided. Indeed the guidance specifically indicates that they should be covered by a school's policy.[378] But, as Meredith says, prescription over matters that might cause offence appears deliberately to have been avoided, and so the decision about these matters is delegated to schools, which are expected to be sensitive to the wishes and mores of local ethnic or religious community groups.[379] In fact, recent research based on interviews with young people from three minority ethnic communities and with focus groups has found a general feeling that sex and relationship education in schools rarely takes account of cultural and religious influences on sexual attitudes and behaviour.[380] There is in fact other guidance to which schools can also turn for ways of addressing the needs of pupils from minority backgrounds within their sex education policies, such as that developed by the Sex Education Forum,[381] which is due to publish the results of a comprehensive study of sex education and minority education groups soon; this is likely to be followed by new guidance from the Forum. But schools are not obliged to consult or have regard to such guidance, unlike that published by the Government.

The Protective Role of Sex Education

It was concern about the overall extent of pregnancy across the teenage population in the UK, highlighted by the SEU's report in 1999, that led to the revised guidance and amendments to the statutory framework made by the Learning and Skills Act 2000, including the requirement that head teachers and governing bodies should have regard to the Secretary of State's published

---

[375] It distiuguishes between primary and secondary school pupils. More detailed guidance as to content at different ages is provided by the indicative attainment targets in Ofsted, *Personal, Social and Health Education in Secondary Schools*, HMI 2311 (London, Ofsted, 2005) 25–6 and 29–30.

[376] DfEE, *Sex and Relationship Education*, DfEE 0116/2000 (London, DfEE, 2000), para 1.14.

[377] Ibid, para 1.25.

[378] Ibid, 18. Note that the governing body of a maintained school must have a policy on sex education: EA 1996, s 404.

[379] P Meredith, 'Some Shortcomings in the Provision of Sex Education in England' in N Harris and P Meredith (eds), *Children, Education and Health. International Perspectives on Law and Policy* (Aldershot, Ashgate, 2005) 105 at 106–7.

[380] RS French *et al*, *Exploring the Attitudes and Behaviour of Bangladeshi, Indian and Jamaican Young People in Relation to Reproductive Sexual Health* (Nov 2005), available at www.dfes.gov.uk/research/data/uploadfiles/RW53.pdf.

[381] See www.ncb.org.uk/sef.

guidance.[382] The SEU reported that some 90,000 teenagers were pregnant in 1997, nearly 8,000 of whom were under the age of 16 (including 2,200 aged 14 or under)—a rate higher than in any other Western European country.[383] But even though the SEU set a target for reduction in pregnancy among under 18s of 50 per cent by 2010, it would be inappropriate merely to use changes in the rate of teenage pregnancy as the basis for judging the effectiveness of sex and relationship education. However, if that *were* to be the basis for evaluation, the evidence would be damning: among the under 16s the numbers becoming pregnant rose in 2000 to 8,115 (8.3 per thousand), fell in 2001 to 7,891 (8 per thousand),[384] but rose again in 2003, to 8,076 (of whom 5,846 were aged 14 or under); and for the under 18s it rose from 41,951 in 2002 to 42,183 in 2003.[385] The latest figures, for 2004, show a small decline in the annual total, however, to approximately 7,500 for under 16s and 41,700 for under 18s.[386] As noted in Chapter 4, the abortion rate among girls becoming pregnant is high. In each of the first two quarters of 2005, some 900 under 16-year-old girls and 9,100 16–19-year-old girls had abortions; the rate for under 16s remained the same in the third quarter but fell among 16–19-year-olds to 8,300 cases.[387]

Although there are no official statistics on teenage pregnancy rates by ethnic group, the Teenage Pregnancy Unit reports that survey evidence suggests that young people from Bangladeshi, African Caribbean and Pakistani communities are 'substantially more likely to be teenage parents than the national average', although the Unit says that that may be partly the result of cultural traditions associated with early childbirth in marriage; but 'various cultural practices' (which are not specified) are also referred to.[388]

Sex education is also concerned with helping to protect young people from sexually transmitted infections (STIs). Here too the evidence suggests that it is not having a sufficiently positive impact, as the prevalence of STIs among young people continues to rise. The UN Committee on the Rights of the Child expressed concern about this increase in its most recent monitoring report on the UK in 2002,[389] but the situation continues to worsen. The Health Protection Agency has reported that young people in the UK are disproportionately affected by chlamydia, gonorrhoea and genital warts and that rates of diagnosis of these

---

[382] See also UN Committee on the Rights of the Child, *Concluding Observations: United Kingdom of Great Britain and Northern Ireland*, CRC/C/15/Add.188, 9 Oct 2002 (Geneva, United Nations, 2002), para 43, in which the Committee also expresses concern about the level of teenage pregnancy in the UK.

[383] Social Exclusion Unit, *Teenage Pregnancy*, Cm 4342 (London, TSO, 1999), 12.

[384] *Health Statistics Quarterly 17* (2003).

[385] *Health Statistics Quarterly 26* (2004), table B

[386] *Health Statistics Quarterly 29* (2006), table 4.1.

[387] Ibid, table 4.2.

[388] Teenage Pregnancy Unit, *Guidance for Developing Contraception and Sexual Health Advice Services to Reach Black and Minority Ethnic (BME) Young People*, paras 1.4 and 1.5, available at www.teenagepregancyunit.gov.uk.

[389] UN Committee on the Rights of the Child, *Concluding Observations: United Kingdom of Great Britain and Northern Ireland*, CRC/C/15/Add.188, 9 Oct 2002 (Geneva, United Nations, 2002), para 43.

diseases 'continued to increase among young people in 2004'.[390] Women aged 16–19 showed the highest rates of gonorrhoea and genital warts diagnosis.[391] Moreover, new episodes of genital warts, the most frequently disagnosed of the STIs in the UK, rose between 2003 and 2005 by 11 per cent in the case of men and 6.9 per cent among women.[392]

In the Netherlands, where the teenage conception rate is much lower than in the UK but has been increasing, as has the incidence of STIs among young people, a study has rejected 'a simplistic mechanical model where teenage conceptions are the direct outcome of specific deficiencies in sex education', finding instead that 'contextual factors have a far more important role to play'.[393] They include greater parental involvement in sex educational provision to their children, stronger family structures (for example, there are relatively few lone parent families in the Netherlands) and greater school responsiveness to parents' wishes. This study also draws parallels with the UK, citing the extension of sex education after the Education Act 1993 as not leading to reductions in conception rates among teenagers. Nonetheless, it could be the case that, but for effective sex education in schools in the UK, the picture might be even worse, although cultural trends in relation to sexual behaviour would be countering its effects. For example, over the decade 1990–2000 the total number of sexual partners that people would have during their lifetimes increased, as did the proportion of men who experienced homosexual sex; and the average age at which sexual intercourse first occurred fell from 17 to 16.[394] Realistically though, the figures on teenage pregnancy and STIs suggest that the legislation and guidance on sex and relationship education has had little impact, notwithstanding the potential of sex education 'as an essential building block for securing improved sexual health both for this and future generations'.[395]

The Effectiveness of Sex Education

The crucial point is that in order to fulfil its potential, sex education needs to be good, addressing the information and health advice needs of pupils of diverse ages and social backgrounds. Although there is evidence that, among girls at least, the proportion of pupils who regard sex and relationship education as having met their needs increased between 2001 and 2004,[396] there is other evidence that suggests that somewhat uneven progress in sex education has been made since it became compulsory in 1994. The Ofsted annual report for 1995–6

---

[390] Health Protection Agency, *Mapping the Issues: HIV and other Sexually Transmitted Infections in the United Kingdom: 2005* (London, Health Protection Agency, 2005) 4.

[391] Ibid, 4 and 30.

[392] Ibid, 30.

[393] J Van Loon, *Deconstructing the Dutch Utopia. Sex Education and Teenage Pregnancy in the Netherlands* (London, Family Education Trust, 2003) 58.

[394] House of Commons Health Committee, *Sexual Health*, HC 69–1 (London, TSO, 2003), para 70.

[395] Ibid, para 267.

[396] K Wellings *et al*, *Teenage Pregnancy Strategy Evaluation, Final Report* (London, DfES, 2005), available at www.dfes.gov.uk/research/data/uploadfiles/RW53.pdf.

revealed that some teaching was carried out by people with inadequate expertise and that one in eight schools had not met the statutory requirement to have a sex education policy.[397] Its 2004–5 subject report on personal, social and health education draws on evidence from the 1990s, and concludes that since 1997 '[a]chievement in SRE continues to improve although there has been a slight increase in the proportion of lessons where it is unsatisfactory'.[398] Coverage of HIV/AIDS has been a particularly problematic area: a 2002 report noted that education about HIV/AIDS was poor in secondary schools and that the subject was 'receiving less attention than in the past, even though it remains a significant health problem'.[399] A survey of young people found that between 1993 and 2000 young people's awareness of HIV and AIDS decreased.[400] This is serious given that, by the end of 2004, approximately 9,500 16–24-year-olds had been diagnosed with HIV infection,[401] and there are bound to have been many other cases where it was undiagnosed. Effective education about the risks and effects of infection should be paramount. The most recent indications are that pupils' knowledge of sexual health issues including HIV has improved, but that '[d]espite further advice [ie the 2000 guidance], many teachers remain nervous about teaching the topic and deal with it in a superficial manner'.[402] The lack of specialist teaching expertise continues to be a problem affecting the quality of sex education provision.[403]

In fact, the Ofsted reports seem to reveal significant problems. For example, according to the 2002 report, at the crucial stage in children's education, when they reach puberty (key stage 3, ages 11–14), 20 per cent of sex and relationship lessons were unsatisfactory or poor and 'significant weaknesses in knowledge and understanding were apparent in Key Stage 3 work on relationships and sexual health'.[404] Moreover, the House of Commons Health Committee found strong evidence that sex and relationship education in schools is 'frequently starved of time and resources in order to accommodate subjects which are accorded a higher priority by schools because of their National Curriculum status'.[405] The Committee has recommended that sex and relationship education should become a core part of the National Curriculum, to give it the priority it

---

[397] Office for Standards in Education, *The Annual Report of Her Majesty's Chief Inspector of Schools 1995/96* (London, TSO, 1997), paras 87 and 88.

[398] Ofsted, *The Annual Report of Her Majesty's Chief Inspector of Schools 2004/05. Personal, Social and Health Education in Secondary Schools* (London, Ofsted, 2005) (subject report), 1–2, available at www.ofsted.gov.uk/publications/annualreport0405/4.2.12.html.

[399] Ofsted, *Sex and Relationships Education* (London, Oftsed, 2002), paras 38 and 39.

[400] Oftsed evidence, cited in House of Commons Health Committee, *Sexual Health*, HC 69–1 (London, TSO, 2003), para 236.

[401] Health Protection Agency, *Mapping the Issues: HIV and other Sexually Transmitted Infections in the United Kingdom: 2005* (London, Health Protecvtion Agency, 2005) 91.

[402] Ofsted, *The Annual Report of Her Majesty's Chief Inspector of Schools 2004/05. Personal, social and health education in secondary schools* (London, Ofsted, 2005) (subject report) 2.

[403] House of Commons Health Committee, *Sexual Health*, HC 69–1 (London, TSO, 2003), paras 287–292.

[404] Ofsted, *Sex and Relationships Education* (London, Ofsted, 2002), paras 16 and 17.

[405] House of Commons Health Committee, *Sexual Health*, HC 69–1 (London, TSO, 2003), para 282.

warrants[406] a view echoed recently by the children's charity Childline, arguing that it should form part of personal, social and health education, which should be made a National Curriculum foundation subject.[407] This problem was still evident in 2005, when it was reported that in 50 per cent of schools the entire provision of personal, social and health education was squeezed by having to accommodate National Curriculum citizenship 'with no additional time provided'.[408] It was also reported that there were still nearly one in 10 schools that did not have a written sex education policy.[409] A further problem is that sex education is widely regarded as failing to address male perspectives.[410] The House of Commons Health Committee found it to be 'usually very female orientated'.[411] The monitoring of school sex education is clearly important. Although the move towards 'light touch' school inspections from 2005 may have renewed fears, previously voiced by the SEU in 1999,[412] that provision of the subject will not be sufficiently inspected, it will be covered by Ofsted's separate programme of subject inspections.[413]

Many school sex education policies were written several years ago, certainly before the general duty under section 176 of the Education Act 2002 concerning consultation with pupils over decisions affecting them was introduced. Ofsted has noted that pupils have been able to give school inspectors 'significant perspectives on SRE in schools' and its deficiencies—for example, inadequate discussion of homosexuality.[414] The SRE guidance places a strong emphasis on consultation with parents in developing policies, but also acknowledges that the policy should reflect the views of pupils.[415] This is clearly right, in the light of research published in the same year that found that pupils' views did not generally inform decisions about sex education policies at school level and that in most schools 'adult views of what is important in a sex education programme were imposed upon pupils'.[416] The Sex Education Forum has been recommending the involvement of pupils in constructing sex education policies for some years.[417] One difficulty with consultation is, however, that pupils from

---

[406] Ibid, para 286.

[407] Childline, *Alcohol and Teenage Sexual Activity* (London, Childline, 2006) 6, available at www.childline.org.uk.

[408] Ofsted, *Personal, Social and Health Education in Secondary Schools*, HMI 2311 (London, Ofsted, 2005), para 45.

[409] Ibid, para 27.

[410] L Measor *et al*, *Young People's Views on Sex Education. Education, Attitudes and Behaviour* (London, Routledge Falmer, 2000), 159–62.

[411] House of Commons Health Committee, *Sexual Health*, HC 69–1 (London, TSO, 2003), para 297.

[412] Social Exclusion Unit, *Teenage Pregnancy*, Cm 4342 (London, TSO, 1999), para 5.15.

[413] These subject inspections are explained in Ofsted, *Subject and Survey Inspection*, available at www.ofsted.gov.uk.

[414] Ofsted, *Sex and Relationships* HMI 433 (London, Ofsted, 2002), paras 43 and 44.

[415] DfEE, *Sex and Relationship Education Guidance*, DfEE 0116/2000 (London, DfEE, 2000), para 1.3.

[416] L Measor *et al*, *Young People's Views on Sex Education. Education, Attitudes and Behaviour* (London, Routledge Falmer, 2000) 150.

[417] Eg, Sex Education Forum, *Developing and Reviewing a Sex Education Policy. A Positive Strategy* (Factsheet 10) (London, Sex Education Forum/National Children's Bureau, 1994).

some minority religious or ethnic backgrounds might, for cultural reasons, find it more difficult than others to discuss sex education policy in a collective environment. One facet of the state's duty under Article 12 of the UNCRC is to afford children an opportunity to express their views on all matters affecting them and, as Lundy argues, that applies not only to decisions relating to individual children but also when school policies are being developed.[418] Lundy, conceptualising this opportunity as 'space', argues that it must be a 'safe space'. Children must be able to express their views without fear of reprisal or ridicule. It must also be an 'inclusive' space, and here the issue is whether the opportunity to participate is afforded to and facilitated for all, regardless of their background,[419] not least in view of the duty on states to ensure that rights such as that in Article 12 are enjoyed without discrimination on the grounds of race, colour, sex, birth or other status, and so on.[420] The right *not* to participate as a matter of choice should also be respected, but different ways for views to be expressed may need to be sought to assist those who feel inhibited, not least in view of the right to privacy under Article 8 of the ECHR.

LANGUAGE AND LINGUISTIC RIGHTS

The International Legal Context

The recent 30th anniversary of the Soweto uprising and its brutal quelling has served as a reminder of the considerable cultural and political importance that the language of instruction in education may possess. On 16 June 1976, black students in the township marched to protest against a law which compelled them to learn in Afrikaans and were fired upon by the police. Unofficial estimates put the eventual death toll at 500. The resistance to teaching Afrikaans in schools was symbolic of the political struggle for freedom.[421] Even in the more settled, modern European context, the language of instruction in schools can be a very contentious matter. It is an important issue of minority rights and freedom of choice.

Linguistic choice within the education system is not a concern for the majority of the population in England, whose first language and language spoken at home is English. In Wales, a minority are Welsh speakers but, as discussed below, English–Welsh bilingualism is firmly established and catered for within the education system. For some minorities, however, language within education is of great significance. The education system may face demands that, in order to respect and uphold the cultural integrity of minority groups, ethnic or religious,

---

[418] L Lundy, '"Voice" is not Enough: the Implications of Art 12 of the United Nations Convention on the Rights of the Child for Education', paper presented at the SLSA conference, Liverpool, 31 Mar 2005.

[419] Ibid.

[420] UNCRC Art 2.

[421] See B Hirsch, *Year of Fire, Year of Ash: Soweto—Roots of a Revolution* (London, Zed Books, 1979).

it should play a part in the preservation of a minority's mother tongue. Indeed, language rights are integral to notions of minority rights and to rights to self-determination.[422] For example, Article 27 of the International Covenant on Civil and Political Rights provides that:

> In those States in which ethnic, religious or linguistic minorities exist, persons belonging to such minorities shall not be denied the right, in community with the other members of their group, to enjoy their own culture, to profess and practise their own religion, or to use their own language.[423]

Although expressed negatively, this provision is accepted by the Human Rights Committee as conferring a right; moreover, it places an obligation upon the state to protect a minority's identity 'and the right of its members to enjoy and develop their culture or language'.[424] This provision can therefore be regarded as aiming to provide minorities with 'cultural space'.[425] It is clearly capable of extending to the issue of education through the medium of a minority language.[426] Thornberry argues that Article 27 seems to connote a positive obligation on states parties to take necessary measures to assist minorities[427] to preserve their values and that the degree of intervention and support required is in inverse proportion to the level of the minority's own resources.[428] It is nevertheless unlikely, on that basis, that Article 27 could be construed as requiring mother tongue teaching to be provided to all minorities; and in any event the rights in Article 27 are not absolute.[429] But there is general provision under other areas of international law for minorities to receive 'adequate opportunities' to be taught their own language or to receive mother tongue teaching. For example, the UK appears to accept that minority ethnic communities or 'visible' minority groups are covered by the Framework Convention for the Protection of National Minorities,[430] which not only provides for each person belonging to such a community to have a right to learn his or her minority language, but also, where there is 'sufficient demand' within the area in

---

[422] See, eg, K Knop, *Diversity and Self-Determination in International Law* (Cambridge, Cambridge University Press, 2002).

[423] GA res 2200A (XXI), 21 UN GAOR Supp. (No 16) at 52, UN Doc A/6316 (1966), 999 UNTS 171, which came into force on 23 Mar 1976.

[424] Human Rights Committee, General Comment No23(50). The Rights of Minorities (Art 27) 08/09/04 CCPR/C/Rev.1/Add.5 (1994), paras 6.1 and 6.2.

[425] See P Thornberry, *Indigenous Peoples and Human Rights* (Manchester, Manchester University Press, 2002) 132–3.

[426] P Thornberry, *International Law and the Rights of Minorities* (Oxford, Clarendon Press, 1991) 188.

[427] A term which itself is capable of different meanings: ibid, ch. 16.

[428] Ibid, 185–6.

[429] See K Knop, *Diversity and Self-Determination in International Law* (Cambridge, Cambridge University Press, 2002), ch 8, discussing the Human Rights Committee's ruling in *Sandra Lovelace v Canada* (Communication No 24/1977, formerly Communication No R6/24), GAOR, 36th Sess., Supp No 40, UN Doc A/36/40 (1981) 166 (merits), where it was held, inter alia, that a valid restriction on the rights of minorities 'must have both a reasonable and objective justification and be consistent with the other provisions of the Covenant, read as a whole': ibid, 174, cited in Knop at 369.

[430] See E Craig, 'Accommodation of Diversity in Education: A Human Rights Agenda?' (2003) 15 *Child & Family Law Quarterly* 279.

which they live, to have 'adequate opportunities' to be taught the language or 'for receiving instruction in this language', although without prejudice to their learning, or being taught in, the official (national) language.[431] As regards the right to education within the International Covenant on Economic, Social and Cultural Rights, under Article 13, language is not referred to specifically, although it has been argued that in relation to the Article's requirement[432] that the stated objectives of education include upholding the liberty of parents to select (non-state) schools for their children and to ensure that education is in accordance with their religious or moral convictions, 'the language of instruction is particularly important'.[433] The fact that, under the UNCRC, a child of indigenous origin or belonging to a minority is not to be denied the right to enjoy his or her own culture 'or to use his or her own language'[434] and that the education of the child is to be directed to, inter alia, '[t]he development of respect for the child's . . . own cultural identity, language and values',[435] certainly implies that importance is attached to the preservation of minority languages, even if mother tongue teaching is not specifically guaranteed. However, it should be noted that, where EC law is concerned, Directive 77/486/EEC merely requires that the teaching of the mother tongue and culture of the family of origin to migrants is promoted, in contrast to the requirement that migrants receive intensive tuition in the, or an, official language of the host state.[436]

Thus the overall position across international law and, within its more limited sphere, EC law, is that there is recognition of the need for coverage of minority languages within education, in the form of either mother tongue teaching or the opportunity to learn the language in school, but no firm obligations that would guarantee such provision, nor are there detailed recommendations. Specific recommendations for more prescription in these areas have, however, been made by a panel of experts assembled on behalf of the Organisation for Security and Co-operation by Europe's High Commissioner on National Minorities. These are the Hague Recommendations and they call, in relation to primary and secondary education, for some or all of the curriculum to be provided through the medium of the minority language and for the minority language to be taught 'as a subject on a regular basis', although they acknowledge that the realisation of this will depend upon the availability of trained teachers.[437]

---

[431] Council of Europe, Framework Convention for the Protection of National Minorities, ETS No 157. See also the UNESCO Convention Against Discrimination in Education, (1960), 420 UNTS 93, Art 5; the Document of the Copenhagen Meeting of the Conference on the Human Dimension of the CSCE, *Conference on Security and Co-operation in Europe* (CSCE) (Vienna, CSCE, 1990), para 34; and the UN Declaration on the Rights of Persons Belonging to National or Ethnic, Religious and Linguistic Minorities (1992), UN Doc A/47/49 (1993).

[432] Art 13(3).

[433] A Edwards, 'New Roma Rights Legislation in Bosnia and Herzegovina: Positive, Negative or Indifferent?' (2005) 9 *International Journal of Human Rights* 465 at 468–9.

[434] Art 30.

[435] Art 29(1)(c).

[436] Noted in Chap 4 at p 210 above, and see p 421 below.

[437] The Hague Recommendations Regarding the Education Rights of National Minorities (1996), available at www.osce.org/documents/hcnm/1996/10/2700_en.pdf.

Jones and Warner make the point that if minorities cannot learn their own language through formal schooling or classes in their communities 'they lose not only their language but part of their identity . . . their language transmits their cultural norms and values and it emphasizes their group feelings'.[438] But it is under threat in an integrated system. A schools system that exemplifies those concerns is that in Israel. It rests on separate systems of Jewish schools (ranging from secular to Ultra Orthodox) and Arab schools. Hebrew is the language of instruction in the former, while the medium is Arabic (with Hebrew taught as a second language) in the latter. According to Goldstein, such arrangements help societal subgroups in Israel to maintain their traditions, culture and linguistic identity, and they respect the liberal value of enabling parents to choose a particular form of education for their children; but they also generate 'significant problems in creating a common civil society'.[439] It is clear that education in the majority national tongue plays a crucial role in the integration of minority groups into mainstream culture and society. Ensuring that children acquire an appropriate level of competence in the majority language is seen as critical to the maintenance of good communication and to maximising equality of opportunity and social cohesion. As Edwards, commenting on the position of the Roma within Bosnia and Hertzegovina, which offers an extreme example, comments, while it is important to acknowledge the importance of teaching and use of minority languages in terms of minority rights and dignity, the Roma need to learn the official languages 'as a means to their full integration and acceptance within a fractured society'.[440] This has also become the official view of the inclusion of minority languages in the Netherlands. Over the past 30 years, policy in that country has shifted from an emphasis on education in the immigrant minorities' own language and culture towards a more integrationist approach, reaching the current premise that 'one's own culture is at most something private and must not stand in the way of integration', leading, inter alia, to the ending of any teaching in the mother tongue.[441]

As noted in Chapter 4 and above, EU Member States are under an obligation towards children of EU migrants, contained within Directive 77/486/EEC, Article 3, to 'promote, in co-ordination with national education, teaching of the mother tongue and culture of the country of origin'. The UK Government's response to this has been to recommend to LEAs that they should explore ways in which such provision could be made, but not to regard themselves as under an obligation to deliver it.[442] Indeed, according to research by Ackers and Stalford, there is a

---

[438] C Jones and R Warner, 'Language and Education' in Minority Rights Group, *Education Rights and Minorities* (London, Minority Rights Group/UNICEF, 1994) 18 at 18.

[439] S Goldstein, 'Multiculturalism, Parental Choice and Traditional Values: A Comment on Religious Education in Israel' , in G Douglas and L Sebba, *Children's Rights and Traditional Values* (Aldershot, Ashgate, 1998) 118 at 131.

[440] A Edwards, 'New Roma Rights Legislation in Bosnia and Herzegovina: Positive, Negative or Indifferent?' (2005) 9 *International Journal of Human Rights* 465 at 472.

[441] R Rijkschroeff *et al*, 'Educational Policies on Migrants and Minorities in the Netherlands: Success or Failure?' (2005) 20 *Journal of Education Policy* 417 at 424–5.

[442] Department for Education and Science/Welsh Office, DES Circular 5/81, WO Circular 36/81, *Directive of the the Council of the European Community on the Education of the Children of Migrant Workers* (London/Cardiff, DES/Welsh Office, 1981), para 7.

prevailing attitude throughout the EU that 'mother tongue teaching is not a priority for the child's educational development in the host country'.[443] The UK has only acknowledged that the provision of English language tuition, including provision appropriate to the needs of children who speak little or no English, is an obligation required by the Directive (in Article 2).[444] Ackers and Stalford believe that in practice the UK is in fact complacent about this obligation, perhaps because the children of many EU migrants have some capability in English.[445]

Linguistic Diversity and Provision in the UK

Before considering whether the ECHR may convey any rights in relation to mother tongue teaching or the possibility to study one's own minority community's language in the UK, it is necessary to consider the country's linguistic diversity and the current provision. The language by which children should be taught in schools in England is not legislatively prescribed, but in practice almost all teaching is through the medium of English. This can present problems for pupils whose first language is not English. As was noted in Chapter 1, there is considerable diversity in ethnicity and national origin within Britain, particularly as a result of immigration from Africa and Asia in the post-war period, and one consequence is wide linguistic diversity, especially in particular in urban areas of England. While English is the principal first language spoken in all parts of the UK, some citizens are bilingual, and for a substantial minority (although there are no complete national statistics) English is a second or additional language. National Census (2001) planning included a survey to identify languages into which census leaflets should be translated. It identified 24 different languages ranging from Albanian/Kosovan through to Vietnamese. In 2003 the Department for Work and Pensions drew up a similar list for translation of its information for clients: Bengali, Punjabi, Gujerati, Urdu, Arabic, Classical Chinese, Somali, French, Polish and Tamil.[446] Many members of immigrant or ethnic minority groups have English as their first language, but a significant number do not. A major health survey found that across England as a whole, the proportion of the main ethnic minority populations who spoke English as their principal language varied widely across the different groups. It was as low as 55 per cent among those whose origin was Indian, 45 per cent among those of Pakistani origin, 41 per cent in the case of those of Chinese origin and 20 per cent in the case of persons of Bangladeshi origin.[447] Within some of the different groups there was also a range of languages spoken: for example, 32 per cent of

---

[443] L Ackers and H Stalford, *A Community for Children? Children, Citizenship and Internal Migration in the EU* (Aldershot, Ashgate, 2004) 250.

[444] Art 2. Circular 5/81 (n 442 above), paras 4–6.

[445] L Ackers and H Stalford, *A Community for Children? Children, Citizenship and Internal Migration in the EU* (Aldershot, Ashgate, 2004) 246.

[446] Central Office of Information.

[447] Health Survey for England, The Health of Minority Ethnic Groups '99 (1999), available at www.archive-official-documents.co.u/document/doh/suvery99/hse99-t14-27.htm.

those of Pakistani origin spoke Punjabi and 20 per cent spoke Urdu. This means that even if children have English as their first language, many will need to speak another language at home: this is the case for 30 per cent of schoolchildren in London.[448]

The only truly indigenous language in England apart from English is the Cornish language (*Kernowek*, *Kernewek* or *Curnoack*). It is estimated that there are 3,500 fluent speakers of this language.[449] It is recognised as a minority language under Part II of the European Charter for Regional or Minority Languages, which the UK has signed and ratified.[450] Part II sets out the objectives and principles to be applied to minorities by the states parties, but only Part III, which contains the measures to be taken to promote the use of the language in public life, sets out detailed obligations on education. Cornish shares about 80 per cent of its basic vocabulary with Breton and 75 per cent with Welsh, which are among the other Celtic languages within the Brythonic group to which it belongs. The Manx language on the Isle of Man is another. Although the last native Manx speaker died in 1974, interest in the language has since revived. In the 2001 Census 2.2 per cent of the population of the island were identified as Manx speakers.[451] This Census also found that 21 per cent of the population of Wales aged 3 or over (or 580,000 people) could speak at least some Welsh, while 16 per cent could speak, understand and write in the language.[452] The Welsh language, which is in more frequent in use in western parts of Wales, is protected under Part III of the European Charter for Regional or Minority Languages. In relation to primary and secondary education, the states parties undertake to make education or a substantial part of education available in the relevant language; to provide for the teaching of the relevant language as an integral part of the curriculum; or to provide education in the minority language, or teach the language in the curriculum, to those children whose families request it and whose number is 'considered sufficient'.[453] Similar obligations apply in relation to technical and further/higher education, and there is also a duty in relation to pre-school education.[454]

The law in Scotland is not covered in this book, other than selectively for comparison. It may be noted here that in Scotland two national languages other than English, Gaelic and Scots, survive although the latter is only found in the form of dialects spoken in different parts of the country, despite being classed by the Scottish Executive as a 'living language'.[455] There are no reliable data on the precise extent of Scots usage, but it is covered by Part II of the European Charter for Regional or Minority Languages. However, unlike Gaelic, it is not covered by

---

[448] See P Baker and J Eversley (eds), *Multilingual Capital* (London, Battlebridge, 2000).
[449] http://www.cornwall.gov.uk.
[450] ETS No 148 (Strasbourg, 5.XI1992). The UK signed on 2 Mar 2000 and ratified on 27 Mar 2001.
[451] http://www.isleofman.com/locallife/features/man_language.asp.
[452] National Statistics, *Statistical Bulletin 2001 Census of Population. First Results on the Welsh Language*, SB 22/2003 (Cardiff, Statistical Directorate, Wales, 2003).
[453] European Charter for Regional or Minority Languages, n 000 above, Art 8(1)(b) and (c).
[454] Ibid, Art 8(1)(a), (d), (e).
[455] Scottish Executive, *Scotland's National Cultural Strategy*, available at http://www.scotland.gov.uk/nationalculturalstrategy/docs.

Part III. The 2001 Census found that that there were 92,396 people, or 1.9 per cent of the population, who could speak or read the Gaelic language, write in it, or understand it.[456] Although few people speak it, Gaelic is treated as an important aspect of national culture to be promoted as part of the Scottish Executive's National Cultural Strategy.[457] Moreover, the promotion of Gaelic education, Gaelic culture and the use and understanding of the Gaelic language are among the functions of the *Bórd na Gàidhlig* (the *Bórd*) provided for by the Gaelic Language (Scotland) Act 2005.[458] The *Bórd* is given a specific duty to prepare a national Gaelic language plan, covering these matters, and is empowered to require public authorities to prepare their own Gaelic language plans.[459] Provision in relation to Gaelic education continues to be the responsibility of the Scottish ministers, but the *Bórd* is given the power to provide guidance to them.[460]

There is no prescribed National Curriculum as such in Scotland. Instead, the Scottish Ministers are under a duty to define priorities in educational objectives for school education.[461] One of the current priorities is 'to promote equality and help every pupil to benefit from education, with particular regard to . . . Gaelic and other lesser used languages'.[462] Each Scottish education authority must publish an 'annual statement of educational improvement objectives' which must include an account of the ways or circumstances in which they will provide or seek to develop Gaelic-medium education.[463] Moreover, in complying with this duty the authority must have regard to any Gaelic language plan it has published and any education guidance published by the *Bórd*.[464] The number of primary schools providing Gaelic-medium education increased from 45 (1,080 pupils) in 1993–4 to 58 (1,925) pupils in 2002–3,[465] and in relation to one school on the island of Skye there has been a proposal by a Gaelic-language group (including 'incomers' from England) to the Highland Council that the school should become Gaelic only.[466] But within Scotland courses leading to qualifications in Gaelic are still taken by only small numbers of people.[467] Inclusion of the Scots language within the school curriculum is also encouraged.[468]

[456] Cited in Scottish Executive Education Department, *Education and Training in Scotland 2003: National Dossier* (Edinburgh, Scottish Executive, 2003), para 1.4.2.
[457] Strategic objective 2.
[458] Gaelic Language (Scotland) Act 2005, s 1.
[459] Ibid, ss 2 and 3.
[460] Ibid, s 9.
[461] Standards in Scotland's Schools etc Act 2000, s 4.
[462] Education (National Priorities) (Scotland) Order 2000 (SI 2000/443), art. 3(3).
[463] Standards in Scotland's Schools etc Act 2000, s 5(2).
[464] Ibid, s 5(4A), inserted by the Gaelic Language (Scotland) Act 2005, s 9(3).
[465] Scottish Executive Education Department, n 456 above.
[466] D Lister, 'We want our school to be Gaelic only, say English', *The Times*, 3 Feb 2006.
[467] In 2004, only 230 people entered for a 'higher' (typically taken at the age of 18) in Gaelic; and at intermediate levels 1 and 2 (normally taken by 14–16-year-olds) the numbers sitting Gaelic were 11 and 57 respectively: Scottish Qualifications Authority (SQA), *Annual Statistical Report 2004* (Glasgow, SQA, 2005). The SQA plans to axe qualifications in subjects taken by very small numbers of people, but has confirmed that its Gaelic qualifications will continue.
[468] Scottish Executive Education Department, n 456 above, para 1.4.2.

It is necessary at this point to mention briefly the special languages that are used for communication by and with people with various disabilities, such as Braille for blind people and sign language for people who are deaf or have severe impairment of hearing. These languages are both taught and used as the medium of teaching but their provision belongs within the framework of special education and disability law discussed elsewhere in this book. It is also important to note that under that framework, discussed in Chapter 6, a pupil cannot be classed as having a 'learning difficulty' where that difficulty is 'solely because the language (or form of language) in which he is, or will be, taught is different from a language (or form of language) which has at any time been spoken in his home'.[469] Consequently, any provision made on account of that difficulty will not be special educational provision. Care will, however, be needed where a such a child makes inadequate educational progress, since there could be other non-language-related causes of learning difficulty.[470] Where a child definitely has special educational needs, special provision for bilingual help may be needed for his or her parents if their first language is not English, to ensure that the LEA can meet its obligations to involve them and the child in the process of identifying and making suitable provision for the child.[471]

As noted earlier in this chapter, children for whom English is an additional language may be granted temporary exemption from the National Curriculum, at the discretion of the head teacher, in order to receive special language support.[472] But the main source of provision specifically to help children who have recently arrived in the country is the Education Standards Fund (ESF), which includes the ethnic minority achievement grant (EMAG), discussed in Chapter 4. In one school that has benefited from EMAG funding in recent years English was an additional language for as many as 57 per cent of the pupils.[473] EMAGs have also been used to meet the cost of extra assistance required for the education of asylum-seeker children within schools, including the hiring of interpreters, providing mother tongue teaching and the translation of school books. As noted in Chapter 4, there is some evidence that pupils are making progress under such arrangements despite initial language barriers, although staff may in some cases not be fully up to date in their knowledge and understanding of the linguistic, educational and cultural needs of the asylum-seeker pupils.[474] Provision is also made for translated versions of various documents, whether about education generally or about specific pupils, to be made available for parents whose first language is not English.

---

[469] Education Act 1996, s 312(3) (emphasis added), which applies in both England and Wales.

[470] Department for Education and Skills (2001), *Special Educational Needs Code of Practice* (London, DfES, 2001), para 6.14.

[471] Ibid, para 8:56.

[472] Education Act 2002, s 93; the Education (National Curriculum) (Temporary Exceptions for Individual Pupils) Regulations 1989 (SI 1989/1181).

[473] Office for Standards in Education, *Managing the Ethnic Minority Achievement Grant. Good Practice in Secondary Schools* (London, Ofsted, 2004).

[474] Office for Standards in Education, *The Education of Asylum-Seeker Pupils*, HMI 453 (London, Ofsted, 2003).

Information on published examination results or on school admission policies falls into this category.[475]

Within state schools, the possibility of learning another language exists under the National Curriculum, as noted above, at Key Stages 3 (ages 11–14) or 4 (ages 14–16). However, the teaching of Cornish does not take place within this framework at present. According to a survey approximately five years ago this subject was provided in 12 primary schools and four secondary schools in Cornwall, but there is currently no GCSE qualification in it, although pupils may sit special Language Board examinations.[476] Cornish language teaching will need further funding and support, plus a nationally recognised qualification equivalent to GCSE, if it is to make any real advances within the county in which it survives.

Turning to Wales, there is a national action plan, *Iaith Pawb* (Everyone's Language), which aims to increase the use of Welsh, leading to a 'bilingual Wales'.[477] Various initiatives for increasing its use among young people and within the education system are currently being funded. Welsh is well-absorbed into the national culture in Wales. Not only are road signs, public notices and official publications bilingual (English and Welsh), but Welsh is also recognised as an official language within which business may be conducted in the Welsh Assembly (indeed there is a duty to treat the languages as equal there[478]) and in legal proceedings.[479] It is also recognised for the purposes of Part III of the European Charter for Regional or Minority Languages. Grants for bilingual education are made by the Welsh Language Board, which advises the Welsh Assembly. Approximately 27 per cent of primary schools in Wales are mainly Welsh-medium schools and a further 5 per cent teach in Welsh some of the time. This means that in 68 per cent of primary schools in Wales the subject is taught as a second language only. Among secondary school pupils, some 14.4 per cent are taught in Welsh as a first language and 84.5 per cent as a second language.[480] Although parents have no statutory guarantee of a place in a Welsh-medium school, location appears to be the only obstacle,[481] and even then travel is generally possible. Moreover, if the parents prefer a Welsh-medium school that is further from their home than an English-medium school, it is unlikely that the LEA could successfully invoke a particular statutory exception to the duty to meet transport costs, namely that 'suitable arrangements' can be made for the child to attend a nearer school than the one preferred.[482] It is likely to be accepted

---

[475] See the Education (School Information) Regulations 2002 (SI 2002/2897), which make specific provision for translated versions, including including translations into Braille.

[476] http://www.cornwall.gov.uk/cornish/GOSW/education.htm.

[477] The Welsh Assembly has a power to do anything it considers necessary to support the Welsh language: Government of Wales Act 1998, s 32.

[478] Ibid, s 47.

[479] Welsh Language Act 1993, s 22.

[480] National Statistics, *Welsh in Schools*, SB 12/2003 (Cardiff, Statistical Directorate, 2003).

[481] K Williams and B Rainey, 'Language, Education and the European Convention on Human Rights in the Twenty-first Century' (2002) 22 *Legal Studies* 625 at 626, n 2.

[482] Education Act 1996, ss 444 and 509: see Chap 4.

for this purpose that for a child of a Welsh-speaking family an English-medium school may not be suitable.[483]

Welsh as a National Curriculum subject is taught in every state school in Wales, either as one of the core subjects for ages 5–16 in Welsh-speaking schools[484] or as one of the other foundation subjects in non-Welsh speaking schools.[485] There is comparable provision to that made in England (above) in relation to temporary exemption from part or all of the National Curriculum (for example, in the case of pupils whose first language is neither English nor Welsh[486]) and the modern foreign languages that may be offered at a school as part of the National Curriculum.[487] The provision in Wales may be compared with that in the Irish Republic, where national policy aims to promote bilingualism in society and, in particular, the greater use of the Irish language at school and its maintenance as the primary community language in the *Gaeltacht* areas.[488] The Minister of Education in Ireland is empowered to establish a body to plan and co-ordinate the provision of textbooks and aids to learning and teaching through Irish[489] (although the study of Irish is not compulsory in all schools). There are just over 100 Irish language schools, or *gaelscoileanna*, which receive state funding.[490]

The predominance of English within education in England is uncontroversial and has not resulted in legal disputes. Within Wales and Scotland, there is sufficient autonomy of government for indigenous national languages to be given support and recognition within education law and policy, and to meet most parents' aspirations as regards mother tongue teaching, but without disturbing the overall primacy of English. In *Belgian Linguistics* the European Court of Human Rights held that while the first sentence of Article 2 of Protocol 1 (A2P1) to the ECHR 'does not specify the language in which education must be conducted in order that the right to education should be respected', the right 'would be meaningless if it did not imply . . . the right to be educated in the national language or one of the national languages, as the case may be'.[491] But, as noted in Chapter 2, the Court did not consider that linguistic preferences regarding teaching could amount to religious or philosophical convictions within the terms of the second sentence of the Article, and held that (on the basis of the *travaux préparatoires*) the object of that sentence was 'in no way to secure respect

---

[483] *R (Jones) v Ceredigion County Council* [2004] ELR 506, which gave consideration to the Education Act 1996, ss 444 and 509.

[484] Defined as a school where more than half of the subjects taught (only including religious education and all National Curriculum subjects other than English and Welsh) are taught in Welsh: Education Act 2002, ss 105(7) and 106(4).

[485] Ibid, ss 105((2), (3) and 106(2), (3).

[486] Education Act 2002, s 114; the Education (National Curriculum) (Temporary Exceptions for Individual Pupils) (Wales) Regulations 1999 (SI 1999/1815).

[487] Education (National Curriculum) (Modern Foreign Languages) (Wales) Order 2000 (SI 2000/1980) (W141).

[488] Education Act 1998 (Ireland), s 6.

[489] Ibid, s 31.

[490] D Glendinning, *Education and the Law* (Dublin, Butterworths, 1999), paras 2.61–2.63.

[491] *Belgian Linguistics Case (No 2)* (1979–80) 1 EHRR 252, para 3. See further U Kilkelly, *The Child and the European Convention on Human Rights* (Aldershot, Ashgate, 1999) 81–84.

by the state of a right for parents to have education conducted in a language other than that of the country in question'.[492] It rejected, in all but one case, complaints that the failure to meet the linguistic preferences of French-speaking families for their children to be taught in French within the Flemish-speaking area of Belgium amounted to discrimination under Article 14 in connection with the right to education.[493] More recently, however, when Greek Cypriots living in northern (Turkish) Cyprus complained that there were no school facilities for their children to be taught though the medium of Greek beyond primary school, the Court concluded that the absence of appropriate secondary school facilities meant that there had been a violation of A2P1, since Greek-medium teaching was available only in southern Cyprus and to access such education there would have a significant impact on the complainants' family life.[494] That decision hints at a more pluralistic approach, but its wider impact is likely to be limited, given the particular circumstances, political and social, to life in Cyprus. As Dunbar argues, this decision does not establish a general right to minority language education;[495] but, in his view, the underlying principle applied by the court could be applied in future 'where children from a linguistic minority who do not speak the language of the school are forced into majority-language education'.[496] As yet, no cases asserting minority linguistic rights in education have been brought within the courts in Great Britain under the HRA 1998. On the whole, the Strasbourg jurisprudence on linguistic rights has so far not offered much encouragement to any potential complainants.[497] Moreover, there is also the matter of the UK's reservation to the second sentence of A2P1,[498] which means that resource constraints are likely to weigh heavily.

Where there is provision of separate schooling in response to linguistic diversity, as in Wales, it will support rather than prejudice human rights. In this regard it should be noted that the UNESCO Convention Against Discrimination in Education specifically sanctions it (and also where it is established on the basis of religion) as not giving rise to discrimination, provided there is no compulsion to be admitted to a school within that separate system and if the education provided conforms to the standards prescribed by the authorities.[499] It also provides that the state must 'recognize the right of members of national minorities to carry on their own educational activities, including the maintenance of schools and, depending on the educational policy of each State, the use or the teaching of their own language', subject to the same two conditions as regards non-compulsion and standards plus a further one that 'this right is not

---

[492] *Belgian Linguistics Case (No 2)* (1979–80) 1 EHRR 252, para 6.

[493] See Chap 2.

[494] *Cyprus v Turkey,* App no 25781/94 (2002) 35 EHRR 731 at paras 277–280 and 292.

[495] R Dunbar, 'Is There a Duty to Legislate for Linguistic Minorities?' (2006) 33 *Journal of Law and Society* 181, at 189.

[496] Ibid, 189–90.

[497] See in particular *Belgian Linguistics Case (No 2)* (1979–80) 1 EHRR 252. See further K Williams and B Rainey, 'Language, Education and the European Convention on Human Rights in the Twenty-first Century' (2002) 22 *Legal Studies* 625.

[498] Namely that the UK only accepts the obligation in so far as it does not prejudice the provision of efficient education or the avoidance of unreasonable expenditure.

[499] UNESCO Convention Against Discrimination in Education, 1960, 429 UNTS 93, Art 2(b).

exercised in a manner which prevents the members of these minorities from understanding the culture and language of the community as a whole and from participating in its activities, or which prejudices national sovereignty'.[500]

Provision in respect of minority languages seems to be dependent upon whether the language in question is a national language, as in the case of Welsh in Wales or Gaelic in Ireland. Those languages are considered to be part of the established cultural heritage of the nation that is deemed worthy of protection, with education having a key role to play. The same recognition has not been accorded to the many other minority languages, such as those of African and Asian communities within the UK. There has been little positive intervention to support these communities' traditional languages. Indeed, at a time of growing political demands for minority communities to become more proficient in the English language, as a means to their greater integration and in the interests of social cohesion, there seems little likelihood, in the case of the languages that are not (at least not until the recent past) indigenous to the UK, of either state funding for minority language schools or the mandatory inclusion of mother tongue teaching. Of course, the practicability of including all the myriad languages present among families resident in the UK clearly militates against such provision, particularly when the inclusion or non-inclusion of any particular language might give rise to complaints of discrimination. Craig notes that the UK's position has been that 'responsibility for minority language education lies with the communities themselves'.[501] There are, for example, as many as 900 community supplementary schools in London, and over 2,200 in England as a whole, primarily engaged in minority language teaching and cultural or religious activities. Their work is mostly funded via annual community subscriptions; LEA support is 'minimal'.[502]

RELIGION IN STATE EDUCATION

Introduction: the Role of Religion in Education

The UK is not a country where religion is excluded from the state education system. There is no constitutional requirement to separate religion and state in the matter of education, unlike in France and the United States (although religious traditions and secularity have nonetheless come into legal conflict in these countries, most notably over religious dress worn by pupils or teachers in France[503] and the display of religious symbols or articles of faith, such as the Ten

---

[500] Ibid, Art 5(1)(c)(i).
[501] See E Craig, 'Accommodation of Diversity in Education: A Human Rights Agenda?' (2003) 15 *Child & Family Law Quarterly* 279. L Ackers and H Stalford, *A Community for Children? Children, Citizenship and Internal Migration in the EU* (Aldershot, Ashgate, 2004) 249.
[502] T Issa, 'Children's Home Languages in the Classroom' (2006) 225 *Childright* 24 at 26; see also QCA, www.qca.org.uk/10007_10032.html.
[503] See p 363 above.

Commandments, and the teaching of creationism, in the United States[504]). Moreover, there is no tradition of religious neutrality such as one finds in the German Basic Law[505] and in the Belgian Constitution, which states that '[t]he community organizes neutral education. Neutrality implies notably respect for the philosophical, ideological, or religious conceptions of all parents and pupils'.[506] In Belgium this principle gives rise to state funding for schools that uphold a particular religious, philosophical or educational viewpoint.[507] In the UK, some religious minorities, such as Muslims, have traditionally faced difficulties in establishing schools within the state sector, a problem that is however beginning to ease. Moreover, the pervasive religious ethos in the state system as a whole has been a Christian one, although the appropriateness of this today is questioned, partly on the basis of the growing secularity of British society as a whole but also, contrastingly, on the basis that British society is increasingly pluralistic and that no one religious ethos should predominate, a view that during the 1970s and 1980s led to a multicultural approach to religious education and collective worship, which in turn fostered a reactive reinforcement of the traditional law. Even before the Human Rights Act 1998 there were concerns that the UK's laws on religious education and collective worship might not be fully compliant with the ECHR. This is an issue considered below.

The presence of religiously-affiliated schools within the state education system in England and Wales, giving parents the choice of a denominational educational environment for their child (as discussed in Chapter 5), might be regarded as obviating the need for religion to play a part in the rest of the state sector. As discussed in earlier chapters, there are around 7,500 denominational schools. They are classed as voluntary controlled (mostly Church of England), voluntary aided (mostly Roman Catholic, but with some Jewish, Muslim and other schools) or foundation schools with a religious character. Over 13,000 of the 21,000 state schools (excluding special schools) in England are community schools, which have no religious affiliation, although even in that secular environment these schools are required to provide religious education and to ensure a daily act of

---

[504] See in particular the Supreme Court decisions in *Edwards v Aguillard* 482 US 578 (1987), rejecting as unconstitutional provision for creation science to be taught whenever evolution was covered, and *Stone v Graham* 449 US 39 (1980) and *McCreary County v Am. Civil Liberties Union*, 354 F3d 438 (6th Cir, 2004), where the posting of the Ten Commandments in school buildings (and in areas accessed by the public in court buildings in the latter case) was similarly found to be contrary to the Establishment Clause in the Constitution. See also CJ Russo, 'Evolution v Creation Science in the US: Can the Courts Divine a Solution?' (2002) 3 *Education Law Journal* 152; Idem, 'The Ten Commandments in American Public Schools: An Enduring Controversy' (2003) 4 *Education Law Journal* 90; Idem, 'Religious Neutrality in Public Schools and Elsewhere: An Assessment of the Supreme Court's Approach to Posting the Ten Commandments in Public Places in the US' (2006) 7 *Education Law Journal* 21; RD Mawdsley, 'Values Orientation in American Public Schools', 14 *Education & the Law* 77; and C Hamilton, *Family, Law and Religion* (London, Sweet and Maxwell, 1995), ch 8.

[505] Grundgesentz (Basic Law), Art 4, s 1.

[506] Constitution of Belgium (revised), Art 24 (formerly 17), s 1.3.

[507] J De Groof, 'Regulating School Choice in Belgium's Flemish Community' in PJ Wolf and S Macdeo (eds), *Educating Citizens. International Perspectives on Civic Vlaues and School Choice* (Washington, DC, Brookings Instituion Press) 157.

collective worship.[508] Indeed, these duties, which represent the legacy of the Christian Church's historical involvement in schooling, are among few to have continued since the Education Act 1944, under which religious instruction was in fact the only compulsory school subject. They were tightened up under the Education Reform Act 1988, although mostly to mollify religious leaders who were concerned that the introduction of the National Curriculum with its prescribed content would marginalise religious education and hasten the 'slide towards secularism'.[509] As noted above, religious education was specified as an element of the 'basic curriculum' to be provided in state schools.[510] Indeed, it should extend beyond the age of 16, although in practice provision for this age group is poor and many schools fail to meet their legal obligation.[511] It has not been included within the National Curriculum, partly because it is not suitable for prescription by the Secretary of State in the same way as the various secular subjects, but also because parents have a right to withdraw their child from it 'and it was felt that it would be inappropriate to introduce this complication into the newly prescribed list of subjects'.[512]

Notwithstanding its inclusion within the statutory basic curriculum, religious education has tended to become marginalised within the education system. The principal reasons are the absence of prescribed attainment targets for religious education (although there is now non-statutory framework guidance[513]); the partly separate inspection arrangements for that subject;[514] and the dominance of the National Curriculum and the demands and pressures it places upon schools. It has been claimed that some head teachers do not take the subject seriously.[515] While the 'spiritual' development of pupils was identified as a function of state education under the Education Act 1944,[516] continues to be so,[517] and is one of the matters on which the Chief Inspector of Schools has always had to report to the Secretary of State,[518] it has had a lower profile than

---

[508] SSFA 1998, ss 69 and 70; EA 2002, ss 80 and 101.

[509] S Maclure, *Education Re-formed* (London, Hodder and Stoughton, 1988) 17.

[510] See now EA 2002, ss 80 and 101.

[511] See QCA, *Religious Education and Collective Worship. An Analysis of 2003 SACRE Reports* (London, QCA, 2004), available at www.qca.org.uk/15093.html, 3.

[512] Maclure, n 509 above, 17.

[513] DfES, *Religious Education: The Non-statutory National Framework* (London, DfES, 2004).

[514] Initially under the Education (Schools) Act 1992, s 13, later consolidated within the School Inspections Act 1996, s 23 and now in the Education Act 2005, ss 47–50. 'Denominational education' is distinguished from religious education provided under an 'agreed syllabus', which is used in all community schools and some voluntary controlled schools. Denominational education, typically found in voluntary aided schools, is to be inspected by inspectors hired by the schools (the 2005 Act requires the governors first to consult with a prescribed person) rather than by registered inspectors hired by Ofsted. The minister said that '[r]eligious education in Church schools has been subject to different arrangements for over 150 years . . . It would have been a very great break with that long-standing agreement to have required Church schools to use secular registered inspectors for the inspection of their own denominational provision': HL Debs, Vol 536, Col 684, 2 Mar 1992.

[515] Children's Legal Centre, 'Religious Education: A Non-statutory National Framework', *Childright* No 212 (Dec 2004), 18.

[516] Being something towards which a local education authority was under a duty to contribute: EA 1944, s 7.

[517] EA 1996, s 13 (the LEA's duty); EA 2002, ss 78 and 99 (matters that the school curriculum must promote in respect of pupil's and society's development).

[518] EA 2005, ss 2(1)(e) and 20(1)(e).

other aspects of the school curriculum, particularly in secondary schools. Indeed, in his 1995–6 annual report on schools, the Chief Inspector of Schools, referring to pupils' spiritual, moral, physical and cultural development, commented that '[p]upils' spiritual development . . . remains problematic for most schools and this is often the least satisfactory of the four areas of development'.[519] Primary school provision of religious education has consistently been more effective than that made by secondary schools, however, as the Ofsted subject report in 2004–5 confirms.[520] What also emerges from that report is that religious education plays an important role in developing value systems: it was found to make 'a considerably better contribution to pupils' spiritual, moral, social and cultural development than any other subject'.[521] The issues that are covered in religious education in many schools, highlighted below, show why this broader role for religious education has developed. Indeed, that role is set to expand further under the non-statutory framework guidance published by the Government in October 2004, which emphasises the contribution that religious education can make, not only to the four types of personal development noted above, but also to citizenship, PSHE (personal, social and health education), key skills and the connection between beliefs, values and the arts.[522] Importantly, the framework seeks to encourage a thoughtful and reflective approach to religion, religious belief and diversity of faiths, as well as to absence of faith. The subject report shows that, overall, religious education has improved from its position of being one of the weakest subjects in the curriculum in the 1990s. It has also become more popular at key stage 4, with 20,000 more pupils taking a GCSE in religious studies in 2004 than there were in 1997; A level entries in the subject also rose, by 3,000, over this period.[523] Girls outnumber boys among candidates, particularly (by more than 2:1) at AS and A level.[524] What is not clear from the report is how far this growth in popularity in religious education is spread evenly across all faith groups represented among pupils.

The law on religious education and collective worship is complex and is spread across three separate Acts of Parliament.

Religious Education

The Education Act 1944 provided for an 'agreed syllabus' for religious education to be drawn up for the area, and this continues to be the case under the current legislation.[525] This syllabus is to be followed by community schools and by

---

[519] Office for Standards in Education, *The Annual Report of Her Majesty's Chief Inspector of Schools 1995/96* (London, TSO, 1997), para 86.

[520] Ofsted, *The Annual Report of Her Majesty's Chief Inspector of Schools 2004/05. Religious Education in Secondary Schools* (London, Ofsted, 2005).

[521] Ibid.

[522] DfES, *Religious Education: The Non-Statutory National Framework* (London, DFES, 2004).

[523] Ibid, 3.

[524] See QCA, *Religious Education and Collective Worship. An Analysis of 2003 SCARE Reports* (London, QCA, 2004), available at www.qca.org.uk/15093.html, App 2.

[525] Schools Standards and Framework Act 1998, Sched 19.

foundation and voluntary schools which have not been designated as having a religious character. Foundation and voluntary controlled schools which do have a religious character are also to follow the agreed syllabus, save in the case of children whose parents who want their child to be taught in accordance with the trust deed or the tenets of the religious denomination concerned.[526] The reverse is true in the case of voluntary aided schools with a religious character; in other words, the assumption is that the pupils will be taught religious education that accords with the school's trust deed or its denomination, but parents can opt for the agreed syllabus to be followed in relation to their child.[527]

The agreed syllabus is to be drawn up by a local conference of representatives. Under the Education Reform Act 1988, there was in effect a transition period running from 1988 to 1994 during which all existing syllabuses had to be reconsidered by the local conference.[528] Any new syllabuses must now be drawn up by, and may, at the instigation of the LEA, be reconsidered by, the conference.[529] The conference is to comprise persons representing various groups:

(i) Christian and other denominations that, in the opinion of the LEA, 'will appropriately reflect the principal religious traditions in the area';
(ii) representatives of the Church of England, in England only;
(iii) teaching association representatives; and
(iv) LEA representatives.[530]

The conference is distinct from the local standing advisory council on religious education (SACRE) which, inter alia, advises the LEA on the agreed syllabus. Any of the SACRE's representative groups[531] (apart for the LEA group) may require a review of the agreed syllabus to be carried out by the conference.[532]

The 1988 Act introduced the requirement, still in force, that '[e]very agreed syllabus shall reflect the fact that the religious traditions in Great Britain are in the main Christian whilst taking account of the teaching and practices of the other principal religions represented in Great Britain'.[533] This wording was and remains curious, since it appears to represent an attempt to justify on some factual basis the emphasis the law is placing on Christianity. Cooper argues that the specific promotion of Christianity as a result of the ERA 1988 reflected a general attempt by the Christian Right and conservatives to castigate multi-culturalism as jeopardising a sense of English culture and Christian identity.[534]

---

[526] Ibid, para 3.

[527] Ibid, para 4.

[528] EA 1996, Sched 31; The Education Act 1993, s 254, reinforced this by requiring the conference to be reconvened within 6 months of the coming into force of the section.

[529] EA 1996, s 375 and Sched 31.

[530] Ibid, Sched 31 para 4.

[531] There are to be four of these groups, corresponding exactly with the categories that apply in respect of the local conference: EA 1996, s 390(4).

[532] Ibid, s 391.

[533] Education Reform Act 1988, s 8(3). See now EA 1996, s 375(3).

[534] D Cooper, *Governing Out of Order. Space, Law and the Politics of Belonging* (London, Rivers Oram Press, 1998) 50–71.

However, the Government's guidance in 1994 suggested that while Christianity should 'predominate', there should be coverage of other religions as well.[535] Essentially though, this was and remains a matter for local interpretation. The non-statutory guidance issued in 2004 adopts a theme of 'learning about religion', which 'covers pupils' knowledge and understanding of individual religions and how they relate to each other as well as the study of the nature and characteristics of religion'.[536] Given that the leaders of Buddhist, Christian, Hindu, Jewish, Muslim and Sikh faiths signed a joint statement in February 2006 backing teaching about other faiths and committing faith schools to using the non-statutory guidance, which at key stages 2 and 3 prescribes knowledge, skills and understanding of not only Christianity but at also at least two other religions and the projection of a 'secular world view, where appropriate', the emphasis on a more ecumenical approach is reinforced. Yet, as the non-statutory guidance itself acknowledges, the extent to which the recommended approach is applied will remain a matter for local conferences and for local faith communities and schools.[537] Whether the joint statement might pave the way for conversion of the guidance into statutory guidance remains to be seen.

Parents may withdraw their children from religious education at a school and may have their children receive a particular form of such education away from the school premises but during school hours (provided it is at the beginning or end of a school session).[538] This applies not only to community schools but also foundation and voluntary schools. It may noted that in 2005 some of the trustees of an independent Islamic school in Brent sought unsuccessfully in the High Court to prevent the school's conversion to voluntary aided status, partly out of concern that the right of withdrawal would apply and it would be possible for parents to require that their children were 'not given an education in accordance with the tenets of the particular religion, that is, in this case, Islam'.[539] The action failed essentially because the relevant statutory procedures for conversion were held to have been properly operated and the court could find no legal basis, such as irrationality, for intervention. The right of withdrawal may have renewed significance in relation to voluntary schools, given the fact that the Government is keen to see admission to such schools not entirely restricted to children of the religion on which the schools is founded.

The element of choice provided for by the statutory right of withdrawal reflects the right of parents to determine their child's religion and religious upbringing as a facet of parental responsibility.[540] Any dispute between individual holders of parental responsibility in relation to a child would have to

---

[535] Department for Education, *Religious Education and Collective Worship*, Circular 1/94 (London, DfE, 1994), para 35.

[536] DfES, *Religious Education: The Non-Statutory National Framework* (London, DFES, 2004) 10.

[537] Ibid, 10.

[538] SSFA 1998, s 71(1), (3), (4).

[539] *R (London Borough of Brent) v FED2000 and Others* [2005] EWHC Admin 2679, [2006] ELR 169 (QBD), para 8.

[540] For the purposes of the Children Act 1989, s 3(1). See *Re J (Child's religious upbringing and circumcision)* [1999] 2 FCR 345, per Wall J at 353; R White, P Carr and N Lowe, *The Children Act in Practice* (3rd edn, London, Butterworths LexisNexis, 2002), para 3.18.

be resolved within the Children Act 1989 framework.[541] As regards the child's position, recent research suggests that even pre-teenage children are capable of forming their own coherent views on issues of religion affecting them and recommends that adults responsible for children's religious socialisation should listen to them.[542] But there is a potential conflict between the child's rights and those of the parent in this context. While children's right to freedom of thought, conscience and religion is protected by Article 14 of the UNCRC,[543] states parties are required to 'respect the rights and duties of the parents and, when applicable, legal guardians, to provide direction to the child in the exercise of his or her right in a manner consistent with the evolving capacities of the child'.[544] While there is some recognition of children's independence over this matter in the light of their 'evolving capacities', parents are effectively able to choose their child's religion; and the right of withdrawal from religious education may be consistent with that position, even though there is an inconsistency with Articles 12 and 13, which concern the child's right to express his or her views and be heard in relation to various matters.[545] It is also consistent with the obligations of the state under the second sentence of Article 2 of Protocol 1 to the ECHR to respect the right of parents to ensure the teaching of the child in accordance with the parents' religious and philosophical convictions[546] (and the comparable right within Article 13(3) of the International Covenant on Economic, Social and Cultural Rights[547]); and with the protection from encroachment on religious freedom for the purposes of Article 9.[548] Barry argues that 'the parents' freedom of religion is deployed as a cloak for the exertion of power over their children'.[549] But children also have rights under Article 9[550] and so there is a potential conflict between that right and the parents' right under Article 2 of Protocol 1 which, as Lundy explains, has not yet been judicially considered.[551]

---

[541] Children Act 1989 ss 8, 10. As would also be the case with disputes over withdrawal from sex education (discussed below): see A Bainham, 'Sex Education: a Family Lawyer's Perspective' in N Harris (ed), *Children, Sex Education and the Law: Examining the Issues* (London, National Children's Bureau, 1996) 24 at 34–6.

[542] G Smith, *Children's Perspectives on Believing and Belonging* (London, National Children's Bureau, 2005) 67.

[543] UNCRC, Art 14.(1).

[544] Ibid, Art 14(2).

[545] J Fortin, *Children's Rights and the Developing Law* (2nd edn, London, LexisNexis, 2003) 42 and 346–7.

[546] See Chap 2, especially pp 67, 72–5. See also J Fortin, n 545 above, 356; U Kilkelly, *The Child and the European Conventionon Human Rights* (Aldershot, Ashgate, 1999) 73.

[547] See UN Committee on Economic, Social and Cultural Rights, *General Comment 13. The Right to Education (Article 13 of the Covenant)*, E/C12/1999/10 (General Comments), para 28.

[548] See *Hoffman v Austria* (1993) 17 EHRR 293.

[549] B Barry, *Culture and Equality* (Cambridge, Polity, 2001) 201.

[550] See in this context *CJ, JJ and EJ v Poland*, App no 23380/94, Commission on Human Rights, where the Commission considered independently both the father's and his two children's claims that a breach of Art 9 occurred as a result of the way that the school handled the withdrawal of the children from religious instruction, and in particular how the school recorded matters in the children's school reports. The claims were deemed inadmissible, but the Commission reaffirmed the authority of the state to require a course in religious knowledge provided certain exemptions were granted.

[551] L Lundy, 'Family Values in the Classroom? Reconciling Parental Wishes and Children's Rights in State Schools' (2005) 19 *International Journal of Law, Policy and the Family* 346 at 358–9.

Further potential problems with the right of withdrawal are, first, that its exercise is potentially stigmatising and exclusionary for children and their families, as research in Ireland (where a similar rights exists) has shown,[552] and as the Ontario Court of Appeal noted in a case in which the Canadian Charter of Rights and Freedoms was held to have been infringed by various prescribed religious practices within the curriculum, notwithstanding the right of withdrawal.[553] Another difficulty is that the lack of a specific obligation on the school to make alternative arrangements could be discriminatory against religious minorities, although the cost implications of making separate alternative provision for every faith might be raised in justification.[554] However, common alternative arrangements for all opted-out pupils are often made in denominational schools that cater for other faiths. They might take the form of moral education or cover the study of the history of religion or ethics. Such an arrangement in Finland, which was compulsory, although parents had a right to withdraw their children from it, was held by the Human Rights Committee to uphold religious freedom for the purposes of the Universal Declaration of Human Rights[555] provided it was 'given in a neutral and objective way and respects convictions of parents and guardians who do not believe in any religion'.[556]

A further problem with the right of withdrawal arises where religious education forms part of a broader subject that includes moral/ethical and religious education, as was introduced in Norway in 1997. The law there permitted exemption from parts of the teaching that comprised religious activities, although not religious knowledge. The subject, known as the CKREE, included religious practice, such as learning prayers, in addition to the imparting of religious knowledge. Some humanist parents and their children complained, inter alia, that the arrangements were not compatible with Article 18 of the International Covenant on Civil and Political Rights, which contains a similar guarantee of religious freedom to that in Article 9 of the ECHR, and also requires states parties to 'undertake to have respect for the liberty of parents and, when applicable, legal guardians to ensure the religious and moral education of their children in conformity with their own convictions'.[557] The Human Rights Committee concluded, inter alia, that the Norwegian opt out was impracticable as it imposed 'a considerable burden' on persons in the complainants' position 'insofar as it requires them to acquaint themselves with those aspects of the

---

[552] A Mawhinney, 'The Irish Primary Education System: a Neglect of Human Rights', paper presented at the Socio-Legal Studies Association Annual Conference, University of Liverpool, 31 Mar 2005; Idem, 'The Opt-out Clause: Imperfect Protection for the Right to Freedom of Religion in Schools' (2006) 7 *Education Law Journal* 102.

[553] *Re Zylberberg et al v Director of Education of Sudbury Board of Education; League for Human Rights of B'nai Brith Canada et al, Intervenors* (1988), 65 OR (2d) 641; (1988) 52 DLR (4th) 577.

[554] P Cumper, 'School Worship: Praying for Guidance' (1998) EHRLR 45 at 52.

[555] UDHR, Art 18.

[556] *Erkki Hartikainen v Finland*, Communication No 40/1978, UN Doc CCPR/C/OP/1 at 74 (1984), para 10.4. See further *Erkki Hartikainen v Finland*, Communication No 40/1978 (20 June 1983), UN Doc Supp No 40 (A/38/40) at 255 (1983) (response from Finland on views). See also H Cullen, 'Education Rights or Minority Rights?' (1993) 7 *International Journal of Law, Policy and the Family* 143.

[557] ICCPR, Art 18(4).

subject which are clearly of a religious nature, as well as with other aspects, with a view to determining which of the other aspects they may feel a need to seek—and justify—exemption from'; and withdrawing children from part of the teaching would cause difficulties which would deter people from exercising their opt out right.[558] Consequently, 'the system of exemptions does not currently protect the liberty of parents to ensure that the religious and moral education of their children is in conformity with their own convictions'.[559] The fact that the parents had to give reasons for withdrawal, which created a further obstacle for them, and that children experienced a conflict of loyalty when the right was exercised, were other factors in the ruling.[560]

Collective Worship

Parents have also long held a right to withdraw their child from collective worship at school and, as with the corresponding right in relation to religious education, it is unconditional and no reasons will have to be provided.[561] There is only limited evidence on the utilisation of this right; it shows that less than 1 per cent of secondary school parents had exercised it.[562] One recent survey suggests that a propensity to withdraw children might vary across different religions: it was found in one Roman Catholic school that most Muslim children were withdrawn from Christian acts of collective worship but almost all Hindu children participated in it.[563] The extent to which parents may feel any objection to collective worship may depend upon the particular religious emphasis placed within it. In its requirement for a daily act of collective worship in schools the ERA 1988 adopted a broadly Christian emphasis, which continues, as is also found in the requirement on religious education.[564] There must be a single act for the whole school or separate acts for different school groups or age groups,[565] which should generally be 'wholly or mainly of a broadly Christian character', in that it/they should reflect 'the broad traditions of Christian belief without being distinctive of any particular Christian denomination'.[566] The requirement as to

---

[558] UN Human Rights Committee, Communication No 1155/2003: Norway, 23 Nov 2004. CCPR/C/82D/1155/2003 (Jurisprudence), *Views of the Human Rights Committee under the Optional Protocol to the International Covenant on Civil and Political Rights* (2004), para 14.6.

[559] Ibid.

[560] Ibid, para 14.7.

[561] SSFA 1998, s 71. Previously EA 1944, s 25, re-enacted in ERA 1988, s 9(3). But note that sixth formers will be given a right to withdraw themselves from such worship, under the Education and Inspections Bill 2006 (new clause, to amend SSFA 1998 s 71).

[562] Office of HM Chief Inspector of Schools/OFSTED, *Religious Education and Collective Worship 1992–93* (London, HMSO, 1994), para 42.

[563] G Smith, *Children's Perspectives on Believing and Belonging* (London, National Children's Bureau, 2005) 34.

[564] See now SSFA 1998, s 70. The requirement that the act be at the start of the school day, in EA 1944 s 25, was lifted when the ERA 1988 came into force.

[565] SSFA 1998, Sched 20 para 2.

[566] ERA 1988, s 7, now found in the SSFA 1998, Sched 20. This also provides that from time to time acts of collective worship do not have to comply with the above requirements, provided most of them do. Generally the act of collective worship is to take place on the school premises; the governors can, if they consider it desirable, make appropriate arrangements for it to take place elsewhere 'on a special occasion' : ibid, para 2(6).

Christian collective worship applies to community schools and in foundation schools without a religious character, except that the local SACRE may grant an application by the head teacher that it is not appropriate for it to apply in the case of his or her school, or in the case of any class or description of pupils.[567] This enables the SACRE, which also advises the LEA on religious worship in community schools, to modify or lift the Christian collective worship requirement in response to an application by a school where, for example, the school has many non-Christians. Indeed the SACRE is required, when considering the head teacher's application, to have regard to 'any circumstances relating to the family backgrounds of pupils'.[568] Although annual figures show only a small number of new determinations on this issue by SACREs (for example, just 31 in 2003, many of which were renewals of previous arrangements), they give no indication of how many modifications or departures may already be in operation across the country.[569] However, the fact that the DfES interprets 'wholly or mainly' in the statute to mean that it would be sufficient if 51 per cent of the acts of worship are Christian and 49 per cent of them concentrate on other faiths[570] means that many schools would not regard it as necessary to make an application. In voluntary schools the character and content of collective worship are determined by governing bodies and/or trust deeds.[571]

The same argument concerning discrimination that has been raised in relation to the required Christian emphasis within religious education has been made in relation to the law on collective worship, although it has been argued that '[t]he majority status of Christianity and the cost to the state if it had to provide a comprehensive range of alternative forms of collective worship' might satisfy the test of 'reasonable and objective justification' to discrimination for the purposes of Article 14.[572] However, as noted above, exemptions from the requirement for Christian collective worship may be granted, in relation to individual schools, by the SACRE.[573] Such an exemption can be granted only at the behest of the head teacher rather than the parents. Indeed, when (as the statute requires) the head teacher first consults with the governing body, the latter only has a discretion (but not a duty) to consult parents.[574] Not least in view of the applicable human rights obligations plus the general tenor of the

---

[567] SSFA 1998, Sched 20, paras 1–4. The application is made under EA 1996, s 394, as amended by the SSFA 1998, Sched 30, para 97. A dis-application decision must be reviewed within 5 years: (EA 1996, s 395). The head teacher must consult with the governing body before making an application: s 394(5).

[568] EA 1996, s 394(2).

[569] See QCA, *Religious Education and Collective Worship. An Analysis of 2003 SACRE Reports* (London, QCA, 2004), available at www.qca.org.uk/15093.html, 20.

[570] www.teachernet.gov.uk/management/atoz/c/collectiveworship/index.cfm?code=main.

[571] SSFA 1998, Sched 20, para 5.

[572] R Adhar and I Leigh, *Religious Freedom in the Liberal State* (Oxford, OUP, 2005) 242.

[573] See generally S Poulter, 'The Religious Education Provisions of the Education Reform Act 1988', (1990) 2 *Education and the Law* 1–11; A Bradney, 'Christian Worship?' (1996) 8 *Education and the Law* 127; C Hamilton and B Watt, 'A Discriminating Education—Collective Worship in Schools' (1996) 8 *Child & Family Law Quarterly* 28; C Hamilton, 'Freedom of Religion and Religious Worship in Schools' in J De Groof and J Fiers (eds), *The Legal Status of Minorities in Education* (Leuven, ACCO, 1996) 165; P Cumper, 'School Worship: Praying for Guidance' [1998] EHRLR 45.

[574] EA 1996, s 394(6).

legislation, it would seem arguable that a failure by a governing body to consult with parents over such an issue, including taking into account their views, would make the matter judicially reviewable. Notwithstanding the fact that parents' rights have been allowed to eclipse children's over the matter of religion in education, there should also be consultation with children, in view of the general statutory duty concerning consultation with them.[575]

The term 'worship' is not defined but clearly imports some form of devotional activity. It would, moreover, probably be considered contrary to the spirit, tradition and intention of this provision for such devotion to be other than religious or spiritual in nature. The official guidance has long stressed the association to be made with reverence or veneration of a divine being or power.[576] However, even with the emphasis that the legislation places on Christian belief, that does not necessarily mean that Christ has to be the specific object of the worship, even where no application to modify or lift the requirement in relation to the school has been granted. As we have seen, the acts have to be only 'broadly Christian' and reflect the 'broad traditions' of Christianity. This matter was considered by the High Court in *R v Secretary of State for Education ex parte R and D*,[577] where parents argued, inter alia, that the Secretary of State had wrongly rejected their complaints that the pupils at the school were not practising worship and/or that the school's multi-faith worship was illegal as it was not broadly Christian. McCullough J explained, first, that 'act of collective worship' in the statute referred to the 'totality of events' when pupils were assembled, 'rather than each of the successive incidents' which took place.[578] With regard to the act of worship, the Secretary of State had indicted that what was required was reverence or veneration of a divine or supernatural power. But the complainants contended that to meet the statutory requirement the power had to be identified as God, of a broadly Christian character. The Secretary of State had said that it was not necessary to make such identification, but the court considered that he had indicated separately his satisfaction that on most occasions the object of worship at the school was God of a broadly Christian character.[579] The court accepted that the Secretary of State had been entitled to take this view, given that the prayers given 'reflected Christian sentiments' and that in any event not all Christian prayers mention Christ or the Trinity by name.[580] Moreover, the Christian character of the act of worship 'would not be lost by the inclusion of elements common to Christianity and to one or more other religions'.[581] That judgment therefore helped to clarify the position, and while it would not have satisfied all the critics of the Christian emphasis placed by the law, it supported the broader, inclusive approach adopted in many schools.

---

[575] EA 2002, s 176, discussed at pp 58–60 above.

[576] Department for Education, *Religious Education and Collective Worship*, Circular 1/94 (London, DfE, 1994). This guidance is still in force, but is supplemented by information on the "teachernet" website at www.teachernet.gov.uk/management/atoz/c/collectiveworship/index.cfm?code=main.

[577] [1994] ELR 495.

[578] Ibid, 499D.

[579] Ibid, 501H.

[580] Ibid, 502D–F.

[581] Ibid, 502H.

Some questions remain incompletely resolved, however. For example, if the law requires an act of *collective* worship, does that preclude *individual* forms of worship, albeit in a communal setting? If the head teacher decided to incorporate a period of private prayer or contemplation within a school assembly, would that meet the statutory requirement regarding collective worship? Meditation is a practised activity within many religions, but is it worship, and sufficiently within the broad traditions of Christianity?

The questions would become academic if the view of the (now former) Chief Inspector of Schools, David Bell, held sway. Mr Bell has argued that the requirement for an act of worship should be abolished as it is out of step with an increasingly secular society. It seems very unlikely that its abolition would infringe human rights under the ECHR, although it would be interesting to see how a court might determine whether collective worship is a facet of 'education' for the purposes of Article 2 of Protocol 1. Even on the basis that it is, there appears to be no obligation under the ECHR for the state, through the education system, to provide for collective worship in schools.[582] Cultural diversity makes it increasingly difficult, at least in the context of religious worship, to strike the kind of appropriate balance between individual/groups rights and the wider collective interest that some advocate in relation to education.[583] The abolition of collective worship might offer the only effective means to greater religious neutrality and end complaints of discrimination within the current law, although if schools chose to continue with collective worship they would have to be even more careful, in the absence of a statutory framework. Given that many schools, indeed a majority, fail to provide a daily act of collective worship—at least 75 per cent of secondary schools in England in 2003–4[584] and 54 per cent in Wales in 2005[585]—it appears to be a classic case of a statutory duty 'honoured in the breach' and a provision that is becoming increasingly nugatory. One of the reasons that collective worship has become so problematic for schools is that many teachers refuse to participate in it. Indeed, the official guidance makes allowance for this by advising that where there are insufficient willing teachers the head teacher must take steps to find others, including a senior pupil, who are not employed at the school to undertake the task of leading collective worship.[586] In most state schools teachers have the right to refuse to take part in collective

---

[582] See A Blair and W Aps, 'What Not to Wear and Other Stories: Addressing Religious Diversity in Schools' (2005) 17 *Education & the Law* 1 at 5.

[583] See, eg, A Blair, 'Negotiating Conflicting Values: the Role of Law in Educating for Values in England and Wales', (2002) 14 *Education & the Law* 39 at 52–3.

[584] Ofsted, *The Annual Report of Her Majesty's Chief Inspector of Schools 2003/04* (London, TSO, 2005), para 123. (Collective worship is not reported on in the annual report for 2004/05.) This is precisely the same figure as that given for 1995/96: Ofsted, *The Annual Report of Her Majesty's Chief Inspector of Schools: Standards and Quality in Education 1995/96* (London, TSO, 1997), para 86. The evidence from SACREs is that up to 100 per cent of secondary schools may be failing fully to meet the requirement: QCA, *Religious Education and Collective Worship. An Analysis of 2003 SACRE Reports*, available at www.qca.org.uk/15093.html.

[585] BBC survey, covering 149 secondary schools, available at http://news.bbc.co.uk/1/hi/wales/4552382.stm.

[586] Department for Education, *Religious Education and Collective Worship*, Circular 1/94 (London, DfE, 1994), paras 146–148. The head teacher is advised by the guidance to take advice from the LEA or SACRE where appropriate.

worship or to teach religious education, without suffering any damage to their employment status and without discrimination in terms of pay or promotion.[587] They also enjoy special statutory protection (additional to that under general discrimination or human rights law) against disqualification from being a teacher on the grounds of their religious opinions or for attending or not attending religious worship.[588]

THE INDEPENDENT SCHOOLS SECTOR

The anomaly resulting from the exemption of independent schools from the general statutory requirements on the curriculum, noted above, continues notwithstanding the introduction of prescribed standards for independent schools under the Education Act 2002, Part 10. These standards are part of the process of tightening up on the independent sector in the face of evidence that 'the . . . system of registration, deriving largely from the 1944 Act, has not done enough to force [the worst independent] schools to improve, or close'.[589] The prescribed standards partly concern the curriculum, although they also cover matters such as premises and accommodation, pupil welfare, pupil development, the suitability of proprietors, and the handling of complaints.[590] A school proposing unsuitable provision could be refused registration by the Secretary of State or, in Wales, the National Assembly (the maximum penalty for running an unregistered school is a £5,000 fine, up to six months in prison, or both), while its failure to meet the prescribed standards could lead to immediate removal from the register if there were a risk of serious harm to pupils or if the required remedial work were not carried out in a timely fashion.[591] However, so far as education and the curriculum are concerned, what characterises the prescribed standards is their generality and lack of detailed specificity, certainly compared with the National Curriculum (see below). When introducing these standards the Government committed itself to 'minimise regulation', so that areas such as the spiritual, moral, social and cultural development of pupils would be matters for schools (and indirectly parents, through choice of school) so long as the aim was that pupils, on leaving school, would be 'likely to become well adjusted citizens'.[592]

---

[587] EA 1996, s 146; previously EA 1944, s 30. 'Reserved teachers'—those employed in denominational schools as teachers of religion (see SSFA 1998, s 58)—are excepted from this protection.

[588] See *Ahman v Inner London Education Authority* [1978] QB 36.

[589] D Bell HMCI, 'Standards and Inspections in Independent Schools', Address to the Brighton College Conference on Independent Schools, 29 Apr 2003.

[590] The Education (Independent School Standards) (England) Regulations 2003 (SI 2003/1910) and the Independent School Standards (Wales) Regulations 2003 (SI 2003/3234 (W314)), made pursuant to the Education Act 2002, s 157.

[591] EA 2002, s 165. Appeals in respect of registration and other decisions lie to a tribunal established under the 1999 Protection of Children Act: EA 2002, ss 166 and 167.

[592] DfES, *Draft Regulations for Registration and Monitoring of Independent Schools* (London, DfES, 2001), 4.

The curriculum in independent schools has been a subject of concern, particularly in some schools operated by religious bodies.[593] For example, a report by Ofsted in 2003, based on the inspection of independent schools by the Independent Schools Council (which had responsibility for inspections of many of these schools), commented:

> In a minority of independent schools with a religious basis there is still insufficient time allocated to the secular curriculum and the balance is unsatisfactory. Many of these schools have a pattern of religious studies in the morning, with a secular curriculum delivered in as little as two hours in the afternoon and with limited learning resources. The creative and aesthetic areas of the curriculum are often poorly represented.[594]

In the past, these kinds of curricular regimes largely escaped interference, save where the Secretary of State was under a duty to serve a notice of complaint on the proprietor because, inter alia, 'efficient and suitable instruction is not being provided at the school having regard to the ages and sex of the pupils attending it'.[595] The difficulty was that although there was non-statutory guidance for inspectors, there was no prescribed curriculum content for these schools, or even broad aims, set out in law. Moreover, judicial guidance was extremely limited. The judgment in the one case of significance, *R v Secretary of State for Education and Science ex parte Talmud Torah Machzikei Hadass School Trust*,[596] could, however, have continuing relevance, since the central issue in relation to the suitability of religious independent schools continues to be the balance, in the education of the children who attend them, between the twin aims of preparing the children for life within their own particular faith community and equipping them for later life in wider society.

The fact that parents have chosen to send their children to such schools, often at some expense, means that the religious ethos and values of the school are likely to be very important to them. They see them as a means of preserving the integrity and values of their particular faith community and their way of life. In judging the suitability of the Talmud Torah school the Secretary of State therefore needed take account of his duty, when exercising his functions, to have regard to the general principle that children are to be educated in accordance with the wishes of their parents, which has been discussed at various points throughout this book.[597] As Woolf J recognised, that included a duty to have regard to the parents' religious preferences. Indeed, there is the duty under the second sentence

---

[593] See J Fortin, *Children's Rights and the Developing Law* (2nd edn, London, LexisNexis, 2003) 347–53.

[594] Office for Standards in Education, *Annual Report of Her Majesty's Chief Inspector of Schools: Standards and Quality in Education 2001/02* (London, Ofsted, 2003), para 445.

[595] Education Act 1996, s 469(1)(e). The other grounds (in subs (1)) related to the unsuitability of the premises, the inadequacy or unsuitability of the accommodation, the proprietor's or any teacher's unfitness for their role (not being a 'proper person' to undertake it), or failures for the purposes of the Children Act 1989 concerning the welfare of a child boarding at the school.

[596] *The Times*, 12 Apr 1985, also reported in LexisNexis. See p 443 below.

[597] EA 1996, s 9.

of ECHR, Article 2 of Protocol 1 (A2P1), to ensure that the right of parents to ensure the teaching of their children in accordance with the parents' religious and philosophical convictions, a duty which, as we saw in Chapter 2, supports the right of religious and other groups to found private schools. Indeed, more recently in *Costello-Roberts v UK* the European Court of Human Rights has confirmed that the 'fundamental right of everyone to education is a right guaranteed equally to pupils in State and independent schools, no distinction being made within the two' and that other Convention rights might be engaged in independent school education.[598] Articles 3 (freedom from torture or inhuman or degrading treatment) and 8 (right to privacy and family life) were specifically mentioned, but others such as Article 9 (freedom of religion) may also be applicable.

Although the Convention was not enforceable in the UK courts at the time of the *Talmud Torah* case, the duty in the second sentence of A2P1 was nevertheless referred to by Woolf J in his judgment. In any event, Woolf J accepted that the Secretary of State was 'perfectly entitled to have a policy setting down a minimum requirement which he will normally apply to all schools irrespective of the background of the children sent to that school'. As regards the central question whether the education provided at this Hasidic school was suitable, therefore, it was held that the school might meet this requirement by primarily equipping the pupils for a place in their own particular religious community, as opposed to the wider community, provided they were left with the capacity to choose some other way of life later on. The court in fact rejected the assertion that the Secretary of State had acted unlawfully in making a notice of complaint. Nevertheless, Woolf J was disapproving of the specification of a minimum number of hours for secular subjects. He also considered that the Secretary of State should not have expected that music and drama would be part of the curriculum, as 'drama is not acceptable to the community on religious grounds and instrumental music is only tolerated on special occasions, such as weddings'. Still, the overriding message of the decision is that total or substantial exclusion of the secular curriculum found in other schools, state or private, was likely to render the education unsuitable because the curriculum should enable students from all religious minority backgrounds to participate in wider society.

Henricson and Bainham doubt the conduciveness of religious schools to 'providing children with open futures',[599] but this basic test of suitability is still being applied by inspectors, as happened when another Jewish school was inspected after the 2002 Act came into force.[600] But in addition there are now various prescribed elements to the curriculum that set benchmarks, although somewhat vague and generalistic ones, for the aims and content of independent schools' curricula. Provision must 'give pupils experience in linguistic, mathematical, scientific, technological, human and social, physical and aesthetic

---

[598] Case No 89/1991/341/414 [1994] ELR 1, at paras 27–28.

[599] C Henricson and A Bainham, *The Child and Family Policy Divide. Tensions, Convergence and Rights* (York, Joseph Rowntree Foundation, 2005) 79.

[600] Office for Standards in Education, *Akiva School*, inspection report, 28 Jan 2004, available at www.ofsted.gov.uk/reports/manreports/1430.htm.

and creative education'; be appropriate to the age and aptitude of pupils (including those with special educational needs statements); provide for pupils to 'acquire skills in speaking and listening, literacy and numeracy'; offer careers guidance; and (like the curriculum for state schools: above) prepare pupils for the 'opportunities, responsibilities and experiences of adult life'.[601] Even more bland is the requirement that the curriculum provide for 'all pupils to have the opportunity to learn and make progress'.[602] Broad objectives are specified for teaching, such as enabling pupils to 'acquire new knowledge' and 'increase their understanding' via 'well planned lessons'.[603] Parents have a contractual right to expect that the education provided meets their reasonable expectations as regards the values, curriculum and approach in education offered by the school and to a reasonable standard of education.[604] The last of these will clearly be easier to test in relation to preparation for public examinations such as GCSE or A level than in respect of the rather vague standards prescribed by the regulations.[605]

Where are the aims of tolerance and respect for others and other moral values that are important, given the cultural diversity of the wider society that schools may be expected to play a key role in preparing pupils for life within? In fact, there is limited provision in that regard. There is a broad framework for the spiritual, moral, social and cultural development of pupils[606] that includes not only encouraging responsible behaviour and helping pupils to distinguish right from wrong, but also inculcating 'an appreciation of and respect for their own and other cultures in a way that promotes tolerance and harmony between different cultural traditions'. But that does not in itself reflect the broad standard in Woolf J's dictum of preparing pupils to adopt, in later life and by choice, a way of life that is different from the traditions of their own particular faith or cultural community. However, there is a reference within the prescribed standards to the need to 'provide pupils with a broad general knowledge of public institutions and services in England'. There is also a requirement that pupils be shown 'how they can contribute to community life', but as 'community' could be construed narrowly this does not necessarily safeguard against an insular approach. The prescribed standards are also tolerant of the principal language of instruction being other than English, provided pupils are give lessons in written or spoken English.[607] In apparent recognition of the sensibilities of minority groups on the subject of sex education, it is not specifically mentioned; instead, there is a duty to provide 'personal, social and health education which reflects the school's aims and ethos'. Given the current concerns over young people's sexual health and the

---

[601] SI 2003/1910, n 590, Sched, para 1(2).

[602] Ibid.

[603] Ibid, para 1(3).

[604] *Mount v Oldham Corporation* [1973] 1 QB 309 (CA); *Price v Dennis*, 29 Jan 1988 (CA).

[605] See *Buckingham et al v Rycotewood College*, Warwick Crown Court, 28 Feb 2003; and G Hackett, 'Private school pays out for poor teaching', *The Sunday Times*, 10 Nov 2002, reporting an out-of-court settlement of £30,000 in a case where it was alleged that poor teaching of Latin A level resulted in a much lower pass than might reasonably have been expected and thereby reduced a girl's employment prospects.

[606] N 590 above, Sched, para 2.

[607] See below, including the exception to this requirement where the school provides education for pupils who are temporarily resident in England.

risks to it, discussed above, this seems to be a serious omission. The way that the law balances the rights of young people and their parents, including those from minority ethnic or religious groups, over questions relating to sex education was considered earlier.

So far as language is concerned, the prescribed standards include a requirement that the school must have and implement effectively a written policy on the curriculum and appropriate plans and schemes of work which, if the principal language of instruction is a language other than English, must, as noted above, provide for 'lessons in written and spoken English', apart from where the school 'provides education for pupils who are all temporarily resident in England and which follows the curriculum of another country'.[608] So various international schools in England would be exempt from this requirement. Otherwise, all pupils who are mostly not being taught through the medium of English must receive appropriate English language teaching. In Wales, Welsh is added to English for the above purposes.[609]

Overall, therefore, the standards prescribed for independent schools, while going much further than the regulation of the educational provision in non-state schools in much of the rest of Europe,[610] fall some way short of requiring the instillation of common values or culture of the kind that opponents of multiculturalism and supporters of provision leading to a greater sense of common, national identity (above) might advocate. This helps to preserve the distinctive culture and ethos of independent schools, and their freedom, and that of parents, to maintain their religious and cultural traditions through the education of their children. Their right is also associated with basic liberalism that rests on freedom of choice. Of course, while the majority culture has been prepared to surrender a degree of its dominance where children's education is concerned, it continues to able to set limits of acceptability even in the Human Rights Act era, as was illustrated by the *Williamson* case on corporal punishment in independent Christian Fellowship schools;[611] and see also the decision on similar facts of the Constitutional Court in South Africa, where Sachs J (giving the court's judgment) noted that there is an underlying problem in open and democratic societies that seek to respect human dignity, equality and freedom, including religious freedom, namely 'how far such democracy can and must go in allowing members of religious communities to define for themselves which laws they will obey and which not', since 'such a society can cohere only if all its participants accept that certain basic norms and standards are binding'.[612] Indeed, there are some indications that the body responsible for monitoring standards in

---

[608] Education (Independent School Standards) (England) Regulations 2003 (SI 2003/1910), the Sched, para 1(2)(d), made under the Education Act 2002, Part 10.

[609] Independent School Standards (Wales) Regulations 2003 (SI 2003/3234 (W314)), the Sched, paras 1 and 2.

[610] See C Glenn and J De Groof, *Freedom, Autonomy and Accountability in Education* (Vol 2, Utrecht, Lemma, 2002). Portugal and Sweden are noted therein (at 330–1) to include a framework for democratic values to be imparted in non-state schools.

[611] See pp 396–9 above.

[612] *Christian Education South Africa v Minister of Education*, Case CCT 4/00 [2001] 1 LRC 441, at para 35.

independent schools, Ofsted,[613] might under the influence of the previous Chief Inspector, have been keen to see in the independent sector a broader approach to the curriculum, more consistent with that in the state sector.

Recently, the schools run by the Exclusive Brethren, an offshoot of the Plymouth Brethren, have come into the spotlight. They have been largely praised by the Chief Inspector even though this community is one of the most separatist of all the minority faith groups. The Exclusive Brethren keep themselves separate from other people, including other Christians, because they regard the world outside their community as a place of wickedness. There are around 15,000 Exclusive Brethren in Britain.[614] The families do not have televisions, radios or computers and are not permitted to read newspapers or fiction or use mobile phones. There is a strict dress code (for example, women must wear blue or white scarves). Members are not allowed to go to university, as this is considered to expose them to 'unhelpful influences'.[615] Children are often educated within the Brethren community, although some attend mainstream schools. The Focus Learning Trust has been established to maintain Exclusive Brethren schools. There are 31 of these schools, all of which cater for 11–17-year-olds. In most cases they were originally formed from tuition centres where children who were otherwise educated at home were brought together. The schools have offered full-time education since September 2004. The Chief Inspector of Schools presented a largely favourable report on these schools in February 2005, noting that Focus Learning was providing 'good support to its schools' and that '[t]he quality of teaching, most of which is done by experienced practitioners, is generally good, but the amalgamation of small schools has caused problems in finding suitable accommodation'.[616] Critics of the schools argue that they do not prepare children for life outside their community if they later decide on a different way of life. That is the basic test articulated by Woolf J in the *Talmud Torah* case (above), and in the past it has been given some weight by Ofsted. In response to the Chief Inspector's favourable comments about the schools, the Executive Director of the National Secular Society was quoted as saying that it was 'alarming that Ofsted, in its keenness to accommodate religion, appears to have suspended its critical faculties'.[617] Yet, as noted elsewhere, the Chief Inspector has raised concerns about faith schools' pupils not understanding their position as members of a wider society and has been critical of some Muslim schools. So the evidence is somewhat contradictory as to how far a departure by independent faith schools from majority norms in the teaching and the curriculum, which underlines their separateness from other schools, will be tolerated.

---

[613] Or, more particularly, the Chief Inspector for England or Wales, although other bodies may also be approved to inspect independent schools: Education Act 2002, ss 162A, 162B, 163 and 164 inserted or substituted by the EA 2005, Sched 8.

[614] www.bbc.co.uk./print//religion/religions/christianity/subdivisions/brethren.

[615] Ibid.

[616] Ofsted, *The Annual Report of Her Majesty's Chief Inspector of Schools, 2003/04* (London, Ofsted, 2005), para 290.

[617] T Halpin, 'Top marks for sect schools that shun the modern world', *The Times*, 21 Mar 2005.

ACADEMIES AND CREATIONISM

For independent schools that want to change status in order to receive state funding but are resistant to changing their curriculum, or at least to the extent that would be required if, for example, they acquired aided or foundation status, one option (if private finance can be secured) might be to apply to become an academy.[618] Although classed as independent schools and thus not covered by the National Curriculum or the other elements of the prescribed basic curriculum applicable to schools classed as maintained, namely sex education and religious education,[619] academies must nevertheless have a curriculum that meets basic requirements concerning a balanced and broadly based curriculum equivalent to those that apply to maintained schools, but 'with an emphasis on a particular subject area, or particular subject areas, specified in the agreement' (ie, the agreement between the Secretary of State and the proprietor under which the latter agrees to operate the school and the Secretary of State agrees to contribute funding).[620] The DfES 'Standards' webpages confirm that academies[621] 'are not bound by the National Curriculum and are free to adopt innovative approaches to the content and delivery of the curriculum'.[622] Academies can be run as faith academies and the relative curricular freedom probably heightens their attractiveness to potential sponsors with a religious commitment. The private sponsor of an academy would have to contribute only £2 million to attract government funding of 10 times that amount.

The Vardy Foundation established an educational charity with a strong Christian ethos which has provided sponsorship for two academies in the north of England (one in Gateshead and the other in Middlesbrough). The schools are not faith schools as such, but are described as having a 'non-denominational Christian' basis.[623] They do in fact follow the National Curriculum, but what is considered controversial about the Foundation's schools is that creationism—the idea that the origins of man and other living things lie in the creation as depicted in the Book of Genesis—is taught within them. According to Harris, the Vardy schools 'accord equal importance to both creationism and theories of evolution'.[624] One Vardy academy's website explains that the theory of evolution is taught in science but says that '[t]he National Curriculum specifically states scientific data can be interpreted in different ways and produce different theories (eg theory of evolution)' and that 'the Biblical view of creation is taught in RE

---

[618] Academies are discussed in Chap 3 at p 120 above. An independent school belonging to the Headmasters' and Headmistresses' Conference, which comprises the top-ranked independent schools, announced in Feb 2006 that it would be joining the state sector as an academy: T Halpin, 'Private school joins the state sector', *The Times*, 6 Feb 2006.

[619] This is because they are not within the definition of 'maintained school' to which those curriculum requirements apply: see EA 2002, s 76.

[620] EA 1996, s 482(1), as substituted by the EA 2002, s 65.

[621] They are always referred to in Government literature as 'Academies', with a capital 'A', whereas schools are just 'schools'.

[622] www.standards.dfes.gov.uk/academies.

[623] www.emmanuelctc.org.uk/AcademysFAQ.htm.

[624] J Harris, 'What a creation . . .', *The Guardian (Saturday)*, 15 Jan 2005.

lessons'.[625] The implication is that while it may be quite legitimate for the theory of intelligent design, based on the idea that life on earth was designed by an unknown intelligent force, and reportedly described by the academic Fuller as a scientific rather than religious theory,[626] to be covered within curriculum science, there is a risk that in conjunction with the presentation of creationism elsewhere in the curriculum the widespread scientific importance and credence attached to the theory of evolution might be underplayed. Dawkins and the Bishop of Oxford, who write critically about the creationist approach adopted by the Vardy Foundation, state that '[t]he evidence for evolution is so overwhelming that we can reconcile it with young earth creationism only by assuming that God deliberately planted false evidence, in the rocks and genetic molecules, to trick us'.[627] The Vardy Foundation's plan to establish another such academy near Doncaster was rejected by the LEA, reportedly in the light of considerable community opposition to its approach.[628]

The situation with the Vardy academies raises an important issue about the divide between science and religion within the school curriculum. Whilst, as discussed above, in most state schools the science curriculum is closely regulated, that is not true of religious education, as we also saw. In the United States, the Establishment Clause in First Amendment to the Constitution, in effect proscribing state sponsorship of religion,[629] has been invoked to curb attempts to promote creationism within the school curriculum. Creationism or the theory of intelligent design are sometimes presented as a critical alternative to the theory of evolution, but the teaching of them in public sector schools has more or less consistently been struck down by the US courts in decisions going back as far as 1925, the first two of which concerned a state statute that forbade the teaching of evolution.[630] While the courts regarded such a ban as unconstitutional, a subsequent statute, in one of these states, that required a balance (involving equal amounts of curriculum time) between evolution and creation science was also struck down.[631] This was because it failed the test established in *Lemon v Kurtzman*[632] for the Establishment Clause, namely that in order to be constitutional a provision must have a secular purpose; its primary or principal effect must not be one that advances or inhibits religion; and it must not foster 'an excessive government entanglement with religion'.[633] In this case

---

[625] www.emmanualctc.org.uk/AcademysFAChtm (5 Dec 2005).

[626] See S Jones 'UK academic gives evidence in intelligent design case', *The Guardian* 25 Oct 2005, 17.

[627] R Dawkins and the Bishop of Oxford, 'Questionable foundations', *The Sunday Times* (News Review), 20 June 2004, 12.

[628] BBC News, 'School plan axed after protests', 14 Oct 2004. See also J Harris, 'What a creation . . .', *The Guardian (Saturday)*, 15 Jan 2005.

[629] 'Congress shall make no law respecting an establishment of religion, or prohibiting the free exercise thereof'.

[630] *Scopes v State*, 278 SW 57 (Tenn 1925) and *Epperson v Arkansas*, 393 US 97 (1968).

[631] *McLean v Arkansas*, 529 F Supp 1255 (ED Ark 1982).

[632] 403 US 602 (1971).

[633] Ibid, at 612–3. See CJ Russo, 'Evolution v Creation Science in the US; Can the Courts Divine a Solution?' (2002) 3 *Education Law Journal* 152 at 155. Russo points out that in a 1997 decision the *Lemon* test was modified, with the third element, 'entanglement', applied as a factor in assessing the

and another, in the Supreme Court, which arose from Louisiana, where the state statute forbade coverage of one theory without that of the other,[634] the court considered that the statute's purpose was in part to advance religion by altering the curriculum in schools. Russo, writing in 2002, says that the effect of these rulings, plus the lower court litigation until then, is not necessarily that all coverage of alternative cultural beliefs to the theory of evolution should be excluded from biology teaching in the US, but that they would have to be treated as 'supplemental to the primary instruction on evolution'; yet he questions whether their inclusion might undermine 'the study of a legitimate secular topic'.[635] That view is clearly premised on the idea that religion and science are separable in this context.

Some, however, see the boundary as less than clear cut where theories of intelligent design are concerned. This has been well illustrated by *Kitzmiller et al v Dover Area School District et al,* [636] which concerned a complaint by eight families in Pennsylvania against the Dover Area School Board's declaration that students should be read a disclaimer in the ninth grade biology class stating, inter alia, that Darwin's theory was 'not a fact' and had gaps, that 'Intelligent Design is an explanation of the origin of life that differs from Darwin's view', and that '[w]ith respect to any theory, students are encouraged to keep an open mind'. The families contended that the Bible's view of creation was being promoted and that the board's regulation was unconstitutional. Cornelius and Selfridge predicted that the board's policy would be taken to promote the idea of a creator, which would be in violation of the Establishment Clause. They argued that although alternative theories to Darwin's ideas about macro-evolution (that evolution accounts not only for changes to species but also the emergence of new species) are being developed by some scientists, the attack on evolution theory is drawn mainly from those who prefer a religious explanation, so that 'any attempt to undermine its teachings will immediately implicate religious motivations' and place evolution theory 'above reproach'.[637] These comments were prompted by the latest of the lower court decisions on this issue. It arose from a school board policy requiring the placing of stickers in science textbooks in North Georgia, stating: '[t]his textbook contains material on evolution. Evolution is a theory, not a fact, regarding the origin of living things. This material should be approached with an open mind, studied carefully, and critically considered'. The stickers had been placed following a campaign, including a petition with 2,300 signatures,

---

effect of the statute (the second element): *Agostini v Felton*, 521 US 203 (1997), cited in CJ Russo, 'Religious Neutrality in Public Schools and Elsewhere: An Assessment of the Supreme Court's Approach to Posting the Ten Commandments in Public Places in the US' (2006) 7 *Education Law Journal* 21.

[634] *Edwards v Aguillard*, 482 US 578 (1987).

[635] CJ Russo, 'Evolution v Creation Science in the US; Can the Courts Divine a Solution?' (2002) 3 *Education Law Journal* 152 at 158.

[636] *Kitzmiller et al v Dover Area School District et al* (USDC MD Penn), 20 Dec 2005, Judge Jones.

[637] LM Cornelius and JL Selfridge, '"Studies Carefully and Critically Considered": Evolution Battles Return to the Spotlight' (2005) 47 *School Law Reporter* 61 at 63.

attacking the presentation of 'Darwinism unchallenged'.[638] The court considered that the sticker had a secular purpose but, due to being placed prominently at the front of textbooks and carrying a message explicitly endorsed by the school board, 'sent a message that the School Board agrees with the beliefs of Christian fundamentalists and creationists' and the board had 'effectively improperly entangled itself with religion by appearing to take a position'.[639] However, the court specifically declined to resolve the question whether science and religion were mutually exclusive.[640]

Subsequently, when judgment was issued in *Kitzmiller et al v Dover Area School District et al*,[641] the court examined the issue of whether intelligent design (ID) was science. It found that it was not, primarily on the ground that it failed 'the essential ground rules that limit science to testable, natural explanations'.[642] Moreover, it rested partly on dualism, namely that by showing flaws in evolutionary theory it might thereby confirm the validity of the theory of ID. The court concluded that 'ID is not science and cannot be adjudged a valid, accepted scientific theory as it has failed to publish in peer-reviewed journals, engage in research and testing, and gain acceptance in the scientific community'.[643] The theory of evolution, on the other hand, met these conditions and was 'good science'.[644] This represents a somewhat orthodox view of science as a field of investigation, but it enabled the court to confine ID to being no more than 'an interesting theological argument' and a 're-labeling of creationism'.[645] As regards the question of constitutionality, the court found that the ID policy would be viewed by the objective student as a strong official endorsement of religion, in particular because the disclaimer singled out evolution from the entire biology curriculum and undermined it in order to put ID in a favourable light. The objective adult member of the Dover community was also thought likely to perceive an endorsement of religion. The court also found the policy to fail the *Lemon* test (above), since the purpose was not secular but to advance religion, and that was also its effect.

Given the national control of much of the secular curriculum content in England and Wales for maintained schools, only the position of academies is really analogous to that in the US schools. While it has been argued that the independent 'trust' schools currently proposed by the Government[646] may have sufficient curricular autonomy to teach creationism as part of their science curriculum,[647] it is not clear whether their freedom will go that far. Either way,

---

[638] See G Younge, 'Evolution textbook row goes to court', *The Guardian*, 9 Nov 2004, 12.

[639] *Selman v Cobb County Sched. Dist.*, 390 FSupp.2d 1286, 2005 WL 83829 (NDGa), at 24, 25; see also *Freiler v Tangipahoa Parish Bd. Of Educ*, 185 F3d 337 (5th Cir, 1999) (challenge to oral disclaimer regarding evolution).

[640] *Selman*, n 639 above, at 1.

[641] *Kitzmiller et al v Dover Area School District et al* (USDC MD Penn), 20 Dec 2005, Judge Jones.

[642] Ibid, 70.

[643] Ibid, 89.

[644] Ibid, 136.

[645] Ibid and 43.

[646] See p 134 above.

[647] Joint Committee on Human Rights, Ninth Report, Session 2005–06, *Schools White Paper*, HL 113, HC 887 (London, TSO, 2006), para 28.

there is an argument that, in the case of academies such as the Vardy schools, the fact that parents have chosen to send their children there knowing that they place an emphasis on particular Christian ideas means they should have no grounds of objection over the curriculum content. Leaving that aside, the question remains whether, given that these schools also open their doors to those of other faiths, they should be permitted to adopt such an approach as creationism in an area of the curriculum over which parents may have no right of withdrawal (and no statutory right of complaint).

A further question is whether it can be right to permit one relatively small group of children to be presented with a view of something so fundamental to basic biology that is different from that offered to the majority of pupils, particularly one that does not accord with normative scientific principles.[648] In fact, Darwin's theories are generally included at key stage 4 within GCSE syllabuses (although not at earlier key stages), which means that academy and maintained school pupils should be exposed to them. Indeed, the AQA syllabus for Biology for 2007–8 states that candidates should use their skills, knowledge and understanding of how science works to, inter alia, 'suggest reasons why scientists cannot be certain about how life began on Earth'; 'interpret evidence relating to evolutionary theory'; 'identify the differences between Darwin's theory of evolution and conflicting theories'; and 'suggest reasons for the different theories'. The scientific basis to this curriculum implies that scientific theories such as those of Lamarck might come into play as an alternative to Darwin, but not creationism. This is particularly so, given that a Government minister, in a debate in the House of Lords on creationism teaching, gave an example of a key stage 3 religious education syllabus which had a unit entitled 'Where did the universe come from?' and included the conflict between science and religion, and implied that it was in the context of religious education, rather than science, that creationism should be covered.[649] More recently, however, a different Government minister, in a Parliamentary Written Answer, has indicated that pupils in mainstream schools may be able to debate issues such as creationism and intelligent design in key stage 4 science lessons when considering the prescribed issue of 'how scientific controversies can arise from different ways of interpreting empirical evidence'.[650] Furthermore, it was revealed in March 2006 that two other examination boards' GCSE Biology syllabuses will contain modules in which pupils will need to be aware that creationism is a contradictory perspective to the theory of evolution.[651] The *Times Educational Supplement*'s

[648] On this, see the separate articles by Steve Fuller and Harry Brighouse under the joint heading 'Schools for the Enlightenment or Epiphany?' *The Times Higher Education Supplement*, 23/30 Dec 2005, 20–1. See also S Baird, 'Teach two origins of life based on evidence, scientists demand', *The Times*, 22 June 2006, 20, reporting the signing of a statement by national science academies from 67 states (the Royal Society signed for the UK) calling for science courses to be properly scientific rather than concealing or avoiding evolution theories or confusing them with theories not testable by science.

[649] HL Debs, Vol 649, Cols 187–189, 11 June 2003, per Baroness Ashton of Upholland (Under-Secretary of State).

[650] HC Written Answers, Vol 443, Col 520w, 27 Feb 2006, Jacqui Smith MP.

[651] G Paton, 'And God created a rumpus', *Times Educational Supplement*, 10 Mar 2005, 1.

disparaging view is that if, by including the controversy concerning creationism within the curriculum, the examiners want to increase interest in science, 'a module on *Star Trek* would be better and more scientifically sound'.[652] Also, the Archbishop of Canterbury has said, via a newspaper interview, that he is not comfortable with the teaching of creationism in schools, because creationism is 'a kind of category mistake, as if the Bible were a theory like other theories. Whatever the biblical account of creation is, it's not a theory like other theories'.[653] These developments suggest that the debates over the inclusion of creationism in the school curriculum, particularly in the science curriculum, are likely to intensify, since pupils are increasingly likely to receive lessons in which coverage is given to this subject.

CONCLUSION

The basic issue that has been explored within this chapter is the fundamental question which Gutmann expresses in the following simple terms: '[h]ow can civic education in a liberal democracy give social diversity its due?'[654] Beyond the role that education performs in imparting knowledge, preparing for adult citizenship and training in skills lies its broader civilising role that, in a socially and culturally diverse society, is dependent upon the inculcation of values considered to have particular importance to basic citizenship. Yet there is a conflict that much concerns liberal theorists such as Gutmann. It centres on the question of how far should the autonomy and independence of particular social groups, perhaps identified primarily on the basis of their culture or religion, be upheld in the interests of freedom and liberty and ultimately justice and (group) rights, when to do so threatens to weaken the very democratic values which education must be seen to reflect, either by supporting practices that are regarded as antithetical to them or simply by virtue of the special treatment or exemption that is afforded. As we have seen, multiculturalism in education is at the centre of this debate, since at two extremes are the views, first, that it provides a basis for minimising societal fissures resulting from diversity and, secondly, that it deepens them by weakening the bedrock of common citizenship. Also at issue is the position of the individual child or young person, for whom education on matters such as the arts, citizenship or sex is important in establishing their capacity for autonomy and freedom of thought and choice that are competences embedded within notions of liberal society,[655] but whose parents or community may find unacceptable for cultural or religious reasons. Research has shown that children

---

[652] Opinion (Editorial), 'Creation debate out of bounds', *Times Educational Supplement*, 10 Mar 2005, 22.

[653] A Rusbridger, '"I am comic vicar of the nation"' interview with Rowan Williams, Archbishop of Canterbury, *The Guardian* (G2), 21 Mar 2006, 6, at 11.

[654] A Gutmann, 'Civil Education and Social Diversity' (1995) 105 *Ethics* 557 at 557. See also Idem, *Democratic Education* (Princeton, NJ, Princeton University Press, 1987).

[655] See J Rawls, *Political Liberalism* (New York, Columbia University Press, 1993) 199.

of all faith backgrounds are generally very positive about diversity among pupils in school and co-exist well in the school environment, normally feeling unhappy about diversity only when they are threatened by racist behaviour.[656] This shows that there is a firm foundation upon which education can contribute to the development of a tolerant and integrated, while diverse and pluralistic, society. However, it is important to note that the children covered by the research were still quite young; social grouping is more likely among older pupils, not just on the basis of gender but also on that of race, which can make this particular role of education more challenging.[657]

In practice, few disputes between families and schools seem to arise over the content of education. This could partly be because diversity is accommodated to a tolerable extent, so far as most individuals and social groups are concerned, within the main part of the statutory school curriculum, combined with parents' statutory right to opt out their children from some of the more sensitive aspects of education. A further factor is that those pupils whose families hold religious, philosophical or cultural views of a more fundamentalist nature constitute a very small minority of the school population, and many of them will be educated within a significantly mono-cultural environment, such as at a private or state denominational school. Of course, there are some instances, as illustrated by the *Begum* case,[658] where apparent culture clashes occur and require legal resolution, but they tend to be relatively rare. Given the right of parents to have their child educated within a faith-based school, with an increasing likelihood that it will be in the public sector if the Government's policy of supporting Muslim and other independent schools to seek maintained school status bears fruit, disputes are likely to centre on the freedom of such schools in terms of their ethos and curriculum, as in *Williamson*.[659] The state's regulation of these matters within the independent sector is at present relatively weak, as we have seen, but pressure is mounting for greater control. This arises out of concern that some of these schools are sufficiently different and culturally distinctive to reinforce social divisions at a time when there are perceived to be risks that they may deepen. As the UK population becomes ever more diverse, and minority groups become more confident and assertive, claims around issues of religious freedom and cultural autonomy are likely to increase. Human rights norms may provide states with a 'framework to meet the challenges of multiculturalism',[660] as McGoldrick suggests, but they do not provide all the answers as regards how best to resolve conflicts in this field. This is particularly so in the UK and elsewhere in Europe, in view of the deference shown by the courts, both nationally and internationally, to

---

[656] G Smith, *Children's Perspectives on Believing and Belonging* (London, National Children's Bureau, 2005) 27.

[657] See C Wright *et al*, *'Race', Class and Gender in Exclusion from School* (London, Falmer, 2000) 68–9, 86–7.

[658] *R (Begum) v Headteacher and Governors of Denbigh High School* [2006] UKHL 15; [2006] 2 WLR 719; see above.

[659] *R (Williamson) v Secretary of State for Education and Employment and Others* [2005] UKHL 15; [2005] ELR 291; [2005] 2 AC 246; see above.

[660] D McGoldrick, 'Multiculturalism and its Discontents' (2005) 5 *Human Rights Law Review* 27 at 35.

the state's power and autonomy over education policy. In the US, the experience of working out and applying constitutional norms across a range of judgments over aspects of teaching has raised as many questions as it has resolved and continues to generate major legal and philosophical debate about the relevant issues.

Accommodation of all of minorities' culturally-based wishes as regards the education of their children is clearly going to be impossible, which leads to the perhaps unavoidable conclusion that conflict is inevitable. Moreover, there is potentially a triangular conflict, if children from minority communities want to participate in an activity that is regarded as unacceptable by their families or communities. In one school in the North of England researchers observed a school assembly where some Christian hymns had been sung with 'no enthusiasm'. The whole school, which included Muslim children, was invited, for the finale, to sing 'Chitty Chitty Bang Bang'. The researchers found that the children, including most of the Muslims, 'joined in with great gusto', but the researchers also reported that some children had said that they only 'mouth' the words of songs, in order to keep out of trouble. Although in their mosques music is regarded as un-Islamic, the teachers at their mosque had said that miming would be permitted.[661] While the parents' views on this issue were not discussed by the researchers, this pragmatic accommodation of minority interests seems to show that, notwithstanding the still incoherent approach of education law in the UK towards social diversity, there are practical ways of working through some of the difficulties that are presented. Nevertheless, the established legal framework governing the school curriculum fails to provide a clear indication of the weight attached to particular rights, including those of children themselves. Moreover, the curriculum within independent schools is still far less regulated than that of public sector schools. Notwithstanding arguments about segregation and elitism that still surround private education, if parents can meet their obligation to ensure that their child receives a 'suitable' education by sending him or her to a school either in the public or private sector, and if all schools are seen by government as having an equal role in education for responsible citizenship, the disparity between the two sectors, in terms of the curricular requirements applicable in them, seems unjustifiable.

---

[661] G Smith, *Children's Perspectives on Believing and Belonging* (London, National Children's Bureau, 2005) 34–5.

8

Conclusion: Education, Law And Diversity—Goals And Challenges

THE ORGANISATION OF education is one of the key functions of the democratic state. Within England and Wales, its roles in instilling particular values and developing various skills within generations of children and young people have, particularly over the past three decades, been the subject of political scrutiny and legislative intervention. Over the past decade this social reproductive aspect to education has increasingly been linked both to ideals concerning the realisation of citizenship and the achievement of national economic goals via the 'skills economy' as much as to its enabling role in the fulfilment of a critical social purpose for the individual and his or her social and economic empowerment. The centrality of education to modern social and economic development is reinforced by its well established and increasingly elaborate legal framework. Indeed, education has become one of the most developed areas of state governance in England and Wales, re-shaped by complex structural reforms and the subject of considerable central regulation and control. This has affected, indeed re-configured, relationships both between the various agencies responsible for provision and between those agencies and the recipients of education and its stakeholders, particularly parents.

The heterogeneity of modern society presents a particular challenge for education policy and legislation. This book has been particularly concerned to identify ways in which education and its legal framework have responded to social change and the problems, particularly the inequalities, which have arisen and persist. As we saw in Chapter 1, not only is there considerable social and economic inequality within the UK, but society has become ethnically and religiously very diverse. Education has a potentially vital role to play in preparing children and young people for life within such a society, and as a force for minimising social stresses and maximising social cohesion. It is also viewed as a force for combating social disadvantage, which is both a cause and a consequence of a lack of educational achievement. Education policy post-1997 has not merely reflected a belief in education's potential to ameliorate relative disadvantage or social exclusion; it has also been premised on the belief that without raising standards there is little chance of reducing the achievement gap between different individuals and social groups. The policy preoccupation with educational standards that much of recent education legislation reflects is partly predicated on the purported measurability of qualitative improvement in general in this sphere.

Within the general policy push towards improvements in attainment levels, there are many legal and policy initiatives that are targeted at specific areas of disadvantage, in addition to those aimed at preventing discrimination and promoting formal equality, as discussed in Chapter 4 in particular. Education enhances life opportunities for the individual and contributes to the community benefit. But there is no guarantee that a universal service, even one from which everyone is intended to benefit as of right, will be capable of operating on the basis of equality among all persons from all social groupings. As we have seen, there are multiple causative factors in relation to social disadvantage, including a person's financial or employment circumstances; their ethnicity, gender or sexuality; their resident status in the UK; and their physical or mental abilities and capacities. Such factors can and do affect access to education. They can also affect the capacity to exercise choice in respect of provision and/or a particular institution; to learn; and to succeed. As we saw in Chapters 4 (on access to education) and 6 (on special educational needs), governments have increasingly faced demands and social imperatives to improve equality of opportunity across all sectors of education. Elaborate legal protections and asymmetrical initiatives targeted at the disadvantaged have been developed, especially those concerned with combating unfair discrimination and reducing financial barriers to participation in education, measures achieving varying degrees of success.

So wide-ranging and diffuse are the problems to which such responses are directed that the legal and administrative frameworks have tended to become immensely complex. Their aims are, however, relatively modest, in that they are not seeking to effect major structural changes to society through a real redistribution of power in favour of those within particular categories of disadvantage. Instead of equality of outcome they are aimed at equality of opportunity, something which has been a particular feature of the post-1997 Labour Government's strategy of offering a helping hand, but not much more, to those deemed capable of self-help.[1] The underlying rationale is that access will improve and levels of achievement will rise, leading to the gradual removal of the entrenched social disadvantages and barriers. However, further measures to equalise opportunities would clearly be possible. For example, as discussed in Chapter 5, the greater use of 'banding' in school admissions policies could widen access to 'good' schools among those from educationally disadvantaged backgrounds. This could be taken one stage further by offering financial incentives to ensure that schools take more pupils from poorer areas,[2] a move that would be similar to the postcode premium from which higher education institutions can benefit, noted in Chapter 4.

---

[1] See, eg, R Plant, 'Supply Side Citizenship?' (1999) 6 *Journal of Social Security Law* 124; R Lister, 'Citizenship, Exclusion and "the Third Way": Reflections on TH Marshall' (2000) 7 *Journal of Social Security Law* 70.

[2] As suggested by J Le Grand, 'The Blair Legacy: Choice and Competition in Public Services', Transcript of Public Lecture, LSE, 21 Feb 2006, available at www.lse.ac.uk/collections/LSEPublicLecturesandEvents/.

Also seen as critical to achievement is the engagement of parents with their children's education. However, rights of participation and choice in this regard are problematic for a number of reasons. One of these concerns the independent rights of children in connection with their education, an issue which has been considered at various points in this book. Perhaps the most important aspect concerns the participation of children, both individually and collectively, in the various decisions that fall to be made. Such decisions can have critically important consequences and yet children's views are still not systematically sought. We saw, in Chapter 2 in particular, the increasing, but far from comprehensive, recognition of children's rights under Article 12 of the UNCRC in the UK and the failure to ensure that the 'evolving capacities' of the child determine the degree of importance accorded to ascertaining children's views and perhaps the weight to be attached to them. Although progress has been made in recognising children's rights in this field, education is still an area in which the political importance attached to the demonstrable empowerment of parents through choice and representation of interests is treated as the more dominant imperative than that of giving children and young people a voice. As Sachs J commented in the case before the Constitutional Court of South Africa, noted in Chapters 2 and 7, in which a ban on corporal punishment affecting independent schools was challenged on religious grounds but the children's interests were not independently represented before the court, '[a]lthough both the state and the parents were in a position to speak on their behalf, neither was able to speak in their name'.[3] The parent-centredness of education law is reflected not only in the rights of choice and participation but also in parents' responsibilities for ensuring that their children attend school and behave while there, which, as we have seen, have intensified via an increasing range of legal sanctions. Some might argue that if individual children and young people are to benefit from a more independent status in the future, some of this responsibility should be shared by them. Children do, however, have a right to expect that their parents will take seriously this aspect of their upbringing. Perhaps a better approach would be to build on the notion of partnership which is part of the dominant discourse on parent–school relations and to regard the child as a further 'partner' in the enterprise of educating him or her as a future adult citizen.

Although school choice was given a degree of legal effect for largely political reasons in the early 1980s, involving the creation of a competitive market-type system, part of the current rationale for its legal recognition and portrayal as a form of empowerment is to maintain the idea, noted above, that parents have a responsibility to be actively involved in their children's education. The parent's need to exercise choice in order to maximise the child's opportunities illustrates how parent participation is instrumentalised as a form of governance.[4] However, choice can always be rationalised as beneficial to the individual in the way that it connotes a degree of independence and freedom which is consonant with the

---

[3] *Christian Education South Africa v Minister of Education*, Case CCT 4/00 [2001] 1 LRC 441, para 53.

[4] See N Harris, 'Empowering Parents: Rights of Choice and Participation' (2005) 68 *MLR* 925.

basic idea of liberalism and the free society. Either way, it has become a dominant issue within education law and has implications for both individual and collective or group rights in education, including those surrounding the issue of respect for cultural beliefs and preferences. It has been explored in this book as part of the wider discussion of the right to education itself and its manifestation, along with that of related rights such as those concerned with privacy/family life and freedom of religion, within international legal norms. There has also been discussion of its effects in terms of the nature and quality of the education to which there is entitlement. As we have seen, issues concerned with choice are central not only to the relevant provisions of the ECHR, but also the myriad provisions in domestic education law that affect crucial aspects of education that are of particular concern to parents and children, including school admission, the curriculum and provision for those with special educational needs. As we saw in Chapter 5, a huge majority of parents attach considerable importance to school choice. The evidence suggests that this desire may be at its strongest among the less advantaged, which Le Grand argues is not surprising, since 'the middle class already do well out of the unreformed no-choice NHS and education system'.[5] The Government seems to recognise that any expansion of choice would hinder its goal of reducing exclusion and widening citizen engagement, should choice inequality intensify. For example, it acknowledges in the 2005 White Paper that 'we need . . . to ensure the benefits of choice are available to all'.[6] Thus there is an assumption that choice can be linked to notions of social justice through its democratisation, broadening opportunities to enjoy it. At present, as Parsons and Welsh argue, 'the quasi-market in education does not equally empower all consumers', whereas 'social justice as fairness requires the generality of citizens to have the highest amount of choice, and hence the greatest freedom'.[7]

As we also saw in Chapter 5, choice may also be rationalised as a means not only to realising opportunities but, where it is linked to resource allocation, of raising standards. But as resources are finite and their effective allocation is dependent upon state governance in order that collective/national interests, as opposed merely to market forces, are the primary driving force, choice is inevitably limited and cannot be guaranteed for all. The author predicted in 1993, when the shift towards consumerism and the 'managed market' for education under the Conservatives' reforms was largely complete, that 'whatever political changes occur in the future, the rights of education consumers will continue to form a central element in the education system's legal structure', but that '[r]eal consumer empowerment, may . . . continue to prove elusive'.[8] Today, the opportunities for individual choice, based on the exercise of basic social

---

[5] Le Grand, n 2 above.

[6] HM Government, *Higher Standards, Better Schools for All*, Cm 6677 (London, TSO, 2005), para 1.29.

[7] C Parsons and PJ Welsh, 'Public Policies and Practice, Non-liberal Consumerism and Freedom of Choice in Secondary Education: a Case Study of One Area in Kent' (2006) 36 *Cambridge Journal of Education* 237, at 251 and 254.

[8] N Harris, *Law and Education: Regulation, Consumerism and the Education System* (London, Sweet and Maxwell, 1993) 263.

rights, remain limited notwithstanding the active and almost universal support shown towards choice in the various political arenas and despite the increasing number of claims made by parents, desirous of the best educational opportunities for their children (which, in some cases, is linked to choices that are culturally specific). In the analysis of social rights and of human rights protections relating to education in Chapter 2 and at many other points, the contingency of these rights, particularly those linked to choice, was highlighted. It is difficult for individual rights claims, even those centred on moderately strong interferences with basic cultural values, to succeed where the state has acted in a rational way and mindful of the overriding social goals to its policies. So far as choice of school is concerned, despite all recent governments' commitment to extend it there are limits to how far the supply of places at particular schools can be altered on any scale in response to parental demand. Maximising opportunities for choice requires a surplus on the supply side, leading to inefficiencies. If a surplus of places at some schools, those that are the least popular with parents, becomes acute, the inefficiency may lead to pressure to close the school,[9] with the risk of damaging consequences within communities.

Choice of school is also associated, in terms of its effects, with social segregation along the lines of class or race, although, as we saw in Chapter 5, not all the evidence points in the same direction. More clear-cut is the way that school choice reinforces divisions based around social class and wealth. Moreover, in so far as many parents have a choice of selecting a faith-based school, ostensibly on the basis of their own religious identity, and in the light of government policy that a place should be found for a number of independent faith schools within the state sector, segregation on the basis of religion is already occurring on a wide scale. There is now some recognition of the inequity caused by these effects, leading to government encouragement to reduce some of the barriers to entry to denominational schools among those who are not of the relevant faith. Whether, and how far, exhortation to such schools to widen access precipitates firm changes to admission policies remains to be seen.

Choice and participation give an individualised focus to the relationship between citizen and state. But it is also the case that people are part of group identities. These have become more prominent over recent years as the impact of intense national and local governance of state provision on matters relating to the interests of particular sections of the community has fed into debates about cultural identity and social cohesion. The French ban on the wearing of religious dress to school, which caused considerable controversy when introduced in 2004, is reported to have resulted in few departures of Muslim pupils from state schools, but among those that did leave were 10 or so who came to the UK.[10]

---

[9] See Swedish National Agency for Education, *School Choice and its Effects in Sweden* (Stockholm, Swedish National Agency for Education, 2003) 27. See further Chap 5.

[10] According to a report, in the period of 12 months after the ban, 625 pupils arrived for lessons wearing the hijab, of whom 496 agreed to remove it; 45 refused and were excluded (along with 2 Sikhs who refused to remove their turbans): A Sage, 'Headscarf ban is judged success as hostility fades', *The Times* 5 Sept 2005, 31.

They are unlikely to face such a ban here in the foreseeable future. Yet according to a MORI survey in 2005, as many as 35 per cent of the UK public now believe that Muslim pupils should not be permitted to wear headscarves.[11] The *Begum* decision in the House of Lords,[12] discussed in Chapters 2, 4 and 7, has shown how restrictions on pupils' choice of dress may be legitimate if they are proportionate responses to perceived threats posed by expressions of fundamentalist faith to attempts to promote cohesion. At the same time, the schools system has been and continues to be accommodating towards religion. As we have seen, the Blair Government has shown considerable support for faith schools, although their legitimacy is undermined by growing public unease about their impact upon social cohesion. According to a Guardian/ICM poll in 2005, 64 per cent of the public believe that 'the government should not be funding faith schools of any kind'.[13] Fears borne out of the rise in fundamentalism are seen as lying behind this view, which runs against the long tradition of public acceptance that religion is basically a benign influence on education and that its associations with education pose no threat to wider social harmony. Yet the evidence that an increasingly small proportion of the general population adheres to a particular religion or faith and that children are less likely than their parents' generation to do so continues to mount.[14] This growing secularity throws the strong commitment to religious ideals among many minority faith groups into sharp relief.

The interests of minorities demand recognition and protection within education, since the oppression of any group or groups is completely antithetical to the notion of liberal democracy. As the European Court of Human Rights Grand Chamber stated in 2005 in *Leyla Şahin v Turkey*,[15] citing *Young, James and Webster v United Kingdom*:[16]

> Pluralism, tolerance and broadmindedness are hallmarks of a 'democratic society'. Although individual interests must on occasion be subordinated to those of a group, democracy does not simply mean that the views of a majority must always prevail: a balance must be achieved which ensures the fair and proper treatment of people from minorities and avoids any abuse of a dominant position . . .

Yet the state's necessary power over the education of children, who are its future adult citizens as well as being future adult members of their own minority communities, could bring national policies and legislation into conflict with minority wishes. Indeed, they could be perceived by some minorities as posing a threat to their own traditions and values systems and therefore undermining their cultural integrity. The legal and rights frameworks have yet to provide an

---

[11] 'Multiculturalism thrives, poll says', *The Times*, 11 August 2005, 24.

[12] *R (Begum) v Headteacher and Governors of Denbigh High School* [2006] UKHL 15; [2006] 2 WLR 719.

[13] M Taylor, 'Two thirds oppose state aided faith schools', *The Guardian*, 23 August 2005, 1.

[14] See D Voas and A Crockett, 'Religion in Britain: Neither Believing nor Belonging' (2005) 39 *Sociology* 11. The authors found that 'in Britain, institutional religion now has a half-life of one generation' (ibid, 21).

[15] App no 44774/98, Judgment (Grand Chamber) 10 Nov 2005, para 108.

[16] Judgment of 13 Aug 1981 (1982) 4 EHRR 38, para 63.

entirely coherent means of resolving such conflicts. Ten years ago Bainham commented, in relation to areas of law affecting the family: '[e]ducation law is perhaps the area in which there has been least sensitivity to cultural pluralism'.[17] Barry argues that within liberal democracies education is an area where there is a presumption of equal opportunity, but '"cultural dispositions" do not trump reasonable demands on people for conformity with universalistic standards'.[18] Some, such as Ahdar and Leigh, see the state's attempt to broaden the engagement with different religions in education in order to ensure inclusion as essentially assimilationist.[19] However one perceives the broader position, it is the case that, as we saw in Chapter 7, the accommodation of minority cultural preferences within the curriculum in the state sector is limited and the opportunities for upholding individual faith- or conviction-based choices remain restricted and primarily based on withdrawal from a relatively small number of, albeit the more culturally sensitive, areas of provision. The Human Rights Act 1998 has yet to have a strong impact in this context, partly because there remain many as yet untested areas, but also, as we saw in Chapter 2, because, as the Strasbourg and UK judgments to date have shown, the ECHR offers relatively little assistance to parents wishing to challenge aspects of their child's schooling and provides the relevant public authorities with considerable latitude and scope for justifying any restrictions by reference to wider social and economic concerns.

The UN's Special Rapporteur on the right to education has argued that '[d]iversity is the cornerstone of education. It manifests itself in intercultural community life and respect for differences in people'.[20] This positive view of diversity seems to reflect a belief that, by engaging with it in a way that promotes human rights and egalitarian values, education can serve vital social ends, which the Special Rapporteur refers to as 'democratization and anti-discrimination' which are 'essential to a dignified life'.[21] Yet diversity presents education with a range of challenges. It opens up difficult questions about how state policies and national legislation should respond to it. In terms of the normative overriding goals of education to promote opportunity and prepare for citizenship on an equal basis for all, it needs to adhere to some basic notion of equity and justice that minimises or corrects disadvantage resulting from social or cultural background. In this sense, special arrangements concerned with access, discussed in Chapter 4, are particularly important. Where cultural—including religious or linguistic—diversity is concerned, the education system is faced with competing demands to support group rights and individual or collective cultural preferences, something acknowledged by the multicultural approach discussed in

---

[17] A Bainham, 'Family Law in a Pluralistic Society' (1995) 22 *Journal of Law and Society* 234 at 243.

[18] B Barry, 'Second Thoughts—and Some First Thoughts Revived' in P Kelly (ed), *Multiculturalism Reconsidered* (Cambridge, Policy, 2002) 204 at 219.

[19] R Adhar and I Leigh, *Religious Freedom in the Liberal State* (Oxford, OUP, 2005) 261.

[20] UN Commission on Human Rights, 61st session, Economic, Social and Cultural Rights, *The Right to Education. Report submitted by the Special Rapporteur on the Right to Education, Mr. Vernor Muñoz Villalos*, E/CN4/2005/50, 17 Dec 2004, para 70.

[21] Ibid.

Chapter 7, but also to provide a common framework of values and knowledge in order to ensure both social solidarity and personal participative capacity.

How far and in what ways education should play a role in integrating minorities, acting as a unifying force, and combating the segregation that results from the expression of personal wishes, including those based on personal faith or beliefs, is a crucial question at the present time and is likely to continue to be so for the foreseeable future. As Knights argues, these policy issues surrounding education 'can be seen as a microcosm of the broader debate about diversity at the three levels of state, group and individual'.[22] But this has gone beyond an issue of philosophical debate into a matter of hard policy choices and difficult compromises. They are rendered the more problematic by the intense legalism surrounding the modern education system, including the increased regulation of the private sector of education, although, as we have seen, across a range of different aspects of educational provision the apparently sharp lines drawn by parts of the primary and secondary legislation are often revealed, in the face of judicial scrutiny, to offer less certainty than expected. The possibility of human rights challenges based on the assertion of individual or group rights creates the risk of greater uncertainty over the balance between competing interests. The influence of human rights litigation, including that in the domestic courts under the Human Rights Act 1998, has, notwithstanding some important decisions, necessarily been relatively limited so far, as noted above. However, the challenges and decisions to date have served to intensify debates surrounding the accommodation of minorities' rights within a mass (but increasingly less uniform) education system, a system whose role in realising individual ambitions and national social and economic goals has probably never before been viewed as so important.

[22] S Knights, 'Religious Symbols in the School: Freedom of Religion, Minorities and Education' (2005) 5 *European Human Rights Law Review* 499 at 506.

Index